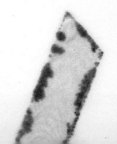

THE HISTORY OF
FANNY BURNEY

FRANCES BURNEY

by Edward Francesco Burney

THE HISTORY OF
FANNY BURNEY

BY

JOYCE HEMLOW

OXFORD
AT THE CLARENDON PRESS
1958

Oxford University Press, Amen House, London E.C.4

GLASGOW NEW YORK TORONTO MELBOURNE WELLINGTON
BOMBAY CALCUTTA MADRAS KARACHI KUALA LUMPUR
CAPE TOWN IBADAN NAIROBI ACCRA

———

PRINTED IN GREAT BRITAIN

PREFACE

AT Dr. Burney's death in 1814 his correspondence and papers went by his own wish to his daughter Frances (Madame d'Arblay), whom, among the members of his family, he had chosen as his editor. At the deaths of her sisters Susan Phillips in 1800 and Esther Burney in 1832, of her husband General d'Arblay in 1818 and of her son Alexander d'Arblay in 1837, successive sections of manuscripts were to fall into Madame d'Arblay's possession, augmenting her own accumulations, the writings and correspondence of a lifetime. In accordance with the editorial policies that she pursued in the last twenty years of her life, she destroyed parts of the family papers, but the hoards were steadily enlarged and diversified with current correspondence until her death in 1840.

In her will she bequeathed her father's correspondence (with the exception of her own share of it), together with all the papers that remained in the Doctor's handwriting, to her nephew Dr. Charles Parr Burney with permission to edit and publish them or commit them to the flames at his own judgement. But her own hoards, described as 'the whole of my own immense Mass of Manuscripts collected from my fifteenth year whether personal or collateral consisting of Letters Diaries Journals Dramas Compositions in prose and in rhyme', she left to her niece Charlotte Barrett, giving her 'full and free permission according to her unbiased taste and judgment to keep or destroy them', stipulating only that Charlotte should eventually bequeath 'whatsoever she had not disposed of or annihilated' to her son Richard Barrett, Madame d'Arblay's godson, grandnephew, and residuary legatee.

This voluminous bequest of manuscripts, augmented by the additions mentioned and by the papers of Madame d'Arblay's sister Charlotte Ann Burney Francis Broome (1761–1838) and by those of her children Marianne Francis (1790–1832), Clement Francis (1792–1829), and Charlotte Francis Barrett herself and by those of the Barrett descendants, came down more or less intact in the Barrett family until the year 1924, when a huge portion of the d'Arblay–Barrett papers was sold.

This section, including about 3,000 letters, a manuscript of *Evelina*, unpublished plays, the manuscripts of the so-called *Diary and Letters of Madame d'Arblay*, and many unprinted journals, did not remain long in England, but was shortly acquired by a collector of rare books and manuscripts, Mr. Owen D. Young of New York City, who had the archive catalogued, and encased in blue morocco fire-proofed boxes. In 1941, partly by gift and partly by purchase, the d'Arblay–Burney–Barrett material was transferred from Mr. Young's Collection to the Henry W. and Albert A. Berg Collection of the New York Public Library, where it is carefully kept in all possible security. This last event is described by Dr. John D. Gordan, the Curator of the Berg Collection, in 'A Doctor's Benefaction: The Berg Collection of the New York Public Library', *The Papers of the Bibliographical Society of America*, xlviii (4th quarter, 1954), 308–11.

The residue of the d'Arblay–Burney–Barrett archive, consisting still of over 2,000 letters, remained in the possession of Miss Ann Julia Wauchope, the great-granddaughter of Charlotte Barrett (and the great-great-grandniece of Madame d'Arblay) until the year 1952, when it was placed in the British Museum. The acquisition is described by Dr. C. E. Wright in 'The Barrett Collection of Burney Papers', the *British Museum Quarterly*, xviii (June, 1953), 41–43.

Dr. Burney's papers and correspondence, as bequeathed by the provisions of Madame d'Arblay's will to Dr. Charles Parr Burney, remained, presumably, within the Burney family. In recent years, however, Dr. Burney's correspondence as edited by Madame d'Arblay and supplemented by the personal papers and juvenilia of Dr. Charles Burney, Jr., the Greek scholar (1757–1817) and by the correspondence of Dr. Charles Parr Burney (1785–1864), an accumulation numbering over 2,500 items, has come to rest in the Collections of Mr. James M. Osborn of Yale University.

The Burney manuscripts are thus concentrated in three major Collections: the Berg Collection of the New York Public Library; the Barrett Collection, which, with other Burney papers previously acquired, is in the British Museum; and the Osborn Collection in New Haven. The first collection includes chiefly d'Arblay papers, the second Broome and

Barrett papers, and the third the papers of Doctor Burney and his son Charles, the Greek scholar; but all three collections contain a cross-section of Burney manuscripts covering roughly a century—the years 1750–1850. Detached segments of the Burney correspondence, for instance the Francis side of the Francis–Piozzi correspondence, the Twining side of the Burney–Twining correspondence, the Malone side of the Burney–Malone correspondence, the d'Arblay side of the d'Arblay–James Burney correspondence, and the Burney side of the Burney–Lowndes correspondence, have made their ways respectively to the John Rylands Library, Manchester; the British Museum; the Folger Library, Washington; the Pierpont Morgan Library, New York; and to a family collection, the possession of John R. G. Comyn, Esquire. These and other collections are listed in the Bibliography of Manuscripts (Appendix), but there are probably many additional collections, both in private hands and in libraries, of which no count is here taken. I have made no attempt, for instance, to list the letters still in the hands of booksellers, through whose agency most of the great transfers of Burney manuscripts have been made.

The great flow of eighteenth-century material, broken in pieces by various vicissitudes, has drifted in huge segments and in smaller ones far from its native shores, and one can only look forward to the day when the jagged pieces on both sides of the Atlantic are fitted together and the lively and heroic saga of the Burneys is made available to all in printed form.

J. H.

McGill University
September 3, 1956

ACKNOWLEDGEMENTS

FOR financial support that made research in the Burney manuscripts possible I wish to record my thanks to the Committee on Research at McGill University, who hazarded the first investment in the venture; to the Humanities Research Council of Canada for several summer grants; to the John Simon Guggenheim Memorial Foundation for one of the Canadian Fellowships (1951); to the administration of McGill University for leave of absence (1951–2); and to the Nuffield Foundation for a study grant for the summer of 1954.

The History of Fanny Burney, based largely on unprinted parts of Madame d'Arblay's journal–letters, notebooks, unpublished works, and voluminous correspondence, and on other unpublished sections of other Burney papers, owes its existence to the owners and curators of the Burney manuscripts. My debts are incalculable, but I wish to thank, first of all, Dr. John D. Gordan, the Curator of the Berg Collection, and the officials of the New York Public Library for the privilege of reading the Burney manuscripts in their possession and for their permission to quote from them. I am very grateful to Dr. Gordan and to the librarians and cataloguers in the Berg Collection, Miss Adelaide Smith, Miss Beatrice Landskroner, and Mrs. Charles Szladits for their unfailing hospitality and for all the help they accorded through many onerous but pleasant months of reading in the Berg treasury room.

It gives me great pleasure to remember Miss Ann Julia Wauchope of Bushey Heath, Hertfordshire, the great-granddaughter of Charlotte Barrett, who in the late summer and autumn of 1951 allowed me to read through the Barrett Collection of Burney Papers then in her possession and to take great sections of it to London to read and copy. I am grateful to her for allowing the archive to be microfilmed and for many pleasant hours in a library rich in Burneyana—first editions, portraits, miniatures, family mementoes, and a voluminous store of very valuable manuscripts. I owe much to her gentle and modest but unrivalled knowledge of Burney matters and to her own careful work on some of the problems in the manuscripts. Such visits were the privilege of a lifetime.

My book owes much to the generosity of Mr. James M. Osborn of Yale University, who has given me permission to read and to quote from his acquisitions of Burney manuscripts. I wish to thank him and Mrs. Osborn for their friendly hospitality and for luxurious weeks of reading in their delightful home.

I am grateful to the late Mrs. Atherton Cumming and to her daughter Miss Elmer Cumming of St. Albans, Hertfordshire, for a pleasant day's reading in a grangerized edition of *Diary and Letters of Madame d'Arblay* and to the present owner, John R. G. Comyn, Esquire, for permission to quote from the Burney–Lowndes correspondence there; to the late Miss Mabel Burney and to her sister Miss Gertrude Burney for the opportunity to see a group of Burney portraits; to Mr. and Mrs. William Woods of Corfe Castle, Dorset, for their hospitality, helpful information, and permission to read transcripts that they had made of Burney letters; to Mr. Richard Border of Pulborough, Sussex, for making transcripts of Burney letters in his collection; and to Mr. John Owen Ward for transcripts of Pacchierotti's letters to Fanny Burney, also in Mr. Border's possession. Many owners of private collections have helped enormously by their obliging hospitality, permission to read and to quote from manuscript material, and their promptness in replying to troublesome letters and requests: Dr. and Mrs. Percy A. Scholes of Oxford; Mr. and Mrs. Donald F. Hyde of Somerville, New Jersey; Miss Stella M. Alleyne of Cuckfield, Sussex; the late Canon d'Arblay Burney, Harworth Vicarage, Doncaster; Professor Frederick W. Hilles, Chairman of the Department of English at Yale University; Mr. Brooks Shepard, Librarian of the School of Music at Yale University, and Mr. John Sparrow, Warden of All Souls College, Oxford.

For kindness to a wandering researcher, promptness in replying to requests for information, and for permission to quote from manuscripts, I wish most particularly to thank the Keepers of Manuscripts in the John Rylands Library, Manchester, and the Pierpont Morgan Library, New York City. Useful lists of letters were instantly supplied by the Manuscripts Division of the Henry E. Huntington Library, California;

the Folger Library, Washington; the Boston Public Library; Princeton University Library; and the Cambridge University Library. Help or advice of various kinds was accorded by Dr. C. E. Wright, the Department of Manuscripts, the British Museum; Dr. Richard Hunt of the Bodleian Library, Oxford; J. M. G. Blakiston, Esq., Librarian at the College, Winchester; Mr. Herman W. Liebert, Research Assistant, and Mr. Robert F. Metzdorf, Curator of Manuscripts, Yale University Library; and by Mr. H. E. Bocking, Curator of the King's Lynn Borough Museum. Mr. Kenneth M. Hamilton, M.A., Deputy Keeper and Assistant Librarian of the Public Library, Armagh, kindly extended the library hours during my hurried visit there in 1951. The Librarians of the British Museum were put to extra trouble in the summer of 1954 in counting over the partly catalogued and unmounted papers of the Barrett Collection. Her Majesty's Librarian Sir Owen Morshead has kindly answered questions about Windsor Castle and the royal *entourage* of 1785–91. I am delightfully indebted to him for a memorable tour of the Castle in 1951 and the most authoritative lecture possible on what it was like in Fanny Burney's time.

I acknowledge levies on the scholarly proficiencies of A. E. Malloch, Slava Klima, Stephen Porter, Curtis Cecil, Alan Heuser, S. E. Sprott, Professors Raymond Klibansky, Henry Alexander, and R. S. Walker.

For aid in establishing biographical facts and dates not supplied by the manuscripts I am much indebted to the custodians of records (including parish records and county archives) who gave advice, conducted searches, or answered troublesome requests for information: the College of Arms; Miss Katharine M. Longley, B.A., Assistant Archivist, Surrey Record Office, Kingston-upon-Thames; the Hon. Secretaries of the Catholic Record Society, the Society of Genealogists, and the Huguenot Society of London; the librarians of the Public Record Office; Dr. A. E. J. Hollaender, Archivist of the Guildhall Library, London; Mr. D. T. Piper, M.A., Assistant Keeper of Manuscripts, and Mrs. B. Isherwood Kay, Archivist and Librarian, the National Portrait Gallery; Mr. Philip Grierson, M.A., F.S.A., Librarian at Gonville and Caius College; Mr. John H. Harvey, F.S.A., F.R.S.L.; Mr. G. F. Osborn; Mr. Leslie Hall; Mr. A. L. Dorer; Mr. W. Le Hardy, M.S., F.S.A.;

Mr. H. Oswald Brown, LL.B.; Mr. D. E. Howell James, LL.B.; the Rev. Canon R. L. Whytehead; the Rev. Canon A. W. Douglas; the Rev. W. A. Aitken; the Rev. Norman de Langdale; and the Rev. F. G. Gunn. I wish particularly to thank Dr. Gwendoline Leigh for her generous interest in the various problems and her persevering and successful searches in the records.

I am indebted to Mrs. F. W. Emus for many pleasant mornings in the house, garden, and grounds of 'The Hermitage', Great Bookham, Surrey, where the d'Arblays once lived; to Dr. Marie Stopes for an afternoon in the famous 'picture room' in Norbury Park, Dorking; to Mr. C. C. Fagg for a visit to Juniper Hall, Mickleham, Surrey; and to Messrs. P. M. Goodchild and Son for a view of the house once occupied by Dr. Burney and his family in the High Street, King's Lynn.

Besides the kindnesses, indulgences, and advantages mentioned, I have still others to record in the preparation of the manuscript, an eighteenth-century study that owes its existence directly or indirectly to Professor George Sherburn, to whom it is most gratefully and respectfully dedicated. Any merit it may have is owing to his sage counsel; all its faults arise from what he disapproves.

I am grateful for the knowledgeable and energetic advice of Professor James Lowry Clifford of Columbia University, who among the manifold cares of his eighteenth-century kingdom has found time to read chapters concerning Dr. Johnson and Mrs. Thrale–Piozzi; to Professor Hélène Larivière of McGill University for reading the chapters set in Paris and Brussels; to Sir Owen Morshead for his kind concern about the chapters on Windsor and Kew; and to Miss Ellen Thibaudeau, M.A., for really herculean labours on matters stylistic and textual, and on proof-reading.

Finally I must thank my mother, who has patiently borne with the long process, learning, as she said, 'more about Fanny Burney than [she] had intended'.

CONTENTS

LIST OF PLATES

ABBREVIATIONS

THE following libraries and manuscript collections are cited in the footnotes in brief form:

A.L.S. (Armagh)	indicates a reference to the Burney MSS. in the Public Library, Armagh, Ireland;
A.L.S. (Barrett)	to the Barrett Collection of Burney Papers in the British Museum (Egerton 3690–708);
A.L.S. (Berg)	to the Burney MSS. in the Henry W. and Albert A. Berg Collection of the New York Public Library;
A.L.S. (Bodleian)	to the Burney MSS. in the Bodleian Library, Oxford;
A.L.S. (BM)	to the Burney correspondence in the British Museum other than that included in the Barrett Collection of Burney Papers;
A.L.S. (JRL)	to the Burney MSS. in the John Rylands Library, Manchester;
A.L.S. (Osborn)	to the Burney MSS. in the Collections of Mr. James M. Osborn of Yale University;
A.L.S. (PML)	to the Burney MSS. in the Pierpont Morgan Library, New York.

The following printed books are cited in the footnotes in brief form:

Burford Papers	refers to *Burford Papers, being Letters of Samuel Crisp to his Sister at Burford . . .* , ed. William Holden Hutton (1905).
Clifford	refers to Professor James Lowry Clifford, *Hester Lynch Piozzi (Mrs. Thrale)* (Oxford, 1941).
Diary	The reference is to *Diary and Letters of Madame d'Arblay*, ed. Charlotte Barrett (7 vols., 1842–6). Among several succeeding editions that by Austin Dobson (6 vols., 1904–5) is here cited.
ED	refers to *The Early Diary of Frances Burney, 1768–1778, with a Selection from her Correspondence and from the Journals of her Sisters Susan and Charlotte Burney*, ed. Annie Raine Ellis (2 vols., 1889). The edition here cited is that reprinted by Bell (2 vols., 1913).
Manwaring	refers to G. E. Manwaring, *My Friend the Admiral, the Life, Letters, and Journals of Rear-Admiral James Burney, F.R.S.* (1931).

Memoirs   refers to *Memoirs of Doctor Burney, arranged from his own Manuscripts, from Family Papers, and from Personal Recollections* by his daughter, Madame d'Arblay (3 vols., 1832).

QL   refers to *The Queeney Letters, being letters addressed to Hester Maria Thrale by Doctor Johnson, Fanny Burney, and Mrs. Thrale–Piozzi*, ed. the Marquis of Lansdowne (New York, 1934).

Scholes   refers to Dr. Percy A. Scholes, *The Great Doctor Burney* (2 vols., 1948).

Sermoneta   refers to the Duchess of Sermoneta, *The Locks of Norbury, the story of a remarkable family in the XVIIIth and XIXth centuries* (1940).

Thraliana   *Thraliana, the Diary of Mrs. Hester Lynch Thrale (later Mrs. Piozzi), 1776–1809,* ed. Katharine C. Balderston (2 vols., 1942).

Members of the Burney family are referred to by initials:

AA   The Reverend Alexander Charles Louis d'Arblay (1794–1837).

CAB
or
CBF   Clement Francis and, widowed in 1792, in 1798 married Captain
or
CBFB Ralph Broome.

Charlotte Ann Burney (1761–1838), who in 1786 married

CB   Charles Burney (Mus.Doc.), 1726–1814.

CB, Jr.   Charles Burney (D.D.), 1757–1817.

CF   Clement Robert Francis, 1792–1829.

CPB   Charles Parr Burney (D.D.), 1785–1864.

EB
or
EBB   Charles Rousseau Burney.

Esther Burney (1749–1832), who in 1770 married her cousin

FB
or
FBA   General Alexandre Jean Baptiste Comte Piochard d'Arblay.

Frances Burney (1752–1840), who in 1793 married Lieutenant-

HLT
or
HLTP Thrale and, in 1784, Gabriel Piozzi.

Hester Lynch Salusbury (1750–1822), who in 1763 married Henry

JB   James Burney, Rear-Admiral, F.R.S. (1750–1821).

M. d'A   M. Alexandre d'Arblay (1754–1818), as above.

MF   Marianne Francis, 1790–1832.

SEB
or
SBP   Captain Molesworth Phillips.

Susanna Elizabeth Burney (1755–1800), who in 1782 married

SHB   Sarah Harriet Burney, 1772–1844.

I

'THE OLD LADY'

(1752–1767)

I always loved my own children & my Brothers the better for
their love to each other, as the want of brotherly love & affection have been regarded as sure marks of a bad heart from the
Time of Cain to the present writing.
DR. BURNEY to his daughter, Charlotte.[1]

FANNY BURNEY began her career as a diarist and journalist
when she was very young, for the young Burneys began to
keep diaries and write journal-letters as soon, seemingly,
as they could write at all, certainly in their early teens. As this
practice was by no means approved by their elders it had to be
pursued fugitively, and much of the early scribbling was consigned by command, or by caution, to the flames. The first
recorded bonfire of Burney manuscripts was that which blazed
in the paved play-court of Dr. Burney's house in Poland Street,
London, on June 13, 1767, when on her fifteenth birthday
Fanny obediently burned her novel 'Caroline Evelyn' along with
'Elegies, Odes, Plays, Songs, Stories, Farces,—nay, Tragedies
and Epic Poems'—all the writings of her first fifteen years.[2] If
one may judge from later journals this holocaust was something
of a loss to biographers. Very serious and significant events in
the life of this child and of other children in the house had
occurred before then, but for that history one must turn to other
records, the best of which seems to be Dr. Burney's own Memoirs.[3]

Pertinent fragments of these Memoirs go back to eight years
before Fanny's birth, the London years of 1744–8, when the
young Charles Burney of Shrewsbury, lately come from Chester
with the composer Arne, lived in the Arne household in Great
Queen Street.[4] His work with Dr. Arne took him to the London

---

[1] A.L.S. (Barrett) from CB to CBF, 8 Dec. 1790.
[2] *Memoirs*, ii. 121–71. Also A.L. (Berg) from FBA to EBB, 1 July 1815.
[3] About 120 fragments (Berg) and 6 (Osborn) cut from the 12 original *cahiers*
of the Memoirs together with the mutilated remains (Osborn) of one of the *cahiers*
(*c.* 23 pp.). Also fragments (Barrett) and *c.* 6 fragments (BM), Add. MS. 48345.
[4] *Memoirs*, i. 1–10; Scholes, i. 1–34.

B

pleasure-gardens, including Vauxhall, and to Drury Lane, where he played in the band (of which his master was the leader) at a time when there or in Covent Garden Garrick was playing Hotspur, Quin, Falstaff. In the green-room and music-room the young man witnessed scenes scarcely less amusing and memorable than those on the stage: Garrick's imitations and antics, and the recurrent altercations between Dr. Arne and the singer Mrs. Clive, who, singing out of tune and time, insisted on placing the blame on the orchestra. Finally the irascible leader, unable to bear more, undertook to administer a spanking, emerging from the encounter, to the glee of his apprentice, without a wig, his face all bloody with scratches, and his long point ruffles torn and dangling over his nails. 'It may seem strange & ungrateful', Dr. Burney added in his eighties, 'not to have spoken with more respect and regard of my master Arne, than I have hitherto done, but I had too much reason to complain of his selfishness.'[1]

Even before 1748, however, when the contract with Arne was formally broken, young Burney had been employed for months at a time by Fulke Greville, who, in search of a musician 'fit company for a gentleman', used to reimburse the master liberally for the loan.

Though at this time partly ruined at the gaming-tables and the race-ground at Newmarket, Fulke Greville was still, by birth, education, fortune, and figure, a somewhat dazzling personage. Nothing in the 'buckish scales of the day', said Madame d'Arblay, could compete with his grandeur or the fame he had acquired as 'the best and most graceful gentleman'.[2] In the autumn and winter of 1747–8 he engaged Burney's services at Bath, where the young musician soon gained great credit with Greville's friends, the Earl of Holdernesse, Lord Cowper, and others, by playing Scarlatti. He had an opportunity to see the humours of deep play at hazard and as many as 1,000 guineas at a time on the tables. He saw the famous Henry St. John, Viscount Bolingbroke, carried early in the morning in a chair to take the waters, and Beau Nash, the tyrannical Master of Ceremonies, with his white hat under his arm and his shirt open on the coldest day of winter.[1]

Even more profitable than the interval at Bath were the long

[1] See p. 1, n. 3.   [2] *Memoirs*, i. 11–146.

days at Greville's family seat, Wilbury House, in Wiltshire.
Here on loan in the autumn of 1747 the young musician met
Mr. Samuel Crisp,

a man of infinite taste in all the fine arts, an excellent scholar, &
who having resided many years in Italy, & being possessed of a fine
tenor voice, sung in as good taste as any professed opera singer.[1]

Mr. Crisp had brought from Italy 'the first large pianoforte that
was ever constructed, even at Rome' but had parted with it on
the persuasion of Mr. Greville (and 100 guineas).[1] Dr. Burney
remembered that its touch was very imperfect, but that slow
pieces like the 'Dead March' in *Saul* and pathetic strains from
the Italian operas could be executed upon it with 'a magnificent
and new effect'. In the evenings he gained 'considerable credit'
in showing it off to an accomplished company—the Duke of
Hamilton, the Duchess of Queensberry, Lord Talbot, and Mr.
Crisp. There was opportunity in the mornings for 'tranquil
study & practice', and Mr. Crisp, who preferred music to the
joys of the hunt, also remained indoors, probably then, as later
with the Doctor's children, mingling instruction with arch and
informed comment.[1]

　These apprenticeships and their associations led to at least
four friendships later extended to the Doctor's children: the
lifelong friendship of Lady Crewe, Fulke Greville's daughter;
that of Garrick, the idol of their early years; that of the Earl of
Holdernesse, under whose patronage young Charles was to
enter the Charterhouse; and that of Mr. Crisp, whose influence,
over Fanny especially, was incalculable.

　In September, 1748, the indentures binding Burney to Dr.
Arne—articles that had still three years to run—were transferred
with all their limiting and binding clauses to Mr. Greville. 'He had
been so accustomed to have me with him', Dr. Burney recorded,

that he wished to appropriate me to himself entirely, by buying off
the remaining three years of my engagement; and this being proposed & negotiated at a period when Dr. Arne was out of cash, the
transfer of my Indenture was concluded at Michaelmas, this year for
£300: when I was entirely domesticated with Mr Greville, and
accountable to him alone for my time.[1]

If, as Madame d'Arblay suggests, there were clauses forbidding

[1] See p. 1, n. 3.

marriage in articles that had three years to run and if it is understood that already (by the autumn of 1748) young Burney had
not only met the girl of his desires ('I always . . . had an ardent
passion for her person')[1] but was bound to her by honour in
love, then one will be prepared for the difficulties to follow. Up
to this time the apprentice had not chafed in his dependence:
'The desire of independence to his fortune was excited by the
loss of it to his heart.'[1] There were 'secret conflicts' between the
'nameless species of obligation to Mr. Greville' (probably, at
the very least, a gentleman's agreement to abide by the indentures
purchased for their remaining term of three years) and a new
and—as we now know—very urgent obligation that made it
difficult to wait that term.

The cause of all these tumults was Esther Sleepe of the parish
of St. Mary le Bowe, whom Burney had met at a dance at his
brother's house in Fetter Lane. Esther Sleepe was very lovely,
as a miniature of her by Gervase Spencer still witnesses, but she
was not more lovely, we are repeatedly told, than she was intelligent and good. The daughter of a James Sleepe of Foster
Lane,[2] Esther had on the Sleepe side 'nothing to boast from
parental dignity, parental opulence, nor—strange, and stranger
yet to tell—parental worth'.[1] Such was Madame d'Arblay's
honest admission on the matter. The male line of this Sleepe
family was extinct before 1832,[1] but its humble status is perhaps
indicated by that of the impecunious, illiterate, but sweet-
natured man-of-all-work, James Sleepe (possibly a son of the
above James), who lived for some twenty years as a dependant
in one or another of the Burney households until his death
about 1794. Throughout the lifetime of Fanny Burney, James
and his indigent daughters, Esther and Frances, who lived for
a time at No. 38 Little Britain near Aldersgate Street, were the
objects of frequent charities from the Burneys.[3]

[1] See p. 2, n. 2.
[2] Information as given by the Rev. Richard Allen Burney, Rector of Rimpton
(son of Charles Rousseau and Esther Burney Burney, grandson of Dr. Burney), in
an application to the College of Arms for Arms as granted on 8 Aug. 1807 (Grants
24, 253).
[3] According to references in A.L.S. (Barrett) from CBFB to FBA, 5 July 1791,
and A.L.S. (JRL) from FBA to JB, 25 Apr. 1794, this James Sleepe was born in
1714 and died in 1794. See also Manwaring, p. 286, where James Burney the
Admiral (1750–1821) refers to this Hetty and Fanny Sleepe as his cousins, and
A.L.S. (Osborn) from CB, Jr., to CPB, 4 Jan. 1807.

In 1747 Esther Sleepe was twenty-four years old,[1] Charles
Burney, twenty-one, and it will scarcely be expected that prudential motives could triumph over so much beauty, love, and
such high spirits. On her mother's side, moreover, Esther was
descended from admirable Huguenot stock and had seemed to
inherit none of the deplorable qualities to be seen in her worthless father. From her maternal grandfather, a M. Dubois who
had come to England at the Revocation of the Edict of Nantes,
she had learned French and very likely inherited the bright
intelligence that along with her beauty had served to captivate
young Burney. An extant letter from a second admirer preserves
still other tributes to her 'numberless graces & perfections' and
'Engaging Person & behaviour'.[2] Esther's mother, a Roman
Catholic, was the beloved maternal grandmother of the early
diaries whom Fanny later compared to Mrs. Delany as 'a pattern of a perfect fine lady, a real fine lady, of other days'.
'Benevolence, softness, Piety & Gentleness are all resident in her
Face.'[3] Susan also spoke of the mildness, sweetness, and humility,
'pictured in the countenance of our beloved Grandmother
Sleepe'.[4] The mysteriously reprehensible Mr. Sleepe (Esther's
father) was not, in short, 'more wanting in goodness, probity,
and conduct' than her mother was 'perfect in all'.[5] Some part
at least of the gentle training that Mrs. Sleepe gave her daughter was recorded, dutifully and delicately stitched in a sampler
(now over 200 years old),[6] signed in cross-stitch,

Esther Sleepe is my name and in my youth wrought the same
& by this work you may plainly see what care my parents took of me.
November the Last in the year 1732.

The piece, now the colour of the ivory keys of an old keyboard,
is covered with aphorisms in variegated shades.

Let not the flesh seduce thy soul but remember these things well
and learn to spell.

[1] See Note A, p. 492.
[2] A.L.S. (Osborn) from J. Pitt to Esther Sleepe Burney, [c. 1750].
[3] Diary, v. 94; Memoirs, ii. 302; and Diary MSS. (Berg), pp. 1771–3.
[4] Journal (Barrett), July 1789.
[5] See p. 2, n. 2.
[6] In the possession of Miss Ann Julia Wauchope, the great-granddaughter of
Charlotte Francis Barrett to whom Madame d'Arblay's voluminous papers were
willed.

Whatever the methods of 'improvement', the results were good. In 1748 Esther Sleepe, according to the Journal of the Worcester Burneys, was 'a Lady of great strength of mind, possessing a taste for literature, with an engaging manner, & much beauty'.[1]

Charles, who had his own way to make in the world, unaided except by such a patron as Fulke Greville, could hardly expect that proud patron to yield up the best years of the contract to a disadvantageous alliance with the humble Sleepes. Both in 1748 and 1749, apparently because of the indentures to Greville, it was impossible for the lovers to marry without giving offence. In 1749, however, marriage became necessary. It took place in that year, tardily, and not in 1748 as has been supposed. It is recorded under the date June 25, 1749, in the registers of the notorious St. George's Chapel, Hyde Park Corner, where so many of the clandestine marriages of the time took place.

> Charles Burney & Esther Sleep, of St Mary le Bow, London.

A child, Esther, had been born in the previous month, May, 1749 (for the laws of nature and arithmetic will admit of no other year).[2] The young couple settled down with their infant daughter in the City. It is possible that the initial error that hastened the marriage may have influenced Burney through later years to protect his own daughters within compensating bounds of rigorous propriety—in short, somehow to conquer original sin. Whatever the reasons, Burney was eventually to be the kind of father who could not with any ease of mind allow a daughter under forty or fifty to go unchaperoned in a stage-coach.

Finally married, the young man directed his energies to a career in the City as a musician and teacher of music. The family increased in size: James, later Admiral Burney, was born on June 13, 1750, and a son, Charles, on June 3, 1751.[3] All was

---

[1] *Memoranda of the Burney Family, 1603–1845* or *The Journal of the Worcester Burneys* (98 pp. in typescript), the possession of Dr. Percy A. Scholes, to whom I am indebted for a transcript.

[2] The *month* is given in A.L.S. (Berg) from FBA to EBB, 21 June 1819, and in the reply (Barrett), 19 July 1819. The *year* is suggested as that preceding 13 June 1750, when James Burney was born. See also Scholes, i. 57 n.

[3] See the registers (Harleian) of St. Dionis's Backchurch, London, and the MSS. registers of St. James's Church, Piccadilly, and of St. Margaret's and the Chapel of St. Nicholas, King's Lynn.

going well until in 1751 the father succumbed to a fever that left in its wake consumptive symptoms for which the doctor prescribed change of air. Happily the post of organist at St. Margaret's Church in King's Lynn was then open and, through the influence of Sir John Turner, Burney secured the post. In the winter of 1751–2 the young musician went to King's Lynn, where he was to remain about nine years. The family soon followed and settled in a house called St. Augustine's in Chapel Street, later removing to another in High Street. In one of these houses, probably in the former, on June 13, 1752, Frances Burney was born. On July 7 she was baptized in the fisherman's church nearby, the Chapel of St. Nicholas.[1]

There were already three children in the house, aged three, and two, and one, though the baby Charles was buried in the parish of St. Nicholas on October 12, 1752, when Fanny was only four months old. The burial of a second Charles, born presumably in 1753, was recorded on January 5, 1754. Susanna Elizabeth came next (January 7, 1755), and, about two years later (December 4, 1757), the third Charles, who lived to fair renown in Greek scholarship. Before the family left Lynn an eighth child, Henry Edward, relinquished a brief hold on life and was buried in May, 1760.[1] The ninth, Charlotte Ann, was born on November 4, 1761, after the family had returned to London.[1] In those days it was not far sometimes from the cradle to the grave; not long between birth and death. In twelve years Esther Sleepe Burney had borne nine children and buried three, and it is not surprising that even the Norfolk air that had cured and invigorated her husband should have failed to sustain her through so rapid a series of events and that she in turn should have shown consumptive symptoms.

Though the Burney children were very young in this period, some of the associations formed by their parents in King's Lynn were to impinge closely on their lives and to become part of their conditioning destiny.

There was, first of all, Miss Dorothy Young, whose kind arms welcomed Fanny into the world and who long retained great influence over that little girl. Miss Young was unfortunately

---

[1] See p. 6, n. 3.

deformed in person, but possessed of a mind 'the seat of every virtue', of unconquerable patience, and of feelings

so sensitive, that tears started into her eyes at every thing she either saw or heard of mortal sufferings, or of mortal unkindness—to any human creature but herself.[1]

A second friend, affording an antithesis to the first in appearance and, as it later proved, in disposition, was the wife of a wine- or corn-merchant of considerable fortune, Mrs. Stephen Allen, 'the most celebrated beauty of Lynn', who was later to become Dr. Burney's second wife.

Her beauty was high, commanding, and truly uncommon: and her understanding bore the same description. She had wit at will; spirits the most vivacious and entertaining; and, from a passionate fondness for reading, she had collected stores of knowledge which she was always able, and 'nothing loath' to display.[1]

She had found a model, Dr. Burney later observed, in the 'virtue & Intellectual power' of his first wife,[2] for Esther Sleepe Burney, he recalled in 1796, was 'not only possessed of beauty in form & feature, but of a heart & intellects as perfect, perhaps, as nature ever bestowed on a female in private life'.[3]

These were days of 'improvement'. Mrs. Allen, Miss Young, and the Burneys formed the nucleus of 'a bookish little coterie' that met every week to read current works like the *Ramblers*. At home the Burneys read history, voyages, poetry, and 'as far as Chambers' Dictionary, the Philosophical Transactions, and the French Encyclopedia'.[1] Fanny could remember how her lovely mother with the 'masculine understanding' began to form her children's taste for reading, how she 'delighted to find time, amidst all her cares' to guide them to the best authors, how she read and commented on passages to be learned by heart. 'I perfectly recollect,' she wrote at seventy to her sister Esther,

child as I was, and never of the party, this part of your education. . . . I recollect, also, your spouting passages from Pope, that I learned from hearing you recite them before—many *years* before I read them myself.[4]

---

[1] See p. 2, n. 2.   [2] See p. 1, n. 3.
[3] Draft of A.L.S. (Osborn) from CB to Ralph Griffiths, 2 Nov. 1796.
[4] *Diary*, vi. 400–2.

James's genius was for mathematics, and, being a boy, he was sent to the Lynn Grammar School, where for a few years he studied under the famous Eugene Aram, known from Thomas Hood's poem and Bulwer-Lytton's novel. Aram, having murdered a shoemaker for a trifling property some ten or twelve years previously, often dilated and discoursed most fearsomely, as James afterwards used to tell, on murder. The crime was detected and Aram brought to justice in 1759, though unfortunately for the object-lesson it was night, and the boys presumably asleep, when he was led away in the cold and fog with 'gyves upon his wrist'. After school hours or on holidays, no doubt, the boys ran about the old town, sometimes to the wharves where the fishing-boats were moored, or past the Hanseatic warehouses and down the narrow paved lanes to the quays along the Ouse. Though the heavy wine-trade with Flanders belonged to the previous century, there were still activities along the river front, ships with rigging to be climbed, and merchantmen and sailors to be admired. It must be safe to assume that as the ships stood out high and bold on the river they led the long, long thoughts and aspirations of boys like James Burney and George Vancouver to the sea. Whenever James had any money, he ran to the bookstall, as his father told long after, for a penny's worth of reading in *Roderick Random*.[1] All in all it was not long before Burney was telling influential friends in high places that he had a son 'destined for the sea'. A berth was soon found on the man-of-war the *Princess Amelia*, 'where there was a regular school for younkers to pursue their naval studies and go on wth their education'.[1] James was then ten years old, a 'younker' indeed, but if school there must be, what active and intrepid boy brought up by the sea would not like a school on board a man-o'-war?

And what of Fanny and her first eight years in King's Lynn? She was not the oldest and did not require as yet much attention for her education, though unobserved she listened, and memorized Esther's lessons from beginning to end. She was to have a most extraordinary memory and already she was unobtrusively, attentively, memorizing by ear. 'She was wholly unnoticed in the nursery', her father said, 'for any talents, or quickness of study.'

[1] See p. 1, n. 3.

Indeed, at eight years old she did not know her letters; and her brother, the tar, who in his boyhood had a natural genius for hoaxing, used to pretend to teach her to read; and gave her a book topsy-turvy, which he said she never found out![1]

She was not among the youngest, or delicate like Susan, requiring much physical attention. She was in the middle, and led, one may believe, a happy life in an unthwarted and as yet undirected development of her own. Fanny's turn was always to come.

Meanwhile, as Dr. Armstrong had predicted, the Norfolk air and long rides to pupils in the great houses round about had restored Mr. Burney's health and 'fixed his constitution'. With the responsibility he had begun to feel for his children and their 'future establishment', he was thinking again of London and scarcely needed, perhaps, letters like that of Mr. Crisp about the folly of planting his youth, genius, hopes, and fortunes against a north wall. Was not London

the centre of riches, luxury, taste, pride, extravagance,—all that ingenuity is to fatten upon? Take, then, your spare person, your pretty mate, and your brats, to that propitious mart, and, 'Seize the glorious, golden opportunity'.[2]

In 1760, then, Mr. Burney gave up his post at King's Lynn, but not without some regret.[3] London might rob him of quiet evenings and 'domestic converse', and in nine years he had made congenial friends, among them notably the 'scientific' Mr. William Bewley of Great Massingham.

In 1760, however, the die was cast. A house was found in Poland Street, then a fashionable neighbourhood, and very soon Mr. Burney had 'pupils of rank, wealth, and talents' sufficient to fill every hour of the day and, incidentally, his purse. He renewed his associations with the Grevilles and people he had met in former times at Wilbury House, and he could entertain his Norfolk friends, Lords Orford, Eglinton, and March, General Lord Townshend, and others, when they came to London.[2] Mrs. Burney shared her husband's 'uncommon powers of pleasing'. 'I am thoroughly convinced she was fitted for any situation, either exalted or humble, which this life can furnish.'[2] Her ill health, however, marred the new life that seemed

[1] See p. 1, n. 2.   [2] See p. 2, n. 2.
    [3] A.L.S. (BM) from CB to Arthur Young, 1 Aug. 1786.

auspicious both socially and professionally. She had been declining for more than a year, and the birth of the ninth child,
Charlotte Ann, may have been the final exaction on her strength.
Although there had been a temporary improvement from the
waters of the Bristol Hotwells, there was a sudden relapse and
on September 27, 1762, she died.[1]

During the last painful week of her illness, the children,
Frances, Susan, and Charles (then aged ten, seven, and four),
were sent to Mrs. Sheeles's boarding-school in Queen Square,
to be out of the way. Upon the arrival of the sad news the
intensity of Frances's grief was so great that Mrs. Sheeles afterwards declared 'that of the Hundred children she had had the
care of, she never saw such affliction in one before—that [Fanny]
would take no comfort—& was almost killed with crying'.[2]
Fanny never forgot the last melancholy week of September,
1762. Long afterwards she remembered a Mrs. Quinn, as a girl
at school,

chattring & playing with me by every opportunity one day:—&,
on the next, when I had been dejected by some hints of the illness
of my dear mother, her much amazing me, by bluffly saying 'lord,
how dull you are today! You were very agreeable yesterday,—but
if I'd known you'd have grown so stupid, I should have left you to
yourself.'[3]

She had been taught, probably by her Roman Catholic grandmother, to pray for the souls of the dead, and for a long time
the little girl continued to pray for her mother and that she
might be good enough to join her.[3]

When the funeral was over the young widower brought his
young family of six home to Poland Street. For a while he
avoided friends who might recall his loss too poignantly. He
taught music all the day and in the evenings he translated
Italian, choosing Dante as an author whom he had not read in
former happier times with his wife. He was still only thirty-six
years old, with a bright musical, literary, and social career all
before him. Recovering his zest for life, he was to express his
devotion to his wife's memory in the extraordinarily gay and
tender care he took of their children. He always thought, very

---

[1] This date is given by Dr. Burney in his Memoirs (Berg).
[2] Diary MSS. (Berg), suppressed pages, box ii; see also ED, 1. xlv–xlvi.
[3] A.L. (Berg) from FBA to CB, 4 Mar. 1799; A.L. (Berg) to EBB, 18 May 1819.

humbly, that he could not take her place in 'forming their minds', but his tender solicitude for their health and welfare was maternal as well as fatherly, and resulted in and easily accounted for their devotion to him. Even when they were grown up, and far away from home and feeling ill, or forsaken, or betrayed, they imagined that if they could once feel his commiserating arms and pitying eyes they would be well again.

The family was amply provided, besides, with kindly relatives. Dr. Burney's sisters, the amiable Aunt Becky and Aunt Ann (or Nanny) of the early diaries, were no doubt as helpful in infantile crises as later in teen-aged dilemmas. Mrs. Burney, Dr. Burney's mother, was also in London, if not earlier than 1764, then certainly in that year, and the house she shared with her daughters in York Place, Covent Garden, became very popular with the young Burneys for tea in the evenings. Fanny was even more attached as a little girl to her maternal grandmother, sometimes invoked later in comparisons with Mrs. Delany: 'I do not know whether you ever saw my darling Grandmother . . . but I think you once did: Imagine her, then, before you, with all the polish of high life & Education, & you will *see* Mrs. Delany as well as read her words.'[1] Her grandmother's life was like Mrs. Delany's, 'a system of Goodness, & an overflowing of Kindness!'[1] Like her, she belonged to 'the true old school of innate politeness and true humility of mind'. 'It is that true & lovely species of Humility', said Susan, 'that so far from debasing *exalts* the character of the few that possess it.'[2] Probably the 'rectitude' or 'straightforward morality' that the Doctor was so happy to remark in Fanny and Susan especially—the natural probity 'that wanted no teaching'—stemmed in great part from this source and influence and memory.

Among the friends who visited Dr. Burney 'as soon after his heart-breaking loss as he could admit any friends to his sight' was the great Garrick. Such were Garrick's spirits in these years that he could put off tragedy and put on comedy like a cloak. As soon as the young Burneys were old enough to go to the theatre—and that seemed to be from the age of three or four—he frequently offered them his wife's box at Drury Lane, and before they could read they saw him on the stage as Lear, Hamlet, Bayes, and Abel Drugger. He used to call at Poland

[1] See p. 5, n. 3.   [2] See p. 5, n. 4.

Street in the morning, and to the delight of the children he brought his spaniel Phil along and stopped to play with them whether their father was at home or not. Sometimes for their amusement he would represent lofty, expansive, bombastic characters, and then transform himself into little, mean, sneaking, cringing ones like Abel Drugger.[1] Sometimes he took off 'the old puppet show Punch, placing himself against a wall, seeming to speak through a comb, & to be moved by wires'.[2] Garrick seemed to think the laughter of children worth his best comic efforts, and he was, as they rightly judged, the most comic and lively mimic in the world. In the early diaries Charlotte was his Dumpling Queen or Piety in Pattens; Charles, Cherry Nose because of the brightness of his complexion; and the spaniel, Slobber Chops, all tenderness without ideas! 'Nobody', Dr. Burney observed, 'talked such pretty nonsense, as our great Roscius, to children & lap-dogs',[2] and the children in turn worshipped even 'the shadow of his shoe-tie'.[1] He was an idol, and his influence is not difficult to trace or imagine. He encouraged them in their enjoyment of the ridiculous and taught them the art of mimicry as based on a careful observation of *nature*. Before they could read they acted over parts they had seen him play; when they could read, they got parts with the utmost facility for their private theatricals, the company of players augmented in lively fashion by their talented cousins, the Worcester Burneys. Their interest in drama and the standards of acting that they formed from Garrick's performances lasted their lives long.

In all this the sage and serious child Fanny was the aptest pupil. Even in old age she could illustrate and enliven social anecdotes with comical and well-practised talents for mimicry. Her father remembered that she had

a great deal of invention and humour in her childish sports; and used, after having seen a play in Mrs. Garrick's box, to take the actors off, and compose speeches for their characters; for she could not read them. But in company, or before strangers, she was silent, backward, and timid, even to sheepishness: and, from her shyness, had such profound gravity and composure of features, that those

---

[1] *Memoirs*, i. 165–72; ED, see index. For Charles's recollections of Garrick's 'matchless entertainment', see A.L.S. (Berg) from CB, Jr., to FBA, 18 Sept. 1817.

[2] See p. 1, n. 3.

of my friends who came often to my house, and entered into the different humours of the children, never called Fanny by any other name, from the time she had reached her eleventh year, than The Old Lady.[1]

By all accounts there was a great deal of fun and laughter among the young Burneys, for though their feelings were deep their spirits were high (that being the composition of a Burney). One of their playmates, a Miss Betsy Folcher, afterwards remembered Fanny very well: '*You* were so merry, so gay, so droll, & had such imagination in making plays, always something new, something of your own contrivance.'[2] An incident of Fanny's tenth year arising from a day's play with the children of a perruquier, who lived next door, illustrates her disposition towards both merriment and gravity, two co-existent and permanent strains in her character, as well as the power of ratiocination that made her in later years, in a manner, the head of the family. Dr. Burney told how each of the children had donned a magnificent peruke,

and danced and jumped about in a thousand antics, laughing till they screamed at their own ridiculous figures. Unfortunately, in their vagaries, one of the flaxen wigs, said by the proprietor to be worth upwards of ten guineas—in those days a price enormous—fell into a tub of water, placed for the shrubs in the little garden, and lost all its gorgon buckle, and was declared by the owner to be totally spoilt. He was extremely angry, and chid very severely his own children; when my little daughter, the old lady, then ten years of age, advancing to him, as I was informed, with great gravity and composure, sedately says; 'What signifies talking so much about an accident? The wig is wet, to be sure; and the wig was a good wig, to be sure; but its of no use to speak of it any more; because what's done can't be undone.'

Whether these stoical sentiments appeased the enraged perruquier, I know not, but the younkers were stript of their honours, and my little monkies were obliged to retreat without beat of drum, or colours flying.[1]

The wig is wet long remained a tag applicable to Burneyan disasters admitting of no remedy.

As the young family rallied a little from the blow of 1762 and grew a few years older, their father began to make plans for

---

[1] See p. 1, n. 2.   [2] FBA, *Memoranda Book for 1806* (Berg).

their education. In that year he managed to 'make interest' for
James with Colonel, afterwards General, Carey, whose foster-
son, Sir Thomas Adams, commanded a frigate, the *Boston*.[1] A
letter must have been sent to Admiral Montagu requesting a
transfer from the *Princess Amelia*, for the Admiral's letter to Dr.
Burney about 'the very ingenious good Boy' is still extant.[2] The
transfer was made. James sailed with the *Boston*, and afterwards
with the *Niger*, 'where he was rated and perfectly well treated
till Feby 1765'.[1]

In the boarding-schools for girls and in the great houses that
Dr. Burney entered as music-master he had noted that, according to the educational ideals of the day, 'learning French, for
females was absolutely necessary'.[1] Concluding from his observations that the language could best be learned in France, he
determined to send his own daughters to that country while
they were still young enough to acquire a perfect accent. He
could afford to send only two, and he chose his eldest daughter
Esther, then fifteen, and the nine-year-old Susan, whose weak
lungs, he hoped, might be benefited by the mild air of France.
There was some danger, he professed to think, that Fanny
because of her 'tender veneration' for her Roman Catholic
grandmother might easily turn to the Roman Catholic Church
if she were in favourable surroundings. It is possible also that
Esther and Susan, whose bright talents turned early to music,
may have seemed to the teacher of music more promising than
the silent shy Old Lady, the second daughter, whose talents had
not yet appeared. At the breaking up of Mrs. Sheeles's school
in June, 1764, Dr. Burney set off gaily with his two daughters,
but on June 13 he sent a long letter to the twelve-year-old
Fanny at home, telling her about the journey to Paris, 'poor
Sukey's cough', and the help that the kind Lady Clifford had
given in getting the sisters settled.[3] Esther was to remain in
Paris two years before, in the summer of 1766, her father returned to fetch her home; Susan may have remained for a year
or two longer.

Intellectually, as Madame d'Arblay points out, this first
Paris journey marked a milestone in her father's life. The change

---

[1] See p. 1, n. 3.
[2] A.L.S. (PML) from J. Montagu to CB, 16 Sept. 1762.
[3] 2 A.L. (Berg) from CB to FB, 13, 18 June 1764. See ED, i. xlvii–l.

of scene, the exciting artistic and intellectual life of the French capital, the stimulus afforded by the works of the French Encyclopedists that he brought back with him or had ordered to be sent after him as they appeared—all these acted in the study in Poland Street like a leaven. His mind, filled with literary works, stirred with literary ambitions of his own. He began with a translation of d'Alembert's *Elemens de Musique*, turned to Rousseau's musical *Dictionnaire*, and finally, with Garrick's encouragement, brought out an adaptation of *Le Devin du Village* (1766). It was probably during this time that Fanny, following along in the wake of this intellectual activity, taught herself French and made her translation, be it known, of Fontenelle. The manuscript still exists, about 130 pages of it, wrapped in a cover of creamy buff with the stately title-page, '*Entretien sur la pluralité des mondes* par Monsieur de Fontenelle Murdered into English by Frances Burney'.[1]

An event of 1763 or 1764 that must be marked large in Fanny's calendar was the first visit of Mr. Crisp to Poland Street. He was tall, handsome, elegant, kind, accomplished. He had 'bright, hazel, penetrating, yet arch eyes; an open front; a noble Roman nose'. He was 'by birth and education a gentleman, . . . in mind, manners, and habits yet more truly so'. 'His address was even courtly.' He was

profound in wisdom; sportive in wit; sound in understanding. A scholar of the highest order; a critic of the clearest acumen; possessing, with equal delicacy of discrimination, a taste for literature and for the arts; and personally excelling, as a *diletante*, both in music and painting.[2]

The Burneys never could say enough in praise of this man, this beloved 'Daddy Crisp'. Fanny came to love him more than anyone else outside her immediate family and she became to him in turn 'the dearest thing on earth'.[2] The encouragement and influence of this paternal virtuoso became a major factor in Fanny's development.

In 1747 Crisp was an affluent and affable member of the cultivated circles into which, as a musician, Burney had a sort of *entrée*. The friendship formed at Wilbury House was lasting,

---

[1] In the Berg Collection.
[2] *Memoirs*, i. 47–55, 172–84, 207–10, 315–24. Cf. Annie Raine Ellis, ED, i. xxvi–xxxviii.

PLATE I

SAMUEL CRISP

by Edward Francesco Burney

though for about sixteen years, covering Burney's marriage and residence in King's Lynn and the travels of the older man to Rome, they had seen little of each other. During this period Crisp had become embittered by his failure as a dramatist, by loss of fortune, and by increasing afflictions from gout. When he could no longer afford to entertain the gay and privileged world that flocked to the house he had fitted up at Hampton with paintings, *objets d'art*, and musical instruments, he retreated over mud roads leading across a wild common, ploughed fields, and fallow ground, not to a wild beast's lair, as Macaulay said, but to the house of his friend Christopher Hamilton, who lived in the dilapidated mansion of his fathers at Chessington near Kingston-upon-Thames in Surrey.

Hamilton, really a ruined spendthrift, welcomed paying guests, 'gentlemen of a certain age, who [had] quitted the world, and who in this chateau met only at meals, and afterwards at a game of cards'.[1] Mr. Crisp, who with the prospect of ruin crossed the wild common to join the ruined company, was, according to Dr. Burney, 'the only reader and polished man among them, who c^d amuse and instruct others'.[1] Later when the young Burneys visited Chessington Hall, it was frankly a boarding-house managed by the deceased Hamilton's sister and her niece, the ignorant but good-hearted Catharine Cooke. The boarders, a somewhat spiritless succession of decayed spinsters or lamed gentlemen, seemed to inhabit a remote multiplicity of odd-shaped rooms in the far reaches of the gables. In the later days when the house unwittingly harboured ladies of certain fame, including Mrs. Jordan, it was again visited by very distinguished persons—on one occasion, at least, by the Duke of Clarence.[2] Mr. Crisp by his tenure and status had all the weight and importance of a *capo di casa* and, while he lived, helped Mistress Hamilton to maintain the ancient dignities of the house.

To what extent he was embittered by his experience of the gay world that had flocked about him in his prosperity but could not find a way to help him in his distress is not clear. In after years he taught Fanny rather thoroughly what conduct could be expected from that Yahoo, man. For the present he

---

[1] See p. 1, n. 3.
[2] Copy of A.L. from FBA to SBP, 20 Mar. 1798, in a Letter Book (Osborn) in General d'Arblay's hand.

wished to see no living example of that Yahoo—except Dr. Burney, and to him 'alone was confided the clue for a safe route across the wild common to Chesington Hall'.[1] In 1763–4 when Dr. Burney made his first visits to Chessington he found the spacious garden a wilderness of old fruit-trees, beans, peas, flowers, and weeds, though there were still box-walks, an orchard, a dove-cote, and a 'ruined summer house with a pleasant view of Epsom, and an extensive prospect'.[2] Somewhere near was the mulberry tree around which Fanny danced when she heard that Dr. Johnson had read *Evelina*. Nearby was a small ivy-clad church in which one Burney at least was married. Chessington Hall was to become dear old 'Liberty Hall', and after 1770 there was scarcely a year in which some Burney needing change of air or an opportunity to write did not spend several months there.

Mr. Crisp's first visit to Poland Street must have been an exciting event, for there were long quiet days there in 1764–6 with Esther and Susan in Paris; Charlotte in King's Lynn; Charles, presumably, at some grammar school; Garrick on the Continent; and Dr. Burney often abroad 'either usefully or ornamentally' from seven in the morning till morning again. When the Doctor was at home he was in his study, and his delight in books new and old and his literary industry were not lost on the little mime, the Old Lady, who had formed her own system of education. She never found loneliness or leisure irksome when she, too, could read and scribble. These years are of no little importance for the development of Fanny Burney's mind. In her early teens she read a large number of books current in her day from which she imbibed the stock ethical ideas of her society, ideas that she later transposed, 'put into action', in her novels and plays in a way that not even Richardson had managed before her.

Her self-imposed curriculum included, besides the study of French, and, later, of Italian, a course of reading such as that appearing, for instance, in Lady Sarah Pennington's *An Unfortunate Mother's Advice to her Absent Daughters* (1761):

Mason on Self Knowledge	The Female Spectator
Economy of Human Life	The Rambler
Seneca's Morals	The Adventurer

[1] See p. 16, n. 2.   [2] See p. 1, n. 3.

Epictetus
Cicero's Offices
Collier's Antoninus
Hoadley's ⎫
Seed's |
Sherlock's ⎬ Sermons
Sterne's |
Fordyce's ⎭
Rollin's Belles Lettres
Nature Displayed
The Spectator
The Guardian
Rollin's Ancient History
Kennet's Antiquities of Rome
Hooke's Roman History
Hume's History of England
Robertson's History of Scotland
Milton's Poetical Works
Pope's Ethic Epistles

The World
Cicero's Familiar Letters
Pliny's Letters
Fitzosborne's Letters
Epistles for the Ladies
Freeman's Letters
Vicar of Wakefield
Telemachus
Salmon's Geographical Grammar
Potter's Antiquities of Greece
Pope's Homer
Thompson's Works
Young's Works
Mrs. Rowe's Works
Langhorne's Works
Moore's Fables for the Female Sex
Tales of the Genii
Cotton's Visions
Dodsley's Collection of Poems

As the commonplace book that can be extracted from Fanny's early diaries indicates, she had conscientiously read almost everything on such lists and much besides. The aim of these lists was *Instruction*, especially *moral* instruction. One must, however, *delight* in order to teach, and among the writers, or rather booksellers, who tried to fashion children's books for this purpose was John Newbery (1713–67), the philanthropic bookseller in St. Paul's Churchyard, next Ludgate Street. Fanny seemed to know about twenty of his fat little flowery gilt-edged volumes with their stories of Giles Gingerbread, Goody Two Shoes, Mr. Thomas Trip, Peter Puzzlewell, and Woglog, the great Giant.[1] All good children were invited to come to the Bow and Sun and buy, for the books were made for 'all young gentlemen and ladies who were good or intended to be good' or for 'every little boy who would become a great man, and ride upon a fine horse' and 'every little girl who would become a great woman, and ride in a lord-mayor's gilt coach'.

> New Books we know require a puff,
> A title to entrap the eyes,
> And catch the reader by surprise

[1] Some of Newbery's compilations survive in the BM, e.g. *The Circle of the Sciences* (1745?), *The Twelfth-Day Gift* (1767), and *Fables in Verse* (1765). See also Charles Welsh, *A Bookseller of the Last Century* (1885).

but, once trapped, the little readers were often instructed in manners and morals as well as in history and science.[1]

History was a study highly esteemed as affording both instruction and moral instruction (and Fanny studied all the standard histories of her time); sermons were widely read; and after them in importance, as prescribed for young ladies, came books on female conduct, or courtesy books, of which there were forerunners in the sixties and not a few earlier, though they began to appear in far greater numbers in the decades following (1770–1820). Among such works one widely prescribed for the young miss was James Fordyce's *Sermons to Young Women* (1765), a work quoted by Fanny on more than one occasion.[2]

The novel was forbidden. Though Lady Pennington ventured to recommend *The Vicar of Wakefield*, reading lists in courtesy books rarely included romance. Such writings, said the preacher, 'carry on their very forehead the mark of the beast'. They are the most pestilential fruit of that 'evergreen tree of diabolical knowledge', the Circulating Library. Dr. Burney's was a liberal household, intellectually, and though it has been said that *Tom Jones* was the only novel in his fine library, that is, in the formal bookshelves of his library and study, there must have been other bookshelves in the house, and on them, most certainly, novels. The allusions in the Burney diaries and letters to novels, novelists, and characters and situations in novels prove that Fanny read not only the eighteenth-century novels that have survived as classics but a swarm of novels and curious works, half novels, half courtesy books, now completely forgotten.

Young ladies of the second half of the eighteenth century, both fictional and real, could be divided into two classes: those who were amenable to Fordyce, and those, like Lydia Languish, Lydia Bennet, and the intractable Misses Houghton in Clara Reeve's *School for Widows*, who were not. Our 'Old Lady', the teen-age Fanny, with her dutiful and conscientious heart, reading along alone, unassisted and uninstructed, was probably on the side of the preacher. She preceded the brilliant mockers by a decade or two, and her satire, when it came, was directed against absurdities in conduct or manners rather than in books.

---

[1] See p. 19, n. 1.

[2] Some account of the courtesy books that FB read is given in an article by the author, 'Fanny Burney and the Courtesy Books', *PMLA*, lxv (Sept. 1950), 732–61.

At this early age she read the serious current literature of her age concurrently and took it seriously.

Fanny's acquaintance with Mrs. Chapone and her *Letters on the Improvement of the Mind* (1772) was to come later, as were her introductions to Hannah More, Mrs. Trimmer, Mrs. Barbauld, Arnaud Berquin, Madame de Genlis, and other writers on the education and conduct of young girls. A journal-letter of 1779 provides a glimpse of her in a circulating library at Brighton perusing Edward Moore's *Fables for the Female Sex* (1741). Here, as in Fordyce, the utility of Virtue is the persuasive. Thus Moore counsels the nymph to eschew immodesty. Modesty is the better lure.

> When Caelia struts in man's attire,
> She shews too much to raise desire;
> But from the hoop's bewitching round
> Her very shoe has pow'r to wound.

Two old yellowed pages written in a round childish hand, still extant in miscellaneous scraps of papers once belonging to Fanny,[1] may be hers, and, if so, they show her early toil over some old book of conduct.

Lessons of conduct & sentiments

. . .

SPIRITS	The spirits should be ever under the dominion of the understanding.
UNENVIOUSNESS	. . .
HONESTY	. . .
VISITING	To be *well* Timed & of proper length should be chiefly considered.
	When Discourse *flags*, before it *fails*, company should separate. . . .

. . .

GOOD MANNERS should be uninterruptedly cultivated. They chiefly consist in softness & attention. Their influence is universal—dispelling or banishing mauvaise Honte, grossness, personal reflections, absence of mind, & all impertinence. Promoting & encouraging observance; humility; & the art of pleasing.

. . .

DELICACY	. . .
INSTRUCTION	To hear Good Counsel, to read Moral Lessons. . . .

[1] Among *Miscellaneous: about 417 pieces of MS. (1772–1828)*, folder iv (Berg).

The courtesy literature was to come to life in Fanny's novels and plays when she placed the courtesy-book morals realistically in action. The great theme of *Evelina* and *Cecilia* (and, with some differences, of *Camilla* and *The Wanderer*) was the entrance of the young lady into the world, her conduct, embarrassments, diffi- culties, and triumphs. Like Fanny and her sisters and cousins, the heroines of her novels and comedies were motherless (except for Camilla, whose mother was in Spain when most needed). They were unadvised in times of crises except for the distant help of elderly monitors like Mr. Crisp. This, of course, in- creased the hazards of the plot, the terminal point of which was happy marriage. The forwarding action was felicitous behaviour on the part of the heroine—modesty, delicacy, sensibility, charity, prudence, fortitude, and all courtesy-book virtues. The retarding action was infelicitous behaviour—coquetry, affectation, singu- larity, artifice, levity, imprudence, and other courtesy-book sins. The young hero combined the roles of monitor and lover, at once the judge of conduct and the prize for good conduct. He was something of a conduct-meter most disconcertingly sensitive not only to error, especially that indicating flaws in character, but also to the unfortunate or accidental appearance of error.

Fanny's own life and the young lives about her suggested the predicament, her sense of fun and adventure supplied the perils and embarrassments, and her experience and observation were to give them verisimilitude. One source, however, of the prin- ciples on which the plot was carried forward or retarded was the courtesy literature, and these books of practical or applied ethics supplied, besides, staid and forthright sententious matter like that in Mr. Villars's letters to Evelina.

Already by her fifteenth year Fanny had written a novel, 'The History of Caroline Evelyn', which seems to have con- cluded with the birth of an infant daughter Evelina. Though the first part of the story was allegedly burned, Evelina's pre- dicament, 'the unequal birth by which she hung suspended between the elegant connexions of her mother, and the vulgar ones of her grandmother'[1] and the 'contrasts and mixtures of society' to which she would be exposed, was to linger in the author's memory supplying much food for further thought and scope for further invention.

[1] See p. 1, n. 2.

Another event of the early years, later reflected in *Evelina*, was a journey of 1767 to Bristol.[1] To Fanny's great joy her father took her along with him to the Hotwells on a three days' visit that he implied in his Memoirs was her only visit there, and the brief tour was to set the scene geographically and in part socially for Book III of *Evelina, or, the History of a Young Lady's Entrance into the World.*

Let the account of the first fifteen years close with a little girl in her father's study (for he would always have his young creatures about him), but a little girl early hurried out into the world by the surge of happy young life all around her—a thoughtful child (the Old Lady), for she had no one to think *for* her—a little mime, observant and shy, but, when safe in the nursery, gay, frolicsome, and more inventive than her play-fellows in childish sports—a silent observer, who began to see the comedy of life as she saw it on the stage, in a series of scenes —a little girl much loved but much neglected, described by her father:

> In state of childhood, innocently gay,
> Thy voice & looks c^d folly well display;
> Could affectation see where'er it lurk
> In face or limb, of Christian, Jew, or Turk.
> Though neither wise nor learn'd thyself, could'st see
> Each subject true of risibility:
> The pedantry & petulance of wits,
> The vulgar ignorance of clown & cits,
> The lies & cant of tradesmen thou couldst trace
> As well as coxcomb's, or Coquet's grimace.[2]

[1] Memoirs (Osborn).
[2] *To my Daughter Fanny, 1797.* A poem of 48 verses (copies in both Berg and Osborn Collections).

II

A DECADE OF COMPLICATIONS

(1768–1778)

Better to dwell in a corner of the housetop.

THE joys of childhood can hardly be permanent, and various events already preparing in the Burney family were to bring on complications for the future.

There was, first of all, Dr. Burney's second marriage, which was to enlarge the family circle and carry the Burneys back, for the summers at least, to King's Lynn. In April, 1763, less than a year after Mrs. Burney's death, Mr. Stephen Allen 'by too great labour & anxiety in his mercantile pursuits, became consumptive & died'.[1] After this, Mrs. Allen and her family spent the winters in London while in the summer groups of Burneys went to King's Lynn. Dr. Burney's visits with the beautiful and vivacious widow rapidly developed into something more than regard, and though he was rebuffed in 1764 because of the ardour of some precipitate love-verses, in 1766–7 he was an avowed and ardent suitor for the widow's hand.[1] In spite of the professional hurry of fifty or sixty music lessons a week besides 'school scholars' he managed to spend Monday evenings 'in Great Russell Street at Mrs. Allen's, out of sight of her imperious mother'.[1] Difficulties arose when the imperious one—also the mother of Mrs. Arthur Young, called by the young Burneys the Sibyl because of her grim and ugly temper—opposed the match. The Allens regarded Dr. Burney as a fortune-hunter, for Stephen Allen had left his widow in 'a state of affluence'.[1] The loss of a large part of the fortune gave the lover an opportunity to prove that it was the lady's 'person' that he desired and not her dower. The marriage took place on October 2, 1767, though it was kept secret for some time because of the continued opposition of the Allen family.

The union did not at once result in a single enlarged household. The new Mrs. Burney was the mother of three children:

[1] *Memoirs*, i. 189–98; also Dr. Burney's Memoirs (Berg).

Maria, aged sixteen; Stephen, twelve; and Elizabeth ('Bessy'), six.[1] For over two years Mrs. Burney continued to live in the dower house opposite St. Margaret's Church in King's Lynn, though as before she made visits to London in the winter, and the Burneys came in groups to King's Lynn in the summer. Dr. Burney expected that the children of each former marriage would be 'loved and regarded' alike by the new partners.[2] How well Dr. Burney so 'blessed by his own feelings' was able to keep his share of the contract appears in the testimonials of his stepdaughter Maria, who long remembered his 'kind Indulgence', 'parental Care', and 'affectionate Conduct'.[3] Unhappily Mrs. Burney was crowned with no corresponding success in her steprole, though the unfortunate aspects of her character took a little time to appear.

The young people, however, got along very well, and the alternate visits and separations fostered journal-writing. 'Hetty's Letters and your Papa's', Maria wrote in 1768, 'Lord why they are common Entertaining Lively witty Letters such as d^n Swift might write or People who prefer the beautiful to the sublime but *you now* . . . well well Fanny's Letters for my money.'[4] Of all the Burneys Maria loved Fanny best, perhaps because though Fanny had more inventive fun and merriment about her than the others, she also had a natural rectitude and reserve of heart and mind and, seemingly, the wisdom, prudence, and sense of an Old Lady. To Fanny Maria confided all her wildest secrets, and in later life the long and tedious tale of her unhappiness.

In addition to the Allens there were, for the *dramatis personae* of the early diaries, the grandmothers already mentioned, two Burney aunts, a Burney uncle, and the nine gay and talented Burney cousins by then living at Barborne Lodge near Worcester. There was also the new connexion with Arthur Young and his family, for Martha Allen, his wife, was Mrs. Burney's sister.

---

[1] The dates of birth as given in the parish registers of St. Margaret's Church, King's Lynn, are: 20 July 1751, 25 Sept. 1755, and 13 Nov. 1761, respectively.

[2] See p. 24, n. 1.

[3] A.L. (Barrett) from Maria Allen Rishton to CB, 1 Nov. [1796]; and A.L.S. (Barrett) to FBA, 24 Dec. 1796. Also ED, i. 273–8.

[4] A.L.S. (Berg) from Maria Allen to FB, 1768; A.L.S. (Barrett) to FB, 15 Oct. 1769. See also A.L.S. (Berg) to SBP, 12 Aug. 1793.

In March, 1768, Fanny had begun a formal diary:

—to *whom* dare I reveal my private opinion of my nearest relations? my secret thoughts of my dearest friends? my own hopes, fears, reflections, and dislikes?—Nobody![1]

So, for a few years, the journal was addressed to Nobody. She was not yet sixteen, and May 30 had been 'such a charming day! and then last night—well, you shall have it all in order'.

Last night, while Hetty, Susey, (Charlotte) and myself were at tea, mama and Miss Allen not being returned from Harrow, and Papa in his study busy as usual, my cousin Dick was gone, that lively, charming, spirited Mr. Young enter'd the room. O how glad we were to see him. . . . Hetty sat down to the harpsichord and sung to him—mama soon returned, and then they left it. *Well, and so*—upon the entrance of fathers and mothers—we departed this life of anguish and misery, and rested our weary souls in the Elysian fields—my Papa's study—there freed from the noise and bustle of the world, enjoy'd the . . . *harmony* of chattering, and the melody of musick![1]

One of the highest luxuries of these times was, as Maria Allen later put it, 'sitting in Elegant undress over a few dying Embers in my bedchamber relating the disasters of the day and afterwards sleeping three in a bed in a charming warm night in July'.[2] In the morning when the girls were dressing for an expedition to Greenwich (Fanny had not slept all night and was up at five o'clock),

who should rap at the chamber door but—(my cheeks are crimsoned with the blush of indignation while I write it)—Mr. Young! . . . poor Miss Allen was in a miserable condition—her Journal, which he wanted to see, in full sight—on her open bureau. He said he had a right to it as her uncle.[1]

Fanny and Esther also kept diaries, though they hid them away, for the proclivity in the house to journal-writing was by no means approved by 'the Higher Powers', unless it were by Mr. Crisp. Yet when the young people were separated the youthful confidences were continued in dramatic epistles constructed to strike the attention and to amuse. Danger was the spice of life, and Maria, who wrote very daringly about the most tender and secret matters, was often in a panic lest the pages meant for Fanny and Susan should fall under some scathing or avenging

[1] ED, i. 1 ff.   [2] See p. 25, n. 4.

eye. 'I tell you no news', she wrote when she returned to Lynn:

I refer you to my *very Entertaining* Little history of anecdotes which will arrive in Poland in a short time. You will be *amazed* at the Brilliancy of sentiment Elegance of Expression Depth of thought and reasoning Containd in the *hole*—[1]

A year later she was writing distractedly about packets dispatched from Lynn.

I am quite terrify'd lest they should be Lost I think they must be somewhere about your house—or else the servant who carried them lost them—how could she be such a little simpleton to send them in separate parcels—if they are found pray let them come with my Gown.[1]

'Well but, now for the Greenwich party', wrote Fanny. 'We set out at about ten or eleven—the company was, mama, Mr. Young, Miss Allen, Stephen, and your most obsequious slave.' She could not recall any of the conversation except that relating to 'happiness and misery, sensibility and a total want of feeling', when her mother turning towards her said, 'Here's a girl will *never* be happy! *Never* while she lives!—for she possesses perhaps as feeling a heart as ever girl had!'[2] This was a discouraging compliment, if indeed at sixteen or approaching sixteen a girl can believe that she will never be happy.

The Journal to Nobody then jumps abruptly to King's Lynn, where most of the family, including Dr. Burney himself, had gone for the summer. Fanny was writing in the Cabin or Look Out at the lower end of a long garden extending from the churchyard of St. Margaret's along Mrs. Allen's house and down to the river front. Ships could be sighted from the Look Out as they sailed up the river. Sometimes they docked at the water-gate below, and the conversation of the sailors and porters, clearly audible from the Cabin, may have supplied part of the robust material that later surprised some of the gentle readers of *Evelina* and made them think of Fielding. Sometimes the ribaldry along the quays was such as to send the occupants of the Look Out flying to the quiet end of the garden facing the calm church and churchyard of St. Margaret's. Fanny was 'tolerably happy'; she liked the 'land of her nativity' and some-

[1] See p. 25, n. 4.   [2] See p. 26, n. 1.

times defended it in mock arguments with Maria and Hetty, who were pining for London.

Her pen followed the streams of consciousness. She wished Kitty Cooke would write and say how 'dear, dear, beloved Mr. Crisp does'. 'My papa always mentions him by the name of my *Flame*. Indeed he is not mistaken—himself is the *only* man on earth I prefer to him!' From *flame* her mind went to true love: 'I scarce wish for anything so truly, really, and greatly, as to be *in love*—upon my word I am serious.' Only she did not wish for love in return. 'I carry not my wish so far as for a *mutual tendresse*. No, I should be contented to love *Sola*.' (This wish the God of Love granted twice if not thrice before she found in her handsome chevalier *mutual tendresse*.) She had been sobered by a chapter on Eternal Misery in the sententious *Series of Genuine Letters between Henry and Frances* by the Griffiths, and in this mood she heard a bell tolling 'most dreadfully loud and solemn' for a funeral. 'Indeed I never heard anything so dismal.' On another day the bells rang again, but this time very merrily, and from the garden Fanny could see the great doors of St. Margaret's flung open and a bride and bridegroom appear. *He* looked gay and happy; she, grave but not sad; 'and, in short, all was happy and charming'. Yet, what 'a prodigious mob', thought Fanny, and 'what a *gauntlet* for any woman of delicacy to run!'

Well of all things in the world, I don't suppose any thing can be so dreadful as a publick wedding— . . . and Mr. Bewly said that when *he* was married, his lady and self *stole* in to the Church, privately as possible, and ashamed of every step they took.[1]

The topic had its fascination, but when later Hetty gave a little account of an Amorosa so forward in love's cause as to write a declaration on her glove and give it to her music-master, their cousin Charles Rousseau Burney, Fanny was brought to a pause, unable to avoid the conclusion that 'upon the whole, the most dignified thing for an exalted female must be to die an old maid'.[1]

During one of the summers at King's Lynn (perhaps in this summer of 1768) Fanny was confirmed. Many years later in arranging for her son's confirmation she recalled her own.

[1] See p. 26, n. 1.

I remember well that, when I was preparing . . . I had such an idea I should undergo an examination, & I was so fearful of some *wry* question that might discountenance me, That I learnt nearly the whole common prayer Book by heart!—Besides reading the Bible *quite through* 3 times! I was so indefatigable, I rose to nothing else; & never went to rest while I could procure light for my labours. Alex would not be much led to imitate me, if he knew that, after all this hard work—the fat clumsy stumpy worthy Bishop of Norwich clapt his hand upon my head, & off it, as fast as he possibly could, & never made a single interrogatory, nor uttered a single doubt or demur upon my fitness or unfitness for his blessing.[1]

Now Fanny was sixteen, and she observed the life around her, listened, and reflected, and no one suspected as yet that she had a memory like a tape-recorder, a mind like a *camera obscura*. And she had a strong sense of duty. 'I make a kind of rule, never to indulge myself in my two *most* favourite pursuits, reading and writing, in the morning.' It was best in the morning to ply her needle with the others, 'by which means my reading and writing in the afternoon is a pleasure I cannot be blamed for by my mother'.[2] Finally at liberty she could retreat to her 'sweet Cabin'.

I cannot express the pleasure I have in writing down my thoughts, at the very moment—my opinion of people when I first see them . . . there is something to me very unsatisfactory in passing year after year, without even a memorandum of what you did, &c. And then, all the happy hours I spend with particular friends and favourites would fade from my recollection.[2]

She wrote happily on, therefore, until one day she was over-taken by the catastrophe lying in wait for young diarists, for, 'negligent fool', she left a sheet of her diary on the pianoforte, where, as her mother reported, it was found by her father, who read it and put it in his pocket. Fanny was in 'sad distress' for days, then, gathering courage,

'Pray Papa,' (I said,) 'have you got—any *papers* of mine?'
'Papers of yours?' said he—'how should *I* come by papers of yours?'
'I'm sure—I don't know—but—'
'Why do you leave your papers about the house?' asked he, gravely.

[1] A.L.S. (owned by Dr. Percy A. Scholes) from FBA to CB, Jr., 10 July 1816.
[2] See p. 26, n. 1.

I could not say another word—he went on playing on the piano forte. Well, to be sure, thought I, these same dear Journals are most shocking plaguing things—I've a good mind to resolve never to write a word more. However, I stayed still in the room, working, and looking wistfully at him for about an hour and half. At last, he rose to dress—Again I look'd wistfully at him—He laugh'd—'What Fanny,' said he, kindly, 'are you in sad distress?' I half laugh'd. 'Well,—I'll give it you, now I see you are in such distress—but take care, my dear, of leaving your writings about the house again— suppose any body else had found it—I declare I was going to read it loud—Here, take it—but if ever I find any more of your Journals, I vow I'll stick them up in the market place.' And then he kiss'd me *so* kindly—[1]

This lesson on the perils incident to keeping diaries made its impression, and Fanny took counsel with her mother's friend, Miss Dorothy Young, and was promptly advised 'very seriously and earnestly' to give up 'these same dear Journals'. 'Heigho-ho! Do you think I can bring myself to oblige her?' Yet the diarist heard the objections through, if not without demur.

She says that it is the most dangerous employment young persons can have—that it makes them often record things which ought *not* to be recorded. . . . 'If you drop it [the Journal], and any improper person finds it, you know not the uneasiness it may cost you.'

'Well but, dear ma'am, this is an "if" that may not happen once in a century.'

'I beg your pardon; I know not how often it may happen; and even *once* might prove enough to give you more pain than you are aware of.'

'Why, dear ma'am, papa never prohibited my writing, and he knows that I *do* write, and *what* I do write.'

'I question that. However, 'tis impossible for you to answer for the curiosity of others. And suppose any body finds a part in which they are extremely censured.'

'Why then, they must take it for their pains. It was not wrote for *them*, but *me*, and I cannot see any harm in writing to *myself*.'

'It was very well whilst there were only your sisters with you to do anything of this kind; but, depend upon it, when your connections are enlarged, your family increased, your acquaintance multiplied, young and old *so* apt to be curious—depend upon it, Fanny, 'tis the most dangerous employment you can have. Suppose now, for example, your favourite wish were granted, and you were *to fall in*

[1] See p. 26, n. 1.

love, and then the object of your passion were to get sight of some part which related to himself?'

'Why then, Miss Young, I must take a little trip to Rosamond's Pond.'

'Why, ay, I doubt it would be all you would have left.'

Well, my (Nobody) I *have* read part of my Journal to Miss Young and what's more, let her choose the day herself. . . . I assure you I quite triumph! prejudic'd as she was, she is pleas'd to give it her sanction,—*if it is equally harmless every where*—nay, says she even approves of it.[1]

This was *carte blanche*. Fanny scribbled on happily, taking as her themes the books she was reading (just then, Plutarch's *Lives*), her critical comments and reflections, the comings and goings of the Burneys and Allens and their friends, and presently youthful parties in Poland Street and young romance. Many pages of the juvenile journals were given to descriptions of the varied company who came to call on Dr. Burney. At first the three men who interested themselves most in the children got most attention, Arthur Young, Garrick, Mr. Crisp, and, later, one of the most delightful of all the wits and scholars who came to St. Martin's Street, the Reverend Thomas Twining. The juvenile journals brought many figures of the time vividly to life and served as practice-ground for even greater portraits to come. Already in her sixteenth year Fanny had learned to record direct speech, even long conversations, an art by no means easy. Such recording requires, to begin with, attention, concentration, and memorization. No wonder that already the young recorder was dubbed *the silent observant Miss Fanny*.[2]

At the end of the summer vacation, when Dr. Burney and his daughters returned to London, life at Poland Street followed its former pattern, though with some changes, for the winter of 1768 seems to mark the entrance of Esther and Fanny into the world.

Near by in Poland Street there lived an accommodating and light-hearted widow, by name Mrs. Pringle, who often invited the Misses Burney to dances and parties at her house. She also invited 'droll and entertaining' young men at whose gallantries and *bons mots* Fanny was 'ready to die with laughter', and among them Alexander Seton, a charmer of quite superior sense and

---

[1] See p. 26, n. 1.   [2] ED, i. 39 n.

cleverness. These were merry proceedings, and out of them romance was developing, especially between Hetty and young Seton, who never knew his own mind while she was free. For about two years Esther and Fanny were left pretty much to themselves, and their adventures probably furnished material for Evelina's unchaperoned début into the London world.

In this year Mrs. Burney, in moody despair of surviving the coming ordeal of childbirth, bequeathed the unborn infant, Richard, to the 'Pity & Protection' of the sixteen-year-old Fanny.

You will ev'ry day become more & more capable of the Task—& you will, I *do* trust you will, for your *same* dear Father's sake, cherish & support *his* Innocent child—tho' but *half* allied to you. My weak Heart speaks in Tears to you my Love . . .[1]

On November 20, 1768, Richard Thomas (the beautiful Dick) was born, and Maria wrote a hoaxing letter to Fanny conveying

Master Newcomes' affectionate Love to his sister Fanny is Extremely obliged for her kind letter which was delivered to him the minute he made his first appearance in the World. . . .[1]

In January, 1769, Susan was sent to King's Lynn to recuperate from a dangerous illness, and Fanny, Esther, and the Doctor were alone in Poland Street. This, if Susan were only there, was the life that Fanny liked best. 'We are still only us three together.'

How forcibly do I feel to whom I owe all the (earthly) happiness I enjoy!—it is to my father! to this dearest, most amiable, this best beloved—most worthy of men![2]

In June, 1769, the most worthy of men took his degree at Oxford, and though Fanny feared that he would think her impertinent, she could not forbear celebrating the 'Day of Days' with some verses *To Doctor Last,* concluding:

> For I never can think of a Doctor, not big
> As a Falstaff, and not with a full bottom'd wig,
> And the sly air Fame gives an at*e*rney;
> Not more at the bag did the citizens stare
> Of Harley, when Harley was made a Lord Mayor,
> Than I at the thin Doctor Burney.

[1] A.L.S. (Berg) from Mrs. Burney to FB, 13 Oct. 1768; and A.L. (Berg) from Maria Allen to FB, [20 Nov. 1768]. Partly printed, ED, I. lxvi–vii.
[2] See p. 26, n. 1.

> O! may Wisdom, which still to Good Humour gives birth,
> May fatness with dignity, goodness with mirth,
>   Still attend you, and speed your town journey!
> And O! till the hour that Death us shall part
> May Fanny a corner possess of the heart
>   Of the owner of her's, Doctor Burney.[1]

The Doctor and his friends had a very hearty laugh over these verses, and when later he asked her for an extra copy and she made *mille façons* (a way young girls had, Mr. Crisp said) about her trash, her father said, 'It's very sufficient for the occasion, and for your age'.[1]

The summer in King's Lynn with its compulsory round of dull visits could not compare for freedom and fun with the winter and the pleasant parties in Poland Street. Had it not been for the sorrow of parting with Susan and Maria, who 'looked weeping after us till the road turned', she would have been wholly happy to return to the 'ever dear house, in charming London'.[1]

The year 1770 opened with a long-anticipated masquerade in which Fanny, in a fancy dress of pink persian, made such an impression on a young man in the guise of a Dutchman that he promptly sent her tickets for the next Chelsea Assembly, proposing to wait on her next evening to know whether he might 'exist again or not'. The Doctor said that she must return the tickets but that she might 'let him come to tea, as he deserved civility', and then they 'might see more how to judge him'. Fanny was terrified. Left to answer the note herself, she sent a point-blank refusal that she did not risk showing to her father. 'As they thought him serious I determined to be so too.' That ended that, for she did not as yet wish to exchange her life in Poland Street for life with the 'Dutchman', or any man. Later, at a Benefit, the young man looked 'very, very dejected', but Fanny softened not. 'However he contrived to hand me to the coach.'[1]

In this winter Esther and Fanny slowly made up their minds about Alexander Seton. The young man was very eligible, but though he continued his 'insinuating address', he did not come forth with an offer. Fanny was much concerned.

If the sincerity of this man equal'd his sense, wit, polite and insinuating address, I would not wish Hetty a happier lot than to be his. . . .

[1] See p. 26, n. 1.

Mr. Seton is artful: I have seen that: . . . for his unworthy trifling with so sweet, so amiable a girl as Hetty. . . . I know he is agreeable to a superior degree; and I believe he is as artful as agreeable.[1]

Meanwhile, plans that the Doctor was making for a tour through France and Italy to collect materials for a History of Music caused a reshuffle in the household arrangements. It was decided that Fanny must go to King's Lynn while her mother came to Poland Street. Hetty was to go on a vacation to Chessington, and their gifted cousin Charles Rousseau Burney was to take over the Doctor's pupils. As the girls rightly anticipated, their mother's not being acquainted with Mrs. Pringle put an end to their intimacy with that family. A dance lasting until three o'clock in the morning proved to be a farewell to all that set. Mr. Seton was more flattering than ever that April night as he handed Hetty to the coach. Mrs. Pringle accompanied the Burneys to her house next door, and

poor Hetty passed an uneasy night, racked with uncertainty about this Seton, this eternal destroyer of her peace! *Were* he sincere, she owned she could be happier in a union with him than with any man breathing:—indeed, he deserves her not; but the next morning, when she had considered well of every thing, she declared were he to make her the most solemn offer of his hand, she would refuse him,—and half added—*accept of Charles!*[1]

With Susan Fanny was happy enough at Lynn.

We work, read, walk, and play on the harpsichord—these are our employments, and we find them sufficient to fill up all our time without ever being tired.[1]

She read French with Susan, having taught herself that language 'for the sake of its bewitching authors', and she was studying besides Smollett's *History of England.* She had family letters to read—'a word & a wish of kindness & affection' sent by her father on June 6 from Dover ('Continue to Love me & to believe that I Love you', he had said)[2] and, even more absorbing, Esther's letters telling of her decision to marry her cousin, the dextrous harpsichordist, Charles Rousseau Burney. The marriage took place on September 20, 1770, at St. Paul's Church, Covent Garden, in the presence of Ann Burney (Aunt Nanny), Catharine Cooke, and Mrs. Burney's friends, Robert

[1] See p. 26, n. 1.   [2] A.L.S. (Barrett) from CB to FB, 6 June 1770.

and Mary Bruce Strange. In the autumn Fanny was writing in a very subdued manner from Poland Street.

Hetty, my dear Hetty, has given herself away from us. She has married at last her faithful Charles. God send her happy! He is one of the worthiest young men living. I am come up to town to spend a little time with them.[1]

This event marked the end of a decade, the decade in Poland Street with its early bereavement, its merry, laughing, loving, carefree girlhood. Until the year 1770 such discipline as Fanny knew for the employment of her time was of her own devising. Up to her nineteenth year she had had unusual freedom 'following my own vagaries, which my papa never controls'.[1] With a stepmother conspicuously in charge, everything was to be different. Mrs. Burney had bought a large house in Queen Square, and to Fanny's grief Mr. Crisp had ruled that they were 'quite to drop Mrs. Pringle, that we may see no more of Mr. Seton'. Mr. Crisp was doubtless determined to protect Fanny from an experience such as Esther had known under the easy chaperonage in Poland Street. They must cut the good-natured Mrs. Pringle forever. 'On my side', said Fanny, 'how unwillingly!' Apart from the ingratitude, 'I must also own that since we have droped her acquaintance, we have never made any half so lively and agreeable'.[1]

On November 16 Fanny was writing from the charming new house in Queen Square with its delightful prospect of Hampstead and Highgate. The spacious house made a new way of life, for the Allens (including the imperious grandmother) could now come on visits, and the young Burneys and Allens could be brought under one roof.

Scarcely, however, were the two families united when the unfortunate aspects of the second marriage began to appear. In her old age Madame d'Arblay pasted over, cut away, crossed out, and thoroughly obliterated all the unfriendly references to her stepmother that she could see in journals that she thought might be published. With these heavy burnings, scorings, and deletions, the juvenile diaries give unblemished impressions of unvaried happiness, and it has scarcely been noted that Fanny's testimonials of bliss occur when her stepmother was absent on

[1] See p. 26, n. 1.

visits to Lynn or elsewhere. Such entries may be epitomized in that of 1772: 'We are still without mama. We live in the most serene comfort possible.'[1]

A few veiled but antagonistic references to 'the Lady' that the editor of the early diaries allowed to appear in an appendix[2] give some warning of a situation that emerges with startling violence from the unedited papers. The gentle Susan referred to a 'long & bitter slavery begun almost in childhood' and to her stepmother's power of 'ill-treating by rudeness & coarse speeches'. 'I know her tenaciousness of opinion, her petulance, her inflammatory powers, & malignancy, & dread them.'[3] Fanny, long after, labelled a packet of letters to be destroyed: 'Extraordinary incomprehensible account of the *early* character of one who turned out our Family Scourge!'[4] Charlotte thought Precious ought to be 'indited for living'.[5] 'Madam is as spiteful as usual', wrote young Charles. 'The Devilish particles in her composition act with their usual powers.'[6] When at court Fanny thought the cruel and abusive German, Mrs. Schwellenberg, her stepmother's 'exactest Fellow,—gloomy, dark, suspicious, rude, reproachful'.[7] Susan and Fanny could scarcely believe that there could be *two* such persons in the world, but from the close of 1770, when Mrs. Burney bought the house in Queen Square, there was, as a sombre and ominous backdrop to all the scenes of merriment, a poor unhappy 'sulky madre' envying youthful happiness.[7] 'Precious', Mr. Crisp wrote to his sister, Mrs. Gast, 'should cry out, with the Devil in Milton, when he first view'd the happy pair in Paradise, *Evil, be thou my Good!*'[5] Through the seventies and eighties one unhappy Burney or another seemed always to be supplied with some characteristic tale or 'long story of malignancy in the Lady of the Manor'.[8] The references sometimes matched the complaints of Arthur Young and others about the Sibyl of Bradfield, his wife Martha

---

[1] See p. 26, n. 1.
[2] e.g. ED, ii. 288.
[3] Susan Burney's Journal (Osborn, copies, Armagh), 20 July 1787, Feb. 1789.
[4] In *212 A.L. or portions of A.L. (only a few signed) to Fanny Burney* (Berg).
[5] *Burford Papers*, pp. 82–84.
[6] A.L. (Osborn) from CB, Jr., to FB, Nov. 1781.
[7] Diary MSS. (Berg), pp. 1608, 2743–9.
[8] Diary MSS. (Berg), pp. 1608–19, 1685–1704. Also A.L. (Barrett) from FB to SBP, 31 Aug. 1782.

Allen, Mrs. Burney's sister. 'Lamentable it was', wrote Arthur Young in his *Autobiography*, 'that no enemy ever did me the mischief that I received from the wife of my bosom by the grossest falsehoods and the blackest malignity.'[1] In 1787 Arthur Young's daughter paid a long visit to her aunt, Mrs. Burney, and Susan, wondering at the length of the visit, could only conclude: 'that poor Girl is removed from such horrible scenes of rage & anarchy, that to live even wth the Lady must seem peaceful & happy to her—as I believe she does not experience from her such kind of conduct as *we* were favoured with, nor c^d it equally affect her if she did'.[2] A portrait of the Lady later emerged in Mrs. Ireton, one of the Furies in *The Wanderer*.

Difficulties arose for Fanny when, in the years to follow, her diligent service to her father, as amanuensis or nurse, provoked her mother's jealousy and resentment. By 1775–6 Mrs. Burney thought herself 'the most miserable woman that breathes',[3] and her misery arose, according to Fanny and Susan, from envy and jealousy of the enjoyment the young Burneys always found in one another and of their share of their father's affection and attention. 'The least appearance of comfort with any part of the family, she regards as *cabal*, & therefore becomes suspicious, sour & violent from the moment any new meeting takes place.'[4] There did indeed seem to be a great deal of caballing, or, to use their mother's accusing terms, *treason* or *sedition*, 'snug talks' in which they indulged their grievances and their dislike of her.[4] Sometimes they worried over the safety of letters 'full of Treason', and sometimes when away they were not above soliciting the Burney unhappy enough to be left at home for 'some pretty little bits of sedition'. Mr. Crisp developed a great relish for them and so did Mrs. Thrale.[5] One such bit was supplied by Charlotte in 1781:

M^rs *precious* has had her eldest son in Town for this week past, & tho' it was a year & a half since they were together before, . . . there

---

[1] Ed. M. Betham-Edwards (1898), p. 429; also pp. 339, 358–9, 438. Also ED, i. 98–99, 121, 271. Also A.L.S. (Barrett) from SHB to Mary Young, 7 Oct. 1792. Also Fanny Burney's account of her visit to Bradfield in 1792, Diary MSS. (Berg), suppressed pages, box v, part ii. [2] See p. 36, n. 3.

[3] 2 A.L.S. (Berg) from Maria Allen Rishton to FB, 1 Jan. 1775, 24 Sept. 1776.

[4] See p. 36, n. 8.

[5] 2 A.L.S. (Berg) from FB to SBP, 15 Jan. 1781, 17 Sept. 1782; 2 A.L.S. (Barrett) to HLT, 19, 25 Nov. [1782].

has not an hour passed that they have not been upon the point of a quarrel, from the incessant disputes they had together—. . . for as she never scruples saying 'the thing that is not,' if she had nothing else left to say, in order to *prove* that black is white, she'll cry 'Nay—don't be warm—I only say its my opinion—To be sure Dr Johnson said long ago, to my certain knowledge, that such was *his* opinion—but its no matter'.

The other day after they had been arguing near an hour about the Laws of England, he *for* them & she *against* them, she said that as to Our Laws they are so weak one can have no reddress for any Insult whatever; a blackguard may kick you into the kennell & you can't punish him!

'Yes, answered the son, but I think it better than French Government never the less'—'Oh! you do—well I confess I am rather surprised that you should wish to be rolled in the kennell every time you go out!' I have just met with a description of a Lady by Swift, wch I think quite suits her—. . .

> All her spirits in a flame
> When she knows she's most to blame![1]

If, therefore, there were malignancy, ill humour, petulance, self-pity, desire for attention, captiousness, suspicion, violence, and rudeness on one side, there was some malice on the other, and, whether unavoidable or not, a kind of closed compact or united front, which, as it excluded the unhappy Lady from all the secrets and the fun, must have increased her jealousy, suspicion, and resentment.

There was very soon, therefore, an unfortunate alignment of sympathies in a house now indeed divided against itself. Mrs. Burney's sarcastic rudeness had provoked silent resistance, had driven the young people, children and stepchildren alike, into a conclave bound together by mutual sympathy and love, and at first a shocked dismay. They withdrew from the unhappy new presence in the house, happy only when they were together, and engaged, as the stepmother thought, in sedition and treason against her. They continued their own lives, pursued their former interests, but apart from her, retreating when possible to their father's study, to cold rooms in distant parts of the house far from the fire in the parlour or living-room where the loud, noisy, and demanding presence entertained her Lynn

---

[1] A.L.S. (Barrett) from CAB to Mr. Crisp, 8 Feb. 1781.

friends, quarrelled with the younger children, exacted attendance or pity for her ills or long hours of reading for her amusement, and broke in upon one's reveries with abuse or sarcastic
and spiteful remarks. 'She's such a queer fish,—to be sure, for
a sensible woman, as she is', remarked Catharine Cooke with a
striking lack of euphemism:

for, you know, for such a good soul as the Doctor to have such a wife,
—to be sure there's something very disagreeable in her, Laughing
so loud, & hooting, & clapping her Hands,—I can't love her, a nasty
old cat,—yet she's certainly a very sensible woman.[1]

The Cabal, as the joyless lady thought it, was soon enlarged by
close friends of the Burneys like their Worcester cousins, Mr.
Crisp, Kitty Cooke, and later Mrs. Thrale, and even Mrs. Locke
of Norbury Park.

With all that could be said of Mrs. Burney's faults as originating chiefly in ill health, 'nerves', 'that impracticable Temper',[2]
and perhaps some sense of inadequacy or unpopularity, no one
ever doubted her affection for the Doctor or his for her. She was
capable of unselfish action where he was concerned, and in the
great family crises to come she acted nobly and disinterestedly.
Her good qualities were 'manifold and charming', as Madame
d'Arblay later thought it just to say;[2] and perhaps it was chiefly
in the common stress of the common day that the poor lady
failed. But these failures, along with social infelicities ('Laughing so loud, & hooting, & clapping her hands'), made additional difficulties for young ladies like Fanny and Susan at their
first entrance into the world.[3]

If, finally, the Lady and her stepchildren had one interest in
common or entered into any conspiracy, it was to keep the day's
history of their dissensions and discomforts from the Doctor's
knowledge or notice. He believed that birds in the nest should
agree, and he quoted Nurse Ball, who had brought him up.
'Nurse Ball used to say in her great proverbial wisdom, that
"'twas a sorry bird who bewrayed his own nest". And people
who are perpetually telling the failings of their relatives, & at

---

[1] Diary MSS. (Berg), p. 651.
[2] Two drafts of A.L.S. (Berg) from FBA to the Rev. Stephen Allen, [1832].
[3] Diary MSS. (Berg), 18 June 1788. Cf. A.L.S. (Berg) from FB to HLT, Dec.
1781: 'But hear now the character of the *Head Lady* given by Mrs. Shirley,—
"She is really a very violent, noisy, agreeable woman." '

variance with them, always lessen my opinion both of their
wisdom & goodness of heart.'[1] This was a check-rein, for children, stepchildren, and wife alike feared the Doctor's gloom or
displeasure. 'The little, very little Time he has to spare for
domestic concerns', Fanny once wrote to Mrs. Thrale,

> I would rather wish less than more, were it to be embittered by com-
> plaints, or even insinuations of discomfort. Surely we should profit
> little from the example he has himself set us of patience & sweetness
> at *all* Times, to prefer our own convenience to his *dearest tranquillity*.[2]

'The Family of the Burneys are a very surprizing Set of People',
remarked Mrs. Thrale, patently amazed that Dr. Burney, a
comparatively poor man, should be as much beloved at home
as if he were rich—a rich Linen-draper! 'Nobody is so much
beloved.'[3]

By dint of hard winter-travelling the Doctor reached his
family on Christmas eve, 1770, and after a short delay he went
off to consult his 'Guide, Philosopher, & Friend', Mr. Crisp,
remaining at Chessington to write up his travels.[4] *The Present
State of Music in France and Italy or the Journals of a Tour through
these countries undertaken to collect materials for a General History of
Music* appeared, according to Fanny, on May 3, 1771, and
already in June she was happily recording the honours her
father had gained by it.[4] A second happy event of 1771 was
James's return with the East Indiaman the *Greenwich* from
Bombay. At that time there was great excitement about Cook's
expeditions of discovery, and James longed to transfer from his
merchantmen and men-of-war to the new scientific enterprise.
Dr. Burney was able to make interest for his son with the famous
or notorious Earl of Sandwich, First Lord of the Admiralty,
who had always proved friendly and helpful. At Hinchinbroke
James was introduced to Captain Cook, Sir Joseph Banks, Dr.
Solander, and Dr. Hawkesworth, and in July, 1772, he set sail
as Able Seaman with Cook's second expedition. In November
of the same year he was made second lieutenant of the *Adventure*.
James was as yet in these early days

honest, generous, sensible, unpolished; . . . very careless, and pos-

---

[1] A.L.S. (Barrett) from CB to CBF, 8 Dec. 1790.
[2] A.L.S. (JRL) from FB to HLT, n.d.   [3] *Thraliana*, i. 399.
[4] A.L.S. (Osborn) from CB to Mr. Crisp, 19–24 Dec. 1770; also *Memoirs*, i.
226 and ED, i. 115–24.

sessed of an uncommon share of good nature; full of humour, mirth, and jollity.[1]

These events in the men's world touched and gratified Fanny because, being the reward of great effort, they gratified her father. In the girlhood world of Queen Square, meanwhile, a compelling interest was astir in a new romance, that terminating in Maria Allen's elopement with Martin Folkes Rishton. Fanny and Susan had been apprised of this affair, scene by scene, in secret communications from Maria since 1770.[2] Having gained permission to travel, to go to Switzerland ('and by myself too'), Maria dispatched 'charming pacquets' of journals from Paris and Geneva with full accounts of all her affairs. Fanny and Susan knew that, against the wishes of parents and guardians on both sides, the lovers had again opened a correspondence, then that they had met, and finally that at Ypres on May 16, 1772, they had married. Hoping to remarry in England, they returned almost immediately, Maria masquerading as Miss Allen, Rishton as her lover. 'Good Heaven! what a romantic life has this beloved friend lived!' exclaimed Fanny. 'What scenes we shall have!' Such scenes!

On deliberation it seemed less terrifying to confess to Mr. Crisp than to tell the truth at home, and on June 7 Maria and Susan set off for Chessington, leaving Fanny at Queen Square to bear the brunt of the inquiry there. The report on this expedition includes one of the most amusing of the Chessington scenes.[3]

'Why what's all this?' said [Mr. Crisp].
Kate claw'd hold of her [Maria's] left hand, and shew'd him the Ring.
The air was then rent with expletives current in the reign of the good Queen Anne, but very painful to sensitive ears of 1772. He then turned to Susan.
'Susettikin,' sd he, 'You know all this affair—is it so?'
'Yes Sir—Indeed—'
'She is really married,' sd he, arching his eyebrows with such a stare of astonishment.
'She is upon my honour.'

[1] See p. 26, n. 1.
[2] A folder of 32 letters (Berg) from Maria Allen Rishton to FB and SB, 1768–74, partially printed, ED, i. 107–9, 113 n.–115, 136–7, 140–3, 164–5, 180–4.
[3] ED, i. 175–84, 202–4, 265–81, 312–13, 319–21; ii. 37–38, 41–42.

But here, according to Susan, Maria again intervened:

'No—No—No—Indeed—Nothing—Nothing at all—its all the lyes of that impudent little toad'—(meaning *me*).

However, the bride still hid her face in agonies, confirming what Susan had said. The man of the world knew what questions to ask and what measures to advise. He undertook to frame a letter to Mrs. Burney—a letter surely worth reading, did it survive—and for the benefit of the young Burneys he took occasion to expatiate on the ruin that could befall through clandestine actions, private or secret marriages, or affairs kept from relatives. What if the marriage certificate should be lost? What if the man should deny the marriage? Why then, as Fanny suggested, conning over such a situation, one could only, like Evelina's mother, die oneself and leave a motherless child to make its own way in the world. Maria's experiences may have provided some images for the fancy that was to produce one of the liveliest accounts of eighteenth-century girlhood extant in English literature.

There was no easy forgiveness for Maria in Queen Square, but presently the high-spirited girl was driving away in a smart whisky with her sportsman-farmer to the life she had chosen on a Norfolk farm. She did not yet know that she had married a bashaw, whose possessive nature was to cut her off from Burneys and Allens alike until with another great ado she ran away from him. Mrs. Burney's judgement was right, though ill-expressed. Surely, wrote Maria, it was not right

to tell my Husband every vice fault or foible I had ever been guilty of since my Infancy for she never would have forgiven herself if she had destroyed the Happiness of those it was her first duty to promote. I am afraid Rishton will never forget it.[1]

But Fanny loved the impetuous, self-willed Maria chiefly because, with all her wild and original spirits, she had an affectionate heart.

In the years 1770–3 there were many other jaunts to Chessington, including that of 1771, when a group of young Burneys and Allens took Jenny Barsanti along and put on the

[1] See p. 41, n. 2.

play *The Careless Husband* in order to give Mr. Crisp an opportunity to judge the singer's talents for acting. Fanny, who had
not been there for five years, found it

a place of peace, ease, freedom, and cheerfulness, and all its inhabitants are good humoured and obliging, and my dear Mr. Crisp
alone would make it, to us, a Paradise.[1]

In about a year she was rejoicing, as well she might, that her
design upon the correspondence of Mr. Crisp had succeeded to
her wish. He could say more in three lines, she observed, than
she herself could in a hundred; yet the practice in writing lively
and dramatic journals to so cultivated a critic, the encouragement derived from his full enjoyment of her efforts, and his
occasional criticisms of her methods and style ('You are devilish
long-winded, Fan, pray mend that fault')[2]—all this was to
serve as a pattern in the secret enterprise that she was soon to
begin in earnest: the series of imaginative letters from Evelina
to Mr. Villars (another old gentleman in the country), which,
with his replies, constituted the epistolary novel *Evelina*. Prévost's
Doyen de Killerine, with whom Fanny had 'fallen in love' in 1769,
provided a literary model of a Monitor and Confessor currently
exercised over the errors and follies of the youth in his care.
Though Fanny's work was not to approach Prévost's in depth
of passion, scope of experience, or its quality of compassion, its
central situation may have lent literary reinforcement to the
structure of the book taking form naturally from her own
situation.

The new commitment to Mr. Crisp changed the nature of
Fanny's diaries. They were no longer addressed exclusively to
Nobody, but tended to take the form of actual letters, long
journal-letters, written for Mr. Crisp or for Susan. The thought
of giving pleasure to these two spurred her best efforts in light
and lively writing. As declining health kept Mr. Crisp away
from the town, he grew more avid for news of Dr. Burney and
his world and his creatures. 'In this situation, my dear Fanny,
assure yourself, one of my principal regales, is the Queen Square
Journal, and I heartily wish I could procure it three times a
Week.' So much did he relish the matter that he refused to be

[1] See p. 26, n. 1.
[2] See p. 41, n. 3.

'a Critic or Schoolmaster or observer of composition—the deuce take them all!' Yet he sometimes offered some criticism:

If once you set about framing studied letters, that are to be correct, nicely grammatical, and run in smooth periods, I shall mind them no otherwise than as newspapers of intelligence. . . . There is no fault in an epistolary correspondence like stiffness and study. Dash away whatever comes uppermost; the sudden sallies of imagination, clap'd down on paper, just as they arise, are worth folios, and have all the warmth and merit of that sort of nonsense that is eloquent in love. Never think of being correct when you write to me.[1]

And again in the same strain:

You cannot but know *that trifling, that negligence, that even incorrectness*, now and then in familiar epistolary writing, is the very soul of genius and ease; and that if your letters were to be fine-labour'd composi- tions that smelt of *the lamp*, I had as lieve they travelled elsewhere. So no more of that, Fanny, and thou lov'st me. Dash away, what- ever comes uppermost; and believe me you'll succeed better, than by leaning on your elbow, and studying what to say.[1]

So rich was she in material that he had decided to call her Jessica.

You riot in provisions of all sorts, and have nothing to do, but to choose, or reject; and your Cookery is at your fingers' ends, and to do you justice has the true relish, and is highly season'd; all this I give you credit for.[1]

Mere letters will no longer do.

Send me a minute Journal of every thing, and never mind their being trifles—trifles well-dressed, are excellent food, and your cookery is (with me) of established reputation.[1]

Fanny wrote hundreds of pages, a volume of journal-letters, before all was done, for Mr. Crisp alone. She had, as he said, extraordinarily rich and varied material in the exotically diversified stream of musicians, artists, and savants who came to wait on her father. Her records were marked increasingly by dramatic effects, a sly subtlety of characterization, economy, ease, and skill.

Evenings at Covent Garden and Drury Lane and Garrick's morning visits continued as before.

The day after we were happy indeed, for we saw Garrick, the

[1] See p. 41, n. 3.

inimitable Garrick, in Bayes! O, he was great beyond measure! . . . never in my life did I see any thing so entertaining, so ridiculous,— so humorous,—so absurd!¹

Fanny saw Garrick again 'exquisitely great' as Lear and 'sublimely horrible' as Richard III, 'so truly the monster he performed'. 'It is inconceivable how terribly great he is in this character!' And yet, 'never was character so well entered into' as that of Abel Drugger.

> Never could I have imagined such a metamorphose as I saw; the extreme meanness, the vulgarity, the low wit, the vacancy of countenance, the appearance of *unlicked nature* in all his motions.[1]

In the years 1770–3 she went with family groups occasionally to the pleasure-gardens, Ranelagh, Marylebone Gardens, or Vauxhall; to the opera, to concerts, benefits, and rehearsals. Yet nothing could exceed the rapture of the evenings when the opera singers and composers came to her father's house and sang their sweet Italian airs to the accompaniment of the harpsichord. In instrumental music Charles Rousseau's performances struck all hearers with astonishment. The Italians, who gave most of their attention to the voice, sometimes laughed aloud with amazement and pleasure. Esther also won her share of acclaim when, to the astonishment of Sacchini, she played the overture to his new opera, then unprinted, but half of which she had got by ear at the rehearsals. The peak of the evening was reached when Millico sang. 'Never', said Fanny, 'have I known pleasure so exquisite, so heartfelt, so *divinely penetrating*.'[1]

Young Charles, at the Charterhouse since 1768, reviewed all these pleasures and many others in a long rhyming letter addressed to Fanny:[2]

Dear Sister,

. . . .
Whilst you are *flirting* ab^t town,
In linnen or in silken gown;
Whether to Drury Lane you croud,
And at Dear Garrick laugh aloud; . . .
You laugh at Bayes, or weep at Lear,
Hate Richard, but applaud the Play'r; . . .

[1] ED, i. 163, 186, 194–215, 264–5.
[2] A.L.S. (Osborn) from CB, Jr., to FB, 3 May 1774.

> You laugh if Ranger trip the scene:
> In heart, as countenance serene; . . .
> Or else Miss Ford's box is bespoke
> To hear Ned Shuter crack a joke: . . .

> At Ranelagh, or perhaps Vauxhall,
> You shine or pelse upon the Mall.
> Or else dear Millico to see,
> You croud the upper Gallery. . . .

As for Charles himself at sixteen,

>   I now at college
> Fag hard in search of further knowledge. . . .
> Berdmore is really very strict,
> And will sharp punishment inflict,
> On Idleness—& therefore I
> Wholly to Greek my mind apply.[1]

On quiet days, meanwhile, Fanny and Susan also sought further knowledge. They had been trying to master a treatise by Diderot on the theory of music, a subject on which later Susan was '*capable de juger en professeur*',[2] or so said Pacchierotti. They were reading Italian and, as before, the English poets and the 'best French works', including Voltaire. Fanny read, or rather studied, the standard histories of her time (Hume, Rollin, Rapin, Stanyan, Smith's *Thucydides*) and, in 1771, Nathaniel Hooke's *The Roman History from the Building of Rome to the Ruin of the Commonwealth* in four volumes, followed by Middleton's *History of the Life of M. Tullius Cicero*.[3] She read travel tales and heard them at first hand from voyagers like her brother or travellers like Richard Twiss, Bruce of the Nile, and others who seemed to accept and honour Dr. Burney by virtue of his *Tours* as a member of their will-o'-the-wisp profession.

In the summer (August 29, 1772) Mrs. Burney gave birth to a third daughter, Sarah Hariotte (as spelled in the parish register). The child was baptized on September 29 in the parish of St. Nicholas at King's Lynn, the second Burney novelist to be baptized in that Chapel of Ease.[4] Unlike her brother, the beautiful Dick, she had inherited no beauty except luxuriant hair. (Mr. Twining saw her at five years of age as 'a little thing

---

[1] See p. 45, n. 2.   [2] ED, I. lxxiv.
[3] See p. 26, n. 1.
[4] See the parish registers of St. Nicholas, King's Lynn.

buried under a great periwig, that turned out to be Queerness. I am glad you won't suffer that hair to be cut.')[1] Somehow the stars had crossed. Brought up, as Maria said, 'in a perpetual state of Warfare',[2] she developed what would now be called personality problems. For many years she was known as 'poor Sal', Mrs. Burney's 'poor little neglected Girl, Sally', half-ruined already, it was feared, in temper and manners, though everyone felt that she was improving or would soon begin to improve.[3]

Before this (in July, 1772) the Doctor had set out for Germany to collect additional materials for his History of Music. He returned in December with travel tales, like those of his Alpine journey, to make porcupines of all who heard them, but with the hardships of winter travelling, 'over-work and over-hurry', he came down, as soon as he reached home, with the 'merciless pangs of the acutest spasmodic rheumatism'. It was at this time, apparently, that Fanny began her onerous service as amanuensis. According to her later accounts, her father never lost any 'fragment of leisure'.

Every sick or failing pupil bestowed an hour upon his pen. Every holiday for others, was a day of double labour to his composition. Even illness took activity only from his body, for his mind refused all relaxation. He had constantly, when indisposed, one of his daughters by his side, as an amanuensis; and such was the vigour of his intellect, that even when keeping his bed from acute rheumatism, spasmodic pains, or lurking fever, he caught at every little interval of ease to dictate some illustrative reminiscence; to start some new ideas, or to generalize some old ones; which never failed to while away, partially at least, the pangs of disease, by lessening their greatest torment to a character of such energy, irreparable loss of time.[4]

The amanuenses were more than willing. It would have been 'out of all nature', monstrous, repugnant to all ideas of filial piety, duty, and gratitude, to grudge such service, or in memoirs or diaries to dwell on the work of scribe and copyist. It is not from Fanny herself, therefore, but from the complaints and dissatisfaction of people like Stephen Allen that one hears 'how

[1] A.L.S. (BM) from the Rev. Thomas Twining to CB, 6 Oct. 1777.

[2] A.L.S. (Barrett) from Maria Allen Rishton to FBA, 24 Dec. 1796.

[3] *Burford Papers*, pp. 58–60; Maria Rishton's letters, 1774–96; Susan Burney's Journal (Berg), 27 July 1788.

[4] *Memoirs*, i. 224–33, 244–7; Scholes, i. 198–260; ED, i. 221–2.

close the Doctor kept Fanny to writing'.[1] Not that Stephen
cared about Fanny and the Doctor. He was giving voice, rather,
to the unhappy jealousy and resentment of his mother, who
needed constant companionship to drive away the 'foul fiend'
and who felt neglected and much put upon in the management
of the household with only young Charlotte as her right hand.

The work on *The Present State of Music in Germany, the Netherlands, and the United Provinces* went on through the winter of 1772,
and on May 2, 1773, it appeared. The German *Tour* had cost
the author 'sickness, fatigue, exorbitant expense, and poignant
bodily suffering' but among the compensations for all this was
Baretti's report that Dr. Johnson had pronounced Dr. Burney
'*one of the first writers of the age* for travels'. It later appeared that
Dr. Johnson had skipped a bit over the great pipes of the
Netherlands; yet such praise gave Dr. Burney great pleasure
and spurred him on.[2] Subscriptions gave proof of public interest
in the great work planned, *A General History of Music*, and before
the summer vacation of 1773 author and copyist were again
at work.

Maria Rishton, however, had other plans for the scribe
Fanny.[3] Though still in disfavour with her mother over the
elopement, she wished to obtain the Doctor's consent to Fanny's
paying a long visit to Teignmouth, where Maria and her husband had secured a cottage for the summer. It was impossible,
Maria said, that Fanny could be 'a person of such immense
consequence' that she could work on the History alone while
her father was absent in Lynn—and that in the dog-days—
unless, of course, she was 'to be the Authoress' and only 'allow
the Dr. the merit of it'. 'I own that will be noble.'[3] The Doctor
might have used a copyist for the pages produced when he left
Lynn during his own vacation and went quietly off to his friend
William Bewley at Great Massingham, where, as he wrote Mr.
Twining,

I am at work upon the *opus magnum*, in Peace and Quiet, for I can
do nothing at it in London on acct of Eternal Interruptions, nor at
Lynn for eating & drinking.[4]

[1] See p. 37, n. 3.   [2] See p. 47, n. 4.
[3] ED, i. 201 n., 212 n.–213 n., 224 n.–225 n., 228–62, 273 n.–278 n., 279. The
originals are in the Berg Collection.
[4] A.L.S. (BM) from CB to the Rev. Thomas Twining, 30 Aug. 1773.

As to the Doctor's chief objection—Fanny's travelling alone—Maria, who had travelled by herself since she was sixteen, had noticed that the stage-coach was not the conveyance for '*Bucks* or *Mackeronies*'. One was likely to meet there only reputable tradesmen, their wives or daughters, or perhaps a mantua-maker or a milliner.

I must say with a deep sigh—we don't Live in an Age for Adventures—Nor have we the men spirit enough to be knight errants—[1]

She wondered that the Doctor had not thought of Fanny's travelling on a cow and feeding on her milk, as she herself had longed to do ever since she had read his Italian *Tour*. Finally she wrote to her stepfather himself saying that she would take his consent as a mark of the kind partiality that he had ever shown her and that she would never forget. Here she struck the right note. The Historian of Music yielded, and early in July (Fanny was now twenty-one) she set off alone in a post-coach for the Oxford Inn at Exeter, where the Rishtons had sent a whisky to meet her.

Once at Teignmouth Fanny began a journal for Susan, which was to fill a *cahier* of about one hundred pages (some thirty pages in print). Fanny had had practice enough in copying, if not in writing, *Tours*, and this journal, lent to Mr. Crisp, who begged to lend it to his sister and others, was the first of her diaries to go into private circulation.

The holiday came to an end in late September, when the Rishtons brought Fanny to London. A little loneliness had crept into Maria's letters to Fanny: 'Indeed I *feel* it no Joke parting with one whose loved society I have enjoy'd so long.' 'I hope there is so firm a friendship in our hearts . . . that no ill nature or Insinuations can ever lessen it.'[2] The year ended in Queen Square with a bout of family nursing. Fanny had sat up three nights with her 'poor mother', who with such attentions had turned 'exceedingly kind'. The faithful and affectionate Dorothy Young had been sent for. 'I love her much', said Fanny, 'and hope we shall keep her some time.'[3]

In 1774 Fanny neglected her Journal to Nobody. 'Almost two months have elapsed without my recording one anecdote!'[4]

[1] See p. 48, n. 3.   [2] See p. 41, n. 2.

[3] See p. 26, n. 1.

[4] *Memoirs*, i. 288–93; ED, i. 279–83, 313–14, 328.

She also neglected her correspondence with Maria. 'Are you sure, James, Miss Burney did not give me any letter or parcel?' 'No indeed, ma'am.' 'Well then she is a false perfidious girl, and so much for her.'[1] The commonplace-book is almost bare, and there were no critiques of books, plays or players, concert performances or operas, no records of expeditions to pleasure-gardens, theatres, or exhibitions, though no doubt they still filled a part of Fanny's life. For Mr. Crisp, indeed, she wrote a description of the Otaheitan Omai, the noble savage brought from his southern island with Cook's expedition; a report of the coarse conversation of Dr. Shebbeare ('As to Susy and I, we never presumed to open our lips for fear of being affronted!'); and a full account of the puppyisms of the Spanish traveller, Richard Twiss. These went a little beyond the mark in Queen Square when, with the fearsome trio Mrs. Allen, Mrs. Young, and Mrs. Burney all present, he talked about Spanish and Italian ladies easy of access, fandangos, bull-fights, and *billet-doux*, asked Dr. Burney if in Italy he had been accosted by *una bella ragazza*, asked Fanny what assemblies she frequented and whether she had read *La Nouvelle Héloïse*, and recommended a Dictionary of Love. 'Even my gentle and candid father says that *he has quite mistaken the thing*, and that he shall never see a *table-cloth* in his house again, or be invited ever more to the tea-table.'[2]

All this while, Dr. Burney, occupied with professional engagements during the day, was working indefatigably at night on his History. According to Mr. Crisp's predictions on the consequences of such 'downright idiotism' ('How true is it, that he that increaseth knowledge, increaseth sorrow!'),[2] the Historian came down with a rheumatic illness, and in September and part of October, 1774, he went to Chessington to repair his 'spare Frame' and to write. To Fanny's great joy he took her with him, no doubt to copy out new sections of the History, but, restored by 'dear Old Liberty Hall' (that 'dear, dear place') to her 'old original rattling spirits', she proceeded with a new design of her own. In December when she closed the entries in her diary for the year, she remarked on their paucity, explaining obscurely that she was already 'in arrears with some *new* ones'. She had neglected the Diary not only for her father's History but for a

[1] See p. 48, n. 3.   [2] See p. 26, n. 1.

new, secret, and engrossing interest, though as yet no one except Susan knew what this was, or indeed that there was anything unusual afoot.

In 1774, when difficulties arose over the title of the property in Queen Square, Mrs. Burney with her usual resourcefulness found a large dwelling in St. Martin's Street, Leicester Square, the house once occupied by Sir Isaac Newton.[1] Though there were some regrets for Queen Square and its wide prospect 'ever verdant and smiling, of Hampstead and Highgate', the family were disposed to be pleased with the house in St. Martin's Street and its convenient location in the vicinity of the Opera House and 'nearly in the centre of the town'. The Doctor and Fanny, returning from Chessington on October 8, came directly to this house, which she said they proposed calling *Newton House* or *The Observatory* or 'something that sounds *grand*'.[2]

Newton House was torn down in 1925,[3] but Constance Hill's impressions of the interior serve to clarify some of the geographical allusions of the Burney diaries.[4] One would be struck first, she said, by 'the fine old oaken staircase' ascending by shallow steps to the drawing-room with its 'three lofty, recessed windows' overlooking St. Martin's Street, its deep cornice, and highly ornamented ceiling. She noticed folding doors opening from the drawing-room into the library, which served also as a music-room. Here the Merlin harpsichord must have stood, another harpsichord or two, and the pianoforte. It was here that Dr. Johnson on his first visit bent his great head and wig so closely over the keys of the pianoforte that the performers (Susan and Hetty) could scarcely avoid striking him or, what was more difficult, keep their countenances, from the oddity of their situation, or rather, of his.[5] It was not his great rough friendly heart that kept him from understanding music. When the piece was finished he kissed Hetty and then pored over the books, shelf by shelf, 'almost touching the backs of them with his eye-lashes, as he read their titles'.

Beyond the library was a small room known as Sir Isaac Newton's Study, which the Doctor appropriated and filled with

[1] See p. 26, n. 1.
[2] See p. 49, n. 4.
[3] Scholes, i. 263–71.
[4] *The House in St. Martin's Street* (1907), pp. 1–5.
[5] ED, ii. 152–8; *Memoirs*, ii. 86–101.

the materials of his science. Above, there were large bedrooms
and Dr. Burney's powdering-closet; above this again, a closet
appropriated to the younger children as a play-room, the room
in which, according to Dr. Burney, a large part of *Evelina* was
written. Below on the ground floor and facing the front was a
small panelled dining-room or 'parlour' with an old-fashioned
fireplace. On the top of the house was Newton's observatory,
from which during the Gordon Riots Susan—her knees all
'knicky-knocky like the Frenchman's in Harlequin's Invasion'
—watched a yelling mob build a huge bonfire of furniture in
Leicester Square and smaller fires in St. Martin's Street itself,
while away across to the City flames ascended from Newgate
Prison, a distiller's house on Holborn Hill, and from another
holocaust in Bloomsbury, where the sky was all red with flames.[1]

Of all places in the house the play-room and the observatory
were at the greatest possible distance from the parlour on the
ground floor below. 'To every action, there is an equal and
opposite reaction.' The more the turmoil, unpleasantness, and
demands increased below, the farther, ascending, one might
escape in one's mind to the free world of the imagination.
'Better to dwell in a corner of the housetop' than with a glower-
ing woman in a wide house. Up above, one might indeed remember the real world below, the words, actions, and grimaces
of men, and the ethical codes the best of them had evolved for
the rest to live by. In the early twenties oneself, one might think
of the entrance of the young lady into the world and in that
world, an ideal lover. Fanny's brief experience in the world, her
observations, and the imaginative conjurings of play-room and
observatory were soon to mingle in *Evelina*.

[1] Journal-letter (Barrett), July–Aug. 1790.

PLATE II

CHARLES BURNEY (MUS.DOC.)
by Sir Joshua Reynolds

MRS. BURNEY
by Gervase Spencer

FANNY BURNEY
Miniature by John Bogle

SUSAN BURNEY
by Edward Francesco Burney

III

NOVELIST

(1776–1778)

Distant as you may think us from the great world, I sometimes
find myself in the midst of it, though nobody suspects the
brilliancy of the company I occasionally keep.

FANNY BURNEY, 1777[1]

ERHAPS only in the dead of night was the house on St.
Martin's Street quiet and peaceful. In the Doctor's study
a candle often burned until 'two, three, four, five o'clock in
the morning',[2] and in the play-room or the bedroom shared
by Susan and Fanny another candle burned very late. Perhaps
only Susan heard intermittently through the dead watches the
soft sound of a quill moving rapidly over odds and ends of paper
and knew that Fanny was again scribbling about Caroline
Evelyn's daughter and her entrance on the great and busy stage
of life. This topic engrossed Fanny, and it was scarcely less
interesting to Susan and Charlotte, and later to many young
ladies in their teens and early twenties, who, like Dr. Burney's
daughters, were about to venture into London society. And it
was to prove no less interesting to gentlemen well out of their
teens, who had long since ventured.

An old family document[3] supplies data for a refutation of
Croker's accusations that Madame d'Arblay could not have
been (as she never claimed to have been) seventeen when she
wrote *Evelina*. It states that in fact *Evelina* was begun when she
was still younger; that in the very year (1767) that 'Caroline
Evelyn' was burned, Fanny 'composed in her own imagination
the story of *Evelina* & wrote scraps of it'; that Mr. Villars,
Lady Howard, Miss Mirvan, Sir John Belmont, and Madame
Duval were all principal personages in 'The History of Caroline
Evelyn' and had passed from that work to its successor. In the
summer of 1770, when the Doctor was in Italy, she was able

---

[1] ED, ii. 150. [2] ED, i. 269–71.
[3] Charlotte Barrett's notes (Barrett) for a reply to Croker's attacks on Madame
d'Arblay in the *Quarterly Review*, xlix (Apr. 1833), 97–125.

to regale Susan with scenes for the new work. In 1771 'she transcribed her father's *Tour* & continued her own writings'. In 1772, when the Doctor set out for Germany, 'she arranged and connected the disjointed scraps & fragments in which *Evelina* had been originally written' and formed from them a continuous narrative. After her father's return in 1772 and for the next year she was kept unusually busy as amanuensis; yet, as her defender goes on to say, 'at night, & in occasional solitudes', the adventures of Evelina 'kept offering themselves, in various scenes, situations, dialogues, and incidents, to her imagination'.[1] Only occasionally, with all the avocations of that house, literary, domestic, and social, did she have the opportunity to write down the pieces long '*pent in her head*'.[1] Chessington offered the best opportunity and it was probably in the autumn of 1774 when Fanny was there with her father that nine of the long journal-letters that agree with that calendar year were written.[2]

Though the dates of some of Evelina's journal-letters correspond to the calendar year of 1775 and were probably written then, in the long diary of the year no mention is made of the novel. The diary of 1775 is interesting, however, for its full accounts of life in St. Martin's Street and for stylistic developments that were to be reflected in *Evelina*. The *dramatis personae* are now introduced by short and effective character-sketches, and the descriptions of the evenings, when cast in dialogue, read like lively scenes from a play.

Susan and Fanny were charmed by the young opera star Rauzzini and the sublime Signora Agujari ('O, Mr. Crisp, she would heal all your complaints—her voice would restore you to health and spirits . . . so sweet, so mellow, so affecting!'). There were the visits of the Reverend Thomas Twining (Aristotelian Twining)—a man of infinite kindness, good humour, and drollery, a man of learning (said Fanny), 'very fond of music, and a good performer both on the harpsichord and violin'. For tea in the evenings there were relatives like Aunt Nanny, vainly hoping, as she frankly admitted, that she 'should meet

---

[1] For a document similar to but briefer than the above see 2 pages boxed with Diary MSS. (Berg), 1839.

[2] ED, i. 322–8. For a comparison of the dates of Evelina's letters with those of the calendar years see Sir Frank D. Mackinnon, ed. *Evelina* (Oxford, 1930), 'Chronology of the Story', appendix viii.

with no foreigner'. There were family friends like Dr. Ogle, the Dean of Winchester, also a man 'of drollery, good humour, and *sociality*'; Sir Joshua Reynolds and his sister, who lived near by; and in the mornings, if not in the evenings, still that 'most entertaining of mortals', Garrick. There were pages on the Man Mountain, James Bruce, 'the tallest man you ever saw in your life—at least gratis'. ('When he returns—if he should overlook *me*!' said Mr. Twining in a pretended fright, 'if he should think the chair Empty! I shall be crushed. It will be all over with me!'). Guests appearing at one time or another at the Burney concerts included Prince Orloff, ex-lover of the Empress Catherine of Russia; occasionally Jemmy Twitcher, the Earl of Sandwich himself, of famous name and character, as browned and 'weather-proof as any sailor in the navy'; and, by way of contrast, His Excellency, Count de Guignes, once a remarkably handsome man, but now grown 'monstrous fat', whose august departure (much inconvenienced by the dearth of lackeys at St. Martin's Street) provided one of the Burneyan jokes: '*Mes gens! où sont mes gens? Que sont ils donc devenu? Mes gens! Je dis. Mes gens!*'[1]

Small wonder that the St. Martin's Street journals were eagerly awaited in quiet Chessington. Mr. Crisp began to see new qualities and new worth in Fanny's conversation pieces:

If specimens of this kind had been preserved of the different *Tons* that have succeeded one another for twenty centuries last past, how interesting would they have been! infinitely more so, than antique statues, bas-reliefs, and intaglio's. To compare the vanities and puppyisms of the Greek and Roman, and Gothic, and Moorish, and Ecclesiastical reigning fine gentlemen of the day with one another, and the present age must be a high entertainment, to a mind that has a turn for a mixture of contemplation and satire; and to do you justice, Fanny, you paint well.[2]

What Mr. Crisp had now begun to prize was the play of the comic spirit, satire with its slight flips of the whip, implicit sting, and corrective force. This, too, was a tendency and a purpose to emerge again in *Evelina*.

There came the tender month of May, 1775, when Fanny good-naturedly accepted an invitation to tea at her sister's in

[1] ED, ii. 1–147; also *Memoirs*, ii. 9–68; A.L.S. (Barrett) from FB to Mr. Crisp, Mar. 1775; Susan Burney's Journal (Barrett), 1780.   [2] ED, ii. 143–4.

Charles Street. Esther had urged that it would be charity on Fanny's part to come, since Esther herself, in order to oblige their grandmother, was dutifully entertaining one of their grandmother's friends, a Mrs. O'Connor, along with that lady's deaf-and-dumb daughter, Miss Dickenson, and Mr. Thomas Barlow, a young man who had boarded with Mrs. O'Connor for two years. Aunt Becky and Aunt Ann and the grandmother also came to the party in Charles Street on May Day, 1775.

The evening went along as stupidly as was expected, not much enlivened after supper by a game of cross-questions. After some thought Mr. Barlow phrased the query that he wished to put. What quality did Fanny think most requisite in love? 'Constancy', she replied promptly, with fleeting thought perhaps of the fascinating but fickle Mr. Seton, or perhaps of the ideal lover that only she knew about, Evelina's lover, Lord Orville.

At eleven o'clock the coach arrived and Fanny rose to go, offering to set her grandmother down on the way. Mrs. O'Connor gave an urgent invitation to all the company to visit her the following week, and Mr. Barlow took occasion to hope most particularly that Fanny would make one of the party. Mrs. Burney then took affectionate leave of her granddaughters, giving Fanny, according to her custom, 'a kiss and her blessing', a ceremony that Fanny strongly felt ought to have ended there. But no, her aunts must kiss her in turn, and after them, Mrs. O'Connor, then the mute, and finally, in eager sequence, Mr. Barlow! After this Mr. Barlow watched the carriage out of sight and then went home to write his declaration. He experienced a mighty contest between his 'ardorous Pen' on the one hand, and, on the other, the dread 'of being accused of Adulation'. Mr. Barlow had never seen such an engaging girl, so lively and good-natured a countenance, but Fanny took not a moment to deliberate. She felt her heart 'totally insensible', as unmoved by Mr. Barlow and his epistle on this fine May morning in her twenty-third year as she had been in former times by Mr. Tomkin (the 'Dutchman') or by a certain Mr. Bloomfield with similar aspirations. 'I am too spoilt,' she wrote, 'too spoilt by such men as my father and Mr. Crisp to content myself with a character merely inoffensive. I should expire of fatigue with him.'

Since, however, she was not 'an independent member of society', she felt that she must show Mr. Barlow's letter to her father, but the Doctor, with the responsibility of four dowerless daughters, would not be hurried into a refusal. Fanny must consider.

Mrs. O'Connor meanwhile had called at Charles Street with such an account of the virtues, excellencies, pretensions, and the serious and honourable intentions of the young man, that Hetty was quite won over, and, as chief advocate, won still others to the cause—the grandmother, the maiden aunts ('Ay— when Fanny is *like us!*'), and, as a fell stroke, Mr. Crisp. If Fanny knew that 'villanous Yahoo called Man' as well as he did, she would regard Mr. Barlow's honest action and 'tender and respectful and submissive' letter in a very different light.

Ah! Fanny, such a disposition promises a thousand-fold more happiness, more solid, lasting, home-felt happiness, than all the seducing exterior airs, graces, accomplishments, and addresses of an artful (worldly man).[1]

He asked Fanny to consider the dismal and woeful plight of the indigent spinster.

Look round you, Fan; look at your aunts! *Fanny Burney* won't always be what she is now! Mrs. Hamilton once had an offer of £3,000 a-year, or near it; a parcel of young giggling girls laugh'd her out of it. The man, forsooth, was not quite smart enough, though otherwise estimable. Oh, Fan, this is not a marrying age, without a handsome Fortune!—Suppose you to lose your father,—take in all chances. Consider the situation of an unprotected, unprovided woman![1]

His advice proceeded from his regard and concern for her and his 'deep knowledge of the world'. Mr. Crisp has written 'such a letter!', Fanny confided to her Diary. 'God knows how I shall answer it!' Everyone was now against her except her 'beloved father'.

Presently a second letter came from Mr. Barlow's 'ardorous Pen', and eventually he paid a formal call in St. Martin's Street. He could scarcely speak, but fifty years could not make him more certain of his heart:

'I have seen Madam, a great many ladies, it is true—but never—'

[1] ED, ii. 47–86; A.L.S. (Barrett) from FB to Mr. Crisp, 22 May 1775.

'You do me much honour . . . but I must desire you would take no further trouble about me—for I have not at present the slightest thoughts of ever leaving this house.'

'*At present*? . . . No, I would not expect it—I would not wish to be precipitate—but in future—'

'Neither now or ever, Sir, . . . have I any view of changing my condition.'

'But surely, surely this can never be! so severe a resolution—you cannot mean it—it would be wronging all the world!'

. . . He looked very much mortified.[1]

'I was never so happy as when he left the house', Fanny later wrote to Mr. Crisp. But an evil crisis followed in a few days when her father again urged her not to be peremptory or precipitate. She was reduced to ceaseless weeping, ate nothing, moped,

and passed the whole day in more misery than, merely on my own account, I ever did before in my life, except (when a child) upon the loss of my own beloved mother, and ever revered and most dear grandmother.[1]

In a later interview the parent relented.

After supper I went into the study, while my dear father was alone, to wish him good night; which I did as chearfully as I could, though pretty evidently in dreadful uneasiness. When I had got to the door, he called me back, and asked some questions concerning a new Court mourning gown—kindly saying he would assist Susey and me in our fitting-out, which he accordingly did, and affectionately embraced me, saying, 'I wish I could do more for thee, Fanny!'

'Oh, Sir;' cried I, 'I wish for nothing! only let me live with you.'

'My life!' cried he, kissing me kindly, 'Thou shalt live with me for ever, if thee wilt! Thou canst not think I meant to get rid of thee?'

'I could not Sir; I could not!' cried I; 'I could not outlive such a thought!' and, as I kissed him—O! how gratefully and thankfully! with what a relief to my heart! I saw his eyes full of tears! a mark of his tenderness which I shall never forget!

'God knows,' continued he, 'I wish not to part with my girls! only, don't be too hasty!'

Thus relieved, restored to future hopes, I went to bed, light, happy, and thankful, as if escaped from destruction.[1]

Mrs. O'Connor wondered that a girl with so much good nature in her looks could be so cruel, or, rather, that a girl

[1] See p. 57, n. 1.

should know her own mind so well. 'Oh, Fie, Fie!' But the
Doctor, who had four dowerless daughters to marry or provide
for and two sons to educate, never once named Mr. Barlow
again. 'I thank Heaven!' sighed Fanny. She could now write
quite debonairly to Mr. Crisp. What were her objections?
There was nothing against the young man's 'character, disposition, or person—they are all good':

but he is not used to company, or the world; his language is stiff,
studied, and even affected. In short, he does not *hit my fancy*.

> 'I do not like you, Dr. Fell,
> The reason why I cannot tell.
> But I don't like you, Dr. Fell.'

And she signed all letters on the subject with the BURNEY
written large. 'I AM QUITE FIXED.'[1]

Meanwhile the work in the study went on. The completion
of the first volume of *The General History of Music* in 1775 ('with
my paw too!') must have cost the amanuensis many an hour's
work. Fanny's letter of June 1, informing Mr. Crisp that her
father would arrive within a week, and an extant letter from
the Doctor, dated Chessington, August 2, suggest that he may
have spent almost three months there in completing the great
task.[2] Nowhere, so good a place to write. From Chessington he
had been ordered to Buxton for September and, after three
weeks of the waters there, he tried sea-bathing at Cley in
Norfolk. He had come home in mid-October in good health,
Fanny reported, though his hand was 'still *obstinately bent*' from
rheumatism.

The long period at Chessington had placed the first volume
of the History 'in great forwardness', and while the Doctor was
trying curative waters, his friend Mr. Twining toiled over the
manuscript. The 'long cessation' that Fanny speaks of on
October 30 may refer to the time that Mr. Twining had taken
in his minute and scholarly examination of the work.[2] 'It is
now *rough* written', she went on to say, 'to the end of the first
volume, Preface and Dedication inclusive.' As usual she made no

---

[1] See p. 57, n. 1.
[2] A.L.S. (Cambridge University Library) from CB to —, 2 Aug. 1775; ED, ii.
77–78, 85–89, 101–2, 134–5. Also 7 A.L.S. (BM) from the Rev. Thomas Twining
to CB, 21 Aug.–3 Dec. 1775; and 16 A.L. and A.L.S. (Osborn) from CB to TT,
28 Feb.–24 Dec. 1775.

mention of the help that she gave, counting it nothing, no doubt, in comparison with all that her father gave her; but that she may have recopied the roughly written manuscript in fair batches for the printer may be inferred from Mr. Crisp's suggestion of December 30 that now, since the first volume of the History had gone to the press, Fanny might be allowed a holiday, might come with Jem to Chessington.

> Surely my little friend Suzette can at *any time*, much more at such a pinch, make out a list of subscribers as well as yourself. My love to her, and beg her to undertake it.[1]

Mr. Crisp, for one, thought Fanny's work on the History not without very good effects.

Ches. Nov[r]. 19

Dear Fanny,

>   That I wish for the remnant of your evening concert, is saying nothing. You have learn'd from that Rogue your father (by so long serving as amanuensis, I suppose) to make your descriptions alive,— send the remainder, therefore, without a moment's delay;—while breathing and warm.[1]

In 1776 Fanny had more leisure for writing than she had had for many a year, and her neglect of the diary and correspondence (even that with Mr. Crisp) indicates the degree of her absorption in Evelina's adventures. Not only the completion of the History but also the absence of the family on summer travels and visits gave quite unusual opportunities for writing. In the spring Mrs. Burney had gone to Lynn and Stanhoe for her health and on her return, though 'no *common* eye could discern she had been ill', she kept to a previous plan and set off in July for the Bristol Hotwells with further plans for two months in Wales.

Dissensions had grown rife of late in the troubled house in St. Martin's Street as the unhappy Lady grew still more unhappy.[2] There was not a member in the two families, the angry and resentful Presence must have thought, who with their intense and independent avocations would willingly sacrifice

---

[1] See p. 59, n. 2.

[2] 2 A.L.S. (Berg) from Maria Allen Rishton to FB, 1 Jan. 1775, 24 Sept. 1776, and A.L. (Barrett), 24 Dec. 1796. Cf. Susan Burney's Journal (Barrett), July 1789.

a day or an evening chatting in high and animated style with
her and her particular acquaintance before the parlour fire,
who would willingly read to her or attend when she was not
feeling precisely in spirits. One had to be at death's door to
gain the proper attention, and so one must prolong one's illnesses and convalescence as much and as pathetically as possible.
There was no conversation to be had, only music. And then the
eternal scribbling—not only in the study, but in chilly bedrooms, closets, and the observatory on the roof. Surely it showed
a lack of 'civility' and 'respect' to creep away from the parlour
fire to read and write alone or, worse still, to meet in hilarious
and treasonable groups in far corners of the house. Such warfare
developed that by September, 1776, even Maria was moved to
take her mother's part.

How comes it things are come to so dreadful a pitch between all of
you and my Mother—I have such letters from her they freeze my
very soul—even *mine* who *thought* nothing coud ever vaporize me—
I knew you never coud live all together or be a happy society but
still bad as things used to be when I was amongst you they were meer
children falling out to what they seem to be now. . . . You know
the force of her *expression*. And indeed I believe she writes from the
heart when she says she is the most miserable woman that breathes—[1]

In July, 1776, however, after a visit to Maria at Stanhoe
Mrs. Burney set off for the Bristol Hotwells accompanied by
the Doctor and, as little handmaiden or errand-runner, the
unwilling Charlotte.[2] Mrs. Burney's fifteen-year-old daughter
Bessy had been sent to Paris in the previous year to complete
her education. James, lately returned from America, sailed
away in August, 1776, with Captain Cook on a three-year
voyage.[3] Susan had accompanied Esther on a long summer's
visit to Worcester; Charles and Dick were somewhere on
schoolboy holidays, and the troubled house in St. Martin's
Street was deserted for the summer and at peace. Except for
little Sarah, Fanny was quite alone,—'at large and at liberty!'[1]
Now she could write anywhere—in the library, the study, or
the observatory on the roof—and she need not hide her written
pages.

It was fun now to develop the story of Evelina and the

[1] See p. 60, n. 2.   [2] ED, ii. 128–9, 140–2.
[3] ED, ii. 133–4; also Manwaring, pp. 24–70.

difficulties she encountered or brought on herself through her ignorance of life, and the quandaries and embarrassments in which she found herself by reason of the arrogance of the upper classes and the low vulgarity of certain members of her family. Susan and Charlotte had delighted in Evelina's scrapes and embarrassments and sympathized with her perverse luck in either failing to encounter Lord Orville, that embodiment of all wistful dreams, or else in meeting him unexpectedly in the most unpropitious circumstances. The proud and affected misses and the fops and beaux, the Mr. Lovels and the Sir Clement Willoughbys, were just such characters as the Burneys had often seen on the stage and had themselves acted in private theatricals. Fanny's versions, they might have conceded, were as interesting and as much fun as anything in Murphy, Colman, or Garrick. The Branghtons with all their low squabbles, loud laughter, and little meannesses were even better than the sportive pictures of absurd characters that Fanny had always liked to draw from life: being drawn from nature, they exhibited a more concentrated essence of innate vulgarity than could be easily found in particular instances in real life. According to eighteenth-century concepts of art such universals were to be hailed as truer to nature than the single example. But in the universal is the particular, and so true were these pictures and so unerring Fanny's gifts of delineation that she won the astounded acclaim of her age for 'just representation of life and nature'.

By the time the family returned in September or October to St. Martin's Street, adventures had accrued sufficient to fill a second volume of the history of Evelina. Fanny does not say when the wish to see her work in print—'a wish—as vague, at first, as it was fantastic'—took form,[1] but the practice (almost the habit) of book-making that she had known for the last five years in her father's study must have been sufficient by the momentum of its progress and procedures to carry her on to the press. The second volume, written that summer, had still to be transcribed, and, since her writing was known to booksellers and compositors, the volume must be copied in a feigned hand.[2] If the manuscript of Evelina were to be sent forth in the hand-writing of the *Tours* and the *History of Music*, and the great

---

[1] *Memoirs*, ii. 126.
[2] ED, ii. 161–4; A.L. (Barrett) from FB to Mr. Crisp, 28 Mar. 1777.

Doctor Burney suspected or derided by some scurvy lampooner like 'Joel Collier' as the author of the history of a young lady, what a horror! And what the 'Joel Colliers' could have made of that![1]

If, however, Fanny herself were to be suspected, the horror would be scarcely less, for if it were 'perdition' for a girl to read a novel what must it be for her to write one? Fanny knew also that the intellectual young lady was in some degree suspect. It was considered highly probable that the woman who took to writing novels and relaying the passions of men knew too much about them, and that such young ladies were likely to leap the conventional pales if they had not already done so. 'An *Authoress* must always be supposed to be flippant, assuming & loquacious', Fanny complained. 'And, indeed, the dread of these kind of censures have been my principal motives for wishing *snugship*.'[2] She also knew that scribblers of all kinds were subject to lampoons or mention in coarse pamphlets, and she shrank from such publicity. Every thought, in short, that one could have on the matter pointed to the need for secrecy. This was awkward, for in such a large and stirring family it was difficult to be 'snug'.

The fear of discovery, or of suspicion in the house, made the copying extremely laborious to me; for in the day time, I could only take odd moments, so that I was obliged to sit up the greatest part of many nights, in order to get it ready.[3]

And so she worked on in the chilly nights of November and December in remote corners of the house where fires were not usually lit. The candles burned low in their sockets as she wrote, for she worked with her father's speed and intensity, unheeding; she wrote on, cramped with the cold, bent almost double, with her near-sighted eyes close to the page, her nose almost touching the table;[4] and, seeing the neat pile of beautifully written material mount to the proportions of volumes, she began to consider which publisher to approach.

The young Burneys met in conclave on this problem, entering

---

[1] George Veal (?), author of the parody, *Musical Travels through England* (1774). See *Memoirs*, i. 258–60; Scholes, i. 272–5.

[2] Diary MSS. (Berg), suppressed fragments, box ii.

[3] See p. 62, n. 2.

[4] A.L. (Berg) from Mr. Crisp to FB, [1780–2]; *Diary*, i. 138.

into the quaint sport with 'more amusement than surprise', and after some consultation

Mr. Dodsley was fixed upon; for Dodsley, from his father's,—or perhaps grand-father's,—well chosen collection of fugitive poetry, stood foremost in the estimation of the juvenile set.

Mr. Dodsley, in answer to the proposition, declined looking at any thing that was anonymous.

The party, half-amused, half-provoked, sat in full committee upon this lofty reply; and came to a resolution to forgo the *éclat* of the west end of the town, and to try their fortune with the urbanity of the city.

Chance fixed them upon the name of Mr. Lowndes.[1]

Negotiations by letter ensued. The bookseller obediently sent his replies by messenger to Mr. King, and afterwards to Mr. Grafton, at the Orange Coffee House, where in 1776 they were picked up by Charles (presumably home from the Charter-house on a Christmas vacation), and later by Edward Burney, to be carried to St. Martin's Street, and then past 'the Lady', who was all unaware of the mischief afoot, to the seditious group met in palpitating conclave. This was a 'frolic' a little more ambitious than usual.

The first letter that Fanny sent to her publisher is still extant.

As Business, with those who understand it, makes its own apology, I will not take up your Time with reading Excuses for this address but proceed immediately to the motives which have induced me to give you this trouble.

I have in my possession a M:S. novel, which has never yet been seen but by myself; I am desirous of having the 2 first volumes printed immediately,—and the publication of the rest, shall depend wholly on their success.

But, sir, such is my situation in Life, that I have objections un-conquerable to being known in this transaction;—I therefore must solicit the favour of you to answer me the following queries, which I hope you will not think impertinent.

1st whether you will give a candid and impartial Reading, to a Book that has no *recommendation* to previously prejudice you in its favour?

Secondly, whether if, upon perusal, the work should meet with your approbation, you will Buy the Copy of a Friend whom I shall

[1] *Memoirs*, ii. 121–71.

commission to wait upon you, without ever seeing or knowing the Editor?

I shall be obliged to you to direct your answer to Mr. King, to be kept at the Orange Coffee House till called for, in the Haymarket.[1]

The bookseller's reply survives in a folder labelled

> Some of the Original Letters
> of Mr. Lowndes
> The Bookseller—
> To the Anonymous Author
> of Evelina
> with 2 letters of that Author.[2]

Sir

I've not the least objection to what you propose & if you favour me with sight of your MS I'll lay aside other Business to read it & tell you my thoughts of it at 2 Press's I can soon make it appear in print for now is the time for a Novel

Fleetstreet   Yr obedt Servt

Dec. 23, 1776   Thos Lowndes[2]

At this juncture, as Madame d'Arblay records in her *Memoirs* (1832),[3] Charles was muffled up 'by the laughing committee, in an old great coat, and a large old hat, to give him a somewhat antique as well as vulgar disguise; and was sent forth in the dark of the evening with the two first volumes [though from the tenor of the correspondence, the second volume was in outline only] to Fleet-street, where he left them to their fate'. He may have carried along a letter, a draft of which still survives:

Sir,

The frankness, with which you favoured me with an answer to my Letter, induces me to send you the M:S. with the firmest reliance on your candour.

The plan of the first Volume, is the Introduction of a well educated, but inexperienced young woman into public company, and a round of the most fashionable spring Diversions of London. I believe it has not before been executed, though it seems a fair field open for the Novelist, as it offers a fund inexhaustible for Conversations, observations, and probable Incidents.

The characters of the sea captain, and *would be* French woman, are

---

[1] See Note B, p. 492.   [2] See Note C, p. 492.
[3] See p. 64, n. 1.

intended to draw out each the other; and the ignorance of the former, in regard to modern customs, and fashionable modes, assists in marking their absurdity and extravagance.

I shall send you the second volume with all the expedition in my power, if that which is now under your examination, makes you desirous of seeing it,

I am,

s^r

Your most obd^t servant[1]

The conspirators awaited the result in 'trances of impatience', and in a few days a missive appeared in the Orange Coffee House, addressed to Mr. King 'To be left till called for'. Thomas Lowndes wasted no words.

Sir

I've read & like the Manuscript & if you'll send the rest I'll soon run it over.

Decr. 29   Yrs obed^t

1776   T. Lowndes[2]

This was encouraging, though the artist was 'much mortified that a multiplicity of perverse engagements' had caused a delay of a few weeks in the second volume.[1] 'There, the Heroine, as you will find, descending into a lower circle, now partakes of a round of *summer Diversions*', which, though of a more vulgar cast than those of the spring, are still 'productive of Incidents'. Pressed for time, Fanny suggested publishing in instalments, two volumes at a time.[1] On January 17, 1777, Mr. Lowndes replied:

Sir,

I have read your Novel and cant see any reason why you shou'd not finish and publish it compleat I'm sure it will be your interest as well as the Booksellers, you may well add One Volume to these & I shall more eagerly print it. I returnd one in a similar state to a Lady on Thursday who has before favour'd me with the Production of her Pen I w'd rather print in July than now to Publish an Unfinish'd book this I submit to your Consideration and with wishes that you may come into my Way of thinking I'll restore the MS to the Gentleman that brought it.

Fleetstreet   Y^r Ob^t Servt

Jany 17, 1777   T. Lowndes[2]

[1] See Note B, p. 492.   [2] See Note C, p. 492.

The decision plunged the new author in sloughs of despond. In her diary she duly recorded what the publisher had said with a pertinent comment:

Now, this man, knowing nothing of my situation, supposed, in all probability, that I could seat myself quietly at my bureau, and write on with all expedition and ease, till the work was finished. But so different was the case, that I had hardly time to write half a page in a day; and neither my health nor inclination would allow me to continue my *nocturnal* scribbling for so long a time, as to write first, and then copy, a whole volume. I was therefore obliged to give the attempt and affair entirely over for the present.[1]

Yet she could only acquiesce, and in a style acquired as amanuensis to her father she replied:

Sir,

I am well contented with the openness of your proceedings, & obliged to you for your advice.

My original plan was, to publish 2 volumes now, & two more next year: I yield, however, to your Experience in these matters, & will defer the publication, till the work is completed—though I should have been better pleased to have *felt the pulse* of the public, before I had proceeded.

I will write to you again, when I am ready for the press. In the mean Time, I must beg the favour of a line, directed as before, to acquaint me how long I may delay printing the Novel, without losing the proper season for its appearance.

I am, s^r

Y^r humble serv^t[2]

The work was probably delayed through January and February, but in March, luckily, Fanny was again allowed to make a long visit to Chessington, where she could write under ideal conditions.

All the household are kind, hospitable, and partial to me; there is no sort of restraint; every body is disengaged, and at liberty to pursue their own inclinations; and my Daddy Crisp, who is the soul of the place, is at once so flatteringly affectionate to *me*, and so infinitely, so beyond comparison clever in *himself*, that were I to be otherwise than happy in his company, I must either be wholly without feeling or utterly destitute of understanding.[1]

She was again at liberty to pursue her inclinations and again,

---

[1] See p. 62, n. 2.   [2] See Note C, p. 492.

as on a previous occasion, her pen ran serenely on with the resolution of Evelina's difficulties.

> Distant as you may think us from the great world, I sometimes find myself in the midst of it, though nobody suspects the brilliancy of the company I occasionally keep.[1]

Susan knew that this company comprised Lord Orville, Lord Orville's sister (the Lady Louisa), Mrs. Beaumont, Sir Clement, and the rest, who in the third volume of *Evelina* had assembled at the Bristol Hotwells. Mr. Crisp noted that Fanny had her father's intentness and energy. He worried over her 'murtherous stooping' and gave dire warnings, evidently without effect. He thought that she was writing merely journal-letters, which in time he hoped to read.

From this 'loved spot' she was all too soon hurried away by family duties. Her uncle was expected in town, and fearing that he would be displeased at finding that she had made a visit to Chessington at the time when she was invited to Barborne Lodge, she hurried home before he should arrive in London. Mr. Crisp felt the loss: 'You can't imagine how we miss'd you as soon as you were gone—There was a Void, which still continues.' He was none too well pleased with 'old Barebones', who had taken Fanny away, and his letters began to sound a little lonely. 'So now write a long account, a journal of yourself, and all your proceedings . . . a most minute, and particular account.' Since he could not himself go to London she should send him part of the 'turtle feast', which, to do her justice, had 'all the full relish'.[2]

To her father's pleasure and satisfaction ('no small consolation and pleasure to me') she arrived in time to meet her cousins James and Becky and her uncle Mr. Richard Burney, who had made up his mind to carry her back with him to Barborne Lodge near Worcester. 'And he would not be denied; nor let my father rest, till he obtained his leave.'[3] Before Fanny left, however, she wished to clear away a small matter very much on her conscience, and, penetrated by her father's 'parting embrace', she spontaneously confessed that she had sent a manuscript to Mr. Lowndes,

[1] ED, ii. 149–51.   [2] ED, ii. 158–210.
[3] See p. 62, n. 2.

earnestly, however, beseeching him never to divulge it, nor to demand a sight of such trash as I could scribble; assuring him that Charles had managed to save me from being at all suspected. He could not help laughing; but I believe was much surprised at the communication. He desired me to acquaint him from time to time, how *my work* went on, called himself the *Pere confident*, and kindly promised to guard my secret as cautiously as I could wish.[1]

The Doctor forbore to ask 'its name, or make any enquiries'.

I believe he is not sorry to be saved the giving me the pain of his criticism. He made no sort of objection to my having my own way in total secrecy and silence to all the world. Yet I am easier in not taking the step, without his having this little knowledge of it, as he is contented with my telling him I shall never have the courage to let him know its name.[1]

And so at the beginning of April Fanny set off for the long family visit. Her Worcester Journal gives a lively account of her cousins, among them, Edward Francesco, who had begun the study of art in London; the rodomontading dancing-master, Richard; and Becky, 'gay as the morning of May, and wild as the wind of March'.[1] The Journal also described the private theatricals staged on that visit—*Tom Thumb* and *The Way to Keep Him*—and the cleverness of James, Richard, and Edward in various foppish roles. At the arrival of the audience for the evening Fanny was almost incapacitated by self-conscious shyness and at first did very badly. 'Indeed, had my extreme terror lasted longer, I should have hated heartily the very thoughts of acting ever after.' As usual she was backward in public; but that when alone with her cousins she contributed original and comical inventions of her own in her old way is shown by the shrewd guesses that Bessy Burney later made about the authorship of *Evelina*. In 1778 Bessy was to write cautiously to Susan about a conjecture that had come into her head: 'I think I know a person not *one hundred* miles from Leicester Square very capable of writing such a novel—Indeed 'tis so clever and so much in her style!' Yet Susan was warned not to mention this notion, for Bessy well knew how 'extremely delicate' Fanny was about her performances. 'I never knew her allow any but her most particular and intimate friends to be the better for her uncommon abilities in this way.'[2]

[1] See p. 62, n. 2.   [2] ED, ii. 220-1.

When the Worcester visit came to an end (presumably in
July) Fanny returned to St. Martin's Street. As in the preceding
summer, the family were widely scattered, and Fanny and
Charlotte, now a gay and lively girl of sixteen, seem to have
had the house to themselves until at the close of August Mr. Crisp
and his sister Mrs. Gast arrived to carry Fanny off to Chessington. 'My mother is gone to Paris', wrote Charlotte on August 25,

my father to Mr. Thrale's at Stratham—Fanny to Chessington—
Susey to Howletts—Dick to Hindon—and Jemm to Otahieta—so
they are pretty well dispersed *methinks*, and I am left at home to keep
house, unless somebody should run away with me, as Mr. Crisp says.[1]

This was a propitious turn of events for Fanny, and in September she completed the third volume of *Evelina*.

Dr. Burney's friendship with the Thrales had developed
rapidly since his introduction to Streatham in 1776. Before long
(before 1778, as he recorded in his Memoirs) he was to receive
a salary of £100 a year from Mr. Thrale for dining at Streatham
once a week and remaining for the evening, departing as early
as he wished in the morning.[2] Part of the time was spent over
Queeney's music lessons, though at Streatham conversation
easily won over music as a social asset. The Doctor seems to
have spent the summer in rounds of visits to Streatham,
Hinchinbroke, Garrick's villa at Hampton, and other hospitable
homes, and in excursions to the seaside.

Mrs. Burney had gone to Paris to visit her sixteen-year-old
daughter Elizabeth (Bessy) Allen, who, though apparently
quite unimprovable, had been sent abroad to complete her
education. The summer's visit was abruptly concluded when
Bessy, instead of returning with her mother as was planned,
eloped with an adventurer, Mr. Meeke. Returning alone,
Mrs. Burney stopped at Streatham under the impression that
her husband was still there. 'Greater, & more real Distress',
reported Mrs. Thrale to Dr. Johnson, 'have I seldom seen.
Poor Thing!'[3] Bessy had been a favourite, 'much indulged and
spoiled', and Mrs. Burney shrank from the triumphant sympathy

[1] ED, ii. 284; and A.L. (JRL) from CB to HLT, Nov. 1777.
[2] Memoirs (Berg); *Thraliana*, i. 136–7; letters (JRL).
[3] A letter from HLT to Dr. Johnson, 18 Oct. 1777, printed in *The Letters of
Samuel Johnson with Mrs. Thrale's Genuine Letters to him*, ed. R. W. Chapman (3 vols.,
1952), ii. 556a–b; and Dr. Johnson's reply, 22 Oct. 1777, ii. 557.

of her stepchildren in St. Martin's Street. This was the second elopement in her family, and the ungrateful blow was hard enough without additional mortifications. Mrs. Burney had intended, said Dr. Johnson, 'to enjoy the triumph of her daughter's superiority'. 'The consolations of (Burney's) girls must indeed be painful.' 'There is in this event', continued the great moralist, 'a conflagration of the soul.'

Every avenue of pain is invaded at once. Pride is mortified, tenderness is wounded, hope is disappointed. Whither will the poor Lady run from herself?[1]

The reply to this query emerges in a letter from Dr. Burney to Mrs. Thrale.

You are very good ('but 'tis a way you have') to try to comfort poor Madam after her unfortunate Campaign on the Continent. She changed her Resolution, & came to London the day after her Landing, & the Day following we went together into Surry, for a week. She is now in Town, but invisible: 'Tis humiliating to tell melancholy Stories ab^t one's Self, & more so to hear people pretend to pity one, when we know they have no more feeling than *Punch*. I hate to think of the Trick that has been played her, & still more to talk about it.[2]

The Doctor, still unaware of the blow in store for him through the wild acts of one of his own children, tried to comfort his wife with verses for her birthday, October 20.

> May black Ingratitude no more torment
> Or Reminiscence petrify the heart![3]

Fanny's sly comment on the affair was given to Madame Duval, the noisy old grandmother in *Evelina*, who was of the opinion that Evelina, too, 'greatly wanted the polish of a French education'. Madame Duval

particularly instanced a Miss Polly Moore, daughter of a chandler's-shop woman, who, by an accident not worth relating, happened to be sent to Paris, where, from an awkward, ill-bred girl, she so much improved, that she has since been taken for a woman of quality.[4]

The peace of the summer was indeed broken. Bessy Meeke settled for a time at Geneva, though at various awkward crises in her troubled affairs she was to make unheralded descents on

---

[1] See p. 70, n. 3.
[2] In a Letter Book (JRL), Nov. 1777.
[3] Osborn.   [4] *Evelina*, i. xvii.

England and St. Martin's Street. At a time ten years or more hence Fanny shuddered with repugnance in giving her 'a salute' of welcome, noticing that Bessy's trepidation was soon followed by gathering boldness, 'daring spirit & exertion'. 'Afflicting to me—& *shocking* was her sight—& still more her manners & her courage.'[1]

Meanwhile, in the same month, October, 1777, a second catastrophe was preparing, not at Paris as before, but at Cambridge, where the wayward Charles had been pilfering books from the University Library. Charles, having completed his studies at the Charterhouse in April, had entered the University as a member of Caius College, and an entry in William Cole's *Alphabetical Collections for an Athenae Cantabrigienses* will tell what happened there in October, 1777.

Berney,—Caius College, 1777. Undergraduate. Son of Dr. Berney, Mus: D[r] who has so learnedly & pleasingly entertained the Public with his Musical Travels & Treatise on that Science, was admitted at Caius College, under M[r] Squire, & was very studious & industrious: insomuch, that he was admitted into the Public Library, tho' an Undergraduate. But Mr. Tyson of Benet calling on me this Day Thursd. Oct: 23. 1777, told me, that he & the Master of Eman: being in the Library, found some Books ill used, & which could not have been returned in that Condition without the Schole Keeper's observing it: so concluded it must have been done in the Library: whereupon an Order was given, that none under M[r] of Arts sh[d] be permitted to come there. Marshall the Schole Keeper accordingly acquainted Mr. Berney with the Order, who regularly came every Day & stayed till the Doors were closed. He however [after this] occasionally got Books out in Mr. Tilliard's Name, & sending them back, on some occasion the Man observed that several Books were misplaced: & in searching for them that a great Number had been taken away, chiefly classical Books of Elzevir Editions; whereupon he began to suspect Mr. Berney, & complained to Mr. Whisson, the Under Librarian, who advised him to be quiet, & contrive to get into his Chambers, & see if he could discover any of the lost Books: The Bedmaker said, it would be difficult, as her Master was very studious, & hardly ever 10 Minutes out of his Room at a Time, except at Dinner Time: he got in at that Time, & found about 35 Classical Books in a dark Corner, which he had taken the University Arms out of, & put in his own in their Place; & the Tutor being

[1] Fragments (Barrett) of FB's Court Journal; also letters (Berg) from Maria Allen Rishton to FB, 1775–83.

spoke to, he went into Hall the Day it was first discovered to him &
then disappeared: & this Week a Box of Books belonging to the
Library was sent from London, whither he had sent them. What
further will be done is unknown. I pity his Father, who must sensibly
feel the Stroke; as the young man can never appear again in the
University & so his views in this way utterly overturned.[1]

Thus all indeed seemed utterly lost, all the efforts of the years
sunk in disgrace. The young man, banished from home, was
soon to be found, for whatever the reason, in Shinfield, where
he remained for nearly a year while new plans were devised for
him. A volume of occasional verse written at this time reflects
the sylvan scenes of Berkshire and a romantic despair much at
variance with anything before heard about or from that studious
but merry-natured boy.[2] In a long autobiographical poem
(addressed to one of the distinguished Wollastons, a friend of
his Charterhouse days) Charles reviewed the 'poignant horrors'
of his 'wretched Fate', bewailing in couplets his banishment
from home,

> Torn from my Father, Brothers, Sisters, Friend,
> Can my anxiety e'er know an end?
> Must they, ye Gods, the grief I scarce can bear,
> Must they with me the heavy burden share?

'A Parent's rage, a Parent's grief' fills many another couplet.
The fault is his own, his help in Almighty God:

> 'Tis He alone can point the road to Fame,
> Can clear from vile disgrace my spotted name; . . .
> O let thy goodness point the better way;
> Thence by thy grace upheld, ne'er let me stray![3]

The Doctor, writing to the Reverend Thomas Twining in
mid-December,[4] had not at that time seen his son since the
University dismissed him, nor did he then feel that he could
ever see him again. It seemed to him that the boy was 'lost for
ever', and, ill physically and unable as yet to fight off the 'foul
fiend' Despair, he could think only of desperate expedients.
Charles, having irretrievably dishonoured his name, must
change it and take on another; having ruined his prospects in
England, he must go to the Continent, begin again if possible,

---

[1] In MS. (BM); also Scholes, i. 344–8.
[2] See Note D, p. 492.
[3] See Note E, p. 492.
[4] See Note F, p. 493.

or if not, carry on his nefarious life far away. The incredulity, anger, shame, and affright at St. Martin's Street can be imagined without the help of diaries that Madame d'Arblay later destroyed. The despairing letters that Doctor Burney wrote to his Cambridge friend, the Reverend Mr. Twining, have probably been destroyed also, but Mr. Twining's replies reflect the Doctor's unhappy confidences and deliberations, and, in the light of events, go far beyond them in mercy and wisdom, though it must at once be said that, as soon as the Doctor recovered a little from the blow, he acted as wisely and as indefatigably in Charles's cause as if he had never despaired of it.

Mr. Twining had never seen the 'unhappy boy' but he refused to condemn his error as irretrievable.

It seems to me essential to shew the young man all the tenderness, affection & encouragement that *can* be shewn him consistently with the letting him also see the greatness of his error, & the pain it has occasioned to yourself, & all his friends.[1]

As to consolation: 'God forbid I shou'd insult you with reasons & arguments, common or uncommon, why you shou'd not feel what you *must* feel.' But there was still hope. That was the point that Mr. Twining wished to make.

I repeat it—all seems to me to depend upon his being made to see the consequences of his conduct in a light that will make him shudder, & to see at yᵉ *same time*, that it is clearly in the power of his *future* conduct to reduce this unhappy step to a mere youthful indiscretion, that will either be forgot, or remembered without a stain.[1]

This advice was inspired and it fell on congenial ground in St. Martin's Street, where the family rallied and reclaimed the boy by love and kindness, a service of goodness later requited in full.

The foolish crime was to cling relentlessly to Charles, to cut him off at first from a career in the Church, to continue for years to rise like an ogre barring all advancement that depended on preferment and patronage. It was to take, in short, almost a lifetime to live down, though it *was* lived down, if not entirely forgotten by those of malicious memory. The long letter on the episode that Madame d'Arblay wrote at the close of her

[1] See Note F, p. 493.

brother's distinguished career (1817) in reply to queries put by
his son must perhaps be the definitive statement on the matter.[1]
Charles Parr Burney was apparently the only person in the
world to be kept in ignorance of his father's fault. How weary
Madame d'Arblay was of the old unhappy story that had
hounded her brother through his life, and to some extent the
family also, and that would not die. It is true that there was a
Fault.

Yet this, my dear Charles, was punished—& ought not, therefore,
to exasperate even an Enemy;—was pardoned & ought not, therefore, to cover any longer with blushes either his Family or his
Friends. AND—it was public, therefore you cannot hide it. . . .
I have many reasons—many!—for believing the origin of that
fatal deed to have been a Mad rage for possessing a library, and that
the subsequent sale only occurred from the fear of discovery. But he
never sought extenuation, nor except from you, ever troubled himself much about concealment: all he coveted was this:
To have his fault considered as JUVENILE as SINGLE & corrected
and as such he always looked back to it with regret, he held himself
entitled to look forward without shame—Imitate, therefore, &
adopt his philosophy; leave Anonymous writers to Themselves, &
detraction to contempt.[1]

After the Doctor had consulted Dr. Johnson and Mr. Twining
(who in turn consulted Dr. Parr) and had canvassed the question
as to whether a degree from a Presbyterian College would prove
a bar to ordination in the Church of England, Charles was sent
either late in 1778 or early in 1779 to King's College, Old
Aberdeen. How hopes were blasted! But the problem was
settled for a while. In 1779 all went well, though sisterly epistles
to Charles from St. Martin's Street seemed to temper prescripts
with somewhat doubtful hope. Susan was unable to say whether
James had been informed in family letters about the change
from Cambridge to Aberdeen and the reason for it, but she
ventured to hope

that we all may have the greatest dependance on your present &
future conduct . . . I have the satisfaction of hoping that you feel as
we do a very eager desire that you may become in *all particulars*

---

[1] For the request see A.L.S. (Berg) from CPB to FBA, 7 Feb. 1818. For Madame
d'Arblay's replies see a Letter Book in General d'Arblay's hand (Barrett), being
copies of Madame d'Arblay's letters written at Bath in 1815–17.

worthy our dear Father's kindness & protection, & consequently deserving of that peace and prosperity which I hope you will one day enjoy.[1]

Susan long believed that Charles bore the disappointments resulting from the crime but too well—'I sh^d grieve more for him—but not be the less satisfied, if he felt them more deeply.' Later she was astonished at the 'excess of his good fortune'.

Heaven keep him worthy of it—if he ever can *be* so—& may no levity or imprudence overturn his fair hopes, wch if realized will indeed fill me with everlasting surprise![2]

Fanny, in whom Charles confided many of his giddy escapades, thought him wild and careless enough in his youth, always, poor fellow, lacking 'penetration into Character, & foresight into events',[3] but the help and the support they were to give each other in recurrent crises in their lives were to become bonds that were not 'leaseholds ever to be broken'. Buoyant in spirit, 'facile, good-humoured, & open to conviction', Charles listened gratefully to prudential advice, even when he forgot it, and it was 'an excellent part' of his character, Fanny said, that he never forgot any kindness shown him. Charles's gay and careless youth, his levity, and his debts were one day to furnish copy for the career of Lionel Tyrold in Madame d'Arblay's novel *Camilla*.

Madame d'Arblay later destroyed the diary and all the letters that she could find bearing on 'family matters and anecdotes' for the years 1776–7 ('I have destroyed it in totality'),[4] but oblique references of later years point to intercessions that she made for Charles, while the *Memoirs* of her father include some of her recollection of final stages in the publication of *Evelina*.

Fortunately, the third volume had been completely written and transcribed at the beginning of November, 1777, and early in that month the packet was prepared for the bookseller.[5] Her first envoy, now dismissed from the University, was, as the *Memoirs* correctly put it, in the country, but a 'newly trusted

[1] Quoted by Katharine C. Balderston, *Thraliana*, i. 360, n. 3.

[2] Journal-letters (Berg) from SBP to FB, 5–12 Jan. 1790, with similar comments, Journals, 1787–91.

[3] A.L. (Barrett) from FB to CAB, 6 Aug. 1784; A.L.S. (Berg) to HLT, [1781]; Diary MSS. (Berg), p. 5110.

[4] See ED, ii. 136, 148, 284.   [5] See p. 64, n. 1.

agent' appeared in Edward Francesco, one of the Worcester cousins, who carried the manuscript to Fleet Street. No doubt there were 'transports' of joy over the acceptance, though they must have been cut short very soon by news of the plight of 'Mr. King' of the 'old great coat, and a large old hat', the wild, gay-hearted boy now cooling his heels 'in the country'.[1] Sorrow and dismay, almost Miltonic, must have sat on the countenances in conclave as they thought that, unless parental anger could be softened, Charles might never again share in the life of St. Martin's Street.

Readers of *Evelina* were soon to be exclaiming about Fanny Burney's knowledge of life. How could a girl who had scarcely left her father's house know so much about the world and human nature? The varied life in King's Lynn, Poland Street, York Place, Queen Square, Chessington, Bristol, Teignmouth, and Worcester, the variety of visitors, personalities, and creatures in St. Martin's Street itself 'from my *Mo*, and my *Do* to the cat and Charlotte's Sparrow'[2] supply part of the answer. The rest lies in her observation and imagination, in the ethical works that she read, and her reflections. 'But *where*, Miss Burney, *where* can, or could you pick up such characters? *Where* find such variety of incidents, yet all so natural?' 'O, Ma'am, *any* body might find, who thought them worth looking for!'[3]

[1] See p. 64, n. 1.
[2] ED, i. 278.
[3] Diary MSS. (Berg), pp. 843-4.

IV

EVELINA

(1778)

I never yet heard of a novel writer's statue;—yet who knows?
—above all things, then, take care of thy head, for if that
should be at all turned out of its place by all this intoxicating
success, what sort of figure wouldst thou cut upon a pedestal?
Prens y bien garde!

DR. BURNEY to Fanny[1]

THE composition of the first draft of *Evelina* had not been
difficult. The episodes in Evelina's world had taken form
readily in Fanny's imagination, and she had only to write
them down graphically and naturally in the unbowdlerized
idiom of the early journals—the familiar style that had always
pleased her sisters and Mr. Crisp well enough.[2] In 1776, however, after she had begun to think of an audience much wider
than the family group, and at the beginning of 1777, when
Mr. Lowndes had approved her work for publication and when
she thought that it would be read at least by misses in boarding-
schools, she grew dissatisfied with the first informal drafts. She
perceived for one thing that her novel, written with such speed
and secrecy and designed merely for her own enjoyment and
that of her sisters, was colloquial in style and therefore lacked
elegance.

A manuscript of one of the early drafts of *Evelina* is still
extant,[3] a priceless possession in itself, and of peculiar interest
in showing various stages in composition. As this manuscript
indicates, the speech employed in the first drafts was often that
of everyday life at Lynn Regis or Poland Street, broken by
picturesque dialectal expressions and tags picked up in the

[1] *Memoirs*, ii. 121–71. Diary MSS. (Berg), pp. 658, 686, 709.

[2] ED, i. 267–70; ii. 41–42.

[3] In the Berg Collection, the NYPL. This manuscript, consisting of 208 holograph pages, is not complete. It is not the first and not the last draft of the novel,
but the manuscript of some intermediate stage or stages of composition. It is
clearly legible and shows revisions throughout. One folio in the vertical 'feigned
hand' of the final draft may be seen in the Pierpont Morgan Library. A hand-
made title-page survives in the grangerized edition of the *Diary* (as in Note B,
p. 492).

theatre and the City, which the Burneys incorporated in their own speech—odd words or the idiom of foreigners learning English, or phrases from plays they knew well. Thus they amused one another; but this would never do in print. As the revisions of the extant manuscript show, Miss Burney eliminated such expressions from the conversation of Evelina, Lord Orville, and the other 'gentles', and concentrated the vulgar idiom in the speech of the lower classes. With these strokes she brought out contrasts in birth and character, and avoided the monotony of the sentimental novel of the day; she raised her work above the level of *Betsy Thoughtless* and its kind, and added to it refinement of manner along with refinement of expression—in brief, *elegance*, a quality by no means lost on her young contemporaries. 'So much wit, so much *sport*, such humour, such *Life*!' 'So much Elegance in it too! I know not how to say enough of it!'[1] The elegance, however, was not lightly attained. The first text, produced characteristically at headlong speed, was the spontaneous ebullition of a fun-loving spirit and probably read much as the Burneys spoke. 'The sudden sallies of imagination, clap'd down on paper, just as they arise, are worth folios', Mr. Crisp had said,[2] and though this advice might apply very well to 'familiar epistolary writing', to letters and journals to be circulated only among friends, Fanny judged that a book would require more care. Thoughts of the criticism her work must brave, of notices or reviews with the usual contemptuous remarks about 'the commonplace trash that novels abound in' and about their vulgarity, spurred her to fresh efforts, or, more specifically, to revisions in the diction. A new critical faculty emerged. It was almost as if the stern but delicate, spidery, and informing hand of a professor in stylistics had gone over the girlish text. Thus the colloquial and somewhat broken style of

Home early. I cannot but be hurt at the opinion this man entertains of me—though I deserve no better—yet he is himself, the most agreeable, & seemingly the most amiable man in the world—well! I can't help it—but I think I have done assemblies!—This morning was set apart for *seeing sights*—such as the Tower—the abbey . . .[3]

[1] Diary MSS. (Berg), pp. 1261–2; ED, ii. 221; *Diary*, i. 48; ii. 46, 60–66.

[2] See p. 78, n. 2.

[3] Vol. i, letter xii. This collation and those to follow are made between the manuscript of *Evelina* (Berg) and a first edition of *Evelina* (of which the Berg Collection has three copies).

is changed to—

I cannot but be hurt at the opinion he entertains of me. It is true, my own behaviour incurred it—yet he is himself the most agreeable and, seemingly, the most amiable man in the world, and therefore it is, that I am grieved to be thought ill of by him: for of whose esteem ought we to be ambitious, if not of those who most merit our own?—But it is too late to reflect upon this now. Well, I can't help it;—However, I think I have done with assemblies!

This morning was destined for *seeing sights*, auctions, curious shops . . .[1]

A comparison of the original section with the printed text will show the trend of the improvements: the clarifying of occasional ambiguous phrases, pruning of unimportant or superfluous details, tightening of the sentence structure, replacing of direct, artless, and informal effect by one of greater finish, dignity, and elegance. The manuscript text reads:

Feb. 11, London Tuesday

My dear Sir,

We came Home from the Ridotto so late, or rather so early, that I cᵈ hardly persuade myself to go to Bed, Indeed we did not go— you will be frightened to hear it—till past Eleven—but nobody does —a terrible reverse of the Order of Nature! We sleep with the sun, & Live with the moon—the Captain went with us. The Room was magnificent—the decorations brilliant & the company splendid— Though I should have told you, I objected to going very much—but Maria Laughed me out of any scruples—& so, once again, unfortunately for me I went to an assembly!

Miss Mirvan danced a minuet—who with I know not.—In our walks—we saw Ld. Orville—he was quite alone—but did not observe us. As he seemed of no Party, I thought it was not impossible he might join us—& though I did not wish to Dance at all—yet as I knew more of him than of any body else in the Room—why I thought it would be preferable to me to Dance again with him than with an entire stranger. To be sure, after all that had passed, my thoughts had no probability to strengthen them—but I am obliged to mention them, on acct. of what followed. Maria was soon engaged—& presently after, a Gentleman, much dressed, who seemed about 30— came & asked *me* to dance—Now Maria's partner was of Mrs. Mirvan's acquaintance—for she had told us that at a Public assembly no girls should dance with strangers. I blush to tell it you—but I told

---

[1] See p. 79, n. 3.

him I was engaged.—For then, I th^t I was still at liberty to Dance in case of accident.[1]

For the letter that was to be printed, however, Evelina managed a much more polished account.

Tuesday, April 12.

My dear Sir,

    We came home from the ridotto so late, or rather, so early, that it was not possible for me to write. Indeed we did not *go*, you will be frightened to hear it,—till past eleven o'clock: but nobody does. A terrible reverse of the order of nature! We sleep with the sun, and wake with the moon.

    The room was very magnificent, the lights and decorations were brilliant, and the company gay and splendid. But I should have told you, that I made many objections to being of the party, according to the resolution I had formed. However, Maria laughed me out of my scruples, and so, once again—I went to an assembly.

    Miss Mirvan danced a minuet, but I had not the courage to follow her example. In our walks I saw Lord Orville. He was quite alone, but did not observe us. Yet, as he seemed of no party, I thought it was not impossible that he might join us; and tho' I did not wish much to dance at all,—yet, as I was more acquainted with him than with any other person in the room, I must own I could not help thinking it would be infinitely more desirable to dance again with him, than with an entire stranger. To be sure, after all that had passed, it was very ridiculous to suppose it even probable, that Lord Orville would again honour me with his choice; yet I am compelled to confess my absurdity, by way of explaining what follows.

    Miss Mirvan was soon engaged; and, presently after, a very fashionable gay-looking man, who seemed about 30 years of age, addressed himself to me, and begged to have the honour of dancing with me. Now Maria's partner was a gentleman of Mrs. Mirvan's acquaintance; for she had told us it was highly improper for young women to dance with strangers, at any public assembly. Indeed it was by no means my wish so to do; yet I did not like to confine myself from dancing at all; neither did I dare refuse this gentleman, as I had done Mr. Lovel, and then, if any acquaintance should offer, accept him: and so, all these reasons combining, induced me to tell him—yet I blush to write it to you!—that I was *already engaged*; by which I meant to keep myself at liberty to dance or not, as matters should fall out.[2]

---

[1] Vol. i, letter xiii, MS. of *Evelina* (Berg).
[2] Vol. i, letter xiii, *Evelina* (1st ed.).

Additions to the original manuscripts include reflections or sentiments, such embellishments as 'Can you, *like patience on a monument* smile in the midst of disappointment?', and, as time went on, comments on current plays or operas, including praise of Pacchierotti as Evelina's experience expanded in the wake of Fanny's own. Finally she amplified the manuscript by character-sketches, which through long practice in her journal-letters she had learned to fashion as brief introductions to personages whom she was shortly to exhibit in action. The compact character-sketch preceding specimens of comic dialogue became a characteristic of the later diaries, and may be seen in the series of pen pictures that in Letter XVII (Vol. I) introduces the Branghtons, and in the sketch that in Letter XI (Vol. I) describes Lord Orville.

His conversation was sensible and spirited; his air and address were open and noble; his manners gentle, attentive, and infinitely engaging; his person is all elegance, and his countenance, the most animated and expressive I have ever seen.

Some care had to be taken with Lord Orville's language lest by a rough accent he should disturb this picture; and his utterances are, like himself, the last word in elegance though rather pontifical for modern taste:

'My dearest Miss Anville,' said he, taking my hand, 'I see, and I adore the purity of your mind, superior as it is to all little arts, and all apprehensions of suspicion; and I should do myself, as well as you, injustice, if I were capable of harbouring the smallest doubts of that goodness which makes you mine for ever: nevertheless, pardon me, if I own myself surprised, nay, alarmed, at these frequent meetings with so young a man as Mr. Macartney.'[1]

A comparison of passages in manuscript with their printed counterparts will show that undignified expletives like 'Faith' are removed from Lord Orville's utterances, and that he no longer 'wears himself out', but 'fatigues himself'. Sir Clement Willoughby's speeches are also repaired, relieved of abruptness, and augmented as he assumes importance as the villain of the piece. (' "The letter," cried he, gnashing his teeth, "you shall never see more!" ') The conversation of the fop, Mr. Lovel, already close to the language of the stage, is further rounded out with catchwords, mild oaths, and ejaculations. Such re-

[1] III. xvi.

visions helped to individualize character. And always by the
removal of awkward narrative detail or naïve observation,
Evelina becomes something above the schoolgirl, and the novel
is rendered pleasing to mature readers.

In the vulgar scenes too the dialogue sometimes seemed to
demand more cautious or judicious phrasing than that of the
first draft. 'Mr. Brown pulling Polly towards him sd. she must
sit on his Lap' is decorously changed to 'seated on a window,
with Mr. Brown at her side, sat Miss Polly'.[1] The manuscript
states that in the Marylebone Gardens Evelina is to be seen—
'gracious Heaven! . . . in company with 2 women of the Town!'
In the printed text she is 'with two women of such character!'[1]
By the insertion of additional speeches the scenes from low life
were often run to the length of acts in a play: ' "Miss must try
if she can't get a good husband," said Mr. Branghton, "and then
she may stay and live here." ' And later, the subject of the opera
being introduced: ' "Miss will think us very vulgar," said Miss
Branghton, "to live in London, and never have been to an
Opera; but it's no fault of mine, I assure you, Miss, only Papa
don't like to go." '[2]

Great care had to be taken with Evelina's speech, comments,
and sentiments, not only because she was the heroine, but
because the plan of the epistolary novel caused other characters,
situations, and events to be known chiefly through her pen. She
set the tone, therefore, for most of the work. In the final draft of
Evelina's letters the artless and feckless remarks of the schoolgirl
were in some measure restrained. The earlier text reads:

I am always to do wrong! Mrs. Mirvan & Maria have been all the
Town over—& *so* entertain'd!—while I, like a Fool, was moping at
Home. And at an auction in Pall Mall—who shd. they meet, but
Lord Orville! Well he sat next to Mrs. Mirvan, & talked a great deal
to her—but she gave me no account of their conversation—& either
he did not recollect with whom he had seen her or did not think or—
I suppose, care about it—but he never enquired after me—& Maria,
who sat on the other side of her mother, he did not seem to know.

But I shall never again have an opportunity of seeing London—
how could I be such a Fool!—but, I was rightly served for indulging
my ill-humour—Well—I do think I never will again—I shall certainly be the happier for always combating my spleen—

[1] II. xiv.   [2] I. xvii.

Thursday night

Just returned from the play—& within a few Boxes of us, sat Lord Orville—but he did not see us the whole evening. Well—adieu—it is too late to write more.[1]

In Evelina's mind the success of the evening depended on a meeting with Lord Orville, but in the printed text there is less peering about for his lordship than in the manuscript and more attention to the entertainment in hand.

I thought I had done wrong! Mrs. Mirvan and Maria have been half the town over, and so entertained!—while I, like a fool, stayed at home to do nothing. And, at an auction in Pall-mall, who should they meet but Lord Orville! He sat next to Mrs. Mirvan, and they talked a great deal together: but she gave me no account of their conversation.

I may never have such another opportunity of seeing London; I am quite sorry that I was not of the party; but I deserve this mortification, for having indulged my ill-humour.

Thursday night.

We are just returned from the play, which was King Lear, and has made me very sad. We did not see any body we knew.[1]

Some of the charm that won for *Evelina* the indulgence of aged eighteenth-century critics like the Dowager Duchess of Portland or Mrs. Delany was perhaps owing to this revision in diction. Before her work went to press, in her determination to make Evelina genteel and well-bred, just such a young lady as the matchless Lord Orville could approve, Fanny Burney turned Pygmalion. Evelina speaks no more of *Horse-Laughs*, therefore, but of *loud laughter*; refers not to the *parlour* but to the *drawing room*; not to *every fright* in it but to *whoever was old or ugly*; not of *home strokes* but of *sarcasms*. She decided to say that Lord Orville *made choice* of her rather than that he *fixed* upon her, and she gave over some of the colloquialisms of the day, 'Monstrous provoking!', and 'Lord, how *horrid slow* the man drives!' There is a difference between the Evelina who said 'I was so mad at this sneering speech that I had hardly patience to make any reply', and the one who wrote more carefully 'I was so much disconcerted at this sneering speech that I said not a word.' Like most people who grow up in places where dialectal expressions are preserved, Fanny Burney had at least two levels

[1] See p. 79, n. 3.

of speech at her command; and one of her tasks before sending
Evelina to the printer was, as we have seen, to make a greater
differentiation between the idioms of the upper and of the lower
classes. She transposed the speech of the 'gentles' (and especially
of Evelina) from the levels she had acquired at Lynn Regis,
Poland Street, or even at St. Martin's Street, where people from
different strata of society met, to that which she imagined was
spoken in London drawing-rooms, which she did not yet know
very well. Nothing surprised her contemporary readers more
than the *range* of life depicted in *Evelina* unless it was the realism
or verisimilitude of many of the characters. Her success in both
depended in large part on her attentive ear and the pains she
took to provide her personages with their characteristic speech.

Some of these revisions were made, no doubt, in transcribing
the fair copy in the feigned hand. Two volumes were ready for
the press at the end of December, 1776, while the visit to
Chessington in March, 1777, must have taken Fanny far along
in the third volume, though she was again delayed by the three
months' visit to Worcester. Late summer and autumn of 1777
in deserted St. Martin's Street and at Chessington probably
sufficed to complete the first draft of the third volume. Since,
however, she wrote rapidly and in a colloquial style, scribbling
from what may be termed an auditory memory of scenes and
dialogue 'long pent in her head', there was much work still left
in revising and copying. The latter presented special difficulties
since it must be done at night when she could work unobserved.
The October nights were getting cool; Susan with the incipient
trouble in her lungs could never have stood these nights of
writing added to the tasks and demands of the day, but Fanny
had her father's constitution and his ability to recover from
physical and mental exhaustion. Some of the phrases that she
penned in her Memoir of him were equally applicable to
herself: 'His Fancy was his dictator; his Spirit was his spur;
and whatever the first started, the second pursued to the goal.'[1]
Now she worked with her near-sighted eyes close to the paper,
her slight body stooped and cramped with the cold. 'That
murtherous stooping . . . will be your bane', said Mr. Crisp.
She was thinking of a Preface.

Many authors, she knew, wrote resounding prefaces, and

[1] *Memoirs*, i. 233.

novelists especially thought it necessary to write *apologias* for their art. Since her preface was to appear with her book anonymously, she might venture to touch on a most pertinent matter, the disrepute of Novels and Novelists. No one '*is so much disdained by his brethren of the quill, as the humble Novelist*'; but '*perhaps not one can be named of which the votaries are more numerous*'. Thus the general situation; now the injustice of it and a vindication of herself for following her great precursors, Rousseau, Johnson, Marivaux, Fielding, Richardson, and Smollett. '*No man need blush at starting from the same post, though many, nay, most men, may sigh at finding themselves distanced.*' And then the hopelessness of the attempt to condemn the new species of writing, and the good use to which it might be put:

Perhaps were it possible to effect the total extirpation of novels, our young ladies in general, and boarding-school damsels in particular, might profit from their annihilation: but since the distemper they have spread seems incurable, since their contagion bids defiance to the medicine of advice or reprehension, and since they are found to baffle all the mental art of physic . . . surely all attempts to contribute to the number of those which may be read, if not with advantage, at least without injury, ought rather to be encouraged than contemned.

The work here presented, she goes on to say in effect, is not a Gothic novel depicting fantastic regions, not one of the current sentimental pieces in which *Imagination* luxuriates and *Reason is an outcast*. All her effort will be to copy *what is*. '*To draw characters from nature, though not from life, and to mark the manners of the times, is the attempted plan of the following letters.*'

For this purpose, a young female, educated in the most secluded retirement, makes, at the age of seventeen, her first appearance upon the great and busy stage of life; with a virtuous mind, a cultivated understanding, and a feeling heart, her ignorance of the forms, and inexperience in the manners, of the world, occasion all the little incidents which these volumes record, and which form the natural progression of the life of a young woman of obscure birth, but conspicuous beauty, for the first six months after her Entrance into the world.

There is then a Dedication to the Authors of the Monthly and Critical Reviews, 'Magistrates of the press, and Censors for the public', who are asked to be just and, if not lenient, at least mindful that they too were 'all young writers once'. Then comes the dedicatory ode to the Author of her being. The verses to this Author

> far more dear
> To me than light, than nourishment, or rest,

had come into her head in the 'Dead of the night' at Barborne
Lodge on the first night of her long visit there, when she thought
of her father's affectionate farewell and his kindness about the
literary secret confided to him that day.

> Obscure be still the unsuccessful Muse,
>   Who cannot raise, but would not sink, thy fame.
>
> If in my heart the love of Virtue glows,
>   'Twas planted there by an unerring rule;
> From thy example the pure flame arose,
>   Thy life, my precept—thy good works, my school.

There was a crookedly printed title-page: *Evelina or a Young
Lady's Entrance into Life*,[1] afterwards revised to *Evelina, or, the
History of a Young Lady's entrance into the World*. The loss of the
diary for 1777, and contradictions between the story as recollected by Madame d'Arblay in the *Memoirs* and extant drafts
of letters written to Mr. Lowndes, but perhaps never sent, make
it difficult to say when the packet was finally carried to the
bookseller. The suspense was short. Very promptly (within a
few days, as Madame d'Arblay remembered)[2] Mr. Lowndes
made his famous offer:

Sir,
    I've read this 3d Vol & think it better than 1 & 2d. If you please
I'll give you Twenty Guineas for the Manuscript and without loss
of time put it to Press.

Fleetstreet,   Yr Obedt Servt
Nov. 11,   Thos Lowndes[3]
1777

According to the *Memoirs* of 1832 the sum was accepted with no
less alacrity and with 'boundless surprise at its magnificence'.[2]
These seem to be the roses of memory, for a somewhat thorny
letter drafted at the time indicates that the author was by no
means satisfied with the terms. Apparently Fanny had put a
price of thirty guineas on her labours. 'I should not have taken

---

[1] See facsimile, Constance Hill, p. 98; the original is in the possession of J. R. G.
Comyn.   [2] See p. 78, n. 1.
[3] Lowndes Letters (Barrett) as described in Note C, p. 492.

the pains to copy & correct it for the Press, had I imagined that
10 Guineas a volume would have been more than its worth.'[1]
She had planned to submit the manuscript to a referee,[1] possibly
Mr. Crisp, but the dire news from Cambridge or some other
family vicissitude may have prevented the plan. The letter,
perhaps, was never sent. Lowndes had the novel for twenty
guineas, and by the middle of January it was in print—in three
volumes that he now wished to have read for a list of errata
before binding. Fanny could not have the printed sheets appear
in St. Martin's Street, but she had taken the precaution to tell
her aunts about *Evelina* ('They will, I am sure, be discreet,—
indeed, I exacted a vow from them of strict secresy'),[2] and the
old ladies allowed her to use their address as a place less exposed
to perilous accident.

In January a parcel addressed to Mr. Grafton arrived at the
new address. Inside Fanny found the following letter:

Mr Grafton
    Sir
    I take the Liberty to send you a Novel wch a Gent. your acquain-
tance said you wd hand to him I beg with expedition as 'tis time it
should be published & 'tis requisite he should revise it or the
Reviewers may find a flaw

                    I am

Fleetstreet   Yr obedt servt
Jany 7, 1778   Thos. Lowndes[3]

The aunts insisted that she read aloud as she looked for errors.
'*Of course*, they were all prodigiously charmed with it', but
Fanny felt she could place no reliance on critical faculties so
biased by kindness and partiality for the author. Lowndes,
having got the manuscript, was rushing it into print, scarcely
waiting, as the author feared, for the corrections. Moreover, he
had sent her a faulty copy.

Sir,
    I am extremely sorry to have kept the press waiting, but I did not
receive yours of the 10th till this Instant. I hope you have not gone
on with the 2d volume, without the corrections:—
    I will send you the conclusions before the End of the week: but I
must beg you to let me have a waste sheet of the last of the 3d. volume

   [1] Included in the grangerized *Diary* (described in Note B, p. 492).
   [2] ED, ii. 213–19.   [3] See Note C, p. 492.

as the set from which I correct is incomplete. You will be so good as to give it to the bearer.

> I am,
>> sr,
>>> yr. ob^d serv^t.

Pray let the sheet you send be put in a cover, & wafered, & without any direction.[1]

When the list of errata was completed, the 'newly trusted agent' carried it to Mr. Lowndes.

The next dramatic scene was probably the breakfast table at St. Martin's Street when Mrs. Burney, securely in possession of the morning paper, favoured the family with items of interest, among them a notice inserted by Lowndes about a new novel, *Evelina*. Accustomed as she was to Treason, she did not seem to observe the extraordinary effect of the announcement—the crimson face of the authoress and the meaningful glances of Susan and Charlotte.[2] The joke went on through February and March, when the aunts read the book to Richard Burney without giving away the secret of its authorship and, unknown to him, the authoress listened to his comments and criticisms.

The winter of 1777–8 was not a happy one. On February 22 Dr. Burney wrote to Mrs. Thrale that he had a cold, that he had been 'snivelling & sulking at Home all the Morning'.[3] Presently, as the *Memoirs* record, he was dangerously ill with acute fever. Fanny shared 'the assiduous attendance upon the invaluable invalid',[2] and one has only to turn from the language of the *Memoirs* and edited *Diaries* to the private correspondence, the letters of Maria Rishton, for example, to learn of the rages, jealousies, sulkiness, and malignity that such attentions provoked in 'the Lady'.

No sooner had Dr. Jebb pronounced the Doctor out of danger than he was called to attend Fanny. 'Severe mental suffering from a Family calamity',[4] mental excitement, overwork, all added to the 'eternal avocations of this house', had combined to bring on one of the feverish illnesses to which she was from this time subject. At the end of March she began to recover from

---

[1] See Note B, p. 492.   [2] See p. 78, n. 1.
[3] A.L.S. (JRL) from CB to HLT, 22 Feb. 1778.
[4] Diary MSS. (Berg), 30 Mar.–23 June 1778 (pp. 648–58); scrap, series of letters (Berg) from FB to SBP [1778].

an indisposition 'long and dangerous'. 'Susy, Charlotte, Hetty, & my Aunts vied in good offices,—& my beloved Father was hardly himself till my recovery was out of doubt.'[1] For a long time she was unable to walk, read, write, or dress herself. Chessington was the place fixed on for change of air; and in May, Susan and her Cousin Edward accompanied her there, supporting her one on each side in a post-chaise all the way, and applying smelling salts when she seemed in danger of fainting. The tendency to faint continued for weeks; her eyes were still weak, and she could neither read, work, nor write for twenty minutes together. After a while she could 'stump' out into the garden by herself, though she could not keep pace at first even with Daddy Crisp. At the end of June, however, when her father visited Chessington, she was almost restored and quite able to enjoy the praise of *Evelina*, which had been making its way during this interval, though, as she adds, 'the length of my illness, joined to severe mental suffering from a Family calamity which had occurred at that period, had really made me too weak for a joy mixt with such excess of amazement'.[1]

All this while the two confederates, Susan and Charlotte, kept faithful watch at St. Martin's Street, excitedly reporting to Chessington the perils, escapes, and vicissitudes of *Evelina* and finally the discovery of the secret.[2] Sometimes the accomplices carried on hoaxes of their own. Without divulging the secret, Susan sent a copy of *Evelina* to Miss Coussmaker, whose comment is still extant.

Good God! My Dearest Susy I hope Evelina will not have such an effect on you as it has on me . . . I cannot tell you how it has affected me but I have never been well since, some part of the discovery is so tragical that I declare it worked me as much as the death of Desdemona or Belvidera though the subject is totally different— and how mortifying it is to think that so few nay I hardly know any Lord Orvilles or Evelinas to be found & so many Sir C Willoughbys —I prefer their characters by far to either St. Preux or Julie though they seem more natural. . . . I cannot hear any body talking of not having read it with any patience & yet 'Twas pitiful, 'twas wondrous pitiful. . . . Not any one character in La Nouvelle Heloise gave me half the Idea of nobleness, generosity, & goodness this book has.[3]

[1] See p. 89, n. 4.   [2] ED, ii. 220–54.
[3] A.L. and A.L.S. (Barrett) from Miss Catherine (or Mrs. G. O. Coussmaker?) to SBP, Howletts, n.d. and 7 Sept. 1778.

This reaction to *Evelina* seems typical of the novel-readers of the age. Later, when Miss Coussmaker had learned the name of the *incognita*, she rejoiced that she had come off with such flying colours in her criticisms. She praised the work ('infinitely beyond my Ideas of a Novel') on three counts:

There is not only *true wit* & humour in it, But the *true* pathetic! Many parts of it excites all the tender feelings that a good tragedy wd. do. And the letters of the worthy good old clergyman too would have done honour even to the pen of a Johnson.[1]

The three components here listed may explain the phenomenal success of *Evelina* in its age. It succeeded for its *wit and humour* (still tolerated), the *true pathetic* (now frequently called the *false pathetic*), and moral *observations* (now likely to be disdained). In a discarded preface[2] Fanny Burney had asked pertinent questions. 'Will maxims of conduct have any weight, where their Inditer is unknown?' 'Will opinions of right & wrong be heeded, where their promulgator has no party?' The answer, of course, is 'No', but not for the reasons suggested. A third query, scribbled by quill and candlelight, 'Will the World value the notions of Those of other Times?', has a more winsome interest and may gain some hospitality or toleration even for old 'maxims of conduct' and 'opinions of right & wrong'. But whatever weight the 'maxims' and 'opinions' may carry now, they impressed eighteenth-century readers, many of whom thought the serious part of the book as good as the comic and realized that the cream of the seriousness was in Mr. Villars's letters.

These monitory letters from the worthy old gentleman at Berry Hill, if read in sequence, will soon be recognized as a compact courtesy-book covering a surprisingly full list of the stereotyped topics treated in such works, many of which were also epistolary in form. *Affectation, artifice, coquetry, imprudence* receive due emphasis. Thus at a public assembly when Evelina did not know how to dismiss a persistent follower, she pretended that she was engaged to Lord Orville for the next dance. When her graceless pursuer, destined, as she said, to be the scourge of her artifice, had the cunning to mention the alleged engagement to Lord Orville himself, 'the fair artificer' was

---

[1] See p. 90, n. 3.
[2] See (Berg) *Miscellaneous: about 417 pieces of MS.* (*1727–1828*), folder iv.

ready to 'sink for shame' and, to the consternation of all, did indeed burst into tears. Nor did Mr. Villars in his role of moral commentator fail to point out how much more deserved this mortification was than others incurred more innocently through ignorance of the world.[1]

Like the authors of the courtesy-books and writers from Jean de Meun onwards who took some notice of the conduct of the young lady, Mr. Villars found it necessary to descant upon Prudence. Evelina often had cause to lament her lack of thought and foresight: 'Alas, my dearest Sir, that my reflections should always be too late to serve me! dearly, indeed, do I purchase experience!' And she went on to express a concern shared by Mr. Villars: 'Much I fear I shall suffer yet more severely, from the heedless indiscretion of my temper, ere I attain that prudence and consideration, which, by foreseeing distant consequences, may rule and direct in present exigencies.' Mr. Villars as well as Lord Orville worried over her private though well-intentioned meetings with so young a man as Mr. Macartney, and they had again to deplore her indiscretion, when, having been separated from her chaperons at an opera, she allowed the designing Sir Clement to entice her into his carriage. Her adventures there taught her to repent 'heedless imprudence' and to beware of snares. Evelina's mother, Mr. Villars said, had been 'led to destruction by her own imprudence, the hardness of heart of Madame Duval, and the villainy of Sir John Belmont'. When Sir Clement's villainy began to appear, the aged monitor cautioned circumspection: 'The slightest carelessness on your part, will be taken advantage of, by a man of his disposition.' The old gentleman was filled with misgivings as he was persuaded to consent that Evelina 'quit the protection of the hospitable and respectable Lady Howard' and accompany her noisy old grandmother to London. His counsel might have come straight from the courtesy-books: 'Do not, by a too passive facility, risk the censure of the world, or your own future regret.' Finally the monitor advised her to be prudent in the choice of friends, and, adopting the sentiment and almost the words of the courtesy-books, he concluded:

Remember, my dear Evelina, nothing is so delicate as the reputation

---

[1] I. xiii, xv.

of a woman: it is, at once, the most beautiful and most brittle of all human things.[1]

The monitor finally descanted on the dangers of the unbridled imagination.[2] Evelina's painful disappointments could always be traced to the beguiling pictures suggested by that untrustworthy painter, the Imagination. 'Her glowing pencil, dipt in the vivid colours of her creative ideas', painted tender and thrilling possibilities in Lord Orville and in addition, said Mr. Villars, 'all the good and rare qualities, which a great length of time, and intimacy, could alone have really discovered'. '*Imagination* took the reins, and *Reason* slow-paced, though sure-footed, was unequal to a race with so eccentric and flighty a companion. How rapid was then my Evelina's progress through those regions of fancy and passion whither her new guide conducted her!'[2] The old gentleman concluded his counsel with a prayer for the kind of girl he wished Evelina to be.

May thy manners, language, and deportment all evince that modest equanimity and chearful gratitude, which not merely deserve, but dignify prosperity! May'st thou, to the last moments of an unblemished life, retain thy genuine simplicity, thy singleness of heart, thy guileless sincerity! And may'st thou, stranger to ostentation, and superior to insolence, with true greatness of soul, shine forth conspicuous only in beneficence![2]

'*That man is* ALWAYS *right*', said Dr. Burney, 'in his advice and judgement of things.'[3] Yet the moral burden of *Evelina* was by no means confined to the conduct of the young lady; it included also a model of gentlemanly conduct and one that brought about at least one known instance of reform. When the coxcombical Richard Burney, one of the Worcester cousins, was recovering from an illness at Brompton, his aunts had read him *Evelina* without divulging the enormous secret of its authorship. All through this illness he had 'penetrated us by his patient & most amiable behaviour'; but the greater wonder was that 'since his recovery he has *more* than kept his Ground, by having wholly discarded all the foibles that formerly tinged his manners, though they *never*', the loyal chroniclers affirmed, 'affected his Heart'. And all this reform was based on the

---

[1] II. viii; also, I. xxiv, xxviii; II. vi, xviii; III. vi, xiv.
[2] III. vi, xii.   [3] ED. ii. 242–3.

example of Fanny's hero! There was something in the character and manners of Lord Orville 'so *refined*, and so polite', and something in his compliments so *new* as well as so *elegant*, which Richard had never seen in any book before. 'I think I can't read it too often,' he told the giggling Susan and Fanny, 'for you are to know that I think it very edifying.' Only he wished very much to know who the author could be—'such amazing knowledge of characters,—such an acquaintance with *high* and *low* life,—such universal and extensive knowledge of the world'. Richard knew of no one who could have written such a book except his uncle Dr. Burney. Aunt Ann then told Fanny that she must tell him the secret. Well then, he must *kneel* and make a vow that 'he will never tell *any* body in the world'. When he protested, by all that he held sacred on Earth or in Heaven, that he would not tell, she gave him a slip of paper on which were penned the cryptic words NO MAN. Though he studied the message, it was the odd expression on Fanny's face that at length revealed how the affair stood. He blushed violently. Fanny thought it 'utterly impossible for astonishment to be greater than his was at that moment'. 'I believe I must now kneel indeed!' he said. She made him rise instantly; but the involuntary homage paid by the lively and foppish Richard to his cousin, as he knelt to her before the fire, is as charming and dramatic a scene as might have occurred in the book itself had Lord Orville been less stiff. Lord Orville, whose character, Richard said, he studied 'every day of his life', was a new model; and his unbiased judgement (formed before he knew his cousin had written the book) remains valid for the young generation of the seventies.[1]

Launcelot and Gawain, however, are dead, and with them their 'olde courtesye', and with that also the eighteenth-century courtesy-books and many of the principles and tenets on which they were based. One may pass over the *models of behaviour* and the *maxims of conduct* and 'the notions of other Times, and choose another Tale'. There is still much left, for the 'opinions of right & wrong' encroach very little on the lively and lifelike episodes that remain perennially fresh and young and gay. The realistic delineation of comic character and situation was a contribution to the comedy of manners or to the

[1] MSS. (Berg), printed for the most part in ED, ii. 215–19 n.

novel of manners and is perhaps the part of Fanny Burney's achievement that now wins widest acclaim. Hear the 'Holborn beau' condescending to fall in love with Evelina:

'My dear Ma'am, you must be a little patient; I assure you I have no bad designs, I have not upon my word; but, really there is no resolving upon such a thing as matrimony all at once; what with the loss of one's liberty, and what with the ridicule of all one's acquaintance,—I assure you, Ma'am, you are the first lady who ever made me even demur upon this subject; for, after all, my dear Ma'am, marriage is the devil!' . . .

'Why, really, Ma'am, as to your being a little out of sorts, I must own I can't wonder at it, for, to be sure, marriage is all in all with the ladies; but with us gentlemen it's quite another thing! Now only put yourself in my place,—suppose you had such a large acquaintance of gentlemen as I have,—and that you had always been used to appear a little—a little smart among them,—why now, how should you like to let yourself down all at once into a married man?'

I could not tell what to answer; so much conceit, and so much ignorance, both astonished and silenced me.

'I assure you, Ma'am,' added he, 'there is not only Miss Biddy,—though I should have scorned to mention her, if her brother had not blab'd, for I'm quite particular in keeping ladies secrets,—but there are a great many other ladies that have been proposed to me,—but I never thought twice of any of them, that is, not in a *serious* way,—so you may very well be proud,' offering to take my hand, 'for I assure you, there is nobody so likely to catch me at last as yourself.'

'Sir,' cried I, drawing myself back as haughtily as I could, 'you are totally mistaken, if you imagine you have given me any pride I felt not before, by this conversation. . . .'

While Madame Duval was seating herself in the coach, he said in a voice of *pique*, 'Next time I take the trouble to get any tickets for a young lady, I'll make a bargain beforehand that she sha'n't turn me over to her grandmother.'[1]

Many of Evelina's journal-letters, it will be observed, are cast like acts in a lively comedy of manners. Both Arthur Murphy and Richard Brinsley Sheridan later thought that the author who could write such scenes ought to attempt comedy; and before 1786 producers in Paris had adapted the novel as both a play and an opera.[2] Fanny Burney had set many of the scenes in pleasure-grounds like Ranelagh or the Marylebone Gardens,

[1] II, xix.   [2] Diary MSS. (Berg), p. 2470.

and filled her stage with a cross-section of the eighteenth-century types. Thus she could show a wide variety of contrasting characters in action and draw on an additional source of laughter in their impact on one another. With her apt ear for idiomatic speech she was able to set them talking in natural, convincing dialogue. These scenes, lively as they were, had not been designed solely to amuse, but were everywhere tinged with satire. There was much fun in them, but they served also to castigate what she disliked in the manners of high and low alike. The self-revelatory dialogue exposed the pride, vanity, vapidity, conceit, and affectation she discerned in the upper classes; the vulgarity, squabbles, litigiousness, parsimony, violence, loud laughter, ignorance, and lack of feeling that she associated with low life. 'In the sportive way of holding up Ignorance, Conceit & Folly to ridicule, I thought I discovered your attentive Ear, & observing Eye', Mrs. Burney later said, and at Streatham also it was said that she 'hit off the City Manners wonderfully'.[1] 'No writer so young and inexperienced had ever seen so deeply into character', said Dr. Johnson, 'or copied the manners of the time with more accuracy.'[2] What seemed to impress her contemporaries was the realism of her sketches, their variety, their sportiveness, fun, and humour. For all this, and for the boisterousness of which Mrs. Montagu complained, her critics, including Lord David Cecil, have been tempted to compare her to Fielding.[3] The rough action of the scenes in which Captain Mirvan appears and the occasional use of caricature point to Smollett. Fanny had said in the Preface to *Evelina* that her great precursors had 'culled all the flowers' before her; yet in the minute and exact delineation of what goes on in the mind and heart of a young lady 'at her first entrance into the world' they had left a fair flower for her. 'One excellence is, that it is not *copied*', wrote Mr. Twining; 'it is fairly an *original* novel, both as to characters, & manner of writing.'[4] As Dr. Burney noted, 'Evelina is in a new style too—so perfectly natural and innocent.'[5] By associating with youth errors and shortcomings

---

[1] Diary MSS. (Berg), p. 685.

[2] Dr. Burney's Memoirs (Berg); also *Memoirs*, ii. 121–71.

[3] 'Fanny Burney's Novels', *Essays on the Eighteenth Century, presented to David Nichol Smith in honour of his seventieth birthday* (Oxford, 1945), pp. 212–24.

[4] A copy of A.L. (Osborn) from the Rev. Thomas Twining to CB, 12 Mar. 1779.

[5] ED, ii. 231.

natural to youth, Fanny Burney created a character at once convincing and sympathetic; and in depicting a heroine lifelike in her imperfection the new realist surpassed even her four great predecessors, who tended to draw paragons for that role.

As we have seen, Fanny Burney pleased her eighteenth-century readers in a third respect by adding tears to their laughter. Men as well as women blubbered over the reunion of father and daughter. Mr. Twining thought the 'cit family' excellent, but 'the *serious* & *pathetic* part' struck him most. 'The account of the meeting between Evelina & her father has great force, strong *male* painting, & has some strokes of nature.' Everyone must feel them strongly and own them to *be* nature. At the risk of making Miss Burney ill and pale, he wished the Doctor to tell her how he had *cried* over the closing scenes, 'tho' I believe', he added, 'it will make her laugh'.[1] Sir John Belmont's agonized remorse over the 'injured Caroline', the scenes of 'filial tenderness' and reconciliation, had moved readers almost as much as the death of Desdemona or of Belvidera; and the eighteenth-century reader had no higher praise than this to bestow. 'Thou hast made thy old Father Laugh & Cry at thy pleasure', wrote Dr. Burney.[2] Everybody had been brought to 'Laugh & Cry!' Lady Hales told Susan how she had 'been reading Evelina to Madame de Ferre, the Governess, & the children, & that the meeting with the Father made them all *sob* so much, she was obliged to leave it off'.[3] This was the age of sensibility. The lordly librarians in the full-powdered wigs knew that misses preferred 'crying volumes'. 'Misses must cry or it's nothing.' A crying volume, Sir, 'brings me more money in six months than a heavy merry thing will do in six years'. 'Write for the white handkerchief, dear Webb, an' you love me.'[4] Fanny Burney also knew what the eighteenth century required in a novel, and the *Critical Review* marked the three principal components in *Evelina* with approval: Readers '*will weep* and (what is not so commonly the effect of novels) *will laugh*, and *grow wiser*, as they read'.[5]

[1] See p. 96, n. 4.   [2] See p. 78, n. 1.
[3] Diary MSS. (Berg), p. 659.
[4] See Samuel Jackson Pratt, *Family Secrets* (5 vols., 1797), i. 384–90; and Thomas Bridges, *The Adventures of a Bank-note* (4 vols., 1771), iii. 3–4.
[5] xlvi (Sept. 1778), 202–4. The italics are mine.

The playful comedy and the monitory morals were the warp and woof of *Evelina*; the tears of sensibility are the time-marks in its texture, and are as inerasable as the ruffles, snuff-boxes, and the high head-dress of the drawing-rooms on royal birth-days. These three elements are woven inextricably through all Fanny Burney's works, though in each work they appear in different proportions. Happily in *Evelina* comedy predominated. Though it may be said that the comedy of manners is the great asset of this novel and the main cause of its permanent attrac-tion, Fanny had one other gift—one most necessary to novelists and story-tellers—the ability to tell a story. The central story of her novel was the love between Lord Orville and Evelina, from its inception through its tentative unfolding, growth, and resolution. In the third volume Fanny had no need to resort to comic scenes, *sententiae*, or extraneous sources of interest to depict the tension between the two lovers or to keep the reader interested in the outcome. *Evelina* is a period piece filled with lively dramatic scenes, but not only that: despite its stereotyped plot-devices, in the delicate tension of the scenes between Lord Orville and Evelina it constitutes a love story of persistent and enduring strength.

The welcome accorded *Evelina* by the literary world, the Wits, and the Great is a romance in itself and one of the most cherished of the Burney legends. The anonymous work, which had appeared at the end of January, by June had won great popularity. It was being read by everyone and had been favourably described in the *London Review* and the *Monthly Review*.[1] Fanny's confidants kept with increasing difficulty the uneasy secret of its authorship. It quivered a dozen times a day at the tips of their tongues; and at Chessington Fanny herself, recovering from her long illness, awoke to read reviving letters from Susan and Charlotte about the outstanding success of their frolic. When in July she learned from her sisters that her father had discovered that *Evelina* was her work, she began to worry over his reception of the dedicatory ode.

My dearest Sir,

I have just received from Susan an account of a little *Embarrass* you have been in, upon the affair of my *schtoff*; and I know not how to thank you for the kind manner in which you guard my secret:

[1] vii (Feb. 1778), 151; and lviii (Apr. 1778), 316, respectively.

indeed from every soul, but yourself, who is acquainted with it, I have taken a solemn promise never to reveal it, without my consent.[1]

As she had said in the Ode, she had power to *sink*, but not to raise, his fame; and, for that reason among others, she wished to remain incognita. She hoped the *sincerity* of the stanzas would recommend them to him, 'for I may truly say they *flowed from the Heart*, since I wrote them, in the very fullness of it, in the Dead of the very Night that I owned to you my secret'.[1] In his Memoirs the Doctor said that it was Susan who confessed to him 'with a trembling voice, that the book was written by her sister Fanny, with a determination never to own the sin she had committed'.[2] It was, however, Charlotte who had watched him read the account in the *Monthly Review* and been asked to procure the work from the bookseller's, and who had seen him, when it came, quell the tears that arose at the dedication to himself. 'I opened the first Vol. with fear & trembling', he wrote long afterwards in his Memoirs,

not supposing she w^d disgrace her parentage; but not having the least idea, that without the use of the press, or knowledge of the world, she c^d write a book worth reading.[2]

He was at once 'struck & astounded' by the 'good sense & good writing in the letters of Mr Villars', and before he had read half-way through the first volume all his fears had given way to delight.[2] By June 23 he had reached the conclusion that Lowndes had had '*a devilish good Bargain* of it—for the book will *sell*—it has real merit, and the Review alone would sell it'.[3]

Fanny knew nothing of these changes of opinion and she trembled at the thought of her father's arrival at Chessington (June 23). 'I thought she w^d have fainted,' he wrote later,

but I hastened to take her by the hand & tell her that I had read part of her book with such pleasure, that instead of being angry, I congratulated her on being able to write so well. this kindness affected her so much that she threw herself in my arms, & cried *à chaudes larmes*, till she sobbed.[2]

'I have read your book, Fanny,' he said gently, 'but you need not blush at it—it is full of merit—it is, really,—extraordinary!'[4] Her tears then gave way to 'a gayer pleasure—a pleasure more

[1] A.L.S. (Berg) from FB to CB, 20 July 1778.   [2] Memoirs (Berg).
[3] ED, ii. 222–4.   [4] See p. 78, n. 1.

like his own'[1] and 'the poor humble author I believe never was
happier in her life'.[2] Fanny reviewed the episode: 'I had
written my little Book simply for my amusement, I printed it,
by the means first of my brother Charles, next of my cousin
Edward Burney, merely for a frolic, to see how a production
of my own would figure in that Author like form.'[3] She had
hardly dared to hope that anyone except her sisters, to whom alone
she had read her compositions, could be partial enough to like
them. In a letter to Miss Coussmaker she confessed to having
thought that Evelina's 'only admirers wd be among school
girls'. She had 'destined her to no nobler habitation than a
circulating library'.[4]

Despite the rumours about persons great and humble who
were sitting up all night to finish *Evelina*, she still wished to
remain unknown. She feared the odium attached to the term
'novelist'. Yet, as she said, '*every body* longs to tell *one* body!', so
that the 'Blabbation' of her scribbling went on apace.[5] Dr.
Burney's pride in her performance was not tinged with Fanny's
delicate notions. 'Poor Fan's *such* a prude.'[2] *Evelina* was a work
no one need blush at—and therefore he did not scruple to tell
Mrs. Thrale, Miss Coussmaker, Lady Hales, and many others,
that it was his daughter, Fanny, who had written *Evelina*, and
that this was the more remarkable because, unlike her sisters,
she had not been given the advantages of a formal education or
of travel abroad. Mrs. Thrale came second, but soon took first
place as a publicity agent; and Fanny was not long in realizing
that her hope for secrecy was desperate. And she protested:
she herself had never told anybody outside her own family,
'nor half the bodies in it'. 'I really thought myself as safe, and
meant to be as private, when the book was at Mr. Lowndes's,
as when it was in my own bureau.'[6] Such over-delicacy, Mrs.
Thrale said, might make her unhappy all her life. 'Poor Miss
Burney! so you thought just to have played and sported with
your sisters and cousins, and had it all your own way; but now
you are in for it! But if you will be an author and a wit, you
must take the consequences!'[6] When Fanny saw that she was

---

[1] See p. 78, n. 1.   [2] See p. 99, n. 2.
[3] Diary MSS. (Berg), p. 658.
[4] Copy of a letter (Berg) from FB to Miss Coussmaker, n.d.
[5] Diary MSS. (Berg), pp. 712, 832.
[6] *Diary*, i. 96–100, 137–9.

to be known as an Authoress, a Scribbler, or perhaps a Wit like
her own Mrs. Selwyn, whom everybody disliked for her mascu-
linity, she was ill all night and could not sleep. Nor did the
painful feelings depart as Mr. Crisp said they ought 'when the
salts of general applause [were] held continually under their
nose'.[1] 'I part with this, my dear, long loved, long cherished
snugship with more regret than any body will believe, except
my dear sisters who *Live with* me, & know me too well & too
closely to doubt me.'[2]

Before the close of 1779 *Evelina* went through four editions,
'traversing all London amongst the literary and the fashionable
alike'. In the review of *Evelina* (the *Critical Review*, September,
1778) it was asserted that 'the purchasers of novels, the sub-
scribers to circulating libraries, are seldom in more elevated
situations than the middle ranks of life'. Yet by July, 1778,
according to a letter from Mr. Lowndes, the Great World was
sending to him for *Evelina*. Polite ladies feared being quite
'unfashionable for not having read it'.[3] The booksellers at Bath,
Brighton, and Reigate were also embarrassed by the demand
for *Evelina*, which could not be kept upon the shelves. Other
dealers found great faults in Mr. Lowndes. Thus Mr. Bowen,
the bookseller at Brighton, to Mrs. Thrale: —'O ma'am, what
a Book thrown away was that!—all the Trade cry shame on
Lowndes, not, ma'am, that I *expected* he could have known its
worth, because that's out of the question,—but when its *profits*
told him what it was, it's quite scandalous that he should have
done nothing!—quite ungentleman like indeed!'[4]

Everyone had read *Evelina*: Mr. Jessop, a schoolmaster
'living in a remote part of Ireland'—'a man of the finest taste,—
a man of great profundity,—an extraordinary scholar';[5] the
anatomy professor at Cambridge, who 'never read novels', but
who for all that insisted that his friends read this one;[6] Mr.
Bewley's friend Mr. Everard, 'who could never be induced to
read these novels in his life', but who was found 'nailed to his

---

[1] See p. 100, n. 5.
[2] Diary MSS. (Berg), suppressed pages, box ii.
[3] A.L.S. (Barrett) from Thomas Lowndes to Mr. Grafton, 2 July 1778. For a
paraphrase see A.L.S. (Berg) from FB to CB, 20 July 1778; Diary MSS. (Berg),
p. 679.
[4] Diary MSS. (Berg), p. 1040.   [5] *Diary*, ii. 48.
[6] Diary MSS. (Berg), pp. 752-3.

chair' at sunrise with Volume III of *Evelina* in his hand;[1]
Dr. Barnard, the Provost of Eton, who sang its praises;[2] Lady
Radnor and other representatives of the Great World, who had
secured copies;[3] Miss Hales, 'a formal old maid', who thought
it 'destruction for a girl to read a novel'; Mrs. Horneck, who
thought novels 'generally, so bad, that they are not to be read',
but who had seen 'nothing like this since Fielding';[4] Mr. Sheridan, who declared publicly at the club that it was '*superior* to
Fielding';[5] Mr. Edmund Burke, who had sat up all night to
read it; and finally Dr. Johnson, a name in literary criticism to
end all lists. When at Chessington Fanny heard that he had said
there were 'things and characters in her book *more* than worthy
of Fielding!', she danced a jig around the mulberry tree.[6]

'I often think, when I am counting my laurels,' she wrote
sportively to Susan, 'what a pity it would have been had I
popped off in my last illness, without knowing what a person of
consequence I was!—and I sometimes think that, were I now
to have a relapse, I could never go off with so much *éclat*!'[7]
'It's wonderful,' Mr. Crisp said, 'wonderful!'[8] 'With all his
powers of speech, his choice of language, and his general variety
of expression', he could think of no other comment when at last
he was informed by Dr. Burney that Fanny was the author of
Evelina, the novel that she and Hetty had been roguishly reading
to him and that was being read all over London for the preceding five months.[6]

Hetty had wished above all things to read the novel to Mr.
Crisp, but Fanny, unable to resist the opportunity to observe
his reaction and to obtain his unbiased opinion of it, sent
excuses to her sister, and herself began on the first two volumes.
Though she was breathless and tremulous with embarrassment
and therefore *mauled* the book in the reading, she could see that,
though Mr. Crisp 'by no means treated it with the praise so
lavishly bestowed upon it from other quarters', he was 'even
greedily eager to go on with it'.[8] His 'ill humour' on being told

---

[1] 3 A.L.S. (Osborn) from William Bewley to CB, 16 Sept. 1778, 29 Mar. 1779,
5 Nov. 1781.
[2] *Diary*, i. 339.
[3] Diary MSS. (Berg), p. 659.   [4] Diary MSS. (Berg), pp. 843–4.
[5] Diary MSS. (Berg), p. 873.   [6] See p. 78, n. 1.
[7] *Diary*, i. 40–41.
[8] *Diary*, i. 28–31, 44–45, 52–53.

(rather inaccurately) that he must wait for Hetty to bring the third volume was the 'delightful' proof of his interest.

Fanny had shown in *Evelina* how artifice will bring its own punishment in mortification. Just so at Chessington the ruse about the third volume led its authors into a *scrape*, as they would have called it, one day when their stepmother appeared for a short visit,

for Mr. Crisp, before my mother, very innocently said to Susan, 'Oh, pray Susette, do send me the third volume of *Evelina*; Fanny brought me the two first on purpose, I believe, to tantalise me.'

I felt myself in a ferment; and Susan, too, looked foolish, and knew not what to answer. As I sat on the same sofa with him, I gave him a gentle shove, as a token, which he could not but understand, that he had said something wrong—though I believe he could not imagine *what*. Indeed, how should he?

My mother instantly darted forward, and repeated, '*Evelina*—what's that, pray?'

Again I *jolted* Mr. Crisp, who, very much perplexed, said, in a boggling manner, that it was a novel—he supposed from the circulating library—'only a trumpery novel.'

Ah, my dear daddy! thought I, you would have devised some other sort of speech, if you knew all!—but he was really, as he well might be, quite at a loss for what I *wanted* him to say.

'You have had it here, then, have you?' continued my mother.

'Yes—two of the volumes,' said Mr. Crisp.

'What! had you them from the library?' asked my mother.

'No, ma'am,' answered I horribly frightened, 'from my sister.'

The truth is, the books are Susan's, who bought them the first day of publication; but I did not dare own that, as it would have been almost an acknowledgment of all the rest.

She asked some further questions, to which we made the same sort of answers, and then the matter dropped. Whether it rests upon her mind or not I cannot tell.[1]

Susan and Fanny had then to devise replies to Mr. Crisp, who later wished to know why he could not mention *Evelina* without being joggled. At last he learned the true reason:

'Why you little hussy,—you young devil!—an't you ashamed to look me in the face, you *Evelina*, you! Why, what a dance have you led me about it! . . . Oh you little hussy, what tricks have you served me!'[1]

[1] See p. 102, n. 8.

He perhaps never realized his own part in the production of the famous novel, and his amazement seemed to equal that of the age. How had she found time to write so much unsuspected? Where and how had she picked up such varied materials? 'It's wonderful!'

V

THE WITS AND 'THE WITLINGS'

(1778–1780)

Suffice it to have said,
Where'er the power of Ridicule displays
Her quaint-ey'd visage, some incongruous form,
Some stubborn dissonance of things combin'd,
Strikes on the quick observer.

AKENSIDE, *The Pleasures of Imagination*, iii.

Evelina, which was to win for its author a place among the wits, had been introduced at Streatham by Dr. Johnson. Chatting with Mrs. Thrale and Dr. Burney, over dishes of tea one evening, he chanced to recollect a conversation of the preceding evening. ' "Madam", he cried, see-sawing on his chair,'

'Mrs. Chol'mley was talking to me last night of a new novel, which she says has a very uncommon share of merit—*Evelina*—She says she has not been so much entertained this great while as in reading it—and that she shall go all over London in order to discover the author—'

'Good G—d cried Mrs. Thrale—why somebody else mentioned that book to me—Lady Westcote it was I believe—*The modest writer of Evelina*, she talk'd to me of.'

'Mrs. Chol'mley says she never met so much modesty with so much *merit* before in any literary performance,' said Johnson.

'Why,' said [Dr. Burney] quite cooly and innocently—'Somebody recommended it to *me* too—I read a little of it, which indeed seem'd to be above the common class of works of this kind.'[1]

Mrs. Thrale was not long in procuring the book, and in the following week, Dr. Burney heard her opinion of it. ' 'Tis *very* clever I assure you', and not 'a mere sentimental business',

there's a vast deal of humour and entertainment in it—the second volume is *charming*—there is such a family, silversmiths on Snow Hill, that diverted Queany and me beyond measure! . . . I wish'd it had been longer. . . . I am sure there's a great deal of human *life*

---

[1] ED, ii. 220–54; for Fanny's versions of the discovery, *Diary*, i. 23–153; *Memoirs*, ii. 121–71.

in this book, and of the manners of the present time. It's writ by
somebody that knows *the top and the bottom*, the *highest* and *lowest* of
mankind—It's very good language, and there's an infinite deal of
fun in it.[1]

Dr. Burney now ventured to think that there would be no
impropriety in acknowledging the book. Susan agreed, if a little
doubtfully:

'Why, indeed, Fanny would not come to any discredit if she was
known as the Authoress, shy as she is about it.'

'*Discredit!*' repeated my father, 'no indeed,—*just the reverse*—
'*twou'd be a credit to her, and to me, and to you*—there is great goodness
of heart and great purity of manners in all that relates to her
heroine. . . . [Lord Orville] seems to me a *model* for a young man—
as Villars is for an old one—'[1]

And in short, on one of his visits to Streatham in July, the
Doctor told Mrs. Thrale about the 'poor humble author'[2] of
the clever book.

'Why—it's *well enough* [said Doctor Burney]—but I have something to tell you about it.'

'Well, what?'

'Has Mrs. Cholmley found out the author?'

'No—not that I know of—'

'Because I believe I have—tho' but *very* lately—'

'Well, pray—let's hear,' said she eagerly—'*I want to know him of
all things.*'

'And so then' continued my father, . . . 'I told her 'twas *our
Fanny's*—'[1]

On the Doctor's next visit to Streatham, Mrs. Thrale talked
of nothing but *Evelina*, plying him with questions about the
authoress ('How did she get it printed without discovery?'),
and when she had heard all, concluded,

'L[d]! D[r] Burney! we must be acquainted—do bring her with you the
next time you come to Streatham.'[2]

Fanny was still at Chessington, where on July 25 the Doctor
arrived 'in full health, charming spirits, and all kindness,
openness, and entertainment'.[1] He had promised to take Fanny
to Streatham on his way back, and on Monday, July 27, he
returned there with 'Fan in his hand'. The Streatham group

---

[1] See p. 105, n. 1.   [2] Dr. Burney's Memoirs (Berg).

included or came to include, besides the Thrales, Arthur
Murphy, Lord Mulgrave, and Sir Philips Jennings Clerke;
Dr. Johnson and the Johnsonian circle: Edmund Burke, Windham, Boswell, Sir Joshua Reynolds and Garrick (already well
known to Fanny); Sir William Weller Pepys, Mrs. Montagu
(Queen of the Blues), Mrs. Boscawen, and other bluestockings,
with a long list of personages slightly less distinguished, among
whom may be numbered the gay and varied company at Bath
and Brighton.

Fanny was in 'a kind of twitter', though 'highly flattered' and
'highly delighted' at the prospect of being introduced at
Streatham. She was always (even after her years at court) shy
and self-conscious when required to act a brilliant part in
public, as if on a stage, but when she felt herself on familiar
ground, she had all the Burney charm and attractiveness of
manner. She was twenty-five years old when *Evelina* was
published, twenty-six at her introduction to Streatham; Mrs.
Thrale was thirty-nine; her eldest daughter, Hester Maria
(Queeney), about fourteen. The visit of 1778 was a prelude to
a friendship with Mrs. Thrale of some five years' duration and
to a long association with Queeney, afterwards Lady Keith,
which ended only with Madame d'Arblay's death some sixty
years later.

Though it is quite useless to speculate on the consequences
of action that might have been taken or to quarrel with the
facts of biography, it may nevertheless be observed in passing
that Dr. Burney's fond determination to push his daughter into
the uncongenial limelight and her consequent introduction to
Streatham Park had, with many advantages, serious disadvantages. With all that Streatham had to offer in itself, in picturesque
materials for journalizing, in further introductions, and widening avenues of experience, there were on the debit side not only
the toll on free time and the virtual attempt at adoption that
both the Doctor and Fanny stoutly resisted and that may be
forgotten, but also the ruinous effect of the public betrayal on
the fun-loving imaginative quality of her work. What she might
have done if she had been left to her own secret, happy, inventive way is a matter of tempting and vain speculation. Anonymous, she had been free; known, she must take greater care
than before not to disgrace her father or herself, and the ticklish

allowance that she felt must henceforth be made for Mrs. Grundy and the moral and social climate about her tended to inhibit her old spontaneous inventiveness. 'I should certainly have been more finical, had I foreseen what happened', she remarked after the 'blabbation' about *Evelina*;[1] and again, in connexion with her play 'The Witlings': 'I would a thousand times rather forfeit my character as a writer, than risk ridicule or censure as a female.'[1]

In *Cecilia* Fanny was to make the proud Mr. Delvile speak characteristically enough, for his type, on the moral and social status of novelists and readers of novels:

'But what Bill at all,' cried he, with much surprise, 'can a young lady have with a bookseller? The Spectator, Tatler, and Guardian, would make library sufficient for any female in the kingdom, nor do I think it like a gentlewoman to have more.'[2]

So much for reading books, and now, for writing them:

'Let me counsel you to remember that a lady, whether so called from birth or only from fortune, should never degrade herself by being put on a level with writers, and such sort of people.'[2]

Fanny well knew that though novelists, actors, singers, or musicians were often invited to the houses of the great, they were still 'such sort of people', as Lord Chesterfield put it, 'fiddlers, pipers, and *id genus omne*'.[3] Dr. Burney told how poor Piozzi, on being hired for a month in one of the great houses in England, was baited and teased as a monkey might be, and had finally to barricade himself in his room in order to gain peace and security.[4] The favour with which Dr. Burney himself was received can be attributed partly to his achievements but chiefly to his powers of conversation and the extraordinary charm of his manners and address. The great Doctor's status was an exception, and it was not necessarily shared even by members of his own family. Fanny Burney was the daughter of a music-teacher (albeit the great Dr. Burney), a scion of the humble Sleepes and herself a novelist. Though in the Never-never land of the *intelligentsia*, where talents without rank or gold were

---

[1] Diary MSS. (Berg), pp. 667–9; *Diary*, i. 160–3.
[2] *Cecilia, or Memoirs of an Heiress* (5 vols., 1782), ii. 25–26.
[3] *Letters to his Son*, 6 June 1751; 27 Sept. 1749.
[4] See p. 106, n. 2.

sufficient, she had many advantages, in the Great World where birth, breeding, privilege, and wealth provided other criteria of judgements, she was conscious of many disadvantages.

Mr. Thrale was a wealthy brewer and a Member of Parliament. His wife, Hester Lynch Salusbury, liked to trace her descent from Adam de Saltzburg, who came to England with the Conqueror, but though some of the links connecting her with this Adam seem to have been lost, she could indeed trace her lineage to illustrious Salusburys of the Crusades and the Wars of the Roses and to the celebrated Katherine of Beraine, granddaughter of an illegitimate son of Henry VII.[1] To distinction of birth she added learning, wit, talents, something of the arrogance of rank and wealth, good nature, and great kindness towards those she loved. 'I have known many Genius's, & Famous & charming people, from fifteen years of age, when I first knew her', wrote Charlotte Burney some thirty years later,

& I have never met with any one with manners & conversation so captivating, her wit is so sweet temper'd, her humour so spontaneous & comic, her observations so original, her repartee so ready & brilliant, her quotations & allusions so impressively applied, such a luxuriant playfulness of Fancy, & of her shining qualities she seems unconscious, there is no arrogance, she is as artless, easy, & unaffected as if all her companions were her equals![2]

Mrs. Thrale had visited St. Martin's Street in March, 1777, and Fanny, who shared Charlotte's impressions, would not have been in such 'a twitter' as she drove along the dusty midsummer road with her father to Streatham, had it not been for this business of being known as an authoress. Had she realized how unfavourable Mrs. Thrale's first impressions of her were to be, she would have been still more uneasy. 'The Doctor is a Man quite after my own Heart', said the daughter of the Salusburys; 'if he has any Fault it is too much Obsequiousness.'

His Daughter is a graceful looking Girl, but 'tis the Grace of an Actress not a Woman of Fashion—how should it? The Burneys are I believe a very low Race of Mortals. Her Conversation would be more pleasing if She thought less of herself; but her early Reputation

---

[1] Clifford, pp. 3–46.
[2] A.L.S. (Barrett) from CBFB to Charlotte Barrett, 21 May 1810.

embarrasses her Talk, & clouds her Mind with scruples about Elegancies which either come uncalled for or will not come at all: I love her more for her Father's sake than for her own, though her Merit cannot as a Writer be controverted. . . . She is a girl of prodigious Parts.[1]

No such thoughts were allowed to ripple to the surface, needless to say. Fanny was invited to return for a week, and after that for many weeks and for months at a time between the years 1778 and 1782, until Mr. Crisp began to think that, like Dr. Johnson, she was to be domiciled permanently at Streatham. Mrs. Thrale was delightful, and Fanny hastened to set down her pen-picture before flaws should appear to mar it.

She has talents to create admiration, good humour to excite love, understanding to give entertainment, and a heart which, like my dear father's, seems already fitted for another world.[2]

Gradually Fanny was reassured, and as her shyness and self-consciousness wore away, and her 'prodigious parts', arts of mimicry and entertainment, and love of the ridiculous, in short, the comic spirit, emerged, she was soon at home among the wits. 'If this rogue is like her book', Mrs. Thrale had predicted, 'how will she trim all of us by and by!' And then, as Mrs. Thrale saw her prophecy coming true: 'Miss Burney looks so meek and so quiet, nobody would suspect what a comical girl she is.'

'Oh, she's a toad!' cried Dr. Johnson, laughing—'a sly young rogue! with her Smiths and her Branghtons!'

And then directly to Fanny:

'What a Holborn beau have you drawn!' . . . 'Mr. Smith is the man!' cried he laughing violently. 'Harry Fielding never drew so good a character!—such a fine varnish of low politeness!—such a struggle to appear a gentleman! Madam, there is no character better drawn anywhere—in any book or by any author.'[2]

Mrs. Thrale, eager to provide copy of similarly ludicrous portraits, insisted on visiting a ridiculous family in the neighbourhood, that of a clergyman, Mr. Tattersall, whose absurd rage for building temples and summer-houses in a crowded garden was to appear eventually in Mr. Dubster of *Camilla.*

---

[1] *Thraliana*, i. 368.   [2] *Diary*, i. 66–118, 263; also *Memoirs*, ii. 172.

'Themes of mere ridicule offer everywhere', Fanny commented.
'I could write some tolerable good sport concerning this visit,
but that I wish to devote all the time I can snatch for writing,
to recording what passes here.'[1] What she wished to record was
Dr. Johnson's entertaining conversation, his *bon mots*, and his
amazing kindness to her, and her Streatham Journals of 1778–82
are rich in Johnsoniana.

The great Lexiphanes in his 'large, full, bushy wig' and
'snuff-colour coat' played out his immortal part at Streatham
as the fearsome Challenger of every loose and foolish thought
and inaccurate expression. Fanny had met him on his visit to
St. Martin's Street in March, 1777, and her first impressions
of him are well known.

He is, indeed, very ill-favoured! Yet he has naturally a noble figure;
tall, stout, grand, and authoritative: but he stoops horribly; his back
is quite round: his mouth is continually opening and shutting, as if
he were chewing something; he has a singular method of twirling his
fingers, and twisting his hands: his vast body is in constant agitation,
see-sawing backwards and forwards: his feet are never a moment
quiet; and his whole great person looked often as if it were going to
roll itself, quite voluntarily, from his chair to the floor.[2]

All this, she said, was quite forgotten at a second meeting, while
at Streatham she learned that Dr. Johnson had 'more fun, and
comical humour, and love of nonsense about him, than almost
anybody' she ever saw.

I mean when with those he likes; for otherwise, he can be as severe
and as bitter as report relates him. Mrs. Thrale has all that gaiety of
disposition and lightness of heart, which commonly belong to fifteen.
We are, therefore, merry enough, and I am frequently seized with
the same tittering and ridiculous fits as those with which I have so
often amazed and amused poor Kitty Cooke.[3]

In the diaries of 1778–83 we can still catch fragments of the
conversations and echoes of the laughter at Streatham. The
dinner parties there were brilliant. Fanny delighted to tell how
the wits 'flashed away' with allusions and sarcasms gay, forcible,
and splendid. 'Oh, Fanny, set this down as the happiest period
of your life', advised Mr. Crisp. 'Where will you find such
another set?'[3] 'Everything was most splendid and magnificent',

---

[1] See p. 110, n. 2.   [2] *Memoirs*, ii. 86–100; also ED, ii. 153–8.
[3] *Diary*, i. 70–79, 210–17, 321–3.

reported Mr. Crisp on the one occasion that he was a guest there, 'two courses of 21 Dishes each, besides Removes . . . everything in plate, of which such a profusion, and such a Side Board: I never saw such at any Nobleman's.'[1] The menus included pineapples (besides grapes, melons, peaches, and nectarines) from the hothouses and kitchen gardens, and perhaps no one except Mr. Blakeney had ever been known to find fault with Streatham hospitality.

'I am glad, Mr. Thrale,' continued this hero, 'you have got your fireplace altered. . . . Admirable dinners—excellent company— *très bon* fare—and, all the time, "Signor Vento" coming down the chimney!'[2]

In November 1778 Streatham was the scene of a champagne party.[3] There were about ten guests besides Fanny, Dr. Johnson, the Thrales, and Lady Ladd, 'own sister to Mr. Thrale', who Mrs. Thrale thought would wear 'Pink in her Coffin'.

She is a tall and stout woman, has an air of mingled dignity and haughtiness, . . . dresses very youthful and gaily, and . . . chooses to be much more lively than her brother; but liveliness sits as awkwardly upon her as her pink ribbons.[4]

After dinner a Miss Moss played and sang 'to the great fatigue of Mrs. Thrale' and of Dr. Johnson, who refused to leave his wine for the song, and in the evening nearly everyone strolled upon the gravel walks before the windows. Fanny 'was going to have joined some of them' when Dr. Johnson stopped her and asked how she did.

'I was afraid, sir,' cried I, 'you did not intend to know me again, for you have not spoken to me before since your return from town.'
'My dear,' cried he, taking both my hands, 'I was not sure of you, I am so near-sighted, and I apprehended making some mistake.'[4]

Then the great man drew her 'very unexpectedly towards him' and kissed her. When the others went he drew a chair for her close to his own at the window, and 'thus *tête-à-tête* we continued', writes the diarist, 'almost all the evening' and 'almost' (as the manuscript has it, though not the printed *Diary*) 'almost in the Dark'. 'We have no candles at Streatham till we go into the Library', she explained.[3] The Doctor talked to her about his journey to the Hebrides and was good enough to wish that she had been along—'quite gravely, I assure you!', added Fanny for the benefit of the appreciative Susan.[1] This conception of Fanny in the Western Isles and Scottish Highlands must have amused them still more on the appearance of Rowlandson's caricatures, for the Burney sense of the ridiculous did not spare the Burneys themselves. Dr. Johnson was indulgent to the young,[2] and his kindness to unassuming youth is nowhere better illustrated than in his indulgence to the young Burneys. Perhaps in return Fanny afforded him some happiness in times like this when she listened with such gratifying attention.

Presently they were disturbed. 'By degrees, however, our party encreased: . . . Mr. Embry ventured to approach us nearer—& then Mr. Seward came & flung himself on the back of my sofa.'[3] When all except the house guests had departed Mrs. Thrale joined the group and 'we had a *most nice* general conversation' until the candles were brought and everyone repaired to the library. For some time Miss Burney had fancied 'the folks had all drunk too much champagne!' for Mr. Seward, who usually was 'as shy as any *Girl* can be', actually took 'advantage of the *Dark*' to detain her forcibly from joining the company.[3] It was perhaps at this time and perhaps because of the champagne that Lady Ladd had her historic fall. The conversation in the library was upon current politics and made, as Fanny thought, 'but melancholy reporting'.

Next morning the events of the preceding afternoon and evening were reviewed. As usual at breakfast, 'Dr. Johnson was quite in a sportive humour', full of mirth and jollity. Mrs. Thrale informed the Doctor that, like him, Lady Ladd had unfortunately fallen down and hurt herself woefully.

'How did that happen, madam?'

'Why, sir, the heel of her shoe caught in something.'

'Heel?' replied he; 'nay, then, if her ladyship, who walks six foot high' (N.B. this is a fact), 'will wear a high heel, I think she almost deserves a fall.'

---

[1] See p. 112, n. 4.

[2] Cf. *Diary*, ii. 287: 'He was always indulgent to the young, he never attacked the unassuming, nor meant to terrify the diffident.' Also Dr. Burney's Memoirs (Berg): 'Dr. Johnson was more indulgent and kind to her [Fanny] than to any female author after my acquaintance with him.'

[3] See p. 112, n. 3.

'Nay, sir, my heel was not so high!' cried Lady Ladd.

'But, madam, why should you wear any? That for which there is no occasion, had always better be dispensed with. . . .'

'However,' continued he, 'if my fall does confine me, I will make my confinement pleasant, for Miss Burney shall nurse me—positively!' (and he slapped his hand on the table), 'and then, she shall sing to me, and soothe my cares.'[1]

> She shall sing me a song,
> Of 2 Day's long,
> The Woodcock & the sparrow;
> Our little Dog has bit his Tail
> And he'll be Hang'd to-morrow.[2]

In the early days of their acquaintance Dr. Johnson had suggested that Fanny write a comedy, a farce called 'Streatham' and Fanny had been delighted with his sense of the burlesque. 'How little did I expect at a distance, from this Lexiphanes, this great & dreaded Lord of English literature, a turn so comic & diverting for burlesque humour!'[3] 'While we were thus alone one Evening we made an extempore Elegy, Dr. Johnson, Mrs. Thrale and myself *spouting* it out alternately, for Miss Thrale is no versifier, not even in this miserable way. The *occasion* was to *make fun* of an Elegy in a Trumpery Book we had just been reading, so I will try to recollect it.'

I

> *Here's a Woman of the Town,*
> *Lies as Dead as any Nail!*
> *She was once of high renown,—*
> *And so here begins my Tale.*

II

> *She was once a cherry plump*
> *Red her cheek as Cath'rine Pear,*
> *Toss'd her nose, & shook her Rump,*
> *Till she made the Neighbours stare.*

III

> *There she soon became a Jilt,*
> *Rambling often to & fro'*
> *All her life was nought but guilt,*
> *Till Purse & Carcase both were low.*

---

[1] See p. 112, n. 4.　　　　　　　　　　[2] See p. 112, n. 3.
[3] *Diary*, i. 101–2; Diary MSS. (Berg), p. 754.

IV

But there came a country 'Squire
He was a seducing Pug!
Took her from her friends & sire,
To his own House her did Lug.

V

Black her eye with many a Blow,
Hot her breath with many a Dram,
Now she lies exceeding low,
And as quiet as a Lamb.

So if any 3 people can do worse—let them![1]

As the records of Streatham indicate, the Doctor was often kind, even though his gallantries may have been a little ponderous and awkward—especially when they came into collision with high head-dresses—and a little absent-minded and precarious. A description of his attentions to a newly-married young thing who was dining at Streatham may be apocryphal, but is characteristic.

After dinner was ended, Dr Johnson tapped the Bride on the shoulder, saying 'My dear, should you like to see me feed the swans?' . . . 'Child, did you ever hear of a Black swan?'

The little bride had heard that there were such things, but when they got to the Park the conversation turned to Miss Burney.

'Ay child,' said he, 'I don't know that an introduction to Miss Burney would do you much good; for you look as if you took more pains with the outside of your head than the inside,'—then seemingly conscious that he had spoken rudely & unprovoked; he added, 'And your time has not been thrown away,—for it is a very pretty head—and very well dressed.'

Presently he said, 'My dear, would you like to see a Kamschatka Dog?' and upon her answering in the affirmative, he walked with her to the stables and shewed her *Lion* (brought to England by Lieut. Burney). He then ordered the carriage which was to carry him back to London to be got ready, and when it was prepared he got into it & set off, without taking leave of the Streatham party & without even recollecting the young lady whom he left alone to find her way back from the stables as she could.[2]

[1] Diary MSS. (Berg), pp. 1506–7.
[2] A holograph (Barrett), signed H. S.

The accounts of Chessington that the Burneys gave determined Mrs. Thrale also to become a favourite with that
Mr. Crisp,[1] and in September, 1779, the Thrales seem to have
made their first visit to Chessington. What surprised Mrs. Thrale
most

was the elegance of Mr. Crisp in language and manners; because
that, from the Hermit of Chesington, she had not expected.

And what most to Mr. Crisp caused a similar pleasure, was the
courteous readiness and unassuming good-humour, with which Mrs.
Thrale received the inartificial civilities of Kitty Cooke, and the old-
fashioned but cordial hospitality of Mrs. Hamilton; for these, from
a celebrated wit, moving in the sphere of high life, he also in his turn
had not expected.

The Thrales, however, were all much entertained by the place
itself, which they prowled over with gay curiosity. Not a nook or
corner; nor a dark passage 'leading to nothing;' nor a hanging
tapestry of prim demoiselles, and grim cavaliers; nor a tall canopied
bed tied up to the ceiling; . . . nor a window stuck in some angle
close to the ceiling of a lofty slip of a room . . . missed their scrutinizing eyes.

They even visited the attics, where they were much diverted by
the shapes as well as by the quantity of rooms . . . of all sorts of forms
that could increase their count. . . . They peeped, also, through little
window casements, of which the panes of glass were hardly so wide
as their clumsy frames, to survey long ridges of lead that entwined
the motley spiral roofs of the multitude of separate cells . . . and
afforded . . . a view, sixteen miles in circumference, of the adjacent
country.[2]

The visits of the Thrales to Chessington thus yield additional
glimpses into the old mansion Liberty Hall, where much of
Evelina and still more of *Cecilia* were written, and additional
vignettes of the people, Streathamites and Chessingtonians,
with whom Fanny spent so much of the time between 1778 and
1783. 'You will have great comfort in Mr. Crisp's conversation,'
wrote Mrs. Thrale to Fanny, 'long may you keep him!'

But 'tis a foolish thing to attach oneself to old men as you & I do,
one has a moral certainty of losing them, and I see by my own
murmuring over Mr. Scrase now, that I shall not take his Death
easily when it comes.[3]

[1] ED, ii. 255–61.
[2] *Memoirs*, ii. 182–90. For the date see A.L.S. (Osborn) from HLT to CB,
27 Aug. 1779.   [3] A.L.S. (Berg) from HLT to FB, 5 July 1780.

Gout, from which Mr. Crisp had suffered for some time; apoplexy, which was soon to strike down the Master of Streatham; death, which in not more than half a dozen years was to carry away all three men—Mr. Thrale, Mr. Crisp, and Dr. Johnson—was to bring an abrupt end to a period that seemed for the present to pass like the scenes in a play.

How many times had the Burneys, in winter, spring, summer, and autumn, traversed the mud roads over the wild common to Chessington! Sometimes the postilions missed the path, and, as to the Lane, it was 'utterly impracticable for any carriage but a stout all enduring cart or wagon'.[1] It was as safe, said Maria Rishton, as Hook Lane.[2] 'The Roads just now are dreadful', wrote Fanny in February of 1781 to Mrs. Thrale, who had wished to come *sousing through Gascoyne Lane* to see her. It had taken two farmers' daughters six hours to go seven miles 'in a little light sort of caravan, which they called a *shay cart*'.[1] Fanny herself had arrived only after 'sundry perils by *Land & by Water*', and the common was 'so little better than a large & dirty pond' that she had not been able to leave the old Hall.[1] George Cambridge later told Fanny that though he saw the house as soon as he came upon the common, he was very proud of his sagacity in finding it.

'How did you find the Roads?'
'O pretty well: never above the Horses legs.'[3]

All this kept neither paying guests nor visitors away. At first the Thrales came alone, but later, on one occasion at least, they came by the mud road in a coach-and-four bringing the old Philosopher, Dr. Johnson himself, across the wide common, the ploughed fields, and fallow ground to Chessington.

Before this, however, Mr. Crisp, who 'was of the old school in the forms of good breeding', thought that he must return the 'civility' of the Thrale visit 'whatever might be the inconvenience to his health; or whatever his disinclination to such an exertion'.[4] As soon as his gout subsided a little, he set off,

---

[1] A.L. (Berg) from FB to CB, May 1793. Also A.L.S. (JRL) from FB to HLT, 14 Feb. n.y.; and A.L.S. (Berg) from FB to HLT, 17 Aug. 1782.
[2] ED, i. 126.
[3] Diary MSS. (Berg), pp. 1709–11, 1755.
[4] See p. 116, n. 2.

and Fanny, who was then at Chessington, accompanied him. Dr. Burney was already at Streatham.

Dr. Johnson, in compliment to his friend Dr. Burney, and by no means incurious himself to see the hermit of Chesington, immediately descended to meet Mr. Crisp. . . . The meeting, nevertheless, to the great chagrin of Dr. Burney, produced neither interest nor pleasure; for Dr. Johnson, though courteous in demeanour and looks, with evident solicitude to shew respect to Mr. Crisp, was grave and silent; and whenever Dr. Johnson did not make the charm of conversation, he only marred it by his presence; from the general fear he incited, that if he spoke not, he might listen; and that if he listened—he might reprove.[1]

No sufficient stimulus to conversation emerged; and Dr. Johnson spoke not. So many wits and witlings! And yet among them Mr. Crisp lost the 'opportunity for developing and enjoying the celebrated and extraordinary colloquial abilities' of the great man. Later in the evening (too late) Dr. Johnson felt like talking, and his mind now ran on Mr. Crisp.

Sir, it is a very singular thing to see a man with all his powers so much alive, when he has so long shut himself up from the world. Such readiness of conception, quickness of recollection, facility of following discourse started by others, in a man who has long had only the past to feed upon, are rarely to be met with.[1]

Finally there came the great day, September 20, 1780, when Mr. and Mrs. Thrale, Queeney, and Dr. Johnson himself came in a coach-and-four to Chessington. 'At Eleven everybody was prepared & in high expectation', wrote Susan to Charlotte. (Though Susan was to return to St. Martin's Street in a few days, and though her father thought it ridiculous that she should send a letter, fortunately she could not resist writing.)

At Eleven everybody was prepared & in high expectation. Mr. Crisp quite beauish—Patty Payne all elegance—Mrs. Ham & Miss Cooke in their best *becomes*—Fanny & I *as we could*—because you know when we came here we did not expect the *Quality*—The Telescope adjusted & examined every 5 minutes, or *moments* rather—but twelve o'clock came—*One* o'clock, & no appearance on the common —at half past one we began all to despair—except *Fanny*—I was afraid & so was Mr. Crisp, something might have happened to Mr. Thrale.

[1] See p. 116, n. 2.

The telescope was removed, the window shut down, and then William espied a coach on the common. At three minutes past two the travellers arrived.

Fanny & my Father ran out to receive them, & I after, & received such a Salute from Dr Johnson after he had kissed Fanny, that I was half afraid he had pull'd down all my hair, for he put his two great hands on each side of my head to draw me towards him in a very awkward but very goodnatured manner—Mr Thrale too performed upon Fanny & me the same operation—but with somewhat more Gentleness.—In the hall my Father introduced them to Mr. Crisp—who looked uncommonly well.

Mrs. Thrale and Fanny, Mr. Thrale and Mr. Crisp, entered into close conversations. Dr. Johnson was in a very good humour, but did not talk a great deal. With the exception of Queeney, who was 'as usual—cold—grave, indifferent, & silent', everyone was in very good humour, Mr. Thrale in 'uncommon spirits'.

He brought a magnificent present of Fruit . . . and made the most pressing invitations possible to Mr. Crisp to come & spend some time at Streatham, or Brighthelmstone—said he w^d do *everything* he was able to make it comfortable to him—& wanted badly to make him & my Father promise to take a Coach or two Post Chaises to go there with Fanny & me for as long a time as they could immediately—[1]

He prowled curiously about the old mansion, invading the kitchen, the attic, and, by accident, the room of a 'Sequestered old lady', 'whom mortal man had not for many years beheld'.[2] At something after four they had all got into the coach and had taken leave, when 'as we stood still to see them off—*Goodbye Susey*, cried Dr. Johnson *twice* to me—how comically good-natured!' But for Dr. Burney's disapproval of such useless scribbling, Susan could have written '3 pages of particulars about this visit'.[1]

Dr. Johnson was often in mirthful and sportive humour. 'I took Fan in my hand & went to Bolt Court', wrote Dr. Burney to Mrs. Thrale in November of 1778, 'where the good soul rec^d

---

[1] A.L.S. (Barrett) from SB to CAB, 22 Sept. [1780]; *Burford Papers*, p. 46; Clifford, pp. 190–2.

[2] A.L.S. (JRL) from FB to Mr. Thrale, 20 Dec. [1780]. Printed, Clifford, p. 191.

me with open arms, & was so pleasant & comical!—but you
know him when he is off the great Horse, & condescends to
tittup on a little Welch Kephel.'[1] The great Doctor was often
complacent and kind, but not invariably so, as many people
had learned to their embarrassment and woe. 'Oh, sometimes
I think I shall die no other death', said Mrs. Thrale, 'than
hearing the bitter things he says to others.'[2] Fanny's account of
the 'grand Battle upon the Life of Lyttelton' is well known[3] and
according to her letters to her father from Brighton in 1782,
she again found cause to regret Dr. Johnson's belligerence and
its effects:

I am quite sorry to see how unmercifully he attacks & riots the
people. He has raised such a general alarm, that he is now omitted
in all cards of invitation sent to the rest of us. What pity that he will
never curb himself! nor restrain his tongue upon every occasion
from such bitter or cruel speeches as eternally come from him![4]

Fanny feared that, as a result, Dr. Johnson did not 'spend his
time very agreeably',

for he is dreaded too much to get any conversation, except by accident; & he has had no invitation since my arrival, but to one
Dinner, at single speech Hamilton's. He has therefore passed most
of his Evenings alone, & much to his dissatisfaction. He has, however,
so miserably mauled the few who have ventured to encounter him,
that there is little wonder they wave the ceremony of any meetings
they can avoid.[4]

In 1783, however, she thought Dr. Johnson 'much softened'.
'Why I am now', said he, 'come to that Time when I wish all
bitterness & animosity to be at an end.'[4]

    The Burneys were perhaps more fortunate than most people
in their encounters with the great man. ('My heart goes out to
Burney.' 'I love all of the race which I do know, and some that
I do not.' And to Susan: 'I think one should love *you*, too, *if one*

    [1] A.L.S. (JRL) from CB to HLT, 6 Nov. 1778.
    [2] *Diary*, i. 129.
    [3] *Diary*, i. 497–502; ii. 234–7. For additional details see the Diary MSS. (Berg),
pp. 1843–7, or an article by the author, 'Dr. Johnson and Fanny Burney—some
additions to the Record', *Bulletin of the NYPL*, lv (Feb. 1951), 55–65. I am indebted
to the NYPL for permission to reprint parts of this.
    [4] A.L.S. and A.L. (Berg) from FB to CB, 3, 8 Nov. 1782, respectively. Diary
MSS. (Berg), pp. 1843–7; *Diary*, ii. 234–7.

did but know you'! '*Goodbye, my little love*.')[1] In the end Dr. Burney found the old Philosopher as 'good-natured as a family mastiff, whom you may safely pat & stroke at the fireside, without the least fear of his biting you. The utmost he will do if you are a little rough with him is to growl.'[2]

Apart from strong family feeling, there seemed no trait more characteristic of the Burneys from their childhood up than their perception of and delight in the ridiculous. The friends they made—Lady Clarges, Mrs. Lambert, or the daughters of Thomas Payne, the bookseller—were characterized by their turn for 'nonsensical sport and jollity', 'fun and ridicule', their gifts for 'discerning characters' and 'relating ridiculous circumstances in a laughable manner'.[3] Comic idiosyncrasies often supplied the gleeful subject-matter of the early diaries, and for their lives long whatever was odd, queer, quaint, affected, or fantastic seemed to suggest a letter to some other member of the family. 'Foibles make all the charm of society', Fanny made Mrs. Arlbery say in *Camilla*. 'They are the only support of convivial raillery, and domestic wit.'[4] Thus Kitty Cooke's 'oddments' had contributed largely to the gaiety of Chessington. 'In her thoroughly unrivalled Dialect, there is a queerness, an originality, a ridiculous yet meaning oddity, that would raise a laugh "even in the ribs of Death." '[5] This was not to condemn the good creature, for hers was not the oddity of affectation. 'If ever any mortal had to look back upon an entirely *guiltless* existence for herself, & *useful* & benevolent one for others, I should think her that mortal', wrote Fanny at the close of Miss Cooke's life. 'I cannot forget while I live the innumerable kind offices I owed to her upon every visit to once so dear—now so utterly desolate Chessington.'[6]

The Burneys had keen ears for variations in dialect, odd expressions, or the incongruous speech of the foreign visitors who came to St. Martin's Street, singers and musicians whose grasp of English idiom was not yet secure. They prized whimsical or humorous letters like those of Mr. Twining, Christian

---

[1] *Diary*, ii. 54; ED, ii. 255–61.
[2] A.L.S. (Osborn) from CB to the Rev. Thomas Twining, n.d.
[3] Diary MSS. (Berg), pp. 1176–8; ED, ii. 142; A.L. (Berg) from SB to CAB, 29 Jan. [1780].
[4] (5 vols., 1796), iii. 84.   [5] A.L.S. (Berg) from FB to CB, May 1793.
[6] Fragment of a letter (Barrett) from FB to SBP, n.d.

Latrobe, or Jacob Bryant, the antiquarian, or idiomatic recordings like Maria Rishton's transcript of the Norfolk wife's lament.

The publication of *Evelina* had made the author's delight in
the ridiculous evident, and Mrs. Thrale and others were ready
to supply new copy. Fanny had been encouraged by Mr. Crisp
to consider her excursions into the Great World as field trips
on which she might cull and select specimens and examine them
as 'the blood globules circulating in a frog's foot, when seen
through a microscope'.[1] She may also have had in mind her
father's verses about the 'Moving Scene':

> The whole's a *comedy of Errors*
> More full of ridicule than terrors,
> In which the Characters are found
> In whim & humour to abound
> Sufficient to supply wth mirth
> The wight most dolorous on earth.
>
> Let's now therefore take the good we find
> Nor be to present comfort blind
> But laugh at each mundane mutation
> Till time ordain our own Migration.[2]

In December, 1779, Fanny Burney was assuring Mr. Crisp that
Miss Birch and other characters in her journal were not imag-
inary, as he supposed, but transcripts of real life. 'I never mix
truth and fiction.'[3] 'The world, and especially the Great World,
is so filled with absurdity of various sorts, now bursting forth in
impertinence, now in pomposity, now giggling in silliness, and
now yawning in dulness, that there is no occasion for invention
to draw what is striking in every possible species of the ridiculous.'[3] Like Meredith's Comic Spirit she had come to survey
the world as a 'full field', and whatever she saw that seemed to
'wax out of proportion, overblown, affected, pretentious,
bombastical, hypocritical, pedantic, fantastically delicate' was
likely to move her laughter and almost as often her pen.
Whether or not she had, like that famous Comic Spirit, the
sage's brows or the sunny malice of a faun lurking at the corner
of half-closed lips, she was often enough, as she said, surprised

---

[1] *Diary*, i. 149–53.

[2] In a notebook (Berg) entitled *Characters extracted from various writings of my
dearest father.*   [3] *Diary*, i. 311–12.

in 'the full grin' and found it impossible to 'keep her countenance'. Mrs. Vesey's manipulation of her cushions, ear-trumpet,
and 'Brass Ears, & *silver* Ears, & Glass Ears, & Ears of all sorts!'
was an occasion in point.[1] The Comic Spirit, it is true, often
looked 'humanely malign', and the 'oblique light' it is wont to
cast on unshapely variations from the norm is often cruel, as
also are some of Fanny's *exposés* of the folly of affectation or the
sin of pride.

Her long visits with the Thrales at Brighton and Bath widened
the field for her observation, and the Brighton and Bath journals
were rapidly filled with pen-pictures of the company encountered on the Steyne or the Parades, in the assembly-rooms,
private drawing-rooms, or booksellers' shops. It would be
difficult to find a more accurate illustration of the play of the
comic light about its victim than in her unconscious delineation
of herself as she contemplated Mr. Blakeney. She began as
usual with an introductory character-sketch and then proceeded with the samples of conversation.

I must now have the honour to present to you a new acquaintance,
who this day dined here—Mr. Blakeney, an Irish gentleman, late a
commissary in Germany. He is between sixty and seventy, but means
to pass for about thirty; gallant, complaisant, obsequious, and
humble to the fair sex, for whom he has an awful reverence; but
when not immediately addressing them, swaggering, blustering,
puffing, and domineering. These are his two apparent characters;
but the real man is worthy, moral, religious, though conceited and
parading.

. . . His whole conversation consists in little French phrases, picked
up during his residence abroad, and in anecdotes and story-telling,
which are sure to be re-told daily and daily in the same words.

Having given you this general sketch, I will endeavour to illustrate
it by some specimens; but you must excuse their being unconnected,
and only such as I can readily recollect.

Speaking of the ball in the evening, to which we were all going,
'Ah, madam!' said he to Mrs. Thrale, 'There was a time when—
tol-de-rol, tol-de-rol (rising, and dancing, and singing), tol-de-rol!—
I could dance with the best of them; but, now a man, forty and
upwards, as my Lord Ligonier used to say—but—tol-de-rol!—there
was a time!'

[1] *Diary*, ii. 233–9; also Diary MSS. (Berg), Dec. 1783, including suppressed
fragments; and A.L.S. (Berg) from FB to SBP, 23 June–7 July 1783.

'Ay, so there was, Mr. Blakeney,' said Mrs. Thrale, 'and I think you and I together made a very venerable appearance!'

'Ah! madam, I remember once, at Bath, I was called out to dance with one of the finest young ladies I ever saw. I was just preparing to do my best, when a gentleman of my acquaintance was so cruel as to whisper me—"Blakeney! the eyes of all Europe are upon you!"—for that was the phrase of the times. "Blakeney!" says he, "the eyes of all Europe are upon you!"—I vow, ma'am, enough to make a man tremble!—tol-de-rol, tol-de-rol! (dancing)—the eyes of all Europe are upon you!—I declare, ma'am, enough to put a man out of countenance!'

Dr. Delap, who came here some time after, was speaking of Horace.

'Ah! madam,' cried Mr. Blakeney, 'this Latin—things of that kind —we waste our youth, ma'am, in these vain studies. For my part I wish I had spent mine in studying French and Spanish—more useful, ma'am. But, bless me, ma'am, what time have I had for that kind of thing? Travelling here, over the ocean, hills, and dales, ma'am— reading the great book of the world—poor ignorant mortals, ma'am, —no time to do anything!'

. . . After this, Dr. Johnson being mentioned,

'Ay,' said he, 'I'm sorry he did not come down with you. I liked him better than those others: not much of a fine gentleman, indeed, but a clever fellow—a deal of knowledge—got a deuced good understanding!'

Dr. Delap rather abruptly asked my Christian name: Mrs. Thrale answered, and Mr. Blakeney tenderly repeated,

'Fanny! a prodigious pretty name, and a pretty lady that bears it. Fanny! Ah! how beautiful is that song of Swift's—

> "When Fanny, blooming fair,
>   First caught my ravish'd sight,
>   Struck with her mien and air—"'

'Her face and air,' interrupted Mrs. Thrale, 'for "mien and air" we hold to be much the same thing.'

'Right, ma'am, right! You, ma'am—why, ma'am—you know everything; but, as to me—to be sure, I began with studying the old Greek and Latin, ma'am: but, then, travelling, ma'am!—going through Germany, and then France, and Spain, ma'am! and dipping at Brighthelmstone, over hills and dales, reading the great book of the world!'[1]

Over fifteen pages of the *Diary* are given over to accounts of

---

[1] *Diary*, i. 292–311, 465–8.

Mr. Blakeney. With 'the solemn stiffness of his person, the conceited twinkling of his little old eyes, and the quaint importance of his delivery', he seemed like 'some pragmatical old coxcomb represented on the stage', though no character in any comedy had ever made Fanny laugh 'more extravagantly'. 'He dines and spends the evenings here constantly, to my great satisfaction. . . . However, I have never told you his most favourite story, though we have regularly heard it three or four times a day!—And this is about his health.'

'Some years ago,' he says—'let's see, how many? in the year '71 —ay, '71, '72—thereabouts—I was taken very ill, and, by ill-luck, I was persuaded to ask advice of one of these Dr. Gallipots:—oh, how I hate them all! Sir, they are the vilest pick-pockets—know nothing, sir! nothing in the world! poor ignorant mortals! and then they pretend—In short, sir, I hate them all; I have suffered so much by them, sir—lost four years of the happiness of my life—let's see, '71, '72, '73, '74—ay, four years, sir!—mistook my case, sir!—and all that kind of thing. Why, sir, my feet swelled as big as two horses' heads! I vow I will never consult one of these Dr. Gallipot fellows again! lost, me, sir, four years of the happiness of my life!'[1]

'And all the old phrases were repeated with so sad a solemnity, and attended to by Mr. Hamilton with so contemptuous a frigidity', says the reporter, 'that I was obliged to take up a newspaper to hide my face.' This Mr. Blakeney often convulsed her with laughter; and yet it was his manner more than his words that made him 'so peculiarly ridiculous'. In 1781 Fanny Burney described a very gay party at the Thrales' in Grosvenor Square. 'Mr. Blakeney was just as absurdly pompous as at Brighton; and, in the midst of dinner, without any sort of introduction, or reason, or motive, he called out aloud,'

'Sweet are the slumbers of the charming maid!'
A laugh from all parties, as you may imagine, followed this exclamation; and he bore it with amazing insensibility.

'What's all this laugh for?' cried Dr. Johnson, who had not heard the cause.

'Why, sir,' answered Mrs. Thrale, when she was able to speak, 'Mr. Blakeney just now called out,—nobody knows why,—"Sweet are the slumbers of the virtuous maid!"'

'No, no, not *virtuous*,' cried Mr. Boswell, 'he said *charming*; he thought that better!'

[1] See p. 124, n. 1.

'Ay, sure, sir,' cried Mr. Blakeney, unmoved; 'for why say *virtuous*?—can we doubt a fair female's virtue?—oh fie, oh fie! 'tis a superfluous epithet.'

'But,' cried Mrs. Thrale, 'in the original it is the *virtuous man*; why do you make it *maid* of the sudden, Mr. Blakeney?'

'I was alarmed at first,' cried Dr. Delap, 'and thought he had caught Miss Burney *napping*; but when I looked at her, and saw her awake, I was at a loss, indeed, to find the reason for the change.'

'Here, sir! my lad!' cried Mr. Blakeney to the servant; 'why, my head's on fire! What! have you got never a screen? Why, I shall be what you may call a *hot-headed fellow*! I shall be a mere *rôti*!'[1]

Mr. Cator also, because 'he prated so much, yet said so little, and pronounced his words so vulgarly', often surprised the Comic Spirits at Streatham 'on the full grin'; for Fanny observed that Mr. Seward was as much off guard as she herself, 'having his mouth distended to its fullest extent every other minute'.[2]

Such were the 'slim feasting smiles' and the volleys of silvery laughter that in the diaries and letters of Fanny Burney followed all those who, like Mr. Blakeney and Mr. Cator, allowed themselves to run into variations or aberrations of normal behaviour. Such laughter, according to Bergson, is 'the punishment of society inflicted on eccentric types'. Laughter is the leveller of manners, the whip to conformity.

Ridendo castigat mores; but the laugher, like all castigators, is likely to be feared, and so it proved with Fanny Burney. While readers of *Evelina* and *Cecilia* laughed at the Holborn beau, Miss Larolles, the Branghtons, and the rest, they cringed as well. 'I don't know, ma'am, how it is,' said Pacchierotti, 'but you have made, indeed, all the people, not only for the young, but at the same time for the old, quite afraid of you.'[3] Pacchierotti was thinking at the time of Miss Catherine Bull, who had herself told Dr. Burney that she should be 'dreadfully afraid' of his daughter. The Doctor's hostess, Lady Mary Duncan, 'professed the same ridiculous fear' and to Fanny's regret neglected to send her the invitations she coveted most—those for the evenings at her home when Pacchierotti sang.[3] Miss Palmer and Mrs. Cholmondeley had both wished and feared to meet the

[1] See p. 124, n. 1.
[2] *Diary*, i. 498–502.
[3] *Diary*, ii. 147–52.

author of *Evelina*, and Miss Palmer's uncle was frightened at
the thought of Miss Burney's company, 'because she must be
such a very nice observer, that there would be no escaping her
with safety'.[1] After reading Fanny Burney's second book
Mrs. Thrale had remarked more seriously that even if she had
more virtue than Cecilia, 'she should half fear the censures of
such an insight into the deepest recesses of the mind'. 'Since I
have read this volume, I have seriously thanked Heaven that
all the litter of mine was in sight; none hoarded in holes, nor
hastily stuffed into closets.'[2]

'The joke is', Fanny wrote to Susan from Streatham, 'the
people speak as if they were afraid of me, instead of my being
afraid of them.'[1] When she read Baretti's invective concerning
Mrs. Thrale, she 'half-shuddered' in recalling what he had said
to her after the discovery of *Evelina*: 'I see what is it you can do,
you little witch—it is, that you can hang us all up for laughing-
stocks; but hear me this one thing—don't meddle with me. I see
what they are, your powers; but remember, when you provoke
an Italian you run a dagger into your own breast!'[3]

During the visits, dinners, teas, routs, and *bas-bleu* parties of
1778 until her entrance to the court in 1786 polite tribute to
Fanny Burney usually included a profession or mock profession
of dread. The Bishop of Winchester, Dr. Willis, Mr. Owen
Cambridge, Mr. Burke, and Sir Joshua Reynolds confessed
their fear of her in half-jesting, half-serious gallantries. When
Fanny Burney had remarked to Dr. Johnson that it was not for
nothing he was feared, the Doctor had laughed and replied
'they would fear *you* if they knew you!'[4] Later he told her that
Sir Joshua Reynolds had said that 'if he were conscious to himself of any trick, or any affectation, there is nobody he should
so much fear as this little Burney!'[5] Sir Joshua in turn had
sportively suggested to Miss Burney a cause for Mr. Gibbon's
taciturnity: 'He's terribly afraid you'll snatch at him for a
character in your next book!'[6] The fear of being put into a book
acted as a check-rein to some of the novelist's tormentors at
court. Sometimes Dr. Willis slyly wielded this weapon in her
defence.

[1] *Diary*, i. 107–9.
[2] *Diary*, ii. 84–85; i. 118.
[3] *Diary*, iv. 32.
[4] *Diary*, i. 89.
[5] *Diary*, i. 185.
[6] *Memoirs*, ii. 239.

'Why—I have been thinking of that . . . and, indeed, this thought, all along, has made me, as you may have observed, rather cautious and circumspect, and *very* civil. I hope it has not been thrown away.'

'Well, anybody's welcome to me and my character,' cried Miss Planta, 'and that's always the answer I make them when they tell me of it.'

'Upon my word,' said Mr. Willis, affecting great solemnity, 'I cannot say quite so much: on the contrary, I never go out of the room but I think to myself, How have I behaved to-night? Will that do? Will t'other tell well? No, no; not well! not well at all!—all in the wrong there. But, hang it!—never mind!—she's very—humane —she won't be hard upon a trifle!'[1]

The gentle Bishop of Winchester could understand that Fanny Burney was not afraid of him because 'I am afraid of her, that's all!'[2] Mr. William Burke thought it not very politic to be playing cards and have Miss Burney 'listen to our follies'.[3] Mr. Owen Cambridge complimented her in terms that did justice to himself as well: 'Nay, I give you my word, if I was not conscious of the greatest purity of mind, I should more fear you than anybody in the world . . . you know everything, everybody . . . so wonderfully well!'[4]

Even when allowance is made for gallantry and doting flattery, the general drift of remarks indicates the impression that Fanny Burney made on her contemporaries as a judge and critic of manners. Mrs. Thrale and Fanny Burney come to the rooms to 'comment upon others!', remarked the Master of Ceremonies of the Brighton Assembly in 1779—an observation that gave pause at least to Miss Burney: 'I think I am most safe—& I *know* that I am most easy—in resting a quiet Spectator!'[5] It was politic and natural for her to be quiet in company, 'a poor sheepish wretch' as she described herself to Susan, 'among strangers whom I *fear*'.[6] In large gatherings she seems to have been silent, shy, attentive, and watchful—attitudes that Lady Hesketh, for one, evidently found disconcerting. Nothing was so formidable, she remarked pointedly, 'as to be in company with silent observers'—a comment that promptly served to bring Fanny into the conversation. As the diaries reveal,

[1] *Diary*, iv. 353–4.   [2] *Diary*, ii. 184.
[3] *Diary*, i. 176.   [4] *Diary*, ii. 219.
[5] Diary MSS. (Berg), p. 1062. Cf. *Diary*, i. 378.
[6] Diary MSS. (Berg), p. 738.

Lady Hesketh had some reason to feel uncomfortable, for, just as she perhaps divined, Fanny was in fact putting her down as 'tittle-tattling, monotonous, and tiresome'.[1]

The apprehension and uneasiness raised by the flick of the whip of ridicule or laughter illustrate its social sting and explain its potency as a corrective force. Fanny Burney has sometimes been credited with only hit-and-miss purposes and methods and merely accidental successes. Yet there is more of purpose, plan, and method in her achievement than has been supposed. In her early years she liked to draw ridiculous figures and situations for the entertainment they might afford her father, Susan, Charlotte, Mr. Crisp, and others; and though *Evelina* was written chiefly though not entirely to promote amusement, just as *Cecilia* was written mainly though not entirely to promote morality, it must be pointed out (though it were to damn 'poor Fan' forever) that in her works she did not evoke laughter merely for fun or for art's sake but for its potential corrective force. 'She taught Morality by her writings' was the clause in her epitaph that she would have prized. After the publication of the *Memoirs of Doctor Burney* in 1832, when at the age of eighty she had to defend herself from the charge of sarcasm directed at her stepmother, she says that she is conscious of none throughout the work; then she adds significantly, 'By this I mean against any Individual; for against vices & follies, taken abstractedly, satire, in a moral writer, is almost a duty'.[2] In her later works the proportion of the incompatible ingredients *morality* and *entertainment* is regrettably reversed; yet the risible episodes that enlivened *Evelina*, parts of *Cecilia*, and even *Camilla* were not purely or merely spontaneous and unpremeditated, but served the moral purpose that matured with her maturity.

The comic or satiric spirit that played over some of the social scenes in which Evelina appeared was not, of course, lost on contemporary readers. Many of Evelina's letters moreover— the spirited entrances of fops and affected young ladies, the lively idiomatic dialogue, the shifting locale of the action—both in form and content resembled lively scenes in the comedy of manners. All this suggested that Fanny might succeed as a

---

[1] *Diary*, i. 445.
[2] Two drafts of letters signed (Berg) from FBA to the Rev. Stephen Allen [1833].

dramatist. 'You must set about a comedy', said Mrs. Thrale, 'and set about it openly; it is the true style of writing for you.' 'I declare', she continued a few months later,

'I mean, and think what I say, with all my heart and soul! You seem to me to have the right and true talents for writing a comedy; you would give us all the fun and humour we could wish, and you would give us a scene or two of the pathetic kind that would set all the rest off. If you would but try, I am sure you would succeed, and give us such a play as would be an honour to all your family. And, in the grave parts, all your sentiments would be edifying, and such as would do good,—and I am sure that would be real pleasure to you.'[1]

Dr. Johnson, according to Mrs. Thrale, thought the same, and she was sure he would be at Fanny's service 'in anything in his power'.

'We'll make him write your prologue; we'll make him carry your play to the managers; we'll do anything for you;—and so, I am sure, he readily will.'[1]

Encouragement to write comedy came next, and very impressively, from Richard Brinsley Sheridan himself, whom Fanny met at an evening party at Mrs. Cholmondeley's. In due course the usual compliments began. Sheridan had 'expected to see in Miss Burney a lady of the gravest appearance, with the quickest parts'. *Evelina* was 'a most surprising book'. And what, if he might ask, was Miss Burney about now?

SIR JOSHUA.—Anything in the dialogue way, I think, she must succeed in; and I am sure invention will not be wanting.

MR. SHERIDAN.—No, indeed; I think, and say, she should write a comedy. . . .

SIR JOSHUA.—She has, certainly, something of a knack at characters; —where she got it, I don't know,—and how she got it, I can't imagine; but she certainly has it. And to throw it away is—

MR. SHERIDAN.—Oh, she won't,—she will write a comedy,—she has promised me she will! . . .

SIR JOSHUA.—Ay, that's very right. And you (*to* MR. SHERIDAN) would take anything of hers, would you not?—on sight, unseen?

What a point-blank question! who but Sir Joshua would have ventured it!

MR. SHERIDAN [*with quickness*].—Yes, and make her a bow and my best thanks into the bargain. . . .

[1] *Diary*, i. 98, 148–9.

F.B.—Mr. Sheridan, are you not mocking me?

SHERIDAN.—No, upon my honour! this is what I have meditated to
    say to you the first time I should have the pleasure of seeing
    you.[1]

At Streatham in the following month (February, 1779)
Fanny met Arthur Murphy, 'the most intimate in the house,
amongst the Wits, from being the personal favourite of Mrs.
Thrale', 'the man of all other strangers' whom she had 'most
longed to see'. She soon noted that

for gaiety of spirits, powers of dramatic effect, stories of strong
humour and resistless risibility, [he] was nearly unequalled: and
they were coupled with politeness of address, gentleness of speech,
and well-bred, almost courtly, demeanour.[1]

His quietness and gentleness were reassuring, and Mrs. Thrale
charged Fanny to be agreeable.

'He may be of use to you, in what I am most eager for—your
writing a play: he knows stage business so well; and if you will but
take a fancy to one another, he may be more able to serve you than
all of us put together. My ambition is that Johnson should write your
prologue, and Murphy your epilogue; then I shall be quite happy.'[1]

The conversation at the tea-table might have been arranged,
though Mrs. Thrale insisted on her innocence.

'If I,' said Mr. Murphy, looking very archly, 'had written a
certain book—a book I won't name, but a book I have lately read—
I would next write a comedy.'

'Good,' cried Mrs. Thrale, colouring with pleasure; 'do you think
so too?'

'Yes, indeed; I thought so while I was reading it; it struck me
repeatedly . . . comedy is the forte of that book. I laughed over it
most violently: and if the author—I won't say who (all the time
looking away from me)—will write a comedy, I will most readily,
and with great pleasure, give any advice or assistance in my power.'[1]

The wits, including some of the dramatists, were of one mind.
'I cannot tell what might not be expected from Evelina, was she
to try her Genius at Comedy.'[1] Mr. Crisp alone saw difficulties
and objections.

I need not observe to you that in most of our successful comedies
there are frequent lively freedoms (and waggeries that cannot be

---

[1] *Diary*, i. 161–211; *Memoirs*, ii. 174.

called licentious, neither) that give a strange animation and vigour
to the style, and of which if it were to be deprived it would lose
wonderfully of its salt and spirit. I mean such freedoms as ladies of
the strictest character would make no scruple, openly, to laugh at,
but at the same time, especially if they were prudes (and you know
you are one), perhaps would shy at being known to be the authors of.[1]

'In scenes where gay men of the world are got together', such
strokes, Mr. Crisp said, were 'natural and expected'. Only
'fine-spun, all-delicate, sentimental comedies' dispensed with
the spice of licentiousness, but they were 'such sick things, so
void of blood and spirits', that Mr. Crisp thought they might
well be called *Comédies Larmoyantes*.[1] Though, with the prece-
dents of the Restoration apparently in mind, he seemed to
think salacious ideas necessary to comedy, he had noticed that
such ideas could be suggested by means other than filthy
diction. 'That is a rock the female must take care to steer clear
of.' 'I will never allow you to sacrifice a grain of female delicacy
for all the wit of Congreve and Vanbrugh put together.'

Bawdy speech was not a rock against which Fanny Burney
was likely to dash and, as she herself had shown, salacious
ideas are not the sole source of laughter. The definitive work on
laughter has not yet, perhaps, been written, but if Mr. Crisp
had been well enough to come to town and see Sheridan's
brilliant performance, *The School for Scandal* (1777), or even
The Rivals (1775), with their debts to the comedy of humours,
their satiric parody and caricature, the lightning and surprising shifts of attitudes that underlie so much of the glittering
wit, he must have acknowledged that impurities are not necessarily ingredients of highly successful comedy. With the world
to choose from, Fanny took for the subject of her comedy the
new matter in hand, the *literary world*, and particularly the
literary and critical pretensions and pseudo-learning of a set of
bluestockings.

By February 3, 1779, she had gone so far with her general
plan as to be unable, as she told Dr. Johnson, to make use of
Arthur Murphy's advice about the *rules*.[2] In March and April
she was hard at work, for the most part at Streatham, and her

---

[1] *Diary*, i. 149–53, 163–6, 261–4.
[2] Diary MSS. (Berg), p. 1000; *Diary*, i. 211–312; Susan Burney's Journal
(Barrett), 3–6 Aug. 1779.

neglect of letters and of journal-letters marks her absorption in the task. By the first of May one draft of the play was completed, read by Dr. Burney, and read by Fanny herself to Mrs. Thrale, who seemed slightly taken aback by the stringent satire on 'the scribbling Ladies'.[1] Early in May, Murphy read Act I and, according to both Fanny and Mrs. Thrale, commended it very liberally, with high praise for the dialogue. Late in May Fanny accompanied the Thrales to Brighton, where they were soon joined by Murphy, and a Dr. Delap, rector of Lewes, another scribbler, who was writing a tragedy, *Macaria*. Murphy, proceeding with the second act of 'The Witlings', was struck, as the readers of *Evelina* were, by Fanny's merciless powers of observation. 'Miss Slyboots!—that is exactly the thing!'[2]

Fanny had wished above all things to carry her play to Chessington, read it herself to Mr. Crisp, and hear his comments. In this she was superseded by her father, who, as soon as he could free himself from the winter's engagements, insisted on taking the play to Chessington himself and reading it to Mr. Crisp.[2] Charlotte and other members of the family there present laughed loyally and violently over Bob, the son of Mrs. Voluble, over Dabbler, Codger, Mrs. Wheedle the milliner, and others, but Dr. Burney and Mr. Crisp thought the subject-matter, the literary pretensions and pride of a set of bluestockings together with a satire in the manner of *Satiromastix* on the laborious literary efforts of a pedestrian writer, Dabbler, perilously pointed, perhaps presumptuous in so inexperienced a writer and likely to provoke resentment, if not retaliation.

The butt of the criticisms was not here the jostling vulgarity of the lower middle classes and the follies of fops, rakes, and affected young ladies, a satire that the wits and witlings could comfortably enjoy, but a surprisingly sharp satire on the affectations of the witlings themselves and especially of the *bas bleus*. Mrs. Thrale said that she could recognize herself in the villain of the piece, Mrs. Smatter, but Mr. Crisp and Dr. Burney recognized Mrs. Montagu, the Queen of the Blues. By a further coincidence, Mrs. Smatter, like Mrs. Montagu, had great wealth and a nephew somewhat in her power as her prospective

---

[1] *Thraliana*, i. 381, 401.   [2] See p. 132, n. 2.

heir. She was made the object of scorn for pride of wealth, for boasted learning that proved mere pretence, and for literary pronouncements that were shown up as banalities. As usual Fanny's chief butt was affectation, but here, the affectation of learning among the so-called learned ladies, Mrs. Sapient, Mrs. Voluble, and Mrs. Smatter. Mrs. Smatter's villainy consisted further in pride manifested in her refusal to allow her nephew to marry the heroine Cecilia, who had lately lost her fortune, until finally the blue tyrant is brought to terms by the use of the most effective of all literary weapons, the lampoon.

The lampoon was a method of attack much to be dreaded. No one was exempt from its menace. Once, at Bath in 1780, Mrs. Thrale with her usual impetuosity had accepted an invitation from a Mrs. Macartney, a woman of a most notorious character, whom Mrs. Thrale had mistaken for a respectable lady of the same name.[1] Fanny had been assured by Captain Bouchier, who, being a man, 'scrupled not to visit at a House where gaiety & entertainment abounded', that this Mrs. Macartney was 'one of the worst women Breathing, a Drunkard notoriously, an assistant to the vices of others, & an infamous practicer of all species of them herself'. She kept a 'superb house', gave 'most elegant Entertainments', and was 'countenanced by people of character & Rank'. The Bath Queen was a wretch, Miss Bowdler said, who endeavoured 'as much by dispersing obscene Books, to corrupt youth and to assist already corrupted maturity in the prosecution of vice'. 'Her face carries an affirmation of all this account', said the horrified Fanny. 'It is bold, hardened, painted, snuft, leering & impudent! just such a face as I should Draw for Mrs. Sinclair!' She was decked out in thin muslins plentifully adorned with 'red Bows and Ribbons'. Her short basque and coat 'lined throughout with pink' were so arranged as to 'half conceal half her old wrinkled neck,—the rest was visible to all Beholders'. A very Mrs. McDevil! as indeed she was nicknamed in Bath. Yet Mrs. Thrale had allowed herself to be 'drawn into a very intimate conversation with this gay lady, & entered into her affairs & views, & listened to her complaints of ill usage with the utmost sociality & interest', unhappily concluding by accepting an invitation to the 'superb house' for herself, Miss Thrale, and Miss Burney.

[1] Diary MSS. (Berg), pp. 1137–42.

After Fanny had reported all that she had lately heard about this Queen, Mrs. Thrale instantly agreed that 'it was totally improper to make such an acquaintance and that some method must be devised to put an end to it without making the visit'. They were of the same opinion from the moment they had the same information, Fanny is careful to say, but they did not quite know how to back out. This creature, it seemed, would not be slighted with impunity, and only lately she had put 'a mortifying paragraph into the Morning Post about Sophy Streatfield merely for her refusing to visit her'. In a few days 'Mrs. Macartney came in a chair—we were all denied & she left us a card for each, a disagreeable affair! I wish it may end quietly.' Yet since her resentment was likely to be expressed in lampoons and libels, there was some danger in resistance. Mrs. Thrale then decided that she would go alone to return Mrs. McDevil's call, offering excuses 'very civilly' for Miss Thrale and Miss Burney, who had had a previous engagement, which they had forgotten. Mrs. Thrale was perhaps fortunate in finding the Bath Queen 'Drinking Rum & sugar', and all ended amicably.[1]

Such incidents explain why Fanny Burney was so 'shocked, mortified, grieved, and confounded' at the mild reference to her as 'dear little Burney' in the pamphlet *Warley: a satire*.[2] As she made Censor remark in 'The Witlings', 'one satire will be the prelude to another'.[3]

I was for more than a week unable to eat, drink, or sleep, for vehemence of vexation. . . . All that I can say for myself is, that I have always feared discovery, always sought concealment, and always known that no success could counter-balance the publishing my name. . . . But pray Heaven may spare me the horror irrecoverable of personal abuse! Let them criticise, cut, slash, without mercy my book, and let them neglect me; but may God avert my becoming a public theme of ridicule! In such a case, how should I wish *Evelina* had followed her humble predecessors, to the all-devouring flames, which, in consuming her, would have preserved her creatress![2]

She could expect to be ridiculed publicly in rude and coarse pamphlets, as Dr. Burney himself was in an obscene parody of

---

[1] See p. 134, n. 1.   [2] *Diary*, i. 127–8, 158–71, 180.
[3] 'The Witlings, a Comedy', survives in a manuscript of 126 pages meticulously copied in Fanny Burney's hand. The possession of the Berg Collection, the NYPL.

his *Tours*, George Veal's *Musical Travels through England*.[1] Even
Lady Mary Duncan, whose social position was much securer
than that of Fanny Burney, and who, unlike Dr. Burney, could
hardly be derided for sycophancy, had to buy up a whole
impression of a ludicrous caricature of herself and Pacchierotti
in order to prevent her name from being bandied about with
that of the Italian singer, whom she had befriended. 'Her Ladyship was much hurt by it', wrote Fanny to her father from Bath.
''Tis very scandalous that these Caricatures should be permitted, & that to *avoid* public notice should be more Expensive
than to seek it.'[2] The power of the lampooner is epitomized in
'The Witlings' by Dabbler, who could condemn his victim 'for
life to Irony & contempt'.

LADY SMATTER. Alas, how dangerous is popularity: O, Mr.
   Dabbler, that I could but despise these libels as you do!
DABBLER. We men do not suffer in the world by Lampoons as the
   poor Ladies do; they indeed, may be quite—quite ruined by
   them.[3]

The villain of 'The Witlings' is therefore brought to capitulate
through fear of the lampoon. Unless Lady Smatter will agree to
the marriage of hero and heroine, the witlings will see to it that
daily epigrams upon her shall appear in the press. Her name
shall be hooted about the streets by ballad singers, and a puppet
in her likeness shall perform in the Patagonian Theatre. Lampoons shall appear in all the coffee houses, one of which will
run thus:

> Yes, Smatter in the Muse's Friend,
> She knows to censure or commend
> And has of Faith & Truth such store
> She'll ne'er desert you—till you're poor.
>
> At Thirty she began to read,—
> At Forty, it is said could spell,—
> At Fifty, 'twas by all agreed
> A common school Girl she'd excell.

---

[1] This work was printed in 1774, reprinted in 1775, 1776, 1785, and 1818.
See *Memoirs*, i. 258–60; and Scholes, i. 272–5.
[2] See A.L.S. (Barrett) from FB to CB, May 1780.
[3] See p. 135, n. 3.

This lady with study has muddled her head,
Sans meaning she talk'd, & sans knowledge she read
And gulp'd such a Dose of incongruous matter
That Bedlam must soon hold the Carcase of Smatter.
With a down, down, derry, down.

A club she supported of Witlings & Fools,
Who, but for her dinners, had scoff'd at her rules;
The reason, if any she had, these did shatter
Of poor empty-Headed, & little-soul'd Smatter
With a down, down, derry, down.[1]

These and other lines pointed so directly and unmistakably at
the *bas bleus* and especially at Mrs. Montagu, Queen of the
Blues, that the whole piece might be taken as a lampoon on the
learned Queen and her associates. Dr. Johnson had encouraged
Fanny in an attack on the Queen of the Wits.

Down with her, Burney!—down with her!—spare her not!—
attack her, fight her, and down with her at once! You are a rising
wit, and she is at the top; and when I was beginning the world, and
was nothing and nobody, the joy of my life was to fire at all the
established wits! and then everybody loved to halloo me on. But
there is no game now; everybody would be glad to see me conquered:
but then, when I was new, to vanquish the great ones was all the
delight of my poor little dear soul! So at her, Burney—at her, and
down with her![2]

Dr. Burney and Mr. Crisp were no fonder of Mrs. Montagu
than Dr. Johnson was, but they in no wise shared his eagerness
for hardy combat and so withdrew their one ewe lamb from the
fray. Mr. Crisp scolded her roundly. Follies of a general nature
were the right matter for comedy, he told her. The characteristic
follies of the age would furnish 'a profusion' of what she
wanted, 'without descending to the invidious and cruel practice
of pointing out individual characters, and holding them up to
public ridicule'.[3] Dr. Burney also stated that his 'chief & almost
only quarrel' was with the members of 'the Blue Stocking Club
party', and he thought that 'not only the whole piece, but the
plot had best be kept secret'.[4] With drastic revising, the play
might be remodelled, but it was not 'hard fagging' of this kind

[1] See p. 135, n. 3.   [2] *Diary*, i. 115.
[3] See p. 132, n. 2.
[4] A fragment of a letter (Barrett) from CB to FB, post-dated, 1779.

that produced *Evelina*! Mr. Crisp remarked, 'It was the ebullition of true sterling genius—you wrote it because you could
not help it.' Mr. Crisp inclined to the view that 'little entertaining elegant histories', that is, novels rather than plays,
would give Fanny scope to range as she pleased. From general
follies she could 'pick, cull, select' whatever she liked, and she
could then be as minute as she wished.[1]

'The fatal knell, then is knolled', wrote the playwright, 'and
"down among the dead men" sink the poor *Witlings*—for ever,
and for ever, and for ever!—I give a sigh, whether I will or not,
to their memory!' And yet her mortification was not 'at throwing away the characters, or the contrivance;—it is all at
throwing away the time,—which I with difficulty stole, and
which I have buried in the mere trouble of writing'. For some
time Sheridan continued to inquire about the comedy, but
some twenty years were to elapse before his expectations and
those of Murphy and Mrs. Thrale were realized and Fanny
produced in 'A Busy Day' the comedy that they felt she could
write. For the present,

'there are plays that are to be saved, and plays that are not to be
saved!' so good night, Mr. Dabbler!—good-night, Lady Smatter,—
Mrs. Sapient,—Mrs. Voluble,—Mrs. Wheedle,—Censor,—Cecilia,
—Beaufort, and you, you great oaf, Bobby!—good-night! good-
night!'

[1] See p. 132, n. 2.

VI

CECILIA

(1780–1782)

Heavens! what a life of struggle between the head and the heart!
Cecilia, v. x. 6

THE publication of *Evelina*, which introduced Fanny Burney into the Streatham group and thus into the London world, put an end to her fortunate and spontaneous habit of writing for its own happy ends. No one can know, of course, what work she might have produced if she had been left to her own quiet ways. The protests that she made on being thrust into public notice indicate that one of the genial conditions of her growth had been the screen that shielded her from the disapproval or opprobrium easily incurred by the wit or novelist. Anonymity had afforded temporary security and made for uninhibited writing. She had launched her first craft on a lee shore.

In *Cecilia*, however, Miss Burney must meet the full tide of public criticism. Where the earlier novel had been based on the girlish adventures and dreams of Poland Street and St. Martin's Street and took ten years to develop, *Cecilia* was the product of Streatham, Brighton, Bath, and the larger world, which at this time Fanny was getting to know, but which she was allowed no time to assimilate. Finally, the new work was not a spontaneous but a forced production, written largely because Dr. Burney thought that the new author should seize and capitalize on the shining hour of her first success. *Cecilia*, in short, took form under pressures of time and compulsion that had never entered into the composition of *Evelina* and, as Fanny's complaints to her sisters indicate, the book often proceeded with great travail.

I go on but indifferently,—I don't write as I did, the certainty of being known, the high success of Evelina, which, as Mr. Crisp says, to fail in a 2ᵈ would *tarnish,*—these thoughts worry & depress me,

—& a desire to do more than I have been able, by writing at unseasonable Hours, & never letting my Brains rest even when my *corporeal machine* was succumbent.[1]

Dr. Burney and Mr. Crisp had allowed her no respite; having condemned her play, they urged her first to begin and then to hurry on with a novel. Mrs. Thrale insisted that she visit Streatham and accompany parties to the watering-places. Fanny herself wished to journalize, but for a time she attempted to satisfy all demands at once, and we have as a result the first outline of *Cecilia* and a volume of Streatham, Brighton, and Bath Journals.

Early in April, 1780, Mrs. Thrale obtained Dr. Burney's permission to have Fanny at Bath ('I can't go without her & there's an End').[2] The Thrales took a house at the corner of the South Parade overlooking the Avon,[3] and Fanny, Queeney, and Mrs. Thrale went to plays, the pump-room, and countless evening parties, where they met the bluestockings Mrs. Montagu and Mrs. Carter, Mr. Anstey (author of *The New Bath Guide*), the Bowdlers, the infidel Miss W—, Beau Travell, the poet Edward Jerningham, the wit Lord Mulgrave, and, finally, Mrs. Macartney (nicknamed Mrs. McDevil), the notorious Bath Queen. They made a satiric visit to an alderman, Mr. Ferry, in order to see furniture that emerged and dropped out of sight through trapdoors and the mechanical eagle that swooped from the ceiling to remove the table-cloth. There was a merry walk home across the meadows. 'Indeed we laughed all the way.'

Mr. Crisp was very glad to have Fanny in the 'midst of the Bath circle'.

Your time could not be better employed, for all your St. Martin's daddy wanted to retain you for some other purpose. You are now at school, the great school of the world, where swarms of new ideas and new characters will continually present themselves before you,

which you'll draw in,
As we do air, fast as 'tis ministered![4]

[1] A.L.S. (Berg) from FB to EBB, 7–8 Jan. 1781.
[2] 3 A.L.S. (Osborn) from HLT to CB, 1780. Cf. A.L.S. (Barrett) from FB to Mr. Crisp, Bath, 13 Apr. 1780.
[3] Clifford, pp. 182–6; *Diary*, i. 323 ff.; and the Diary MSS. (Berg).
[4] *Diary*, i. 342–4.

Just so had 'old Sarah Marlborough' read men and cards, not books. Yet the old monitor could not refrain from jogging Fanny's memory and conscience about a character-sketch that she had sent him and a plot that he thought would present a large field for unhackneyed characters and give ample scope for satire and ridicule. Just now Fanny had little time for writing anything except the memoranda from which the Bath Journal of 1780 (some hundred pages) was afterwards constructed. She had scarcely a moment to herself.

In June the Gordon Riots reached Bath. 'We saw the flames & heard the shouts together, one whole dreadful night.'[1] Mr. Thrale, dubbed a papist and threatened because in 1778 he had voted in Parliament for the Bill for the Relief of Roman Catholics, was in immediate danger. In the morning (June 10) the family set out for Brighton, choosing a devious route in order to avoid crowds, travelling in a coach-and-four with two postilions and two footmen on horseback, intending, Fanny said, if the rioting grew worse, to embark for Holland. Frantic with fears for the Burney families in London, Fanny could take little joy in the leisurely progress of the route. The Thrales arrived in Brighton on the 18th. With the news that reached them there of the bonfires and pillage that marked the rioting not only in London but in Leicester Fields and St. Martin's Street itself, Fanny felt even worse. At Brighton they may have received Susan's horrific journal of the lurid sights she watched from the observatory, and her explanation of the acute peril the Burneys were in because of threats to a Roman Catholic china-dealer who rented some part of Dr. Burney's premises at the back, and because of proximity to the Orange Street Chapel that the rioters for a time mistook for a Catholic chapel.[1] Fanny was happy when Mrs. Thrale took her to London on June 23 and consented to leave her at home. Long absence had made her feel almost 'an *alien* of late'. She was not ungrateful to the Thrales, but she explained to her father: 'As I should not even *wish* to leave them when they are in sickness or in sorrow, if I also stay with them when they are in Health & in spirits, I am

---

[1] A.L.S. (Osborn) from HLT to CB, 19 June 1780; letters (Berg) from FB to SB and to CB, dated Southampton, Portsmouth, or Brighton, 14, 18, 20 June 1780; Scholes, i. 372 ff.; and for a very vivid first-hand account of the riots, Susan Burney's journal-letter (Barrett), June 1780.

neither *yours* nor *my own*, but *theirs*.'[1] The letters marked Fanny's decision to remain a Burney, rather than accept the hospitality of the Thrales and become a permanent appendage to their household.

In August Dr. Burney with Fanny and Charlotte, and later Susan in exchange, spent about five weeks at Chessington, and Fanny promised Mr. Crisp to return in the winter and work hard on the novel.[2] It was at this time that the Thrales with Dr. Johnson visited Chessington with invitations to Fanny (and *en passant* to Mr. Crisp and Dr. Burney) to accompany them to Brighton, but Fanny felt that she must decline. In late October and in November she was at home incognita—'only stumping out, muffled up & early now & then of a frosty & dry morning into the Park'.[3] The illness of Mr. Thrale delayed her return to Chessington, but for part of December and through January and most of February she was there at work on the early and miscellaneous fragments that were to become *Cecilia*. At the end of January a draft of the first volume was completed.[4]

By February she was worn out by weeks of hard work and longed to return to London.

One way or other my Hand scarce rests an Hour in the whole Day. Whenever this work is done—if ever that Day arrives, I believe I shall not write another word for 3 years! however, I really believe I must still publish it *in part*, for I begin to grow horribly tired, & yet am by no means *near* any thing *bordering* upon an end. And the eternal fagging of my mind & Brains does really much mischief to my Health.[4]

She chafed at the separation from Mrs. Thrale and especially from Susan, whose engagement to one of the heroes of Cook's last expedition, Lieutenant Molesworth Phillips, waited only Dr. Burney's consent. The 'eternal book' that kept her from home at such an exciting crisis had become 'a drudgery'. In mid-February, with the first volume of *Cecilia* scarcely finished, she fell ill of her chief enemy, a lurking fever. Mr. Crisp believed that her 'close application' to writing had 'contributed not a

---

[1] See p. 141, n. 1.

[2] *Diary*, i. 443; *Burford Papers*, pp. 43–47. Dr. Johnson sometimes called Charlotte *Miss Sophy* from the analogy *Susan and Sophy* Thrale. See A.L.S. (Barrett) from SB to CAB, 22 Sept. [1780].

[3] A.L.S. (Berg) and A.L.S. (Barrett) from FB to Mr. Crisp, 13, 18 Nov. 1780.

[4] A.L.S. (Berg) from FB to SB, 3 Feb. 1781.

little to her present Illness', for she was like her father, he said, 'indefatigable and ardent in all her pursuits'.[1] Mrs. Thrale with excitable kindness drove over the winter roads to Chessington, viewed Fanny's state with alarm, and on her return undertook to upbraid Dr. Burney

& told him that your anxious earnestness to oblige him had caused much of the Illness we lamented—Why says he I did tease her to write while she was away &c that the Book so long expected might at length be done.[2]

Before the end of February Daddy Crisp, far from well himself, accompanied Fanny in a chaise across the bare frozen common to the doors of St. Martin's Street. Mrs. Thrale was waiting on the doorstep with a physician that she had brought along to prescribe remedies.[1] Fanny knew that her father would be disappointed that the novel was unfinished.

He will expect me to have just *done*, when I am so behind hand as not even to see land!—yet I have written a great deal, but the work will be a long one, & I cannot without ruining it make it otherwise. . . . I am *afraid* of seeing my father. Think of a whole volume not yet *settled*, not yet begun! & that so important a one as the last! . . . I cannot sleep half the night for planning what to write next Day, & then next day am half dead for want of rest![3]

Obviously all was over with the book for a time. Though 'the vile & irksome fever' was soon conquered, it threatened to return. March was almost sped before Fanny was up and about again at St. Martin's Street, paying frequent visits to the Thrales in Grosvenor Square, busy with dinners and assemblies, and soon much concerned with the sorrows and changes that followed Mr. Thrale's death in April—agitations that, with new troubles nearer home, put her health again in 'a state of precariousness'. Her 'slight machine' was not made for 'rough encounters', the old gentleman at Chessington noted, but he bided his time. Just now, he conceded, Mrs. Thrale had the first claim.[4]

---

[1] *Burford Papers*, pp. 58–60.

[2] A.L.S. (Barrett) from HLT to FB, 20 Feb. [1781] with Madame d'Arblay's annotation.

[3] A.L.S. and A.L. (Berg) from FB to SB, 19 Feb., and n.d.

[4] *Diary*, i. 463 ff.; ii. 1–56; Diary MSS. (Berg), p. 1371. Mr. Thrale died on 4 Apr. 1781.

During most of 1781 domestic joys and distresses filled Fanny's mind. Charles Burney, though now an M.A. from Aberdeen, tarried long in the north after he was expected at home. In love again, he was filling pages with love verses. He was again in debt and his light-hearted gaiety savoured, the family thought, of levity. They almost foresaw and certainly feared what happened in December when the Bishop of London refused him ordination.[1] James, on the other hand, had returned in October, 1780, with the remnant of Cook's last and tragic expedition, sailing up the Thames as 'Master & commander of the ship "The Discoverer", of which he went out first Lieut'.[2] But even so patronage did not come his way, and his next ship, a miserably armed brig, was much below his captain's dignity.[3] His sisters worried over his independent and Whiggish attitudes and the vicissitudes of patronage scarcely less than over the dangers of the sea—and these, Fanny knew, were not slight:

wretched weather, much danger, infinite sickness, & no prize! but he is *safe* now . . . in the Humber, *50* of his men sick with Fevers, from wet, hard watching, & fatigue![3]

In the summer Fanny worried over Esther's health, her careworn state, and her cares—too many children on an income insufficient to support them. In August she helped nurse both Esther and a newly born infant that lived only a few weeks.[4] Somehow she managed to go on with the Streatham Journal, her passages at arms with Crutchley, Johnsonian annals, and the last of the immortal days there.

In September she again succumbed to fever. 'Why, what a

---

[1] 2 A.L.S. (Berg) from FB to SB, 15, 19 Dec. 1781. For details about Charles's career at this time see his own correspondence (Osborn) including A.L.S. to the Earl of Findlater (a request for a loan), Aug. 1781, and A.L. to FB, Nov. 1781 (telling about taking testimonials to the Bishop of London's secretary. 'And when I have got that business over, I shall go—to the masquerade. But tell it not in Gath!—My Father . . .'); also the Burney–Twining correspondence (BM); *Burford Papers*, pp. 72–73; and A.L.S. (JRL) from FB to HLT, [1781].

[2] Two copies A.L.S. (Osborn) from CB to the Rev. Thomas Twining, 23 Oct., 7 Nov. 1780.

[3] A.L.S. (Barrett) from Mr. Crisp to FB, 26 June 1781; A.L.S. (Berg) from FB to SBP, 12 Feb. 1782; Manwaring, pp. 112–79; *Burford Papers*, pp. 49–52; A.L.S. (JRL) from FB to HLT, [1781] and A.L. (Barrett) to SB, 11 Nov. 1781; but, more significantly, the correspondence of Rear-Admiral Burney (PML) and a review of James's democratic principles and thwarted career in A.L.S. (Osborn) from CB to CB, Jr., 31 May 1808.

[4] *Burford Papers*, pp. 59, 64; Diary MSS. (Berg), p. 1507.

slight piece of machinery is the terrestrial part of thee, our
Fannikin!' wrote Mr. Crisp a few years previously—'a mere
nothing, a Blast, a Vapour, disorders the Spring of thy Watch;
& the Mechanism is so fine, that it requires no common hand
to set it a going again.'[1] This time she was attended at Streatham
by the physician Sir Richard Jebb, advised to leave off 'asses
milk as too *nourishing*', blooded ('a thing I mortally dislike'),
and required to exist on 'Turnips, with a little dry Bread, &
odious rennet whey', thus avoiding, as she gratefully believed,
'another long and tedious Illness'.[2] Except for Charles, 'not one
of us c^d boast of much strength', Susan remarked. Fanny, with
a constitution that, like her father's, enabled her to live almost
eighty-eight years, was often feverishly ill. 'She has no radical
complaints', Susan explained.

If she has no particular fatigue or any anxiety of mind to cope with
she is lively, active, & well—but her Frame is certainly delicate &
feeble—She is quickly sensible of fatigue & cannot long resist it &
still more quickly touched by any anxiety or distress of mind.[3]

In the first week of November the novelist left Streatham for
Chessington. On the 22nd Mrs. Thrale was giving her opinion
of the new novel—expecting to cry herself blind over it—''tis so
excessively pathetic'.[4] Mr. Crisp, who had at last won over
Streatham, had made up his mind to keep Fanny till the book
was finished, but by December she was again chafing at the
bit. 'I *have* hinted to him a design of eloping', she told Susan,
'but his arguments were *rage*, & his *rage*, at the same Time, I
must own, was *argument*.'[5]

This time it was Susan's approaching marriage that diverted
Fanny's heart and mind from her work. Dr. Burney, fearing
that there might not be '*de quoi manger* very plentifully', had at
first opposed the match,[6] but by December the Captain's

---

[1] A.L. (Barrett) from Mr. Crisp to FB, 5 Dec. 1779.
[2] A.L.S. (Barrett) from FB to Mr. Crisp, 2 Oct. 1781; *Burford Papers*, pp. 68–71
(10 Nov. 1781).
[3] Susan Burney's journal (Berg), Feb. 1791.
[4] *Diary*, ii. 53–54 (Nov. 22 should be Nov. 12).
[5] Four letters (Berg) from FB to SB, 2, 15, 19, 22 Dec. 1781; *Diary*, ii. 55; also
A.L.S. (Barrett) from FB to HLT, 16 Dec. [1781]; A.L.S. (Berg) from HLT to
FB, 20 Dec. 1781.
[6] A.L.S. (Barrett) from FB to SB, Dec. 1781; but cf. A.L.S. (Berg) from HLT
to FB, 23 Apr. 1781.

relatives, the Shirleys, had evidently come forward, for by then Dr. Burney spoke with satisfaction of their kindness and of plans that seemed to go on 'very smoothly & happily'.[1] He must have been brought to consent to the marriage, which in its tragic ending was to cause Fanny more lasting grief and regret than any other trouble in the Burney saga. But all this was for the future. Phillips was then gay and loving and true, and Fanny was happy at the glad news, though at the same time a little sad.

There is something to me in the thought of being so near parting with you as the Inmate of the same House, Room—Bed—confidence & life, that is not very *merrifying*, though I would by no means have things altered.[1]

She longed to go to St. Martin's Street, but had to throw into the balance the 'villainous draw backs to all comforts' at home, where the jealous and irate stepmother still played her proverbial role. Fanny found it difficult to write there. Again there was the conflict between the head and the heart.

Mr. Crisp will not *hear* of 6 weeks, or *any given* Time, but insists most solemnly upon the propriety & necessity of my staying where I am, till the Book is actually finished. But in this I will be guided wholly by your affairs. If I cannot be of *use* to you, I shall take his advice, as I know well it is my Father's wish equally, & as I know but too well the many interruptions from ill management, inconvenience, & ill nature I must meet with when I go, will retard me most cruelly, & keep me back I know not how long.[1]

On December 15 the 'melancholy news' about Charles and the refusal of the Bishop of London to ordain him had reached Chessington,[2] and Fanny could work no more. ''Tis a vile thing', she lamented, 'that I have such pitiful Brains they will never be content without keeping a correspondence with the Heart, & hanging so upon it, that they catch all its infirmities!'[1] Dr. Burney, realizing the effect of such family disasters on Fanny, desired her to quiet her mind and 'stay peaceably to finish!' 'How to *quiet* it', was another matter,

yet, at the rate I went on, I do believe but for this melancholy affair, I should have written the Finis by this Evening.[1]

---

[1] See p. 145, n. 5.   [2] See p. 144, n. 1.

She wished only to finish the book and go home, and she appealed to Susan for help.

Sweetest Girl, assist *me* now!—What shall I do with my *Father*, to prevent displeasure or cold looks at my return?—they would half break my Heart, after the most kind Letter he has sent me not to *budge* or *fudge*![1]

'I will scrawl Night & Day, if I *can*.'[2] And so she must have done and thus obtained permission to go to London. On December 22 she excitedly wrote to Susan that on Sunday or Monday alike she would be ready.[2] She was back in the fold for Christmas Day and for a family party given early in the New Year (1782), when 'a prodigious Tribe of Burneys' were invited to dine at St. Martin's Street. 'Mighty disagreeable arrangement for Susan', she commented, 'but hardly to be avoided.'[3] The wedding took place at St. Martin-in-the-Fields on January 10. Molesworth Phillips, seaman, sportsman, and gentleman-farmer, was, according to Mr. Crisp, 'a fine made, tall, stout, active, manly-looking young fellow as you shall see. I think Susan has great luck.' 'He seems perfectly to adore her, which She returns very properly.' The honeymoon was spent at Chessington, though in February Phillips was ordered to join a recruiting party at Ipswich. Susan's letters, for a time 'full of Content',[4] were not for over ten years to be filled with sorrow. All who knew her paid tribute to her talents in music, both vocal and instrumental, and to her judgement and taste in all the arts. In intelligence—in almost every way—she, more than her brothers and sisters, resembled the Doctor. The marriage made no interruption in the flow of confidences between Susan and Fanny. Besides 'alives' (short reports on health and the like), they continued to exchange long, confidential journal-letters and sometimes undertook to dispatch them regularly at the end of every month. As Pacchierotti had observed, there seemed to be '*but one soul—but one mind*' between them.[4]

Apparently Fanny had accompanied the wedding-party to Chessington, but had returned to St. Martin's Street before January 22. In the interval arrangements had been made for

---

[1] See p. 145, n. 6.   [2] See p. 145, n. 5.
[3] A.L.S. (Berg) from FB to HLT, [Jan. 1782].
[4] *Burford Papers*, pp. 74–81; ED, i. lxxiv.

the publication of her book. So casually and so often does the name *Payne* occur in the Burney letters—the visits of Patty and Sally Payne to St. Martin's Street and Chessington, James's new 'Beauism', his visits to Castle Street, and his *devoirs* to Sally (ending later in marriage)—that one is hardly surprised to learn that 'honest Tom Payne', 'Old Payne', as the Doctor called him, was to publish Fanny's new work. Fanny had noted that when the publisher had visited Chessington in February, 1781, he seemed to be looking for an opportunity to speak to her in private, but since she was then too ill to discuss business he wrote to Mr. Crisp about the new work, which he did not doubt would be excellent.[1] Apparently the Doctor closed the contract. An old receipt shows that the copyright of *Cecilia* was sold to Payne and Cadell for £250.[2] When Fanny later realized that, whereas Lowndes had printed 500 copies at first, Payne and Cadell had issued 2,000, she was very indignant. Perhaps neither the Burneys nor the Paynes suspected even then how well the £250 was invested, or that, like Lowndes, 'honest Tom Payne' was to get a good novel at a bargain. Mr. Crisp thought the price fair enough, indeed, 'a pretty Spill' for a girl to earn in a few months only by sitting quietly by a good fire and consulting nothing but her own brains.

You see how triumphantly she goes on. If she can coin gold at such a Rate, as to sit by a warm Fire, and in 3 or 4 months (for the real time she has stuck to it closely, putting it all together, will not amount to more, tho' there have been long Intervals, between) gain £250 by scribbling the Inventions of her own Brain—only putting down in black and white whatever comes into her own head, without labour drawing singly from her own Fountain, she need not want money.[3]

What could be simpler?

Through the London winter Fanny was seen occasionally at concerts or operas, but for the most part 'denied' to everyone except Mrs. Thrale and Hetty. In February she is too 'dreadfully busy', as she says in a letter to Susan, to 'write to any human Being but yourself for any pay, so horribly aches my

---

[1] 2 A.L.S. (Berg) from FB to SBP, 19 Feb. 1781; 16 Aug. 1782.
[2] Dated 19 Dec. 1782 (Berg).
[3] See p. 147, n. 4.

Hand with copying'. On February 12 she had 'just finished that drudgery to the 1st volume'.[1]

She was often seized with 'fits of terror' about her work. 'But for my Father', she wrote Mrs. Thrale, 'I am sure I should throw it behind the Fire!—as, when he knew nothing of the matter, was the case with many of its Predecessors; all, indeed, but Evelina.'[2] 'But for my Father' may be taken as the operative phrase for *Cecilia*. Dr. Burney and Mr. Crisp had insisted that she begin; and now the novel, written at headlong speed, was too long; but she was allowed no time to write a short one. She complained later that her book was advertised in the newspapers before she had begun to copy or revise the fifth volume and while the end was still unwritten.[3] Mrs. Thrale could twit her that, like Dr. Johnson himself, she was plagued for copy by her booksellers (i.e. publishers).[4] Many pages of the first draft that she had no time to copy still stand among the copied pages in the *Cecilia* manuscript.[5] Apart from the changes in names (Albina Wyerly to Cecilia Beverley, Mr. Vaughan to Mr. Briggs, *et al.*), the revisions are usually curtailments of the text or attempts to avoid circumlocution. If she had been allowed time for a little more excision, or if she had been advised to delete duplicated trends in the plot, *Cecilia* would now be more popular. Incidents, words, and dialogue came easily and rapidly to her. Such fecundity was wonderful, as everybody thought; but it was a pity too that the work had not been subjected to a little more classical pruning and more control. In February of 1782 she found some recompense for her labour in her father's pleasure in the first volume. 'He is quite *infatuated* with fondness for it,—not only beyond my most sanguine hopes, but almost beyond credibility.'[6]

By March, 1782, the first volume of *Cecilia* was in the press and Fanny was at work revising and copying the second and third.[7] Mr. Crisp, who had seen much of the work in the rough,

---

[1] A.L.S. (Berg) from FB to SBP, 12 Feb. 1782; Diary MSS. (Berg), p. 1551.

[2] A.L.S. (Barrett) from FB to HLT, n.d.

[3] A.L.S. (Berg) from FB to SBP (post-dated, June or May), 1782.

[4] A.L.S. (Berg) from HLT to FB, 17 Apr. 1782.

[5] The Berg Collection (the NYPL) has 547 pp. of the holograph manuscript of *Cecilia*, sections of each of the five volumes of the novel.

[6] Diary MSS. (Berg), p. 1552.

[7] *Diary*, ii. 71–75, 80–83, 86–99, 124–6; Diary MSS. (Berg), p. 1551.

was impatient to see the changes. He had questioned the
credibility of the behaviour of the Delviles—a criticism that
Fanny took great pains to refute. She wished her book to be
'true to life'—not a mere sentimental thing—a romance—

I meant in Mrs. Delvile to draw a great, but not a perfect character;
I meant, on the contrary, to blend upon paper, as I have frequently
seen blended in life, noble and rare qualities with striking and incurable defects.[1]

Later she was able to defend the verisimilitude of the Delviles
through the authority of people of rank, who shared their
views and testified that, placed in the same position, they would
have acted in the same way.[1] Nothing could have been more
disturbing to the new realist than that Mr. Crisp should have
found her characters unnatural. She found it necessary also to
defend the conclusion, which she thought somewhat new in
fiction, 'for the hero and the heroine are neither plunged in the
depths of misery, nor exalted to UN*human* happiness. Is not such
a middle state more natural, more according to real life, and less
resembling every other book of fiction?' 'I shall think I have
rather written a farce than a serious history, if the whole is to
end, like the hack Italian operas, with a jolly chorus that makes
all parties good and all parties happy!'[1] Mr. Crisp will find that
she will 'fight a good battle here'. Unless she is allowed an
ending more consonant with human experience, she told him,
'the last page of any novel in Mr. Noble's circulating library
may serve for the last page of mine, since a marriage, a reconciliation, and some sudden expedient for great riches, concludes
them all alike'.[1] The monitor was, for the moment, subdued.
Fanny 'is so deep in her present Work that I quite let her alone
at present', wrote the old gentleman to his sister on May 7.
'I believe the 1st is printed off, and Mr. Payne is about the 2d.
She is now hard upon correcting the 3d which he will have soon;
the whole 5 Vols. are to come out together.'[2] Later he agreed
whole-heartedly with changes she had made. 'How will this
go down?' he had asked himself as he read. 'The tribunal of
the Inquisition itself is not more inflexible than I endeavoured
to be on this occasion. Every other mode of proceeding is only
delusive, and what is called making one's market at home.'[1]

[1] See p. 149, n. 7.   [2] See p. 147, n. 4.

In April the second volume of *Cecilia* was circulating freely in manuscript and everybody except Mrs. Thrale, who preferred the *ton* parties at the beginning, liked it even better than the first.[1] The work was to be printed volume by volume as fast as copy could be supplied. On May 23 Mr. Crisp was proudly announcing that 'great Expectations' were raised about Fanny's book, which was to come out after the royal Birthday. There was the possibility, too, that 'if the work answer'd' Mr. Payne might give an additional £50. 'A pretty Spill (£300) for a young girl in a few months to get by sitting still in her Chamber by a good Fire!'[2]

Cecilia, or Memoirs of an Heiress (5 volumes) came out on June 12, 1782, and sold so rapidly that the booksellers, the lordly gentlemen in the full-powdered white wigs, could not supply their clientèle. Miss Reynolds told Miss Burney that 'the circulating library people have had it bespoken by old customers for months to come'.[3] If the first edition had been kept at 2,000 copies, according to Dr. Johnson's knowledgeable calculations Tom Payne could have made a profit from July to October of £500.[4] Friends of the Burneys began to scold: 'Miss Cholmondeley told me she understood I had behaved like a poor *simple thing* again, & had a Father *no wiser than myself!*'[3]

In 1782 Fanny sometimes accepted invitations to accompany her father, and wherever she went she heard comments on her book. At Sir Joshua Reynolds's in June she had met Mr. Burke and fallen 'quite desperately & outrageously in love'.[5] At another party at Sir Joshua's in July, Dr. Johnson told Fanny that he had read the first volume of her novel and that he considered Hobson 'a very *perfect* character'. He had kind words also for characters like Simkins and Miss Larolles and for the scene in Vauxhall Gardens: 'I have again read Harrel's death, it is finely done,—it is *very* finely done!'[3] 'One likes one part, another prefers another part', reported Mrs. Thrale; 'but *Johnson* says, most judiciously, that the grand merit is in the general *Power of the whole.*'[6]

[1] See p. 149, n. 7.   [2] See p. 147, n. 4.
[3] A.L. (Berg) from FB to CB, July 1782.
[4] Diary MSS. (Berg), p. 1625.
[5] A.L. from FB to SBP, n.d. I am indebted to Professor James L. Clifford for a copy of this letter.
[6] A.L.S. (Berg) from HLT to FB, 31 July 1782.

Meanwhile Susan and Phillips had been begging Fanny to contrive a visit to them at Ipswich. One difficulty was that she could not ask her father for money since she already owed him some, but in mid-July, when the resourceful Phillips secured her an advance of £100 from Mr. Payne, she was on her way. Susan was now pregnant, and Fanny would congratulate her more cheerfully, if (thinking, no doubt, of Esther) she could but stipulate her 'future number'.[1] She wrote gaily in anticipation of delights and enjoyments not to be had at home—bread and butter with her tea, and a blazing fire annihilating all the black coals in the grate. Her enumeration of other luxuries was an oblique comment on life at St. Martin's Street:

If I find myself in good spirits, I shall not have the fear of wrath before my Eyes because I may happen to simper: if I am grave, & have had cause for gravity, I shall not conclude that you will be gayer than usual: if I ask you a common question, I shall not expect a stern look for an answer; if I make you a common reply, I shall not take it for granted you will pervert my words into an affront: if I talk of some favourite friend, I shall not prepare myself for hearing him or her instantly traduced; nor yet if I relate something that has made me happy, shall I know my conversation is the fore-runner of an Head-ache.[1]

If such indulgences are refused, Fanny will only be where she was. From Ipswich she wrote happily to her father and to Mrs. Thrale about Susan's happiness. 'Poor thing, she has been little used to such serene comfort as she now enjoys!' Every day the sisters made 'thankful comparisons of the past with the present'.

Capt. P., when he listens to us, is seized with such fits of alternate indignation against *somebody*, & rapture that *he* was the deliverer, that it is impossible not to be diverted by such eager & honest transitions.[2]

Fanny had asked Susan not to begin *Cecilia* before she arrived, for she anticipated reading it with her as 'one of the most pleasant & heartfelt satisfactions' of her life.[1] The quiet readings were interrupted one day by a letter from no less a person than Edmund Burke. Fanny longed to send it to her father but had

---

[1] Four letters (Berg) from FB to SBP, n.d., 14 July, 9, 16 Aug. 1782.
[2] A.L.S. (Berg) from FB to HLT, 21 July 1782; A.L.S. (Barrett) to CB, 21 July 1782.

no frank. 'For elegance of praise no such a one was ever written before.' No one else except her father, thought Fanny,

could, at a Time of Business, disappointment, care & occupation such as His are now, have found time to read with such attention, & to commend with such good nature, a work so totally foreign to every thing that just now can come Home to his Business & bosom.[1]

Few authors, perhaps, will deny the justice of these remarks, for Burke had indeed taken the trouble to point out and praise the three components already discussed at some length in connexion with *Evelina*, 'the natural vein of humour, the tender pathetic, [and] the comprehensive and noble moral'.

On August 9 Fanny reported her return to St. Martin's Street, where she

found Charlotte alone, & more glad to see me than I ever yet saw her after the longest separations, for she could hardly speak for crying,—I always knew her to be very affectionate, but never before surprised her in such a trick of sensibility.[2]

Fanny resolved for the future to take 'more comfort' in Charlotte's society than her loss of Susan had hitherto given her spirit to attempt. But the honest and affectionate Charlotte, who meant to fill Susan's place, had not as yet 'the *powers*',

our tastes do not naturally accord, our likings and dislikings, are often dissimilar,—we don't admire the same people, we don't read the same Books, we don't search the same amusements, we don't adore the same Pacchierotti,—with *you* all seemed the same as with myself.[2]

Charlotte's turn was to come later.

In 1782 the Doctor published the second volume of his *History of Music* and began the third.

My father is all himself—gay, facile, and sweet. He comes to all meals, writes without toiling, and gives us more of his society than he has done many years.[3]

In July he had gone to Chessington, accompanied by Mrs. Burney and Miss Young. Though they had planned to return in a few days, Mrs. Burney, as Mr. Crisp wrote to his sister, was

---

[1] A.L.S. (Barrett) from FB to CB, Ipswich, 4 Aug. 1782. For Burke's letter see *Diary*, ii. 92–94. [2] See p. 152, n. 1.
[3] *Diary*, ii. 92–99; *Burford Papers*, pp. 82–86.

taken so ill that she could not go back. Her case was thought
'desperate',

insomuch that the famous Dr. Warren, the King's favourite Physician, was sent for hither from London, who when he came gave but
little hopes. She has ever since lain struggling between Life and
Death, and has been thought actually dying more than once: particularly a week ago Mr. Hemming saw her, and said she would not
live till morning; for that the Death Sweats were upon her. How it
will end, God knows. She still lives, but without sleep, and almost
without food. . . . It is absolutely impossible for her to be mov'd,
it seems; as Hemming says she would dye upon the Road; so that
we are in for it to some purpose.[1]

This crisis also passed. Mrs. Burney slowly recovered, con-
valescing through the month of August at Chessington. Mrs.
Gast arrived, and on August 12 Fanny came with her cousin
Edward in a chaise 'well loaded with canvasses, pencils, and
painting materials'. Edward had been invited to paint Mr.
Crisp and Mrs. Gast, and to Fanny's surprise plans had been
laid for a portrait of her own *'pauvre petite personne'*. 'My sweet
father came down Gascoign Lane to meet us, in very good
spirits and very good health. Next came dear Daddy Crisp,
looking vastly well, and, as usual, high in glee and kindness at
the meeting. Then the affectionate Kitty, the good Mrs. Hamilton, the gentle Miss Young, and the enthusiastic Mrs. Gast.'[1]
The unhappy Invalid waited inside. The pleasant scenes over,
Fanny repaired, as she says,

to the *Lady of the Manor*,—not such was here our performance,—she
was cold,—I was civil,—she looked artificial, I felt heartless! Shabby
doings! as Mr. Blakeney says,—that we cannot live apart from those
who love not us, & whom we yet more dislove.[2]

The letters of the summer reveal characteristic tensions and
attitudes.

The Lady Herself is almost well; she will not, however, confess as
much this Twelve month, for she finds the attendance & distinction
of an Invalide the *only* attendance & distinction she has any chance
to meet.[2]

[1] See p. 153, n. 3.
[2] For unpublished details about this family party, the mutilated Diary MSS.
(Berg), Aug. 1782. Also letters (Berg) from FB to SBP, 8, 16 Aug., 17 Sept. 1782.
Cf. A.L. (Berg) from FB to SBP, 24 Aug. 1792. Also A.L.S. (Berg) to HLT, [12
Aug. 1782].

On many occasions Fanny described her mother's unhappiness and 'eternal restlessness'. 'She wants more amusement to keep off the foul fiend than any human being I ever saw.' At Chessington she did not know how to fill up her time.

She goes out to walk, & returns in 3 minutes. She retires to her own Room, & comes back before we recover Breath, she takes up a Book, & throws it down before she has read one paragraph. My father has bought for her a very pretty Garden chair, in which he drags her himself every Day; & though she will suffer him, or any one else, to work like a plough man in pulling it without resting, she always finds it too hot or too cold, & only goes into it, with an air of reluctance, as if she were compelled.[1]

As usual there was a treasonable quarter where none but rebels were welcome, this time the painting-room, where Edward had caricatured the poor Lady '& that with not more keen severity of exaggeration, than acuteness of humorous observation'. How many would 'esteem his sketch invaluable!' But Mr. Crisp had seized upon it and would not give it up for anything that could be offered in return. As for Fanny, she had never found her stepmother more 'supportable' than at this time.

You well know she never behaves so kindly to any of us as when alone with her, her eternal jealousy of our affection & comfort from each other having then less power to torment her.[1]

Meanwhile Edward toiled with loving care over the well-known portrait of Fanny. He succeeded, she thought, too well, and her troubled comments on his efforts are still extant.

I believe if I am not under written, no one would guess he ever saw me, much less that I sat for the Picture called mine. Never was Portrait so violently flattered. I have taken pains incredible to make him *magnify* the Features, & darken the complection, but he is impenetrable in action, though fair & docile in promise. I shall still, however, work at him, for it really makes me uneasy to see a Face in which the smallest resemblance of my own can be traced looking almost *perfectly* handsome. In his 3 portraits of Mr. Crisp he has succeeded beyond all his former works; they are all different, yet all strikingly like, animated, expressive & handsome. I never saw likenesses more agreeable, yet more just. Mrs. Gast is like à faire rire!— which it is impossible not to do when looking at her Picture, which, however, is by no means flattered. His flattery, as I reproach him

[1] See p. 154, n. 2.

eternally, is all for *me*; not only in the phiz, but the back Ground, which he has made very beautiful; & as to my Dress, which I have left to himself, he has never been tired of altering & gracing it. It is now the black vandyke Gown, with slashed lilac sleeves, & very elegant.[1]

Edward probably thought that he was presenting an artistic truth, even if, to make it apparent, he must paint a fairer flesh. What he captured was a modest, elusive, Evelina-like quality, probably that which in its day disarmed Dr. Johnson and charmed old gentlemen like Mr. Crisp, Sir Joshua Reynolds, Jacob Bryant, Owen Cambridge, Windham, and George III, captivated even such honest knuckle-heads as Mr. Barlow, or the shy, retiring Edward Francesco himself.

In late September Fanny returned to Ipswich, but a few weeks after the birth of Susan's child (October 5, 1782) she joined Mrs. Thrale, who had been waiting for her at Brighton, where Fanny remained till near the end of November. For the first time in over two years she could take 'a change of air' without an inquiry from Chessington about the progress of her book or qualms of conscience about disappointing her father. Mr. Belfield's complaints to Cecilia about the pangs and sufferings of the hack writer coincide so exactly with those expressed by Fanny herself in her letters of the previous years to her sisters, that the passage may be considered no less dramatic than autobiographical. It may serve as her final comment on the composition of the *opus* in which it occurs:

. . . to write by rule, to compose by necessity, to make the understanding, nature's first gift, subservient to interest, that meanest offspring of art!—when weary, listless, spiritless, to rack the head for invention, the memory for images, and the fancy for ornament and allusion; and when the mind is wholly occupied by its own affections and affairs, to call forth all its faculties for foreign subjects, uninteresting discussions, or fictitious incidents!—Heavens! what a life of struggle between the head and the heart! how cruel, how unnatural a war between the intellects and the feelings![2]

---

[1] A.L. (Barrett) from FB to SBP, Chessington, 31 Aug. [1782]. Cf. A.L.S. (Barrett) from Charlotte Barrett to FBA, 29 June 1837, referring to 'a little miniature portrait', possibly that painted by John Bogle in June 1783, 'which much more resembles [Madame d'Arblay]'. See A. L. (Berg) from FB to SBP, 28 June 1783; and the reproduction, Plate IIc, p. 53.

[2] *Cecilia, or Memoirs of an Heiress* (5 vols., 1782), v. x. 6.

Yet fame followed fast upon her effort. So reliable a witness as Mrs. Barbauld testified that 'next to the balloon Miss B[urney was] the object of public curiosity'.[1] In the public rooms at Brighton Fanny could feel the pointing fingers. 'Most violent was the staring and whispering as I passed and repassed.' 'That's the famous Miss Burney! That's she!' 'Had any body told her 2 or 3 years ago', remarked Susan, that 'such a *misfortune* would have befallen *her*, the most shy & retired of human creatures, could she even have believed it?'[2] The favour of the 'Blues & the Tons' was contagious. 'Oh, ma'am, you don't know what a favour this is, to see you!' said Mrs. Thrale's milliner. 'I have longed for it so long. It is quite a comfort to me, indeed!'[2] Apparently everyone was reading her book, from the Queen to mantua-makers and tradeswomen, who, seeing all the ladies they served 'quite distracted' about *Cecilia*, procured copies for themselves. Mrs. Twining read it '*twice in a breath. As soon as she had finished she began again.*' 'Who will read our Histories of Music & our commentaries upon *Aristotle* at *this* rate?' archly asked Mr. Twining.[3] Mrs. Chapone also read the novel twice—once for the story, and once more for the moral sentiments. Not even the opera house, which in November, 1782, Dr. Burney found so much improved that he thought himself in Italy ('so much symmetry & Elegance!'), not even the music pleased him more than the praise he heard of *Cecilia*. Everyone there had read *Cecilia*, even his old friend Lady Mary Duncan, who he suspected had read no other book except the Bible.[4]

One evening in December, 1782, at Miss Monckton's fashionable house in Charles Street, Berkeley Square, it seemed to Mr. Burke that Fanny Burney's fame must have reached its zenith. So fashionable was her book and so much was she mentioned that the aged Dowager Lady Galway, who usually kept to her seat by the fire, receiving nobody, hobbled across the room to peek at the little figure who also kept quietly to one

---

[1] Quoted in Constance Hill, *Juniper Hall* (1904), p. 244. Also A.L. (Berg) from FB to SBP, 28 Oct. 1782.

[2] *Diary*, ii. 102–31; Diary MSS. (Berg), Oct.–Nov. 1782; also A.L. (Barrett) from SBP to CB, n.d.

[3] 3 A.L.S. (BM) from the Rev. Thomas Twining to CB, 18 Sept., 28 Nov. 1782, 27 Jan. 1783. Cf. A.L. (Berg) from FB to CB, 8 Nov. 1782.

[4] A.L. (Barrett) from CB to FB, 6 Nov. 1782.

place, and who was so gallantly supported by kind old Sir
Joshua, the witty and satiric Mr. Metcalfe, Miss Monckton
herself, Dr. Johnson, and Mr. Burke. Among them they
managed to tell her that Mr. Crisp's former acquaintance, the
Dowager Duchess of Portland, who had read 'no Modern Book
of entertainment for so long', had praised *Cecilia*; that the aged
Mrs. Delany, who no longer expected any pleasure from novels,
had read it three times; and finally that Mr. Gibbon had gone
through the five volumes in a day. Here were laurels enough!
And Fanny described them in full for Susan's pleasure and the
satisfaction of the old gentleman at Chessington: 'My dear
daddy and Kitty, are you not doubly glad you so kindly hurried
me upstairs to write?'[1]

The time was still good for a novel. 'Good novels amongst the
bad, "*apparent rari nantes in gurgite vasto*". '[2] So artfully, moreover,
was *Cecilia* contrived, that through one or another of its components—the satire on the manners of the times, moral lessons,
the 'tender pathetic', or the story—it seemed to please everywhere.

In the eighteenth century only the lost souls did not weep.
The response of tears was the indication of benevolence and of
the right feeling heart, and the ability of the author to evoke
them was one criterion of success. 'Misses must cry or it's
nothing!' Here *Cecilia* did not fail. 'It has drawn iron tears
down cheeks that were never wetted by pity before', said Mr.
Twining. 'As to myself, Cecilia has done just what she pleas'd
with me; I laughed & cried, (for I am one of the blubberers—)
when she bade me.'[3] There were ladies unnumbered appearing
late at balls and dinners with red eyes and noses; Lord Ferrars,
who 'cried violently'; and many others, who, like the Dowager
Duchess of Portland and Mrs. Delany, read and wept together.
'Oh, Mrs. Delany, shall you ever forget how we cried?'[4]

Fanny Burney knew the literature of her age, the theatre, and
the public who went to weep over Mrs. Siddons as Belvidera or
Jane Shore. She knew at least one source of contemporary tears
and she tended to fashion the crises and harrowing denoue-
ments of her novels on the pathetic finales of the she-tragedies
of Nicholas Rowe and others or on the mad scenes of eighteenth-

---

[1] *Diary*, ii. 132–68.   [2] The *English Review*, i (Jan. 1783), 14–16.
[3] See p. 157, n. 3.   [4] *Diary*, ii. 124–6, 199.

century Shakespeare. How much the stage was in her mind as she wrote such melodramatic scenes is indicated in the closing chapters of *Cecilia*, where the heroine emerges as an Ophelia-like creature of innocence and beauty gone mad with harsh usage and pain, and where her lover (and husband) young Delvile, the immediate source of her late miseries and distress, finds words for his contrition in utterances reminiscent of Hamlet. 'Well, then,—I may grieve, perhaps, hereafter.' Shades of Shakespeare hover again as Delvile stands over the expiring girl so much ill-used of late but 'sweet even in the arms of death and insanity'. Scarcely indeed is the eighteenth-century lover outdone by the Prince of Denmark: 'Peace and kindred angels are watching to receive thee.' In the end Cecilia does not die, or remain mad, or float dead upon the waters, but the reader, having wept tremendously, is the better for having endured such crises—crises that had a functional as well as a cathartic effect, since partly through them the elder Mr. Delvile was constrained to abandon his objections to the marriage and the long woes could close.

Such scenes no longer move us to tears, but may appear over-wrought, hollow, farcical, and falsely heroic. Having their origin in the stage rather than in life, they must be at least once removed from reality. If Fanny Burney had succeeded in depicting emotional crises or great emotions as accurately after 'life and nature' as she had been able to draw minor characters and situations, she would indeed have added many cubits to her stature as a novelist. Even as it was, not all of her high action failed. The Vauxhall scene with its hurrying excitement, its lurid and desperate merry-making in the teeth of ruin, and the abrupt cessation with Harrel's suicide are credible even now.

The laughter that, according to contemporary testimony, made amends for the tears was confined largely to the minor action, where characters like Miss Larolles, Honoria Pemberton, Mr. Meadows, Mrs. Belfield, Hobson, and Simkins afford comic relief, choric comment, and, at the same time, a telling satire on manners. Here, as in the journals, new or absurd personages were introduced by a *character* in the technical sense followed by revealing specimens of dialogue exhibiting the character in action.

Formal character-sketches were sometimes given to a fictional commentator, Mr. Gosport, 'a man of good parts, and keen satire',—one who, 'minute in his observations', like Mrs. Thrale or Miss Burney herself, made 'the *minutiae* of absurd characters' his study.[1] He divided the *ton*-misses into two classes, the SUPER-CILIOUS and the VOLUBLE, and, as 'chronologer of the modes', supplied a sketch of the rude and negligent fop Mr. Meadows and of Captain Aresby, who belonged to the sect of the JARGON-ISTS. The *ton* thus anatomized was made to reveal itself in lively dialogue. Nothing had struck Mr. Burke more in reading Fanny's book than 'the admirable skill' with which she made her 'ingenious characters' known 'by their own words'.[2] Thus the voluble Miss Larolles:

'Lord, my dear creature, who'd have thought of seeing you here? I was never so surprised in my life! I really thought you was gone into a convent, it's so extreme long since I've seen you. But of all things in the world, why was you not at Lady Nyland's last assembly? I thought of asking Mrs. Harrel fifty times why you did not come, but it always went out of my head. You've no notion how excessively I was disappointed.'

'You are very obliging,' said Cecilia laughing, 'but I hope, since you so often forgot it, the disappointment did not much lessen your entertainment.'

'O Lord no! I was never so happy in my life. There was such a crowd, you could not move a finger. Every body in the world was there. You've no idea how delightful it was. I thought verily I should have fainted with the heat.'

'That was delightful indeed! And how long did you stay?'

'Why we danced till three in the morning. We began with Cotil-lions, and finished with country dances. It was the most elegant thing you ever saw in your life; every thing quite in style. I was so monstrously fatigued, I could hardly get through the last dance. I really thought I should have dropped down dead. Only conceive dancing five hours in such a monstrous crowd! I assure you when I got home my feet were all blisters. You have no idea how they smarted.'[3]

Her sprightliest conversation, however, is provoked by the languid fop, Mr. Meadows ('a real and common character'). The reciprocal effect of his absent-mindedness (he is 'so exces-

<hr/>

[1] I. i. 5; III. v. I.   [2] See p. 158, n. 4.
[3] II. iv. 6; IV. vii. 9; I. i. 5; I. ii. 4.

sive absent you've no notion') and Miss Larolles's loquacity is one of the sources of laughter in the comic sections.

The foibles, philosophy, and idiom of the London citizenry were represented in Mr. Hobson, a retired 'man of business' (formerly a bricklayer and a landlord), and his cringing friend Mr. Simkins.[1] According to contemporary testimony Mr. Hobson was drawn with no less verisimilitude than Miss Larolles, and is in his own right and in his role as choric commentator a truly comic figure. Though his function is the somewhat traditional one of the clown in tragedy, he comes stalwart and fresh from the London streets and pleasure-gardens of the seventies—just such a character as Garrick may have acted out for the amusement of the young Burneys on one of his morning visits to Poland Street or St. Martin's Street. Cecilia first caught sight of Mr. Hobson at the Vauxhall Gardens:

A fat, sleek, vulgar-looking man, dressed in a bright purple coat, with a deep red waistcoat, and a wig bulging far from his head with small round curls, while his plump face and person announced plenty and good living, and an air of defiance spoke the fullness of his purse, strutted boldly up to Mr. Harrel, and accosting him in a manner that shewed some diffidence of his reception, but none of his right, said 'Sir your humble servant'.[1]

His criteria of values ('what i'n't fit for business, i'n't of no value'), his shrewdness, litigiousness, natural prejudices (patriotism and contempt for foreigners), his good-heartedness (where his rights, monetary or civil, were not infringed), his sturdy independence, self-indulgence, and the sententious absurdity of some of his choric comment all appear in self-revealing and discursive conversation. In spite of his respect for money he will have no part of the self-denial and miserliness of Mr. Briggs.

'Let every man have his own proposal . . . for my part, I take every morning a large bowl of water, and souse my whole head in it; and then when I've rubbed it dry, on goes my wig, and I am quite fresh and agreeable: and then I take a walk in Tottenham Court Road as far as the Tabernacle, or thereabouts, and snuff in a little fresh country air, and then I come back, with a good wholesome appetite, and in a fine breathing heat, asking the young lady's pardon; and

---

[1] See the study of 'A Man of Business', III. v. 12; also III. vi. 1; v. ix. 2, 4; v. x. 6. Cf. study of 'A Rattle', III. vi. 4; also III. vi. 6–10; IV. vii. 2.

I enjoy my pot of fresh tea, and my round of hot toast and butter, with as good a relish as if I was a Prince.'[1]

He by no means approves of Mr. Briggs, who tries to live on water-gruel.

'When a man's got above the world, where's the harm of living a little genteel? as to a round of toast and butter, and a few oysters, fresh opened, by way of a damper before dinner, no man need be ashamed of them, provided he pays as he goes.'[1]

He is the free-born Englishman:

'For what I say is this, what a man earns, he earns, and it's no man's business to enquire what he spends, for a free-born Englishman is his own master by the nature of the law, and as to his being a subject, why a Duke is no more, nor a Judge, nor the Lord High Chancellor, and the like of those; which makes it tantamount to nothing, being he is answerable to nobody by the right of Magna Charta: except in cases of treason, felony, and that.'[1]

As for a Lord,

'I am one of them that lay no great stress upon that, unless he has got a good long purse of his own, and then, to be sure, a Lord's no bad thing. But . . . nothing, in comparison of a good income. . . . A man's a man, and for one man to worship another is quite out of law.'

A man's a man for a' that:

'I've got a fair character in the world, and wherewithal to live by my own liking. And what I have is my own, and all I say is, let every one say the same, for that's the way to fear no man, and face the d——l.'

If Mr. Hobson were to speak his notion, his last word would be this:

'The best way to thrive in the world is to get money; but how is it to be got? Why by business: for business is to money, what fine words are to a lady, a sure road to success.'[1]

In the opinion of the *Monthly Review*, 'the self-importance of a rich tradesman is represented to the life'; and there was no lack of contemporary testimony to the verisimilitude of Mr.

[1] See p. 161, n. 1.

Hobson.[1] Dr. Johnson supported him 'at the Head of the tribe';[2] Mrs. Thrale had often seen him and his friend the cringing Simkins in the Borough. 'I am confident they were both canvassed last year; they are not representations of life, they are the life itself.'[2] Mr. Twining thought them 'admirable pieces of nature. Characters that every soul must recognize, & nobody has drawn.' He also praised the lawyer from the Egglestons as another 'portrait of *exact* nature': 'not in the whole book, nor in any other book is there a juster piece of natural delineation.'[3]

Mrs. Belfield was 'so grossly natural, so mean in her Ideas, so confined, so determined' as to resemble, according to Mrs. Thrale, 'half the *decent* women of the Borough'.[4] Mr. Hobson with all his absurd sententiousness was not without common sense and a certain square-footed dignity. Mrs. Belfield, according to Fanny Burney's conception, lacked good sense, and appeared in *Cecilia* as the vulgar exponent of ambition and folly.[5] She had encouraged her son to forsake his father's shop and 'proper station' and to rise in the world. The career of young Belfield himself is an extended study based on notions that Fanny had imbibed from current literature, the semi-ethical courtesy-books, didactic works like the *Rambler*, and of late, of course, from conversations at Streatham, where an Old Philosopher sat discoursing with his Mistress and her company on order and subordination versus anarchy and savagery, on reason versus the imagination, genius, or enthusiasm. Young Belfield is a speaking picture of the woes to be incurred by the rebel, the genius, and the enthusiast—a son, said Mrs. Belfield regretfully,

'that I thought to have seen living like a prince, and sending his own coach for me to dine with him! . . . for when he was quite a child in arms, the people used all to say he was born to be a gentleman, and would live to make many a fine lady's heart ache.'[5]

---

[1] lxvii (Dec. 1782), 453–8. Reviews of *Cecilia* appeared in the *Gentleman's Magazine*, lii (Oct. 1782), 485; the *Critical Review*, liv (Dec. 1782), 414–20; and the *English Review*, i (Jan. 1783), 14–16; the *London Magazine*, lii (Jan. 1783), 39–40. For an analysis of the structure of *Cecilia* see Miriam Jeanette Benkovitz, *Fanny Burney, Novelist* (an unpublished doctoral dissertation, Yale University, 1951).

[2] A.L.S. (Berg) from FB to CB, July 1782.

[3] See p. 157, n. 3.

[4] *Diary*, ii. 81–84. Also A.L.S. (Berg) from HLT to FB, 1782.

[5] For scenes in which Mrs. Belfield appears, II. iv. 10; III. v. 2; III. vi. 1; V. ix. 2, 6; V. x. 6. The moral is given to Mr. Monckton, v. ix. 3.

Such were the characters drawn from both high and low life that impressed Fanny Burney's contemporaries by their realism. So exactly were they represented that *Cecilia* seemed to many, as it seemed to Mrs. Thrale, 'a Camera Obscura in a Window of Piccadilly'.[1] 'No character appears (Miss Beverley and Albany excepted) that every day's experience does not discover a similar', wrote Miss Burney's critic in the *English Review*. 'To her own observation she appears to be solely indebted for the characters of the novel. All of them seem fairly purchased at the great work-shop of life, and not the second-hand, vamped-up shreds and patches of the Monmouth-street of modern romance.'[2]

Yet Fanny Burney always affirmed that the characters in her novels and plays were copies of *nature* rather than of *individuals*. As preliminary sketches that have survived often show, she first envisaged her fictitious personages as *types* or *abstracts*, epitomizing some phenomenon of manners, a condition, quality, or set of follies or foibles. If one may judge from the extant scraps of paper showing tentative lists of *dramatis personae*[3] for her later novels and plays and from the internal evidence of *Cecilia* itself, the preliminary cast for the minor action of that novel was almost certainly first filled with such bloodless cyphers as a Miss Rattle, a Miss Voluble, a Miss Supercilious, a Mr. Nonchalant, a Mrs. Vulgarity, and a retired tradesman (a 'rich business leaver-off')—a cast who only later appeared as Honoria Pemberton, Miss Larolles, Miss Leeson, Mr. Meadows, Mrs. Belfield, and Mr. Hobson. Having first conceived the social scene in the abstract, and having thus secured representatives of general or universal truth, she had next to put the shadowy states, faults, foibles, or qualities into action. Here she could rely on her long habits of observation, her keen ears, and her retentive memory, and she succeeded in supplying action and dialogue so credible, natural, and realistic that her readers took many of her characters for what they were not, copies of individuals, and were forever looking about for the originals. As Lady Hales read the book, she thought she could 'hear some people chattering their nonsense at random'.[4]

---

[1] The remark is quoted in a letter from W. W. Pepys to Mrs. Elizabeth Montagu, 22 July 1782. See *Mrs. Montagu, 'Queen of the Blues', her Letters and Friendships from 1762 to 1800*, ed. Reginald Blunt (2 vols., 1923), ii. 121.

[2] See p. 163, n. 1.   [3] In the Berg Collection, NYPL.

[4] A.L.S. (Berg) from Lady Hales and Miss Coussmaker to SBP, 24 July 1782.

'O, . . . said Mrs. Walsingham, . . . I meet her characters every Day: Miss Larolles in particular.'

'O, said Mrs. Pery, I have seen more Miss Larolles's than any character I ever saw drawn in my life.'

'All the Misses that go to see Mrs. Siddons, said Mrs. Walsingham, talk like Miss Larolles, they are so *hot*, & so *delighted*, they *cry* so & find it so *charming*. And then Mr. Meadows—'

'O, the *Meadows* are a tribe as numerous as it is hateful, said Mrs. Montagu.'[1]

Even Albany, who resembles Dr. Burney's Moravian friend Mr. Hutton and who seems to have a literary antecedent in Sir Launcelot Greaves, had a counterpart suggested for him. Mr. George Cambridge knew just such a philanthropist in a benevolent 'old half-pay officer', who wandered about St. James's Park looking for persons in distress and relieving poverty with borrowed funds.[2]

Mr. Briggs, a caricature of a miser (probably suggested by the sculptor Nollekens), the villain Mr. Delvile (said to exist only by virtue of his Ruling Passion, Pride), the exponents of low life, even the members of the lively social set, have all at times been criticized as mere sets of foibles and must, perhaps, yield to the charge. Taken separately, they are not, indeed, great characters, but slight characters are not without very good effect in the large satiric canvas that Fanny wished to paint. In large canvases, like those of Dickens, for instance, the use of caricature makes for greater clarity. It makes also for the ready comprehension on which comic effect must depend. By the photographic depiction of ridiculous foibles, speech, and action, Fanny hoped indeed to amuse the reader, but she intended also to castigate follies. By 1782 she had had an opportunity to observe the social scene at Bath, Brighton, and, to some extent, in the London drawing-rooms, and her second novel mirrors the fashionable people she met there. Cecilia's comment on 'how ill the coldness of their hearts accorded with the warmth of their professions' matches Fanny's impression as given in a journal-letter to Susan: 'My coldness in return to all these sickening, heartless, *ton*-led people, I try not to repress.'[3] She proceeded, therefore, to castigate heartlessness and, after that,

---

[1] Diary MSS. (Berg), p. 1688.   [2] *Diary*, ii. 205–6.
[3] Cf. *Cecilia*, 1. i. 5, with *Diary*, i. 417.

insincerity and affectation. In low life she discerned the same heartlessness and, in addition, selfishness, meanness, turbulence, and frequent recourse to litigation. Her pen-pictures of vulgarity are attacks on such propensities. In spite of the moral purpose, the lively actors of the comic scenes seem to walk straight from life to the page, and they are as entertaining today as they ever were.

The central action of *Cecilia, or Memoirs of an Heiress* follows the adventures of Cecilia Beverley for two years, from the age of twenty-one when she emerged from the country estates of her family to reside with her guardians in London, until she marries young Delvile. The terminal point of the action is marriage. The chief retarding factor is family pride: first, that of the Beverleys (in particular, that of an uncle, who bequeathed Cecilia a fortune of £3,000 per annum on condition that, if she should marry, her husband must take her name); and, secondly, that of the elder Delvile, scion of a noble family, who, though impoverished, values his son's name above Cecilia's fortune or, of course, the happy culmination of young love. This resolution is delayed further by the machinations of a self-interested (if rather unreal) villain Monckton, by the forwardness of Mrs. Belfield, and finally by errors and indiscretions on the part of the heroine herself, who, though closer to the courtesy-book girl than Evelina was, is still subject to human failings.

Now that Fanny was known, her original impulse to draw her heroines from nature seemed almost stultified by the compulsion to invent a novel and a heroine meeting the indispensable qualification for novels and novelists in her time, that is, *moral utility*. She felt that she must draw a model of behaviour, but the twofold purpose, to draw a paragon and to draw from nature, could not be easily reconciled. Moreover, the paragon of behaviour was not without great difficulty made to enter into interesting action. As the *Monthly Review* of 1782 noted, it was odd to see such a girl as Cecilia in the company of the Harrels at Vauxhall. Cecilia had lost the natural youthfulness, demureness, and piquancy of Evelina. Leaves from the courtesy-books cling about her, sometimes making odd contrasts not only with *nature* but also with violent scenes reminiscent of the she-tragedies of the age. Improving paragraphs on reason (with which, we are assured, Cecilia was endowed) scarcely prepare the way for imprudent love, temporary madness, and distresses worthy of Belvidera or Jane Shore. Fanny's inventive muse had frequented quiet and sheltered places, had liked slyness and 'snugness'. But now Fanny had been dragged into the limelight, and Cecilia was the result. Happily, at least, we have the testimony of 'that honest gentlewoman' Mrs. Chapone that Miss Burney was 'more like her first Heroine than her second'.[1]

Through the exigencies of a plot that took Cecilia into the homes of three guardians and on many another round of visits, as well as to assemblies, masquerades, and routs, and on excursions to the opera, the theatre, bookstalls, and the pleasure-gardens of Vauxhall and Ranelagh, the novelist secured an opportunity to depict a varied social scene, a cross-section of the London of her time, still valuable as a genuine record of customs and manners. According to Dr. Johnson, moreover, one could hear in *Cecilia* 'the free full flow of London talk'.[2] The conversational pieces taking place in the City, the comic dialogue of the pump-room (though probably not Cecilia's stilted idiom) may be taken as tape-recordings of contemporary speech.

By the criterion of the age, moral utility, *Cecilia* came off very well. Many young ladies, usually forbidden access to so dangerous a genre as the novel, were allowed to read it. Even the Princesses, as Fanny discovered later, were permitted to read *Cecilia*—at least after it was 'sanctioned by a Bishop's recommendation,—the late Dr. Ross of Exeter'.[3] Even Cecilia's faults were useful, for the sufferings they entailed came tearfully home to the business and bosoms of young ladies and served as warning guides.

The crowning praise of the work was, in Fanny's opinion, that of Mrs. Delany and the Duchess of Portland.

'If you speak of the Harrels, and of the morality of the book,' cried the Duchess, with a solemn sort of voice, 'we shall, indeed, never give Miss Burney her due: so striking, so pure, so genuine, so instructive.'[3]
Mrs. Delany, with the eagerness of fifteen—though 83!—exclaimed:

---

[1] 'Letters from Mrs. Chapone', *A Later Pepys*, ed. Alice C. C. Gaussen (2 vols., 1904), i. 404.
[2] Quoted by Charlotte Barrett in notes (Barrett) for a defence of Madame d'Arblay against Croker's attack.
[3] *Diary*, v. 264.

'*No* Book ever was so *useful* as this; because none other that is so *good*, has been so universally read by young as well as old.'[1]

It was only with the greatest difficulty that Mrs. Delany had gained the unwilling consent of the Duchess to have the authoress presented to her, so chary was she of artists, writers, and their kind. She had 'a prejudice against female novel writers, which *almost* amounted to a *horror of them*'; yet the moral tone of *Cecilia* and unlooked-for modesty in the authoress undermined old prejudices a little. This novel could not be dismissed as the trash common to the circulating libraries or be banned for its immorality. On the contrary, said the Duchess, 'it should be the study of youth Both for Precept & Example'.[1]

'It is so innocent, & as [Mr. Burke] says, so pure, with all its contrasts of gaiety & humour, that if I had now the care of any young persons, it should be the first Book I would put into their hands.'[1]

One citadel at least had been taken. Old prejudices began to give a little, though for the wrong reason. Fanny could scarcely keep the tears from her eyes 'at so solemn a sanction'. This accurate analysis and the appreciation of her purpose by 'characters so respectable, so moral, so high in public estimation, & so aged, with Mr. Burke as their Guide', constitute the last words, as she told Mr. Crisp, 'hear what I may, that I can ever write upon Cecilia'. 'I close forever my Pen as Panegyric Recorder.'[1]

[1] *Diary*, ii. 198–202; Diary MSS. (Berg), pp. 1765–73.

VII

'HOME & BOSOM STROKES'

(1783–1786)

[Men] think themselves free, if they have made no verbal
profession; though they may have pledged themselves by looks,
by actions, by attentions, and by manners a thousand, and a
thousand times!

Camilla, iv. 42–43

THE years between October, 1782, when Fanny joined Mrs.
Thrale at Brighton, and July, 1786, when she was immured
at court, are marked less by satiric observation and invention than by personal experiences and emotion. Disappointed
love and wild love, manifested in scenes as pathetic, lurid, or
tender as those of eighteenth-century drama or romance—love
in various ramifications constituted a tumultuous prelude to
the five slow years at court.

Mrs. Piozzi's love story is a thrice-told tale; yet it emerges
again with startling vigour and abandon in the 200 letters still
remaining of those she wrote for long periods daily, sometimes
twice daily, to her friend and confidante Fanny Burney.[1] 'I
write my mind; a foolish one enough, but tender to a Degree of
Agony.' 'I will continue to pelt you with Letters till I can get
the sight of my sweet angel.' 'If you would but come!' she
pleaded almost continually. '*If you loved me as well as I love you.*'
In 1783 Fanny was the only person in the world (save one) that
she wished to see, the only one within five hundred miles she
could talk to, the only one whose company could console her,
and she referred wistfully to the thick rough-edged packets of
confidential journals that Fanny habitually dispatched to Susan.
Protestations by the dozen could be excerpted to show that up
to August, 1784, affection and confidence were mutual. 'Irresistible Burney! and who was ever like you for warm affection, cool

---

[1] In the Berg Collection, the NYPL. Madame d'Arblay says that she preserved
only those letters (about 200, dated 1780–4) that evinced Mrs. Thrale's 'conflicts,
her misery, & her sufferings, mental & corporeal, to exonerate her from the banal
reproach of yielding unresisting, to her passions'. See Diary MSS. (Berg), pp.
1876, 1890–1907.

Prudence, and steady Friendship!' And one statement more that in the future was to ring very strangely: 'While I retain my senses, I shall retain my love of *you*; all three shall go together!'

Confidences about Piozzi had begun to appear in the letters of October, 1780, written from Brighton, where the Streatham party had gone for Mr. Thrale's health. These were harrowing days with the Master 'so altered, so violent', but Piozzi's music, 'tender & tasteful', had helped 'to sooth sorrow charmingly',— so much so, that the Mistress confessed to seeing the singer 'every day once, & often twice'. 'I am ashamed to say how fond I am grown of Piozzi.'[1] In these early days the odd wishful thought occurred to her that Piozzi might be her brother, the natural son of her father, Mr. Salusbury. This fantasy, no more zealously guarded than other aspects of her great love, was soon spread (probably by Baretti) beyond the shores of England to Milan itself, where in 1783 Piozzi himself heard it and rebuked Mrs. Thrale roundly for originating 'Reports prejudicial to his Honour and his Mother's honour'.[1] The term 'brother', how-ever, soon yielded to that of 'Husband', an appellation Mrs. Thrale began to use over a year before her second marriage in order to impress Fanny with the seriousness of her intentions.

There is no room here to describe the steps and manœuvres by which the desperate woman attempted to free herself from the impediments to a second marriage—obstacles that included family responsibilities, Streatham Place or any place where she must continue to entertain the ageing Dr. Johnson,[1] the objec-tions of the trustees of the Thrale estate and of her daughters' guardians, the condemnation of the London social set, debts or financial difficulties that hindered her freedom of action, and finally, as some people thought, the reluctance of the prospective bridegroom. Difficulties that she could not remove, she ignored. A single drive, one urge, the desire or the need of love, directed her actions wildly, but none the less consistently, to one end. 'Oh what a Bustle is here about loving an honest Man for an honest Purpose!'[1] Fanny Burney knew that all compromises, the abandonment of the continental tour, the temporary banish-ment of Piozzi, and the exile with her daughters in Bath, were only temporary expedients to evade difficulties for the moment

<hr />

[1] See p. 169, n. 1.

insurmountable. 'You have distressed & harrassed yourself',
Fanny wrote her, 'not about *changing* your plan, but merely in
a wild anxiety to obtain approbation for it.'[1] Her purpose, fixed
from the beginning, only grew stronger with opposition. To it
all had to give way, as Dr. Johnson saw, when with a 'laborious
heaving of the ponderous chest, and the roll of the large,
penetrating, wrathful eye', he agitatedly broke forth: 'She cares
for no one!' Perceiving Fanny's frightened face, he added: 'You,
only—You, she loves still!—but no one—and nothing else!'
And then with a half smile, a quip, and a truth that Fanny
probably never understood: 'You she still loves—As—she loves
her little finger!'[2]

Nearly all the aspects of this story have been related very
justly elsewhere.[3] Here perhaps there is room for two incidents—
one to show that Fanny Burney spoke out clearly when called
upon for advice, and therefore played no deceitful or ambiguous
part in the deliberations; and a second, which, focused on the
lurid night of the crisis of November, 1783, in Bath, when the
frightened Queeney agreed to Piozzi's recall, will go far to
explain the consultations between the teen-aged girl and her
mother's friend, consultations that Mrs. Thrale later considered
treasonable.

There was first that Saturday night in January, 1783, when
Mrs. Thrale informed Fanny that her final answer to Piozzi was
to be given next day. Fanny then braced herself for 'the painful
& afflicting—nay tremendous effort' of stating the objections to
the marriage as she saw them. '*Think* a little', she pleaded. All
thought so far had been spent in obtaining approbation for
the plan. 'That approbation will *for-ever* be with held! The
mother of 5 children, 3 of them as Tall as herself, will never be
forgiven for shewing so great an ascendance of passion over
Reason.' Contemporary comments on 'such mighty overbearing
Passions . . . in "a Matron's bones" '[4] indicate that Fanny had
not misjudged public opinion, and she wrote manfully on.
Would Mrs. Thrale not be sorry in the future to have wilfully

[1] A.L. (Berg) from FB to HLT, [Jan.] 1783.   [2] *Memoirs*, ii. 361–2.
[3] See Clifford, pp. 202–31. For a less sympathetic story, but one often supported
by Mrs. Thrale's letters of 1780–4, see the Marquis of Lansdowne, introduction
to *The Queeney Letters, being Letters addressed to Hester Maria Thrale by Doctor Johnson,
Fanny Burney, and Mrs. Thrale-Piozzi* (1934).
[4] Mrs. Chapone's remark, *A Later Pepys*, i. 408.

deprived herself 'of all hope of happiness but one,—that one
so uncertain! so *inadequate* to such a sacrifice!' '*How*, you will
say, can you sacrifice a man to whom you have given such
hopes?—but *how* dear madam, can you sacrifice to that man
all else?' She then enumerated the chief considerations—*Children,
Religion, Friends, Country,* and *Character* (two or three of which in
varying degrees, curiously enough, Fanny herself was to sacrifice
for the sake of love when, a decade later, at an age little short of
Mrs. Thrale's at this time, she was also to reach the age of
defiance). 'All is at stake,—& for what?—a gratification that no
man can *esteem*, not even he for whom you feel it.' Though
she knew that Mrs. Thrale would think this very cruel, she
said it only to save her 'future repentance'. She trusted that Mrs.
Thrale would not show the letter for it was not written out of
any particular enmity to Piozzi, of whom the writer thought
'even *highly*, but who to me is nothing, while you are almost
everything'.[1]

The message was written in great haste and delivered on
Sunday morning, but Mrs. Thrale hurried it back to St. Martin's Street and to Fanny's room almost before the ink had had
time to dry: 'You charge me not to shew it—&, that I may not
be tempted, I return it to you.' 'She then ran out of the Room,
& the House.' Fanny then donned bonnet and cloak and
followed to Argyle Street 'with all the soothing tenderness of
pity & deep concern'.[1] But her concern and pity for Mrs.
Thrale's distress did not change the rational opinion that she,
along with most of the London world, had formed on the matter.
Mrs. Thrale herself understood Fanny's position very well and
sometimes tried to remonstrate: 'You think I am Passion-led!'
'Oh Burney, when you who should teach better, yield to the
stream and think nothing of [Piozzi's] noble mind!'[2] And again,
persuasively: 'Do not be solemn not too solemn sweetest
Burney!'[2]

It must be emphasized, however, that whatever actions of
Fanny's or false reports of her actions were later to inspire Mrs.
Piozzi's epithet *l'aimable Traitresse*,[3] it was not Fanny's failure
to speak out openly when asked and to make her objections
known to Mrs. Thrale herself. Opinions will doubtless continue

---

[1] See p. 171, n. 1.   [2] See p. 169, n. 1.
[3] *Thraliana*, ii. 760, n. 3; also Clifford, p. 447.

to differ about the weight that ought to be given to social, conventional, or maternal obligations versus Love, that is, about the validity of Fanny's judgement of the affair, but the correspondence of the time shows that she played no ambiguous, spineless, or deceitfully easy part. She was not hypocritical, cowardly, or insincere. When called on by Mrs. Thrale, she braced herself to remonstrate; when absent, she either remained silent or attempted a defence. She felt in duty bound to keep the confidences even from Susan and Charlotte who knew no more than all the rest of the world, though that knowledge, in distorted versions, was not little.[1] She tried to act as confessor, consultant, and friend to one madly in love—a thankless and precarious part, unless the consultant happens to approve and concur. Small wonder that the real traitors, those who tactfully held their peace, fare better in *Thraliana* than 'honest Fan'.

Fanny missed Mrs. Thrale 'most woefully'. With her departure for Bath in March, 1783, all the savour of the London parties had fled. There was no one now to shine and flash, to interest the head as well as the heart. With such a loss Fanny had no desire to visit even though 'the people visited have been among the first for talents in the kingdom'.[1] Besides, as we shall presently see, she had begun to suffer more poignantly than Mrs. Thrale realized over a deepening disappointment of her own.

She was bent, therefore, on going to Bath, where for nearly a year Mrs. Thrale kept a room aired and waiting, but Dr. Burney with his implacable disapproval of Mrs. Thrale's hopes and plans would not of course allow Fanny to go. He had a thousand objections 'all founded on arguments unanswerable'.[1] Fanny continued to defend her friend: Mrs. Thrale possessed 'a thousand good qualities which her censurers never could boast'.[1]

Though her failings are unaccountable and most unhappy, her virtues and good qualities, the generosity and feeling of her heart, the liberality and sweetness of her disposition, would counterbalance a thousand more.[1]

She was determined to remember only Mrs. Thrale's 'better Day', and her eulogies place that lady in a fairer light than do the wild, self-pitying, self-willed missives that arrived at this

---

[1] *Diary*, ii. 229–30, 243, 253–4, 268; *QL*, p. 101.

time almost daily, occasionally twice daily, by post or diligence
from Bath. This correspondence,[1] replacing the visit that was
denied, even the most innocuous parts of it that Fanny preserved, gives a close history of the painful conflicts and finally of
the stubborn auxiliary issue on which the Burney–Thrale
friendship was wrecked.

In the autumn of 1783 the Bath concession or truce was
coming to an end. As Mrs. Thrale reminded Fanny a little later,

[Seward] knows as well as *you* know, that I am & have been content
to bear absence, anxiety & affliction, rather than gratify my wishes
at the Expence of my duty; but he knows, too that I do it in hope of
Release, & that I shall at length be dismissed from such misery to a
state of consolation in the World, or Happiness in the next.[1]

The suggestions of the executors that at the proper time she
should bring the young heiresses to London, should try to
retain Streatham Place as a home for them, and superintend
their débuts, made her frantic. She would not have such expenditures and such company forced on her. Until Queeney consented to Piozzi's recall, the mother scolded endlessly about her
teen-aged daughters—'too ignorant to talk, too insolent to learn,
too hard-hearted to sympathize in one's sorrow, and often too
magnificent to join in one's mirth'. She thought herself blameless. 'I never did, never do, and never will say even an ill-
natured Thing to them, which can be construed into ever so
distant a Reproach for my lost Health & Happiness.' She was
wearied with representations about their interests. 'So to
Weymouth on Monday sennight 4:August we will go, and let
'em in God's name meet who they please.'[1]

'*Such a Life*! oh most intolerable, unutterable!' 'My Heart!
how it pants to be free!' Often she felt like the badger she had
rescued on the street, innocent, unoffending, baited and torn to
pieces by dogs; in her case, revilers—the newspapers, 'Card
players' and 'Tea-Drinkers'. 'Let them at least not kill this
innocently-hunted Mortal, who cannot by distance itself escape
their arrows.' She felt herself trampled upon, though making no
more resistance than a 'Down Bed—fit for young Heiresses to
repose on'. When Dr. Johnson suggested that her carriage and
horses could set him down 'very *commodiously*' at Kensington,

[1] See p. 169, n. 1.

she felt herself 'patiently ridden to Death like a Post horse'. And she was not at all well. 'I have a radical & dangerous complaint brought on by Grief, which Happiness alone can cure: that Happiness I have told you twenty Times I shall at last obtain either in this World or the next.' Fanny would be sorry if she could see 'the Ravages sorrow has made in my Person, or feel the Furrows it has ploughed in my Heart'. 'I told you ages ago that Death or Piozzi should be my Lot . . . I told it you not in passion, but in deliberation, and I told you what *I knew to be true*.' 'Marriage or Death', 'Death or Piozzi', 'Heaven or Italy', became the watchwords. Compromise was no longer possible. She must be made to suffer no more.[1] 'Heaven or a Husband' was the alternative, and, confronted with this choice, Fanny and Queeney rapidly capitulated. Though, as Shakespeare observed, 'there was not anie man died in his person (videlicet) in a love cause', Mrs. Thrale seemed prepared to do so. This was the possibility, probability, threat, prospect (whatever it was, let experts in these matters judge) that impelled the frightened Queeney in the autumn of 1783 to consult her mother's friend.

The action that they ought to take, in the two alternatives presented to them, is the subject of most of the correspondence of 1783 and 1784 between Fanny and Queeney published by the Marquis of Lansdowne in *The Queeney Letters*.[2] In October Queeney had apparently written to Fanny that she sometimes thought her mother's peace of mind 'should be purchased at almost any rate'.[3] Only Mr. Seward seemed to think death preferable to Piozzi. Finally in a letter of October 25, and in the letters following, Fanny, unlike Seward, supported Queeney in her decision to resist her mother's wishes no longer. So delicate a matter demanded some euphemism:

Certainly, most certainly, my dear Miss Thrale, I could not join in Mr. Seward's shocking sentence, that you should sooner see the poor self-deluded Mrs. T: in the state he speaks of, than contribute to relieving her from it her *own* way! . . . I should think *you* unnatural & impenetrable, & *myself* savage & barbarous, to carry our antipathy to her views to such fatal lengths. O what a situation it is, where an

[1] See p. 169, n. 1.   [2] See p. 171, n. 3.
[3] Queeney's words are quoted in FB's reply of 25 Oct. 1783, *QL*, pp. 72–74. Also pp. 75–90.

evil so desperate is the *only* alternative that can be yet worse than compliance!

I am amazed at Mr Seward,—I thought him softer minded. His *surprise*, his *aversion*, his *horrour* of such a scheme, were all but *of course*, because he is *Mrs. Thrale's Friend*,—& as such, must revolt from all things that lead to her disgrace & downfall: but to tell her *Daughter* to be passive, though she expire before her Eyes, is surely stretching his sense of propriety into inhumanity.[1]

Like Queeney she had opposed the marriage, but that was now over,[2] and she advised the daughter not only to accede but to accede gracefully: having yielded the great point, she ought not to fail in small attentions that could estrange her from her mother. Though Fanny made no attempt to disguise her regret for what she now took to be the necessity of the marriage, there was nothing in her letters either in expressions of love or admiration for Mrs. Thrale or in disapproval of the proposed step that she had not written and said to Mrs. Thrale herself a hundred times over during the preceding three years. 'I have said all I could say, & she knows all that I think.'[2] Fanny had long ago noted that mother and daughter were so different— the one 'so cold, the other so buoyant'—as to appear each a caricature of the other;[3] but, contrary to Mrs. Thrale's assumptions,[4] she never failed either at this time or later to remonstrate against unfilial behaviour.

Perhaps the caricatures had never appeared more exaggerated than in November of 1783. The increasing frenzy of the October letters[5] had warned Fanny that the crisis was approaching. Mrs. Thrale's endurance was at an end. All this useless misery and expense, Piozzi's 'spotless character traduced', her own endangered, and 'for what? for who?' 'I am not able to bear the Idea of having *nobody* so—I will send for him home.' In November Sophy Thrale was seized with an illness manifested in screaming fits and cold torpors.[5] The child's life was saved, Mrs. Thrale thought, by her timely prescription of a glass of usquebaugh; but, by her own admission, it was Queeney who remained in the sick-room through the screaming fits, while the mother trembled at the door. 'Sophy has such a sister that

[1] See p. 175, n. 3.   [2] *QL*, pp. 85–89, 90–103.
[3] Diary MSS. (Berg), pp. 2448–9. Cf. A.L.S. (Berg) from FB to CB, 20 June 1783.
[4] *Thraliana*, ii. 612; i. 582 ff.   [5] See p. 169, n. 1.

whether I leave her for Heaven or for a Husband, I shall know she is in better and wiser hands than those of your H:L:T.' It has not been the fashion to sympathize with the eighteen- or nineteen-year-old girl, who seemed so wise for her years. But what a night that was, near the close of November, when Dr. Dobson judged Sophy in a condition too critical to leave and Mrs. Thrale in a state scarcely less alarming. Sometimes she fainted, sometimes she laughed, then she cried and said her prayers; and finally she appeared before her daughter with 'spasms on her whole nervous system', tremors and shivers—

Oh, Queeney I shall expire cried I, and never see him more—this with agony scarce endurable—*send for him home* says she; He is 1000 miles off replied I: *Hurry him* quoth Hester, he must hurry indeed cried I again, for I shall die before tomorrow morning. Shall you indeed? says the dear Tit naively, & made up such a Face, that (strange to tell) I burst into an irresistible Fit of Laughter not to be suppress'd. Poor Soul! how she did sit astonished.[1]

Perhaps it was not only magnificence that kept the troubled girl from sharing 'one's mirth'. Perhaps she merely failed to see the joke. But who shall find the right end to such a tangled skein? Mrs. Thrale had now her desire. To the relief of all concerned, one would almost think, Piozzi was 'sent for home'.

New problems, however, seemed to arise because of the difficulty in persuading the exiled lover that all barriers were now in very truth obviated, and he need only return. What was next to pain Fanny Burney and shock the *bas bleus*, the Mrs. Grundys of the town, was not so much marriage to an Italian music-master but the fact that the music-master seemed reluctant to enter into marriage, and consequently that Mrs. Thrale, the mother of four children living (and eight in the grave), presented (to their eyes) the unlovely, unbecoming, undignified, if not disgraceful spectacle of an impassioned woman in impassioned pursuit of an elusive male—a woman in the grip of a passion she could not control. What they objected to was the love *rage* (in Chaucer's language), the *furor* (associated with Dido), or, in the eighteenth-century terminology, the victory of the passions over reason—a course that violated at the same time all *Grundiana*, the *gentle* or courtesy-book conceptions of

---

[1] See p. 169, n. 1.

delicacy, propriety, decorum, and prudence. Fanny could not
forgive Piozzi for putting Mrs. Thrale in such a position.

Mrs. Thrale on her side made a spirited defence. 'The Man
I mean to marry is wise, virtuous, and honourable—let those
who choose on other Principles be ashamed of themselves—I
am not ashamed.'[1] Piozzi's birth she said was equal to her
first husband's. If, however, this was to argue that the social
position of an impecunious Italian music-teacher was equal in
England to that of a wealthy English brewer and member of
Parliament, she could hardly expect her thesis to be accepted.
Piozzi's social status is somewhat defined (at its lowest limits,
one may hope) in an anecdote related in Dr. Burney's unpublished Memoirs.[2] The Doctor, recalling Piozzi's appearance in
England in 1777 and his pleasure in Piozzi's 'manner of singing'
('his taste and expression was new and extremely elegant'),
went on to relate how, through his own recommendation and
that of Lord March, Piozzi was engaged by the Duke of
Ancaster to spend three months at Grimsthorpe, in Lincolnshire,
where he was to teach instrumental music in the morning and
entertain the Duke and Duchess in the evening. The summer was
not a happy one.

He was put to the 2[d] table and kept at a great distance from the
Duke & Duchess. He was expected to devote his whole morning to
L[y] Priscilla and at night was never sent for by the Duke till 9 or
10 o'clock, before w[ch] time he used to lock and barricade his chamber
door with trunks, boxes, and all the lumber he c[d] find that he might
not be forced to quit [it] like an animal to shew his tricks, and when
he came away he protested that he hated the place so much that 'if
he had left an eye behind him, he w[d] not go back to fetch it.'[2]

Another consideration, however, troubled people like the
Burneys, who were not themselves in a social position to find
fault with Mrs. Thrale's choice of a music-teacher. Mrs. Thrale
thought she had managed Dr. Burney very well, but according
to Fanny he never mentioned the situation without groans about
the frailty of human nature. Because, Fanny explained,

he was not called upon for advice, but only told the business in confidence, he treated it with all possible chearfulness & delicacy to *her*,
—but he was not for that reason at all the less shocked that she

<hr />

[1] See p. 169, n. 1.   [2] Berg.

should thus fling away her talents, situation in life, & character;—for thus to quit all her maternal duties is a blot upon it never to be erased.[1]

Though, according to Fanny, Mrs. Thrale 'most eagerly coveted to retain' her daughters, that compromise was not so feasible, all things considered, as to exonerate her in contemporary eyes. 'That such a Mother should desert her Children, & leave them to the mercy of the World, & the errors of youth unprotected & unadvised!'[1]

Furthermore, Fanny had somehow got the idea firmly in her mind that Piozzi lacked a proper sense of Mrs. Thrale's worth and position and of the sacrifices made by everyone for him. His failure at the first summons to weather the snowbanks of the Alps and a chilly reception in England augured ill, she thought. 'Did not my Father travel home through Italy in December?' Piozzi could not, perhaps, have travelled fast, 'but *not at all*—O I much doubt the *ardour* of his desire! And to have Her throw away an affection that absorbs every faculty upon an *Ingrate!*'[1] '*Can* I love him too well?' Mrs. Thrale had asked Fanny. 'Has he not cost me my life almost? Have I not purchased him with my very vitals?' Fanny would have liked the love scene better if these questions had been asked by the lover, not the lass.

I assure you I sometimes feel an indignation at the thought of this graceless & unfeeling return in a Man for whom she sacrifices all that ought to be dear, valuable, or right, that subsides into nothing but *shame & regret* that she can add to so many improprieties a *wilful* blindness to an indifference which ought not only to cure, but disgust her. I thought, indeed,—amiable, accomplished, attractive & excellent as she is, she might have chose her Mate among all Mankind, so she fixed not on one too Young,—but it is not so,—this man is as little worthy of her by a *sense* of her worth, as he is by partaking it.[1]

One is greatly handicapped in arbitrating eighteenth-century love tangles by the failure of the lovers (Boswell, of course, excepted) to write and preserve confidential reports on their feelings and motives. Fanny had an advantage over us in having read (presumably) the letters from Piozzi that Mrs. Thrale often enclosed in a franked cover to St. Martin's Street. She had in

[1] See p. 176, n. 3.

mind also the extensive Thrale correspondence that for the writer's sake she had burned. She may have become unduly prejudiced against Piozzi, but no one in the world was better informed on the subject. Mrs. Thrale's jealousy and worry over the lover's delay are recorded in *Thraliana*.[1] In extant letters to Fanny she betrayed concern only over his health. She has no fear but that absence will make the heart grow fonder; besides, she had not been so unskilful as to let him know of the love-longing that had cost her her health, as she said, and half her wits. Of this she had given but the merest hint, for it had always been her 'Diversion to keep him *jealous of the Cavaliers*'.[2]

There seem to have been misunderstandings and delays. According to a long letter to Fanny in May, Mrs. Thrale had sent her 'summons & final promise' only on April 17, 1784. She waited for the reply, which could be expected on May 9, and set out then on May 10 for London, where she had taken rooms for a week in Mortimer Street. Fanny went there for breakfast every morning and usually remained all day listening to such tales of 'recollective misery' as made her shudder.[3] The person who saw and heard Mrs. Thrale and who would yet think of opposing her wishes 'must either be mad,—or utterly careless about making her so'.[3] On May 16 or 17, 1784, the friends parted in sorrow, on Fanny's side in 'real affliction',[4] which would have mounted to wild grief indeed if she had realized that, though Mrs. Thrale was to live until 1821 (almost thirty-seven years longer), this was the last time they were to spend a week together, spend a day together, or ever to meet again except in a few polite, forced, and formal calls.

On May 20 a tender letter came from Italy. 'He thinks I do love him now.'[2] On June 2 Piozzi set out, and, after seventeen months of absence, arrived in Bath on July 1. 'He lives, he loves me.'[2]

I have seen him, I have rejoyced over him: I have cried, and prayed, and thanked God—and cried again for Joy, a whole Day, & almost a whole Night.[2]

On July 23, 1784, and again on the 25th they were married in 'the Face of God and the whole Christian World, Catholick, and

[1] See p. 176 n. 4.
[2] See p. 169, n. 1.
[3] See p. 176, n. 3.
[4] *Diary*, ii. 258.

Protestant'.[1] On July 25 Mrs. Piozzi wrote to Fanny: 'Wish me Joy my dearest Miss Burney', 'Wish me Joy then generously and like a Friend.' Even His Majesty the King had spoken kindly of her. 'And be not sorry to see your Letter signed by the beloved and long desired name of your affectionate H:L: Piozzi.'[1]

Fanny replied promptly, but unlike Dr. Burney, who wrote 'very sweetly',[1] and Dr. Johnson, who in the end calmed his wrath and resentment, and sent 'Prayers and wishes' for the happiness of both, 'acting with all the Tenderness you can imagine', Fanny seems to have omitted all felicitations for Signor Piozzi and to have included in her good wishes for Mrs. Piozzi's happiness the tactless observation that she had certainly 'deserved' her 'husband's affection'.[2] The remark may have seemed barbed with reminders of the unhappy past, with aspersions on the part that Piozzi had played as a suitor, with overtones of contempt for Piozzi, and, by association, contempt for the whole proceeding—in short with something of a sneer, which Mrs. Piozzi promptly challenged, appending the dignified warning of the married woman, which Fanny would have done well to note:

If I have, as you say, *deserved* my Husband's Affection, I will take Care not to rely on *past Merits*, as many women are apt to do; and will make myself a pleasing companion if possible, and so sincere a Friend that every action of my Life shall convince him that my Heart holds no Fellowship with those who refuse him the Esteem due to his Character & Conduct.[2]

Fanny had not seemed to see the implications of her stand: that her former attitude, compounded of love and regard for Mrs. Thrale alone, was no longer tenable. She forgot, in fact, that she was now writing not to Mrs. Thrale but to Mrs. Piozzi. What might be resented by Piozzi would now be resented by his wife, and the Burneys later conjectured that after her marriage Mrs. Piozzi may have shown her husband letters written by them when their concern was only for her, participating then

---

[1] See p. 169, n. 1.

[2] A rough draft of this letter is boxed with the Diary MSS. (Berg); the letter is missing, but its contents are partially revealed in later references to it and in Mrs. Piozzi's reply, e.g. *QL*, pp. 116–18; A.L.S. (Berg) from HLTP to FB, 6 Aug. 1784; and in a letter from FBA to Mrs. Waddington in R. Brimley Johnson, *Fanny Burney and the Burneys* (1926), pp. 104–7; *Memoirs*, ii. 387–91.

in the resentment that he must naturally have felt.[1] The clause
about esteem for Piozzi was an ultimatum if Fanny had but
realized it. A sketch of Fanny's reply, 'a letter of ice', as she
afterwards described it, is printed in the great Diary.[2] She had
either missed the point, at least the seriousness of the request, or
else she was stubbornly, if logically and consistently, refusing
what Mrs. Thrale required, some kindly message of acceptance
or regard for her husband. Though Mrs. Piozzi's reply was kind ·
('Give yourself no serious concern, sweetest Burney'), it still held
the warning note, 'Love my husband if you love his and your
H:L: Piozzi'.[3] Fanny then wrote the 'kindest letter' that she
could write 'without hypocrisy', and though she later conjectured that this letter perhaps never reached its destination, there
can be few doubts that she may still have withheld her *'esteem &
affection'* for 'a Man I hardly know, & whom I only have heard
of to regret he ever existed!'[2]

Mrs. Thrale did not reply. 'I have never heard from her
since!—never!'[2] Fanny had missed two opportunities to revise
the felicitations in a way that would include the man she thought
Mrs. Thrale's inferior in mental ability and education, as well
as in birth, fortune, and social position. She would not be
hypocritical, and the rift in the friendship came at last not
through treason and hypocrisy but through stubborn, logical,
and quite tactless sincerity. The rift may have widened later,
as the Burneys thought, through some *mal entendu*[4] that quite
falsely attributed to them some of the light remarks or squibs
inspired by the marriage of the wealthy brewer's widow to her
daughter's music-master. Nothing (outside family griefs) was
later to cause Madame d'Arblay more 'acute pain' than the
realization that all the overtures she could make were useless,
that nothing could bridge the gap or recall the past, or ever
make Mrs. Piozzi believe again in her affection and gratitude.

Whatever the complications later, there was difficulty enough
in the present. A man will forgive an injury, Dr. Johnson said,

---

[1] See Note G, p. 493.   [2] See p. 181, n. 2.

[3] See p. 169, n. 1.

[4] e.g. see A.L.S. (Berg) from FBA to CBFB, 28 Oct. 1816: 'I see almost nothing
of Mrs. Piozzi, though I have made every possible overture. Whether she cannot
forgive the sincerest of disapprobation I thought it a duty to manifest—or whether
there is some *mal-entendu*, as I often conjecture, I know not. But I shall always be
ready when she is *willing*.' See also Katharine Balderston, *Thraliana*, ii. 760, n. 3.

more easily than contempt, and Piozzi soon suspected that Miss
Burney was guilty of both. As remarks in *Thraliana* show, he had
not since his marriage received invitations formerly sent by the
Lockes of Norbury Park, and he suspected malign influence
there.

In the spring of 1784 Captain Phillips had settled his family
in Mickleham in a cottage near the bridge crossing the river
Mole to the narrow meadows and heights of Norbury Park
beyond. A path led up the heights to the White House on the
Hill, the country house built in the early seventies by William
Locke for his wife and family.[1] Mr. William Locke was to fill
Dr. Burney's 'Idea of an accomplished man more than any
gentleman' he was 'ever acquainted with'.

The artists all bow down to his Judgement in Sculpture, painting,
architecture, & antiquities—In Music his Taste is nice, refined, &
certain—& in Literature all you'd love—[2]

Susan had rapidly judged Mr. Locke to be

one of the most superior of men in knowledge, taste, & understanding, . . . the most excellent, upright, & perfect of moral characters,
. . . & the *pleasantest*, most chearful & even tempered companion that
can be conceived.[3]

In the winter of 1784 Fanny and Susan had met the Lockes in
London. Mrs. Locke's formal call at St. Martin's Street on
April 23, 1784, marked the beginning of a lifelong friendship
with both Fanny and Susan.[4] Mrs. Locke, much younger than
her husband, was in fact about Fanny's age, and to youth,
quite extraordinary beauty, sensibility, and goodness, Mrs.
Locke added another attribute much prized by the Burneys—
'innocent gaiety' and a quick-sighted perception of the ridiculous.[5] This was indeed the family of families, beautiful Norbury
Park, Elysium, and the Burneys were not alone in their opinion
of it.

Nearly every day through the summer Mr. and Mrs. Locke
took the enraptured Susan for a ride in 'a pretty low phaeton'—
'the sweetest rides that can be'—and on one occasion Mr. Locke

---

[1] See the Duchess of Sermoneta, *The Locks of Norbury* (1940).
[2] A.L.S. (Berg) from CB to the Rev. Mr. Twining, 31 July 1784.
[3] A.L. (Berg) from SBP to FB, 5 June 1784.
[4] See p. 173, n. 1.
[5] Copy (Berg) of a letter from FB to Mrs. Delany (SBP's hand), n.d.

told her how he had met her sister Fanny at Mrs. Montagu's.
'She is indeed *the most interesting creature I ever beheld, or can have
any idea of.*'[1] Thus a new stage was set. Norbury Park replaced
Streatham Place; yet parts of the old setting still remained. On
June 29 Mrs. Thrale was congratulating Fanny on her visit to
'dear delicious Norbury Park', 'a Place which will be as famous
in future Times, as it is delightful in these',[2] and significantly,
the house that in all England Piozzi loved best. But now, though
the Piozzis were in London several weeks in August, no invitations came for them. As a foreigner Piozzi perhaps did not
understand how such things could be—how, though musicians,
actors, entertainers, especially musicians, were often invited to
the great houses, such invitations did not always or necessarily
mean social acceptance. Even in the most democratic of countries and times, to use a crude analogy, one might invite and pay
a gypsy (if one could be found) to tell fortunes at a party and yet
fail to follow this up with invitations to the same gypsy and his
wife, were she ever so estimable, for a week-end. It must have
seemed a paradox to Piozzi that his marriage to a woman of
better birth, social position, and fortune than his own should
have seemed to lower rather than raise him socially. Such
distinctions are elusive; and, looking around for an explanation,
he was not long in thinking of his old enemy Fanny Burney.
Was she not at Norbury Park at this very time? and moreover
writing to his wife in a way that continued to put a slight upon
him? What could be plainer than that, as Mrs. Thrale put it
in *Thraliana*, 'Miss Burney has seduced that Family to hate us'.[3]

Mrs. Thrale had affirmed that she was ready to give up the
'good will of all Mankind' or its 'respectable aggregate'[2] for the
consolations of love, and in some measure she was to know what
that sacrifice could mean. The brilliant creature is reflected
variously in the argus eyes of the past. 'Mrs. Piozzi is the dearest
thing in the world', wrote the youthful Marianne Francis
(Fanny Burney's niece) in 1805, 'so lively, witty, good-natured,
clever, entertaining and affable.'[4] The young Wesleys had
expected to find her 'brilliant, learned & highly bred; but not
enchanting', not one of those who strike 'a true chord upon the

---

[1] Journal-letters (Berg) from SBP to FB, 1784.
[2] See p. 169, n. 1.   [3] See Note G, p. 493.
[4] Journals of Marianne Francis (Berg), 1805.

heart', and yet they found her so.[1] But hear the grating, the ground swell of Grundyism at its most relentless, implacable, and perhaps its most unjust, in the voice of Miss Harriet Bowdler (of famous name) in an impromptu obituary (1821). Miss Bowdler had known Mrs. Piozzi 'as maid, wife, widow and alas in disgraceful 2d marriage & more disgraceful second widowhood, & old age of degrading folly'. But in mercy Miss Bowdler would now 'draw the curtain close'.[2]

Though, as *Thraliana* indicates, Mrs. Piozzi was to make many brilliant public appearances, to shine again at routs and assemblies, though she was to retain many old friends like Arthur Murphy and Mrs. Garrick and to make in the theatrical world new friends like Mrs. Siddons, and though she was to attract many youthful devotees like Clement Francis or the scholarly Marianne, though she was to have many sympathizers and friends and admirers from that day to this, yet the strong tide of Grundyism had set against her. It was an eighteenth-century conviction that this tide could not be resisted triumphantly. The general or universal voice, the World, was likely to be *right*, and the individual who differed from it, *wrong*—a principle that held in dress, conduct, and morals as doctrines about *general nature* held in art and literature. Signora Piozzi was an exotic and lived to be a curiosity. 'Who was that *painted Foreigner*?' Queen Charlotte asked her attendants after having caught a glimpse of Mrs. Piozzi in Windsor Chapel.[3] Fanny cringed, as usual taking criticisms of her friend as much to heart as if they had been levelled at herself or her sisters. 'It is truly vexatious she will descend to singularity so unbecoming. For the paint was nothing to the rest of the glare, though high enough for the Opera Stage!' This thought Fanny kept to herself and Susan: 'I cleared her, as well as I was able, of anything worse than injudiciousness; I *believe* it, indeed, the chief cause of all her errors.'[3]

Mrs. Piozzi's story with its repercussions tends to occupy a disproportionate space in the biography of Fanny Burney. There was great concern at St. Martin's Street over Mrs. Thrale's departure, but new friends appeared and new scenes

---

[1] A.L.S. (Berg) from S. Wesley to —, 1 May, n.y.
[2] A.L.S. (Barrett) from H. M. Bowdler to FBA, 28 May 1821.
[3] Diary MSS. (Berg), pp. 4093–4.

were enacted at Twickenham, Norbury Park, Strawberry Hill, in the drawing-rooms of the *bas bleus*, and finally at St. James's Place, that later proved the avenue to Windsor.

Even at Chessington life did not stand still. The Phillips family had spent the winter in the old retreat, but in April Susan was writing to St. Martin's Street with anxious foreboding about Mr. Crisp's health, begging the Doctor and Fanny for the affectionate messages that seemed to cheer him. As reports grew graver, Fanny hastened to Chessington to help with the last offices and to 'close the Eyes', as she said, of that '*all but* matchless man', the friend and adviser of her girlhood and youth.[1] Mr. Crisp died on April 26. Since Fanny, Susan, and the Doctor were not separated at this time, they had no need to write their grief, and Mr. Crisp's death is marked by lacunae in the manuscripts. One lament from the Old Hall, however, had reached Mrs. Thrale, who had wept for an hour over it.[2] All through the summer Fanny could hear Mr. Crisp's beloved voice.[2]

Dr. Burney, on his part, wrote such lamentations to Colchester that Mr. Twining hardly knew whether to regret or rejoice that he had not known Mr. Crisp. In the next few years the Burneys lost old friends like Mary Bruce Strange and Mr. Bewley of Great Massingham, who died at St. Martin's Street while on a visit to London.

At the close of 1784 a magisterial, a majestic figure was passing from the stage. As reports from Bolt Court grew gloomier, it was known that Dr. Johnson too was 'going on to death very fast'. '*Priez Dieu pour moi!*' he had enjoined Fanny in November, 1783.[3] A year later on one of her visits to Bolt Court he had renewed the solemn injunction, 'Remember me in your prayers'. Afterwards she wished that she had had the courage to ask him 'so to remember' her. One of the last prayers that he made for himself, Dr. Burney said, was 'the most pious, humble, eloquent, and touching, that mortal man could compose and utter'.[3] On December 12 Fanny went to Bolt Court and waited for hours in the little square parlour below. Mr. Langton had at last to tell

[1] 2 A.L.S. (Berg) from SBP to FB and CB, 11 Apr. 1783; and A.L.S. from FB and SBP to CB, Apr. 1783; Diary MSS. (Berg), p. 1796; *Diary*, ii. 208–13, iii. 407; *Memoirs*, ii. 315–24.
[2] See p. 169, n. 1.
[3] *Memoirs*, ii. 358–66, iii. 1–17; *Diary*, ii. 282.

her that in spite of the sprightly message sent to her the evening before ('Tell Fanny—I think I shall yet throw the ball at her again!') the great man could not now see her. How much she had to recall as she closed the annals of 1784.

Dec. 20th.—This day was the ever-honoured, ever-lamented Dr. Johnson committed to the earth. Oh, how sad a day to me! My father attended, and so did Charles. I could not keep my eyes dry all day; nor can I now, in the recollecting it; but let me pass over what to mourn is now so vain![1]

Mrs. Thrale had reminded Fanny that in the normal course of nature the young outlast the old. ' 'Tis a foolish thing to attach oneself to old men as you & I do.'[2] Fanny's losses were very great, but as Mrs. Thrale, Susan, and Mrs. Locke knew, it was not only old men that engrossed her attention in these years, but one young man in particular whom Fanny often met at the *bas-bleu* parties of 1783–5, the son of Richard Owen Cambridge, George Owen Cambridge, later Rector of Elme, Prebendary of Ely, and Archdeacon of Middlesex, and the heir to Twickenham Meadows. Marianne Francis was to describe him in 1808 as 'a very unaffected, pleasant, and charming man, at least as far as good scholar-ship, good conversation, & extensive reading, & a natural stock of dry-humour & love of a joke can make him'.[3] He had much to recommend him, and in 1783 he had Fanny's 'solid good opinion for worth, honour, religion, morals, and domestic virtues'.[4] She wept for Mr. Crisp and Dr. Johnson and carried on sedate conversations with the elder Cambridge, and these griefs and interests, as judged most seemly, were allowed to stand in the journals later sent to the printer. Personal and private matters like unrequited love were, naturally, suppressed. Unpublished manuscripts, however, unpublished letters, suppressed sections of the printed journals, and suppressed packets of journals properly described as Confessions[5] yield up the hidden tale—her agonized heart-searchings, bewilderment, heartache, and bitter repining over

---

[1] See p. 186, n. 3.   [2] See p. 169, n. 1.
[3] A.L.S. (JRL) from Marianne Francis to HLTP, 24 Oct. 1808.
[4] Scraps boxed with the Diary MSS. (Berg), 1788–9.
[5] Packets of journal-letters (*c.* 32 folios), foolscap size, written closely from top to bottom, edge to edge, and addressed to SBP, who in 1784–5 was in Boulogne for her health; also suppressed fragments of Journals for 1783.

the young clergyman who seemed by his manner and actions to intimate thoughts of love, but who did not come forth with the offer of his hand, who did not, and did not, and did not *speak*.

As is usual in such histories all had begun merrily enough. Fanny Burney and George Cambridge had, one would say, much in common. There were hilarious evenings of 'almost riotous gaiety' at Mrs. Montagu's, and again great merriment at the expense of Mrs. Vesey and her hearing-aids ('a collection of silver *Ears* to serve instead of *Trumpets*').

Down dropped her Ear! she stooped to pick it up, & in so doing, brushed from her chair a cushion which she always has removed as she moves herself to sit upon. Mr. G. C. picked that up for her, &, after some apologies, they both sate down with decent gravity.

Fanny could scarcely keep her countenance when, glancing at Cambridge, she 'saw his Face almost convulsed with restrained laughter'. Ridiculous speeches and episodes amused them equally, and in 1783 there was much laughter.

Mr. G. C. was going to speak, when Mrs. Vesey interrupted him, by saying, 'Do you know Mr. Wallace, Mr. Cambridge?'
'No, ma'am.'
'It's a very disagreeable thing, I think,' said she, 'when one has just made acquaintance with any body, & likes them, to have them die.'
This speech set me grinning so irresistibly, . . . Just then my father came in: and Mr. G. C. came, and took the chair half beside me.[1]

In the happy evenings of 1783 it had been a characteristic procedure with him 'to steal round as the Evening drew on, to talk to some one near me, *standing*, & therefore ready to take the first vacated place next me'.[2] These were the happy times when she was '*monopolized* either by Mr. Cambridge or his son,— by the latter so much the most'.[2] The mutual attraction ('He looked so happy! & *you* looked so happy!' said Miss Gregory) and the marked attention of a handsome and eligible young man did not fail to provoke comment and speculation, and presently, to Fanny's horror, a paragraph was published linking the two names. The time had come when, according to all

[1] Letter (Berg) from FB to SBP, June 1783; Diary MSS. (Berg), pp. 1839–42. Printed for the most part in *Diary*, ii. 234.   [2] See p. 187, n. 5.

the rules, Mr. George Cambridge should either have made a declaration or have withdrawn. Yet apparently he did neither; and in the years 1784–6 Fanny suffered 'torturing uncertainties', 'harrass of mind, spirits, and nerves', distress, confusion, suspense, 'silent anguish',[1] and, intermittently, her old feverish illnesses.

Painful scenes succeeded the merry ones, when, stung by the inquisitive watchfulness of Mr. Pepys, Mrs. Ord, and others, Fanny assumed a kind of *hauteur* and for the benefit of the onlookers brought herself to 'rebuff, repulse, or disoblige' the young man when he tried to approach her in the old manner. As Mrs. Thrale said, Fanny Burney was very proud, and she was proud because she was poor.

Pride is the prominent Fault in both their Characters [Fanny's and Piozzi's]: but both will mend of it: when their Situation in Life will be exalted—hers by her Ingenuity—his by his Merit & Talents. They are proud *now* because they are *poor*, & feel their Fortune below their Deserts. when they shall no longer have their Dignity to defend by perpetual Vigilance, they will be more humble, more gentle, & suffer that keen sense of Neglect never practised—to offend them less, as they have less Reason to apprehend it.[2]

Sometimes she was distant and unfriendly towards young Cambridge because she was not sure of his regard and because she knew herself to be at a great disadvantage. She was at a disadvantage because she was dowerless, and her family had not the influence or interest in high places that would secure livings and promotions for young clergymen. She was in her early thirties, three years older than the young man. She knew that she was 'a disadvantageous connection', and therefore it was that she was proud—too proud to betray an unseemly or unsuccessful eagerness or let the curious janglers know how she felt. 'How often have I relinquished all the pleasure of an Evening merely from a watchful eye or curious glance!'[1] In a similar situation a few years later she decided to 'leave comments and commentators to satisfy themselves'. And she lamented: 'Had I done this formerly! But I could not! Other feelings

[1] Diary MSS. (Berg), p. 1825; letters (Berg) from FB to SBP, 28 Feb. 1783–23 Apr. 1786; fragments, boxed with Diary MSS. (Berg), Jan. 1784–22. Mar. 1786.
[2] *Thraliana*, i. 551. Cf. Diary MSS. (Berg), 1783.

impelled me—& I was alive, sufferingly alive to every look,—whisper, glance, or even _possible_ suggestion of misconstruction.'[1] Time went on. George Cambridge did not speak, and for the benefit of the onlookers she often turned from him coldly. One evening she saw the 'deep crimson' that dyed his face when for a second time he failed in an attempt to talk to her. The next evening she suffered in her turn when he made no attempt at all.[2]

It had been Mr. George's custom (with or without an invitation) to follow her on evening visits to Mrs. Thrale, the Lockes, Mrs. Ord, Mrs. Vesey, and even, on one occasion, Mrs. Delany.[2] There was that evening at the Lockes', in 1785, when, at 'the well-known knock at the door', she shook, felt ill, and was forced to smell at her salts,[3] and another evening four years later at Twickenham, when the sound of a door opening forced all the life-blood to her heart.[4] In the summer of 1784 all this was 'even torture'.[3] As late as 1789 (six years from the beginning and two from the end of the affair) Susan feared for Fanny's peace of mind if she ventured to accept Miss Cambridge's invitation to Twickenham and once more find herself

in the society of a Person formerly so very high in her estimation, & who may still retain _some_ power of _electrifying_ her by the tone of his voice—a penetrating look—or by general manner—the agitations which may yet await her fill me with uneasiness.[5]

Very painful also were meetings in St. Martin's Street, where Mrs. Burney, embarrassingly friendly at first ('hooting & clapping her hands'), soon became, as was her wont, 'stern and suspicious'. Offended and neglected, she sat 'patting one hand with the spectacles she held in the other,—as if to proclaim "_I have nothing to do with this conversation_" '[2]—a conversation that ordinarily was wont to proceed somewhat as follows:

'_You must go, then?_' These few words were spoke so as to carry me back to the period the most flattering of our acquaintance,—to the time when his regard for me appeared the tenderest! They were uttered in so soft a tone,—the Eye, the voice, the smile, all in strict harmony— . . . Another Bow—another expressive smile, expressive of pleasure, serenity, & _partiality_—[Says he will call at Mrs. Locke's

[1] Diary MSS. (Berg), p. 3463.   [2] See p. 189, n. 1.
[3] See p. 187, n. 5.   [4] Diary MSS. (Berg), May 1789.
[5] A.L. (Berg) from SBP to FB, 15 Mar. 1789.

this evening.] How *astonishingly* does he deceive me, if he went not from the House impressed with the most flattering sensations towards me. . . . Yet firmly I believe I *am* deceived.[1]

Mrs. Burney's caller Mrs. Bogle thought the two as like as two peas: '*Manner* was so exactly alike, . . . same expression, & same smile! It was perfectly impossible to know which talked & which held his peace!'[1] Fanny weighed the evidence:

He loves me? I said internally, else he would not return in less than a week. No, he means nothing. Yet so interested his air & look, so gay, animated, & undisguised the pleasure he received in our conversation . . ..[1]

Surely he behaved like one who wished to 'engage her affections!' Like many a wiser head Fanny seemed to have mistaken the *manner* for the *man*.

Long documents to this effect are Confessions in the real or perhaps in the eighteenth-century sense, so minute and tortured is the record of every glance and half-glance, thought and half-thought, expression, word and feeling. As Dr. Johnson said of Richardson, one may wish to hang oneself if one reads for the story; one must read for the sentiment.

More curious still was the part played in those years by the elder Cambridge, Richard Owen, author of the *Scribleriad*, something of a wit, and a well-known figure in the London drawing-rooms of the time. Avid for news and excitement, like all the society in which he moved, he was interested in the sensation of 1782-3, the authoress of *Cecilia*. Like Mr. Crisp, Mr. Locke, Jacob Bryant, and others of mature years, he probably found Fanny Burney an interesting young creature, intelligent, quiet, modest and, above all, respectful and *attentive*, willing to listen intelligently and sympathetically to his long discourses. So persistently and fatuously, however, did he hover about, that the 'dreadful idea' had occurred severally to Charlotte Burney, Major Phillips, Mrs. Ord, and Mrs. Thrale that such homage was not inspired by Fanny's book alone.[2] Mrs. Ord feared the attachment was not Mr. George's but Mr. Cambridge's. 'And is not Mrs. Cambridge jealous?' she asked. 'I hope not,' replied Fanny steadily, 'for I shall never refrain giving her

[1] See p. 187, n. 5.
[2] Diary MSS. (Berg), Apr.–Nov. 1783; A.L. (Berg) from FB to SBP, 12 Apr.–23 Nov. 1783.

equal reason.'[1] 'I have no Patience', said Mrs. Thrale, 'with that odd old man.'[2] She thought the son might share his father's oddity. 'One w^d wonder what Fathers are *for* but to keep their sons away from amiable women that they are not, (God knows why) to marry.'[2] What effect it might have had on the romantic notions of a young man to find himself continually ousted and supplanted by his father, must be left to conjecture.[3] Fanny seems to have taken a small revenge in *Camilla* when she brought in a good but foolish and innocuous old father, Mr. Westwynn, leading along his dutiful son Hal by the nose.

Even Mrs. Thrale, to whom one might hopefully look for a diagnosis of these love troubles, fails us here. In those years she was occupied by her own bid for freedom, and she was informed about Fanny's affairs only up to a point. She knew that 'for some—*No Reason*' George Cambridge did not speak.[2] When Fanny told her of his illness, she thought that might be the 'Effect of fire among young Twigs, which burn out, and leave a fine *Pale Ash*'.[2] If Mr. George had kept journals as articulate as those of the practised diarist and novelist, we should know whether any wavering fires had blazed and been quenched by the worldly wisdom of the elder Cambridge, his own self-interest, or the awkwardness of the situation. Fanny with her watchful pride must have been difficult. She was three years older than the young man and perhaps she did not have the beauty to stir his senses beyond the pitch of prudence. The girl (Cornelia Mierop) whom he finally married in 1795 was very beautiful and his junior by thirteen years. Whatever the fires, bitter ashes indeed filled the chronicles of 1786–7.

Who . . . could pardon except on a Death Bed—could, or can pardon such wanton, such accumulating—such endless deceit & treachery? I can use no other words; his conduct has long past all mere impeachment of *trifling*,—it has seemed irrepressibly attached to me,— it has been deemed honourably serious by all our mutual acquaintances.[4]

By February, 1786, Mrs. Ord had decided that Mr. George Cambridge himself had at last seen it necessary to break the acquaintance and that it therefore behoved Fanny for her

---

[1] See p. 191, n. 2.   [2] See p. 169, n. 1.
[3] *Diary*, ii. 218–22.   [4] See p. 187, n. 5.

'interest, & welfare, & *honour*, to shun him utterly'.[1] Susan had
arrived at a similar opinion: Mr. George Cambridge means to
be thought a 'particular & intimate Friend, yet no more'.[2] Yet
Fanny continued to write minute accounts of every meeting,
unwilling to abandon hope.

Meanwhile time had not stood still with others in the Burney
family. In June, 1783, Charles had married a Dr. Rose's
daughter and become headmaster of a school at Chiswick.
While Fanny's fate hung suspended James had had time to sail
to the East Indies, try the climate there, and return to England.
In September, 1785, he married Sally Payne, and was contented
now, as Mr. Crisp had wished, to 'let the Sea rumble and
tumble its Bellyful' and to exchange his hammock for a down
bed.[3] The greatest loss of these years to St. Martin's Street was
the affectionate and dutiful Charlotte, always ready with laughter and puns, 'striking out of stock & stone', as her father
rhymed, 'both wit & humour' of her own.[4] In February, 1786,
she married Clement Francis, a surgeon, who had returned
from India, where he had acted as secretary to Warren Hastings.
'Anon', the family called him, since Charlotte was too shy to
pronounce his name. He took his bride to his old home in
Aylsham, Norfolk, and Dr. Burney penned an affectionate
Epithalamium.

> Blest is thy mind devoid of Art,
> Blest is thy probity of heart,
> Blest is thy temper, cool & steady,
> To acts of kindness ever ready![4]

Lost now was the Queen of 'Chaos's Dingy Empire'—the
study—and an extract from one of Charlotte's characteristic
letters will show that Dr. Burney was not exaggerating her usefulness there.

My Father has been making a new regulation in his study, namely
that of having the large Piano-Forte removed in to the study, in the
place of his large wooden Table, which *arch contrivance* has turned the
tables upon *me*, for I have had the pleasing & *recreative* task of finding

---

[1] Diary MSS. (Berg), suppressed sections, 20 Feb. 1786.
[2] See p. 189, n. 1.
[3] *Burford Papers*, pp. 71–73; *QL*, p. 111.
[4] A poem (Barrett) of 135 verses 'To my Daughter Charlotte on her Marriage
with Clement Francis Esq.', 11 Feb. 1786.

new places (& places at Court are not more difficult to be met with) for every Book & paper, the ponderous weight of which, altogether, had *well nigh* worn the wooden legs of the old table to the stumps— so that I have been in an *abyss of literature* & at the most grievous *non plus* for new plans for these Books & papers, than for time to do anything for myself!—I have been in a situation only to be enjoyed by some of the fogrum codgers of the Royal Society; surrounded by learned papers, & fusty Books, Folios, Quartos, & Duodecimos up to my chin, & not knowing which way to turn for the depth of my Father's literary property that I have had to dig into, & investigate.[1]

With Charlotte's departure early in 1786 all of Fanny's brothers and sisters (Hester, Susan, James, and Charles) had left St. Martin's Street for homes of their own. Her stepbrother, the handsome young Dick, was at school. There were left only the Lady and a stepsister, the sixteen-year-old Sally, who, brought up, as Maria Rishton said, 'in a state of Warfare', gave her stepsisters much to deplore in her temper and manners. Major Phillips and James, still delighting in treason, were glad to hear of Charlotte's escape and the great roaring fires she made in her own house at Aylsham. And Susan, congratulating Charlotte and rejoicing still in her own happiness, wrote with deep pity for the Burney that was left. 'How sorry was I for our dear Fanny when she returned to that solitary Newton House!'[2]

Fanny had found in visits to Mickleham and Norbury Park a congenial refuge from tedious London parties and the buffets of love. Mrs. Locke had soon become a close confidante. 'All your feelings electrify me', she wrote to Fanny, 'for do I not hold the chain? it is so entwined around my Heart, that at every emotion of yours mine vibrates.'[3] 'There is a *viscosity* in their friendship', Dr. Burney had remarked after the long visits his daughters had made at Norbury Park in the summer of 1784.[4] Dr. Burney found 'the soft & insinuating manners' of the female part of the Locke family 'a little too pathetic' and sometimes spoke a little ironically about 'Paradise Regained'. Not so his daughters. To Susan and Fanny the Locke family was perfection.

Fanny found a second congenial refuge from the world in visits to the aged Mrs. Delany. In the summer of 1785, when the Duchess of Portland died and Mrs. Delany fell ill from grief and

---

[1] A.L. (Barrett) from CB to SBP, 25–26 Oct. 1783.
[2] A.L.S. (Berg) from SBP to CBF, 4 Mar. 1786.
[3] See p. 187, n. 5.   [4] See p. 183, n. 2.

age, Fanny interrupted a visit to Norbury Park to nurse her. Since Lady Llanover has succeeded in throwing such a shadow over Fanny Burney's devotion to the gentle old lady,[1] this incident may be best related by a third party, that honest gentlewoman Mrs. Chapone, who introduced the novelist to her friend. In a letter of September, 1785, to W. W. Pepys, she told how

the Sweet Evelina (Miss Burney) left her friends the Lock's to nurse Mrs. Delany in Town, who was ill there of a fever and thrush. 'She has left her delightful friends (said Mrs. Delany to Mr. Boscawen) to devote herself to my infirmities.'—how I love her for it! and how pleased am I to have been instrumental in that friendship between the most amiable of the Aged & of the Young.[2]

And now the tale turns to Windsor. 'You have doubtless heard', continued Mrs. Chapone,

of the noble testimony to Mrs. Delany's worth & their own goodness of heart given by the King & Queen; the Queen desired her acceptance of a house she had furnish'd for her at Windsor; & the King of £300 annuity to supply the expense of removals. She is now gone thither . . .[2]

The King and Queen often visited Mrs. Delany in the house that they had provided for her, and through the old lady's kind manœuvres Fanny Burney was soon presented to them. These encounters are described in detail in journal-letters written to Dr. Burney and Susan in November and December, 1785. In June, 1786, Her Majesty invited Fanny Burney to present herself for an audience or interview, and Fanny knew very well what was coming.

I now see the end—I see it next to inevitable. I can suggest nothing upon earth that I dare say for myself, in an audience so generously meant. I cannot even to my father utter my reluctance,—I see him so much delighted at the prospect of an establishment he looks upon as so honourable. But for the Queen's own word *permanent*,—but for her declared desire to attach me entirely to herself and family,—I should share in his pleasure; but what can make *me* amends for all I shall forfeit?[3]

---

[1] See editorial notes to *The Autobiography and Correspondence of Mary Granville, Mrs. Delany* (6 vols.), vi.   [2] *A Later Pepys*, i. 411–12.

[3] *Diary*, ii. 361–72. Cf. A.L. (Barrett) from FB to SBP and Mrs. Locke, 19 July 1786: 'The Blow was struck on Monday, — & hard it struck, & almost felled me.'

To cut long deliberations short, Fanny was honoured by the royal invitation to replace Miss Haggerdorn as Second Keeper of the Robes. As a subordinate to Mrs. Schwellenberg, she was to assist at the Queen's toilette, to have a footman and a maid and £200 a year. Dr. Burney's pleasure and gratification at this recognition—'a place solicited by thousands and thousands of women of Fashion and Rank'—outweighed his daughter's dismay at the durance in prospect.

What a life for me, who have friends so dear to me, and to whom friendship is the balm, the comfort, the very support of existence![1]

In a letter of June, 1786, to her sister Esther, she reviewed her situation, the cold facts of the case, and put her objections.

The separation from all my friends & connections is so cruel to me,— the attendance, Dress, confinement, are to be so unremitting, . . . I know my situation will be thorny & dangerous, & I know, too, there is nothing upon Earth that make me really happy when deprived of the society of those I love: I think, indeed, there *is* no other happiness.[2]

The unpleasant life in St. Martin's Street where the tyrannical Lady ruled splenetically and maliciously was one determining factor. Another was Fanny's helplessness and dependence in her unmarried plight, but above and beyond all were her father's wishes. As the Doctor had said in another connection: 'A man without family attachments is an awkward & isolated beast; but a woman without a mate is still more insignificant & help-less.'[3] Independence of a kind could indeed be bought with a few unattractive and painful alternatives, described at great length and perhaps with bitter realism in Madame d'Arblay's *The Wanderer; or, Female Difficulties*, which shows the plight of the penniless and unprotected female in eighteenth-century Eng-land. Fanny Burney was not financially in a position to refuse so honourable and glorious a means of livelihood as an invitation to serve at court, unless her father, who must bear the cost of her refusal, had encouraged it. Far from this, the Doctor, greatly flattered and highly gratified, could see only honour and

---

[1] See p. 195, n. 3.
[2] A.L. (Berg) from FB to EBB, June 1786.
[3] A.L.S. (BM) from CB to Arthur Young (congratulating him on the marriage of his daughter), 21 Sept. 1791.

security for his daughter in the appointment. In enraptured dreams he saw not only a daughter at court, but organ-posts for himself, ships for James, schools, degrees, and dioceses for Charles, and Fanny had not the heart to dash such beaming prospects. Thus she concluded in her letter to Esther—

To have declined such a proposal would . . . have been thought madness & folly,—nor, indeed, should I have been *permitted* to decline it, without exciting a displeasure that must have made me quite unhappy.[1]

The joyless relationship with her stepmother was next touched on.

Besides,—since now all my dear dear sisters have deserted my original Home—it has lost so much of what made me love it,—while still it retains *all* that ever made it comfortless or irksome or painful to me,—that, when I weigh together the bad with the good, I am sensible there are a thousand serious & real advantages in the change,—Time only can shew which way the scale will preponderate.[1]

Such were some of the deliberations, and still the man who might have saved her did not speak. He knew that she was to be immured in a castle (for Fanny herself kept Miss Cambridge well informed about the preliminary negotiations), and he did not stir. Circumstances were prison chains and there was no knight errant. With the knowledge that was to come later Fanny wrote an analytic comment on the midsummer crisis of 1786: either the young man had deceived her and the world by his unmeaning pursuit, or, if he had ever thought of 'a permanent union', he had decided against its disadvantages. 'His prudence is stronger than his affection.'

He would prefer to see the Person of whom he thought highest in the world, subdued into the saddest lot that Destiny, without positive calamity, could frame for her!—know her doomed to confinement—Dependence—& Attendance,—banishment from her friends,—hardships to her Health, & the tyranny & caprice & gloom of a companion notorious to the whole world for ill-nature & ill-qualities![2]

Like many a maid left similarly forlorn, she could not but feel that the man was cold at heart. If, for want of rescue by

---

[1] See p. 196, n. 2.
[2] Diary MSS. (Berg), suppressed fragments, 1788–9.

marriage, the offer of a livelihood at court had, perforce, to be accepted,

then I should see, what now I surmise, realized: that, with all the solid good qualities to be desired, with a turn to domestic life, . . . with all the virtues of morals, of good conduct, of upright integrity, honour of character, & principles of Religion,—there is yet a *coldness of Heart, innately* unconquerable, & a *selfishness of disposition* which to nothing can give way.[1]

Since there was no help for it, then let her go to court. At ten o'clock in the morning of July 17, 1786, Fanny left her father's house. In a year Dr. Burney was to move to apartments in Chelsea College, leaving the storied, once-lively house in St. Martin's Street very vacant. One day in July, 1787, Susan returned with her father to look for music. 'Poor old St. Martin's Street house looked very dark & dismal',[2] she thought. Fanny had often found it 'dark & dismal' in its life, and she had no romantic regrets as she drove away.

I wept not then. I left no one behind me to regret; my dear father accompanied me, and all my sisters had already taken their flight never to return. Even poor little Sarah, whom I love very dearly, was at Chesington.[3]

At Queen Anne Street the Doctor and his daughter transferred to Mrs. Ord's carriage, leaving their own to follow as a baggage train. The two older people were in ecstasy, though a little puzzled from time to time by the drooping dejection of the new courtier. On the way from Mrs. Delany's door to the Queen's Lodge, her courage all but failed.

I was now on the point of entering—probably for ever—into an entire new way of life, and of foregoing by it all my most favourite schemes, and every dear expectation my fancy had ever indulged of happiness adapted to its taste—as now all was to be given up—I could disguise my trepidation no longer—indeed I never had disguised, I had only forborne proclaiming it.[3]

She faltered, and the Doctor became alarmed. Before this, Fanny knew, not a doubt had assailed him. She allowed him,

[1] See p. 197, n. 2.
[2] Diary MSS. (Berg), pp. 2078–97. Cf. Susan Burney's Journal (Osborn, copies, Armagh), 20 July 1787.
[3] See p. 195, n. 3.

however, to mistake her agitation for fear of the coming audience. 'Indeed was it not!'[1] 'My mind had no _room_ in it for feelings of this sort.'[2] The Doctor awaited her return from the
audience, too anxious to depart till he had seen her again.
Though she was herself miserable almost past endurance, she
saw no reason for making him so, and used every means to
remove the uneasiness that this day seemed first to awaken in
him. 'Thank God! I had the fullest success; his hopes and gay
expectations were all within call, and they ran back at the first
beckoning.'[1] The Doctor's speaking face was soon 'all fresh
illumined with returning content', gratification, and pleasant
expectations. Later she rejoiced to recollect that she had said
nothing that morning to check his satisfaction. One person, at
least, might be happy. 'It was now, suddenly, & all at once all
my care to increase his delight. And so, henceforward, it must
invariably continue.'[2]

Often disappointed in 'the favour of fortune or patronage of
the Great' the Doctor had felt at first that the whole proposal
might yet prove 'the baseless fabric of a vision'. As events moved
on, his scepticism gave way to incredulous delight; and though
at Windsor he had caught a passing glimpse of his daughter's
distress, his guileless version of the episode shows that, just as
she had surmised, he had been reassured by her assumed cheerfulness. Mrs. Delany had persuaded him to walk with Fanny to
the Lodge,

the approach to wch was so formidable that I feared she would not
be able to get thither. She turned pale, her lips trembled, & she
found herself so ill that it was with the utmost difficulty she reached
the lodge, where she was shown into Mrs Haggerdorn's appartm^{ts}.
This seizure was not a mere panic or fear of approaching her
Majesty's presence, for that she knew to be all gentleness & benignity;
but it was the aggregate of her feelings on quitting her family &
friends with whom she had ever lived in perfect harmony and of
whose cordial affection she had long been convinced.[3]

In the evening, however, the Doctor had found Fanny in
'very good spirits & much pleased & flattered by all that [had]
passed during the course of the day'. Since then he had had a
reassuring letter from her, and, in short, though the Doctor had

---

[1] See p. 195, n. 3.   [2] See p. 198, n. 2.
[3] Draft of a letter (Osborn) from CB to Leonard Smelt, 178[6].

'been so fortunate' as to marry three of his daughters to 'worthy & good Husbands', he had 'never given any one of them away with the pride & pleasure' he then felt.[1]

Even if the Doctor had known in his man's way about the real sorrow, the bitter disappointment that corroded his daughter's life at this time, could he have thought that tarrying longer outside would help? Let the portcullis fall. In the time of George III the royal family and their servants lived in the Upper and Lower Lodges erected just outside the castle walls in a beautiful expanse of countryside;[2] yet figuratively, at least, one may think of grey walls and towers, the clank of iron on stone, and heavy gates swinging shut for five long years.

[1] See p. 199, n. 3.
[2] For an authoritative history of the castle see Sir Owen Morshead, *Windsor Castle* (1951).

VIII

WINDSOR AND KEW

(1786–1791)

I have not yet forgot myself to stone.
Eloisa to Abelard

THOUGH Fanny thought it would be 'foolish, useless, even wicked' not to reconcile herself to her destiny, the first six months at court seem to have been spent in bitter repining. 'I [am] just beginning to educate myself for smiling no more, except for now & then, with a little agreeable fawning-ness, at some poor stale joke,—or little miserable conceit, that, in my inmost mind will make me long to [spit].'[1] By December she seemed to have plumbed the depths of despair. An extant document, with lines crossed out and written over, seems to have been produced in tears at Windsor in December, 1786: 'My Eyes will hardly let me see,—nor my Head hold itself up.'[2] Separation from her family and friends was one source of dis-content, but a second soon appeared in her immediate superior in office, a cruel and savage German with whom she was expected to spend most of her time. She soon saw that she

was expected by Mrs. Schwellenberg not to be her Collegue but her dependant Deputy! not to be her visitor, at my own option, but her companion, her Humble Companion, at her own command! This has given so new a character to the place I had accepted . . . that nothing but my horror of Disappointing—perhaps displeasing my dearest Father, has deterred me, from the moment that I made the mortifying discovery from soliciting his leave to Resign. But . . . kind, good, indulgent as he is to me, I have not the Heart, so cruelly to thwart his Hopes—his views—his Happiness in the Honours he conceived awaiting my so unsolicited appointment. The Queen, too, is all sweetness, encouragement, & gracious goodness to me—& I cannot endure to complain to her of her old servant.

You see, then, my situation; *Here I must remain!* The die is cast,— & That struggle is no more;—to keep off every other—to support the loss of the dearest Friends, & best Society, & bear, in exchange

---

[1] A L.S. (Berg) from FB to EBB, 5 Dec. 1785.   [2] The Barrett Papers.

the tyranny, exigeance, the ennui, & attempted indignities of their greatest contrast, must be my constant endeavour.

. . . Could I have, as my dear Father had conceived, all the Time to myself, my Friends, my Leisure, or my own occupations, that is not devoted to my official Duties, how different would be my feelings, how far more easily accomodated to my privations & sacrifices! Little does the Queen know the Slavery I must either resist or bear. And so frightful is Hostility. . . . Can you read me? I blot and re-write— yet know not how to alter or what to send.[1]

No more need be said. Further developments in the tyrannical character of Mrs. Schwellenberg, the terrifying illness of the King, and the deeper seclusion of the court increased both the painfulness of the situation and the difficulty of escape. All this was for the future. At the beginning of the New Year (1787) the new courtier resolved to conquer fruitless grief and banish discontent. 'I took shame to myself, and *Resolved to be happy!*'[2] She promised to curtail painful recollections and heart-searchings and to write a court-journal from the accumulated memoranda of the previous six months. This journal of about 250 pages was the first instalment of the Windsor Journal, which was to run on for nearly five years and to include (for the parts later printed) about 1,100 pages.

Unlike the family correspondence of these years or the long personal letters resembling Confessions that Fanny wrote for Susan's eyes alone, the Windsor Journal was not a private, but a semi- or mock-private communiqué. It was addressed to Susan and Mrs. Locke but extracts at least, as she knew, would be in public reading in Norbury Park. Though she kept memoranda of the day's events, the journal was usually written up at the close of each month (though sometimes many months later). It was not a day-to-day account but a selection of such incidents as were likely to afford interest or amusement. Though the journalistic style required a chronological pattern, and though the Windsor Journal is in a manner a chronicle, it is more accurately described as a selection of episodes, recollected from memoranda in tranquillity and sometimes described with imaginative force and stylistic effect. When she was amused, as in her meeting with the French novelist Madame La Fîte, or

---

[1] See p. 201, n. 2.
[2] *Diary*, iii. 161–2. Also Diary MSS. (Berg), suppressed parts, Jan. 1787.

when she had spectacular subjects at hand like the opening scenes of the trial of Warren Hastings or the fearsome topic of 1787-8—the King's illness (or delirium, as she thought it)—she wrote with her old enjoyment and effectiveness. Often, however, whether from the joylessness of her situation or the irksomeness of the commitment to write, the journal entries were mere gestures, brief and unrelieved reports. With the visits of the Lockes and Susan to Windsor or St. James's, conversations took the place of journals, and a sentence or two marked the passing of a month.

The journal contract was, it must be added, reciprocal. Both Susan and Mrs. Locke agreed to compile journals in exchange for the monthly packet they could expect from Windsor. Susan's monthly packets of journals[1] incorporated a running commentary on her sister's journal of the previous month, vignettes of her children, of the life at Mickleham and Norbury Park, and long reports on the family visits of the Burneys. In the summer they all came—Dr. Burney, Sarah, and the Lady, Mr. Burney and Esther, James and his children, Charles and the flamboyant Rosette ('diamonded with pink'). Nothing escaped Susan's merciless observation, and much of the domestic life of the Burneys can be read in the pages she wrote to Fanny. The Lady, one learns, was as noisy as ever when happy, but afflicted still with spasms of jealousy and resentment when the attention of the company turned away from her, as it often did turn in so musical a family, to music. One scene, described by both Susan and Mrs. Locke,[2] occurred at Norbury Park, when the poor Lady, much saddened by the applause given to Dr. Burney's rendering of some ancient music and to a duet that he played with Susan, began to tremble and weep, burst at last into hysterical crying, and could only be quieted by her own prescription, ten drops of laudanum. The Doctor performed well, whispered the wicked Captain Phillips to Mrs. Locke on leaving, and 'so did Mrs. Burney'. The old tensions still remained even though all the stepchildren had now left their father's house.

Fanny Burney's Journal of 1786 was an introduction of some 200 pages to her life at court. It furnished Susan and Mrs.

---

[1] In the Berg and Barrett Collections, with copies in the Public Library, Armagh.
[2] In the Barrett Papers, June 1789.

Locke with descriptions of the royal figures, their kindness and
condescension, her associates in service, the duties of attendance,
the evening tea-table, and the equerries, governesses, precep-
tors, and various untitled folk who comprised the company
there. Except for occasional visits of relatives or of such aged
and respectable friends of the court as Mr. Bryant, the antiquary
and mythologist, the staff lived in seclusion. 'Void was the
scene, blank, vacant, drear', but happily visits to Mrs. Delany
afforded some relief. The gentle old lady, living now by the
bounty of the King in a house immediately adjacent to the
Castle, had become 'the bosom repository of all the livelong
day's transactions, reflections, feelings, wishes'.

In January for the Queen's birthday, in Lent, in June for the
King's birthday, and at other times for the Drawing Rooms,
the Court was in residence in London. Though the elaborate
dress required for ceremonials meant more work and later
hours for the Keepers of the Robes, in these seasons Fanny
could sometimes make short evening visits to old friends or
receive members of her family—James with his radical or
Whiggish principles, Charles with his buoyant energy and
hopes, Dr. Burney himself, 'full of spirits, full of Handel, full of
manuscripts, and full of proof-sheets'.[1]

In February, 1788, the Queen indulged Fanny with tickets
for the great trial at Westminster Hall. She went on the second
day and from an advantageous place in the Great Chamber-
lain's box she watched the proceedings, much pained to see
Hastings a prisoner at the bar, and her old idol Burke now, as
she thought, the devil's advocate, but much gratified by long
conversations with Windham and other friends of the family.
She concentrated her attention on the managers, the accused,
and the central drama, her accounts of which were later to
provide historians with first-hand impressions. Her tenacious
memory and the liveliness of her recordings soon made an
impression on the King and Queen, who listened to her reports
as if they had no other sources of information, and in the
succeeding years sent her back for other hearings, including
Hastings's defence in 1790.

Three days at the trial sufficed for forty bright pages of diary.
For the rest the year 1788 resumed its dull monotone, though

[1] *Diary*, ii. 378 ff., iii, and iv.

muted to still sadder tones by the death of Mrs. Delany (the loss of 'all that I dearly loved that remained within my reach').

It was in this dreary epoch that Fanny found at court a mournful comforter in the Queen's Vice-Chamberlain, Colonel Stephen Digby (the Mr. Fairly of the printed diaries),[1] brother of the Dean of Durham and of the first Earl Digby, whose ancient family seat was Sherborne Castle in Dorset. He had married a lady of still higher connexion than his own, Lady Lucy Fox-Strangways, who in January, 1788, died of cancer. Fanny shared the sympathy of all the court when in January the Colonel returned to the Lodge, a widower,—'thin, haggard, worn', grey, with 'some of his front teeth vanished'. Fanny found in the Queen's Vice-Chamberlain a man of 'the most scrupulous good breeding', 'the most acute sensibility', with 'soft and seducing manners' and 'the tenderest social affections', one who, inured to sorrow, could sympathize with the sorrows of others—in short, a man of sentiment. His conversation was, of course, edifying. He liked to descant on such subjects as Death and Immortality, misery, friendship, and 'the necessity of participation to every species of happiness'. He read poetry, sermons, and homiletic literature like Moir's *Discourses* or William Combe's *Original Love Letters* ('They are full of beauties—moral, elegant, feeling, and rational'). He read Falconer's *Shipwreck* seeming himself to feel 'the chastity of silent woe'.[2] 'What a sad *luxury*', commented Susan, 'must it have been to him, to read such passages . . . to one so tremblingly alive all o'er to every tender feeling—to a mind congenial with his own & formed to soften the distress of others by sympathy in it!'[3] This was the setting for trouble ahead.

On July 12, 1788, the court set out for a month's holiday at Cheltenham. The royal family (the King, Queen, and the Princesses) with some of their personal attendants (including Fanny) were accommodated in Fauconberg Hall, a house in a beautiful situation facing the Malvern Hills. Others in the retinue, including Colonel Digby, were lodged about a quarter of a mile away in the town. Since Mrs. Schwellenberg had been left at Windsor, there were no tea-meetings, and Fanny had not

[1] See Note H, p. 493.
[2] Diary MSS. (Berg), pp. 3071–220. Printed with deletions, *Diary*, iv. 1–89.
[3] See p. 203, n. 1.

for a long time achieved so much peace and freedom. At times the Colonel's countenance also 'spoke inward peace'.

I cannot give you our conversation; . . . the Birds that chirped, the meadows that bloomed, the Hills that rose before us, the purity of the air we breathed, the clearness of the fine blue canopy that covered us, the stillness from turbulence . . . made a union of our faculties with our senses. . . . And here, for near two Hours, on the steps of Fauconberg Hall, we remained; & they were two Hours of such pure serenity, without & within, as I think, except in Norbury Park, with its loved Inhabitants & my Susan, I scarce ever remember to have spent.[1]

Though the Colonel was soon heavily afflicted with 'a smart fit of the gout' and with neuralgia that swelled his face to twice its natural size, he by no means proposed to stay in his room in the town. As soon as the 'royals' were safely away for the day, he muffled himself up in a greatcoat, swathed his swelled cheek in a handkerchief, thrust one foot into a gouty shoe, and with the aid of a cane made his way to Fauconberg Hall and then to the ladies' parlour. Columb (Fanny's servant) stared as if confronted by an apparition, and Miss Planta's scream expressed the amazement of all the court at this venture. 'It's the oddest thing I ever knew! It's just such a thing as never was done! to hit just the time when [the court] were all away!'[1]

The tone and the style of the literary works absorbed during these visits were to emerge a few months later in a new literary venture—a series of sentimental tragedies in blank verse, taking as their ostensible subjects unhappy events in early English history. Fanny had always studied history assiduously, and now she found in the histories of Robert Henry and others suitable incidents to develop as she-tragedies. These were sentimental histrionics reflecting the dreariness of her own mind, the pomp and circumstance of court, and perhaps the cabals and political intrigues of the proposed regency. Fanny's first tragedy, *Edwy and Elgiva*, was begun at Kew in October, 1788, when the court was unexpectedly detained for a week because of the King's illness. 'Had not this composition fit seized me, society-less, and bookless, and viewless as I am, I know not how I could have whiled away my being.'[2]

In November, however, as the King's illness became more

---

[1] See p. 205, n. 2.   [2] *Diary*, iv. 118–52.

apparent, all thoughts of fictional or historical tragedy were eclipsed. By November 4 the Monarch was in a state of hurry and volubility 'almost incomprehensible', the Queen in great distress, and all the court uneasy and alarmed. As suspense and fear spread to the antechambers, 'not a voice was heard; not a step, not a motion', only in the royal suites, the hoarse, exhausted, but unceasing voice of the unhappy King: '"I am nervous", he cried, "I am not ill, but I am nervous: if you would know what is the matter with me, I am nervous."'[1] On the next day at dinner the King (in 'positive delirium', as Fanny put it) seized the Prince of Wales by the collar and thrust him against the wall. The Prince and the Princesses burst into tears. The Queen was in hysterics. The musicians were ordered away, physicians called in, and the crisis had to be faced. From the window Fanny saw faithful friends of the King turned away 'in deluges of tears', for now the court was to live in seclusion. On November 9 no one went even to church. 'Not a creature now quits the house.'[1]

Very soon it was decided that the King should be persuaded to leave Windsor for the peace and seclusion of Kew. On November 29 the Keeper of the Robes was hastily packing up, preparing, she said, 'for we knew not what, nor for how long, nor with what circumstances, nor scarcely with what view!'[2] On that day, in gloom and tears as if the end of the reign had come, the court set off for Kew. The White House, or, as Fanny called it, Kew Palace, had not been used before as a winter residence and 'there was nothing prepared for its becoming one'. The parlours were in need of fires and washing; the cold draughty boards of many of the rooms and passages were uncarpeted; the loosely fitting windows not yet stopped with winter sandbags, so that the December winds blowing in were quite enough, Colonel Digby thought, to destroy the Princesses. Yet such was the fearful sense of calamity that all there 'would individually sooner perish than offer up complaint or petition'.[2]

Fanny was finally settled in a room up a tortuous flight of stairs at the end of a long corridor into which bedroom cells (those of the maids and wardrobe women) opened on each side. The room was difficult of access but in itself very comfortable, 'carpeted all over, with one window looking to the front of the

---

[1] See p. 206, n. 2.   [2] *Diary*, iv. 153–202.

house and two into a courtyard'.[1] The drawback was the distance from the Queen. 'The long passage is nearly quite dark—the stairs are winding, dirty, & narrow,—and very high. A *coal hole* is now formed at the bottom, to save trouble & time, on account of the many Fires kept at the top of the House, & the passages leading to these stairs from the Entrance into the House are bleakly cold & miserably neglected.'[2]

In accordance with a new duty accruing to her, the Second Keeper of the Robes rose very early in the morning and made her way to the King's Physicians (now the Willises, father and son) for a verbal report on the King's health to take to the Queen. She next waited anxiously in the draughty passages outside the Queen's rooms until she heard voices within, then delivered the report with such curtailment of distressing episodes as she thought necessary or kind. In retrospections of a later time, the Willises recalled her good-humoured morning face, and there can be little doubt that her cheerful and sympathetic service in the painful and terrifying crises of 1788–9 served to cement the lasting goodwill of the Queen and the Princesses towards her. They were never to forget that to them she was as 'true as gold'.

The court was to remain at Kew for about four months. Isolated from family, friends, and the outside world, the royal attendants had to depend on one another to beguile the uneasy months of waiting. For Fanny this meant, first of all, the fierce old coadjutrix, who, plagued by ill health and the worries and discomforts of the situation, had grown even more fretful and savage than before. Though the evening tea-hours were not observed at Kew, there was still much to endure from her 'unprovoked Harshness', fretfulness, 'Tyranny, Dissension, & even insult'. But for Mr. Smelt, Colonel Digby, and the Willises, Fanny must have 'almost sunk', as she said, 'under the *pressure of vacancy*'. 'I must have died of depression, confinement, ennui, & tasteless existence.' 'What a situation it is . . . to live pent up thus, Day after Day, in this forlorn apartment!—confinement! —attendance!—seclusion!'[2]

The Queen's Vice-Chamberlain, also finding life rather dull

---

[1] See p. 207, n. 2.
[2] A.L. (Berg) from FB to SBP, 14 Feb. 1789; Diary MSS. (Berg), Jan.–Mar. 1789 (pp. 3303–584); also 2 A.L.S. (PML) from FB to JB, 2, 10 Mar. 1789.

at Kew, frequently found his way along the servants' corridor, past the coal-hole, and up the tortuous stairs to the apartment allotted to the Second Keeper of the Robes. In this secluded refuge he established himself to write letters and to read, and the court soon learned where he was to be found when wanted. Fanny marvelled that he should be so careless about appearances, but, remembering the London blue-parties when in self-conscious deference to the watchers she had unhappily offended George Cambridge, she now passed to the opposite extreme and perhaps deferred too little to the gossips. All this time the court had been accumulating evidence that Colonel Digby was to marry a beautiful Maid of Honour, Miss Gunning. 'I'll be hanged', cried Colonel Gwynn, 'if he does not.' Miss Gunning 'loves him prodigious', declared Mrs. Schwellenberg, 'and she has got £10,000!' But Mr. Digby should be 'ree-ely sorprised',

for he bin grown so white as possible, what you call his Head, others his Hair; & his Teeth been all gone, & his skin been so *galler* as possible,—& he got 4 children.[1]

Others could tell a story about the Maid of Honour and the green-eyed monster—how once on Colonel Digby's sudden entrance into the drawing-room, after it was reported that he had been found in Miss Burney's apartment, Miss Gunning reached for her salts and fainted dead away.[1]

Fanny heard these rumours everywhere but failed to give credence to them. 'Why should he be a Hypocrite?' Why, indeed? This was the crux of the matter. Yet infinitesimal signs of hypocrisy began to appear. After all the tender, significant, and flattering remarks the Vice-Chamberlain had made apropos of Moir's chapter on Friendship (which they had lingered over together), it appeared on January 17, 1789, that he had forgotten with whom he had read it. When she saw how careless he was about provoking gossip and how ready to 'brave the world' at her expense, she began to think him deficient in consideration. As for *serious intentions*, she knew that

he could not, in the very Heart of his high Family, & of his Lady Lucy's still higher connections, sustain the idea of braving a torrent of censure from them, & all mankind.[1]

As for herself, a platonic friendship was quite sufficient. 'I covet

---

[1] Diary MSS. (Berg), pp. 3802-4, 3994-8, 4010-30.

no more! All beyond is pain & alarm.'[1] Nevertheless it was the considered opinion of the servants that Mr. Digby came a-courting.

'And all the maids, ma'am, & Columb, & every body says so!'

'Then all the maids,' cried I, '& Columb, & every body are much mistaken. I desire you will tell them so. I only see Mr. D—— as a Friend & acquaintance—for anything further, I should as soon think of the Man in the Moon.'

As for liking Colonel Digby, Columb thought his mistress could not be such a fool. He himself took the liberty of disliking the Colonel intensely and sometimes took independent action in the affair. 'He says he never calls you for him, & he never will.' He always told Colonel Digby that Miss Burney was out '& nobody knows where' and he advised Goter and Miss Planta's maid to do the same. 'Columb quite hates him, ma'am.' And Columb knew why he hated him.

'And why?'

'Because, ma'am, he says he's a villain . . . all the time that he is coming after you in this manner, morning, noon, & night, he pays his addresses to a Lady in Town—a very handsome Lady, ma'am, & a Maid of Honour.'

'Miss Gunning?' cried I.

'Yes, ma'am, that is the very name.'

Columb was scarcely better pleased with other callers.

'[He says] you've a rare pack of old gentlemen coming after you, as ever he see, there's nobody but that old sniffling Gentleman, Mr. Bryant, & old Mr. Cambridge, & t'other old Gentleman with the Horn; that ever he sees.'

'This is Mr. Hutton, who is deaf', added Fanny for Susan's elucidation.

I was now obliged to speak angrily of this liberty in Columb, & express my astonishment at his caring so much about my visitors, be they whom they might.[2]

In March Fanny was writing cautiously that the King was better, that he was walking in the gardens, and though still weak and emaciated 'restored to everything but *strength*'. On March 12 he was able to receive the Address of the Lords and

---

[1] See p. 209, n. 1.

[2] Diary MSS. (Berg), Mar. 1789 (pp. 3735–40).

Commons, in person, on his recovery, and on March 14 the court returned to Windsor. All the town came out to meet the King, recounted Fanny. 'It was a joy amounting to extacy; I could not keep my eyes dry all day long. A scene so reversed!' She had been allowed a visit of a day and a night to her father's apartments in Chelsea, and later in March she was in town again for receptions celebrating the King's recovery.

In June the court set off for a three-months' holiday in Dorset, with a stop at Lyndhurst on the way and plans for a midsummer excursion into Devon—a tour welcomed in the West, with loyal acclamations all along the route.[1] Gloucester House in Weymouth was the abode fixed for the summer, though from there the royal family went on daily excursions or on visits to the great houses round about, including Sherborne Castle. In August they spent ten days at Saltram, described by Fanny as the most magnificent house in the kingdom. As usual, as many personal attendants as possible were housed under the same roof. At Gloucester House Fanny had the attics overlooking the calm waters of the bay; at Saltram, a 'sweet parlour' with a magnificent prospect extending over the sea to Plymouth and Mount-Edgecumbe, though what she liked best here was a wood resembling Norbury Park, with paths slanting down to the water. When the royal family departed for the day, the attendants could spend their time in the wood, in idle strolls along the sands, or on exploratory expeditions of their own— to Mount-Edgecumbe, the docks at Plymouth, or crumbling castles by the sea.

Though Colonel Digby was sometimes in attendance during the summer, Fanny saw little of him, observing that 'his dauntless incaution had now given way to fearful circumspection'.[2] Only later did she learn that from Saltram he had penned Miss Gunning an offer of his hand.

The return to Windsor on September 18 was for Fanny a return to Mrs. Schwellenberg. 'Deadly sunk my heart as I entered her apartment.'[1] Ahead she saw only dreary evenings at picquet, and all chances of any other kind of evening seemed ended when on November 20 Miss Gunning's engagement was announced. Fanny could scarcely believe it (though why not,

---

[1] *Diary*, iv. 289–329. Cf. A.L.S. (Berg) from FB to CB, 26 June 1789.
[2] Diary MSS. (Berg), July, Aug. 1789.

is not clear), and yet felt so little at the news that she could only rejoice in her 'wonderful preservation'. But seeing now in the Colonel 'a man of double-dealing, & selfish artifice', she was very indignant. Her reflections began to savour of the high matter of the tragedies she was soon to take in hand.

He has risked my whole Earthly peace, with a defiance of all mental integrity the most extraordinary to be imagined! He has committed a breach of all moral ties, with every semblance of every virtue![1]

'I don't not like the men neither; not one from them', Mrs. Schwellenberg confided, but this time Fanny seemed to have learned a lesson. 'When may I cease to regret that Duplicity can wear an air so like openness? that Art can assume a character so like Honour? & that selfishness can so fraudulently borrow the appearance of feeling?'[1] 'It was not him I have to thank that he has not broken my Heart! It is Heaven that I have to praise!'[1] For the second time she had been too susceptible to soft artifices, at least soft manners, and too prone to mistake the manner for the man. Later, in her pleas for the 'gentle-mannered' Mr. Hastings, she was, in William Windham's opinion, still ready to make the same mistake. ''Tis amazing', he told her (little realizing how smartly his observations were to come home), ''tis amazing how little unison there may be between *manners* & *character*, & how softly gentle a man may appear without, whose nature within is all ferocity & cruelty.' '*This* is a part of mankind of which you cannot judge,' he told the little Keeper of the Robes, 'of which, indeed, you can scarce form an idea! Well as all *other* classes are known to you—every species of error—folly—vanity—absurdity—you dive into with a perspicuity to which I should instantly submit—but villainy, *masked* villainy is a world unknown to you!' 'Alas!—thought I! —This time twelve month you might have said so! for never has any Mask more completely done its office of Duping!'[2]

Deaf to warnings and curiously apathetic in action, perhaps chiefly for lack of anything else to occupy her, she had seemed to watch the affair objectively, experimentally, as if it were happening to someone else. But this time she had suffered no

[1] Diary MSS. (Berg), pp. 3976–94.
[2] *Diary* iv. 389. The conclusion of Windham's observations and the *double entendre* of Fanny's comment are omitted in the printed diary. See Diary MSS. (Berg), May 1790 (pp. 4134–8).

searing injury and soon found a vent for her outraged feelings in the Confessions and Reflections that she penned to Susan and Mrs. Locke and in the therapeutic blank-verse tragedies that she was presently to resume.

In 1790 Fanny's health and strength failed along with her spirits, and she began seriously to consider ways and means of retiring. No action, however, could be contemplated without Dr. Burney's permission, but this was obtained on a lucky day, May 28, 1790, when, on leave to accompany her father to the Abbey to hear the *Messiah*, she seized the opportunity for a three-hours' conference—'the only conference of that length I have had in four years'.[1] It was an opportune time. The Doctor was all himself ('kind, gay, open'), and fortunately he began to speak of his daughter's seclusion and the discontent of their friends and of certain notables, admirers of *Cecilia*, at never seeing the author. Fanny then confessed her own discontent. She lived like an orphan, she complained, 'lost to all private comfort, dead to all domestic endearment'. She was 'worn with want of rest, and fatigued with laborious watchfulness and attendance'. As she went on, the Doctor's head sank into his chest with dejection and discomfort, but his eyes filled with kind tears as he said:

'I have long . . . been uneasy, though I have not spoken,—but—if you wish to resign—my house, my purse, my arms, shall be open to receive you back!'[1]

This was still the age of patronage, however, and aware of the disappointment that her family must feel at losing their representative at court, she determined in spite of her pride and dislike of solicitation either to win some favours for them or to demonstrate by her failure what her knowledge of the court and her common sense told her—that her powers were void. Out of a sense of family duty, therefore, she forced herself to speak to the Queen about James, his claims on the Admiralty, and his wish for a ship of thirty-two guns or indeed for any employment now that England was at war on the sea. She was also concerned in 1790 with Charles's unsuccessful application for the headmastership of the Charterhouse. In 1791 she helped him

---

[1] *Diary*, iv. 374–400. For Susan's comments on the plans for liberation see Journal-letters (Berg), 1790–1.

complete a memorial 'first designed & sketched by the celebrated Dr. Parr' petitioning the Archbishop of Canterbury to
grant, by his special prerogative, a mandate degree in place of
the normal university degree on which ordination or advancement in the Church seemed in part to depend. The business was
very painful, for the paper must include an explanation of why
such a request was necessary—a review of the old unhappy tale
of the theft of books and the expulsion from Cambridge; in
short, a paragraph 'acknowledging, fully & with contrition,
the ever to be regretted circumstance'. At first when Charles's
scholar-friends, including Dr. Parr, had hit upon the Keeper
of the Robes as a convenient short-cut through the Queen to
the Archbishop, Fanny had represented the impropriety of
such an intervention on the part of one so near the royal
persons, and Charles, 'always facile, good-humoured, & open
to conviction', had agreed. Afterwards, however, as part of her
plan of liberation, she determined to put all to the test by 'a
quiet, but strong solicitation'.

You will not be surprised, when you consider this solution formed
from motives of conscience: that I may really satisfy myself whether
any power is vested in my situation, & its favour, to serve any part
of my family. To ascertain this will contribute highly either to relieve
my *mental* difficulties in pursuing a certain plan should I fail; or to
reconcile my disappointment in relinquishing it, should I succeed.[1]

She promised Charles, therefore, that she would make the
effort.

I did!—I opened the affair,—but surely I will spare our nerves all
round the manner—& the feelings. . . . The next morning I more
explicitly told the brief heads of the unhappy tale,—though I could
not yet explain the particulars,—my voice *would* not give them!—
however, what was necessary to be understood, & made plain that
the interference of the Archbishop was *all or nothing*; the future prospects of a young man already long punished, even to severity, for his
misdemeanour, was said: & I saw I was fully comprehended,—I
believe, too, I awakened some concern & compassion,—but whether
to any effect—I know not. This, however, is certain, I would not go
through such another relation for *any* thing almost, that could accrue
to *myself*.

[1] See Note I, p. 493.

But I am easier & happier in having done it! it seems, in the
present state of my views, a justice due to my family.[1]

The petition, though granted in 1807, was at this time refused. Charles himself, according to Susan, recovered but too
easily from such blows, but the family felt the humiliation
keenly. Dr. Burney 'was obliged to gulp & gulp' before he could
'get the bitter pill down'. And he counselled his son:

Submission & indignation supply hard fare; but we have nothing
else for it. You, my dear lad, have still one revenge in store, wch is to
produce some literary work, wch with diligence & good conduct shall
make your enemies ashamed of their implacability & persecution.[1]

Charles followed this advice with success and prosperity in the
end, though hard work and high living together shortened his
days. He never forgot Fanny's early kindness and in later years
amply repaid all her 'active exertions' on his behalf. The years
at court were strong in invested friendships.

The summer of 1790 proved all petitions on behalf of
Charles and James quite futile, and with these delays it was not
until October that Fanny drafted her resignation and submitted
it for her father's approval. The paper stated simply that she
had found her strength unequal to her duties, but she could not
find the courage to present it until a rapid decline in both
health and strength, whether psychosomatic or not, made the
necessity of the resignation palpable to all.[2] The paper was
submitted in December, but half a year was still to drag on
before she was free.

Meanwhile, other liberating forces were at work, among
them the representations of the Burney friends and connexions,
who began to complain with Mr. Twining that Fanny was now
so seldom seen as to be a rare sight, a *show* like 'the Lincolnshire
ox, or new American bird'.[3] Mrs. Crewe, struck by Fanny's
appearance in the spring of 1790 at Westminster Hall, advised
the Doctor to secure his daughter's release. From Aylsham the
kind-hearted Charlotte, much concerned by all she heard of
her sister's failing health and the strenuousness and fatigues of

---

[1] See Note I, p. 493.   [2] *Diary*, iv. 436–47.
[3] *Diary*, iv. 374.

court service, ventured to write a remonstrance to her father.[1] At the Norfolk assemblies she entered into cabals with Windham, who wished to see what influence a round robin from the Johnson Club might have on Dr. Burney. Charlotte also inquired of the old family retainer James Sleepe, who was staying with her at the time, whether or not he could manage without the little dole that Fanny regularly allowed him from her court salary. As Charlotte had expected from his 'pure, generous, sweet disposition', he insisted that he could manage very well and wrote to Fanny an illiterate but polite and charming letter (still extant) to say so. Many a time the old man had thought as he sat in St. James's Park looking across at the palace windows how glad he would be to give up the money for the pleasure of seeing Fanny again sometimes.[1]

> Heaven free the Encaged
> And appease the Enraged!

became the slogan of a group including Fanny's sisters, who set themselves to caballing in earnest and to good purpose. They consulted on finances (Fanny's future means of support), the possible reaction of Mrs. Burney and the welcome likely to be accorded at Chelsea, the difficulty of persuading such a Tory as their father to address an ungrateful document of resignation to Her Majesty, the propriety and efficacy of such an action could he be brought to take it, the mortifying refusals of petitions on behalf of James and Charles that proved the uselessness of the post to serve the family, and, finally, the possibility of incurring royal displeasure if the real reasons for dissatisfaction were fully stated. The real reason was put succinctly by Susan: the Keeper of the Robes was worn out by and weary of the duties of office.[2]

In the year of waiting Fanny bent her mind again to composition, this time to the series of blank-verse tragedies that she had begun at Kew in October, 1788. On April 4, 1790, after

---

[1] See letters (Barrett) from CBF to FB, 14 Nov. 1790; also 5, 9 July, and 3 Dec. 1791. The sisters wrote caballing letters in the third person, employing codenames for the persons involved. Charlotte was Tatlante; Susan, Bigdumfundus; Windham, Captain Ball or Lysias. Cf. A.L.S. (Berg) from SBP to FB, 12 Mar. 1791: 'The cabal part with Lysias I should have liked immensely'.

[2] A.L.S. (Berg) from CBF to FB, 19 Nov. 1790. Also a sheaf of 13 letters (Berg) from SBP to FB, 4 Apr.–10 July 1791.

parting with Susan at St. James's she turned as a sad resource to the story of Edwy and Elgiva and 'the unconnected speeches, & hints & ideas' that she had jotted down over a year ago.[1] The troubles of the Anglo-Saxon heptarchy were far removed from those of the eighteenth-century court, but a situation sufficiently tragico-sentimental presented itself in the conflict between the youth Edwy, King of the West Saxons, and the monastic reformer St. Dunstan, Abbot of Glastonbury—a story often remembered because of the dramatic scene at the Coronation in 956 when the boy-king, having slipped away from the banqueting hall, was discovered by Dunstan in the company of two women (the younger of whom was by some accounts his wife; by others, his paramour) and hustled by the Saint back to the council-room. The incident admits of many readings, but, as the verbal echoes and the interpretation of Dunstan's character indicate, Fanny followed Hume's version (in the pertinent pages of his *History of England*), though not without some changes in the interests of dramatic motivation, unity, and effect. The edict of excommunication was moved ahead to account for Edwy's consent to the divorce, and Aldhelm (in Hume, St. Dunstan's uncle and tutor) here figures as an adviser to the young king. He is 'that sage Experience', that 'Heart benign', the prudent monitor or guardian who in Fanny Burney's works so often points the moral. He anatomizes Edwy as follows:

> Had years matur'd him ere he reach'd the Throne
> His virtues might have rank'd him first of kings.
> Form'd mildly to command, or nobly yield,
> Fair his intent, his very wishes upright,
> His soul the genuine seat of native honour;
> But of a sensibility so ardent
> His spirit impetuous owns no curb but feeling:
> Reason it leaves behind, impell'd by impulse;
> 'Tis fiery, ev'n to fury, if incens'd,
> 'Tis tortur'd ev'n to madness, if unhappy.[2]

[1] *Diary*, iv. 362, 365, 413, and Diary MSS. (Berg), pp. 4072-192.

[2] 'Edwy and Elgiva', beautifully transcribed on about 145 folios (6 × 4 in.) and sewn together in five separate packets or acts, is preserved in the Berg Collection, the NYPL. Here also are two drafts of a prologue, an early version of parts of the story written in rhyme, and about 50 scraps with corrections in General d'Arblay's hand. A manuscript in his hand (in Emmanuel College Library, Cambridge University) has been edited by Miriam J. Benkovitz, *Edwy and Elgiva* (1957).

Aldhelm presents Edwy's case to the churchmen and pleads the king's need of 'bosom comfort' and 'heart-felt sympathy'. The loss of 'sweet domestic peace' is no less deplored than loss of life itself. Domestic woe, the distraction of Edwy, and the tender and pathetic sorrows of Elgiva eclipse the affairs of Church and State and haunt the action.

In August Fanny recorded she had completed and copied the work.

What species of a composition it may prove she is very unable to tell; she only knows it was an almost spontaneous work, and soothed the melancholy of imagination for a while. . . . Nevertheless, whether well or ill, she is pleased to have done something at last, she had so long lived in all ways as nothing.[1]

Scarcely was this locked away in a strong-box for future correction 'when imagination seized upon another subject for another tragedy'.[1] The second composition, entitled 'Hubert De Vere, A Pastoral Tragedy', though cast in dialogue, had greater affinity to a romantic tale than to a play.[2] Fanny later described it as 'a tale in dialogue' or, as in the sub-title of a revised version, 'A Dramatic Tale'. In all probability it was suggested by some narrative poem like Falconer's *Shipwreck*, which Fanny admired only too much. The scene opens on a heath where a morose hero appears with 'arms folded, his Eyes fixed on the Earth'. He is brooding over 'wrongs and woes', 'Unheard of Wrongs! unutterable woes!' The trouble seems to be that Geralda, 'sunk in the low abyss of Avarice and Vanity', has wedded

> the potent Glanville,
> The Lord of Wealth, as Hubert is of Honour.

The villain of the piece, a former traitor, De Mowbray, somewhat darkly incites a shepherd's daughter, Cerulia, to greet De Vere with 'smiles and blandishments'. Even without such

---

[1] See p. 217, n. 1.

[2] Also in the Berg Collection. The work survives in two drafts: the earlier, entitled 'Hubert De Vere, A Pastoral Tragedy in Five Acts', comprises 126 pages ($9\frac{1}{2} \times 7\frac{1}{4}$ in.), is much corrected (black ink over brown), and much pinned and pasted over with revisions. The second draft (110 pp., $6\frac{1}{2} \times 7\frac{1}{4}$ in.) is entitled 'A Dramatic Tale in Five Parts'.

encouragement this artless maid has been trailing De Vere over the moors. Always he can see

> Between the Trees, beside some bush, or near
> Some stream meandering wild, her gentle Form:
> This delicate Maid would court the assailing storm
> Though trembling, tottering from the rude, bleak blast—

to cross his path. To cut much wandering matter short, De Vere has no sooner in an unguarded moment offered Cerulia the remnant of his heart, when ('Flash, Lightnings, Flash!') Geralda darts forward. Glanville is now dead, and it presently appears that she had married him not out of avarice and vanity but to keep him from betraying her uncle, De Mowbray. 'Conjunction dire!' Geralda was not false, and there is now nothing for Cerulia the village maid but to die, and she dies, hoping she has injured none, and pardoning all. Act V is filled with grim portents of death, Gothic terrors, madness, harrowing farewells, and finally De Mowbray's intimation that he, her murderer, is her father. '*The Village Maids group weeping around: & the curtain drops to the sound of the Church Death Bell.*'

The dramatic action of a third piece, 'The Siege of Pevensey',[1] hinges on various conflicts between Love and Honour or between Private and Public Duty during the course of military manœuvres about the citadel of Pevensey in 1088. The requirement that 'a good Moral' be 'deduc'd from the whole' is amply fulfilled in situations calling forth sentiments on paternal and filial duty. When the Earl of Chester decides that his daughter Adela must go to a nunnery, she is content to

> pass her Days in soft remembrance
> Of all his wondrous patience, sweetness,
> His mild indulgence to her early errours,
> His noble precepts for her rules of life.

The swollen style and the easy solution of the melodramatic dilemmas discourage any serious consideration of the piece as a tragedy; because of its recurrent theme and ostensible purpose it may perhaps best be described as a dissertation on filial piety.

---

[1] In 120 folios (6¼ × 4 in.), written very clearly and legibly on both sides, sewn in 5 packets or acts, the possession of the Berg Collection, the NYPL. Acts III, IV, and V are divided into 16 scenes each; Acts I and II, into 12 and 14, respectively. The manuscript has the appearance of a final draft.

In February and March of 1791 Fanny was very ill. Even in May she was still 'very unwell, low, faint, and feeble'. The Queen had written to Germany for a replacement, and yet there were dreary months of waiting.

So melancholy indeed was the state of my mind, from the weakness of my frame, that I was never alone but to form scenes of 'foreign woe', when my own disturbance did not occupy me wholly. I began —almost whether I would or not—another tragedy! The other three all unfinished! not one read! and one of them, indeed, only generally sketched as to plan and character. . . . The power of composition has to me indeed proved a solace, a blessing! When incapable of all else, that, unsolicited, unthought of, has presented itself to my solitary leisure, and beguiled me of myself, though it has not of late regaled me with gayer associates.[1]

'Elberta', evidently begun about this time, was not carried beyond preliminary jottings including a list of *dramatis personae*, short character-sketches, and scraps of dialogue. The evolution of a she-tragedy may be seen in the fragments:

A Female is mentioned, who wild & unknown is seen roaming about —no one is informed whence she comes—woe is in her voice, terror in her aspect—she never weeps, yet frequently wails. . . . Her fierce harangues . . . her gentle supplication to shadows. . . . She asks how long the children may live without nourishment.[2]

No scrap among the 303 extant memoranda[2] promises any brighter end than gnawing famine, madness, and death, but unfortunately we are spared the finished tale. One has the uneasy impression that Fanny herself was not escaping too soon.

  Though the tragic dramas had been useful psychologically in providing occupational and emotional outlets for the dreary years 1789–91, Fanny's experiments in blank verse,[3] scarcely to be considered as poetry, had a deplorable effect on her prose style. She yielded to a wild rhetoric or sentimental rant that

---

[1] *Diary*, iv. 478–9 (June 1791).

[2] In the Berg Collection, the NYPL.

[3] For observations on Fanny's metrics see E. S. Shuckburgh, 'Madame d'Arblay', *Macmillan's Magazine*, lxi (Feb. 1890), 291–8. As observed here, many of Fanny's verses run to eleven or twelve syllables. Many will not yield to scansion. 'Choriambics, eh? . . . Possibly, of course; but treat them as ionics a minore with an anacrusis, and see if they don't go better?' (Gissing, *New Grub Street*, x.)

she seemed to think suited the themes. This was, after all, the verge of the romantic age.

Three works which I have now in hand seize me capriciously; but I never reprove them; I give the play into their own direction, & am sufficiently thankful, in this wearing waste of existence, for being so seized at all.[1]

The dramas, in short, gave scope to a flamboyant rhetoric, the empty swollen manner that she was henceforth to use on great occasions. The peculiarly hollow, half-romantic, half-sentimental effect of *The Emigrant French Clergy* (1793) and *The Memoirs of Dr. Burney* (1832) owe not a little, one may suspect, to the grand manner and the wild speeches of her blank-verse heroes. One may be thankful that Fanny reserved her *grand style* for special occasions and works, that her informal letters were considered unworthy of it, that her epistolary style, except when highly sentimental matter was in hand, remained unchanged, and that the family letters for some forty years to come were written in her *natural* style—in the realistic, humorous, subacidic, characteristically Burneyan idiom.[2]

Another feverish illness of February and March subsided into languor and weakness.

And—O picquet!—life hardly hangs on earth during its compulsion, in these months succeeding months, and years creeping, crawling, after years.[3]

Even yet the Queen counted on a recovery that would annul the resignation, offered a holiday in the country, and when this was refused sometimes showed displeasure.[4] From Mickleham Susan exhorted Fanny to '*steady, cold persevering firmness*'; the alternative was the '*eternal sacrifice* of what remains of Health & of life—of comfort, & of Friends'.[5] Dr. Burney felt that he should soon reach the stature of Agamemnon, having sacrificed a daughter ('you, my Iphigenia') to the state.[6]

[1] Diary MSS. (Berg), May 1791 (pp. 4272–3).
[2] I am grateful to the University of Toronto Press for permission to use parts of my article, 'Fanny Burney: Playwright', *UTQ*, xix (Jan. 1950), 170–89.
[3] *Diary*, iv. 469–91.
[4] Diary MSS. (Berg), pp. 4263–70; A.L.S. (Berg) from FB to CB, 27 Dec. 1790.
[5] See p. 216, n. 2.
[6] A.L.S. (Osborn) from CB to FB, 5 July 1791.

To cut much like matter short, after the royal birthday cele-
brations of the spring, Miss Burney was at length released

After having lived in the service of

HER MAJESTY

FIVE YEARS

with

TEN DAYS

From July 17, 1786
to July 7, 1791.

She was given a pension of £100 per annum.

IX

A SURREY IDYLL

(1792–1795)

Ah! if peace would come without,
what could equal my peace within?
Diary, v. 222

FOR the remainder of July, 1791, Fanny Burney remained quietly recuperating in her father's apartments at Chelsea. 'Poor Fan is too much fagged to be other than feeble', the Doctor observed.[1] On August 1, she set off with Mrs. Ord in her coach-and-four on a health-seeking, sight-seeing excursion through south-west England. A diary of about thirty pages records their leisurely progress through Farnham, Winchester, Salisbury, and Dorchester to Sidmouth, where they stopped for a week 'all devoted to rest and sea-air'. On August 16 they continued through Exeter, Bridgwater, Glastonbury, Wells, and on to Bath, where they remained for three weeks. Bath now looked, Fanny said, 'a city of palaces, a town of hills, and a hill of towns'. She thought of Mrs. Thrale and sighed over the 'breach with a friend once so loved'.[2]

There was in Bath in this year, however, an interesting group —the Dowager Lady Spencer, her daughters Lady Duncannon and the Duchess of Devonshire, Lady Elizabeth Foster, and *la petite Caroline*, introduced as a little French orphan but believed to be, as Fanny's brother would have put it, 'a little orphan between the Duke and Lady Elizabeth'.[2] On visits of former times to Mrs. Delany Fanny had met Lady Spencer, who now called upon her and introduced her to the Duchess, who also called. Fanny was delighted to return the visits and paid little attention to Mrs. Ord, who bristled and stiffened at the prospect of consorting with such Whigs, to say nothing of the Lady Elizabeth Foster, whose allurements, Gibbon had said,

---

[1] A.L.S. (Osborn) from CB to CB, Jr., 1791; A.L.S. (BM) to Arthur Young, 16 Feb. 1791. Cf. A.L. (Berg) from SBP to CBF, 18 Sept. 1792.
[2] *Diary*, v. 1–50; Diary MSS. (Berg), pp. 4399–420; A.L. (Berg) from FB to CB, 13 Aug. 1791.

could 'beckon the Lord Chancellor from his woolsack'.[1] She was, indeed, alluring, but in spite of all the 'Hervey talents' Fanny would not be won; '_la petite Caroline_ was always in the way'.[1]

Mrs. Ord was dismayed with this high acquaintance among the Whig aristocracy, friends of the Prince Regent, whose private lives, she thought, could so little bear examination. A comparison between the Duchess of Devonshire's accounts of the mad king and those Fanny wrote, or between _The Sylph_[2] and _Cecilia_, will readily illustrate many of the moral and political conflicts of the eighteenth century and contrasts in the attitudes of the upper and middle classes. Though Fanny insisted on speaking loyally and gratefully of the court, the Duchess could allow for her views. Unlike Mrs. Ord, Fanny was also ready to make concessions. She would never, she said, make over into Mrs. Ord's custody and management her opinion of the world. 'She thinks the worst, and judges the most severely, of all mankind, of any person I have ever known.' The time was nearing when Mrs. Ord was to apply this prejudiced rigour of judgement to Fanny herself.

With this holiday Fanny's health improved. On September 10 the travellers left Bath for Dunstan Park to visit Mrs. Delany's niece, Mary Ann Port, now Mrs. Benjamin Waddington. Later they visited Mrs. Montagu, but at Sandleford Fanny parted from Mrs. Ord and went on to Norbury Park and to Mickleham, remaining with Susan for about a month after the birth of her third child, William.

By October 14 Fanny was happily at work in her father's study at Chelsea. 'The day is never long enough, and I could employ two pens almost incessantly, in merely scribbling what will not be repressed.'[1] She was occupied with the revisions of a sentimental poem, 'Willy', a story about two lost children rescued by a dog.[3] The narrative, composed at court in 1786,

[1] See p. 223, n. 2.

[2] For 'Georgiana, Duchess of Devonshire's Diary', see appendix iii, Walter S. Sichel, _Sheridan_ (2 vols., 1909), ii. 399–426. _The Sylph_ (2 vols., 1779) was the work that Lowndes once advertised along with _Evelina_ in order to give the impression that Fanny Burney was the author.

[3] The ballad survives in at least two manuscripts: (_a_) a French translation by M. d'Arblay preserved in a commonplace-book, 1793–7, the possession of Yale University Library; and (_b_) the same translation as meticulously transcribed in a little _cahier_ (Berg).

was intended to furnish William Locke with a subject for a drawing that he had promised her, and, as Susan knew, the poem had been read with tearful appreciation at Norbury Park. For the rest Fanny was revising the tragedies. Her present happy state, she affirmed, would never have suggested such 'tales of woe'; 'but, having only to connect, combine, contract, and finish, I will not leave them undone'.[1] She scribbled on, therefore, easing her mind and heart of the last of lurking aches, disappointments, and hardships—and all this was a prelude to the better days in store.

The first scenes of a drama in which she was to play a part as romantic as any she had devised for her heroines had already startled all Europe with its violence and alarums. Though she did not yet know it, the French Revolution, which was to change so many lives, was already shaping for her a fair but troubled fate.

It was not Fanny Burney's policy to write about politics—a sphere allotted to men by the plan of creation and the advice of the courtesy-book—but allusions and stray remarks in the diaries of 1789–90 indicate that she knew well enough what was in store for monarchies. Though her Court Journal may be taken as a loyal Tory testimonial of devotion to King and Constitution, she at one time suggested to Horace Walpole (who had helped in difficulties over the disposal of Columb's poor little effects and savings) that 'if such was our chance of *justice* with *law*, we must agree never to relate this little history to the democrats abroad, lest we should all be brought forward to illustrate the necessity of universal Reform, and the National Assembly should echo with all our names!'[2] All his life Dr. Burney had been 'loyal to such excellent sovereigns', and, as he said, 'fighting & scolding with Wickites, Foxites—Democrats—revolutionists—Jacobins—& anarchists'.[3] With *Reflections on the French Revolution* of 1790 Burke had recovered his old place in the Burneyan affections. Fanny liked to hear his vehement denunciations of proceedings in France: 'This it is that has made ME an abettor and supporter of Kings!'[4]

The fall of the French Monarchy, the flight of Lafayette, of

[1] See p. 223, n. 2. [2] *Diary*, iv. 406–7, 416–27, 493–5.
[3] A.L. (Berg) from CB to FB, 4 Aug. 1796.
[4] *Diary*, v. 90–98, 115–34.

the Constitutionalists, and of the non-juring priests, the September Massacres, and 'general alarm for the political safety of all manner of people' corroded the year 1792. Though Fanny well knew that some of the widening effects of the Revolution had reached Britain, she did not dream that out of these events a destiny was being wrought for her, nor had she yet learned of their impact on quiet Mickleham. Susan was the harbinger of the new future.

Mickleham, September 1792.
We shall shortly, I believe, have a little colony of unfortunate . . . French noblesse in our neighbourhood. Sunday evening Ravely informed Mr. Locke that two or three families had joined to take Jenkinson's house, Juniper Hall, and that another family had taken a small house at Westhumble, which the people very reluctantly let, upon the Christian-like supposition that, being nothing but French papishes, they would never pay.[1]

Susan went on to tell about one of the refugees, Madame de Broglie, who had come over 'in an open boat, with a son younger than my Norbury, and was fourteen hours at sea'. Susan longed to offer her house and had been 'much gratified by finding Mr. Locke immediately determined to visit them; his taking this step will secure them the civilities, at least, of the other neighbours'. Susan knew how they were likely to be treated on John Bull's Island.

At Jenkinson's are—la Marquise de la Châtre, whose husband is with the emigrants; her son; M. de Narbonne, lately Ministre de la Guerre; M. de Montmorency; Charles or Theodore Lameth; Jaucourt; and one or two more . . . persecuted persons.[1]

The spring and summer of 1792 Fanny spent in rounds of visits—to Susan at Mickleham, Mrs. Locke at Norbury Park, Mrs. Crewe at Hampstead, and to Esther at Titchfield Street, where she spent all July. In August she was nurse to her stepmother, then dangerously ill. On September 24 she set off with Esther and her daughter to Halstead on a fortnight's visit to one of the Worcester Burneys who was married to the Reverend John Hawkins.[2] The clergyman's 'prosing style of conversation' had scarcely prepared Fanny for the animation of the pamph-

[1] See p. 225, n. 4.　　　　[2] Diary MSS. (Berg), pp. 4590–609.

lets that he was writing against Burke's antagonists, Tom Paine and other democrats.

It is impossible to be under the roof of an English clergyman and to witness his powers of making leisure useful, elegant, and happy, without continual internal reference to the miserable contrast of the unhappy clergy of France.[1]

She noted that the day's papers teemed 'with the promise of great and decisive victories to the arms of the Duke of Brunswick'; Fanny hardly wished for the success of the combined forces, so much did she 'tremble for the dastardly revenge menaced to the most injured King of France and his family'.

On October 5 she accepted Arthur Young's invitation to Bradfield Hall, where she found her younger sister Sarah 'living upon French politics and with French fugitives' and 'perfectly satisfied with foreign forage'. Young was now

a severe penitent of his democratic principles, and has lost even all pity for the *Constituant Révolutionnaires*, who had 'taken him in' by their doctrines, but cured him by their practice, and who 'ought better to have known what they were about before they presumed to enter into action'.

Even the Duc de Liancourt, who was then in a small house at Bury, merited, he said, all the personal misfortunes that had befallen him.[1]

But Young, having some real obligation to the Duke, waived political differences and invited him to dinner, and Fanny had an opportunity to meet the handsome, haughty, and distinguished nobleman. 'His manners are such as only admit of comparison with what we have read, not what we have seen; for he has all the air of a man who would wish to lord over men, but to cast himself at the feet of women.' Presently speaking about *Cecilia*, he managed to draw from Fanny more elucidations than even Sarah had ever been privileged to hear. He inquired very particularly about M. de Narbonne and the Juniper colony and said that he wished to meet M. d'Arblay, 'who was a friend and favourite of his eldest son'. Now Fanny had heard the name d'Arblay, and she had learned from the Duke that the charm of the dispossessed Frenchmen outlasted their troubles and could make one forget political biases and prejudices.

[1] See p. 225, n. 4.

The year closed with visits in Norfolk. On October 8 she went to Aylsham to visit her sister Charlotte Francis, who on October 2 had given birth to a son. Urged by Charlotte she went on October 18 to Thornham with plans for a fortnight with Maria Rishton, who was reputedly as 'diverting and comic' as ever. Fanny had scarcely arrived when she learned from a messenger following hard at her heels that her brother-in-law, Clement Francis, had been fatally stricken with apoplexy. She began the return journey at once—at five in the afternoon. Soon it was raining and pitch dark. There was 'not a step of turnpike road' between Thornham and Aylsham, but only rough cross-roads through fields. It was three in the morning before she arrived.

Nothing but eagerness to get to poor Charlotte . . . could have given me courage to proceed, alone, & at such a season—but except when the Horses were left for opening Gates, or when an unseen Hillock mounted the carriage suddenly, I had not even a thought upon the subject.[1]

She found Charlotte with a sixteen-day-old baby in her arms, still very weak and ill, and her husband dead. Fanny remained in Aylsham until December, when the Francis family (Charlotte and her three children) moved to London.[1]

Meanwhile Susan was writing about the charm and brilliance of the society at Juniper Hall.[2] Sometimes she and the Major spent whole days there, and the *émigrés* in turn often came to their house and to Norbury Park. Nothing could be more interesting than the comments of the exiles on French affairs, nothing more touching than their despair and destitution. A friend of M. de Narbonne had now arrived, a M. d'Arblay. He was Adjutant-General to Lafayette, Susan explained, 'the first in military rank of those who accompanied that general when he so unfortunately fell into the hands of the Prussians; but, not having been one of the *Assemblée Constituante*, he was allowed, with four others, to proceed into Holland, and there M. de Narbonne wrote to him'. Susan was prepared to like any loyal follower of the hero Lafayette. She was pleased at the coming

---

[1] A.L.S. (Berg) from FB to EBB, 20 Oct. 1792; A.L.S. (Berg) to CB, 10 Oct. 1792; A.L. (Berg) to Mary Port Waddington, 11 Dec. 1792.
[2] *Diary*, v. 136–210.

of the Adjutant-General and 'more and more pleased with himself every moment that passed'. M. d'Arblay

seems to me a true *militaire, franc et loyal*—open as the day—warmly affectionate to his friends—intelligent, ready, and amusing in conversation, with a great share of *gaieté de cœur*, and, at the same time, of *naïveté* and *bonne foi*.[1]

Susan listened sympathetically to accounts of his misfortunes. He was the officer on guard at the Tuileries on the night the king escaped to Varennes, and had run 'great risk of being denounced, and perhaps massacred, though he had been kept in the most perfect ignorance of the King's intention'. He had been imprisoned with Lafayette at Nivelle, had escaped with his life, but he had lost his fortune and his income. '*Et me voilà, madame, réduit à rien, hormis un peu d'argent comptant, et encore très peu.*'[1]

Meanwhile in London Fanny noted the stiffening of political feeling against the Constitutionalists. They 'are now reviled as authors and originators of all the misfortunes of France',[1] she wrote to Susan, who in return indited charmed letters about the Juniper colony. Mrs. Locke's invitations became more urgent. 'It is quite out of my power', Fanny replied, 'to leave town before the birthday, as I must then present myself at the Queen's house.'

Your French colonies are truly attractive—I am sure they must be so to have caught me, so substantially, fundamentally, the foe of all their proceedings while in power. But the Duc de Liancourt taught me how little we can resist distress, even when self-incurred.[1]

After the Queen's birthday in January Fanny at last came to Norbury Park. And now, since she was within reach of her confidantes, there was no occasion for the letters that might otherwise have given a detailed account of her first meetings with the handsome and accomplished Frenchman who soon came to love her devotedly and idyllically and whom she loved no less devotedly and idyllically to the end of their days. There were here no jealous watchers or enemies of love, but since the handsome lover was penniless and also a Frenchman, a Roman Catholic, and a *Constituent*, there were impediments enough to marriage, and before that came about there was much to be

---

[1] See p. 228, n. 2.

done. As Dr. Burney was later to remark, the charming and distinguished chevalier was 'a mere soldier of fortune, under great disadvantages'.[1] Successive orders confiscating the property of emigrants were to keep him forever impoverished —to begin with, that decree of the Girondists in November, 1792, which classified as *émigrés* all those who had left France in July of that year and did not venture to return. Fanny knew that M. d'Arblay's hopes for employment in England would prove a 'cruel delusion'.[2]

These prospects did not seem more hopeful when in January (1793), with the execution of the 'Fils de St. Louis', Pitt prepared for war with France, sent the French agent out of London, and stood ready to deport emigrants like Talleyrand, Narbonne, or Madame de Staël, who were likely to interest themselves in politics.

Meanwhile Fanny's letters to her father were filled with the sufferings and the *agrémens* of the French colony. Madame de Staël is 'one of the first women I have ever met with for abilities and extraordinary intellect'. M. de Talleyrand 'is a man of admirable conversation, quick, terse, *fin*, and yet deep, to the extreme of those four words'. There were more nonpareils. The Comte de Narbonne and M. d'Arblay are 'two of the most accomplished and elegant men I ever saw'. M. d'Arblay 'for openness, probity, intellectual knowledge, and unhackneyed manners' is one of the 'most delightful characters' she has ever met.[1] On February 29 she was still at Mickleham and, feeling her father's disapproval, slightly on the defensive:

M. d'Arblay is one of the most singularly interesting characters that can ever have been formed. He has a sincerity, a frankness, an ingenuous openness of nature, that I had been unjust enough to think could not belong to a Frenchman. With all this, which is his military portion, he is passionately fond of literature, a most delicate critic in his own language, well versed in both Italian and German, and a very elegant poet. He has just undertaken to become my French master for pronunciation, and he gives me long daily lessons in reading.[1]

Mrs. Grundy, meanwhile, had heard burning stories about Madame de Staël and her pursuit of M. de Narbonne. On

[1] See p. 228, n. 2.
[2] Diary MSS. (Berg), suppressed parts (May 1793, pp. 4826–9).

February 22 Mr. Hutton wrote directly to Fanny about 'a Report given out that she [Fanny] was in the habit of Intimacy and much seeing the blasted character Md. de Staël Daughter of Necker who is in Repute of wicked Democratic Esteem, and ran adulterously after a Mr de Narbonne'.[1] Mr. Hutton, the Burkes, Mrs. Ord, and others had repeated all this to the Doctor, who lost no time in warning his daughters.

If you are not absolutely in the house of Madame de Staël when this arrives, it would perhaps be possible for you to waive the visit to her, by a compromise, of having something to do for Susy, and so make the addendum to your stay under her roof.[2]

Fanny, 'hurt and astonished at the acrimony of malice', tried to contradict the report as 'a gross calumny'. Yet, according to the dicta of the time, a woman's virtue is not in her morals but in her reputation,[3] and in order to avoid the visit she went off in May for a fortnight's stay at the 'once most dear old spot' Chessington. There she might escape insistent and embarrassing invitations and consider another matter much nearer her heart.

The climate of Chelsea was far less favourable to *émigrés* than Mickleham and Norbury Park had been. Fanny could foresee impediments '& a clamour against a *French* man almost overwhelming!' 'Mrs. Ord has been here this moment, so cruelly praying the *Exile of All alike*, that I warmly combatted her, with *the worth of Those I knew*: before la Dana [Mrs. Burney] too,—who, still more barbarously to *me*, was pleased to *beg*, in a whining tone of moderation, That the *Priests* might be exempt, though none other!'[4] Fanny was not very 'placid or composed', therefore, when in the presence of her father or mother French notes were delivered by the servants and French callers announced. There was that '*cart-day*' when Molly came into the Doctor's study carrying a rosebush and a note. Fortunately Fanny concluded erroneously that *le joli rosièr* was from Mrs. Locke and luckily said so before she learned the more romantic

---

[1] A.L.S. (Berg) from James Hutton to CB, 21 Feb. 1793; A.L.S. (Osborn) to FB, 22 Feb. 1793.

[2] See p. 228, n. 2.

[3] The standard dictum of the courtesy-books; but see *Diary*, v. 181–4, and the remark, *Diary*, v. 197: 'I wish the world would take care of itself, and less of its neighbours. I should have been very safe, I trust, without such flights, and distances, and breaches.'

[4] Four letters (Berg) from FB to SBP, 4, 5–9, 11, 14 Apr. 1793.

truth. The Doctor then asked if the note was in Mrs. Locke's hand. Fanny felt 'almost ready to die' but manfully acknowledged that it was a *Thème*, she believed, from M. d'Arblay. 'How fortunate no one else was present! My dear guileless Father alone could so soon have been satisfied, my extreme emotion considered, which made me stammer every word.'[1] *Ce joli rosier* became the subject of her next theme in French. '*C'est si bel si élégant, d'un parfum si charmant, d'un air si riant — que je ne puis rien faire que le regarder, l'admirer.*'[2]

M. d'Arblay's visits to Chelsea provided the most charming chapters Fanny's diary had yet produced in the comedy of manners.[3] Even though the action concerned her so nearly, the delicate play of her observation was humorously objective. The uneasy actors and their uncomfortable prejudices are brought deftly to life and set concretely in the eighteenth-century household.

The time had come, as she thought, when she ought to introduce her chevalier to her father. She ventured to ask him, therefore, if M. d'Arblay might call in the morning or in the evening.

My dear Father evidently disliked both!—the *Constitutionel* is cruelly in the way! He is all aristocratic!—& I am sure there is not fair play to his mind for these instances of constitutional Individual merit!

Finally the Doctor chose the evening—though only by the grudging remark that 'on Friday he should be out'. One evening, then, after the lovers had dined with the Lockes at Portland Place and the Doctor's carriage had arrived for Fanny, and Oliver, the coachman, had handed her in and drawn up the steps, M. d'Arblay, oblivious of English punctilio, leapt over them, got into the coach, and seated himself opposite Fanny. 'I believe Oliver's surprise was equal to my queerness!'

'Where is he to go, ma'am?' cried he.
'To Chelsea,' I answered. And the door was shut—& off we drove.

Fanny had indeed wished to introduce her chevalier but had not counted on 'the wonderful step' of carrying him to Chelsea

---

[1] See p. 231, n. 4.   [2] A.L. (Berg) from FB to M. d'A, 2 Apr. 1793.
[3] See a manuscript (Berg) of 27 folios (55 pp.), dated 8–19 Apr., 3–9 May 1793, separated from the Diary MSS. and entitled 'Concerning her Courtship'.

herself! She was thinking of her father and mother, the Queen,
Mrs. Ord, the servants, and a 'thousand things endless to name!'
The General thought he might at least be allowed to speak.

'Mais! mais!' he cried, a little impatiently, 'laissez-moi parler!
laissez — permettez —'

'Non! non! non! non!' I kept crying—but, for all that he dropt
on one knee—which I was fain to pretend not to observe—& held
up his Hands folded, & went on—

I begged him to say no more then quite fervently—

'Mais — enfin,' cried he, '*pourquoi? pourquoi* faut-il que je me taire
toujours?'

'O mon Dieu!' cried I, 'pour tant de raisons!'—

The *militaire* could ascribe this only to *aversion* on her part and
flung himself back in the coach. Fanny attempted no reply, but
when she saw him 'bending from his little Boudoir', she began
to talk about her father, 'his goodness, & sweetness, & character, & disposition'. The chevalier had expected nothing less
than this of the *grandpère de Cecilia*. He could assume the same
from the Doctor's own writings.

Fanny saw that Sam was as much astonished to see a gentleman leap out of the carriage, as Oliver had been to see him leap
in. A fine figure of a man at that! She found only Sarah in the
parlour, but had the pleasure of finding that M. d'Arblay was
expected, not, it is true, with her, but that passed off unre-
marked. Mrs. Burney had retired with a headache. The Doctor
too was in the bedroom; he seemed languid, looked uncomfortable, but soon appeared. 'The meeting was of cold civility
on the part of my Father,—of the most agitated fervour on
that of M. d'Arblay.' The Frenchman's efforts, however, were
not without effect. Sarah afterwards rapturously sang his
praises. Even Fanny had never seen him to better advantage.
She saw that everything about him pleased the Doctor—'his
style, his manner, his appearance, his gaiety, & his gentleness'—
and yet nothing could make the Doctor forget his being *constitu-
tionnel*—or 'induce him to utter one word in his favour! I should
be else too happy!'

After other visits M. d'Arblay finally requested in a 'public note'
that he might come to tea. 'My father prepared himself drily, &
sans commentaire; my mother was taciturn, but oddly smiling, ...
Sarah flightily delighted.' The guest entered 'early, light, gay,

& palpably in inward spirits'. The Doctor was unlike himself,
'full of reserve & thought', but, said his daughter, 'never insensible to such exertions, was soon brought round to appear more
like himself; &, in a short time, his amiable nature took the
reins from his fears & his prejudices, & they entered into
literary discussions with all the animation & interest of old
friends'. The Doctor brought out his fine editions of Ariosto,
Dante, Petrarch, and Tasso; and when these were appreciated,
out came the select prints, and finally the collection of French
classics. There followed then, Fanny said, 'disquisitions, interro-
gatories, anecdotes, & literary contentions, of the gayest & most
entertaining nature'. 'Though not a word passed between us,'
Fanny reported, 'I received, by every opportunity, *des regards si
touchans, si heureux!*'[1]

When alone the exile relapsed into gloomy reverie, looked
worn, dejected, wretched, and fell to writing elaborate defences
of Lafayette or Talleyrand and others whom he thought unjustly maligned or treated. This led to confession of his faults:
'*Je suis — de mon naturel — plus sensible aux maux de la vie, qu'à ses
plaisirs.*' '*Si — si nous espérons à passer la vie ensemble — il faut vous
avouer tous mes défauts.*' 'I could say nothing to this, you will
believe', said Fanny; 'and he hid his own Face upon my Glove
while he spoke it, & for some minutes afterwards—& then
began a fair & full confession of his defects: "*Je suis brusque
quelquefois. Oh! d'une brusquerie!*"' He 'bent over the Table to
kiss the tip of my little Finger — "*Jusqu'à demain — matin.*"'[1]

Thus April passed away; May was concerned with ways and
means. Marriage required an income; and the combined
financial assets of M. d'Arblay and Fanny Burney amounted
to £120 per annum. This sum had its source in a pension of
£100, which the Queen granted yearly to the former Keeper
of the Robes, and in an annuity of £20 per annum arising from
the invested revenue from *Cecilia*. Indeed all depended on *cette
pension*. In pessimistic moments Fanny feared that it might be
withdrawn; at other times she was more hopeful. Before she had
agreed to an engagement, she had paved the way for it by
speaking about M. d'Arblay's story, situation, and character
to 'a person in the court and in high favour'. 'I should cease to
think Honour & Integrity existed if ever I lost my opinion of

[1] See p. 232, n. 3.

PLATE III

GENERAL D'ARBLAY *at the age of sixty-four*
by Carle and Horace Vernet

their residence in M. d'Arblay',[1] she asserted, knowing that her words would be repeated. She thought it wiser to have this report reach the Queen indirectly than to raise an issue that might force an unfriendly reaction. She had not lived five years at court without learning some diplomacy and she relied on her strong assertion making its impression.

In his study at Chelsea Dr. Burney mused unhappily about anarchy, rebels, democrats, republicans, detestable fellows like Fox, Horne Tooke, or Erskine, and now in Mickleham his two daughters were walking hand-in-glove through the meadows with French Constitutionalists, who more than the Jacobins themselves, he believed, had undermined the French monarchy. He thought of the impression Fanny had formerly made not only at court but on celebrities like Dr. Johnson, Sir Joshua Reynolds, Burke, and Windham, on people like Jacob Bryant, Mrs. Crewe, Mrs. Ord, and countless others, who, in spite of the aberrations they had sometimes allowed themselves, stood firm for Church, State, 'and our excellent Constitution'. How would they now receive Fanny, Madame d'Arblay? Gone were the days when he had proudly taken 'Fan in his hand' and visited Bolt Court, Strawberry Hill, Hampstead, and Farnham, or when he could call on her at St. James's Palace. He remembered Fanny's former triumphs. Now he must see her buried in obscurity, ignored, slighted, and perhaps spoken of contemptuously. Such must have been some of the thoughts that crossed his mind as he penned his objections to the Lockes: 'All the self-denying virtues of Epictetus will not keep off indigence in a state of society without the assistance of patrimony, profession, or possessions on one side or the other ... the alliance w^d probably shut my daughter out of the society in wch she has hitherto been so earnestly sought.'[2] Fanny herself was not ignorant of the cost: 'How the World will blame me at first, I well know.'[3]

In her 'woman's wise' she listened to the arguments pro and con, selecting those that coincided with her own and discarding others, even those of her father. 'Should you put your notion in practice, & discover your way to this retired spot,' she wrote

[1] Diary MSS. (Berg), p. 4411.
[2] A.L.S. (Berg) from William Locke to CB, 3 July 1793; and the reply, Diary MSS. (Berg), pp. 4850–2. [3] See p. 231, n. 4.

to M. d'Arblay from Chessington in May, 'you will find a dilapidated old Dwelling, two worthy, but most uncultivated Inhabitants, &—*une personne*—who leaves it to your own imagination to decide whether or not she shall be glad to see you.'[1] At Chessington there was great curiosity, with a corresponding activity in culinary matters until the unexpectedly prompt appearance of 'the French *top Captain*' sent honest Kitty Cooke hurrying into curls and a silk gown early in the morning.

Though Miss Cooke had not intended to speak a word, 'the gentle quietness of her guest so surprised and pleased her, that she never quitted his side while he stayed'. The chevalier later told Susan disconsolately that the ladies had never left the room and all the conversation had been in English. Up to this time Miss Hamilton and Miss Cooke had thought the stories about the French Revolution a mere 'sham'. Now, when they saw with their own eyes a very quiet representative of 'the French gentry' who had been driven out of his country by villains, they could believe what they had not before credited—that there really had been a Revolution.[2]

In June Fanny was assuring the General with 'a great *Yes!*' that most certainly she could support a retired life.

Situation, I well know, is wholly powerless to render me either happy or miserable. My peace of mind, my chearfulness of spirits, my every chance of felicity, rest totally and solely upon enjoying the society, the confidence, & the kindness of those I esteem & love. These, I am convinced, will at all times be successful; everything else has at all times failed.[1]

She assured him also that though she had had little experience, she was less ignorant of the details *du ménage* than he might imagine. If she can expect patience and encouragement, she will answer for her application.[1] She was no longer the *dumb portrait*, aggravating in her provoking and enigmatical silence.[1] As she explained to Susan on June 11: 'I feel, that as such a man could live, *I* could live, be it how it might.' 'Indeed I cannot endure finding more & more unhappiness, & sadness, with more, & more, & more of worth, excellence, delicacy, & good-

---

[1] 2 A.L. (Berg) from FB to M. d'A, May, 3 June 1793; 4 A.L. (Barrett) from SBP to FB, 10, 22 Apr., 17, 31 May 1793.

[2] See p. 228, n. 2.

ness.'[1] '*Je sais depuis long-tems*', wrote Madame de Staël, '*combien il vous aime.*'[2] There was little left to debate. Though Dr. Burney felt that the lovers were probably condemning themselves to 'a perpetual struggle with penury to the end of their days', he gave a 'cold consent'. He would not, of course, be present at the wedding, and James was invited to take his place.[3] Only six people, relatives and friends in the immediate vicinity of Mickleham, attended Fanny's wedding. Charlotte's offer to come had perhaps arrived too late; and Charles, who could *merrify* or *dignify* any function as occasion required, had gone to Clifton for his health.

So beautiful, however, was the setting for this midsummer wedding in the village church, with its solid Norman tower set so unobtrusively and with such perfect taste among the sloping hills, that one may wish, if not for a modern wedding, for a few modern photographers who could have recorded the scenes. A road, turning sharply away from the old ford at the river, where the Phillips's house is said to have been, ascended the slope, curving between the high stone walls of the gardens, covered at that time of the year, no doubt, with roses, passed between the Running Horses inn on one side and the church of St. Michael on the other, and then along to Juniper Hall and Box Hill. Away across on the other side of the river Mole rose the heights of Norbury Park. As the hour approached the wedding party converged on the church. One may imagine Mr. Locke's shining carriage driving down the hill and along the river to the Phillips's house to call for Susan and the bride. The former messmates Molesworth Phillips and James Burney with the tortured lines on his face and the strange piratical coiffure, were close friends still, and probably walked together to the church. Meanwhile, at Juniper Hall, two elegant and distinguished Frenchmen, the Comte Louis de Narbonne and M. d'Arblay, Adjutant-General to Lafayette, thought of former elegancies as they debated whether to walk or to drive in doubtful style in the shabby cabriolet, the common property of the French colony. They probably walked round the few bends

---

[1] 2 A.L.S. (Berg) from FB to SBP, 4 Apr., 11 June 1793.

[2] See p. 228, n. 2.

[3] 2 A.N.S. (Berg) from M. d'A to JB, 28, 29 July 1793; also A.L.S. (Osborn) from FBA to CB, Jr., 8 Aug. 1793.

and arrived in good time at the old grey church. At sixteen Fanny had written that on such an occasion she would not have the courage to get out of the coach and that she would insist on sitting for an hour or two in the church to revive her spirits.[1] However, when she saw the handsome and accomplished chevalier, she probably forgot the palpitations of sixteen and all the trepidations that had so often made her life miserable since. She was now forty-one; M. d'Arblay, forty. As we have said, this was a wedding of high midsummer.

It has not been the custom to think of Fanny as a courageous revolutionary, braving the world, and yet it took some courage, in the face of all opposition, to marry a man without a profession (at least, one that could be practised in England or even, as the political situation developed, in France), without possessions (or indeed the means to buy a loaf of bread), and without prospects. She was marrying a man who was at once a Roman Catholic, a Frenchman, and a Constitutionalist, and this at a time when the Gordon Riots of 1780 were still very much in living memory, when Catholic Emancipation Bills were yet to be passed, when England was preparing for war with France, when politicians of all shades were rallying to the support of the monarchy and ready to invite those with contrary ideas to leave the country. Unlike M. d'Arblay, Fanny knew very well that his proposal was an invitation 'to walk out together in the wide world, & gain our subsistence by our labour'.[2] '*A supposer que la pension reste,*' commented M. de Narbonne, '*il faudra qu'ils vivent comme — des Paysans! — Et le Monde, et le public — et le qu'en dira-t-on?*'[3] For Fanny all this meant writing. 'Print, print, print', urged Susan. 'Here is a resource, a certainty of removing present difficulties.'[3] Probably many women before this time had undertaken to support themselves and a family by writing, but in any age or clime this is no craven undertaking.

On Sunday morning, July 28, 1793, in St. Michael's Church in the village of Mickleham, Frances Burney and Alexandre Gabriel Jean Baptiste Pieuchard d'Arblay were married. On July 30 the marriage ceremony was repeated according to

---

[1] ED, i. 16–18.
[2] See p. 231, n. 4.
[3] A.L. (Berg) and A.L. (Barrett) from SBP to FB, May, 9 June 1793, respectively. Cf. *Diary*, v. 200–3.

Roman Catholic rites in the Sardinian Chapel in London,[1] so
that Fanny might have legal rights if by a counter-revolution
in France M. d'Arblay should recover his property.

On July 23 Fanny had posted letters to her brothers and
sisters telling them of her plans. The replies, even more affectionate than usual, as such an occasion required, also revealed
frank astonishment. 'I could have lain any wager in the world',
wrote Charlotte, 'that no man on earth could have prevail'd
on you to change your name'—

May you be happy my beloved Fanny!—only half as happy as you
deserve to be, & I shall be contented—but my amazement is unspeakable!—All I have heard of M. D—inclines me to think he can
never forget your Value, if his Memory is good in *this* point, I fear
neither your happiness, nor his—

I am grieved at the hard conflicts I am certain you must have
suffered—the *cloud* you mention I think will certainly pass away, &
since you have *leave* to judge for yourself, if the sacrifice had cost you
your life, our dear Padre would only have blamed you for not knowing how to please yourself—[2]

'When I shall overcome the incredible astonishment at an
event so little thought of, first excited, Heaven only knows!'
wrote Sarah Harriet. As Captain Phillips remarked, nothing
could now be improbable and like him she has made it 'a rule
to lay aside all surprise for the future'.[3] 'Can you conceive any
thing equal to my surprise', wrote Maria Rishton to Susan, 'at
hearing our vestal sister had ventured on that stormy sea of
matrimony.' Maria had tried to compose an Epithalamium
about the Lily of France and Rose of England as she turned
a great bustard on a spit in her Norfolk farm-kitchen, and she
had cried and laughed twenty times that day.

I am dying to see the Othello who has drawn her within his spells—
for she is quite Desdemona & loved him for the dangers he had
passed & he loved her that she did pity them—I must beg you will
send me a description of this Conquering Hero—who has thaw'd
Fanny's Ice . . . and raised 'these Tumults in a Vestal's Veins'.[4]

Maria recalled a youthful performance of *The Drummer* in which

[1] See Constance Hill, *Juniper Hall*, pp. 166–7.
[2] A.L.S. (Barrett) from CBF to FB, 27 July 1793.
[3] A.L.S. (Barrett) from SHB to Mary Young, 2 Aug. 1793.
[4] A.L.S. (Berg) from Maria Allen Rishton to SBP, 14 Aug. 1793; and another
(Barrett) to FBA, n.d.

Fanny as 'the prudish Lady Truman' insisted in the 'Tender
meeting' of the fifth act that her husband, the hero Sir George
(Maria), on his return after an absence of three or four years
when he was believed dead on the field of honour, should
merely kiss her hand. Maria had remonstrated strongly against
so unnatural a reception and threatened to drop the part, but
the play went on when Fanny grudgingly conceded 'a Chaste
Embrace'. 'I hope she does not treat poor M. D'Arblay so
cruelly.'[1]

Charles also hastened to send his felicitations; and there were
also the letters printed or mentioned in the diaries, the congratulations of Madame de Staël, the Comte de Lally-Tollendal,
Madame de la Fîte, la Princesse d'Hénin, le Prince de Poix,
and others. There were graceful letters from the Burkes, from
Queeney Thrale,[2] and finally a letter most anxiously awaited,
as one may guess, a missive from Mrs. Schwellenberg conveying
the good wishes of the King, the Queen, and the Princesses.
Apart from the required £100 that saved the d'Arblays from
beggary until Fanny could get a book written, the tolerance of
the royal family was a social sanction _par excellence_ for her
marriage. Though she was immediately ostracized by Mrs. Ord
and others, her disgrace was not complete and not irremediable
while she could be received at Windsor, appear occasionally in
the royal boxes at the theatre, and be permitted presently to
dedicate a new work to the Queen. It seems never to have
been very fashionable to praise the Germanic Queen and the
wrong-headed, blind, and mad old King (though called in his
time by his people 'the good old king'); yet their leniency
towards their servant Fanny Burney, allied now by marriage to
the enemies of England, was not without some little touch of
magnanimity. Her gratitude towards them and their family
increased a hundredfold and never faltered to her dying day.
And neither, one may add, did the pension.

Fanny had brought all this off, then! And it was not without
some insight that Mrs. Thrale had spoken of Fanny's 'Knowledge of the World' and 'ingenuity of Expedient', had pronounced her 'Skill in Life and Manners . . . superior to that of

---

[1] See p. 239, n. 4.
[2] A.L.S. (Berg) from Hester Maria (Queeney) Thrale to FBA, 12 Aug. 1793.
For the Burkes see A.L.S. (Osborn) from CB to FBA, 25 Sept. 1793.

any Man or Woman in this Age or Nation'.[1] There is a difference between independence, bravery or boldness of spirit, and
boldness in Manners—a distinction that Fanny Burney understood very well, but that her critics or biographers have not
always noticed. Such is the impression she has made by her
discretion, quiet manner, and a few incidents like her refusal
to associate herself with forward or 'fallen' women (more
specifically women of genius with lovers publicly in tow), that
it has hardly been noticed that in action, in her literary career,
in her marriage, and in episodes yet to come, the 'prudish'
Fanny was one of the most unconventional, one of the most
forward women of her age. The woman of brave and independent mind, the rebel and the pioneer, is not always distinguished
by flamboyant challenges to the conventions. This is the little
hoax that Fanny played on many a good old body of that age
and this. As the Duchess of Leinster wrote to her daughter
Lucy Fitzgerald, '*Manner*, my love! is *everything* with him [Mr.
Ogilvie], and indeed with almost everybody.'[1] The study of
manners, of courtesy, its charm, graciousness, and its *utility* was
a subject that Fanny Burney did not neglect.

The d'Arblays secured rooms in a farmhouse, Phenice Farm,
at the top of Bagden Hill, a stiff walk from Norbury Park or
Mickleham and about a mile from Bookham. The house there
has been rebuilt, but the wide fields and the sweeping view to
the northward, the 'beautiful and healthy situation', which
Fanny mentions, are probably little changed. In November of
1793 Mr. Locke had discovered that Mrs. Catherine Bailey,
widow of John Bailey of Bookham, would let Fairfield Place, the
'house, garden, and orchard adjoining Fair Field', and before
the close of that month the d'Arblays moved in. The cottage
still stands on the Pound Piece Plot or the Fair Plot as the
nucleus of a much larger dwelling formed by the addition of
L's and a verandah. The original may be seen as a long narrow
cottage containing on the ground floor a parlour, hall, dining-
room, and scullery. The rooms were not indeed spacious, but
they were quiet, secluded, and peaceful, and opened into a
pleasant garden and orchard. Here Fanny spent some of the
happiest days of her life. Here *Edwy and Elgiva* was revised for
production, *Camilla* was written, a son was born.

---

[1] *Thraliana*, i. 549; Sermoneta, pp. 109–20.

Sometimes the little square parlour was 'laughably crowded' with callers—the Lockes and their visitors and disconsolate French gentlemen like M. de Beaumetz, whose adventures filled one of the most vivid of Fanny's journal-letters.[1] In 1796 William Locke brought Lucy Fitzgerald to call, and she was charmed by Madame d'Arblay's conversational powers.[2] Finally, on a day of fair and happy memory, Dr. Burney drove up unannounced to the house, garden, and orchard adjoining Fair Field, Bookham, to see for himself how his daughter fared in obscurity in a cottage.[3] Dr. Burney's disapproval, that cloud in the Surrey idyll, had soon passed away. Within a month of the marriage he was sending parcels of books to Phenice Farm as indefatigably as he had supplied Chessington—an edition of Milton, which Fanny 'ought not to live without'; for M. d'Arblay, books on gardening; and *Rasselas*, for both.[3] The letters that he wrote to Fanny at Bookham and, later, at West Humble are among the gayest and most entertaining of the Burney correspondence. Fanny in her turn wrote cheerfully and contentedly about her husband and his rural occupations. In March, 1794, he had built a 'winter walk' and a winter arbour as a *but* for the walk.

He has been transplanting lilacs, Honey-suckles, & Jessamines, root, mould & branch, till he has been obliged in the coldest Days, to as completely new attire as Richard may be at Calcutta upon the hottest. . . . But perhaps you will suspect he means, hereafter, to lessen his manual labours by some Orphean magnetism, when I tell you he has lately *composed an air*, to a song of his own writing, which he plays upon his mandoline—& plays in defiance of the poor Instrument's wanting two capital strings.[4]

The Historian of Music probably shivered no more at thoughts of the March arbour than over the sad love-song played on a mutilated mandolin; but the latter he could remedy somewhat, and in the next parcel to Bookham he included 'two capital strings' for the instrument. There were other problems in Bookham. After the deportation of Talleyrand and the

---

[1] A.L.S. (Barrett) from FBA to CB, 8 Jan. 1794.
[2] See p. 241, n. 1.
[3] *Diary*, v. 218–47. Also A.L.S. and A.L. (Barrett) from FBA to CB, 27 Mar., Aug. 1794.
[4] 2 A.L. (Barrett) from FBA to CB, 2 Mar., 2 Aug. 1794.

attacks on Lafayette the Doctor feared that M. d'Arblay might call undesirable attention to himself by publishing a defence of his friends, or that if he were in London he might be tempted into imprudent political arguments. For the moment the more unobtrusively he lived, the better, and the Doctor counselled him to remain quietly in the country and cultivate his garden. Fanny for her part was content to remain 'undisturbed and undisturbing'.

> He works in his garden, or studies English and mathematics, while I write. When I work at my needle, he reads to me; and we enjoy the beautiful country around us in long and romantic strolls, during which he carries under his arm a portable garden-chair, lent us by Mrs. Lock, that I may rest as I proceed. He is extremely fond, too, of writing. . . . These resources for sedentary life are certainly the first blessings that can be given to man, for they enable him to be happy in the extremest obscurity.[1]

Fanny had supposed 'the profession of blood' wholly relinquished, and she was dismayed when in the summer of 1793 the warrior wished to offer his military services at Toulon. She wrote her consent, though she could not utter it. 'I cannot endure that the tenderness of your nature should be at variance with the severe calls of your Honour.'[2] When Pitt refused the offer, Fanny was frankly delighted. The warrior had perforce to exchange his sword for a pruning-hook.

In 1793 Dr. Burney wrote to Fanny about the plight of the emigrant French clergy, of whom there were '6000 now in England, besides 400 laity here and 800 at Jersey, in utter want'.[3] 'Mrs. Crewe, having seen at Eastbourne a great number of venerable and amiable French clergy, suffering all the evils of banishment and beggary with silent resignation', was endeavouring to raise funds for their relief. She had enlisted 'very illustrious and honourable' ladies in her enterprise; and though it was 'hoaxed and scouted by the men, who called it "Ladies' nonsense"', Dr. Burney had consented to act as secretary. With the typical attitude and phraseology that the lampooners

---

[1] See p. 242, n. 3.

[2] A.L.S. (Berg) from FBA to M. d'A, n.d.; A.L.S. (Barrett) to CB, 1794; *Memoirs*, iii. 188–90.

[3] *Diary*, v. 218–28; *Memoirs*, iii. 184–7; A.L.S. (Berg) from CB to FBA, 4 Oct. 1793.

of his time had seized on so mercilessly, the Doctor continued:

> The good Bishop of St. Pol de Leon has heard of my zeal as secretary to the Ladies, from M. Jumard, I suppose, and has inquired my direction, and wished for my acquaintance. I shall wait on this venerable prelate to-morrow.[1]

> The expense, in only allowing the clergy 8s. a week, amounts to about £7500 a month, which cannot be supported long by private subscription, and must at last be taken up by Parliament; but to save the national disgrace of suffering these excellent people to die of hunger, before the Parliament meets and agrees to do something for them, the ladies must work hard.[1]

Mrs. Crewe hoped that Madame d'Arblay would lend her pen to the cause. The d'Arblays subscribed a guinea from their small means and were very willing to help with their pens; but when Fanny asked her father for advice on what to write, unfortunately he suggested a general and abstract theme—an '*éloge* of female benevolence'. Fanny then wrote an essay of twenty-seven pages on this topic, in her best rhetorical style:

> Come forth, then, O ye Females, blest with affluence! spare from your luxuries, diminish from your pleasures, solicit with your best powers; and hold in heart and mind that, when the awful hour of your own dissolution arrives, the wide-opening portals of heaven may present to your view these venerable sires, as the precursors of your admission.[2]

All this, as Charlotte would have said, was not worth the hundredth part of a letter of twelve pages that Fanny had sent to the Doctor about M. de Beaumetz—his adventures and escapes in the 'Iron Reign of Terror'.[3] Yet the eighteenth century liked the pamphlet well enough. The *British Critic* quoted one of its 'many striking passages', and the *Monthly Review* pronounced it 'the most energetic, the most pathetic, the most eloquent charity sermon that ever came under our perusal'. The writer in the *Critical Review* took his assignment a little more seriously than the others. He approved of the plea for charity but was

---

[1] See p. 243, n. 3.
[2] *Brief Reflections relative to the Emigrant French Clergy: earnestly submitted to the humane consideration of the Ladies of Great Britain* (1793), p. 26.
[3] See p. 242, n. 1.

unable to believe that the French clergy were wholly innocent
of political manœuvring. He seemed, morœver, to have been
somewhat taken aback by Fanny's new style, the grotesque
rhetorical robes she was henceforth to don on great occasions,
but in spite of that and of some of the doubtful sentiments about
the holy martyrs in 'this animated charity sermon, as it may
properly enough be called, our advice to the amiable author
may all be comprehended in two words, *Write on*'. The celebrated Miss Burney had not been forgotten. 'We ... have found
our favourite again.'[1]

Dr. Burney saw everything in the pamphlet that he wished.
'I never liked anything of your precious writing more.'[2] He
recommended that 2,000 copies be printed and sold at 1s. 6d.
for the benefit of the dispossessed clergy. Susan learned in
Ireland later that Fanny's work had won friends for the priests
there among those formerly prejudiced against them. It was
even suggested that Fanny attempt an exculpation of the
'grossly calumniated & libelled' Empress of Russia and procure,
incidentally, a handsome Russian pension.[3]

M. d'Arblay had intended to translate the tract, but in spite
of a notice to this effect in the closing pages, he was forestalled
by the Evêque de Troyes, who came forth with the French
version. Madame d'Arblay complained about the Bishop, who
was 'very sorry to have "done this thing"', but who made no
offer to relinquish it.[4]

On the first anniversary of their wedding, Fanny looked back
thankfully over a year that had 'not been blemished with one
regretful moment!'[5] 'Oh my dearest,' wrote Susan from Mickleham, 'I have but to wish that the second year may produce an
aggregate of happiness equal to the portion which has been
granted you during that but closed upon us.'[6] While dark unhappy changes or developments in the character of her
husband, and the beginning of cruel usage were overshadowing
the brightness of her own life, Susan rejoiced the more intensely

---

[1] The *Monthly Review*, xii (Dec. 1793), 475; the *British Critic*, ii (Dec. 1793),
450; the *Critical Review*, x (Mar. 1794), 318–21.
[2] A.L.S. (Berg) from CB to FBA, 23 Oct. 1793.
[3] A.L. (Berg) from SBP to FBA, 14 Nov. 1796.
[4] 2 A.L.S. (Barrett) from FBA to CB, 27 Apr., 9 May 1794.
[5] See p. 242, n. 3.
[6] A.L.S. (Barrett) from SBP to FBA, 28 July 1794.

over Fanny's happy fate. According to her wish the joy of the
d'Arblays remained constant, and was even augmented in
December by the birth of their son, December 18, 1794.[1]

Alexander Charles Louis Piochard (or Pieuchard) d'Arblay
carried the past in his name (Alexander for his father, Charles
for the Burneys, Louis for the Comte de Narbonne, and Piochard d'Arblay for old lost days, rights, and régimes in France).
He was born at an awkward moment just when revolutions had
swept away old patterns of life and means of livelihood without
establishing new opportunities for brilliant young men. But this
lay in the future. Now he was a beloved infant, according to
Susan, a lovely child in a cradle, looking 'truly jolie à manger',
and soon very sociable. Three weeks after his birth M. d'Arblay
had allowed Fanny to hold a pen in her hand just long enough
to thank her father for a very generous 'baptismal present for
the christening of Alexander'. Soon the child came to occupy
a charming place in the journal-letters.

In the years 1794–5 the d'Arblays paid lengthy visits both
to the family at Chelsea and to Charles Burney, now at Greenwich. Sometimes James and his wife came from Kingston to
visit the d'Arblays and the two families walked from Bookham
to Mickleham to visit Susan. The old friendship between Fanny
and Charles seemed to have been strengthened by her marriage
to the personable and intelligent Frenchman, while the indigent
circumstances of the d'Arblays seemed a challenge to Charles's
affection and ingenuity.

Looking about for a source of income Charles thought of
Fanny's plays. In October, 1794, he read *Edwy and Elgiva*, one
of the blank-verse tragedies she had composed at Kew and
Windsor, and asked for permission to show it to Mr. Kemble.
Three days before her child was born, Mr. Kemble had sent
for the play that it might be read to Sheridan. Fanny had but
one copy, had 'intended divers corrections & alterations', and
was in every way unprepared for such precipitancy. Charles, however, went ahead, and superintended the reading in the green-
room. Mrs. Siddons, Bensley, and Kemble himself took the
leading parts, but some of the actors disliked the play and some
of them refused to learn their lines, substituting speeches of their

---

[1] The dates of birth and baptism are recorded in the register of St. Nicholas
Church, Great Bookham, as 18 Dec. 1794 and 11 Apr. 1795 respectively.

own at random.[1] It was produced at Drury Lane on March 21, 1795, and ran for one night only. Fanny told Mrs. Waddington how with her sister Susan, her brother Dr. Charles, and her husband she sat 'snug & retired & wrapt up in a Bonnet & immense Pelice, in Mr. Sheridan's Box',[2] and, in Mrs. Thrale's malicious phraseology, saw *Edwy and Elgiva* 'hooted off the stage'.[3] The painful event is described by Mrs. Siddons:

Oh there never was so wretched a thing as Mrs. D'arblaye's Tragedy —She was at the representation in spite of all I coud say of the ill effects so much agitation as she must necessarily feel would have upon an invalid for she has been extremely ill it seems since her lying in.—I was grieved that a woman of so much merit must be so much mortified. The Audience were quite angelic and only laughed when it was *impossible* to avoid it—Her brother negotiated the whole business, I never saw herself, but she went to my brothers the next day and nobly said, she had been deceivd by her friends that she saw it was a very bad thing, and withdrew it immediately—that was done like a woman of an exalted Spirit.[3]

'How it must gall her Pride! and that *worthy* Gentleman her Brother's Pride', wrote Mrs. Thrale triumphantly.[3] Though Madame d'Arblay suffered some chagrin from this unprofitable event, it was soon forgotten in the most painful and dangerous illness she had yet known. When her baby was a fortnight old it contracted thrush and

communicated it to my Breast—& in short—after torment upon torment, a mild fever ensued—an abscess in the Breast followed—& till that broke 4 days ago, I suffered so as to make life—even my happy life—scarce my wish to preserve! need I say more. . . . But— they have made me wean my child! . . . what that has cost me![2]

By the summer of 1795 Fanny had recovered once more and was able to take stock of the d'Arblay situation. There were now three people instead of two at the Hermitage, and a nurse-maid was now necessary. Expenses had so increased that an increase in income became 'absolutely indispensable'.[4] The war

[1] *Diary*, v. 249–51; Diary MSS. (Berg), pp. 4811–12; A.L.S. (Berg) from CB, Jr., to FBA, 17 Mar. 1795.
[2] Two letters (Berg) from FBA to Mary Port Waddington, Mar. 1795 and 15 Apr. 1795 (Diary MSS.).
[3] *Thraliana*, ii. 916 and n. 1.
[4] Diary MSS. (Berg), June 1795. Cf. *Diary*, v. 283–4.

had sent the prices of food soaring, while the pension rested at £100. The pension was secure, but with England now at war with France M. d'Arblay's hope for employment grew even remoter than before. At Chessington in 1793 Fanny Burney had had to consider not only marriage but ways and means of supporting a family; she had determined to set aside all her 'innate and original abhorrence' to publishing and 'to regard and use as resources' *herself*, that is, her ability to write. The time for this now seemed to have come, and she set to work in earnest on her third novel, *Camilla*.

X

CAMILLA: OR, A PICTURE OF YOUTH

(1796)

I mean this work to be sketches of characters and morals put
in action,—not a romance.
Diary, v. 264

A HYBRID produced by modifications or variations of the
courtesy-book and of the novel of manners, to which
Fanny had already made significant contributions, *Camilla*
may be described as a courtesy-novel. Madame d'Arblay herself
insisted that *Camilla* was not a novel. It was a *work*, she said, in
which she meant to put characters and morals in action.[1] The
principal character was once again the young lady at her first
entrance into the world, and the morals were, for the most
part, those governing the conduct of the young lady. Madame
d'Arblay had adopted the impeccable purpose of the courtesy-
books, and, like Madame de Genlis and other courtesy-writers
of these decades, she set out to enliven dry precepts with narrative or action—right action, which might be rewarded; and
wrong action, which in its disastrous consequences might serve
as a 'warning guide' to youth.

The English political reaction to the French Revolution and
all its works and ways had stiffened the moral postures. In the
closing decade of the eighteenth century Mrs. Grundy seemed
even less disposed to approve of novels than she had in earlier
times—especially French novels or confessions like those of
Rousseau. One had only to look at France! Infidel writers like
Hume or Voltaire were much to be feared, as were all loose and
free ideas menacing the political or domestic *status quo*. Madame
d'Arblay, who had defied the world in her romantic marriage,
knew that this was not a propitious time to try Mrs. Grundy's
patience further. A moral book was good in itself; it might
reassure the good ladies who had dropped her, might show the
court and society in general that she had imbibed no wild ideas

---

[1] *Diary*, v. 264; also letters (Berg) from SBP to FBA; and from CB to CB, Jr.,
June, July 1795.

from her romantic marriage, that her principles were unchanged, and that morality might flourish in a French home. A courtesy-novel would be generally approved for its utility; it would sell, and now that there was a child in the house, the education of youth was a congenial subject.

Madame d'Arblay's family had determined that this time the profits of Fanny's work should accrue not to the progeny of Lowndes and of Payne, but to the son of the author.[1] Dr. Burney, James, and Charles formed a triumvirate insisting that she bring out the work by subscriptions at a guinea and a half each. Fanny acquiesced; the pride that had made her refuse such a plan for *Cecilia* was now subdued by concern for her child.[2] Old friends of the Burneys like Mrs. Crewe, Miss Cambridge, and Mrs. Boscawen were eager to help, and the summer of 1795 saw magnificent efforts for the sale of the book. On hearing of the scheme Mr. Hastings had given 'a great jump, and exclaimed, "Well, then, now I can serve her, thank Heaven, and I will! I will write to Anderson to engage Scotland, and I will attack the East Indies myself!"'[2] The Duchess of Beaufort had just sent in 'a list of nine Dukes & Duchesses!' And Fanny spoke gratefully of the 'uncommon exertions' of Mrs. Locke, Mrs. Waddington, and the Dowager Duchess of Leinster.[1] Mr. Burke subscribed for fifteen sets (five for himself, five for his wife, and five for his son); Mrs. Móntagu bought ten; Mr. Richard Burke took five, as did also Mr. Crewe and Mr. John Crewe. The subscription list—300 names in all—included, besides patrons in high places, many staunch friends of the Burneys like the Reverend Mr. Twining and Lady Mary Duncan. There were old friends like Mrs. Piozzi, Hannah More, Bennet Langton and, not least in point of interest, Miss Edgeworth, Mrs. Radcliffe, David Hume, and Miss J. Austen, Steventon.

Meanwhile Madame d'Arblay had been at work in earnest. Her father's visit had spirited her on in all ways, she reported in August, 1794, 'for this week past I have taken tightly to the *grand ouvrage*'.[3] The birth of her son, the time required to re-

---

[1] 2 A.L. (Berg) from FBA to CB, 15, 21 July 1795; also A.L. (Berg) from CB, Jr., to FBA, 12 July 1795; 4 A.L.S. (Osborn) from FBA and M. d'A to CB, Jr., 1, 10, 18 July 1795, 14 Mar. 1796.

[2] *Diary*, v. 260–9.

[3] *Diary*, v. 246.

cover her health and strength, revisions of *Edwy and Elgiva*,
her dangerous illness of March and April—all these events
interfered with the new book. Yet whenever opportunity offered
she was at work. A letter to her husband on February 3, 1796,
includes a bulletin of progress:

Yesterday I wrote 14 pages & ½. I won't tell you how late I sat up.
You were very good to exact no promises. Come back, & keep me
in order. . . . I am very careful of myself, I assure you, except in the
one article of writing late—but—it is so delicious to stride on, when
en verf![1]

As usual, her readiness in words, dialogue, and invention
enabled her to write at headlong speed. She was now, moreover, spared the fatigue of copying, for, as one extant manuscript of *Camilla* shows, she had a meticulous and devoted
copyist at hand in her husband. A manuscript of 1,370 pages[2]
in his small, clear, and upright hand stands as mute testimony
of his care and devotion. Except for changes in names (Ariella
to Camilla, and the rest) this manuscript shows few corrections,
whereas another of ninety-five pages in Madame d'Arblay's
own hand is marked with the usual drastic revisions and curtailments. Her practice was to revise while copying, and there is no
doubt that if she herself had made the final copy of *Camilla* she
would have eliminated many of the colloquialisms, dialectal
expressions, curious constructions, and grammatical errors that
the *Monthly Review* later objected to at length and that had not
been apparent to M. d'Arblay, in spite of the six hours a day
he religiously devoted to the study of English.

Happy news came in a letter written by Mrs. Schwellenberg
on February 26, 1796:

I do assure you I never took my pen in hand with more pleasure to
informe you I have her Majestys Commands to say she gives leave
for you to Dedicate youre Books to her.[3]

By June 28, 1796, the work was completed and printed in five
volumes by T. Payne at the Mews-Gate and T. Cadell in the

---

[1] A.L. (Berg) from FBA to M. d'A, 3 Feb. 1796.
[2] Both manuscripts, together with work-sheets, preliminary drafts, and lists of
revisions, are in the Berg Collection. An early draft (*c.* 46 ff.) is in the Barrett
Collection.
[3] In the Berg Collection, the NYPL. See also A.L. (Berg) from FBA to CB,
4 Mar. 1796; also postscript to A.L. (Berg) from M. d'A to CB, 11 Mar. 1796.

Strand. In July there was much fuss and flurry over dress as Fanny set off once more to court, this time to present her work to the King and Queen. M. d'Arblay, who carried ten presentation volumes of *Camilla*, ventured only as far as the iron palings, but Fanny was graciously received. She dropped on one knee before the Queen to present her offering, and longed to kneel again when the King entered to receive his copy. He showed his usual interest in the process of making books. Where, when, and why was the work written, and had she seized any characters from life?

None, I protested, from life.
'Oh!' cried he, shaking his head, 'you must have some!'
'Indeed your Majesty will find none!' I cried.
'But they may be a little better, or a little worse,' he answered, 'but still, if they are not like somebody, how can they play their parts?'
'Oh, yes, Sir,' I cried, 'as far as general nature goes, or as characters belong to classes, I have certainly tried to take them. But no individuals!'[1]

Though Madame d'Arblay stoutly denied painting individuals, and though she had answered the King pat with one of the critical tenets of the eighteenth century about *general nature*, yet *Camilla*, even more than *Evelina* and *Cecilia*, is peopled with ghosts, shades of the past, fragments and figments of the walking present. Though her subject was once again the conduct of the young lady at her first entrance into the world, Camilla, unlike Evelina and Cecilia, is placed in a family milieu consisting of a father, mother, uncle, sister, brother, and cousins. It is as if St. Martin's Street were given a rural setting in Mickleham, within reach of Norbury Park (Beech Park) and the visits of Mr. William Locke, Junior, and within calling distance of Mrs. Thrale. Counterparts to many of the incidents are also to be found in the diaries of Madame d'Arblay's youth—Camilla's mirth at a performance of Shakespeare where each actor spoke in a different dialect, and some of the adventures in the public rooms at the watering-places. Her visits to Mr. Dubster's Gothic establishment recall the merry expeditions with Mrs. Thrale to see the absurd 'devices' that Mr. Tattersall had put up in his garden, or the startling knick-

[1] See p. 250, n. 2.

knacks devised by Alderman Ferry at Bath.[1] Camilla's rejection
of a suitor (to be read at length in discarded pages of the work)[2]
is a feverish, highly-wrought, nightmarish version of the attitude
of Fanny herself and her family towards Mr. Barlow. Camilla's
brother, Lionel Tyrold, is the young Charles Burney; the
consternation caused by Lionel's scrapes at the university is a
reflection of the embarrassment and anxiety that Charles at
one time brought to St. Martin's Street. *Camilla* is a phantas-
magoria in which shifting memories of the past are fixed
momentarily as they drift and shape into something new.
Mr. Westwynn and his son Hal are perhaps vengeful shades of
Owen Cambridge and his son George. When Mrs. Tyrold finds
it necessary to go to Spain, the family is bereft of a mother's
counsel, and the conclaves and deliberations that the young set
conduct in times of crisis suggest the youthful conferences at
Poland Street, Queen Square, and St. Martin's Street.

The work-sheets of *Camilla* reveal interesting stages in the
transformation of material from the real to the imaginative
product. A character-sketch for one of the PICTURES OF YOUTH,
preserved on an old scrap of paper, recalls Charles and youthful
escapades now nearly twenty years in the past.

Story   *Family*
> Harry turns out the scourge of his Family . . .
> The Father's grief and shame
> Harry is in perpetual scrapes . . .
> Harry the very torment yet delight of his House
> Debts—late Hours—bad connections—Gaming of Harry
> distract his family
> Frolics, dangers, wild schemes, of Harry occupy & tease &
> please them alternately
> Unfeeling extravagance of Harry . . .
>
> Distress at unexpected Bills.
> Her generosity in assisting them.
> Levity with which distress is forgot.
> He sells an annuity.
> Acct. of Duel—fraud and baseness.

In Mr. Twining's letters, as we know, and probably at St.
Martin's Street also, Dr. Burney had read or listened to

---

[1] Cf. 'Specimens of Taste', ii. 285–307, with *Diary*, i. 66, 388–9.
[2] A manuscript (Barrett) of 46 folios.

arguments, pleas, and intercessions something like those preserved in one of the holograph work-sheets of 1794–6.

He has done wrong, 'tis true but he is young. He has erred—I confess—but he is not incorrigible. Ah, will you, then renounce him?
Which way must he turn? to whom apply? Will you cast him back
upon those very beings whom but to have mingled with has lost y^r
favour? Shall he find evil no longer his dread, but his resource?
Will you let him see himself abandoned by all but those whom he
ought himself to abandon? Will you force him to seek those courses—
or persons—whom you bade him blush ever to have found.[1]

Susan had long harboured sisterly doubts about Charles. 'May
no levity or imprudence overturn his fair hopes, wch if realized
will indeed fill me with everlasting surprise!'[2] Fanny's reflections on levity emerge in her study of Lionel Tyrold, whose
careless gaiety or vicious pranks and misdemeanours involve
his family in financial difficulties. Since *Camilla* was to be 'a
warning guide to youth', Madame d'Arblay went still more
deeply into the sources of Lionel's errors. Mr. Tyrold attributed
his son's crimes not to moral turpitude, 'but to the prevalence
of ill example, & to a *flighty gaiety of levity* that had led him to
treat every serious subject with mockery',[3] and the good clergyman deplored the 'spirit of levity' more than the crimes themselves. The moral to be drawn appears on a holograph scrap of
paper among the 'hints and plots' for the novel: 'There is no
such hardener of the heart as levity; its self-disguises amuse but
beguile the fancy till they deaden all sensation.'[1] In a study of
Camilla, Dr. Marchmont also wished to distinguish between
'youthful inexperience' that time and reason will rectify and
'innate levity' that time will 'harden and embolden'.[3] In the
novel, Lionel's career had a double, even triple, function. In
the play of the moralities he is Levity in action; in the dramatic
or narrative sense he is the Vice impeding and embroiling the
action; historically, he is the young Charles Burney, and,
according to both the *Critical Review* and the *British Critic*, but
too common and 'too just a picture of the conduct of young men

---

[1] Fifty-nine scraps, 200 sheets and slips of paper (Berg) relating to Fanny
Burney's novels and plays.

[2] Journals (Berg), 1790–1.

[3] *Camilla*, ii. 196; iv. 268–9; v. 109, 171–3, 181 (the MS. variant).

at our universities'.[1] Esther Burney agreed laconically: 'Lionel
is cruelly natural I fear.'[2]

Lavinia, Camilla's elder sister, is a faultless maiden, probably
drawn from the courtesy-books. Her place in the counsels and
her serenity recall the 'wifeish Hetty', though she certainly
lacked the talents and the wit of Dr. Burney's eldest daughter.
In the same way Major Phillips may be discerned in the preliminary sketches of the Irish Ensign and in the gay animal
spirits, practical jokes, and impractical schemes of the finished
product, Macderfy. Sir Hugh Tyrold received praise in the
Monthly Review as a character 'quite original'. The reviewer
had seen nothing like his

artless openness, invincible good-humour, a peculiar simplicity
producing easy credulity, an odd confusion of ideas, a profound
respect for learning, accompanied with a humble consciousness of
ignorance, a whimsical fondness for projects, and, above the rest,
an honest kindness of heart, 'with which . . . he was stuffed so full
that no room was left for any thing else'.[1]

He may have been new, if a little insipid. 'There never was such
a Triumph of Heart over Head', wrote Susan, not even in
Uncle Toby.[3]

The hero, Edgar Mandlebert, must rank next to Cœlebs in
Hannah More's *Cœlebs in Search of a Wife* (1809) as the greatest
prig in English literature. His character is modified by the
double part he has to play as monitor and lover. The terminal
point of the action is, of course, marriage. Through the judiciary
vacillations of the monitor-lover, who offers or withholds his
hand according as Camilla's conduct seems or does not seem
to indicate a nature guileless and pure, the main action is protracted through five volumes. Those who knew the Lockes
thought that they could recognize Mr. William in Edgar
Mandlebert, the exacting young man, heir to beautiful Beech
Park, who hoped Camilla might prove worthy of the offer of his
heart, hand, and possessions. The monitor-suitor was anatomized none too sympathetically by Mrs. Arlbery, the satiric
commentator in the work:

Mandlebert is a creature whose whole composition is a pile of

---

[1] xviii (Sept. 1796), 26–40. Also the *Monthly Review*, xxi (Oct. 1796); and the
British Critic, viii (Nov. 1796), 527–36.
[2] A.L.S. (Barrett) from EBB to FBA, 30 July 1796.   [3] See p. 249, n. 1.

accumulated punctilios. He will spend his life in refining away his own happiness: but do not let him refine away yours.

He is a watcher; and a watcher, restless and perturbed himself, infests all he pursues with uneasiness. He is without trust, and therefore without either courage or consistency. To-day he may be persuaded you will make all his happiness; to-morrow, he may fear you will give him nothing but misery.[1]

This was not quite fair. The lover was not inconsistent but judicial. He was a judge of conduct, and the ardour of his pursuit depended on the degree of approval he could bestow on the conduct of the young lady of his desire, the lovely but erring little heroine. In philanthropy and in nearly all the qualities recommended in the courtesy-books of the age he was himself all but faultless, but being a critic, a judge, a monitor, as well as an avenger of feminine errors, he must always appear ungenerous and, therefore, an unsympathetic character. In the end he is made to see how ill his carping behaviour compares with that of the open-hearted Hal Westwynn.

I have lost Camilla! I see it plainly. This young man steps forward so gallantly, so ingenuously, nay so amiably, that the contrast—chill, severe, and repulsive—must render me—in this detestable state—insupportable to all her feelings.[1]

Camilla often seems to reflect a cross-section of experience, thus illustrating the debt of fiction to fact. In mechanical structure the novel, subtitled *A Picture of Youth*, suggests a family of Burneys making their entrance into life from a country vicarage within riding distance of Norbury Park and Streatham. Many of Camilla's embarrassments and adventures arose like Fanny's in her separation from her family (as if Mrs. Thrale had driven up to Norbury Park and taken the beautiful, innocent, and inexperienced Amelia Locke off on a jaunt to a watering-place), though Camilla's love-story was not Fanny's and not Amelia Locke's. A third component in the identity of Camilla lies hidden in an old story drenched in tears, a tale of love long outstanding.

The story concerns Mary Ann Port, Mrs. Delany's greatgrand-niece, who lived with her aunt in St. James's Place and later at Windsor until the old lady's death in April, 1788.

---

[1] *Camilla*, iii. 376–81; iv. 332–3.

Suppressed parts of the court journals and the correspondence of 1786–9 between Fanny, Susan, and Dr. Burney contain many references to the lively 'Friskitten', her youth, 'native liveliness', and growing 'rage for coquetry'.[1] These were dangerous potentials. 'She must be kept *out of the way* of temptation, as she cannot for her life resist it!'[2] The temptations, perhaps the tempters, were officers and equerries, and especially Philip Goldsworthy, then Colonel but later Lieutenant-General in the first Royal Regiment of Dragoons, a man of about fifty, with whom, notwithstanding other flirtations *en passant*, the seventeen-year-old Mary Ann had fallen hopelessly in love.

After a visit of the Lockes to Windsor in the summer of 1787 it had become apparent to the wise that the handsome and talented young William Locke, heir to Norbury Park, was much 'smitten' by Mrs. Delany's beautiful niece just as in the novel Edgar Mandlebert, heir to Beech Park, was by Camilla. 'Marianna Port & Mr. William Lock!' exclaimed Fanny. 'What bliss for my revered Mrs. Delany!—I believe she would almost *die* with joy!'[2] In October of the same year Mrs. Delany, then eighty-seven, set off with Mary Ann on a visit to Norbury Park, no doubt hoping, as the Duchess of Sermoneta observed, 'to bring off the match between her niece and William'.[2] To the great pleasure of all beholders (including the Lockes), William, suddenly cured of his old habits of aloofness, unbent, but Mary Ann was so spoiled by 'gross draughts' of flattery from the officers at court that 'the elegant attentions of Mr. W. were thrown away upon her', and, frankly bored with the visit, she hurried the old lady back to Windsor within four days. '*Norbury*, sweet *Norbury*, wearied her!' Her heart was with the magnificent dragoon, but only, Fanny thought, because she did not suspect Mr. William's intentions. 'But is such a chameleon to be trusted with the happiness of that exquisite family?' That was the rub. When, therefore, Mrs. Locke inquired through Susan about Mary Ann, the evidence is that Susan and Fanny felt compelled to tell something of the truth as they saw it. Very few, they thought, much less the little coquette Friskitten,

---

[1] For specific references: Diary MSS. (Berg), pp. 3068, 3161, 3784–7.
[2] See Sermoneta, pp. 33–41; 4 A.L.S. (Berg) from FB to SBP, 4, 13, 23 Nov., 10 Dec. 1787; also A.L.S. (Barrett) from FB to CBF, 31 July 1781. See also Susan Burney's Journal (Berg), Oct.–Nov. 1787.

could merit Mr. William and that sweet earthly paradise Norbury Park.

The most dreadful principles of *Art* & *policy* & disguise have been instilled into her from her Birth, I believe, by her bad mother. . . . Had she *always* lived with Mrs. Delany, I often think she would have been everything that is desirable. . . . However, 'tis needless to think of this [the Locke marriage] now, as she has a pursuit of her own that seems to have a promising appearance. . . . I warmly hope it will take place, for such steps has she ventured that she will other·wise be deeply mortified, & poor Mrs. D. thinks even *disgraced*.[1]

Meanwhile, Mary Ann, all unaware of what had been won and lost, pursued her perilous course at court, but here too all went amiss, for, as it proved, the equerry had no intention of offering his hand. After Mrs. Delany's death in the spring of 1788, Miss Port left Windsor quite broken-hearted on more counts than one. On a visit to Fanny in July, she 'opened her poor swelling Heart, & almost drowned me in her tears'. And Fanny blamed the Colonel, who knew the world and ought to have discouraged the 'partiality' of an 'inexperienced & lovely young girl . . . *immediately, decisively*, & long before she should have been injured in the world, or hurt in her own bosom'.[2]

In February, 1789, Miss Port's family arranged that she should marry Mr. Benjamin Waddington, a good-hearted gentleman of means.[3] After this, however, she still made tearful visits to Windsor, and long after, even after the births of her children, she wrote to Fanny for news of the faithless courtier she could not forget, and Fanny scolded her roundly: 'Your unwearied solicitude of inquiry after old favourites grieves—& amazes me. My poor Marianne—I would to God the affections of your heart were placed more around you!'[4] Years passed into decades, and still the lovely Mary Ann Port Waddington pined for the apoplectic dragoon, by then in his grave, and she seems to have told some tale of her unhappiness to her daughters. In August, 1812, on Madame d'Arblay's return from France, Emily and Frances Waddington, then in their late teens, wrote

---

[1] See p. 257, n. 2.   [2] See p. 257, n. 1.
[3] Mrs. Locke's Journal (Barrett); A.L.S. (Berg) from FB to CB, 3 Feb. 1789; to SBP, 7 Apr. 1789.
[4] 4 A.L.S. (Berg) from FB to Mary Port Waddington, 4 Jan. 1789, Nov. 1795, 20 Apr. 1799, 17 Feb. 1801; also Diary MSS. (Berg), p. 5137.

curious letters to her, proving, if nothing else, that the true
love-stories of old are no stranger or less sentimental than the
old fictions. Their poor mother was so completely worn down
by twenty years of mental anguish 'that the sight of the *only*
person except her children that she ever *truly loved*' will be 'a trial
that her shattered nerves are ill able to support!' Madame
d'Arblay was the only person who could tell them what their
mother was like when 'alive to the vibrations of hope &
pleasure'.[1] Her daughters had known her only in her unhappy
years.

This is by no means the end of the d'Arblay–Waddington
friendship; there was more for the future, but the progress of
the story to the mid-nineties had provided an improving theme
for a courtesy-work. Madame d'Arblay's great resource was
not now the Imagination that had come into play in *Evelina*,
but Memory, and the examples she could call to mind to
illustrate her moral themes. In 1794–5, when she was again
writing about the entrance of a young lady into the world, the
temptations she must withstand, and the errors and faults she
must avoid, Mrs. Delany's great-grand-niece seemed to be
often in her thoughts and at the tip of her pen. The setting for
the new novel was not, indeed, the court, but the groups of
young people Madame d'Arblay had known at Norbury Park,
Poland Street, St. Martin's Street, Streatham, and the watering-
places. The lover was not Colonel Goldsworthy, but, as everyone recognized, William Locke, and with a few adjustments,
including a happy ending, Mary Ann's history became
Camilla's.

Madame d'Arblay meant, however, to write a courtesy-book,
and a further intellectual process fashioned Camilla according
to the analyses of human nature to be read in the semi-philo-
sophical or educational works, the courtesy-books of the day.
There was first the distinction between the gifts of nature or
natural qualities and those that had to be inculcated by education. Camilla was endowed by nature with glad animal spirits
and a feeling heart. Her natural affections, sensibility, and
benevolence are made apparent by incidents introduced for the
purpose—her generosity to Eugenia, her kindness to a prisoner's
half-starved family, her solicitude for a tortured bullfinch, and,

[1] The Barrett Papers.

finally, her grief at the improvised death-bed scene when her uncle Sir Hugh is seized by the gout. There is a schematic rather than a haphazard presentation of attributes.

Edgar had never yet beheld her in a light so resplendent—What a heart, thought he, is here! what feelings, what tenderness, what animation!—O, what a heart!—were it possible to touch it![1]

This is the crux of the matter; five volumes are devoted to Edgar's efforts to decide whether Camilla's errors in conduct spring from a bad heart, innate levity, or a vicious nature, or merely from the thoughtlessness and inexperience of youth. He has to ascertain also whether she is satisfied with her status in society and willing to play a woman's role at the fireside. 'You must study her,' insisted the arch-monitor, Dr. Marchmont,

you must study her, from this moment, with new eyes, new ears, and new thoughts. Whatever she does, you must ask yourself this question: 'Should I like such behaviour in my wife?' Whatever she says, you must make yourself the same demand. Nothing must escape you.[2]

Thus Camilla is placed under continual observation as she negotiates the untried ways of life. If she runs the gauntlet safely, a husband is the prize. Her mother had misgivings.

I have not a fear for her, when she can act with deliberation; but fear is almost all I have left, when I consider her as led by the start of the moment.[3]

Even Dr. Marchmont had conceded that Camilla was 'the most inartificially sweet, the most unobtrusively gay, and the most attractively lovely of almost any young creature' that he ever beheld.[3] All this, however, is not enough. Camilla must acquire the courtesy-book virtues of propriety, prudence, and fortitude. As her disastrous experiences teach, she must learn to eschew artful practices, coquetry, and precipitance.

In the rectory at Cleves or in the quiet of Sir Hugh's country estate Camilla was comparatively safe, but pitfalls are provided in travels with Mrs. Arlbery to Tunbridge Wells and Southampton. Edgar thought Mrs. Arlbery 'a dangerous acquain-

---

[1] *Camilla*, i. 190–224, 257–65, 354–66; ii. 413 ff.; iii. 397 ff.
[2] Ibid. i. 378 ff.   [3] Ibid. i. 285–6, 358.

tance', or at best an unreliable monitor, guide, or example for
a young lady.

She was a woman far more agreeable to the men, than to her own
sex; . . . she was full of caprice, coquetry, and singularity; yet,
though she abused the gift, she possessed an excellent and uncommon
understanding. She was guilty of no vices, but utterly careless of
appearances, and though her character was wholly unimpeached,
she had offended or frightened almost all the country around, by a
wilful strangeness of behaviour, resulting from an undaunted determination to follow in every thing the bent of her own humour.[1]

Edgar had hoped that Camilla would have chosen other friends,
and yet (and one can almost hear Fanny speak of Mrs. Thrale)
Mrs. Arlbery was one of the first women of the age for 'wit
and capacity'. 'She has an excellent heart, too; though her
extraordinary talents, and her carelessness of opinion make it
sometimes, but very unjustly, doubted.'[1] Singularity was costly.
   At Tunbridge Wells the jealous watcher, all unaware of
extenuating circumstances, soon found cause for distrust when
Mrs. Arlbery's party decided to take tea with the foppish Sir
Sedley, who was confined to his room in a hotel by an injury
sustained in stopping Camilla's runaway horse, thus saving her
life. Sir Sedley, having set aside his affected foppery, conversed
in so pleasantly natural a way that, with Mrs. Arlbery's wit
and the gaiety of Camilla's contribution, the evening sped
rapidly away, though somewhat interrupted at the close by
groans of anguish heard through the wainscot. These originated,
as one may guess, from Edgar Mandlebert, who sat all unseen
beyond the partition, racked with torture at hearing Camilla's
gay voice in a man's room. The party left at half-past eleven,
but then Miss Dennel's screams on tripping over the carpet
brought Edgar forth in time to see Camilla being escorted down
the stairs by the Major! All must now be over with the romance.

To visit a young man at an hotel; rich, handsome, and splendid;
and with a *chaperon* so far from past her prime, so elegant, so coquettish, so alluring, and still so pretty; and to meet there a flashy
Officer, her open pursuer and avowed admirer . . . his love, he told
himself, was past.[2]

---

[1] *Camilla*, ii. 80–82, 100; iii. 84, 347. See also deletions in Camilla MS. (Berg).
[2] Ibid. iii. 176–96, 278–9.

The moral is that innocence is not enough; one must be prudent. Deviations from 'transparent openness', including coquetry, were also severely punished. On Mrs. Arlbery's advice Camilla attempted to win Edgar by arousing his jealousy, and though she meant to disperse her charms indiscriminately, the share bestowed on Hal Westwynn caused that honest young man to fall honestly in love. And now 'not all the guiltlessness of her intentions could exonerate her from blame with that finely scrutinizing monitor', the conscience within. Worse was to come, however, when in order to disabuse Hal Westwynn of his mistake, she turned her attention to the elderly Lord Valhurst, who with this encouragement also made an offer of his hand. Edgar could scarcely believe his eyes.

Has she wilfully fascinated this old man seriously to win him, and has she won him but to triumph in the vanity of her conquest? How is her delicacy perverted! what is become of her sensibility? Is this the artless Camilla? modest as she was gay, docile as she was spirited, gentle as she was intelligent? O how spoilt! how altered! how gone![1]

As Dr. Marchmont saw it, a girl capable of such conduct must lack *chaste purity* and *fidelity*. He advised Edgar to consider whether the net in which Camilla was entangling herself was not that 'of levity, delighting in change, or of pique, disguising its own agitation in efforts to agitate others'. Edgar could only lament for the artless Camilla he had first adored! And by this catastrophe the young reader may see how art and artifice defeat their ends.

   At Southampton Camilla made other mistakes. On a fine summer's day she chose to walk through the town with the forward, vulgar Mrs. Mittin, who behaved in so extraordinary a fashion in the shops along High Street that the merchants took her and her young companion to be shop-lifters, deranged persons, or travellers of light character. The jeweller and the linen-draper, together with a set of wastrels, pursued them along the quay with a view to settling a wager about their characters. Camilla and Mrs. Mittin, beleaguered by their tormentors, took refuge in a bathing-house, where they were espied by, of all people, Edgar and Dr. Marchmont, who chanced to be strolling along the beach. Edgar came to the rescue, and Camilla, aghast with

   [1] *Camilla,* iv. 373–80, 398–405; v. 1–67.

terror, was disposed to listen docilely while he remonstrated strongly against the *impropriety* of her appearance in public with a vulgar person, so ill adapted to ensure her the respect that was in every way her due. Edgar could predict nothing from such companionship but further improper acquaintances and harmful adventures.[1] Camilla must learn prudence in the choice of friends.

A friend more dangerous than either Mrs. Mittin or Mrs. Arlbery was, of course, Mrs. Berlinton, the exponent of wayward and unregulated sensibility, at first, perhaps, the shade of Sophy Streatfield.

She possessed all that was most softly attractive, most bewitchingly beautiful, and most irresistibly captivating, in mind, person, and manners. But to all that was thus most fascinating to others, she joined unhappily all that was most dangerous for herself; an heart the most susceptible, sentiments the most romantic, and an imagination the most exalted.[2]

'Nothing steady or rational had been instilled into her mind by others; and she was too young, and too fanciful to have formed her own principles with any depth of reflection, or study of propriety.'[2] In short, Mrs. Berlinton lacked principle and her career is meant to illustrate the *progress of dissipation*. Edgar considered her as dangerous as a sunken rock, and, as he feared, it took Camilla some time to discover perfidy under so fair a surface. Finally perfidies appeared—the hollowness of sentimental pacts of friendship, a growing addiction to the faro table, and a romantic alliance ('unhallowed leagues and bonds') with the villain Bellamy, the wicked adventurer who had forcibly abducted Camilla's sister, the heiress Eugenia, and carried her off to Gretna Green. When his melodramatic death put an end to this infatuation, Mrs. Berlinton was snatched from utter ruin not by 'rational piety', as was most desirable, but by 'protecting, though excentric enthusiasm'.[2]

Camilla had to learn prudence also in the management of money. Her monitors watched for manifestations of compliance and good taste. Once, having peeped in at a door, the monitor-lover was aghast to see Camilla at a monkey-show, but transported to rapture when, after explaining that her presence there

[1] *Camilla*, iv. 215–37.
[2] Ibid. iii. 137–52, 234–5, 339–40, 381–91; v. 291–312, 551–2.

was quite accidental and unavoidable, she asked him to judge for her in matters of taste and conduct.[1] This was that requisite in a young lady—*compliance*.

Mr. Tyrold was satisfied that Camilla's principles were established upon 'adamantine pillars of religion and conscience', but, worried by the 'partiality' to Edgar that she failed to hide, he attempted to supply guidance on the affairs of the heart. In a letter of eighteen pages[2] praised by the *Monthly Review* as the *gem* of the work, by the *British Critic* as 'a masterly performance', and quoted at full length in the *Critical Review*, Mr. Tyrold gave some cautions about the behaviour of the young lady in tender situations and pointed out the attributes that he would like to see in his daughter—modesty, delicacy, discretion, prudence, and fortitude.[2]

The same letter introduced a second problem closely allied to the conduct of the young lady, namely, the formal education she ought to have: its extent, nature, and aims. As Madame d'Arblay observed truly (and not only for her own time):

the proper education of a female, either for use or for happiness, is still to seek, still a problem beyond human solution.[2]

After the publication of *Émile* the courtesy-books of the eighteenth century tended to merge into educational treatises. Among such works was Madame de Genlis's *Adèle et Théodore*, in four volumes, which had been read aloud at both Norbury Park and Chelsea and which in the eighties Fanny had praised for its 'many good directions about education'.[3] In general aim and purpose *Camilla* was not unlike this work, though Madame d'Arblay was not of course dependent on Madame de Genlis for her interest in the conduct and education of young ladies.

Eugenia's career seems to illustrate the mistakes likely to be made in human or social relationships by the female Latinist, student, pedant, or recluse. The absorption of the little cripple in books robbed her of a practical knowledge of people and of the world, so that she was easily, even tragically, betrayed in affairs of the heart, while the unkind comments of the young

---

[1] *Camilla*, iii. 221–63.

[2] Ibid. iii. 58–76. Reviews appeared in the *Monthly Review*, xxi (Oct. 1796), 156–63; the *British Critic*, viii (Nov. 1796), 527–36; the *Critical Review*, xviii (Sept. 1796), 26–40.

[3] *Diary*, ii. 129, 263, 288–9; iii. 12–17, 309; v. 78, 112–13.

rascal Clermont Lynmere, whom Sir Hugh intended for her husband, illustrated the typical reaction of the young man of the age to a scholarly wife.[1] Like Lovelace, Clermont was afraid of appearing a dunce in his own house.[2] Latin was a disadvantage to a young lady. A little music, a little drawing, and a little dancing were sufficient; and these should be only slightly pursued so as to distinguish a lady of fashion from an artist. Rousseau's ideal woman was supplied in '*l'aimable ignorante! Heureux celui qu'on destine à l'instruire! Elle ne sera point le Professeur de son mari, mais son disciple.*'[3] According to Mrs. Thrale, Dr. Burney would not allow Fanny to continue lessons in Latin under Dr. Johnson, 'because then She would have been as wise as himself forsooth, & Latin was too Masculine for Misses'. 'A narrow Souled Goose-Cap the Man must be at last', remarked Mrs. Thrale,[4] though apart from this incident there was little to show Dr. Burney illiberal in regard to the intellectual pursuits of his children. He was sympathetic to the *bas bleus*, the 'old sweethearts' of his seventies, Miss Carter, Mrs. Chapone, Mrs. Boscawen, Hannah More, and even Mrs. Montagu; but such an attitude was not general. The learned woman, it was widely felt, was for ever appearing 'out of her sphere and latitude', and, as Jane West observed, 'like the bear in a boat, encountering an element on which she had no business to embark'.[5] 'If you happen to have any learning,' Dr. Gregory advised his daughters, 'keep it a profound secret, especially from the men.'[6] The book hidden furtively under long gloves or spreading skirts was symbolical of female education in Fanny Burney's day. Madame d'Arblay thought that a curriculum should improve the 'Heart as well as the Head'; manners had to be formed and morals taught.

Eugenia's tutor, Dr. Orkborne, is a caricature of a pedant marked by ignorance of or indifference to social usages or the

---

[1] The chapter, 'Tuition of a Young Lady', *Camilla*, i. 96–108.

[2] Cf. Lovelace in Richardson, *Clarissa Harlowe* (ii), *Works* (1883), v. 191–2.

[3] *Emile* (Amsterdam, 1762), iv. 199.

[4] *Thraliana*, i. 502. Cf. Fanny Burney's remarks, *Diary*, iv. 223: 'My father himself likes and approves all accomplishments for women better than the dead languages.'

[5] *Letters to a Young Lady, in which the Duties and Character of Women are considered, chiefly with a reference to prevailing opinions* (1806), p. 310.

[6] 'A Father's Legacy to his Daughters', *Chapone's Letters, Gregory's Legacy, and Pennington's Advice* (1830), p. 144.

graces. His awkwardness and unsociability were thrown into high relief by the polite address of a second scholar, Dr. Marchmont, who, unlike the first, united

deep learning with general knowledge, and the graceful exterior of a man of the world, with the erudition and science of a fellow of a college.[1]

A galaxy of minor characters in *Camilla: or, a Picture of Youth* serves principally to set off contrasting qualities in the heroine, for, as Mr. Twining observed, if the novel is to be a prose Epic it must concern itself largely with the adventures of its major character and pursue its chief theme (in this novel, Camilla's education and improvement) to the end.[2] Paragons and patterns like Lavinia Tyrold or the Lady Isabella Irby threw the heroine's defects and errors into high relief, while faulty characters like Indiana, Miss Dennel, or Miss Margland made her virtues shine the more brightly. Edgar longed to present Camilla to object-lessons in good conduct like the Lady Isabella Irby—'a model for a woman of rank in her manners, and a model for a woman of every station in her mind'.[3] The exotic Indiana, on the other hand, supplied a contrast in selfishness, hard-heartedness, lack of sensibility and charity, that gave an added lustre to Camilla's naturally good qualities and inculcated virtues.[3] Miss Dennel, married at fifteen years of age to a young squire of twenty-seven, exhibited comical failures in filial and marital duty, supplying another set of contrasts and recalling in some ways the Branghtons of *Evelina*.

Then, turning to Camilla, 'Dear,' she cried, 'how grave you look! Dear, I wonder you don't marry too! When I ordered my coach, just now, I was ready to cry for joy, to think of not having to ask papa about it. And to-day, at breakfast, I dare say I rung twenty times, for one thing or another. As fast as ever I could think of any thing, I went to ringing again. For when I was at papa's, every time I rang the bell, he always asked me what I wanted. Only think of keeping one under so!'

'And what in the world said Mr. Lissin to so prodigious an uproar?'

---

[1] *Camilla*, i. 303; v. 140–2.
[2] Cited in A.L.S. (Berg) from FBA to CB, 6 July 1795.
[3] *Camilla*, iii. 355. Cf. i. 190–224, 257–65.

This independent conduct, as Mrs. Arlbery suggested, was likely to bring on its own punishment, for 'Mr. Lissin, who is a country squire of Northwick, will soon teach her another lesson'.[1]

Though in *Camilla* there were no characters among the idle rich as amusing as Miss Larolles or Mr. Meadows, Madame d'Arblay still drew satiric pictures of *ton*-led people, their supercilious airs and mental vacuity. Lord Newford is an insolent tonnish young man; Lady Alithea Selmore is a ton-queen, who on the Pantiles at Tunbridge Wells or in the Rooms at Southampton superseded Mrs. Arlbery and was in turn superseded by the youthful and beautiful Mrs. Berlinton.[2]

As in *Evelina* and *Cecilia* Madame d'Arblay's satire on manners included strictures on the vulgarity of low life—untidiness, meanness, stinginess, bad taste, the tendencies to haggle, squabble, and to litigate.[2] These personages from the lower levels of society are sometimes anatomized in formal sketches, though, as of old, their characteristics emerge more amusingly in self-revelatory dialogue.

'Mr. Dubster, if I'm not ashamed of you! how can you forget yourself so? talking to gentlemen at such a rate!'

'Why what should hinder me?' cried he; 'do you think I shall put up with every thing as I used to do when you first knew me, and we used to meet at Mr. Typton's, the tallow chandler's, in Shug-lane? no, Mrs. Mittin, nor no such a thing; I'm turned gentleman myself, now, as much as the best of 'em; for I've nothing to do, but just what I choose.'

'I protest, Mr. Dubster,' cried Mrs. Mittin . . . 'Where's the use of telling every body he's a tallow chandler? and as to my meeting with you there once or so, in a way, I desire you'll mention it no more, for it's so long ago, I have no recollection of it.'

'No! why don't you remember —'

'Fiddle, faddle, what's the good of ripping up old stories about nothing? when you're with genteel people, you must do as I do; never talk about business at all.'[3]

A character-sketch of Mrs. Mittin, developed into a *character* in the technical sense, is a masterly delineation of folly, but, for

---

[1] *Camilla*, ii. 258; iii. 147, 340–2; v. 221–8.
[2] See 'Specimens of Taste', *Camilla*, ii. 285–307; 'Traits of Character', iii. 343–74.
[3] *Camilla*, iii. 365–6, 340–2.

all its anatomizing penetration, it scarcely brings the busy vulgar little person to life as vividly as her own conversation.

'Well now, young ladies . . . I'm going to tell you a secret. Do you know, for all I call myself Mrs. I'm single?'

'Dear, la!' exclaimed Miss Dennel; 'and for all you're so old!'

'So old, Miss! Who told you I was so old? I'm not so very old as you may think me. I'm no particular age, I assure you. Why, what made you think of that?'

'La, I don't know; only you don't look very young.'

'I can't help that, Miss Dennel. Perhaps you mayn't look young yourself one of these days. People can't always stand still just at a particular minute. Why how old, now, do you take me to be? Come, be sincere.'

'La, I'm sure I can't tell; only I thought you was an old woman.'

'An old woman! Lord, my dear, people would laugh to hear you. You don't know what an old woman is. Why it's being a cripple, and blind, and deaf, and dumb, and slavering, and without a tooth. Pray, how am I like all that?'

'Nay, I'm sure I don't know; only I thought, by the look of your face, you must be monstrous old.'

'Lord, I can't think what you've got in your head, Miss Dennel! I never heard as much before, since I was born. Why the reason I'm called Mrs. is not because of that, I assure you; but because I'd a mind to be taken for a young widow, on account that every body likes a young widow; and if one is called Miss, people begin so soon to think one an old maid, that it's quite disagreeable.'[1]

In *Camilla*, as in *Evelina* and *Cecilia*, different classes mingle and jostle together and the comedy often arises from their impact on one another. But though the components of *Camilla* are similar to those of *Evelina*, their proportions are reversed. The didactic and moral sections of the new work outrun the satiric or comic parts. In the end, however, *Camilla* fails in its moral purpose, and for two reasons. Readers interested in applied ethics will hardly turn to tenets, concepts, and principles translated into juvenile action. The total effect of *Camilla*, unlike that of many contemporary works written for the guidance of youth, is puerile rather than aphoristic. Teen-agers, on the other hand, who might be interested in the characters or the love-story are discouraged by the immoderate length of the plot, the rhetorical language, and the moralizing. The action,

[1] See p. 267, n. 3.

vacillating repetitively on a slight theme, is protracted to five volumes. Though contemporary reviewers commended Madame d'Arblay's fertility in the invention of characters, praising some of the characters as 'portraits of real manners', they rightly thought that the work was too long in proportion to its matter.[1]

Dr. Burney, who had worried over plans for Fanny's book, the advertisements, the sale, and then the reviews, 'never felt so zealous for the defence of any of her writings'.[2] Though the reviews sometimes devoted as much as fourteen pages to the book and quotations from it, and though they treated it with great respect as the work of a major writer, Dr. Burney was disturbed by adverse criticism. The observation that *aliquando bonus dormitat Homerus* and that Madame d'Arblay too drowsed at times 'riled' him, he said, for he had not found any part of the book tedious even on a third reading. A Mr. Batt also ventured some adverse criticisms in the Doctor's hearing.

I flew at him like a Tiger—& among other things sd if the book was not a *perfect monster*—it had certainly intrinsic merit & originalness which sufficiently blazed like the sun to render me & many others unable to see its spots.[2]

Madame d'Arblay confessed to being 'a good deal chagrined' by the critics. 'The panegyric is entangled, and so blended with blame as to lose almost all effect.' Yet she could afford to be philosophical. The sale, she learned, 'had been one of the most rapid ever known for a Guinea Book: it is 4 times that of Evelina, and nearly double that of Cecilia'. The publishers had given 1,000 pounds for the copyright (affirming that a similar price had never yet been given), and the subscriptions were expected to clear another thousand.[2] Madame d'Arblay could remember the days when novels made their way without the help or hindrance of learned pens, and so it had again proved. Novels 'will be judged by the various multitude, not the fastidious few'.[3]

They want no recommendation for being handed about but that of

---

[1] See p. 264, n. 2.

[2] A.L.S. (Bodleian) from CB to CB, Jr., 3 Aug. 1796; six letters (Berg) from CB to FBA, 12, 14, 16 July, 6, 23 Sept., 2 Dec. 1796. See Diary MSS. (Berg), pp. 4938, 4972 (Feb. 1797); A.L.S. (Berg) from FBA to Mary Port Waddington, 2 Oct. 1796.   [3] *Diary*, v. 297–301.

being new, and they frequently become established, or sunk into oblivion, before that high literary tribunal has brought them to a trial.[1]

In any case, as Fanny herself seemed sometimes to forget, *Camilla* was not a novel but a *work*. 'I mean this work to be sketches of characters and morals put in action.' In the advertisement to the French translation of 1798, it was confidently asserted that

le Lecteur y retrouve Miss Burney dans une foule de vérités de sentiment mêlées à ses récits, dans une philosophie douce, aimable, toujours en action, toujours pleine de leçons utiles pour tous les âges.[2]

The *Monthly Review* also pointed out the usefulness of the work: 'We may principally recommend it to the world as a *warning* "picture of youth;"—as a guide for the conduct of young females in the most important circumstances and situations of life.'[3] This conclusion had compensated Madame d'Arblay, as she said, for all the unfavourable comments and strictures.[1]

She had succeeded only too well in her purpose. In spite of the winsomeness and grace of the heroine, in spite of lively sections and some comical and realistic characterization, *Camilla* has shared the fate of the category to which it aspired— warning guides, books of sermons, courtesy-books, and histories of manners. 'The second title, *a Picture of Youth*, is well, very well chosen', commented Charles the Greek scholar, 'for the work is much better calculated to instruct and improve the rising generation, than *Cecilia*, or even *Evelina*. It must become a Family Book!'[4]

Camilla: or, a Picture of Youth will keep its place as a courtesy-novel on a dusty though 'improving' shelf, which, however neglected, contains nevertheless some charming old reading: Fénelon's *De l'éducation des filles*, Dr. Gregory's *A Father's Legacy to his Daughters*, Lord Halifax's *The Lady's New-Year's Gift*, Mrs. Chapone's *Letters on the Improvement of the Mind*, Madame de Genlis's *Adèle et Théodore*, and other legacies, gifts, and letters from the past concerned with ethical ideals for the young lady— part of the perennial legacy of the wise to the young.

---

[1] See p. 269, n. 3.
[2] *Camilla, ou la peinture de la jeunesse* (2nd ed., Paris, 1798).
[3] See p. 264, n. 2.
[4] A.L.S. (Osborn) from CB, Jr., to M. d'A, 17 July 1796.

'CRUELLY BLASTED'

(1797–1800)

She [Susan] was the soul of my soul from my first
remembrance in life!
MADAME D'ARBLAY, 1800[1]

IN spite of the faults found in *Camilla* Charles was able to
report in October that in less than three months only 500
copies of the work remained of the 4,000 printed, and in
November that nearly all the 4,000 copies of *Camilla* had been
sold.[1] With the proceeds the d'Arblays could now begin the
project nearest their hearts—a house of their own. Shortly after
their marriage Mr. Locke had designated a beautiful plot of
ground on his property, a small field and a site for the house
that they might some day hope to build. The Frenchman
thought he had a lease good for ninety-nine years and he did
not foresee legal complications that would force him to sell his
house when Norbury Park itself was sold.

In the autumn of 1796 the well was dug, the foundation laid,
and the framework prepared. M. d'Arblay had drawn twenty
plans for the house,[2] and Fanny thought the consultations with
the carpenter extremely comic because of her husband's dearth
of English words and the carpenter's dearth of ideas. The gentle
chevalier, both architect and builder, worked like a labourer
through the summer of 1797 and by November Camilla Cottage
was habitable. Moving-day was an event—one of the happiest
of days in the lives of all three d'Arblays.

So bewitched were we with the impending change, that, though
from six o'clock to three we were hard at work, without a kettle to
boil the breakfast, or a knife to cut bread for a luncheon, we missed
nothing, wanted nothing, and were as insensible to fatigue as to
hunger.

M. d'Arblay set out on foot, loaded with remaining relics of things,
to us precious, and Betty afterwards with a remnant glass or two;

---

[1] Diary MSS. (Berg), box viii; *Diary*, v. 292–354.
[2] A plan for the interior of the house is extant in the Berg Collection, NYPL.

the other maid had been sent two days before. I was forced to have a chaise for my Alex and me, and a few looking-glasses, a few folios. . . .

My mate, striding over hedge and ditch, arrived first, though he set out after, to welcome me to our new dwelling; and we entered our new best room, in which I found a glorious fire of wood, and a little bench, borrowed of one of the departing carpenters: nothing else. We contrived to make room for each other, and Alex disdained all rest. His spirits were so high upon finding two or three rooms totally free for his horse (alias any stick he can pick up) and himself, unincumbered by chairs and tables and such-like lumber, that he was as merry as a little Andrew and as wild as twenty colts. Here we unpacked a small basket containing three or four loaves, and, with a garden-knife, fell to work; some eggs had been procured from a neighbouring farm, and one saucepan had been brought. We dined, therefore, exquisitely, and drank to our new possession from a glass of clear water out of our new well.[1]

The effort that went into the writing of *Camilla* and the building of Camilla Cottage had brought the d'Arblays to a bench before their own fireside. Though this seemed 'a Paradise', further spurs to literary invention made themselves felt everywhere in the cold floors, empty rooms, and untapestried walls. Almost immediately Fanny turned happy thoughts to the work that since the publication of *Evelina* she had been encouraged to attempt—a comedy. In January, 1798, she informed her father that she was immersed in 'a scribbling business that fills all my scribbling ideas, & takes me up all I can exist from my little occupying Alec', but that 'the fear of raising expectation' made her unwilling to expand upon the subject.[2]

In visits to London in 1797–8 she joined groups of Burneys in theatre parties and on two occasions sat by 'royal favour' in her old place in the royal boxes.[3] On those evenings she saw Mrs. Cowley's *The Belle's Stratagem* and at least five new plays— *The Heir at Law, Cheap Living, The Castle Spectre, Secrets Worth Knowing,* and *He's much to Blame,* the work of the contemporary playwrights George Colman (the younger), Frederick Reynolds,

[1] See p. 271, n. 1.

[2] A.L.S. (Barrett) from FBA to CB, 18 Jan. 1798.

[3] A.L.S. (Barrett) from FBA to CBFB, 5 Apr. 1798. See also letters (Berg) from FBA to SBP and a Letter Book (Osborn) in General d'Arblay's hand. According to Genest the dates of the first nights were respectively: 15 July, 21 Oct., 14 Dec. 1797, 11 Jan., 13 Feb. 1798.

Matthew G. Lewis, Thomas Morton, and Thomas Holcroft, respectively.[1]

Madame d'Arblay's new comedy, 'Love and Fashion',[2] at least in the disposition of the characters and their relations to one another, had its source, however, not in contemporary drama, but in *As You Like It*, where the younger of two brothers, in the role of the bad Duke, banishes the elder, the good Duke Senior, to the forest. In 'Love and Fashion' the good Lord Exbury, forced by his son's debts to give up his town house, goes to visit his brother Lord Ardville, but finding himself unwelcome there is forced to retreat to an unpretentious house in the country. He is followed by his daughter, his ward Hilaria Dalton, and a faithful servant (an eighteenth-century Adam willing to serve without wages). Lord Exbury has two sons, the elder the profligate and spendthrift Mordaunt, who has ruined him, and the younger the exemplary monitor-lover, Valentine. Though all this is, mechanically speaking, vaguely Shakespearean, the Argument and the principles in dispute were those suggested in Fanny's own Forest of Arden. The main issue here debated had entered into the choice she herself had made five years earlier between love in rural poverty and a loveless fashionable life in London. For all her happiness Fanny had apparently not forgotten the unfriendly reactions to her marriage, and the piece may easily be read as a *retort courteous* to Mrs. Ord and others who had cut her.

The burden of the Argument is given to the heroine Hilaria, who throughout the play wavers between the proposal of the wealthy but aged Lord Ardville (the wicked brother and villain of the piece) and that of Valentine, who can offer only young love and a competence. The fop, Archy Fineer, plays the devil's advocate, at strategic moments reminding his cousin Hilaria of the equipages, nabob muslins, the faro table, and the widow's jointure that would be hers with the wealthy marriage. Hilaria's state of indecision is revealed in successive soliloquies. She begins to see beauty in the landscape and, overhearing a

---

[1] See p. 272, n. 3.

[2] The manuscript of this play is in the Berg Collection, the NYPL. The script (236 pp.) is carefully copied into a notebook ($7\frac{1}{2} \times 4\frac{1}{4}$ in.) covered with marble paper. This has the appearance of a final draft. Boxed with it are 29 scraps of paper from a first draft. There are revisions scribbled in a Memorandum Book of 1801.

rustic love-scene between a Woodcutter and a Haymaker, perceives that country people may be objects of envy. Favourable fluctuations such as this are periodically counteracted, however, by gifts from Lord Ardville, and it is not until the last scene, when Valentine himself appears with a sturdy sermon on the criteria by which a husband should be chosen, that Hilaria is brought to conquer the 'Tyrant Fashion'. The moral is that the suitor's disposition, principles, humours, age, and character should be looked into. Not

for the gratification of bye-standers, the applause of lookers on—are we to chuse the friends of our bosoms—the Partners of our days.[1]

When Lord Exbury chimes in, 'Has a man hands, & shall he fear to work for the Wife of his choice?', Lord Ardville can only hide his discountenanced head and make his nephew Valentine his heir.

The first theme of 'Love and Fashion' is, therefore, an indictment of the *mariage de convenance*, and, as a subsidiary thesis, Fanny's usual castigation of the vices and follies of fashionable life. Lord Ardville, Miss Exbury, Archy Fineer, and Mordaunt are made to betray in their own lively dialogue what Madame d'Arblay most wished to condemn—arrogant vanity and selfishness, affectation, ill-nature, and hard-heartedness. In the closing scenes the votaries of fashion are punished and love triumphs.

In an involved subplot a triangular relationship is developed among the servants: Dawson, a confirmed braggart; Davis, who appears in a preliminary list of *dramatis personae* as a Mr. Exaggerator; and Innis, a lady's maid who ambitiously copies all the vanities and follies of her betters. Attached to Lord Ardville is a sycophant Mr. Litchburn, who includes in his character that of a Mr. Literal ('one who answers always to the word, never to the meaning'). The servants at Windsor or Kew may have supplied some of the ideas for this group, though their terror of a ghost in a haunted cupboard and the resolution of this mystery reflect the reaction of the realist, Fanny, to Gothic drama and romance.

Whatever excites terror . . . ought to be traced to its source. . . . Like all other reported apparitions, it wanted but investigation, to be metamorphosed into fraud, or mistake.[1]

[1] See p. 273, n. 2.

The rustic scenes include an encounter between the profligate Mordaunt and Kate, a haymaker, wherein Audrey puts the eighteenth-century Touchstone in his place. The woodcutter's honest wooing, staged in its view of domestic bliss as an object-lesson for Hilaria, must mark a nadir in sentimental mawkishness and banality. Such scenes were meant as arguments for the country versus the town or for domestic life versus fashionable life.

The happiness of true Love is domestic Life; the very existence of Fashion is public admiration.[1]

At the close of 1799 the enterprising Charles, always eager to help Fanny, had shown her comedy to Thomas Harris, the Manager of Covent Garden Theatre, and on October 30 he wrote a jubilant report: 'Huzza! Huzza! Huzza! Mr. H[arris] admires the Fable—& will bring it into use in the month of March!'[2] The manager had suggested cutting down the underplot, especially the sentimental scenes between Davis and Innis, Mordaunt and Kate, as well as the long moralizing soliloquies of Valentine and Hilaria. He was delighted with Archy Fineer, Litchburn, and Hilaria (as 'quite drawn from Nature') and he offered £400 for the manuscript. Dr. Burney, remembering perhaps the humiliating reception of *Edwy and Elgiva*, objected strongly, but Charles and Fanny would perhaps have gone on had not a new family tragedy eclipsed every thought or possibility of producing the comedy in March, 1800. Mr. Harris returned the manuscript, agreeing to a year's postponement.[2]

In the troubled annals of the Burneys no period was free from anxieties and certainly not the years 1797–1801, which saw Susan's death, the death of Mrs. Burney, Charlotte's unfortunate marriage to the irascible Ralph Broome, the elopement of James and his half-sister Sarah Harriet, the rising power of Napoleon, and the beginning of Madame d'Arblay's long exile in France.

In June, 1795, Susan had 'left Mickleham—Norbury Park—Bookham—every spot most dear to her, to go and live in London'. In the despondent letters that she wrote to Fanny it

---

[1] See p. 273, n. 2.
[2] A.L.S. (Berg) from CB, Jr., to FBA, 30 Oct. 1799. Also *Diary*, v. 459–61, vi. 419; and 3 A.L. (Berg) from FBA to EBB, 19 Nov. 1799, [1800], 18 Mar. 1801.

patently appeared that all happiness in her marriage had
ceased four years earlier and that her health was again in
jeopardy. The boisterous Captain was now or was soon to be
'the cruel Major' or 'the Temps', whose unreasoning rages
frightened the children and the servants.[1] Marital infidelity,
so conspicuous in his second marriage, had probably ruined the
first one, though at this time at least Susan seemed to suffer
most from her husband's sadistic pleasure in separating her
from her precocious son, the fine child-prodigy Norbury, born
at Norbury Park in November, 1785. It was not unusual for
boys to be sent away to school (as Norbury was) at the age
of seven or eight, but even in the holidays Susan was seldom
allowed to see her son, at least to see him alone. In 1794 the
Major took him to Dublin and placed him under a tutor—
Mr. Maturin. Susan noticed that only letters sent in care of the
tutor reached the boy, and she suspected her husband of inter-
cepting others.[2]

At the outbreak of the Irish rebellion, moreover, the Major
resigned his commission in the English forces. Susan, who had
the task of confessing the resignation to her father before he
should hear it from Sir Joseph Banks or others, found the ordeal
'sufficiently painful', for the Doctor was already annoyed by the
failure of the Major to pay his debts.[3] An extant legal document
shows that in 1795 Dr. Burney had advanced £2,000 on a
mortgage of £3,000 on Phillips's property at Belcotton in
County Louth.[3] The Major then owed the Doctor £160 interest,
but he did not keep his interest day with even 'a lying-excuse'
or 'apology for so uncommon a delay'. 'What a savage!'[3] Of
the family, Fanny and Esther alone could drink a toast to good
Husbands. 'Who besides can you give it to without exciting a
sigh?' Fanny was writing just then about Maria Rishton's
troubles with her despotic Norfolk squire, but her deepest sighs
were for Susan.[4]

---

[1] *Diary*, v. 261. See also copies of Susan Burney's Journals (the Public Library,
Armagh), partly printed in R. Brimley Johnson, pp. 119–335.

[2] 2 A.L.S. (Berg) from SBP to FBA, 13, 26 Nov. 1795; Diary MSS. (Berg), pp.
4952, 5037; A.L. (Berg) from FBA to Mary Port Waddington, 19 June 1795.

[3] A Bond of Indemnity (Osborn); 3 A.L.S. (Berg) from CB to CB, Jr., 2 Nov.,
14, 20 Dec. 1799; A.L.S. (Osborn) to CB, Jr., 6 July 1801; Diary MSS. (Berg),
p. 4979.

[4] Diary MSS. (Berg), p. 4986. Also A.L.S. (Berg) from FBA to EBB, 29 June
1797.

In August, 1796, Phillips returned from a visit to Ireland with a determination to take his family back with him. 'Secret afflictions' at heart and uneasy forebodings, perhaps, about her fading health caused Susan to shrink from what was to her a dreary exile, separation from her family and, as she doubtless considered, from the arts and civilization. Fanny waited anxiously at Bookham for news, and on several occasions left on secret missions to London to try to comfort Susan, to rouse her from despondency, and to encourage her in the wifely attributes of submission and compliance, the marital duty that the Burneys thought she should not shirk. Finally Susan acquiesced. On September 15, 1796, she was able to reassure Fanny.

The terrible struggle is over—I think I shall be capable of submitting as you would have me—not from *mere* despondence—but from something better.[1]

In the same month the Doctor wrote gloomily to Fanny about Susan's health, the journey, the voyage, and the season before her. He feared that the 'half mad & unfeeling' Major meant 'to travel to the sea side in a strange kind of open carriage, wch is constructed with a basket that is to contain the whole family!' The Doctor had seen the contraption, and even though he had little hope of 'working upon' the Major's 'wrong-headed & tyrannical spirit', he intended to remonstrate if this plan were put into effect.[2] In October Susan wrote accounts of her journey to the sea, 'the desolate Isle of Anglesea', Holyhead, the voyage, and her arrival in Dublin, where at last she was permitted to see Norbury alone for five or six minutes.[3] There were letters about Dublin and the journey to Belcotton in County Louth.[4]

In the next two years Susan wrote to her sisters about the Major's flagrant pursuit of Jane Brabazon,[3] but it was only with the greatest difficulty that they could elicit details about her failing health and strength or about the unfinished farmhouse

[1] A.L. (Berg) from SBP to FBA, 15 Sept. 1796; correspondence (Berg) between FBA and SBP, 1795–6; A.L. (Berg) from FBA to M. d'A, Sept. 1796.
[2] A.L.S. (Berg) from CB to FBA, Sept. 1796.
[3] See p. 276, n. 1.
[4] 3 A.L.S. (Berg) from SBP to FBA, CB, and CBF, Oct., Nov., and 9 Dec. 1796, respectively.

at Belcotton, the farmstead, the flat and dreary country, as she thought it, facing the desolate sea. On all subjects except that of health, Fanny and the Doctor said, Susan's word was gospel. Madame d'Arblay wrote to her sister with 'constant dread of not writing to *her* alone'. 'The flames that would blaze forth at sight of any thing I could write naturally would be tremendous.'[1] Sometimes the sisters adopted the ruse of writing about one another in the third person, the trick they had employed when Fanny was at court. 'Grief & indignation for that beloved of our Hearts never subside,—but astonishment is *all gone* for him who produces them.'[1]

Scarcely had Susan departed when, at Chelsea, Mrs. Burney, long referred to in the Burney letters as the Patient, again suffered violent hæmorrhages from the lungs.[2] On October 20, 1796, she died. Dr. Burney's grief and sense of loss, his pity for her sufferings and his tributes to her virtues are reflected in his Memoirs and more vividly still in his letters of the time to such friends as the Reverend Mr. Twining, Christian Latrobe, and Ralph Griffiths.[3]

No expectation of these events, is sufficient to fortify the mind against harrowing afflictions, whenever they arrive. The being bereaved of a bosom friend & rational companion of 30 years, who had virtues, cultivation, & intellectual powers, sufficient to make home not only desirable, but preferable to places where amusement is sought & promised; add to this a similarity of taste and coincidence of opinion in all matters of wch the discussion is apt to ruffle the temper and alienate affection, & who can calculate my loss?

Christian Latrobe, a frequent visitor at Chelsea at this time, wrote of what Mrs. Burney's friends must miss in her hospitality and 'pleasing & profitable Conversation'.

All her friends have to lament the loss of a most worthy, sensible and affectionate friend, possessed of a rectitude of sentiment not often matched.[4]

---

[1] A.L.S. (Berg) from FBA to EBB, 29 June 1797; A.L. (Barrett) to EBB, 14 Sept. 1799; and A.L. (Barrett) to SBP, 17 Aug. 1797.

[2] A.L.S. (Barrett) from SHB to Mrs. Arthur Young, 20 Oct. 1796. Cf. joint A.L.S. (Barrett) from Mrs. Burney and Miss Young to the same, 19 July 1796.

[3] A.L.S. (Osborn) from CB to Christian Latrobe, 10 Nov. 1796; A.L.S. (Bodleian; draft, Osborn) to Ralph Griffiths, 2 Nov. 1796; and A.L.S. in Diary MSS. (Berg) to the Rev. T. Twining, 6 Dec. 1796.

[4] A.L.S. (Osborn) from Christian Latrobe to CB, 29 Oct. 1796.

All the Burney stepchildren (except Susan) arrived at Chelsea, shocked and unhappy. Yet their reactions probably resembled Fanny's:

Affliction, indeed, I felt not,—it was impossible where so unearned— but concern I felt, in various ways, both for herself & my Father. The better, also, rises highest after the worse part can no more displease.[1]

She had the justice to chronicle her stepmother's last generous act of devotion to the Doctor.

She charged Sally and her maid both not to call my father when she appeared to be dying; and not disturb him if her death should happen in the night, nor to let him hear it till he arose at his usual time.[2]

Long afterwards she could review her own unhappy relationship with her stepmother with a little more moderation, though the perspective of the years did not change the facts.

Her Temper alone was in fault, not her heart or intentions. But for that impracticable Temper, I should always have loved her as I did at first. . . . But of this no more, Peace to her Manes, & rest to her Soul! Such is my truly sincere prayer,—& such I uttered it—Sarah can tell you—over her Coffin.[3]

In the winter the Doctor began to read and destroy old letters, 'the record of past happiness'.

My dear & ever to be lamented companion & I, have often been separated by travels . . . but though corporally distant, we have never been long mentally asunder; wch you will readily believe, when I tell you, that I have destroyed near 500 letters of my own writing to the dear soul, during absence; and wch in her kindness and partiality, she had thought worth preserving. And these, I am certain, produced an equal number from her.[4]

Madame d'Arblay returned with her family for a fortnight at Christmas and helped her father with the reading and sorting— the first steps in the editing of the Burney papers.

The next family concern to command Fanny's attention was Charlotte's plans for a second marriage and her plea that Fanny gain the consent of the Doctor and James and persuade

---

[1] Diary MSS. (Berg), p. 4946.   [2] See p. 271, n. 1.
[3] See Note J, p. 494.   [4] See p. 278, n. 3.

them to draw up the marriage settlements. At his death in 1792 Clement Francis had left his widow and three children (Charlotte, Marianne, and Clement) well provided for, but in December, 1796, Charlotte, as pretty and gay a widow as she had been a girl, had begun to write to Fanny about a Mr. Ralph Broome, one-time Captain in the Bengal Army, and the witty author of *Simpkin's Letters* and other political pamphlets. Esther knew only 'the exterior' of the gentleman, which was not striking either for 'elegance or gentility'.[1] She knew that Broome had been unhappily married to a Miss Jeffereys, now dead, and that before this, having spent some time in Bengal, he had had a natural daughter by an Indian lady of high rank and that this daughter, now about seventeen, had been educated in England. Maria Rishton was amazed at Charlotte's giving up 'an affluent independence' for so 'disgusting a Being both in mind and person'.[2] Fanny understood that Broome's first attraction was 'the Fame of his sportive genius', but how, she added, 'that can operate against all charm of manner, all sympathy of taste, & all liberality of kindness—can only be attributed to that eternal wonder-raiser, the wanton God who pierces Hearts'.[3] Esther could only credit the choice to 'the total want of common sense & reason'.[3]

On Charlotte's plea, however, Fanny set off on her diplomatic mission and at first made some progress. A reference to *Simpkin's Letters* brought a smile to the Doctor's face, a smile almost immediately erased by a recollection of Broome's latter-day republicanism. When the Doctor had had time to verify his impressions about Broome's stock-jobbing politics and Jacobinical principles, and when in the business of the marriage settlements he and James were met with evasions and flimsy excuses, they refused their consent. Charlotte's infatuation, however, carried her beyond her family's warnings and objections, and on March 1, 1798, her old friend Mr. Hoole gave her away in marriage at Marylebone Church.[4] In spite of Fanny's representations about Charlotte's 'perfectly spotless,

---

[1] Diary MSS. (Berg), pp. 5103–8, 5128; A. L.S. (PML) from FBA to JB, 19 Nov. 1793; copies of letters (Letter Book, Osborn) from FBA to Ralph Broome and to JB, 1797–8.

[2] A.L.S. (Berg) from Maria Allen Rishton to FBA, 12 Jan. 1803.

[3] 2 A.L. (Berg) from FBA to SBP, 12 Mar., 13 May 1798.

[4] A.L.S. (Barrett) from CBFB to FBA, 1 Mar. 1798.

nay, exemplary life up to this period', it was some time before
the Doctor could bring himself to see her,[1] and unhappily his
fears were soon justified. The juvenile journals of Charlotte and
Marianne Francis,[2] like Daisy Ashford's *The Young Visiters*,
reveal more about their elders than they themselves could
realize—the magnificent and memorable proportions of their
stepfather's rage on discovering that the servant Frank had
brushed his coat with the shoe-brush, his habitual fretfulness and
paroxysms of rage, his 'fractious and gloomy temper', his premature senility, and the howling days of his last illness and death
at Bath on February 24, 1805. Fanny could never condemn
Charlotte,

this perfectly *good* soul who can never have any errour of Heart,
whatever she may have of Head; never any of design, whatever she
may have of execution.[3]

'Poor infatuated thing! What a life of quiet enjoyment has she
thrown away thus thanklessly!'[4]

After Mrs. Burney's death Fanny rejoiced that the family
could at last feel welcome at Chelsea, and she was especially
glad 'to see our worthy & dear James once again there upon
his own proper & deserved footing'.[5] Soon, however, she began
to see 'with something beyond grief' that in spite of the presence
of her stepsister, Sarah Harriet, there was for the Doctor at
Chelsea 'almost nothing but solitude' or the alternative, 'a
species of dissention to which he has little been accustomed in
his daughters'.[6] The cause of the dissention was the Doctor's
indignation at the unfilial, if not unnatural, behaviour of Sally
and James, for no sooner had that strange tar gained free access
to his father's dwelling than ample reason appeared for Mrs.
Burney's having closed the doors against him.

In August, 1798, Sarah Harriet, author of the novel *Clarentine*
(1796), was twenty-six years old. James, then forty-eight, had
in 1785 married Sally Payne, by whom he had had three

---

[1] See p. 280, n. 1.
[2] In the Barrett and the Berg Collections, respectively. Cf. A.L.S. (Berg)
from CPB to his mother Mrs. Charles Burney, Jr., 24 Jan. 1804; A.L.S. (Barrett)
from CBFB and Charlotte Francis to FBA, [1804].
[3] See p. 280, n. 3.
[4] A.L.S. (Berg) from FBA to CB, 20 May 1801.
[5] A.L. (Barrett) from FBA to SBP, 12 Nov. 1796.
[6] Diary MSS. (Berg), pp. 5111–12; also pp. 5098–9, 5128–9.

children, Katherine, who had died as a little girl, Martin (best known by Lamb's descriptions of him), and Sally, born in November, 1796. They lived in a house in James Street (Buckingham Gate), bequeathed to him by his father's friend John Hayes. Whatever the reason, James was so unhappy at home that he had already parted from his wife twice.[1] In the nineties he had seemed to spend much time with his half-sister. Together they had visited Charles at Clifton, Madame d'Arblay at West Humble, and they had gone on excursions elsewhere. On his return from a vacation at Margate or Ramsgate he had spent the day at Chelsea, staying on till midnight without going home to inquire about his little daughter, then in precarious health. The Doctor blamed not only James but Sally, often treated her coldly or addressed her with 'bitter raillery or Harshness', quite unable to utter the real fears underlying his discomfort.[2] In September, 1798, James again proposed leaving his wife, children, and home, taking lodgings near Chelsea Hospital, and boarding with his father.[2] He left this proposal on his father's desk, and the Doctor finding it late at night sat up for hours composing a refusal to a request that James himself could only suppose 'would be attributed to an improper Attachment to his sister'. In the morning the Doctor was still 'disordered and agitated' but quite determined: 'I will never suffer any such impropriety or countenance such proceedings.'[2] The next day at Chelsea James read his father's reply, went home to pack up his papers, and on the following day the couple eloped. James looked 'wretchedly', Sarah, 'happy & flighty'. She left the traditional notes to all concerned: 'I trust I am gone to be happy & comfortable.'[2]

On September 2, the day the fugitives left, Maria Rishton, then staying at Chelsea as a temporary refuge from the Norfolk squire whom she was now deserting,[3] sent a servant all the way to West Humble with a hurried letter describing the late events

---

[1] A.L.S. (Osborn) from CB to CB, Jr., 18 Sept. 1798; A.L.S. (Berg) from FB to EBB, 5 Oct. 1798.

[2] For full accounts of these events, see 7 long letters (Barrett) from Maria Allen Rishton to FBA, 2 Sept.–Nov. 1798. Also 2 A.L. (Berg) from FBA to SBP, 13–15 Dec. 1798; to EBB, 22 Nov. 1798.

[3] For the long tale of Maria's marital difficulties see a packet of some 30 letters (Barrett), written in the years 1796–8 (some, later) to FBA. Also Diary MSS. (Berg), pp. 5057–8.

and beseeching Fanny to come to Chelsea. The Doctor had gone on Friday to his old friend Lady Mary Duncan at Hampton, and Maria was alone. Over the week-end she wrote two long reports on all she had seen and all she had heard about James and Sally, with pleas to Fanny for counsel on how to present their action to the world. In these letters and those of October and November, in the Doctor's letters to Madame d'Arblay, hers to Susan, Esther, and Charlotte, and theirs in reply, there are many references in the next five years to the 'Recluse Man and the maiden' and their wanderings (first to Fetter Lane, then to Bristol, and finally to a shabby dwelling, 21 John Street, near Fitzroy Square), and, after a while, hopeful deliberations on how they might be reclaimed.

In this biography, at least, it will not be necessary to dwell on a tale told in former times by Mrs. Burney from which both Maria and Stephen Allen had recoiled in horror and which they had refused to believe, though it had made a strong impression on the Doctor.[1] James and Sally had long been friends, but they were lately, as all the family knew, almost inseparable companions. On Maria's arrival at Chelsea the Doctor had confided to her 'his *dreadful* apprehensions about their uncommon Intimacy', apprehensions that now '*shook* him with agony'.[1] Shortly after his return from Hampton, he drove out to West Humble for such consolation as the d'Arblays could give him.[2] For the first time in his life, he said, he had been made to fly from his home, 'now made wholly comfortless & dejecting to him'. Madame d'Arblay perceived that he had been secretly but deeply wounded for a long time by the cavalier attitudes of James and Sally. 'God forgive them!—is all I can, or dare say—& preserve this most beloved & reverend parent to forgive them too!' The Doctor wished to speak of the present 'heavy evil' but once and to allude to it no more. 'He struggled only, he said, to forget it!' Fanny noticed with great concern that any mention she made of the subject 'not only caused immediate change of countenance, but a mixture of gloom & agitation [that] rested on his spirits the rest of the day, and I always found that his night afterwards had suffered from it'.[3]

---

[1] See p. 282, n. 2.   [2] See p. 281, n. 6.
[3] Ten letters (Berg) from FBA to SBP, n.d., 13–15 Dec. 1798; 12 Mar., 14 Apr.,

For many months Fanny herself was not proof against the shocking ideas Mrs. Burney had suggested. The d'Arblays put off going to town for fear of seeing James.

I felt half dead with the very idea of meeting his Eyes—&, unavoidably, finding my own sink under them, & my hand, that used so heartily to come forth for the mutual grasp, find itself inevitably passive & all but shrinking from his touch![1]

Such had been her opinion of James's principles and probity that she had thought him 'utterly incapable of leading another astray'. 'I have even wished him *dead* ere such an action had sullied his fair character!'[1] Yet the horror that first overwhelmed the minds of the Burneys was quickly and loyally stifled as they united to condemn what was quite enough on its own count— James's failure in duty to his wife and children, Sarah's failure in feeling for her father—'the rash selfishness', as Fanny put it, 'with which they have broken through all duties and ties to others for their own singular caprice & inclination'.[1] 'For, take the deed in its best colours,—'tis *dark*—dark!—though not, I humbly hope—*black!*'[1] Nor had Fanny ever let her father suppose that she had 'imagined the evil of so deep a nature'.[1] She wished James to know that, though she thought his action indefensible, he was not alienated from her 'general affection'. As for Sally,

Poor wretched girl! she is more detestable in this business, because younger, & therefore more unpardonable for total unfeelingness; but she is less culpable in—by far! for James *has* principles, & knows he has led her, as well as himself, into a defiance of all right.[1]

The runaway pair remained together for five years, though doors were invitingly held open for Sally's return. Fanny wrote offering help and was thanked for her 'readiness to serve & advise'. 'Should any occasion present itself, [I should] sooner apply to you than to any other human being.' This was in 1799. 'The Recluse Man & maiden' became reconciled to Esther and her family more quickly, however, than to Fanny, whose rational judgement and devotion to her father made her just now an uncomfortable accuser. She would prove

8, 26 May, 29 June, 28 July–1 Aug., 19 Sept., 12 Oct. 1799, including copies of letters from JB and SHB; 3 A.L. (Berg) from FBA to EBB, 5 Oct., 2, 22 Nov. 1798, 24 Mar. 1799; and 2 A.L.S. to CBFB, 21 Mar., 22 July 1799.

[1] See p. 283, n. 3.

a staunch friend, they well knew, when their thoughts should
turn to right action. It was bitter work blaming those she would
have preferred 'to love & defend'. She wished James no worse
punishment than that 'acute bitter remorse' which might bring
him to himself before a sorry retrospection should embitter his
old age.[1] She offered to plead their cause (when and if they
wished) and with her usual courage she ventured a remonstrance, marked with the characteristic Burneyan tone: 'If,
therefore, it will amuse you to suppose me taking a similar dance
from my family & home with Richard—smile as you may, but
be just in thinking how it might strike you, unexplained.'[1]

Meanwhile friends of the Burneys were asking embarrassing
questions. 'Where is Sally?' And the Burneys agreed on a
'front' or a façade, first devised by Madame d'Arblay: 'To their
great regret James had separated from his wife, and since the
Doctor expected Susan and her family at Chelsea, Sarah had
gone to keep house for James for the present.' The Doctor
choked at the speech and could not bring himself to utter it.
He feared that the fugitives would 'disgrace him by their conduct in his old age';[2] and he could not forgive their last 'barbarous piece' of unfeeling selfishness, the attempt to lure away
his trusty housekeeper and nurse, Molly.[3] From experience he
knew that Fanny would soon approach him, olive branch in
hand, and he warned her:

I never intend to write to either again—& I desire you, Fan, . . .
never . . . try to bring abt a reconciliation & union again. Nothing,
I think can incline me to live under the same roof wth people to
whom I must be so hateful.[3]

Meanwhile the Burneys had begun to realize that in Ireland
Susan was rapidly wasting away. There were great difficulties
in determining the real state of her health and the causes of the
Major's refusals or delays in allowing her to attempt the journey
home and, finally, in financing the voyage (that is, in offering
gifts or additional loans of money where so much was already
owing).[4] Ideas about wifely duty were now relinquished. 'She

---

[1] See p. 283, n. 3.   [2] See p. 282, n. 2.
[3] A.L. (Berg) from CB to FBA, 26 Oct. 1798.
[4] Four letters (Berg) from FBA to CB, 15, 18, 26 Oct. 1799, 7 Jan. 1800; 4 A.L.
(Berg) to EBB, 28 Sept., 15–18 Oct., 19, 28 Nov. 1799; A.L.S. (Berg) to Major
Phillips, 12 Oct., 1799; and letters (Berg) to SBP, 1798–9.

was unhappy', the Doctor admitted, '& did not with all her virtues make others happy where she was chained.'[1] He had now made up his mind to receive her at Chelsea and for the time that he had left 'among the living, to enjoy her sweet temper, tender heart, sound judgment, exquisite taste, integrity, & acquirements!'[1]

In reply to insistent inquiries, Susan had at length admitted her doubts of outliving the coming winter. 'What reasons she must have to use such words!'[2] Fanny grew frantic with fear. In October, 1799, she wrote to Esther that she had M. d'Arblay's permission to write word that if the Major could not allow Susan to

set out immediately—or did not think her well enough—I should forthwith make a journey to Ireland—& see & nurse her myself. And this most religiously I mean to do, if he is still obdurate. My wretchedness at the thoughts of her consuming away to a lingering death in *that* prison with *that* gaoler conquers every obstacle of cowardice & of expence that oppose my voyage. I should never be happy again not to make this *attempt* to save her.[2]

'*Try* at least to sleep', she wrote to Susan,

try to *repeat* something by heart—that has often helped me in my days of toil & nights of watchfulness. If you have no regular poems ready, try *songs*, Italian airs, and overtures & sonatas. *Pray* try, my Susan, my Eyes ache to think of yours![3]

Charles had written with his usual gay flourish to the Major offering to pay the whole expense of the journey from Belcotton to Greenwich and to provide beef and birch for the two boys at his school. James offered to meet Susan on her landing and conduct her safe to her journey's end. The Lockes, almost equally terrified for Susan's health, had sent a draft of £100 and later one of £50 to be used in settling debts that might prevent the family's setting out. Negotiations were difficult and had to be carried on in such a way as to ingratiate the senders with the Major and reconcile him to their plans and hopes.

[1] In the Osborn Collection are 7 A.L.S. from CB to CB, Jr., 24, 25, 30 Dec. 1799, 6, 8, 9 Jan. 1800, 6 July 1801; 6 A.L.S. to FBA, 19, 29 Oct., 1, 19 Nov., 1, 25 Dec. 1799. Also A.L.S. from CB, Jr., to CB, 27 Dec. 1799; to Mrs. Burney (his wife), 9 Jan. 1800; and A.L.S. from CPB to the same, 9 Jan. 1800. Also 3 A.L.S. from FBA to CB, Jr., 6, 19 Dec. 1799, [Jan. 1800].
[2] See p. 285, n. 4.   [3] A.L. (Berg) from FBA to SBP, 17 Dec. 1797.

Finally consent was given and arrangements were made. On October 22, 1799, Susan wrote to her father: 'The Maj^r will not longer detain me, when I *can* go, I am sure I shall.'[1] Still she delayed, trying to gather strength, and it was December before she could be moved to Dublin. Meanwhile Charles had offered to meet her with his carriage at Parkgate or Holyhead. And the Doctor worried. 'Now dear Chas. do inquire directly whether she will land at Park-Gate, or Holy-Head—if you sh^d go to one of the places, & she land at the other, how miserable it w^d make you both!'[1] After Christmas Charles and his son set off, and the brief letters or reports he posted back to his father and other members of the family are the dramatic records of his journey and Susan's journey's end.[2] On December 27, when he had arrived at the White Lion, Chester, he was informed that the yacht had been driven into Holyhead and was there fast bound. He travelled for ninety miles through the Welsh mountains in the snow and ice of December, only to find at Holyhead that with the shifting of the wind the yacht had put off to Parkgate and that Mrs. Phillips had not come ashore, though the Major had several times. 'Well, I swallowed it,—& pon honour, without a blaspheme!'[2] The roads were now so heavy that he was obliged to take four horses, and on December 31 he had again reached the White Lion, Chester. An express to Parkgate brought the reply that Susan was in lodgings there and would remain for several days. On December 30, after the yacht had put in at Parkgate, she managed to write a letter to her father: 'Oh my beloved Father—once more I tread on English Ground, once more I breathe the blessed air you breathe.'[2]

On January 2 Charles wrote that he was under the same roof with the dear, dear Susan and that he did not intend to lose her again now that he had 'gotten her under cover, on English ground'. So agitated was she on seeing him, so weak, enfeebled, and 'sadly reduced' (racked with a violent cough and wasted with dysentery), that she seemed already 'stepping into the Grave'. At first Charles had the unhappy impression that she

---

[1] 3 A.L.S. (Berg) from CB to CB, Jr. (including copies of Susan's letters), 2 Nov., 14, 20 Dec. 1799.

[2] The letters (Barrett) from CB, Jr., to the family include: 5 A.L.S. to CB, 27 Dec. 1799, 1, 6, 8, 10 Jan. 1800; 2 A.L.S. to FBA, 2, 6 Jan. 1800 (with a postscript from Major Phillips). Also A.L.S. from SBP to CB, 30 Dec. 1799; and A.L.S. from Molesworth Phillips to William Locke, 6 Jan. 1800.

could not live two days. In the hope, however, that she might gain some strength if left to herself in quiet, he determined to take the Major and the young people to Liverpool for the weekend. 'We are all very merry in a comfortable little Lodging', the Major wrote to the d'Arblays, but scarcely had the sight-seers returned when tragedy fast followed. Charles went on with the story:

On our return last night [Sunday, January 5], I found the dear Patient feeble;—but up,—& apparently better. She was truly rejoiced to see me return; & much delighted at my having executed some commissions for her, as she termed it so cheaply & nicely. I left her about ten.

She passed a sad night. The complaint in her Bowels, which had torn her to pieces for several weeks, and had reduced her to a shadow, raged violently.

This morning, while we were at breakfast the maid, Susan [Adams], came & called out the Major, & Fanny [Phillips], with a face of alarm,—& with tears. They went upstairs—but returned in about ten minutes;—& thought the fright produced more by [the maid's] fears, than real danger.—Fanny at least did. The Major was silent on the subject; but, (as he afterwards told me) took Fanny out soon after on the pretence of buying shoes; but in reality to prepare her for what he dreaded.—Susan the maid called me up, a few minutes after they went. I staid an hour by the poor soul's bed; but she knew me not:—she saw me not—she spoke to me not.—

Phillips & Fanny soon returned—and about twenty minutes before two—[1]

The next page is missing, if indeed Charles was able to write it. In other letters he said that he had felt 'the last quiver of her pulse', and that, a 'solitary mourner', he followed 'her poor emaciated corpse' to the grave. 'Phillips declines it:—when his thoughts turn that way, he feels.'[2]

Poor dear Susan! not a tenderer heart,—nor a gentler spirit—nor more rectitude of soul;—nor more correctness of judgement hast thou left behind thee![2]

Now Charles faced the task of writing reports that he well knew would be received with anguish. He could not at first find the courage to write to Fanny ('Alas he knew she was the soul

[1] See p. 287, n. 2.
[2] A.L.S. (Berg) from CB, Jr., to FBA, 8 Jan. 1800; A.L.S. (Osborn) to Mrs. Burney (his wife), 9 Jan. 1800.

of my soul from my first remembrance in life!').[1] Esther, herself struck as by 'a thunder bolt', thought fearfully of the time that the news should reach West Humble.[2] All along, Fanny's fears had been the most frantic, the most urgent and prophetic. Her hopes, however, had revived with Susan's arrival in England, Charles's letters, the Major's postscript about the merry lodging, and a letter she had received from Susan herself. Charles had received her happy reply to his earlier reports, a letter 'full of joy, exultation, and congratulations!'[3] Ten times, he said, he had taken up his pen to reply without being able to go on. In the end the Major wrote to Mr. Locke asking him to unfold the tale to the d'Arblays.

For many days Fanny was unable to shed a tear—and her grief forced her 'into screams for some vent to the mighty oppression upon [her] soul'.[4] Mrs. Locke took Alex away, and on the day (January 9) that the fatal news reached West Humble, the d'Arblays left for London intending a journey through Cheshire and on to the coast to visit the 'loved Remains! & to attend them to their last Home!'[5] At Charing Cross they learned that the Mails were booked till Sunday and that, with the heavy snowfalls, the journey could not be made even with four horses in less than four days. At Chelsea they learned with more bitter grief still that the funeral had already taken place.[5] Charles was the only being on earth Fanny envied. 'O my dear Charles, how heavenly is your consolation compared to mine. I can find none!' 'Could I but have seen her once under this roof—once in her Father's arms—and have closed her loved eyes myself, I should not have dared murmur— not even grieve.'[1]

When the sisters had learned the Doctor's intention of receiving Susan 'in all her feebleness, & shaken state, to nurse her himself', they had seemed to think that it would be again as so often in their childhood—to 'meet his commiserating Eyes

---

[1] A.L.S. (Berg) from FBA to Mrs. Locke, 13 Jan. 1800; A.L.S. (Osborn) from FBA to CB, Jr., [1800].
[2] A.L.S. (Berg) from EBB to CB, Jr., 9 Jan. 1800.
[3] See p. 286, n. 1.
[4] 7 A.L. (Berg) from FBA to EBB, 12 Jan., 11, 26 Mar., Oct., 16 Dec. 1800, [1800], 27 Oct. 1801; Diary MSS. (Berg), p. 5192.
[5] Madame d'Arblay's annotation of A.L.S. (Berg) from FBA to CB, 9 Jan. 1800; also A.L.S. (Osborn) from FBA and M. d'A to CB, Jr., [Jan. 1800].

—& be under his roof & his care—would make him *give her a second life!*[1] It was Susan's death in lodgings within a week's journey of her father's house ('the contrast of reality & expectation, the suddenness of horrour'),[2] together with the villainy of the Major in keeping the family ignorant of the real state of his wife's health, that made resignation impossible.

Saint & angel!—she was all ready—all prepared. . . . To her *Death*— she who was so fit to die—and whose life had so little—till now—to be wished—I could have composed myself ever since I knew her sufferings—had not the close to them seemed so promised and approaching.[3]

In a week she replied to a letter from Mrs. Locke: 'Yes my dearest Friend, I do indeed look up to the sky for her—but it is cloudy & thick—& I never can see Her!!' 'The will of God be obeyed and yielded to!'[3]

For months Fanny's grief was convulsive and uncontrollable. For a year she was unable to receive visitors except the Lockes and her father and sisters. Sympathy, like that of the Queen or of M. de Narbonne, who had heard the news with 'an agony of Tears', renewed her initial grief.[4] Drives that the Lockes arranged through the beautiful countryside revived agonizing associations. It was not until March 26 (on a day that the Lockes were away) that she forced herself to enter Norbury Park, where she had last seen Susan ('it almost brought back my first torture').[4] She knew that she would feel the effects of the tragedy to her dying day ('On that day may it help my own passage!'). For the rest of her life she kept January 6 as a day of remembrance, prayer, and communication.

In February she wrote to James: 'Shall a blow like this strike us, & shall we not write to each other?—Comfort we cannot give. The blow is deadly, irreparable, and it strikes at the root of happiness. O my dear James! who can replace her?'[5] Fanny remained inconsolable and she could not forgive Phillips—'that wretch whom I fervently pray Heaven my Eyes may never be blighted with seeing more'.[4] And she never did see him again,

---

[1] A.L. (Barrett) from FBA to CB, 28 Nov. 1799.

[2] Three letters (Berg) from FBA to Mary Port Waddington, n.d., 3 Oct. 1800, 18 Feb. 1801.

[3] See p. 289, n. 1.   [4] See p. 289, n. 4.

[5] A copy of A.L.S. (Osborn) from FBA to JB, 11 Feb. 1800.

refusing for the rest of her life to go where he might be expected to appear (even though that included James's funeral) or ever again to look on his 'baleful visage'.[1]

Though the Doctor could not dissemble his just indignation at the voyage being deferred for so long, he thought time would punish the Major. 'He'll suffer enough, I trust, by & by, when he misses her virtues, talents, & superior head as well as heart.'[2] By the final arrangements, Fanny Phillips was to come to Chelsea and live with her grandfather ('My kindest love to her and tell her I long to embrace her & transfer as much as I can of my affection for her dear dear mother to her'). Willy was to be put to school at Greenwich, and later, like his father, he followed the sea. Norbury, educated in Ireland, later took high scholastic honours at Trinity College, Dublin,[3] and in the brief life left to him made occasional visits to England to indulge his craving for music, the parts of his nature and the gifts inherited from his mother. The Major was to marry again in less than a year, to desert his second wife and family for a mistress, to be seized occasionally by bailiffs for debt (unless saved by his friends, including James), but to appear largely in later days as a welcome guest at James's house in James Street.[4] His obtrusion there 'must be revolting', said Madame d'Arblay, 'while Memory holds her seat'.

Not one moment's penitence has ever appeared to soften off his crime, or plead for his forgiveness. *Therefore* is it that I hold against him my unalterable horrour. He has never been presented to me in any light of appeasement—a 2ᵈ wife deserted—children by a 2ᵈ Bed abandoned—a mistress openly kept—& the possession of spirits triumphant in boldness![5]

The close of the eighteenth century marked the end of an era for Fanny—the end, she said, of her 'perfect Happiness on Earth' or 'of all happy confidence' in the world. Susan's death of course nullified all plans for the production of the comedy 'Love and Fashion',[1] and it marked the close also of Fanny's long

---

[1] See p. 289, n. 4.   [2] See p. 286, n. 1.

[3] A.L.S. (Folger) from Edmond Malone to CB, 8 June 1808; and 2 A.L.S. (Bodleian) from CB to Edmond Malone, 10 June, 9 July 1808.

[4] See Note K, p. 494.

[5] A.L. (Berg) from FBA to EBB, 11 Dec. 1822. Cf. A.L.S. (Barrett) from Charlotte Barrett to Arthur Young, 7 Dec. 1819.

confidential journal-letters or confessions, for the journals produced from this time were spasmodic, adventitious, or occasional documents often written years after the event described with a view to preserving spectacular parts of the family history for Alex and his son's sons. There was still to be, until the year 1842, a large family correspondence, a series of letters showing, first of all, the impact of the Napoleonic wars on such pawns of fate and politics as the chevalier d'Arblay, his wife, and child.

The first year of the nineteenth century that was to ring such drastic changes passed quietly enough in West Humble. Fanny was only fit for home, she said, until time should blunt her feelings. Some comic relief, however, was supplied by Alex, 'the most *étourdi*, gay, romping, riotous little monkey now living'. 'His disposition is full of enjoyment, & his heart of happiness.'[1] Though he interrupted his mother in her writing on an average of every half-line, she managed to record some of his 'gestes and dictes'. When his father went away, he 'retired to cry under the Bow window—"Nanny, you must never bring the dinner till Papa & Boude come back! never! as long as you live!"' Both mother and son needed the master, 'the one for his *Horseback*, the other for everything'. 'Yesterday, in the high wind & Rain, we seemed desolate without him,—to Day, in this beautiful sunshine, we still seem solitary.'[2] At the ages of six and seven, however, Alex needed great care. Though strong, active, and lively, he was thin enough 'for a caricature of a French baby'. Like Fanny herself he was subject to fevers and often had to be dosed with James's powders. If left alone, 'he would apply himself from morning to night' to reading and arithmetic, and at six years of age he had begun formal lessons (three 'while I am dressing, & at Breakfast we have our rewards'). In her new role the *female usher* applied to her nephew Charles Parr Burney, son of the Greek scholar, for

some hints how to use Ash's Grammar for a pupil in preparation— whether it is to be learnt *by heart* throughout, beginning with the introduction—or with the Grammatical Institutes. . . . I would not

[1] A.L. (Barrett) from FBA to CB, 18 Jan. 1798.
[2] Letters (Berg) from FBA to M. d'A, 3 Feb. 1796, 1 Aug. 1797, 17 July 1800, 29 Nov. 1801, 18 Feb., 18 Mar. 1802; to CB, 4 Mar. 1799; to EBB, 27 Mar. 1801; to CBFB, 29 Oct. 1801. Also Diary MSS. (Berg), pp. 5364–7.

trouble your dear toil-worn Father with an enquiry you can so well answer.[1]

Fanny taught virtue along with formal grammar, often moralizing, as she said, 'about goodness, virtue, & such sort of old fashioned matters', and sometimes recording Alex's comically solemn observations. Though at an early age he began to reject petticoat government in favour of that of his father, uncles, or cousins, a final anecdote will show that his famous mother had made the strongest appeal to his heart.

'And should not *you*, said Sophy, like to die, Alex?' 'Not before Mama,' he replied, & when she laughed, he added 'And not *after* Mama!' She laughed again—but not when he concluded with his full meaning—'but I should like to die just when mama begins to be deaded.'[2]

Domestic affairs, Alex's health and daily lessons, and presently the new turn of events in France gave her fresh worries for the present and turned her mind to the future. Another preoccupation, which, as she afterwards admitted, helped to rouse her from her sorrow, was a very successful attempt at matchmaking.

An *émigré*, Antoine Bourdois, born of respectable parents in M. d'Arblay's native town of Joigny, had seized some propitious moment in the Revolution to rescue or acquire a fortune and, now in West Humble, he consulted M. d'Arblay about a wife. His fortune made a dowry unnecessary, and M. d'Arblay hit upon one of Fanny's nieces, Marianne Burney, the eldest of the five dowerless daughters of Esther and the impecunious Charles Rousseau Burney. With the kindness that in later years Fanny's nephews and nieces learned to associate with her, she sent Esther long and carefully written studies of M. Bourdois's circumstances, understanding, and amiable disposition. Later she invited Marianne for a visit to West Humble. This 'will *fix him*, I will trust, to be always hers'. Unlike Evelina, Camilla, Miss Port, and other heroines real and fictional who have engaged our attention up to this time, Marianne survived the probationary period with flying colours. 'Her own behaviour & demeanour are perfectly what I could wish them—unaffected,

---

[1] A.L. (formerly in the possession of Miss Stella M. Alleyne) from FBA to CPB, 4 Mar. 1801. [2] See p. 292, n. 2.

chearful, & sensible.' Marianne's 'good sense, modesty, & propriety' had won the Frenchman's esteem, but when in spite of all this he had the temerity to express some misgiving about possible coldness in the girl's character, Madame d'Arblay ruled all that a matter that 'ought not as yet to be discussed'. As she remarked to Esther (not to the men), she had ample confidence in Marianne's *consoling propensities*, though she would not have them 'prematurely exercised'. All things in time and order; this was decorum, not denial. Some people call it prudery. In September the couple became engaged, and Fanny sent joyful congratulations to Esther: 'A tender & active Friend, my dearest Hetty, will be given to you, & your whole House.' When after the marriage (October 30, 1800) Esther wrote of her pleasure and relief in the event, Fanny had her reward. 'The idea of *you*, laying your dear head down to rest with relieved solicitude, & cheered feelings & prospects, is indeed truly precious to me.'[1]

Often the absorbing interest of the day was the newspapers with their accounts of the war with France and the growing power of the First Consul. In 1799 Fanny had already made up her mind about Napoleon.

I think him so vindictive, & such a man of blood, that his reign will be severe, &, consequently, short, but what may be effected while it lasts, is curious, agitating, & alarming.[2]

Sometimes M. d'Arblay hurried to London hoping to hear news of his family from travellers from France, but usually returned 'dejected, saddened, disappointed beyond expression'. In August, 1800, he learned that his brother had been fatally wounded eighteen months earlier while fighting with the armies of the Republic. The surprise that he should have died *fighting for the Republic* was almost 'as great a grief as that he should have died, so soon, at all'. 'He was completely by education & principle, an aristocrat', but for French officers there were only three choices: 'Flight, serving the Republic, or the Guillotine'. There was, however, some good news. M. d'Arblay's uncle, M. Bazille, and his wife were still alive in their own

[1] 7 A.L.S. (Berg) from FBA to EBB, June, 10 June, 6 July, mid-July, 26 July, 13, 21 Sept. 1800; A.L.S. (Berg) to CB, 13 Sept. 1800; Diary MSS. (Berg), p. 5306.
[2] A.L. (Barrett) from FBA to CB, 28 Nov. 1799.

house in Joigny, and they had heard of the survival of their nephew with a joy that exceeded all description. Secondly, M. de Narbonne was still in Switzerland and had written to M. d'Arblay repeatedly.[1]

As long as France was at war with England the French exile had determined not to visit his native land; but when, late in 1800, he was informed that for over a year his name had been erased from the list of emigrants and that there was yet some possibility of saving a residue of his property from sequestration, he was shaken in all his resolutions and, as Fanny recorded, 'in a state of fermentation, from doubts and difficulties, and crossing wishes and interests, that has much affected his health as well as tranquillity'. Informed that a part of his property (worth £1,000) was still unsold and that a *procuration* could be sent from any country at peace with France, he set off on November 17, 1800, for Holland, made out the *procuration*, got it properly witnessed and authenticated, and returned on the first vessel he could find. On December 14 he was again at Gravesend. 'He is returned . . . already!'[1] To Esther Fanny confessed that the separation was a trial almost beyond her, 'so woe-worn & woe-prepared' was her mind.[1] For this time, however, all was well; and the traveller was in time for Alex's sixth birthday on December 18, 1800.[1]

With 1801 and the cessation of hostilities between France and England, M. d'Arblay was 'almost in Heaven'. News of the Preliminaries of Peace, concluded between the Consulate and the British Government on October 1, 1801, probably reached West Humble the next day, for on October 3 Fanny was writing to her father about the 'hopes and happiness' it had brought to their hermitage.

M. d'Arblay now feels paid for his long forbearance, his kind patience, & compliance with my earnest wishes not to revisit his native land while we were at war with it. He can now go with honour as well as propriety; for everybody, even the highest personages, will rather expect he should make the journey, as a thing of course.[1]

---

[1] 2 A.L. (Barrett) from FBA to SBP and to CB, 20, 29 Aug. 1797, respectively. Three letters (Berg) from FBA to CB, 2, 12 Nov., 11 Dec. 1801; 4 letters (Berg) to EBB, 16 Dec. 1800; 12, 29 Nov., 17 Dec. 1801. Also A.L. (the possession of John R. G. Comyn) to CB, Jr., 18 Nov. 1800; Diary MSS. (Berg), pp. 5234–7, 5240, 5258, 5310–12; *Diary*, v. 466 ff.

She was telling her father, in effect, that her pension, which, apart from the proceeds of her writing, had been her means of livelihood (and that of her husband), would not *now* be endangered by journeys to France. She had indeed made sure of this by gaining the Queen's approval of M. d'Arblay's visit to his native country as a duty he owed his family. The Queen also approved of her desire to accompany her husband, and, wholly sceptical about the peace lasting for long, Fanny wished to go immediately. Through her husband and his friends she was well informed about events in France, though in the somewhat prejudiced but shrewd and realistic judgement she brought to bear on them she echoed her father rather than the Frenchman. Her objectivity and subacidity often emerged in dry comments (quite unconsciously humorous), marking a contrast to M. d'Arblay's fair hopes, enthusiasms, dejections, and dream-visions. Just now there was great rejoicing over the Peace of Amiens.

Fêtes, joy, and pleasure, will probably for some months occupy the public in France; and it will not be till those rejoicings are past, that they will set about weighing causes of new commotion, the rights of their governors, or the means, or desirability of changing them. I would far rather go immediately, than six months hence.[1]

Fanny's plans were, however, frustrated by Alex, who chose the moment of the blessed Peace of Amiens to become ill of a worm-fever. His mother remained at West Humble to build up his strength with James's powders, red wine, bark, and cold tubs.[2]

M. d'Arblay, however, could wait no longer. On October 28 he went to Gravesend, where he had been told a vessel was ready; but after waiting four days through fair wind and weather, when the passengers worked like deckhands loading ballast, the captain put out in a storm, which drove the vessel into Margate. The next day the ship got to Deal, where 'the sea grew yet more rough and perilous'.

Every thing in the vessel was overset; my poor M. d'Arblay's provision Basket flung down, & its contents demolished; his Bottle of wine broke by another toss, & violent fall, and he was nearly famished. . . . My poor voyager, gave his whole noble strength to

---

[1] See p. 295, n. 1. [2] See p. 292, n. 2.

the pump, till he was so exhausted, so fatigued, so weakened, that with difficulty he could hold a pen to repeat that still—I might be *tranquille*, for all danger was again over.[1]

M. d'Arblay's luck was always consistent; on Friday, however, he wrote to Fanny two lines: 'Nov. 6, 1801.—*Je pars!* the wind is excellent—*au revoir*.' On November 7, he was safe at Calais. But what Fanny had suffered through this when she heard the winds blow! '*Ma pauvre tête, autant que mon cœur!*'[2]

After failing to obtain employment as French Commercial Consul in London, he applied for half-pay as a French officer on the retired list and for some of his lost rights and property. There was no hope of his return before Alex's birthday on December 18. Fanny did not expect him to succeed, but she rejoiced at his happiness in seeing France again. M. d'Arblay, more sanguine by nature and perhaps less realistic than his wife, '& full aware of his rights and claims, was deeply mortified & depressed' by the turn of affairs in France, yet not the less determined to persist in attempts to establish himself there.[1]

Il est de mon devoir, comme époux et comme père, de tâcher de tirer parti des circonstances pour nous ménager, s'il est possible, une vieillesse totalement indépendante; et à notre petit un bien-être qui ne nous fasse pas renoncer au nôtre.[1]

The chevalier wrote like a lover still:

Quand reverrai-je donc notre hermitage! Quand presserai-je dans mes bras celle qui remplit tellement mon cœur, celle avec qui seule je puis être heureux! . . . Je lis et relis tes lettres, elles sont ma plus douce consolation. . . . Je t'ai toujours aimée de toute mon âme, de toutes mes forces, et pourtant je ne t'ai jamais tant aimée qu'à présent.[3]

Fanny sighed deeply at thoughts of the new plans—

Our Hermitage is so dear to me—our Book-Room so precious, & in its retirement, its beauty of prospect, form, convenience, & comforts, so impossible to replace—[2]

She had to admit the narrowness of their income, but she was not 'without views, as well as hopes, of ameliorating' their state. This meant, of course, that she was writing again. She asked him to consider all the advantages of their life in a cottage, but

---

[1] See p. 295, n. 1.   [2] See p. 292, n. 2.
[3] A.L.S. (Berg) from M. d'A to FBA, 1 Jan. 1802.

she was prepared, she said, to capitulate if he found the total preponderate in favour of his new schemes. 'I will try *any* thing but what I try *now*—absence!'[1]

In an effort to prolong the quiet life in Camilla Cottage, built by the proceeds of her pen, she had turned to writing again. Ironically enough, though her efforts were to sink out of sight to this day because of the hurry of the French plans, one of them, the comedy 'A Busy Day', was more like her first success, *Evelina*, than anything she had since written.

[1] See p. 292, n. 2.

XII

'A BUSY DAY'

(1801–1802)

But we are different kind of folk
We think not tragic fire & smoak
Equal to Comic wit & Joke.
          ADMIRAL BURNEY'S Prologue[1]

IN 1778 Mrs. Thrale had told Fanny Burney that she seemed to have 'the right and true talents for writing a comedy'.

You would give us all the fun and humour we could wish, and you would give us a scene or two of the pathetic kind that would set all the rest off. . . . And, in the grave parts, all your sentiments would be edifying, and such as would do good.[2]

The modern theatregoer would still be pleased with the fun and humour, but without being less sentimental or less moral than his forerunners he would be willing perhaps to dispense with the moral sentiments and with the pathos (at least what he would take to be an eighteenth-century brand of pathos).

Eighteenth-century sentimental or tragic drama presents in any case certain difficulties, for, with the process known to linguists as degeneration in meaning, words, phrases, or expletives once in high repute for tragedy are now the language of melodrama; therefore, whether or not true pathos or tragedy arises in the situation, the language in its present connotations suggests only melodrama. In the second place, the demand for moral sentiments has long been on the wane. As the manager of Covent Garden Theatre knew in 1799, when he suggested deletions in Madame d'Arblay's 'Love and Fashion', there is a difference between dotting a play with edifying *dicta* and constructing one from which a moral or morals can be drawn. Profiting perhaps from Mr. Harris's criticism, in her next play, 'A Busy Day', Fanny omitted both choke-pears, moralizing

---

[1] In Diary MSS. (Berg), box v.   [2] *Diary*, i. 148; *Memoirs*, ii. 156.

passages, and sentimentally pathetic scenes, and concentrated on the comic element.

For the Burneys Garrick was the authority without peer in the theory and practice of the comic. In addition Madame d'Arblay had lately been reading Goldoni, probably taking stock of a principle that she herself had known and practised in the comic scenes of *Evelina*: 'That any character may be productive of effect on the stage, it has always appeared to me necessary to contrast it with characters of an opposite description.'[1] It was this contrast that Dr. Johnson had noted as the source of the comic in *Evelina*;

for without Lord Orville, and Mr. Villars, and that melancholy . . . Macartney, the Brangtons, and the Duvals, would be less than nothing; for vulgarity, in its own unshadowed glare, is only disgusting.[2]

Such contrasts, with the omission of the choke-pears, resulted in a lively comedy of manners, very much resembling the Holborn scenes of *Evelina*, where ludicrous characters are made to reveal their own absurdities and follies in rapid, idiomatic, and amusing dialogue. 'A Busy Day'[3] is the play that long ago Murphy, Dr. Johnson, and Sheridan had known Fanny Burney could write.

The plot is a love story providing plausible reasons for bringing oddly assorted social groups into the same houses, walks, and gardens. There is again a cross-section of London life. There is again farce with some of the boisterousness of the eighteenth century and, finally, the emergence in some characters of the old comedy of humours.

Eliza Watts, the younger daughter of an opulent, good-hearted, but simple tradesman, has been brought up in India by a cultivated guardian. Her improvement in education and manners is thrown into high relief at subsequent meetings with her sister Miss Watts, a product of the boarding-schools,

---

[1] Garrick's summation of the essentials of comedy is quoted in Elizabeth P. Stein, *David Garrick, Dramatist* (1938), p. 200. Also A.L. (Berg) from FB to CB, 3 July 1800; Carlo Goldoni, *Memoirs* (2 vols., 1828), i. 198.

[2] See p. 299, n. 2.

[3] 'A Busy Day, or, an Arrival from India' survives in the Berg Collection, the NYPL, in five *cahiers* (5 × 8 in.) made by folding and sewing letter-paper (10 × 8 in.). The manuscript (370 pp.), written with great care, neatness, and legibility, has the appearance of a final draft.

though very much the daughter of her vulgar ambitious mother. In India Eliza has become engaged to Mr. Cleveland, the elder nephew and the heir of Sir Marmaduke and Lady Wilhelmina Tylney, who, like the Delviles of *Cecilia*, are to thwart the cause of young love, though their family pride and contempt for 'the cit' are to be subdued in the end by poverty. Their value-judgements are reproved throughout the play by the exemplary attitude of their niece Miss Cleveland towards Eliza's modest merit.

The play opens with the bustle of the arrival from India and a series of accidents that brought Eliza to a gaming-house in London. There Cleveland finds her, and it is not long before Lord John Dervis (an amusing fop) and Cleveland's younger brother Frank also appear. With the arrival of the Watts family and Mr. Joel Tibbs, Mr. Watts's good old friend whom Mrs. Watts now attempts to disown, two-thirds of the cast are already on the stage and have introduced themselves in characteristic and revealing speeches.

Enter MISS WATTS

MISS WATTS. La', Pa' what did you leave us for so? We've been up the wrong stairs, & I dare say Ma'll be blundering on this half hour.

MR. WATTS. Why, my dear, I wanted to see your sister of the soonest, so I e'en put my best foot foremost. . . .

FRANK (*apart to* Lord JOHN). What a vulgar tribe!

LORD JOHN. Confounded vulgar!

Enter MRS. WATTS

MRS. WATTS. Well, I've found my way at last. But I can't think, Tommy, how you could be so rude as to go on at sich a rate, leaving one all alone so . . .

ELIZA. (runs to MRS. WATTS with open arms) . . .

MRS. WATTS. Take care my dear, take a little care, or you'll squeeze my poor new Handkerchief till it won't be fit to be seen. And it cost me sich a sight of money—

Comic dialogues are later to take place between Mrs. Watts and her cousin Mr. Tibbs, who refuses to forget her former penury and low estate; between Miss Watts and Mrs. Watts, exposing their essential vulgarity and parsimony, their obsequiousness to their betters and their quarrels among themselves;

and between Mr. Watts and Mr. Tibbs, with the former expatiating on Mrs. Watts and all his woe. Mrs. Watts, who resembles Mrs. Mittin of *Camilla*, is one of Madame d'Arblay's most entertaining characters. Miss Watts is much like the Misses Branghton of *Evelina* or Miss Dennel in *Camilla*, though her errors in mistaking valets and lackeys for their lords and masters satirize not only her eager ambition but the fine and impressive manners of the servants themselves—a comic theme apparently assisted by Fanny's observations of the lackeys at court or in great houses visited on the royal itineraries.

Before the end of Act I the love story is thrown into confusion by Frank Cleveland's decision to replenish his empty purse by offering his hand to Eliza, who, though 'a cit' and 'a gentoo', is also young, pretty, and an heiress. He loses no time in informing his uncle Sir Marmaduke of his intentions and in persuading Lord John to write a letter on his behalf to Mr. Watts —an action that confounds both Cleveland and Eliza and causes misunderstandings in all directions. Other obstacles to the marriage arise from the inimical pride of Sir Marmaduke and his lady and from the machinations of Eliza's rival, the coquettish and vapourish Miss Percival, also possessed of a fortune; for it soon appears that Sir Marmaduke has called Cleveland home from India to marry Miss Percival and secure her fortune to pay off the mortgages on the estate. As a novelist Madame d'Arblay found no difficulty in placing and removing obstructions in the way of a marriage, but that was not her chief concern here. She was not writing a romantic comedy, but a comedy of manners, and her chief concern was to juxtapose conflicting elements of society in such a way as to make their foibles more conspicuous. As she understood the comedy of manners, her task was not only to exhibit the manners of the great and of the vulgar, but to exhibit the manners of the great as they appeared to the vulgar, and vice versa. Thus she not only shows us Mr. Tibbs, but Mr. Tibbs as he appears to Sir Marmaduke and to Lady Wilhelmina; conversely, we see them through his eyes.

Act II, with its setting in Sir Marmaduke's house, is the usual *exposé* of the pride, haughtiness, selfishness, and hard-heartedness that Fanny Burney had so often associated with characters drawn from the upper classes. Miss Percival appears in an

amusing scene, and the scheming but not ill-natured wastrel
Frank Cleveland instructs his languid friend Lord John Dervis to
write a letter for him.

LORD JOHN. O the plague! how I hate writing! I wish it had never
    been invented, young what, did you say?
FRANK. Friend, to be sure.
LORD JOHN. Do you spell it with an *i*, or an *e*?
FRANK. With both.
LORD JOHN. O the Deuce! I've only put an *e*; Does it signify?
FRANK. Not much. Go on. Why now you've left out Francis.
LORD JOHN. I wish it was all at Jericho, with all my soul! Put it in
    yourself. I'm plaguy tired.

The first scenes of Act III are set in Kensington Gardens,
where on one pretext or another Madame d'Arblay brings on
nearly all the characters except Lord John Dervis, Sir Marmaduke, and Lady Wilhelmina. The Watts family continue their
bickerings and are soon interrupted by Lord John's valet with
the letter requesting Eliza's hand.

MISS WATTS. La, Pa', perhaps the letter's from a lord? Pray let
    me look at it.
MRS. WATTS. No, let me see it first, Tommy, I never see a letter
    from a Lord in my life. (*takes the letter.*)
MR. WATTS. Why how can this here John Dervis be a Lord.
VALET. He's the second son of the Marquis of Wistborough.
MR. WATTS. Son of a Marquis? What John Dervis?
ELIZA. Still I suspect some trick or some impertinence, for Lord
    John Dervis is utterly unknown to me. Will you permit me,
    Madame, to look at the hand?
MRS. WATTS. Dear, my dear, why I ha'n't made out hardly two
    words yet.
MR. WATTS. Well, see but how people are upon the catch when
    one's got a little money! Please to tell his Lordship Lord John
    Dervis—
MISS WATTS. La, pa, don't give him the letter till I've looked at it.
    Why what signifies you holding it ma? You know you can't
    read writing hand. (*takes the letter.*)
MRS. WATTS. Well, I might have made out some of it: snatching
    things away so!

Cleveland and Frank stroll through the gardens, and finally
Miss Percival, thrown into a pretended terror first of the

carriages and then of Mr. Watts in his scratch wig, falls into
Cleveland's arms. There is much stage business of this kind.
Meanwhile Mr. Watts, having drawn Mr. Tibbs to a bench out
of earshot of his wife, dilates on the miseries of his present life.
In a preliminary memorandum Mr. Watts was described as

Mr. Prospero—
An old citizen, who from a running errand Boy grows immensely
rich, & brings up his Daughters to all modern accomplishments:
he is persuaded to take a House in the W. end of the Town, where
he leaves off business, & knows not how to fill up his Time. His
daughters are always ashamed of him. . . . He has no comfort of his
life from inability to enjoy their set. . . . He meets at last an old
fr^d . . . & relates his misery, by degrees, till it all bursts forth in
torrents of lamentations at his acquirement of wealth he knows not
how to manage or use or enjoy.[1]

Implicit in this sketch are the eighteenth-century ideas of the
status quo and a reiteration of the lesson Fanny Burney had
elaborated in the career of Belfield in *Cecilia*.

MR. WATTS. But if you'll take my advice, Cousin Tibbs, you'll
    never be over persuaded by your wife & dartars to leave off
    business.
MR. TIBBS. Why, what a dickins, Tom, a'n't you happy, then, with
    your fine coach to rock you to sleep from one end of London
    to t'other? And your fine House that makes you look like a
    Lodger in it? And your fine servants standing by one, by two,
    by three, to stare an old friend out of countenance?

But Mr. Watts is not happy. He is no longer respected even in
his own house. Once his wife was thankful for a shilling, then
for a guinea, but now she takes her pin-money as a matter of
course. Aylice, who used to be so 'meek, & so mealy-mouthed',
now treats him like a cur. And Peg is no better. 'Being finished
at a boarding school herself makes her so mortal nice, there's
no pleasing her.'

MR. TIBBS. Why then, my dear Tom, if I was as you, I'd mind them
    no more than a cat, but divert myself my own way.
MR. WATTS. Ah, Joel, That's the very thing! I can't divert myself
    no way! Ever since I left off business, I've never known what to
    do. They've made me give up all my old acquaintance, because

    [1] In the Berg Collection there are about 500 holograph scraps showing pre-
liminary sketches of characters, which seemed to be conceived first as *types*.

of their being so mean; & as to our new ones, it's as plain as
ever you see they only despise me: for they never take off their
hats if I meet them in the streets; & they never get up off their
chairs, if I ask them how they do in their own houses; & they
never give me a word of answer I can make out, if I put a
question to them.

MR. TIBBS. Why then don't take off your hat to them; & don't
get off your chair to them; & don't answer them when they
speak to you. That's the way I should treat 'em, if any of 'em
come across me. I should like nothing better.

In Act IV, again in Sir Marmaduke's house, some of the
complications are ironed out. Cleveland has begun to make his
position clear; and when Miss Percival, overplaying her hand,
refuses to pay off the mortgage, Sir Marmaduke is willing to
accept Eliza ('O, hang her Birth! What is her fortune?').
Frank realizes that he is too late with his plans, and Miss
Percival that 'a cit' has made her 'wear the willow'. They can
only console each other, and together they meditate a revenge
that will humiliate both Cleveland and Eliza—that of inviting
Sir Marmaduke, Lady Wilhelmina, Lord John Dervis, and others
to Miss Percival's fashionable apartments in Piccadilly, and of
inviting on the same occasion the vulgar Watts family and
Mr. Tibbs. The behaviour of the second group could bring only
pain and embarrassment to the lovers, and the pride of the
Tylneys would be punished in meeting their new connexions.
The mischievous invitations were, of course, Madame d'Arblay's
device for bringing different ranks of society into the same
room, where contrasting codes of manners (or the lack of them)
could be shown in high relief. The situation was cruel and the
satire was cruel, as it always is when effective. Reflected here
are Fanny Burney's observations on London society in the
seventies and eighties, and it would be difficult to find a more
devastating indictment of the bad manners of high and low alike.

MR. TIBBS. Good lauk, Tom, look at them fine Gentlemen, as you
call 'em! one's lying all along, as if he was sick a bed; & t'other's
gaping at Cousin Peg, as if he was going to take a nap full in
her face!

'If this here behaviour's what they call the thing,' Mr. Tibbs
concludes, 'it's none so difficult. I warrant I could do it as well

as they.' He first 'made free with all them tid bits', and then undertook to 'do after the manner' of John Dervis in genteel conversation. He has only to say 'over again their own last word' and follow that up with 'O the deuce!' or the like. In a farcical scene following, Mr. Tibbs stretches out on the sofa and is not to be dislodged by the comments of Sir Marmaduke, the sarcasms of Lady Wilhelmina, or by Mrs. Watts, who accosts him thus:

MRS. WATTS. Dears! what a sight is here! Joel Tibbs a lying upon this fine couch! Out upon you, Joel!
MR. TIBBS. Tol de rol. (*sings*) . . .
MRS. WATTS. Why, Joel, I say, an't you ashamed?
MR. TIBBS. Hay?
MRS. WATTS. Lolloping so before company!
MR. TIBBS. What?
MRS. WATTS. Why don't you offer the seat to the Lady?
MR. TIBBS. Umph?
MRS. WATTS. Lack a day, why are you turned deaf all o' the sudden?
MR. TIBBS. Deaf? O the doose!
MRS. WATTS. Yes, Deaf; can't you answer? Why don't you get up, I say & make your bow?
MR. TIBBS. My bow? O the Devil!
MRS. WATTS. Dear, if I don't believe you're out of your head! What do you say it all over agen for?
MR. TIBBS. Over agen? O confounded!
MRS. WATTS. Yes; don't you know English, man?
MR. TIBBS. English? O consumed! . . .
SIR MARMADUKE. Pray, Madam, will you give me leave to ask— do you happen to know who that Gentleman is?
MISS WATTS. (*whispering*). Say no, Ma!
MRS. WATTS. Not in the least, Sir. Some poor low Cretur, I suppose.
MR. TIBBS. Some poor low cretur? Fegs, that's pretty high! Why I'm afeard, Cousin Aylice, it's you as has lost your wits!
MISS WATTS. Come this way, Ma! (*Exit hastily.*)

Though there are no contemporary testimonies to vouch for the accuracy of the painting, there can be little doubt that the characters of 'A Busy Day', like those of *Evelina*, were just representations of life. By any standards 'A Busy Day' is a lively and amusing comedy, a satire, an entertaining chapter for the history of manners, a transcript of contemporary idiom, and finally a period piece *par excellence*.

The first draft of still another comedy, 'The Woman-Hater',[1]
is written on the backs of letters sewn together, and some of these,
bearing a postmark as late as November 14, 1801, give a clear
indication of when the play was composed. Madame d'Arblay
seemed to remember that when 'The Witlings' was condemned,
Dr. Burney had suggested she might salvage some of the
characters for another work. Accordingly, Mrs. Smatter here
becomes Lady Smatter, as heartless as she was in 'The Witlings'
and as inaccurate as ever in her quotations. Bob Sapling (the
'great oaf, Bobby')[2] also reappears, and in the absence of
Mrs. Voluble gives a better account of himself. He is much put
upon by his sister Jenny, who informs us that he is a 'great
dunce', unable to read either 'writing hand' or printing.

'The Woman-Hater' combines the comedy of humours with
the comedy of manners and of intrigue. The woman-hater
himself, Sir Roderick, is a 'humorous' character, labelled in
preliminary sketches Sir Peppery. He is the terrible-tempered
Mr. Bangs, and his storms and tantrums are usually excited by
the foibles and literary pretensions of the female sex, which he
has despised since his rejection by Miss Wilmot, who on the
appointed wedding-day had deserted him for Lord Smatter.

The intrigue arises among the groups who hope to inherit
Sir Roderick's fortune. These include his sister Eleanora, whose
unfortunate domestic history and situation seem to belong to
novel, romance, or tragedy rather than to comedy; Sophia,
Eleanora's daughter; a changeling, who is mistaken for the
daughter; Old Waverly the sycophant and his son, who are
distantly related to the rich man; and, finally, an old steward
who schemes for a legacy for Bob Sapling.

The plot is complicated and the entertainment it affords very
uneven. Yet the scenes that now seem to mar the work would
then have been good theatre. Eleanora in her 'Innocence &
Injury', vainly imploring 'compassion & assistance', seems to

---

[1] Two finished versions of 'The Woman-Hater' are extant in the Berg Collection.
The first (*c.* 290 pp.) appears in five *cahiers*, made by folding old letters (a few of
which bear the address West Humble) and the unused Proposal for the printing
of *Camilla* by subscription. Such scraps are very useful in establishing the earliest
limits of the dates of composition. The second version is transcribed into five
cahiers ($8 \times 6\frac{1}{2}$ in.) and has the appearance of a final draft. Boxed with it are 99
bits of paper showing preliminary stages of composition.

[2] *Diary*, i. 259–61.

have strayed from her place in the she-tragedies. Her function is to 'interest the heart', and in an age given to weeping, indeed to being 'half-annihilated' by Mrs. Siddons as Belvidera, Jane Shore, and the rest, Eleanora's role could be counted on as a source of tears. Along with her daughter (and, in the end, her husband) she provides a dialogue of melting tenderness and sensibility that amply fulfils Mrs. Thrale's requirement in comedy of a 'scene or two of the pathetic kind'. Pencilled notes on the list of *dramatis personae* ascribing characters to players give Eleanora to Mrs. Siddons.

For 'fun and Humour' Madame d'Arblay relied mainly on three characters besides Lady Smatter: the choleric Sir Roderick, who belongs to the comedy of humours; Old Waverly, a decrepit beau from the comedy of manners and intrigue; and finally Miss Wilmot, who, like the Misses Branghton of *Evelina*, Miss Dennel of *Camilla*, or Miss Watts of 'A Busy Day', is a transcript from the comedy of contemporary life. With her old Nurse and Bob Sapling, Miss Wilmot enacts the scenes from 'low life' that had gained Fanny Burney such fame in her age as an acute and relentless observer of the ridiculous. Miss Wilmot has been well brought up, but in spite of her education in the courtesy-books and her deceptive silence before her elders, she soon reveals herself as a romp and a hoyden. Her 'first best favourite of all', she assures Lady Smatter, is dancing; and the 'second next best thing', singing; and after that, swinging, running, and jumping. She would like to be a ballad-singer, and her repertoire of ballads from time to time enlivens the play. She would like to make a 'huge gigantic Bonfire' of all 'mopish old Books', to attend puppet-shows and wild-beast shows, and to eat all the tarts at the pastry-cook's. Her obstreperousness finally goads her old Nurse into disclosures calculated to be somewhat subduing:

NURSE. [When mistress ran away she took her own Poppet with her], and . . . old Nick put it into my head to burn the Letter she left for Master, & pop you in young Missy's place, making believe you yourself died up the country. . . .

MISS WILMOT. What, then, i'n't Papa papa?

NURSE. No, Miss. Your own Dad was a very good man, though. He was a Journeyman shoemaker.

MISS WILMOT. A Journeyman shoemaker?

NURSE. Yes, my dear; & he's dead now. . . .

The journeyman's daughter has few regrets for Mr. Wilmot, whom she has long considered 'dismal dull'.

MISS WILMOT. How do you like Papa?
BOB. Not a bit, Miss.
MISS WILMOT. No more do I, Bob; for I'm kept in such subjection, I've no comfort of my life. . . . There's nothing but ordering, & tutoring, & scolding, & managing—and reading!

A separate source of comedy is the vanity and self-deception of Old Waverly, a sycophant and aged coxcomb, suggested perhaps by Lord Ogleby of _The Clandestine Marriage_, often quoted in the letters of the young Burneys. When Sophia, mistaking him for the uncle she hopes to conciliate, addresses him in the Park, his susceptibilities, wishes, and vanity lead him into a gratifying misconstruction:

A young girl coming after me! . . . I suppose she's poor, & so wants me to marry her. . . .
A young Girl! bless me!—they'd think—bless me!

With its well-tried stage tricks and characters 'The Woman-Hater' must have succeeded, one would judge, and succeeded much better than 'Love and Fashion', which Mr. Harris was prepared to produce. Of Fanny Burney's plays 'The Woman-Hater' would have best pleased theatregoers of her time, but 'A Busy Day', an extremely amusing period-piece, with its original scenes and its realistic and satiric comedy would then have provided and could yet provide boisterous and farcical entertainment.

While Fanny sat quietly in West Humble devising comical and farcical scenes for the stage, pot-boilers that might very well have served their purpose, M. d'Arblay in Paris was becoming inextricably involved in French affairs. When attempts to regain his natural inheritance failed, he was encouraged to apply for a _retraite_ and half-pay on the claims of his former military service. Informed that by the decision of the First Consul he could not be placed on the list of retired officers without at least one year's additional service to France and the Republic, he leaped at a tentative offer of a military command in the colony of Santo Domingo, where the natives were rebelling against their French rulers. Fanny could think only of storms and shipwrecks by sea, the pestilential climate, and ambushes in the mountains from 'a ferocious set of irritated, & probably ill used Africans'. 'Indeed, my dearest Esther, the expedition was every way frightful to me.'[1]

The warrior, however, delighted with any opportunity to resume his profession, went on with the negotiations, only stipulating that he could not take up arms against Great Britain. Late in January he returned on furlough to England to say farewell to his wife and child and to procure equipment— 'Maps, Books, Instruments, weapons'. His hopes were high, for he was on active service again. A dispatch confirming his appointment followed, and he was to set out for France on February 16. Before he left England, however, in order to make his position clearly understood, he sat down in the Book Room in Camilla Cottage to indite an honest if somewhat naïve letter to the First Consul, Napoleon himself—a missive referring to his service to the late monarch (*'Enthousiaste de la liberté, je fus encore plus ami d'ordre'*) and concluding with his resolve *'jamais m'armer contre la patrie de mon epouse — contre le pays qui pendant neuf ans nous a nourris'*. Napoleon's gratification at this note was not long in making itself felt. (*'Il m'a écrit un diable de lettre!'* 'However, I ought only to regard in it the husband of Cecilia.')[2] In March M. d'Arblay was informed that his terms could not be accepted and that his commission was annulled. The soldier felt the rebuff keenly.

La cause qu'il assigne à cette disgrace . . . *est ma déclaration de ne point servir contre la patrie de ma femme, qui peut encore être armée contre la République.* Pardon, ma bonne amie, je t'avoue que j'ai été depuis huit jours d'une mélancolie à inquiéter mes amis.[2]

His disappointment damped Fanny's spontaneous feelings of unfeigned relief. She sympathized with his chagrin both over the annulment and 'the cruel and useless expence into which he had been plunged'. Though the cost of the journeys and the martial equipment (about 220 guineas in all) had amounted to more than double the yearly income of the d'Arblays, Fanny had no reproaches: 'If his own mind & spirits will but recover,

[1] Diary MSS. (Berg), pp. 5320–1; 2 A.L.S. (Berg) from FBA to EBB, 3, 22 Mar. 1802; A.L. (Barrett) to M. d'A, 16 Apr. 1802; 4 A.L.S. (Berg) to CB, 17, 18 Feb., 17, 22 Mar. 1802; A.L.S. (the possession of John R. G. Comyn) to CB, Jr., 24 Mar. 1802.

[2] *Diary*, v. 486–93; *Memoirs*, iii. 312–21; Diary MSS. (Berg), pp. 5320–1.

I shall bless God with my whole soul in gratefullest joy that here the mischief ends!'[1] Foremost in her mind was personal gratitude. The sacrifice her husband had made for her feelings and country had robbed him, as she pointed out to her father, 'not only of present profit, but of all future rank & resource in his own country—& in this he has none, & no chance!'[1] To Esther also she put the case:

I shall think my whole life well spent in manifesting my gratitude. . . . I think I must have *buried myself alive*, had a new war broken out, & *he* commanded an expedition against This country.[1]

When M. d'Arblay was warned by the French government that he would do well to remain a year in France before returning to England, and when he expressed his desire still more urgently that his wife and child should join him in his own country, Fanny therefore did not hesitate. 'The whole scheme has a something tremendous in it! But he! what does he not merit from me.'[1] Besides, as she said again and again in her letters to him, she was 'exhausted in spirits and faculties' by the separation. Anything was better.[2]

She saw to the necessary arrangements with remarkable expedition. Camilla Cottage and the garden were put in order so as to bring a higher rent, and were let. A guest at hospitable Norbury Park for the nights, she worked through the days at the Cottage packing away books and papers and preparing for the journey and a sojourn of a year that proved to be ten years.

With the expenses of the year the d'Arblays were in financial straits, but Fanny refused to accept Bourdois's offer of help or to apply, as M. d'Arblay suggested, to Charles.[2] Poverty she could cheerfully bear, but not financial indebtedness. She wished to subsist on their 'simple & actual income', and, for the moving expenses, to wait three months for the quarterly payment of the pension. For the rest she stipulated a place of their own in France. There was nothing she coveted as much as their mutual independence, '*surtout*, now that I shall so much want *Time, at my own free & unaccounted for disposal*'.[3] In other words, she wished for time to write, and on the table before her, as she enunciated the principles that were to govern their lives

---

[1] See p. 310, n. 1.   [2] See p. 310, n. 2.
[3] Sixteen letters (Berg) from FBA to M. d'A, 16 Jan. 1801–28 Mar. 1802.

in France, were two pot-boilers, products of her uninterrupted industry in Camilla Cottage in 1801–2, two very good plays, which might have realized the 'golden dreams' almost realized in 'Love and Fashion', but 'A Busy Day' and 'The Woman-Hater' were packed away in a closet.[1]

There followed then farewell visits to the Queen and the Princesses (even the King appeared for this occasion), to her sisters, and finally to her father who, hardly deceived by her high hopes, felt that it might be long indeed before the d'Arblays should return.

On April 15, 1802, she took Alex to the inn (probably the White Bear) in Piccadilly from which the Dover coach set off. With a brief and hurried farewell to Mrs. Locke, who was sending little Adrienne de Chavagnac along with her, she set off for France. Letters addressed to her father and Miss Planta (the channel to the Queen and the Princesses) give particulars of her journey to Dover, the crossing to Calais, and her arrival at Paris in lilac time, April 20, 1802.[1]

[1] See p. 310, n. 1. I am indebted to the University of Toronto Press for permission to use parts of an article by myself, 'Fanny Burney: Playwright', *UTQ*, xix (Jan. 1950), 170–89.

XIII

THE WANDERER

(1802–1814)

Exiled by Fate

MONSIEUR D'ARBLAY had posted himself at seven o'clock in the morning (April 20, 1802) to watch for the coach from Calais; he had only four hours to wait. '*Ah, qu'elle est longue cette cruelle séparation, et comme je soupire après sa fin!*'[1] At eleven the travellers arrived: a little 'Gothic *Anglaise*', as she called herself, her small charge Adrienne de Chavagnac, and finally Alex, wildly excited over the journey, the arrival, and now the march of soldiers in the Paris streets.

With the Peace of Amiens all war had ceased, and yet the Paris springtime of 1802 was ominously enlivened by the beat of drums, smart military parades, and illuminations. Excitement and suspense marked the prelude of a new outbreak, rather than the end, of strife. At all the *relais* from Calais to Paris Madame d'Arblay had heard people talking about the restoration *du dimanche*. 'The bon Dieu had been lost for Ten years—but Bonaparte had now found him.'[2] The genius of the First Consul was already felt everywhere.

M. d'Arblay had secured comfortable and spacious apartments in the Hôtel Marengo in the rue de Miroménil (No. 1185). The salon was beautifully furnished, large, and airy, and it overlooked the garden of the '*ci-devant* Hotel Beauvais', just then full of lilacs and flowering shrubs.[2] Most of M. d'Arblay's friends were among the *ci-devants*. Many of them had suffered imprisonment or exile, had lost friends or relatives by the guillotine; and nearly all had lost property—rent-rolls, mansions in or near the cities, and villas for 'elegant retirement' in the country. One part, at least, of better times they retained—their charm of manner, grace, and wit. Madame d'Arblay was

---

[1] A.L. (Berg) from M. d'A to FBA, n.d.
[2] 3 A.L.S. (Berg) from FBA to Miss Planta, EBB, and CBFB, 21 Apr., 24 May, 25 June–17 July 1802, respectively. Also Diary MSS. (Berg), pp. 5400–900.

captivated by a society of such elegance. 'Amiability, liveliness, intelligence, gaiety, & good-humour & good breeding mark it in every instance.'[1] Almost every hour from breakfast to supper brought a caller with 'some particular to recommend him'.

'Tis an old friend, or a Brother in misfortune, or a near relation— or a person eminent in late transactions, either of state or in the military—or the wife, mother, or sister of one of these.[2]

She was much touched by a visit from Madame de Lafayette, who, though lamed by an infection contracted in the prison of Olmütz, climbed up three flights of stairs to pay her respects.[3] Later the d'Arblays were guests for a week at her *château, La Grange.* Fanny's letters to Mrs. Locke and the Queen (via Miss Planta) rang with praises of the 'Female Worthies' of Paris for their 'piety, exemplary life', and the 'meritorious discharge' of 'conjugal, maternal, & filial duties'.[4] Perhaps she wished to correct erroneous ideas about the frivolity and immorality of French women—impressions that she knew were held in England and that she had shared—by pen-pictures of the domestic virtues as well as of the hospitality, kindness, charm, and intelligence of those she had come to know.

Visits formal and informal, assemblies, the *Opera Buffa,* and excursions filled the hours that were not given to nursing Alex, who had again succumbed to fever. The establishment of the Consulate was celebrated by a levee, parades, and a review, the sumptuous trappings of which were as new to the *ci-devants* living in France as to the d'Arblays themselves. Early in May, therefore, M. d'Arblay secured admission to the Tuileries for his wife and the Princesse d'Hénin to see the First Consul himself review the troops on the parade-ground.[3] The 'grandeur of the martial scene' saddened Fanny, though her sorrow was as yet only intuitive. She did not see any more clearly than the statesmen of her time that the Napoleonic armies would soon sweep over Europe, and that a Continental blockade would shut out the English shore for a decade.

---

[1] Diary MSS. (Berg), Apr.–Dec. 1802–3.
[2] See p. 313, n. 2.   [3] *Diary,* vi. 1–54.
[4] For sketches of la Princesse de Poix, la Princesse d'Hénin, Madame de Maisonneuve, la Princesse de Beauvau, la Marquise de Tessé, Madame de Lafayette, and others, see Diary MSS. (Berg), box viii; also letters (Berg) from FBA to EBB, 12 Mar. 1819, 22 Nov. 1824.

When before the end of June Alex fell ill for the third time, the d'Arblays moved from the unsavoury airs of Paris to the outskirts. They found a place at Monceau (rue Cisalpine, No. 286) so near the Folie de Chartres, then a public garden, that they could walk into it almost as easily as into another room. This garden, formerly belonging to the Duc d'Orléans, was in a state of ruin, but fresh with uncut grass and lilacs, and both Alex and Fanny recuperated rapidly.[1]

Up to this time M. d'Arblay's affairs had kept him near Paris, but about the beginning of July his aunt, Madame Bazille, and her daughter came to welcome Fanny to France; and shortly afterwards the d'Arblays visited Joigny. This was the exile's return, celebrated sufficiently, said Fanny, to do justice to a Lord Mayor.[2] In understanding, gentlemanly deportment, and arch pleasantry, M. Bazille recalled Mr. Crisp, and all the family were 'agreeable, deserving, & affectionate'.[3] At Joigny, however, there was a social round even more demanding than that of Paris, and Fanny, who had always needed whole days to 'recruit', had not now even half an hour for herself. She found a country town

utterly at war with all that, to me, makes peace & happiness & cheerfulness, namely, the real domestic Life of living with my own small but all sufficient family. I have never loved a dissipated life, . . . but I now far less than ever can relish it, & know not how to enjoy any thing from home, except by decent intervals.[4]

In about a fortnight M. d'Arblay's affairs took him back to Paris, and he settled Fanny and Alex at Monceau for the summer. At Joigny again for the vintage, they met Colonel Louis Bonaparte, afterwards King of Holland. On one day Fanny observed the future rulers; on the next she was shown the sites of burned *châteaux* (like that of the *ci-devant* Princesse de Baufremont at Césy) and shuddered sympathetically over tales of the Revolution. She noted the politeness of the French everywhere, attributing the cordiality of her reception to her husband, though she was often amazed at the reception that *Evelina* and *Cecilia* had prepared for her.[5] To many people, even

[1] See p. 314, n. 1.   [2] See p. 314, n. 3.
[3] See p. 313, n. 2.
[4] A.L. (Berg) from FBA to EBB, July 1802.
[5] Letters (Berg) from FBA to CB, 1802–12.

then, the handsome and distinguished chevalier must have been known only in Napoleon's phrase as 'the husband of Cecilia'.

Before the end of October, 1802, M. d'Arblay purchased a house built on the declivity of a rock two miles from the city at Passy,

an up & down, queer, odd little building, which we entered by the roof, & of which we could only furnish the first floor, but which had two or three magnificent views from the sides of the windows, & from a Terrace . . . built up to our first floor from the garden.[1]

Fanny thought it just the place for such 'odd folk'.[2] She could take modernistic houses in her stride, especially since there was

from one room a superb view of Paris, just far enough off to be picturesque, nay, magnificent; & from another a sweet prospect from the banks of the Seine, of cultivated Hills, whole villas, & beautiful woods & fields.[2]

Fanny was glad to escape the unwholesome air of Paris, 'which, but for the healthiness of the beautiful and delicious walks around it, *i.e.* Les Boulevards, must surely have proved pestilential'.[3] The house at Passy (rue Basse, No. 54) was unfinished, and when the d'Arblays moved there in October, the slow, sleepy village carpenters were still at work. Three months later, M. d'Arblay was forced to send them away because of the bills, while the house was still unfinished, unpapered, and, except for three rooms, unfurnished. The site, nevertheless, was picturesque, retired, and cheerful, and, best of all, the d'Arblays could have the house *à l'anglaise* to themselves.[4]

Meanwhile M. d'Arblay was foiled or frustrated in all his hereditary or military claims and hopes. 'Terrible have been his disappointments in all his expectations here, of a pecuniary sort—but they have not, I bless God, soured his Temper, or affected my happiness, & our home, therefore, with all its wants & privations, is such as I would change for no other.'[5] Fanny saw her father's dismal forebodings realized: 'Our money matters all, all go ill!'[2] The landed property near Joigny could not be recovered. Those who had purchased it from the State during M. d'Arblay's exile added 'such enormous and un-

---

[1] See p. 315, n. 4.   [2] See p. 314, n. 3.
[3] See p. 314, n. 3.
[4] A.L. (Berg) from FBA to CBFB, 6 Apr. 1803.
[5] A.L. (Berg) from FBA to Mary Port Waddington, Aug. 1803.

accountable charges to what they paid for it at that period' that
the price was far beyond anything he could manage to pay.[1] In
April, 1803, however, General de Lauriston had persuaded the
First Consul to grant M. d'Arblay his *retraite*, a pension amounting to 1,500 livres or £62.10*s* annually. 'He expected double!'—
but at least he was under Government protection, though he
could not quit his country during a war. In May he managed
to secure employment as a *rédacteur* in the *Bureau* of the *Ministère
de l'Intérieur*, a post paying 2,500 livres or about £100 per
annum. This was no sinecure.

He attends at his bureau from half-past nine to half-past four
o'clock every day; and as we live so far off as Passy he is obliged to
set off for his office between eight and nine, and does not return to
his hermitage till past five.[1]

Fanny had hoped to return to England in October, 1803, but
on May 18 the Peace of Amiens came to an end. England and
France were again at war. Emigration regulations, a coastal
blockade, and war on the seas made travel difficult or impossible; and now Fanny was in her turn an exile. This was 'a
bitter stroke'. She could only pray that 'Heaven may bless &
preserve my beloved & dearest Father—& return the nations
to peace and me to his arms!' In the meantime 'may Heaven
bless all! all!' till she can come again.[2]

Fortunately at Passy she had for a time the quiet rural
surroundings she liked and life was by no means unhappy in
the house on the rock. Her Memorandum Books[3] of these years
include long lists of 'books read' and 'books read with Alex', and
indicate the intellectual pursuits of a decade. Fortunately the
child's health improved, and his education demanded much
time and thought. M. d'Arblay had started him

in the rudiments of Mathematics, & he made a progress in arithmetic really surprising, but his little head worked so constantly, that
he solved, or invented, difficulties in the night, instead of sleeping.
Alarmed for his health, his Father was forced to remit this species
of instruction or give it sparingly; but Latin, French, writing,
Geography, etc. went on smoothly, while History, English, ortho-
graphy, &, to my best ability, Religion, fell to my share. We had

[1] See p. 314, n. 3.   [2] See p. 314, n. 1.
[3] Berg.

every reason to be content with our little scholar, &, to own the truth, we were not ashamed of the bantling.[1]

Soon, however, the d'Arblays gave him over for three hours in the morning to the village schoolmaster, who soon found the little day-scholar a 'phoenix' for 'application & facility'; and the next spring (1805) at a Commencement in a public hall in the Bois de Boulogne, his famous mother sat wiping away furtive tears—not bitter ones—when before an audience of 700 spectators the diminutive Alex was presented with Thomson's *Seasons* in French prose as the first prize for *bonne conduite*, and adorned with a crown of 'Laurel & oak'; and

the same ceremony for first prize of *Mythology*, & Florian's *Gonzalo* was the Prize. Then the first p. for *Version*, which procured him Voltaire's *Charles 12 of Sweden*; and lastly of *Thème*, which valued him Tasso's *Jerusalem*.[1]

Fanny thought of Susan and the child-prodigy Norbury Phillips; of her brother Charles, that 'Grand Assertor of the Ancient Discipline' at Greenwich; and finally of her father who would have known so well how to appreciate and grace such an occasion. Now she could not even write to her father unless she could find a traveller to smuggle the letter.

In 1805–6 M. d'Arblay had found the long walks between Passy and his *bureau* too strenuous, and before the winter of 1806 the d'Arblays had moved to Paris (this time to rue du Faubourg St. Honoré, No. 100).[2] This was a hard year for Alex, who had become so much attached to the master of the village school that his 'Amante, whenever he elects one', said his mother, 'may esteem herself happy if she meets with similar worship'. (He would stand at the door to watch for M. Chalin, and sometimes get up at six in the morning merely to see him go to mass with his pupils.) The school in Paris had 200 *élèves*, but by 'studious exertions', by 'application & facility' Alex again rose to the top of the class. When the excellence of his day's work was used (perhaps unwisely) as a reproach and a spur to his comrades, they grew mutinous. Apparently the Paris schoolboys lived in revolutionary times to some purpose. One day near the

[1] 2 A.L.S. (Berg) from FBA to CB, 20 Jan., 22 Oct. 1806.

[2] Successive addresses were rue du Faubourg St. Honoré, No. 100; rue d'Anjou, No. 13; and again the Hôtel Marengo, rue de Miroménil, No. 1185.

close of the term, after the master had graded the day's work, as usual giving the firsts to Alex, twelve of the little rioters suddenly shouted out in unison, '*au quatrième d'Arblay! au quatrième d'Arblay!*' In vain the masters (in the way of masters) told the boys that they had only to apply themselves to attain similar results. On the next day they presented a petition to the same effect (i.e. *au quatrième d'Arblay!*) signed by twenty-eight rebels, and they followed this up on the playground with much stronger representations known to schoolboys of all times. He must himself ask to be removed to the fourth form.

Alex took to his heels, but could not escape from such numbers; a tall immense Boy, however, of a higher class, came forward in his cause, & banged all the little Gentlemen in his defence without mercy. This saved him for the moment; but he was so pursued, that at length gave way, & turned *polisson* himself to appease them. This new character—which we did not hear of till some time after by degrees grew so agreeable to him, that he now suddenly dropt all application, &, in a short time, became the idlest & most wanton Boy of the class![1]

Finally, between laughter and concern, the master described the metamorphosis to M. d'Arblay, who must have known what to do, for after two months of idleness Alex applied himself to such effect that at the closing exercises M. d'Arblay and 'la maman' had the great pleasure and satisfaction of hearing that the first prize for general excellence was to go to Alexander d'Arblay, and after that, the first prize for *Memory*, and then for *Geography*, then for *Grammar*, and, finally, the first prizes for *History*, *Version*, and *Thème*. Alex's surprise, awkwardness, and extreme simplicity (his parents had never been able to teach him how to make bows, or present himself), his diminutiveness (it was not until he was sixteen that he took 'the more favourable turn of resembling his father'), the six laurel crowns and the armloads of Racine and Boileau (his prizes) finally brought amused applause not only from the male spectators, but also from the students, the ladies, and finally the *professeurs* themselves. Long before this, 'la maman' in the gallery found her eyes so blinded with tears that she could scarcely use her 'short-sighted glass'. M. and Madame d'Arblay, after receiving congratulations, left the hall to find the little prodigy waiting

[1] See p. 318, n. 1.

on the stone steps, oblivious or unconscious of the honours, but in ecstasy over his new books.

The incidents of the year, however, had taught Alex that the way to get along in the world, to please his fellows and incidentally himself, was to be idle. A few weeks of study before the examinations would suffice to carry off enough prizes to please tutors, parents, and all. And this experiment of 1806 became a habit that was to cause Fanny much bitter worry in the days to come.

Meanwhile Napoleon played his part in the destinies of nations and men. In 1808 he strengthened the Continental blockade, enforcing strict regulations against traffic with England. Travellers with smuggled letters crossed the Channel much less frequently, and for a few years Madame d'Arblay was almost completely cut off from her family. On May days she thought of the English cowslips, even of marrowbones and cleavers, and she knew that her father was now in his eighties.

The news of him that Fanny longed to hear may now be read in the correspondence between his granddaughter, Marianne Francis, and Mrs. Piozzi.[1] In 1808 Marianne reported that her grandfather

was as young and gay as ever, reading & writing without spectacles (which he has never used *yet*) and cheerful and entertaining, and sprightly, and kind, as if he had been *23* instead of *eighty three*.[1]

In 1809 Grandpa still looked 'very gay though pinched with the cold'. In June, 1810, Marianne found her grandfather in better health and spirits than he had enjoyed for ten years, writing and reading the 'smallest hand without spectacles' and as 'industrious & occupied as ever'. Even in 1811, though by then confined to Chelsea, he was 'as full of business as the Sea of Sands, Books, papers, & anecdotes—plagued with a cough but otherwise well'. 'The gold is not become dim, nor the fine gold changed!'[1] 'Here I am, in spite of the old Gentleman and his scythe!' he had written about this time,

and the people I am able to see in the warm weather, tell me I

---

[1] This correspondence is in the John Rylands Library. References to Dr. Burney occur in at least 21 letters between 21 July 1807 and 13 Apr. 1814. Also A.L.S. (Barrett) from MF to Charlotte Barrett, [1809]. Cf. A.L. (Osborn) from CB to FBA, 5 May 1810.

look better, speak, & walk better than I did 'ever so long ago'.
God knows how handsome I shall be bye & bye![1]

For all that, a man cannot always be at his best. Even
Marianne had to admit that though Grandpa '*is* agreeable
when he is kind', he was not like Dr. Johnson, 'sublime' when
he was cross.[1] The reverse side of the picture appears in the
letters of Sarah Harriet, who after the marriage of Fanny
Phillips in July, 1807, returned to Chelsea. She found her father
at the age of eighty-six often enough peevish and perverse and
unreasonable. In 1811 she thought him much injured 'by the
close seclusion he has doomed himself to'.

He wastes, and enfeebles, I think, almost visibly; but he will not hear
the slightest representation from anybody on the subject—and to
fret him would be worse than to see how thin he grows.[2]

Though there were no complaints of the old man's parsimony,
the debts that Fanny Phillips incurred or had to incur while she
lived with her grandfather became a family problem, and Sarah
Harriet seemed to have no money at all except what she could
earn by her novels ('I must scribble, or I *cannot live*'). In 1808
she had published *Geraldine Fauconberg*; in 1810–12 she was
writing *Traits of Nature*, which she hoped would enable her to
take a vacation and for which she was paid £100 a volume. Few
details of the family difficulties reached Fanny in these years,
but as her father passed his mid-eighties she thought day and
night of her return.

In the summer of 1810, however, a new menace in the form
of a metastatic abscess, possibly a cancer, seemed to threaten
not only her return to England but her life. In 1811 she was told
that a surgical operation would be necessary. If one recollects
that at that time anaesthetics had not been discovered, or at
least not put into use, and that operations were performed on
unetherized patients not upon an operating-table but upon an
improvised bed, one may be in part prepared for the horrors
detailed in Madame d'Arblay's closely written quartos on the
subject.[3] Those familiar with her realistic powers of description

---

[1] See p. 320, n. 1.
[2] See 37 letters (Berg) from SHB to Charlotte Barrett, 20 Mar. 1803–1 Mar.
1816.
[3] Detailed accounts of this operation are preserved in (1) A.L. (Berg), twelve
closely written pages from FBA to EBB, 22 Mar. 1812; (2) a copy of this letter

will be prepared, therefore, either to enter the gruesome operating-theatre, feel the cutting and hear the screams, or to turn over the leaf and choose another tale.

There were first the consultations and the advice of a series of eminent surgeons, including M. Dubois, who attended the Empress Josephine, and Baron de Larrey, first surgeon to Napoleon. '*Vous êtes si considérée, madame, ici*,' said he, '*que le public même sera mécontent si vous n'avez pas tout le secours que nous avons à vous offrir.*' The only help was in an operation.

Ah, my dearest Esther, for this I felt no courage—my dread & repugnance, from a thousand reasons *besides* the pain, almost shook all my faculties.

M. d'Arblay's face 'displayed the bitterest woe' but 'with what exquisite tenderness he solaced all I had to bear!' Madame d'Hénin came twice from the country to pay visits of consolation; Madame de Maisonneuve and Madame de Tessé came almost daily, lending every possible aid. 'The kindness I received at this period would have made me forever love France, had I hitherto been hard enough of heart to hate it.' Later Fanny learned that M. Dubois had given his opinion 'that the evil was too far advanced for any remedy; that a cancer was already internally declared; that I was inevitably destined to that most frightful of deaths, & that an operation would but accelerate my dissolution'. Baron de Larrey, however, entertained some desperate hope and was willing to try an operation. '*Vous souffrirez beaucoup!*' His sympathy and his strong personal resemblance to James not less perhaps than his skill lent her the confidence needed.

Weeks passed while the surgeons waited for a summons 'and that, a formal one, & in writing'. '*I* could not give one; *consent* was my utmost effort. But poor M. d'A. wrote a desire that the operation, if necessary, might take place without further delay.'

When, early in a morning in late September, 1811, a message was brought that the surgeons would come at ten o'clock that day, Fanny pretended in her woman's way to have difficulty in

begun by Alexander d'Arblay and completed by M. d'Arblay, together with letters to Baron de Larrey, and official documents (permission to have straw laid, &c., 1, 4 Oct. 1811), boxed with Diary MSS. (Berg), box vi; and (3) a draft, boxed with Diary MSS. (Berg), box viii. See also A.L. (Berg) from FBA to EBB, 10 (?) Mar. 1819.

deciphering the writing while she plotted a way to save her husband 'the unavailing wretchedness of witnessing' what she must endure. She called Alex to her bedside and sent him off with a message to the *chef du Bureau* that the *moment was come* and a request that he write a note calling M. d'Arblay away on urgent business. 'Speechless & appalled, out flew Alex, and as I have since heard, was forced to sit down & sob, after having executed his commission.' Until one o'clock she was occupied with the arrangement of the operating-theatre—two old mattresses and an old sheet placed on a bedstead in the middle of the room. With a message that the surgeons would be delayed until three o'clock, she wandered about the room she had prepared, half sickened at the sight of the compresses, sponges, and lint, but she managed to scribble a few lines to Alex and to her father. At last the clock struck three and she heard four cabriolets drive up in succession and stop at the door.

Nothing could be more ghoulish. Seven black-robed men entered, sombre in mood and dress. When she was ordered by M. Dubois to take off her long *robe de chambre* the degree of prudery appeared. She wished for her sisters—'not one, at so dreadful an instant, at hand, to protect—adjust—guard—grieved me!' Especially she thought of Susan. That angel would have wept. She imagined that to the doctors this was a trivial matter, and she felt defiant. Heartlessness she could not endure. But presently perceiving, by the strained pallor of M. de Larrey's face and the agitation of the others, that they were not unmoved,

I called myself to order, and mounted unbidden, the bedstead. M. Dubois placed me upon the mattress, and spread a cambric handkerchief over my face. It was transparent, however, and I saw, through it, that the bedstead was instantly surrounded by the seven men and my nurse; but when bright through the cambric, I saw the glitter of polished steel, I closed my Eyes. I would not trust to convulsive fear the sight of the terrible incision.

Imagining that the hesitation and deliberation of the doctors proceeded from uncertainty or lack of information, she threw the cambric from her eyes in order to explain the nature of her suffering—how the pain sprang from one point but darted to every part. She was heard politely and attentively and in utter silence. The cambric was replaced; and presently feeling a cross and a circle being traced on her diseased breast she resigned herself to losing the whole organ and interfered no more. The doctors had encouraged her to cry; but now she began a scream that lasted continuously—so excruciating was the agony when the forked poniards of air rushed into the exposed parts. She was keenly aware of the resistance of her flesh to the instrument, the dreadful undercutting to remove the gland, and finally a kind of scraping, or so it seemed, over her breastbone. Though she thought she had fainted for an instant or two, she was still conscious at the end of seventeen minutes, and even heard the final consultation. Was everyone satisfied that the affected parts were completely removed? All, except M. Dubois; and the cutting and scraping and the agonized screams began all over again. Still she was conscious and able to see Baron de Larrey—'His face streaked with blood, & its expression depicting grief, apprehension, almost horrour'. She knew too that when they carried her away, her head rolled and dropped and her arms hung down like lifeless things, there being no force, almost no life within.

Because of her *extrême sensibilité* she suffered violent spasms through the night; yet the wound healed without infection, and she survived and gained strength to live for many a long year. Her fortitude gained her the respect and the friendship of Baron de Larrey, and among M. d'Arblay's friends the name of 'l'Ange'.[1]

With her recovery she began again to think of England. As everyone knew, emigration laws could sometimes be circumvented. If one had an obliging and conniving acquaintance it was possible to obtain a passport not for England directly, but for Canada, Newfoundland, or some point on 'the western continents'. If one could then find a captain willing to make convenient ports of call, one might embark legally from the French shore and land illegally in England. In the spring of 1812 M. d'Arblay heard of an American captain who was to sail from Dunkirk with a clandestine landing at Dover in mind; and Madame d'Arblay, having spent almost ten years in France, determined to take this means of returning to visit her father and her family and to deposit Alex, now a tall, good-looking youth

[1] See p. 321, n. 3.

of seventeen, safely beyond the reach of Napoleon and of conscription in the army destined for the Russian campaign.[1]

She set off early in July but the American captain delayed six weeks at Dunkirk until sailing news about his clandestine intentions got whispered about and brought him his quota of passengers. Only the fear that she would one day arrive too late to see her father again kept her there. 'Oh mon ami! how have you spoiled me for Life without you!'[1] She wandered about the town until friendly gestures towards some Spanish prisoners got her into trouble with the police. She then thought of the manuscript of *The Wanderer* and sent for it in order to pass the time in writing. These papers filled a valise and aroused much suspicion at the customs house. On August 14 the *Mary Ann* put to sea but, since war was now declared between England and the United States, the ship was seized off the Downs and brought to Deal instead of its destination Dover, where Charles's carriage was waiting. On August 16, the travellers landed, but stopped to rest, to wait for Charles, who stayed on at Dover for '*three nights* following, through a mistake', and to write jubilant announcements of their arrival. On the 17th Lucy Fitzgerald (now Mrs. Foley), a sister of the famous Lord Edward, came to call, gave Fanny the latest news about Norbury Park, and arranged an assembly that night.[2] All this together with the sound of the English language ringing continually in her ears kept her smiling all day. On the 19th the travellers set off for Canterbury, where they slept, and the next day, on some common where the driver stopped to water the horses, Madame d'Arblay descried a gentleman on horseback who rode up to their conveyance, looked in, and called her by name. It was Charles, affectionate and gay as of old, and so they proceeded to Chelsea, arriving there at nine o'clock in the evening, August 20, 1812.

She found only servants, and in an almost breathless state demanded to see her father alone.

Fortunately, he had had the same feeling, and had charged all the family to stay away, and all the world to be denied. I found him,

---

[1] *Diary*, vi. 60–83; Diary MSS. (Berg), pp. 5856–8. Also correspondence (Berg) between FBA and M. d'A, 6 July–10 Dec. 1812.

[2] Diary MSS. (Berg), Aug.–Dec. 1812; A.L.S. (PML) from FBA to JB, 15 Aug. 1812.

therefore, in his library, by himself—but oh! my dearest, very much altered indeed—weak, weak and changed—his head almost always hanging down, and his hearing cruelly impaired.... What a change![1]

Long afterwards she remembered that, though when she left for France in 1802 'his elegantly formed person [was] still unbroken by his years', his head now

hung helplessly upon his breast; his voice, though still distinct, sunk almost to a whisper: his feeble frame reclined upon a sofa; his air and look forlorn; and his whole appearance manifesting a species of self-desertion.[1]

Marianne had witnessed the alterations of time only gradually; Fanny saw the ravages of a decade. Seeing the change, she was 'terribly affected' but most grateful 'to the Providence that had propitiated her return, ere that change,—still changed on!—should have become, to her, invisible'.[1] Sarah Harriet told how her father, waiting anxiously on the day he expected Madame d'Arblay from France, walked about the room murmuring to himself—'My HONEST Fanny!'[2] Fanny knew how he had 'kindly, almost comically'

given orders to his immediate attendants, Rebecca and George, to move all the chairs and tables close to the wall; and to see that nothing whatsoever should remain between the door and his sofa, which stood at the farther end of a large room, that could interfere with her rapid approach.[1]

Those who have followed the troubled saga of the Burneys will be glad that the rhythm of events allowed at least the following year and a half to the sensitive old gentleman and to his famous daughter, who could not have borne to lose (at least through any fault of her own) his parting benediction. 'You would see me more than ever all your own', she had written to her husband from Dunkirk, 'after the shortest excursion that procured such peace to my soul!'[3]

Early in the morning James appeared, 'his Eyes filled with affectionate tears'; Charles soon followed, but his joy, though equally strong, was far gayer; in the evening, Charlotte, 'grave & gay too, and almost overpowered with tender feelings'; and finally, Susan's daughter Fanny Phillips Raper, lovelier than

[1] *Memoirs*, iii. 400–9; *Diary*, vi. 82–83.
[2] A.L.S. (Barrett) from SHB to Charlotte Barrett, 1 Feb. 1842; also *Memoirs*, iii. 402.   [3] See p. 325, n. 1.

ever, 'her bloom more bright, . . . & her form more perfect'.[1] 'Kindness & affection such as they all shew would have warmed my heart had it been formed of marble.'[2]

Madame d'Arblay's return was an event. 'Who do you think, my dearest Mrs Piozzi, is come to England?—to my amazement, as much as yours—Madame d'Arblay & her son Alexander!!!'[3] Clement Francis thought that his aunt's arrival had taken nearly twenty years from his grandfather's looks.[3]

During the quiet years in Surrey and the long sojourn in France, Madame d'Arblay's nephews and nieces had grown up, and she now heard about their academic exploits, their marriages, and young families. Norbury Phillips had graduated from Trinity College, Dublin, with 'great reputation, & worth of every kind' and was then preparing for ordination.[4] Charles Parr Burney (son of Charles) had completed his studies at Oxford and now took his father's place in the school at Greenwich. He had married and had a little daughter four or five months old (the Brightblossom of her grandfather's later verses). Richard Allen Burney (Esther's son) was married and had a living in Dorset (and later, at Rimpton in Somerset). James's son Martin was a student in the Temple; and Clement Francis (Charlotte's son) was at Cambridge. Marianne Francis would have made 'a most capital fellow of a College', her mother thought. She would not, of course, have been admitted, but she surpassed her brother and her cousins and, in Dr. Burney's opinion, 'all the parsons & other learned persons at Bath' in erudition. 'All agree she is a *prodige*,' reported Madame d'Arblay, 'though some with praise, some with censure, & all with wonder.'[4] She read Latin and Greek and spoke French, German, Italian, and Spanish, '*chacun comme si c'était sa propre langue*'. She was studying Hebrew and Arabic, she understood geometry and algebra, and was, according to her grandfather, 'a marvellous performer on the Piano Forte'.

She may perhaps be styled a *Bravura* player. But her courage & perseverance in attacking difficulties of every kind, is unparalleled,

---

[1] See p. 325, n. 2.   [2] See p. 325, n. 1.

[3] 2 A.L.S. (JRL) from MF to HLTP, 1, 26 Sept. 1812; and A.L.S. (JRL) from CF to HLTP, 3 Sept. 1812.

[4] A.L.S. (Berg) from FBA and AA to M. d'A, 10 Dec. 1812; also 2 A.L.S. (Osborn) from CB to FBA, 1808, [1810 or 1811]; and A.L. (Barrett) from CBFB to FBA, 18 May 1809.

so that in spite of my civility to her *countenance* I pronounce her to be—a *monster*.[1]

'*C'est un vrai prodige que cette Marianne*', added Alex. With all this she was neither dull nor pedantic, but gay and comical. In 1812 she was at Bradfield, acting as secretary to the blind Arthur Young. Charlotte Francis Barrett and her ultra-Victorian husband Henry Barrett were bringing up a family at Richmond. James's daughter Sally, with her 'lively spirits, & laughing ideas', was just fifteen. 'She is by nature a perfect *espiègle*.'[2] With the exception of the widowed Maria, now living comfortably at Bath, Esther's daughters were all unmarried; one of them, Fanny, was a governess.

To most of these young people the name of Aunt d'Arblay had seemed almost a legend. Shortly after the travellers arrived, Clement Francis and his sister Charlotte Barrett accompanied their mother to Chelsea to spend the evening. Charlotte Broome was now fifty years old; Madame d'Arblay, sixty. Their affection was mutual and to become one of the chief supports of their later years. Just now Charlotte's children were very curious to see their new-found relatives. Alex, they noted, was six feet tall and 'silent & shy & brown & thin, but his countenance very intelligent'.

Clem says that Alec is very forward in mathematics & would shine in any English University. . . . [He] is promised admission into the Polytechnic school in Paris in wch. 300 young men are finished in sciences etc. generally those who have distinguished themselves by previous attainments, & *those only*, in all France, are exempted from the conscription for life, that they may be *literatti & savans* & so on.[3]

And 'Bravo Buonaparte!' was the learned Marianne's comment on this. Later she described Alex as 'a very expressive dark-eyed, intelligent creature—a perfect Bookworm; his nose always in mathematics or Thucydides'.[4]

Those who had known Madame d'Arblay previously said that she had improved rather than lost in appearance. She had, in brief, put on flesh; and flesh became her, giving her face a greater variety of expression than it had had before.[5] She often

---

[1] See p. 327, n. 4.   [2] See p. 325, n. 1.

[3] A.L.S. (Barrett) from Charlotte Barrett to MF, 27 Aug. 1812; and MF to HLTP, as in n. 3, p. 327.

[4] 4 A.L.S. (JRL) from MF to HLTP, 21 Mar. 1811, 26 Sept. 1812, 15 Jan., 14 Apr. 1813; A.L.S. (Barrett) from Sarah Burney to CBFB, 4 Sept. 1813.

[5] Austin Dobson's note, *Diary*, vi. 83.

had a bright feverish colour, looked forty rather than sixty, was
'lively & entertaining', and spoke with a foreign accent—'like
a French woman speaking *remarkably good English*'.[1] Her kind
interest in all the affairs of her nieces and nephews quite won
their hearts, and they could not have enough of her conversation. Thus Charlotte continued with the evening at Chelsea—
her grandfather's wish that she look over Strange's prints, and
when she said that she had seen them, his insistence that she
sit by him

> peeping at frightful monks' faces painted in the margin of an old
> missal, & then Clem was called to read the newspaper. Mama slept,
> but we pretended to listen & to laugh . . . and then came away.

Thus the visit was tantalizing but still delightful. On the way
home Clement gave his opinion and verdict flatly: 'I really
think Aunt d'Arblay is the most charming woman I ever saw
in my life!'[2]

Since there were no spare rooms in the organist's apartments
at Chelsea, Madame d'Arblay and Alex found lodgings nearby
but later lived in picnic style (that is, sharing the expenses) with
Charlotte at 23 Chenies Street, Bedford Square. Many of her
activities are reported in a series of letters intended to interest
and cheer her father. She had spent a 'most social & chearful &
affectionate day on Tuesday at dear James's, whose hospitable
board was surrounded by all of our tribe he could collect'.[3]
James and his wife were now on the best of terms, and the day
had given her great pleasure. At John Street she heard of 'dreadful illnesses' that Esther had suffered

> & cares that would have subdued any one else, from difficulties of life,
> through the changes of Fashion, & fickleness of the times with re-
> spect to her excellent husband; but the inexhaustible gaiety of spirits
> with which Nature has endowed her, buoy her up against all evils
> that are not either immediate, or domestic. . . . The good Mr
> Burney . . . can *think* as justly as any man, [but] he is so absent &
> inexperienced, that he could never *act* till the season for all that
> should be done would be past by. Poor Esther therefore is often

---

[1] See p. 328, n. 4. [2] See p. 328, n. 3.
[3] Letters (Berg) from FBA to CB, n.d., 10, 18 Sept., 2 Nov., 4, 10 Dec. 1812,
13 Jan., 23 Feb., 30 Mar., 30 Oct. 1813; A.L. (Berg) to CB, Jr., 6 Dec. 1813;
letters (Osborn) to CB, Jr., 1812–13; A.L. (Berg) to Mary Port Waddington, 24
Dec. 1813.

heavily laden, in defiance of the elastic spring, that brings all round again.[1]

In January Mr. Burney's birthday was to be celebrated by a large family-party and a ball. Though Madame d'Arblay now feared the 'vigorous season' more than ever, she wrapped herself up warmly, took a warm carriage, and ventured forth. 'I know not exactly how many fandangos, or pas seuls, I may dance, but I cannot deny myself, upon such an occasion, being once more abroad & amongst them.'[2] Later she told her father of the 'true satisfaction' she had had 'in looking round again at our goodly tribe'. Like Sarah Harriet she wished that he would not shut himself away so completely. He might 'feel his spirits higher' if he could receive the young people sometimes,

& accept their relations or prattling, & be content in return, with sometimes a nod, & sometimes a wry face, just as approbation or dissent might dictate, & nothing more.[1]

Charles was now Vicar of St. Paul, Deptford, and of Herne Hill, Kent, and Chaplain to George III. In November Madame d'Arblay paid a long visit to the rectory at Deptford with the magnificent library containing what his nieces maintained that no one could need—twenty-five editions of Homer and thirty of Aristotle, old prayer-books and missals and rarities reaching the ceiling.[3] Here Fanny learned how in 1807, largely through the efforts of Dr. Martin Davy, Master of Caius, the judgements or orders against Charles at Cambridge were rescinded; that in 1808 the degree of M.A. was conferred on him by Royal Mandate, and in 1812 the degree of Doctor of Divinity.[4] He had lately preached in the royal chapel and he had dined twice with the Archbishop of Canterbury.[5] Marianne Francis, who was already embarrassing her family with strong evangelical leanings, entertained many misgivings about the state of Uncle Charles's soul and the policy of the Established Church.

Did I tell you my uncle Charles's strange good fortune of having

---

[1] A.L. (Barrett) from FBA to CB, 30 Jan. 1813; A.L. (Berg) to M. d'A, 31 Aug. 1812. Cf. *Thraliana*, i. 502–3.

[2] See p. 329, n. 3.

[3] A.L.S. (Barrett) from Charlotte Barrett to MF, 8 Oct. 1812. Cf. A.L. (Berg) from CB to Mrs. Crewe, 2 Oct. 1804.

[4] A.L.S. (BM) from CB, Jr., to William Windham, Aug. 1807; also copies of letters (Barrett) from FBA to CPB, 28 Feb., 14 Mar. 1818.

[5] See p. 325, n. 2.

two livings given to him in *one* day, with power to hold both & reside at neither. The Archbishop of Canterbury & the Bishop of Winchester were the two Delinquents. He now waits for the Prebendary of Ely & the Living at Greenwich—two old Incumbents between them & his nobility away, he will have at [55] more than £2000 a year preferment, after having been but 2 years in the Church. O Tempora O Mores! . . . Not *Theology* but *Scholarship* raise a man to a Bishopric now.[1]

Madame d'Arblay perhaps did not look so critically as this into Charles's triumphs. She had always had confidence in his good faith and good heart; at this time her misgivings were probably confined to his health. He had, indeed, only five more years to live. Already he had attacks of gout (the result of the sumptuous table that Susan used to criticize and of later voluptuous junketings, with the Duke of Norfolk and others, that Dr. Burney complained of).[2] He had violent headaches that gave warning of high blood-pressure and of the fit of apoplexy that struck him down on the eve of another titanic effort of scholarship, which, as Fanny had reason to think, might have been rewarded with a bishopric. In spite of his great strength of mind and physique the struggle had been too strenuous. 'Poor uncle Charles!' So dignified and impressive he looked too in his clerical robes, when he officiated at christenings like those of the Barrett children![3] If he was, indeed, something of a Chaucerian prelate, one may only wish for the story's sake that 'apoplexie had shente not [his] heed'—at least not before he had become a bishop.

In 1812 Charles often placed his carriage at Madame d'Arblay's disposal or escorted her himself to Windsor, Norbury Park, Althorp, Richmond, or Deptford. In the late autumn and winter the damp chill, ill health (the result of her operation together with her usual relapse after over-excitement or over-exertion), and the determination to complete her fourth novel kept her imprisoned in the evenings. According to Clement Francis, she was much in demand with 'visitors, Inquiries & Invitations to such excess, that she leads the life of a besieged

---

[1] Letters (JRL) from MF to HLTP, 21 Nov. 1808, 6 June 1810, 5, 27 May 1811, 26 Sept. 1812, 14 Apr. 1813.

[2] See 2 A.L.S. (Osborn) from CB to CB, Jr., 31 May 1808, 15 Jan. 1811.

[3] A.L.S. (Barrett) from MF to Arthur Young, 23 Jan. 1813; 2 A.L.S. (JRL) to HLTP, 21 Nov. 1808, 15 May 1811.

city'.[1] On a visit with Charles to Sandgate in September, 1813, she walked with William Wilberforce on the ramparts, answered questions about France and the state of religion there, and in turn caught up on English history.[2] So effective was the block-ade that she had learned only recently, for instance, what the name Trafalgar meant or that Nelson was dead.[3]

She made little mention of days spent at Windsor, the 'graciousness, goodness, sweetness' of the Queen and the Prin-cesses, and their confidences about the appalling sorrows and perplexities of the royal household in these years. Presently she was embarrassed by an invitation from the Princess of Wales, who was said to abhor the old Queen as her greatest enemy.[4] She visited Mrs. Locke at Norbury Park and Mrs. Locke's daughter Amelia, now married to John Angerstein. On her way home in a postchaise she met a huge procession turning into Kensington Gardens and was soon informed by 'a clown with a broad grin on his face, " 'tis nothing but the Lord Mayor & *that* gang to *congratify* the princess!" '[5]

Though the family had thought Madame d'Arblay in good health and spirits when she arrived, it soon appeared that her strength was limited. Her husband had known that the effort she made was but the '*triomphe du caractère sur la constitution*' and that a relapse would follow. So it proved. She had Baron de Larrey's orders to avoid dampness, cold, and mental turmoil ('either damp, or fretting would be fatal') and in February she was obliged to keep her room two days out of three.[6]

In March Marianne Francis, who at Bath in 1805 had struck up a great friendship with Mrs. Piozzi, tried to mediate between the estranged friends, first of all relaying her aunt's messages:

My Aunt d'Arblay . . . charges me to say from her, that your early kindness never has been obliterated from her memory, & never can; that she always preserves amongst her favourite hoards, its eloquent expression, & that if you were in town, she could with difficulty refrain from seeing if no part of it still remains.[5]

---

[1] See p. 328, n. 4.
[2] Copy of a letter (Barrett) from FBA to the Princess Elizabeth, 1817; A.L.S. (Osborn) from CB, Jr., to CPB, 19 Sept. 1813; to FBA, 11 Sept. 1813.
[3] See p. 328, n. 5.   [4] See p. 329, n. 3.
[5] In at least 13 letters (JRL) to HLTP between the dates 1 Sept. 1812 and 18 Mar. 1814, Marianne Francis alluded to or pleaded for Madame d'Arblay.
[6] See p. 325, n. 2.

When this conciliatory effort proved unsuccessful, Marianne
tried to appeal to Mrs. Piozzi's sympathies by an account of
Madame d'Arblay's ordeal of the previous year and the un-
certain state of her health. When this also was unsuccessful,
Marianne, pushed on by her mother, made the utmost effort.
As her aunt

was so desirous of something kind & conciliatory, & is, perhaps,
poor thing, in a most *dangerous* state, I think if you can bring yourself
to send anything like a kind message, it would be a most christian
act in you, & give great happiness to her.[1]

This was partially effective. In May, 1813, Mrs. Piozzi was in
London, and on the day of her departure she called without
warning at Chenies Street, and found no one at home. 'I was at
my school', lamented Marianne,

and Aunt d'Arblay had unhappily crawled out for some air, & was
inexpressibly mortified & grieved, she desires me to say, at finding
you had been here, during the *only* absence she had made from here
for so long. She comforted herself though, with the hope that she
might see you the day after, & went the very next day to J——
Street: it was late before she got there, & you were gone! The man
said to Bath.[1]

Apparently Mrs. Piozzi did not intend to be appeased. Either
she was, as she described herself, 'by Nature a rancorous and
revengeful Enemy' or, as is more likely, she credited mischief-
making allegations that the Burneys were the authors of squibs
about her in the newspapers.[2] Psychologically perhaps, having
gone to such lengths at one time in friendship and confidences,
it was difficult to go back. She was still resentful, and Madame
d'Arblay, who like her father wished to live at peace with those
she had loved, must continue to fret. A letter that Marianne
received from Mrs. Piozzi in June contained no mention of
Madame d'Arblay. Marianne had not mentioned the omission
to her aunt. 'I thought she would be so much hurt. I know you
wish her happiness—surely you will not refuse [to send] her
some kind message, if it be but *one* word.'[1]

Madame d'Arblay's next concern was not with the events of
a quarter of a century ago and their results, but with a very
lively, present problem—Alex and his education. She observed

---

[1] See p. 332, n. 5.   [2] *Thraliana*, i. 321; ii. 719, 916, n. 1.

that he had fallen into idle ways and wished him to resume his
habits of early rising and regular study. Though he felt it a little
below the dignity of one who had studied under M. Hugot in
Paris, he was persuaded to undergo an examination at the
school at Greenwich, where Charles Parr took his father's place
as Headmaster. To Fanny's relief he was admitted to the sixth
form and the plan was that if he prospered at Greenwich in the
terms 1812–13 he should proceed in the autumn to Cambridge.[1]
But how? Fees and expenses were a great obstacle, and since
as yet there was no prospect of fairer days in France, Madame
d'Arblay determined to meet the emergency by completing *The
Wanderer*, for which she knew she could get a good price, and,
secondly, to secure a Tancred Scholarship, which she had been
informed had fallen vacant. Charles, with unfailing kindness,
wrote to five of the seven members of the board of electors
(including the Masters of Christ Church, Caius, and the Charterhouse; the Governors of Chelsea and Greenwich Hospitals; the
President of the College of Physicians, and the Treasurer of
Lincoln's Inn). The Governor of Chelsea College was assigned
to Dr. Burney.[1] Fanny herself wrote to one of her most faithful
friends, Lady Keith (*née* Queeney Thrale), asking her or her
husband to write to Lord Hood (the Governor of Greenwich
Hospital), and finally she wrote to the Queen: 'Ah, Madam!—
if I dared solicit your Majesty's permission to supplicate the
intercession of their Royal Highnesses with the Duke of York!'[2]
A word from him would obtain Sir David Dundas, the Treasurer
of Lincoln's Inn. Such were the procedures in the age of patronage. Fanny was much harassed with such business—'exertions of
my own such as I never made before'.[3] Yet the Burneys had
come a long way since such letters had to be written for Charles.
This time the application was unanimously successful. The
Tancred amounted to £120 a year for three years, and Fanny's
relief at the solution of one problem vied with her gratitude to
all those who had helped her.

   She was again jubilant when on his entrance to Cambridge
in October, 1813, Alex won a scholarship in classics.[1] She hoped

---

   [1] See p. 329, n. 3.
   [2] Four drafts of letters (Berg) from FBA to Queen Charlotte, 11, 26 Feb.,
5, 16 Mar. 1813. On this occasion apparently the Queen replied in her own hand.
   [3] A.L. (Berg) from FBA to M. d'A, 29 Apr. 1814; *Diary*, vi. 85–86.

above all things that this victory would turn him from mathematics to literary pursuits, for his 'propensity' to mathematics,
'with his thin person & studious turn & absence of mind, often
make me fear for his health & strength & even existence'.[1]
She thought that mathematics inclined students to 'seclusion,
sauvagerie, & absence of mind'—faults that Alex already had,
though he was so young and *'justement arrivé de Paris'*.[1] She herself approved of scholars like Charles cogitating 'in the *brown
study*, in the morning, & willing to be frisky & agreeable, in
your vulgar tongue in an evening',[2] but her lifelong endeavour
could not make Alex conform to that pattern.

At first everything went well at Cambridge; and then everything went wrong. Alex failed in attendance at chapel, at lectures, and in hall. He failed to complete his assignments and
wasted his time in idleness, chess, and studies unconnected with
what he was expected to do. By Christmas he was in such
disgrace that Clement Francis was forced to tell his aunt that
all Alex's friends thought it better to remove him from college
until he should acquire some steadiness.[3] When the youth
arrived for the holidays, Fanny inquired into the truth. 'Had I
time, or composure', she confided to Charlotte, 'to relate his
own account of his motives for thus braving all order, you could
not . . . forbear smiling at their singularity & simplicity.'[4] She
took active steps, first procuring a tutor to superintend his
studies and a gyp 'who is to persecute at his door in a morning,
to watch him for meals, & to attend to his fires'.[4] She wrote to
the Masters begging leniency for the heedless absent-minded
delinquent, and sent him back again. 'I dare not, alas, be
sanguine! I am fear in every pore! But not without hope!'[4] In
the next term there were good reports from Cambridge.[5] 'God
be praised! that is, indeed, a weight off my spirits!'[4] And now all
was well, and then all went wrong again. In June Fanny sent a
dismal report to her husband. 'Our poor *Alexander* failed wholly
in the Examination—& is quite disconsolate; but I try to spirit
him up by hopes of *next term*.'[6] When she heard that he had

---

[1] See p. 329, n. 3.   [2] A.L. (Berg) from FBA to CB, Jr., 21 Aug. 1813.
[3] A.L.S. (Berg) from CF to FBA, 25 Dec. [1813].
[4] 2 A.L. (Berg) from FBA to CBFB, 16 Feb., 22 Mar.–2 Apr. 1814.
[5] A.L.S. (Barrett) from AA to FBA, 29 Mar. 1814.
[6] 4 A.L. (Berg) from FBA to M. d'A, 29 Apr., 30 May, 9, 24 June 1814; A.L.
(Berg) to EBB, 9 Sept. 1816.

again wasted his 'hours & faculties' on chess, she began to fear
the whist- and chess-players at her brother's in James Street.
She thought it necessary to secure a tutor for the summer to
direct her son's studies and '*non obstant* the expence'.[1]

The expense, however, must be defrayed. With sturdy independence she refused to be indebted to the family, and often
wrote in despair to her husband, who could not bring himself
to the mundane way of life suited to their circumstances.

£300, you tell me, is All you have been able to save!—Alas! my dear
friend, had I listened to your tender urgings, & kept a femme de
chambre, & lived up to 50 or 60£ a month, & spent 5*s* daily on a
carriage—where should we be now? Yet, with all the economy I
have been able to practice, our running small revenue is utterly
insufficient for Alexander & me! But I had indeed hoped that
without us, & without his Education, you would have been able to
save for our reunion.[1]

'My ease, comfort, spirits, & health all hang on living without
debts, & without positive dependence upon circumstances', but
the effort to live within their income was hers alone, she
confided to Esther.

What [M. d'A's] early habits never led him to practice, his generous
heart can with difficulty adopt; but dread of embarrassment, &
horror of debt have preserved to me always, most happily! so much
contentment with privation & forbearance, that I always follow
the safe-footed road to security without pain or reluctance—though
not without care or trouble.[1]

The expense must be defrayed, and she shut herself up,
therefore, to complete *The Wanderer*. In the prefatory pages she
stated that the early part of the work had already crossed the
Channel twice in manuscript; that she had begun it before 1800,
had taken plans of the work to France, and there sketched the
whole work and managed to write three volumes.[2] Early in
January, 1813, she told her father about the 'grand effort of
strength & enterprise' she had in hand.[3] In February she lost
time while she nursed Alex through an attack of influenza and
contracted it herself: 'But how cruel for my great business which
has nearly lain upon the shelf for over a fortnight!'[3] In March

[1] See p. 335, n. 6.
[2] See also *Diary*, vi. 70–71; and A.L. (Berg) from FBA to CB, Jr., 6 Sept. 1814.
[3] See p. 329, n. 3.

she visited Norbury Park, but was allowed to keep all her mornings for writing. In the summer of 1813 she was asking Charles for advice in her negotiations with publishers. The work was finished: 'What fatigues me is copying illegibilities; & that I am now labouring at almost incessantly, & yet but little advanced.'[1] Though she had been delayed by ill health, business and other worries political and personal, she had completed one draft of the novel in less than eight months. But 'tired I am of my Pen! Oh tired! tired! Oh! should it tire others in the same proportion—alas for poor Messrs. Longman & Rees!—and alas for poorer ME!'[1]

The publishers, however, had no misgivings. Colburn offered £1,750;[1] Longman and Rees, £3,000 in all—£1,500 for a first edition not to exceed 3,000 copies, £500 for a second edition of 1,000 copies, and £250 for each subsequent edition up to four.[2] Compared with £20 for *Evelina* or £250 for *Cecilia*, this was munificent. By November 4, Madame d'Arblay was able to send the first volume to the printer. In December of 1813 and January of 1814 she kept close to the proofs, and in March *The Wanderer; or, Female Difficulties* was on the market. Though the publishers had fixed the rapacious price of two guineas, 3,600 copies were positively sold, said Madame d'Arblay, in the first half-year. The sale came to a stand before the second edition was sold out, so that by the terms of the contract the author could have realized £2,000 in all. The publishers were later disappointed if not aggrieved over the outcome,[3] but Madame d'Arblay was not perturbed. 'It was only *their* unreasonable expectations that are disappointed.'[4] After all, they had sold 3,600 copies at two guineas in the first half-year.

Anticipation ran high. 'We can hardly remember an instance', began the reviewer in the *British Critic*, 'when the public expectation was excited in so high a degree, as by the promise of a new novel from the pen of their old favourite, Madame

---

[1] Letters (Osborn) from FBA to CB, Jr., 22 June (?), 2, 3, 15 July 1813; 2 A.L. (Berg), 21 July, 14 Aug. 1813.

[2] Drafts of the indentures, dated 1 Sept. and 1 Nov. 1813, and signed by Martin Burney, are extant in the Berg Collection. The final contract is in the Osborn Collection. But see A.L. (Berg) from FBA to M. d'A, 29 Apr. 1814, in which she says she has received only £500.

[3] See draft of a letter (Barrett) from FBA to Longman & Co., 30 Aug. 1817.

[4] 2 A.L. (Berg.) from FBA to Mary Port Waddington, 24 Dec. 1813, 13–18 Oct. 1814; A.L.S. (PML) from FBA to JB, 10 July 1815.

D'Arblay.'[1] The publishers were plagued by requests and actually gave out advance copies of the first volume to Madame de Staël (then in England), Sir James MacIntosh, and others.[2] Byron had attempted to procure a copy for one of his friends who was ill, remarking 'I would almost fall sick myself to get at Madame d'Arblay's writings'.[3] Fanny became 'inconceivably fidgetted' at such news. 'Expectation has taken a wrong scent, and must necessarily be disappointed.'[4]

The public, remembering the comic-realistic scenes of *Evelina* and *Cecilia*, had expected Madame d'Arblay to focus a *camera obscura* behind the Napoleonic curtain. They might hope, they thought, for a photographic cross-section of Paris—the characters to be met in the Paris streets, shops, salons, theatres, at least a pleasing comedy of manners at the expense of the French. They were curious about the political scene and the new rulers. In short, any observation she would care to make about the France of the preceding decade could not fail to be interesting. And so indeed such observations would have been and so they were—only they were not contained in *The Wanderer*. Unfortunately the new novel, subtitled *Female Difficulties*, dealt with a different subject—the difficulties that a penniless and unprotected spinster might encounter in earning her living in England. The strictures in which the five volumes abounded were levelled not against French but against English failings, especially against insularism, pride, and hard-heartedness. When the nature of the work was realized *The Wanderer* remained on the shelf, though not for this reason alone.

The Wanderer proved a choke-pear in style even more than in subject-matter, though, as critics like Hazlitt and Macaulay were able to see, the failure of the whole arose not from 'a decay of talent, but a perversion of it'.[1]

Though the literary style (or rather, styles) of *The Wanderer* changed with successive topics, various factors contributed to

---

[1] *The Wanderer* was reviewed by John Wilson Croker in the *Quarterly Review*, xi (Apr. 1814), 123–30; by Hazlitt in the *Edinburgh Review*, xxiv (Feb. 1815), 320–8; by Macaulay in the *Edinburgh Review*, lxxvi (Jan. 1843), 523–70. Other reviews appeared in the *Monthly Review*, lxxvi (Apr. 1815), 412–19; and the *British Critic*, i (Apr. 1814), 374–86.

[2] See draft of a letter of protest (Berg) from FBA to Longman & Co., 2 Feb. 1814.

[3] Quoted in a fragment, A.L.S. (Barrett) from J. T. W. Angerstein to FBA, n.d.

[4] See p. 337, n. 4.

make it intolerable. There was, first of all, the influence of the French language, most evident in the continual use of the phrasal genitive ('The bell of Mrs. Maple . . . '), which resulted in a kind of hybrid. Romantic and serious scenes were highly marked by the romantic or sentimental strain of rhetoric developed in the blank-verse tragedies. If this was derived in part from the sentimental verse-narratives of the eighteenth century, it was probably strengthened by the romantic cantos of the nineteenth. Madame d'Arblay's heroic ear was not improved by a son in the house who was able to out-Herod Herod in the French schools of declamation and spent whole evenings declaiming modern French verse and Byron. Finally, in descriptions of scenery, nature, and the like, while she reproduced the uncontrolled tones of some of the romantics, she kept to the old eighteenth-century generalized diction, and spoke still of 'zephyrs' and 'tribes'. This gave a double swelling, present in neither romantic nor eighteenth-century writers, and peculiar to Madame d'Arblay alone. When, however, she was placing characters in action and reproducing speech, she wrote with her old skill. If the question is asked whether or not Madame d'Arblay knew when she was writing well and when ill, the reply must be that she did not know. As Lord David Cecil has remarked, she was not a great artist.[1] From the age of seventeen to eighty-five she could and often did write well, but she could not be depended on to write well when she ought. It is a question whether or not the formal education that might have developed her critical faculties would have quenched the playful originality that made her first novel historically a classic—but these are thoughts for pedagogues to ponder.

Though every reference to *The Wanderer* must serve to poke it further into the shadows, an account of the writings of Madame d'Arblay must nevertheless give some idea of what she meant to say in that work. And once again she insisted on calling the effort 'a work'. 'Pray call it a work. I am passed the time to endure being supposed to write a Love-tale.'[2]

There was first of all in the Preface an *apologia* for the genre of the novel. One would have thought perhaps that in the year 1814, when *Waverley* and *Mansfield Park* appeared, the literary or artistic status of the novel would have been conceded. Yet

[1] As in Chap. IV, p. 96, n. 3. [2] See p. 337, n. 1.

a year later Hazlitt opened a long criticism of the works of Cervantes, Le Sage, Richardson, Fielding, Smollett, Sterne, and Madame d'Arblay with a paragraph in defence of that 'class of writing'. Novels enlarged experience and exercised the moral judgement. As Madame d'Arblay had pointed out in turn in her Preface, the Novel is not necessarily 'a mere vehicle for frivolous, or seductive amusement'.

What is the species of writing that offers fairer opportunities for conveying useful precepts? It is, or it ought to be, a picture of supposed, but natural and probably human existence. It holds, therefore, in its hands our best affections; it exercises our imaginations; it points out the path of honour; and gives to juvenile credulity knowledge of the world, without ruin, or repentance; and the lessons of experience, without its tears.

For the rest *The Wanderer* is an indictment of reprehensible manners, pride, uncharitableness, and insular attitudes and prejudices. Like Fanny Burney's previous works, it includes patterns of perfect behaviour who, after protracted difficulties, emerge in triumph, putting evil or graceless characters to shame. Her contemporary critics, however, no longer praised the faithfulness of her copies from the life of the times. Five years' seclusion at court, eight years at Bookham and West Humble, and ten years' absence in France had placed her almost a quarter of a century behind the day in her description of some phases of contemporary life, which she nevertheless attempted to depict in *The Wanderer*. According to the *Monthly Review* her models of behaviour were out of date.

A new generation has grown up in the saloons of Great Britain . . . and an alteration insensibly progressive has effected considerable change in our idea of the gentleman and the lady . . . but we are glad to see depicted again such society as our matrons remember.[1]

The bulk of the writing in the five volumes of *The Wanderer* is concerned with the DIFFICULTIES OF A FEMALE who without family or fortune had her own way to make in the eighteenth-century world. In her search for employment and protection she was driven from one cruel gentlewoman to another; she slaved over needlework; like Esther Burney, she gave lessons

---

[1] See p. 338, n. 1.

on the harpsichord; and like Sarah Burney and one of Esther's daughters, Fanny Burney, she served as governess or companion; she sewed in a milliner's shop, learned the trade of the mantua-maker, and shared the life of the working girl; and finally, as a fugitive in the New Forest, she encountered woodcutters, farmers, smugglers, poachers, the heartlessness and the characteristic immoralities and vices of the countryside. A systematic *exposé* of society required such an itinerary, but it struck Fanny's contemporaries of 1814 as unreal. According to the *Monthly Review* a person without recommendation could not have gained access to fashionable houses even in the role of seamstress or governess.[1] Times had changed. In short, according to contemporary criticism, the intermingling of different ranks of society, on which Fanny Burney's plots and social *exposés* depended, was no longer possible, and the plot of *The Wanderer* was therefore incredible. Some of Croker's abuse therefore was levelled at the improbability of the plot. Whereas Madame d'Arblay thought that her privileged countrywomen would give some succour, menial work, or protection to a homeless, nameless wanderer, however ungraciously and unwillingly in some instances, Croker thought that they would let such a creature go to prison or the workhouse. If he was right, then there was all the more reason for the lessons in humanitarianism that Madame d'Arblay meant to inculcate and that Croker missed, but of which he seemed in need no less than the proud and irascible ladies indicted in the work. In *The Wanderer* there is a fresh *exposé* not only of the hard-heartedness and family pride so often assailed before, but of tyrannical bullying and bludgeoning of defenceless underlings and dependants. Those who said no such cruelty could exist had not had the experience of living with Mrs. Arthur Young, Mrs. Burney, or Mrs. Schwellenberg.[2] The painting was not, however, wholly dark. Foils to the cruel and abusive conduct are provided in the natural kindness of Admiral Powell, Lord Melbury, the Lady Aurora Granville (possibly suggested by Amelia Locke), the

[1] See p. 338, n. 1.
[2] Cf. Susan Burney's Journal, 1789 (Berg): '[Mrs. Schwellenberg] has the heart and temper of a Fiend, wth the grossness & undissembled violence of the lowest & most vulgar of mankind—she seems to be that sad counterpart of which she so cruelly & continually reminds us.' Cf. also Diary MSS. (Berg), pp. 1608, 2743-9, 3453, 3568-74.

monitor-lover Harleigh, and finally the magnificent old beau Sir Jasper Harrington.

The first purpose of the work is to distinguish between propriety and impropriety, between good and faulty behaviour; to delineate and reward perfect conduct, and to describe and punish its reverse. Were it not for this moral purpose and the consequent tameness of the central character, *The Wanderer* would be a picaresque novel. The Wanderer, unlike a picara, has a full complement of natural and acquired virtues, graces, and accomplishments, as revealed schematically for Harleigh's benefit in a progression of incidents and trials constructed for the purpose. Undesirable behaviour is exhibited in a gallery of females—the three Furies: Howell, Ireton, and Maple; Juliet's seven pupils, including Sir Marmaduke Crawley's hoyden sisters and the daughter of Mr. Tedman, the grocer; a group of workers, including Flora Pierson, the willing victim of seduction; and society women like Mrs. Arbe, patron of the arts but a superficial wit or bluestocking, with vanity in keeping with her talents and behaviour marked by heartlessness, aggressiveness, and caprice. The *British Critic* thought this last character 'well conceived, and drawn with great fidelity and spirit'. Mrs. Ireton's abusive and satiric tirades recall suppressed sections of old manuscripts dealing with the second Mrs. Burney and the life in St. Martin's Street:[1]

'You may think it sufficient honour for me, that I may be at the expence of your board, and find you in lodging, and furniture, and fire, and candles, and servants? You may hold this ample recompense for such an insignificant person as I am? ... And I was stupid enough to suppose, that that meant a person who could be of some use, and some agreeability; a person who could read to me when I was tired, and who, when I had nobody else, could talk to me. ...'

Of the many new tasks of Juliet, that which she found the most severe, was inventing amusement for another while sad and dispirited herself. It was her duty to be always at hand, early or late; it was her business to furnish entertainment, whether sick or well. Success, therefore, was unacknowledged, though failure was resented. There was no relaxation to her toil, no rest for her person, no recruit for her spirits. From her sleep alone she could purloin the few minutes that she dedicated to her pen and her Gabriella.[2]

---

[1] See Note L, p. 494.   [2] Chapters lii, liii.

In the career of Elinor Joddrel, Madame d'Arblay attempted to show the kind of girl who had emerged with the new 'system-forming spirit' of the French Revolution.[1] She is the female revolutionist, a *philosophe* of the new school and, of course, a rebel against antiquated forms and established thought. She comes to grief when, reversing old-fashioned procedures, she approaches Harleigh with a proposal of marriage, and after being rebuffed is found raving wildly in a graveyard and is only with much sermonizing saved from suicide.

The plot of *The Wanderer* provided an opportunity for strictures on rural morality when Juliet fled for refuge to the New Forest.[2] All her life Fanny Burney had travelled through the countryside between London and King's Lynn, Chessington, Aylsham, Mickleham, Teignmouth, and countless other places, and in her pages the eighteenth-century road comes to life. The Wanderer met first a young village girl 'hoydening with a smart footman' and wrangling with her mother; then a solitary cart and a carter, 'who amused his toil by the alternate pleasure of smacking his horse, and whistling to the winds'. 'Why you be up betimes, my lovey! come and Ize give you a cast.' 'Why a be plaguy shy o' the sudden.' Then a pedlar; then a ballad-singer—a good old dame, singing dolorously the antique ballad of the babes in the wood:

> Their little lips with blackberries
> Were all besmear'd and dyed;
> And when they saw the darksome night
> They set them down and cried.

This was the comment of Dr. Burney's daughter on 'dismal old ballads', and on the culture of the farmhouse where, save for an odd volume or two of trials or sundry tracts on farriery, books never found their way. In the morning 'carts, waggons, and diligences, were wheeling through the town; market-women were arriving with butter, eggs, and poultry', and workmen trudging to their work; in the evening the road was nearly deserted.

The labourers were no longer working at the high ways, or at the hedges; the harvest-men were vanished; the market-women were

---

[1] Elinor Joddrel's career is developed in chapters ii, v, vi, viii, xvi–xxi, xxxviii–ix, xl, xlii, lxi, lxviii, lxxxv–vi.

[2] For the commentary on rural life, chapters lxxi–viii.

gone; the road retained merely here and there an idle straggler; and the fields exhibited only a solitary boy, left to frighten away the birds.[1]

An extant letter of 1781 to Mrs. Thrale shows that in spite of contemporary theories about the natural man Madame d'Arblay knew that there was evil as well as good in the country.

And now, in return for your anecdotes from Brighton, let me give you a touch of the morals of Chesington. Master Mumford, a Farmer who lives within half a mile from this House, a man as eminent for the low vices of Drinking, swearing & quarrelling, as any Dean's or Lord's son for those of higher horrour, having broke the Heart of one Wife, & almost the Bones of another, met with a third who to the courage necessary for encountering him, joined the admirable prudence of formally binding him, under a penalty of £100, payable to a Tradesman at Kingston, not to beat her! Do you often hear of a lady's greater discretion in disposing of herself? Yet, to shew the utter vanity of all human precautions for happiness, Master Mumford, though the first year of their marriage is not over, contrives at once to evade the law, & gratify his old propensities, by seizing both her wrists, & making her thump her own Face & Neck! So to which will you give the palm for *rural* ingenuity? How can one endure the Town, after seeing the artless simplicity of the Country?[2]

While the Wanderer at times encountered benevolence at the cottage doors, she was often met with inhospitable rudeness and suspicion. In the woodcutter's hut she found that the parents, apparently poachers, were 'rough to their children, and gross to each other; the woman looked all care and ill humour; the man, all moroseness and brutality'. In her lonely wanderings Juliet ran risks of 'personal and brutal insult', and found even the men who had no evil designs either 'gross or facetious'. She often met suspicion and a species of self-interest much at variance with the famed simplicity and hospitality of the country. Finally Madame d'Arblay takes serious note of the status of women in the country. The rough farmer, for instance,

treated neither his wife nor his daughters ill; he only considered them as his servants: The sons . . . were open, boisterous, and daring;

---

[1] See p. 343, n. 2.
[2] A.L.S. (Berg) from FB to HLT, 2 Dec. [1781].

domineering over their sisters, and mocking their mother; while they nearly shared, with their partial father, both his authority and his profits.[1]

So Fanny Burney, the realist, attempted to refute the romantic theorists by the results of her observation. The proper study of man is man. Human nature must be informed, morals inculcated. Even benevolence, when untutored, is less exalted than 'the cultivated products of religion and of principle'.

[1] See p. 343, n. 2.

XIV

'TERRIBLY MANGLED'

(1814–1815)

Upon public events my very private destiny is entirely
hanging! When, where will the conflict end? and how?
MADAME D'ARBLAY, 1814[1]

THOUGH on April 11, 1814, Napoleon's power was tem-
porarily checked, in the preceding months of the year his
efforts and those of the opposing forces had kept all the
world in 'suspensive uneasiness'. Normal methods of communication between France and England had long been prohibited.
In four months Madame d'Arblay had been able to learn only
twice, and then through circuitous messages, that her husband
was safe and well, and she had no hope of hearing from him
until the dire contest should be over.

The year 1814, marked in the Burney annals by the death of
the great Dr. Burney, was saddened in the beginning by the
tolling of a bell in far-off Ireland and news of the death of
Susan's son, the '*erst* nearly incomparable Norbury'.[2]

He was good, I believe, very good, & very pious, that sweet Norbury,
& therefore fitted for death, however premature & sudden—yet
how early a blossom to be lopped off![2]

In November of the previous year Madame d'Arblay had
moved to 63 Lower Sloane Street, conveniently near Chelsea
College where, in lofty rooms overlooking the Chelsea burying-
ground, the Doctor lived in the solitude he now seemed to
desire, only the silence of books and rumination. When Alexander arrived from Cambridge for the Easter vacation, Madame
d'Arblay sent him 'to pay his duty to his grandfather', promising
to come herself in the evening to celebrate the 'auspicious news
from the Continent'. When Alexander returned with the report
that his grandfather had passed an alarming night and that both

[1] *Diary*, vi. 101.
[2] 3 A.L. (Berg) from FBA to CBFB, 16 Feb., 22 Mar., 11 Apr. 1814. Also
A.L.S. (JRL) from MF to HLTP, 13 Apr. 1814.

James and Charles had been sent for, Fanny hurried to Chelsea. She found the invalid seated in his customary manner, on his sofa, but he no longer seemed to know her.

> Whether or not he recognized, or distinguished me, I know not! I had no command of voice to attempt any inquiry, and would not risk betraying my emotion at this great change since my last and happier admittance to his presence.
>
> His eyes were intently bent on a window, that faced the College burial-ground, where reposed the ashes of my mother-in-law, and where, he had more than once said, would repose his own.
>
> He bestowed at least five or six minutes on this absorbed and melancholy contemplation of the upper regions of that sacred spot, that so soon were to enclose for ever his mortal clay.
>
> No one presumed to interrupt his reverie.
>
> He next opened his arms wide, extending them with a waving motion, that seemed indicative of an internally pronounced farewell! to all he looked at; and shortly afterwards, he uttered to himself, distinctly, though in a low, but deeply-impressive voice, 'All this will soon pass away as a dream!'[1]

This scene must have occurred on April 10. All that night Sarah, with his housekeeper, watched by his side and early in the morning, according to the *Memoirs*, Fanny took her place. Sitting by her father's bedside that day (April 11), she wrote long letters about the changes in him to both Charlotte and Esther.[2] She had planned to accompany Alex to Norbury Park for his Easter vacation, 'but now—stationed here, & known by my dear Father, to whom my services are therefore useful, I would not stir for the universe'.[2] As is usual in such circumstances, the end was nearer than she knew. In the evening, when the sky was lit 'to blazon the glorious victory of England and her allies' and the downfall of Bonaparte, Fanny tried to awaken her father to the exhilarating news and her own joy. But he could not hear the news; could not, would not believe it. Bonaparte was defeated, she tried to tell him, put in captivity, a prisoner on board an English man-of-war! But he turned his head away with an old gesture that she knew expressed incredulity, and she did not dare risk the excitement of convincing him. He could not himself rejoice or any more share

---

[1] *Memoirs*, iii. 419 ff. Also Scholes, ii. 253–75.
[2] See p. 346, n. 2.

her joys. At the high windows of Chelsea College she stood with her brothers watching the mounting fireworks and rockets, saw in all this the promise of peace, prosperity, and her husband's return, yet knew that within the room life was flickering to a close. For an hour after the others had realized that breathing had ceased, Fanny listened for a sign of life. With all the Doctor's own busy cares and achievements he had had so much time and sympathy for those of his children. Now this was over. Just as Sir Joshua Reynolds desired that the last name he should pronounce in public should be that of Michelangelo, Dr. Burney, as Fanny remembered, would have liked to conclude his writings (his studies of music and his memoirs) with some reference to that passage in Haydn's *Creation* where 'order arises, & chaos is no more'.

God said let there be light, & there was LIGHT![1]

On April 19 Dr. Burney would have completed his eighty-eighth year, and on that day his last remains were deposited in the Chelsea burying-ground.[2] After this came the reading of the will. The Doctor had wished to treat his children, grandchildren, and other relations 'with equity and kindness'. He had such a high opinion of their 'rectitude and affection for each other' that it seemed to him unnecessary to appoint executors, but in compliance with the law he chose his sons James and Charles. The will (printed in *The Great Doctor Burney*)[1] might be read, one might almost think, as an improving document, so much care did the Doctor take to explain his fair and helpful intentions and the principles on which he divided his property among his daughters according to their relative needs, and among his sons, grandchildren, relatives, and friends. A principle, not enunciated in the will, but later found by Madame d'Arblay among her father's papers and expounded vigorously by her in his defence (soon enough needed!), was that where education or professions were given to the sons, property that was *personal* rather than *hereditary* might without any injustice be given to the daughters. As he thought Charlotte

[1] See p. 347, n. 1.

[2] 3 A.L. (Berg) from FBA to M. d'A, 20, 22, 29 Apr. 1814; A.L. to EBB, 25 Oct. 1816; A.L. (Barrett) to CBFB, 1 July 1814. See also letters (PML) from FBA to EBB, JB, and Martin Burney, n.d., 28 May, and 31 May 1814, respectively.

well provided for, he made Esther and Frances residuary legatees, as such to share equally in the proceeds from the sale of
the library and in the property remaining after debts and
legacies were paid. Their lifelong attention to their father,
together with their own necessitous if not grinding circumstances, explains his action. 'His own design—Heaven bless him
ever!—has been to do what he himself thought *strictly just* by
All: but peculiarly serviceable by Hetty & me. Blessed be his
immortal spirit, Almighty God!'[1]

James, however, shared no such sentiments. He felt that he
was disinherited as the eldest son, that his father had harboured
old angers and resentments against him for his radical or democratic politics and for the irregularity of his domestic life, and
disappointed, angered, and resentful, he refused to act as
executor. As usual Fanny tried to make peace, insisting that
James share in the proceeds of the sale of the library or in the
interest on a mortgage. Esther also offered to share her good
fortune with James, but this, in view of the long history of her
lamentable circumstances, he refused.[1] Charles, who was 'all
activity & zeal' in the executorship, by no means approved of
such philanthropic readjustments in the directions of the will,
and, without extraneous commentary, he related to Fanny a
dream he had dreamed repeatedly on the matter.

On the 24th of October, a little before midnight, I seemed to be
sitting with our dear Father, in a strange room, but still in Chelsea.
The paper was green, & it was divided into two parts, by some glass
sash windows. He said to me seriously but mildly: 'Why, my son
Charles, it could never be right, for them to put that money into a
channel so different from what I had intended. If indeed, when they
have their own wills to make, they had more than they knew what
to do with, they might fairly have bequeathed as they liked.' On this,
I said that 'James must explain that business' & I called him for he
& Sarah seemed to be in the lower extremity of the room, on the
other side of the intermediate windows—'Pray tell my Father what
this means'—James approached us with a lighted candle which
discovered my poor Father's face—& its complection was of an hue
between mahogany & ebony—but the features more such in semblance, as they were in the last days of his life—but the venerable
locks & the snowy beard, were of a darkened hue—I then awoke,

---

[1] See p. 348, n. 2.

but soon dropped asleep again—only to see the same vision. It has dwelt on my mind ever since. . . .[1]

Whatever may be the significance of green walls, partitions, and darkened hues in the psychology of dreams, or however those versed in Burneyan affairs may be tempted to interpret the vision, Madame d'Arblay took issue in her reply with the main point. Another vision appeared to her mind's eye,

parentally approving the legatees for feeling for the disappointment of the eldest son, & the consternation of the youngest daughter but one; for that venerable form, in leaving to Hetty & to me all that was residuary, bequeathed us both an earnest desire to soften all that might appear *hard* or *partial* in his last directions. . . . For you, my dear Carlos, I thank Heaven I have no reason to nourish scruples or wishes. You are not only far the richest of our Tribe, but you have memorials the most flattering & soothing of that favoured regard which it has so bitterly hurt our poor James to have missed.[1]

In France as in England, 1814 brought great changes. With the entrance of the Allies into Paris and the return of the Bourbons to the throne, royalists like M. d'Arblay, who had refused military service under Bonaparte, could now expect rewards. In May M. d'Arblay received a summons from the Duc de Luxembourg to enter *la Garde du Corps de son Roi*. He had had scarcely time to rejoice in his brightening fortunes when a blow descended from a quarter from which it must have been least expected—Norbury Park. The hospitable Mr. Locke, patron of the arts and artists, who had encouraged the d'Arblays to build Camilla Cottage on his property, had died in 1810. The d'Arblays had no deed or title to the land on which their cottage was built, holding it merely as a ground lease for five pounds a year.

In 1814, therefore, when the younger William decided to sell Norbury Park, the Lockes or their lawyer had to point out to the d'Arblays the painful consequences of building on land for which they had no deed. Mr. William offered to buy the cottage at a price to be set by independent assessors; and since no one

---

[1] Copies of letters (Bath Letter Book, Barrett) from CB, Jr., to FBA, 25 Nov. 1815, and her reply. See also A.L.S. (Barrett) from Maria Allen Rishton to FBA, n.d., and her reply, May 1817; 2 A.L.S. (Berg) from FBA to CBFB and to M. d'A, [1814], 30 May 1814, respectively.

else, certainly, would buy a house without a title, the d'Arblays had no alternative but to sell to him at that price.

M. d'Arblay was very angry and, moreover, much offended that as a gentleman he should have been required to treat with another gentleman through lawyers. In France the conduct of a gentleman required not only the observance of the law but 'conscience and délicatesse'. He wrote a spirited letter to William Locke, which seemed to give some offence, and a series of painful letters passed between the two families,[1] Mrs. Locke and Mrs. Angerstein (*née* Amelia Locke) gently defending William and endeavouring to explain his antipathy to business, which he always transacted even with members of his own family through lawyers. Madame d'Arblay defended her husband; yet, being English, she knew the force of laws protecting property, and she could not forget the great hospitality of that house, the pleasures and benefits conferred on Susan, on herself, and on others in her family for now almost thirty years. With the rational mind that she brought to bear on such problems, she perceived that, whatever Mr. Locke's thoughts or intentions had been, as the law stood she and her husband were in the wrong; and even if they had been in the right, there was still 'my impossibility to act against that Family'.[1] In a consultation with a Mr. Haggitt, who through the administration of landed property had become almost as well versed in law as in theology, she obtained an opinion, which she relayed to her husband as definitive and final. 'Our *fault* must pay its *forfeiture*; i.e. of building before we had secured our right of possession!!' Mr. William Locke, 'as a *Gentleman*, & according to *Law*, acts fairly & honourably in letting us sell the house by This valuation; for *we* can *never* sell it ourselves! *Nobody* would buy of *us* a House without a Title!'[1]

In formal statements that the d'Arblays left about the transaction, it is recorded that Camilla Cottage had cost about £1,300 in materials and labour, though this sum did not include wages or fees for the 'Architect, Designer, Surveyor', M. d'Arblay himself. He would have set the forced-sale price at £1,000;

---

[1] See (Berg) *Arblay, Alexandre, Miscellaneous MS. Material* and *Copies, mostly in General d'Arblay's hand*; letters (Barrett) from members of the Locke family to the d'Arblays, May, 24, 26, 28 May, 9 June, 19 July 1814; and correspondence (Berg) between FBA and M. d'A, Apr.–Nov. 1814.

the assessors arrived at £640 or £650. In the end the d'Arblays accepted £620, and so lost an inheritance for their son, and a refuge they were soon again to need. On a short visit to England in the late autumn M. d'Arblay paid a farewell visit to West Humble. 'What a melancholy business I am employed in. *Je t'assure que de ma vie je n'ai autant souffert — à tout moment j'ai les larmes aux yeux. . . . Je me dis que jamais aucun être sensible a été plus véritablement heureux que je l'ai été dans cette aimable cottage.'*[1]

On May 27 M. d'Arblay, having received official notice of his military appointment in *la Garde du Corps*, returned promptly to France. Among the extant glimpses of him in these four weeks in England is one of a spring morning in Hyde Park, where he walked with his wife and listened to a long account of her presentation to Louis XVIII at Grillion's Hotel in Albemarle Street. This was a tale, of course, that Fanny delighted to tell him, not only because of the recognition and honour accorded to her by the King in her husband's name and in her own, but because for her husband's interests she had overcome the natural *sauvagerie* to which he objected, to make such a public effort so soon after her father's death. Eleven years later she recalled his request of that spring morning that she record the presentation scene for Alex, and the piece now appears in the printed diaries.[2] Parts that seldom occur in the printed diaries are those concerning her appearance. On this occasion she wore a 'black bombazien & crepe' dress with an 'enormous train', a small white cap, and a bouquet of fleurs-de-lis.

From Paris M. d'Arblay wrote optimistically about his future. He was in uniform, mounted, and on duty at the '*palais des Tuilleries, assurément rien de moins fatiguant*'.[3] Fanny was a little fearful, dreading 'the great *audace* after a remission of riding for 22 years', but she tried to be cheerful: 'Your new honours, & the restoration of your old ones, fill me with joy & exultation.' 'A new world is opened to you.'[3] M. d'Arblay had the rank of *sous-lieutenant*, which he thought might quickly be raised to that of lieutenant-general. Soon now he would be able to give Fanny

[1] See p. 351, n. 1.

[2] M. d'Arblay had arrived in England on 29 Apr. 1814 (see Diary MSS., Berg) and left on 27 May. See *Diary*, vi. 103–20; and A.L.S. (Berg) from FBA to Mary Port Waddington, 7 June 1814.

[3] 2 A.L.S. (Berg) from M. d'A to FBA, 3 July, 19 Aug. 1814; and A.L. (Berg) from FBA to M. d'A, 10 Aug. 1814; also A.L. (Berg) to CB, Jr., 6 Sept. 1814.

a carriage '*qui te mettra pour jamais à l'abri des ravages que l'humidité te fait éprouver, et des craintes plus grandes qu'elle ne cesse de me donner*'.[1] He now began to wish that Alex would relinquish his studies at Cambridge and their probable sequel in an obscure curacy for a military career in France—a future far more brilliant and assured. The family could then be united and might live, in a very short time, he felt sure, '*dans la plus grande aisance, eu égard à la simplicité de nos goûts, et à notre peu d'ambition*'. '*Réfléchis y bien*', he begged. '*Réfléchis y bien, mon adorable Fanny!*'

And Fanny reflected, had, indeed, already been reflecting; and the downright realism with which she touched on their actual circumstances and prospects appeared like rude flaws on the gentle material of his devotion and his hopes. As to the title of baroness—'*Dieu m'en garde!* it would forfeit my Fame! I could never pass, living as I live, so parsimoniously & obscurely for your wife!'

In England, also, a Baron, who is newly made, & not a peer of parliament, is reckoned a Dentist, or a surgeon, &c & by no means as much respected, for that title, as a powerful Esquire. A Title, unless of ancient & hereditary descent, is always *gênant*, or *ludicrous*, unaccompanied by state or fortune. I earnestly hope that was an idea *passagère*.[1]

Apart from her scepticism about political rewards and the fluctuations of power, influence, and patronage, she knew that for her chevalier the new opportunities had come too late.

Were M. d'Arblay younger, or less worn with revolutionary events, & the dreadful fatigues mental & bodily, of the last 12 months, there could be no doubt of our destiny, for his character, services, fidelity, & friends would all combine to restore him to his military rank; which his constant refusal to serve the last Dynasty had made him preferably sink into becoming a *chef de Bureau*.[2]

But, 'though still young in all his faculties and feelings, and in his capacity of being as useful to others as to himself', he was now sixty-one years of age.[3]

In spite of frequent letters Madame d'Arblay bore the separation from her husband with much less fortitude than before. 'Alas! I must re-make myself, or be worn out by absence,

---

[1] See p. 352, n. 3.
[2] A.L.S. (Berg) from FBA to Mary Port Waddington, 7 June 1814.
[3] *Diary*, vi. 127–8.

distance, & silence thus united.'[1] She could not, however, leave England until Camilla Cottage was sold and her father's estate settled. Besides such business concerns as could not be settled *in absentia*, there was Alex, who, having acquitted himself badly in the examinations at Cambridge, had come to his mother in Lower Sloane Street, quite prepared to spend the summer as he had spent most of his time at the University—with mathematics and chess. Again a tutor must be found, though even that was not enough. He needed vigilant care such as only she could supply. Every hope for the future 'hangs upon his having a *watchful monitor* & *confidential* Friend, within his reach for the present'. She saw in him

a thousand qualities that—if he escape the Quick sands of his slack & tardy formation,—may end in all that we can wish, & make him once again the pride & comfort of our lives. Such he was, till those fatal 6 prizes turned his understanding into presumption, & his application into caprice. He thought—& still thinks he could, & can, do *what* he pleases *when* he pleases. This perverse secret vanity casts him upon indolence & whim, & he never begins anything, little or Great, in time, or with sufficient diligence to make it even possible to obtain success.[1]

'What can be done!' 'Oh who should have told me The Peace—the blessed Peace should have brought me so cruel an alternative!'[1]

The warrior's solution was that Alex should come with his mother to France and enter a military career to which he would now have good pretensions. But this, whether wisely or not, neither Alex nor his mother wished. 'Can you really think him adapted to a military life?' The point was argued in a long correspondence. Was there 'no credit or prosperity in France for a young man, out of the military line'? Was there nothing else in France, absolutely nothing? And the cultivated Frenchman dryly replied: '*Hélas, non, non*'; there is nothing; for anyone who considers etiquette and duty as insupportable slavery '*ne manquerait pas de rendre sa vie un véritable fardeau*'.[2] Moreover, in his position he must take his son back to serve, or *not at all*.

[1] 4 A.L. (Berg) from FBA to M. d'A, 24, 29 June, 13 July, 10 Aug. 1814. Also Diary MSS. (Berg), pp. 6004–7.
[2] A.L.S. (Berg) from M. d'A to FBA, 5 Sept. 1814; 2 A.L.S. (Osborn) from FBA to CB, Jr., 9 Nov. 1814, and from FBA and M. d'A to CB, Jr., 22 Feb. 1815. See also a passport (Berg) dated 9 Nov. 1814.

Finally the Frenchman wrote his son a 'solemn and beautiful letter' giving him his choice between Cambridge and *la compagnie de Luxembourg*, into which he had entered him, and Alex apparently decided for England and the University. In October M. d'Arblay again appeared in England. 'As we can neither of us consent to live a Divorced life any longer, and so *uselessly*, he has demanded a *congé* for coming over to fetch me to a warmer climate for the winter.'[1] The decision, however painful, was made; Alex was left at Cambridge, and Madame d'Arblay accompanied her husband to France. On November 11 they paid farewell calls at Chelsea, Deptford, and Greenwich. Fanny left with many regrets.

The whole time I spent in England was a period of hurry, disturbance, anxiety, or illness: & it has left me nothing but pardons to beg—that I could find no time for enjoyment or comforts.[2]

The November crossing was rough and stormy, and Fanny suffered severely from seasickness.[3] At Calais, unable at first to walk or stand, she was placed in a great chair and carried to a kitchen fire at an inn by a set of fisher-boys. M. d'Arblay, walking at her side, was stopped by a gentleman offering him a cordial, which might revive the lady. Turning to thank the man, he heard a woman's voice cry '*Gare!*', and turning again saw a carter standing upright in a cart and driving it so recklessly and furiously through the crowd that M. d'Arblay had no time to move before the shaft caught him squarely in the chest with a force sufficient to throw him many feet away. He had then in his turn to be carried to the inn kitchen, where Madame d'Arblay was sitting drying her clothes ('for the fury of the waves had wetted me through all my thick equipment'). He was blooded copiously, as she said, in a salad bowl,[3] and took some days to recover. 'In less than ten minutes', related M. d'Arblay,

I was almost drowned, with my backbone almost broken, and quite knocked down, by the beam of a cart, drawn by a nearly galloping *horsome* very big & stout horse. After five days of tenderest care from my almost dying nurse, we left Calais, but we were not able to go

[1] A.L.S. (Berg) from FBA to CB, Jr., 14 Oct. 1814.
[2] See p. 354, n. 2.
[3] A.L. (Berg) from FBA to EBB, 11 Jan. 1816; copy of A.L. (Letter Book, Barrett) from FBA to Princess Elizabeth, 1814.

beyond Boulogne, in which town we should have been both burnt alive, if we had not been preserved by a kind of miracle.[1]

These rough events were but a prelude to 1815, the most strenuous and calamitous year that the d'Arblays had yet known.

In February M. le chevalier d'Arblay, now *Maréchal de Camp*, and second lieutenant *de la Garde du Roi*, was stationed with an artillery company under the Duc de Luxembourg at Senlis. Fanny had scarcely made up her mind to give up the quiet domestic life she preferred and join him there when the news came that Napoleon had escaped from Elba and was in the south of France. Long afterwards, in recalling the events of the time, she could not but wonder at the apathy with which that news was received in Paris.

A torpor indescribable, a species of stupor utterly indefinable, seemed to have enveloped the capital with a mist . . . I knew the character of Bonaparte; and marvellous beyond the reach of my comprehension is my participation in this inertia. . . . The greatness of his power, the intrepidity of his ambition, the vastness of his conceptions, and the restlessness of his spirit, kept suspense always breathless, and conjecture always at work. Thus familiar, therefore, to his practices, thus initiated in his resources, thus aware of his gigantic ideas of his own destiny, how could I for a moment suppose he would revisit France without a consciousness of success, founded upon some secret conviction that it was infallible, through measures previously arranged?[2]

In the previous year M. d'Arblay had acquired an 'elegant light *calèche*', and Madame d'Arblay was afterwards amazed at the lightheartedness with which they took their delightful morning rides in the Bois de Boulogne even after all Paris was aware that Bonaparte had 'effected an invasion into France'. Ominous events, however, disturbed Fanny less than evidences of her husband's failing health. He was ill, fatigued, emaciated, worn with care. 'Anxiety oppressed all my faculties.' 'Oh what an execrable scourge to mankind is War!'[3]

[1] See p. 354, n. 2.
[2] *Diary*, vi. 143–86. Also A.L.S. and A.L. (Berg) from FBA to AA, 23, 27 Mar. 1815.
[3] Six letters (Berg) from FBA to CBFB, 19, 27 Mar., 20 Apr., 11, 14 June, 3 July 1815.

When Napoleon began an unimpeded progress towards Lyons, the chevalier put his alarm into words. 'More clearly than anyone', wrote Fanny with wifely conviction, 'he anticipated the impending tempest, and foreboded its devastating effects. He spoke aloud and strenuously, with prophetic energy, to all with whom he was then officially associated; but the greater part either despaired of resisting the torrent, or disbelieved its approach.'[1] 'When Bonaparte actually arrived at Lyon the face of affairs changed.'

Consternation began to spread; and report went rapidly to her usual work, of now exciting nameless terror, and now allaying even reasonable apprehension.[1]

According to the d'Arblays, the Marquis de Vioménil and their friend the Marquis Général Victor de Latour-Maubourg were appointed to raise volunteers for defence. The Prince de Poix in command of the company of Guards then on duty at the Tuileries had never served, said Fanny, though with his ardour, courage, and affection for the King he would have 'sacrificed his life to the service of the Crown, if his life would have sufficed, without military skill, for its preservation'.[1] M. d'Arblay was prepared for a similar sacrifice. He had taken on double duty— that of artillery officer in the barracks and of *officier supérieur* in the King's Body Guard at the Tuileries. He no longer had health or strength for such service, as Fanny noted with terror, but an engagement with the troops of the usurper appeared to him 'not only inevitable, but desirable, since not to fight was the same thing as to be conquered'.[2] He feared for Fanny's safety and on March 15 procured a passport that would enable her to pass the frontier.[1] The Princesse d'Hénin had agreed that, if it became necessary to leave, Madame d'Arblay might accompany her. As the usurper approached, hope lessened, and active friends of the King were poised for flight. On March 18 all hope disappeared.

From north, from south, from east, from west, alarm took the field, ... yet in Paris there was no rising, no disturbance, no confusion— all was taciturn suspense, dark dismay, or sullen passiveness.[1]

On Sunday, March 19, the companies of Guards were assembled on the Champ de Mars, and M. d'Arblay, hoping and

[1] See p. 356, n. 2.   [2] See p. 356, n. 3.

expecting that they would be sent from there to the field of battle, had come home to the rue de Miroménil to take leave of his wife. To intercept the conqueror was 'his earnest wish, as the only chance of saving the King and the throne'. Just such an encounter was Fanny's 'greatest dread', though she was always silent upon the subject, for if 'his honour was dearer to him than his life', she also had her sense of duty.[1] When on Sunday, therefore, he admitted that, as he then believed, he was to ride out to battle, and called upon her to exert her utmost courage lest she enervate his, she tried to obey his injunction. 'I suddenly called myself to order, and curbing every feeling that sought vent in tenderness or in sorrow, I resolved that, since I must no longer hang upon him for protection or for happiness, I would, at least, take care not to injure him in his honour or his spirits.'[1]

We knelt together, in short but fervent prayer to heaven for each other's preservation, and then separated. At the door he turned back, and with a smile which, though forced, had inexpressible sweetness, he half-gaily exclaimed, 'Vive le Roi!' I instantly caught his wise wish that we should part with apparent cheerfulness, and re-echoed his words—and then he darted from my sight.[1]

Looking down from the windows to the courtyard below, she saw him 'armed and encircled with instruments of death— bayonets, lances, pistols, guns, sabres, daggers!' Horrified, she had at least 'so much sense and self-control left as to crawl softly and silently away'.[1] The street was empty.

The gay, constant gala of a Parisian Sunday was changed into fearful solitude: no sound was heard, but that of here and there some hurried footstep, on one hand hastening for a passport to secure safety by flight; on the other, rushing abruptly from or to some concealment, to devise means of accelerating and hailing the entrance of the Conqueror.[1]

At the sound of horses' hoofs Fanny, looking from the drawing-room windows, saw her chevalier riding on a great war-horse along the rue de Miroménil, followed by his groom, also mounted, and a cabriolet filled with the baggage and equipment. The war helmet added length to his face, so that he looked wan and meagre from 'suffering & fatigue'.

[1] See p. 356, n. 2.

Yet . . . fixedly calm; & his air announced a firm resolution to die at his post, if at his post he could not live with Honour & Loyalty.[1]

In less than half an hour after M. d'Arblay rode away, the Princesse d'Hénin came to tell Fanny that Bonaparte had already reached Compiègne, that he might arrive in Paris on the next day, and that they must, therefore, set out with all speed. Since her hostess could offer no room for baggage, Madame d'Arblay left her home (like the fugitive that she was) with a hand-basket containing two black gowns and a few necessaries and small valuables. The night was pitch dark; at nine o'clock she got into a fiacre to make a farewell call on Madame de Maisonneuve and her family, and from there she went to the Princesse d'Hénin's. Later she recalled the perturbation and despair, her own and that of her friends, the turbulent deliberations, and the confused decisions that had to be revised with every fresh report. The army had melted away, she was told, and there was no force to offer any resistance to the usurper. It was not known whether the King would make a stand at the Tuileries or flee to the coast and embark for England. Later it was learned that he had left with five or six companies of the *Garde du Corps* to cover his retreat. M. d'Arblay could not again obtain leave, but he succeeded in sending a message to his wife:

Ma chère amie — Tout est perdu! Je ne puis entrer dans aucun détail — de grâce, partez! le plutôt sera le mieux.

A la vie et à la mort,

A. d'A.[2]

At ten o'clock the Princesse d'Hénin, still undecided on what measures to adopt, engaged in distraught altercations with her household and turbulent political discussions with the Comte de Lally-Tollendal. With the news that Napoleon was already approaching Paris, the Princesse ordered horses for a berlin already packed and waiting. Between ten and eleven at night, March 19, they set out for Brussels.

The femme de chambre of Madame d'Henin within, and the valet, Le Roy, outside the carriage, alone accompanied us, with two postillions for the four horses.[2]

---

[1] Diary MSS. (Berg), pp. 6130–40.   [2] See p. 356, n. 2.

The Comte remained behind for the moment but overtook them before morning. Then followed the surreptitious journey to the frontier. On the first night and day they drove through, Fanny thought, Noailles, St. Just, Mouchy, Poix, Roy, and then Amiens. At every town there were precarious negotiations with prefects, who, royalist in sympathy and lacking as yet new orders from Bonaparte, allowed the travellers to pass. Madame d'Arblay, as the wife of an officer in active service for the King, was in the greatest danger, and rather than have her produce her own passport the Princesse d'Hénin expediently represented her as one of her family and on one dangerous occasion as a *femme de chambre*. There was then a dark night-ride over rough roads to Arras.

It was every way a frightful night. Misery, both public and private, oppressed us all, and the fear of pursuit and captivity had the gloomy effect of causing general taciturnity; so that no kind voice, nor social suggestion, diverted the sense of danger, or excited one of hope.[1]

At Arras they were entertained at an elegant *déjeuner* by a magnificent old prefect of marked royalist leanings. The Englishwoman was amazed that there could be time for such cheerfulness, grace, and ease.

The King had been compelled to fly his capital; no one knew where he was seeking shelter; no one knew whether he meant to resign his crown in hopeless inaction, or whether to contest it in sanguinary civil war. Every family . . . with its every connection in the whole empire of the French, was involved in scenes upon which hung prosperity or adversity, reputation or disgrace, honour or captivity; yet at such a crisis the large assembled family met with cheerfulness, the many guests were attended to with politeness, and the goodly fare . . . was met with appetites as goodly as its incitements.[1]

Though the travellers had not been able to learn anything about the destination or activities of the *Garde du Corps*, they here learned that 'defection was spreading, and that whole troops and companies were either sturdily waiting in inaction, or boldly marching on to meet the conqueror'. The streets of Douai, through which they next passed, were hung with white flags or ribands for the Bourbons. The roads, before almost

[1] See p. 356, n. 2.

deserted, were now lively with small parties of troops. 'Sometimes they called out a "*Vive!*—" but without finishing their
wish', and the occupants of the carriage and cabriolet called
out *Vive! Vive!* in return with equal goodwill and equal fear of
completing the sentence. In the suburbs of Orchies a wheel
of the cabriolet gave way, and there was a delay of four hours.
Every inn was filled with fugitives, but

a good Gentlewoman in the neighbourhood heard the *Jeremiades* of the
postillions, &, though in Bed, dressed herself to come down into the
street, & offer us assistance. . . . She made us enter her small parlour-
kitchen, lighted a blazing fire to dry & warm us,—made us basins
of tea; & got each of us a pillow, for which she aired a clean pillow
bear, . . . while she herself sat up to nourish the fire, to watch, from
time to time, the arrival of our carriage.[1]

Fanny had never seen a better creature in her life, one 'more
innocently generous & kind'. Parties of soldiers passed in the
night. Presently a troop of Polish lancers advancing to scour
the country for Bonaparte battered at the door and the window,
demanding admission.[2] The travellers remained quiet, and their
hostess, entering into a parley, sent the soldiers away with the
story that her house was filled up with her relatives who chanced
to be travelling that way. Fanny feared with every blast of
the trumpet that she would be seized and made a prisoner, but
on March 23, 'quitting the tortured, wretched, revolutionary France, so lately the beautiful seat of restored tranquillity
and rising prosperity', they crossed the frontier and entered
Belgium.[1]

At Tournai the fugitives learned at last that the King was at
Lille waiting permission to enter the Kingdom of the Netherlands, but of the Guard there was no word. Fanny sallied forth
by herself, making her short-sighted way through the strange
town in an endeavour to post letters in a basket that she had
heard was hoisted over the walls. At one time she perceived
outriders in royal livery, then a chariot-and-four with the arms
of France, a horse guard and a crowd feebly crying '*Vive le Roi!*'
She plunged into the crowd and followed, for who could tell if
this might be Louis XVIII and an advance part of the guard?
Soon the royal carriage passed out of sight, but returning she

<hr />

[1] See p. 356, n. 3.   [2] See p. 356, n. 2.

found it again in the inn yard. It belonged to the Prince de Condé, she learned, and with him was M. le Comte de Vioménil. Now surely she might hear news of *la maison du Roi*! The Princesse d'Hénin was walking with a gentleman, who, seeing Fanny's distress, escorted her to the Comte, who in the end knew only that the King was now at Gand; of the Guard, nothing. The gentleman, as she afterwards learned, was Chateaubriand who, having written a pamphlet on the restoration that the King had thought worth an army, now thought it expedient to move out of the reach of the Emperor. At Atot later, where the travellers stopped to dine, they again met Chateaubriand and heard the story of his woes under Napoleon.

On March 24 the journey ended at Brussels. Madame d'Hénin drove directly to her cousin Madame la Comtesse de Maurville, who received the travellers not without some fear of the political result. Madame d'Arblay was confined for a few days with 'colds & feverish fatigue', but with the help of James's powders she was soon up and abroad and employed again in her research.

Nothing was known at Brussels, nothing at all, of the fate of the Body-Guard, or of the final destination of Louis XVIII. How circumstances of such moment, nay, notoriety, could be kept from public knowledge,

Fanny could form no idea, and, failing to gather any information in Brussels, she wrote at random to 'almost every town in the Netherlands'. On March 26 she learned that the *maison du Roi* had arrived at Ypres, and finally on the 29th Madame de Maurville received a letter of inquiry from M. d'Arblay himself. The letter was dated March 27, and now Fanny lived 'in a hurry of delight' that almost made her forget her misfortunes and losses—

my papers, keepsakes, valuables of various sorts, . . . left, as I had reason to fear, to seizure and confiscation upon the entry of the Emperor into Paris.[1]

In family letters of the time she made woeful lamentations about the valuables left in the capital—the watch given to her by the Queen, 'all my dear Father's MSS., & all my own, & unprinted works, from *my youth upwards*, with all *my* Letters, &

[1] See p. 359, n. 1.

my Susan's, & our Journals!' And she resolved to emigrate more skilfully the next time.[1]

Letters from M. d'Arblay telling of his misadventures and hardships justified all his wife's alarms.[2] He had left Paris on Sunday, March 19, for Melun, as he thought, where he expected to join an army collected to oppose the invader. At a preliminary review on the Champ de Mars, however, the King, having received 'the fatal news of the desertion of all the troops of the line', began a retreat to the sea coast through Lille, 'which none of la Garde du Corps could reach; for none could change horses, and many had no horses to change, and the roads were bad, and the rain poured almost continually'.[1] On the first lap of the retreat M. d'Arblay had ridden for twenty-six hours; on the next, twenty-three; and on no day less than fourteen. From long riding and watches in the driving rain he was suffering from '*rhumatisme, les douleurs dans la poitrine, et la bile verte*'. In an attempt to gain speed, *la maison du Roi* had abandoned on the way more than half the artillery and nearly all the domestics '*pour avoir moins de bouches à nourrir*'. In number about 2,000, they had only one brush with Napoleon's forces, when they were overtaken near Béthune by 200 lancers of the Imperial Guard. M. d'Arblay had been riding all day to requisition horses for the artillery, which he was unwilling to abandon, and was about to eat an omelette (he had eaten nothing but dry bread dipped in brandy on the route), when suddenly a cry went up, '*aux armes! aux armes! des lanciers, des Grenadiers à cheval de la Garde!*' Cannon, carriages, horses, and men—all were in confusion— but the Duc de Berry found, at least, his voice: '*Vive le Roi! Vive les Bourbons!*' And his cry was repeated a thousand times through all the companies of the royal guards. '*Vive l'Empereur!*' was the reply of the Imperial Guards, as they took to flight. The Duc de Berry suspected, however, that these were but an advance guard, that heavier forces were in the rear, and that the flight was a feint to lure the companies of the King into an ambuscade. He therefore ordered a forward march without giving the troops time to recover their baggage or equipment.

[1] 2 A.L. (Berg) from FBA to M. d'A, 26, 29 Mar. 1815; A.L. (Berg) to CB, Jr., 7–12 Apr. 1815; 2 A.L. (Berg) to EBB, 8–12 Apr., 1 July 1815; 2 A.L.S. (PML) to JB, 27 Mar., 6 Apr. 1815.
[2] 3 A.L. (Berg) from M. d'A to FBA, Gand, 20, 31 Mar., 1 Apr. 1815; A.L. (Berg) from FBA to EBB, 8 Apr. 1815.

M. d'Arblay, hoping that at last some great action was impending, exchanged his war-horse, then tired out with the day's
riding, for his groom's miserable mount (*'la jument noire'*) and,
obeying the command, rode on. Many of the servants managed
somehow to rejoin their masters; but never did our knight see
his Violette or Sancho Panza again. He lost all his expensive
equipment—'Baggage, military Books, & stores, his Horses, &
his Domestic—all, in short, but his weapons & uniform'.[1]
'Quant à moi, pauvre diable, j'ai tout perdu, tout absolument.'[2] *La
maison* then followed the *grande route* to Lille, but, as His Majesty
could not enter the kingdom of Holland with French military
guards, he graciously thanked them for their services, giving
them liberty to disband, to return to their families, or to seek
asylum abroad. Those 'rich enough to provide for themselves,
or disposed to run the chances of other provisions' would still
be welcomed. 'I need not tell you', wrote Fanny to Alex, 'that
your father unhesitatingly left all he was worth in France to
pursue the call of honour, and fly from the irruption of new
tyranny and usurpation.'[3]

And now our knight errant riding on in the rain to Ypres in
his *petit uniforme* was kept waiting on a drawbridge for nearly
seven hours,

mourant de froid, et sans nourriture, à donner au diable le Commandant d'Ypres qui pour toute réponse à notre demande d'être
admis dans cette ville, nous avait écrit sans trop de façon

> *Le Commandant ne veut pas que vous entrez actuellement!!!*[2]

He had lost his *manteau* at Béthune and 'starved, spoliated, and
sleepless', said Fanny, soaked and cold, the chevalier 'must have
remained, he thinks, to perish upon his horse!' had he not been
helped by a party of *l'École de Droit,*

who had gallantly followed the *maison* on foot . . . these youths helped
him off, put him to bed, and waited upon him during two days, in
which he was in a high fever, unremittingly and with a tenderness
they would have shown to a father. Heaven bless them![3]

M. d'Arblay was very ill. 'The terrible expedition has nearly
demolished him—he is changed! changed!' He was given per-

[1] See p. 363, n. 1.　　　　　　　　　[2] See p. 363, n. 2.
[3] *Diary*, vi. 187–250.

mission to retire to England and was proceeding to Ostend to embark as soon as his wife could join him.

But after two days confinement, he grew better, & then went to the *Roi*, at Gand, & only accepted a *congé* for 10 days from M. le Duc de Luxembourg, who is capitaine . . . of the company to which he belongs.[1]

On April 4 or 5, about sixteen days after the dread farewell of the Paris Sunday, he appeared at Brussels. 'Oh, how sweet was this meeting! this blessed reunion!—how perfect, how exquisite!'[2] He had come 'for the recruit of his shattered nerves' and to procure fresh equipment for a new military post. The *Ministre de la Guerre*, the Duc de Feltre, had chosen ten officers of known fidelity to be stationed at ten places on the frontier in order 'to receive, select, or recruit Deserters from Bonaparte, & form them into [royalist] Battalions'.[1] M. d'Arblay was assigned first to Luxembourg, but as this area was under Prussian orders and as Blücher wished him to go, rather, to Trèves, 'thither he went'. He was to have a staff of two or three officers including an *adjoint*, and as aide-de-camp a descendant of Godefroy de Bouillon. The d'Arblays moved to a dwelling in the Marché aux Bois, and nearly all of April and May was taken up with negotiations and preparations for the new post.

Fanny counted the days seized from war and tried to hide her fears. The uncertainty of the political and martial situation and the view of her husband's 'shaken health, diminished strength, & changed appearance' filled her with alarm.[3] When he could find leisure, they rode out again in the morning in a new equipage along the famous Allée Verte. They visited the Palace de Lachen, and one evening they went to the concert hall to a benefit given by the celebrated Angelica Catalani and saw there the Queen of the Netherlands and Marshal Lord Wellington, 'the Hope of the World', applauding everything except 'Rule Britannia'. When Wellington rebuffed an English officer's request for an encore Fanny thought she could see his flair for 'imperious dominion'.[2]

On May 13 when orders came from the Duc de Feltre, M. d'Arblay set off to his post on the frontier. Fanny remained at

[1] See p. 363, n. 1.
[3] See p. 356, n. 3.
[2] See p. 364, n. 3.

Brussels watching the political events and scenes leading to Waterloo and writing long reports on the subject to her husband in Trèves and to her sisters in England. She had been frantic in the spring over a newspaper report about typhus fever at Cambridge and over Alex's failure to give an account of himself. She tried to persuade him to take a room at Richmond and board with his aunt rather than impose on the hospitality of his uncle in James Street, where games of chess, she well knew, were likely to prove more enticing than the college textbooks. Charles, himself engaged in scholarly undertakings that taxed his health and strength, was probably withholding his active interest until Alex could attend chapel and lectures and condescend to learn at the university notwithstanding its alleged backwardness in mathematics when compared to France. George Cambridge, now Archdeacon of Middlesex, took Charles's place as guardian to Alex. Thirty years before he had broken Fanny's heart, but in the difficult years yet to come he was to pay a handsome recompense in friendship towards that absent-minded, eccentric, and hapless young man, Madame d'Arblay's son.

Meanwhile all the world watched Brussels, and all Brussels was at the windows or in the streets. All the Allies were to arrive there with 'Fire & sword!'[1] 'The opening of Hostilities is expected to be inexpressibly dreadful—but, by many, to be decisive! Oh how to be pitied will be the victims of that opening, who never will reap its fruits!'[1] So placid, phlegmatic, and taciturn were the Dutch people with whom Madame d'Arblay lived, and so quiet her own way of life after her husband's departure, that she was awakened by bugle calls and saw regiments marching directly to battle before she realized that the campaign had opened, that on the 15th (twenty-six hours before) Bonaparte had broken into Belgium and had taken Charleroi. She was awakened early on the 16th, however, by a bugle horn in the Marché aux Bois, and so unmoved were the Dutch that standing there among them Fanny could not distinguish between Bourbonists and Bonapartists. Later in the

[1] Letters (Berg) from FBA to M. d'A, 13, 28, 29 May, 3, 11–13, 14–15, 17–19, 22, 24–25, 29 June, 1, 3–4, 6, 10, 13, 17 July 1815; A.L. (Berg) to EBB, 1–3 July 1815; drafts of letters (Berg) from FBA to the Princess Elizabeth, 29 May, 10–20 June 1815.

morning she watched the black-uniformed corps of the Duke of
Brunswick marching by in measured time. She saw the whole
army pass by: the Duke, the uniformed officers, the infantry,
cavalry, artillery, bag and baggage, little dreaming that neither
they nor their chief would in a few short hours 'breathe again
the vital air'.[1]

Curiosity was all awake and all abroad; for the procession lasted
some hours. Not a door but was open; not a threshold but was
crowded, and not a window of the many-windowed Gothic, modern,
frightful, handsome, quaint, disfigured, fantastic, or lofty mansions
that diversify the large market-place of Brussels, but was occupied by
lookers-on. Placidly, indeed, they saw the warriors pass; no kind
greeting welcomed their arrival; no warm wishes followed them to
combat. Neither, on the other hand, was there the slightest symptom
of dissatisfaction.[1]

The experience of fifteen years had taught that Napoleon was
invincible, and on the eve of the battle that had not yet reached
the history books the odds were in his favour. Even as Fanny
wrote she could hear the cannon. What if Brussels should be
taken and pillaged, and the English more severely punished
than any others? As in Paris before, the royalists and the English
prepared for flight. On June 17 news came that the gallant
Duke of Brunswick had been killed, and 'that the two mighty
chiefs, Bonaparte and Wellington, were almost constantly in
view of each other'. Military contingents no longer looked gay
and splendid, but grim, morose, gloomy. And always there
was a dreadful growling noise like distant thunder.[1]

Since land-conveyances of all kinds were requisitioned for
the army, Madame d'Arblay's English friends, the Boyds,
thought they might go by barge to Antwerp. On June 18 ('the
greatest, perhaps, in its result, in the annals of Great Britain!'),
the Boyds, terrified at adverse reports, wakened Fanny at six
in order to set off at eight to board a barge by the waterside.
While their luggage was loading they ordered breakfast at an
inn, but they were soon interrupted by the commotion of a
military arrival. Presently they were told that the barge also
was requisitioned by the English army, that

all was lost—that Bonaparte was advancing—that his point was
decidedly Brussels—and that the Duke of Wellington had sent orders

[1] See p. 364, n. 3.

that all the magazines, the artillery, and the warlike stores of every description, and all the wounded, the maimed, and the sick, should be immediately removed to Antwerp. For this purpose he had issued directions that every barge, every boat should be seized for the use of the army, and that everything of value should be conveyed away, the hospitals emptied, and Brussels evacuated.[1]

The dread reverberations of the cannon made anything credible. Every shot tolled to Fanny's imagination 'the death of myriads' and a carnage in which the English would be the first victims.

Yet, strange to relate! on re-entering the city, all seemed quiet and tranquil as usual! and though it was in this imminent and immediate danger of being invested, and perhaps pillaged, I saw no outward mark of distress or disturbance, or even of hurry or curiosity.[1]

On the 18th the news was hopeful. Even Fanny's phlegmatic host and hostess raised a cry of '*Bonaparte est pris! le voilà! le voilà!*' when they saw passing by in the street 'a general in the splendid uniform of France' mounted on

a noble war-horse in full equipment . . . followed by a crew of roaring wretches, who seemed eager for the moment when he should be lodged where they had orders to conduct him, that they might un-horse, strip, pillage him, and divide the spoil.

His high, feathered, glittering helmet he had pressed down as low as he could on his forehead, and I could not discern his face; but I was instantly certain he was not Bonaparte.[1]

Then the news was very good: Lord Wellington and Marshal Blücher had gained a complete victory. Then again came reports of reverses: the enemy was trying to turn the English right wing; Wellington was in great danger; Brussels might be taken in the morning. On Sunday, with the expectation of fire and sword at the gates, church services were out of the question, though certainly not, said Fanny, the need of prayer. The silence was broken by 'riotous shouts', 'a howl, violent, loud, affright-ing, and issuing from many voices'.

I ran to the window, and saw the *Marché aux Bois* suddenly filling with a populace, pouring in from all its avenues, and hurrying on rapidly, and yet as if unconscious in what direction; while women with children in their arms, or clinging to their clothes, ran scream-

[1] See p. 364, n. 3.

ing out of doors; and cries, though not a word was ejaculated, filled the air, and from every house, I saw windows closing, and shutters fastening.[1]

Fanny had only had time to see all this from the window when someone burst into her room with the announcement *the French were come*! And now Fanny, who had secretly rejoiced at the failure of the barge expedition so that she might remain and write letters to her husband and the more readily receive news from him, grew really terrified. She crammed papers and money into a basket, and, throwing on a shawl and bonnet, 'flew down stairs and out of doors'. She intended to join the Boyds,

but the crowd were all issuing from the way I must have turned to have gained the Rue d'Assault, and I thought, therefore, I might be safer with Madame de Maurville, who, also, not being English, might be less obnoxious to the Bonapartists. To la Rue de la Montagne I hurried, in consequence, my steps crossing and crossed by an affrighted multitude; but I reached it in safety, and she received me with an hospitable welcome. I found her calm, and her good humour undisturbed. Inured to revolutions, under which she had smarted so as she could smart no more, from the loss of all those who had been the first objects of her solicitude, a husband and three sons! . . .

What a dreadful day did I pass! dreadful in the midst of its glory! for it was not during those operations that sent details partially to our ears that we could judge of the positive state of affairs, or build upon any permanency of success. Yet here I soon recovered from all alarm for personal safety, and lost the horrible apprehension of being in the midst of a city that was taken, sword in hand, by an enemy—an apprehension that, while it lasted, robbed me of breath, chilled my blood, and gave me a shuddering ague that even now in fancy returns as I seek to commit it to paper.[1]

On the next day it was learned that the *alerte* that had hurried all Brussels into the Sunday streets was false. 'The French, indeed, were coming; but not triumphantly.' They were prisoners, and in such numbers as to be mistaken by the Belgians for an advancing army. At least, so Fanny explained the error of the previous day. 'I attempt no description of this day, the grandeur of which was unknown, or unbelieved, in Brussels till it had taken its flight, and could only be named as time past.'[1]

[1] See p. 364, n. 3.

Inaccurate news of the battle still kept Brussels in alarm. The Boyds again planned to escape by barge to Antwerp. Fanny was summoned at four in the morning but when at seven she heard from an English officer that 'Bonaparte would have too much to do to be at Brussels that day' [Monday the 19th], she changed her mind and insisted that her friends go on without her. 'Everybody ran away at the late invasion', she wrote Mrs. Locke on June 25—'every person I know except Madame de Maurville.'[1] For anything short of actual rapine Fanny would not change her address for fear of missing letters from Trèves.

And now in the streets she began to see the aftermath of war—officers of high rank in gay and costly attire, French, English, or Belgian, either dying or dead, extended upon biers, carried along in silence; noisy soldiers exulting in the spoils of battle—fine rings, a tall war-horse, 'two Tri-coloured Drapeaux, & two large & beautiful Eagles'.[2] There were prisoners in immense numbers and almost all severely wounded. At first they seemed a set of 'dirty, ragged, coarse Jacobins! in soiled old carter's Frocks', but Fanny later learned that the frocks had been cast over them after they were despoiled of their uniforms by their English captors.[1] Yet the Commander-in-Chief had forbidden pillage. The English also began to arrive, 'on foot, in carts, & on Horse back, grievously wounded also. Never yet, all agree, has there been so bloody a battle fought!' On the 19th there were yet no consistent details, 'but the continued sight of the maimed, wounded, mutilated & tortured victims to this exterminating warfare is shocking & afflicting beyond description!'[2]

'Times of disturbance give even me courage.' And Fanny employed herself, with others, in preparing bandages and went out to render whatever services she could to the wounded. From the soldiers themselves she heard accounts of the field of slaughter. 'Piles of Dead!—heaps, masses, *hills* of Dead!—French, English, Belge & Prussians.' On the 22nd she reported that the wounded were still coming in but that carts were being sent back for 'the sick & maimed prisoners'. On Saturday, June 24, she wrote again to M. d'Arblay about the appalling carnage, happy that he had neither witnessed nor aided in it. 'The

[1] See p. 364, n. 3.
[2] See p. 366, n. 1.

soldiers here themselves say it was murder rather than fighting, on both sides!'[1]

The wretched prisoners are now brought in every hour, in a condition so horrible, the streets seem pestilential as the carriages pass with them! Even all the shopkeepers bathe their faces with eau de cologne to support the effluvia! There were so many English & Belgians wounded & maimed to remove, that the carriages for the prisoners were not at liberty—though ALWAYS in motion, till the blood drying upon them, & their garments, caused, I imagine, this nearly putrid effect. The Dead!—the piles of dead, are now burying, by 3000 peasants!—to prevent a pestilence, so many are employed at a time.[1]

On July 1 the grisly carts were still passing.

Brussels is a walking Hospital! maimed & wounded unhappy *men of War* are met at every step, either entering, carried in carts, from the Field of Battle, or the adjoining villages, to be placed in Infirmaries, work houses, churches, & also at private houses.[1]

'It is not near the scene of battle that war, even with victory, wears an aspect of felicity—no, not even in the midst of its highest resplendence of glory!'[2]

When fear and horror subsided, however, Fanny began to rejoice in the victory and in a proclamation insisting that with Napoleon 'all must be finally & utterly & eternally finished'.[1] If he should succeed in escaping, 'he will again lead us the same dance of death he has so frightfully taught us at this moment'. Now 'Wellington is indeed at the Head of this nether World!' And the Englishwoman gloried in

Wellington's tremendous charge; ordering, all at once, Infantry, cavalry, & Artillery to dash, in one great blow, from the whole line, upon the heights & the plain; but for that shake, it would at least have been a drawn battle; but that grand manœuvre unexpected & abrupt . . . conquered. . . . Immortal Wellington! Vive! Vive! Vive!![1]

She could not but be proud of the accounts of the Battle; 'and pendent from its glory my revived imagination hung the blessed laurels of peace'.[2]

Meanwhile at Trèves a forgotten warrior stayed doggedly

[1] See p. 366, n. 1.   [2] See p. 364, n. 3.

on at his post. On June 20 he had not even heard that Bonaparte had invaded the Low Countries. Apparently he could depend only on his wife for news military and political, but from her he learned that the royalist battles had been fought and won not by Frenchmen but by foreign liberators and, still worse, that a representative French faction had offered *any* sacrifice to recover peace—'resign the Emperor, become a republic, take another and new form of government, or revert to a free monarchy— *anything* for peace, except reinstating the [Bourbons]'.[1] M. d'Arblay had thought only of the cause, never of himself, and now the cause also had passed him by.

Communication was slow. A post left Brussels for Trèves three times a week, but since a letter took six days on the way, Fanny could not send news and receive an answer in less than a fortnight. The d'Arblay correspondence, always a memorial of personal devotion, in these months provides a commentary on the political tensions of the Restoration. Madame d'Arblay gleaned all Brussels for authentic news to write to her husband, knowing very well that nothing except immediate family concerns could interest him as much. (*'O mon amie, tes lettres sont ma vie!'*)[2] His letters in return expressed deep worries over his native land, the treatment that the conquerors (especially the Prussians) might accord the conquered, the status of the Bourbons in the hearts of the people, and whether now, forsaken himself, he might forsake his useless post.

From the first, everything at Trèves had seemed to go badly. *'Ma santé, notre bourse, ma position, tout à la fin allait fort mal.'* With fatigue or exposure the soldier was threatened with rheumatism and *'des douleurs dans la poitrine'*, the effects of his accident at Calais. *'Un autre sujet d'inquiétude très vive a été ma jument noire, qui non seulement a été menacée d'être poussive, mais morveuse.'*[2] The military mission was arduous. The General was often engaged until midnight in questioning deserters, examining suspicious personages (for one might easily conceive the horror he would have in allowing a *'mauvais sujet* to *glisser* through his hands').[3] He was now on full pay, but, as Fanny explained, the expenses

---

[1] See p. 364, n. 3.

[2] Letters (Berg) from M. d'A to FBA, 25 May, 3, 5, 9, 13, 23, 28, 30 June, 6–8, 10, 11, 15 July 1815.

[3] 2 A.L. (Berg) from FBA to EBB and CBFB, 1–3 July, 3 July 1815, respectively.

of military service in France were greater than the remuneration.

For the *ci-devant officiers supérieurs* were commonly chosen from among those rich enough to dedicate their private fortune to the service, not as *chez nous*, to *make* a fortune for private uses & enjoyment.[1]

At this time, moreover, M. d'Arblay had had to make advances to his own staff, 'ruined Gentlemen' like himself, who could not afford the necessary horses and equipment. The mission, however, was honourable, difficult, and important, as Fanny always emphasized in the letters going to England. She had no illusions about its glory or its rewards, but in letters to her husband she ventured to demur only in warnings about health.

I feel & acknowledge every true Frenchman should come forth, according to his powers, to aid his injured King.
According to his powers,—but oh, go not beyond them![2]

Diplomatic arrangements were made meanwhile for the French King to return to his throne without a foreign escort. On July 3, Fanny wrote, Louis XVIII was proceeding to Paris 'amidst the acclamations of the people of every town through which he passes'. She thought the acclamations so changeable that there was 'no honouring them with any full or firm confidence'.[1] To Fanny the important thing was 'that the armies fight no more!'[3] She saw the backstage of the Grand Entry: 'Ah! how melancholy a mixture of shame, repentance, mortification,—or secret vengeance & despair, must sadden the gaiety of the Restoration! France can only be a *happy* séjour for those yet to be born!'[2] And she had now a grievance of her own. It would have seemed appropriate, she thought, that the *maison du Roi* who followed the King in the days of his adversity (or, more specifically, in his desperate flight from the Tuileries in June) should have been invited or summoned to attend him on the grand re-entry. M. d'Arblay had somehow missed that honour and satisfaction, and she thought the omission or neglect 'a real hardship'. 'One of the most faithful subjects of *la maison du Roi*, he ought to have been summoned to escort the King, in common with his comrades, into the capital.' 'I think there must have been some cruel neglect, or mistake in this business',

[1] See p. 372, n. 3.   [2] See p. 366, n. 1.
[3] See p. 364, n. 3.

she confided to Alex, especially when he (M. d'Arblay) had 'written repeatedly for permission to join the King!' The staff at Trèves were restless. 'Nothing less than their born & bred severity of military discipline & order could keep them from gallopping off to join their corps.'[1] On reflection Fanny grew very indignant: 'Indeed, mon ami,—your having no Letter of recall or of direction, I think now, inexcusable, wherever the blame may lie. Who more merited a summons to attend the King upon his entrée?' 'Clouds—if not of danger, at least of ill-will are hovering still in the air.'[2]

Finally even the chevalier's idealistic and exalted spirit was a little subdued. '*Je suis désormais inutile ici, complètement inutile.*'[3] He was now sixty-one years of age. He had served with zeal since he was thirteen-and-a-half years old, for eight years of exile and the ten years of office work in place of the military appointments that he could have had under the Emperor must also be counted as service to the Bourbons. Now if he could obtain half-pay and a letter expressing satisfaction with his career, he would retire.[3]

J'ai d'ailleurs éprouvé, que ma bonne volonté et tout le zèle dont je suis capable n'étaient suffisans pour remplir dans une saison rigoureuse les devoirs d'un général de mon grade. C'est une vérité.[3]

Fanny had hardly time to applaud these sentiments, when an accident, the worst her star-crossed chevalier had yet sustained, sent her hurrying to Trèves.

On July 19 she was writing in her apartment on the Marché aux Bois when the Princesse d'Hénin and Colonel de Beaufort came to tell her that

M. d'Arblay had received on the calf of his leg a furious kick from a wild horse, which had occasioned so bad a wound as to confine him to his bed; and that he wished M. de Beaufort to procure me some travelling guide, that I might join him as soon as it would be possible with safety and convenience.

But what was my agony when I saw that the letter was not in his own hand! I conjured them to leave me, and let me read it alone. They offered, the one to find me a clever femme de chambre, the other to inquire for a guide to aid me to set out, if able, the next day. . . .

<hr>

[1] A.L. (Berg) from FBA to AA, 3–12 July 1815.
[2] See p. 366, n. 1.   [3] See p. 372, n. 2.

No sooner were they gone, than, calming my spirits by earnest and devout prayer, which alone supports my mind, and even preserves my senses, in deep calamity, I ran over the letter, which was dated the fourth after the wound, and acknowledged that three incisions had been made in the leg unnecessarily by an ignorant surgeon, which had so aggravated the danger, as well as the suffering that he was now in bed, not only from the pain of the lacerated limb, but also from a nervous fever! and that no hope was held out to him of quitting it in less than a fortnight or three weeks.[1]

Fanny had remained on the Continent through the sanguinary struggle and frequent separations for just such a contingency. Now it had come; and in a few hours she set off without waiting for the *femme de chambre*, the guide, the necessary passports, or money (having in her hurry missed the banker). She knew that the roads were 'dreadfully infested with robbers & pillagers of all sorts', that private carriages going even to Paris had to be guarded by outriders,[2] and that a few days previously her nephew Charles Parr Burney had relinquished a journey to Luxembourg and Trèves because of the dangers of the routes beset with 'worthless & desperate fugitives' (starving remnants of Bonaparte's army or pillaging parties from the pursuing army of the Prussians).[3] When at the inn she was told that it would be dangerous to travel in a chaise without a guard, she instantly resolved to go by the diligence. Unhappily, however, there was no diligence to Trèves, and the one for Luxembourg had set out the day before and would not go again for a week. Fortunately a friend, the Baronne de Spagen, knew of a diligence to Liège, which though not a direct route was a safe one, and fortunately also she could offer an escort in her brother-in-law, who was going to that city by the night coach. Fanny at once secured a place on the Liège coach; but with various delays, including time to argue with the confidential servant sent by the Princesse d'Hénin to persuade her to give up the hazardous venture or wait until safe arrangements could be made, she arrived at the posting-inn four minutes late. A whole week must pass before she could catch another diligence, but at the book-keeper's suggestion, she offered the coachman

[1] *Diary*, vi. 265–90. Also A.L. (Berg) from FBA to AA, 9 Aug. 1815.
[2] See p. 372, n. 3.
[3] See p. 366, n. 1.

a reward if he could catch the conveyance in the Allée Verte, where it stopped for passengers and parcels.

Off he drove. The diligence was at the appointed place, and that instant ready to proceed!

She rushed into it 'with a trepidation of hurry' and presently looked around for the Comte de Spagen, only learning at Liège that he had come by a previous coach and had now gone off to his estates. There was no diligence from Liège to Trèves, but she was told that at Aix-la-Chapelle she might find a conveyance to take her on her way. She travelled on, therefore, to Aix, but there she could hear of no diligence except one going northward to Juliers at four o'clock in the morning. She wandered about Aix in a mizzling rain, procured a few hours of rest in a miserable room, but fearful of missing the coach, she descended at three in the morning to inquire if it was not soon time to set off. There was still an hour to wait, but at four her vehicle was standing in a heavy rain in the courtyard. At Juliers the passengers alighted at a large inn in 'an immensely long market-place'. Everywhere Fanny noted the effect of the wars— the maimed soldiers, the preponderance of women, children, and old men, and the poverty. At every *relai* she encountered police-officers who were displeased with her passport. At Juliers there were the usual 'gross authority & unfeeling harshness' and the same 'irascible menaces' to send her back.[1] In this exigency she found the name of General Kleist, whom her husband had mentioned in his letters, an effective watchword, and in the end, therefore, she obtained a passport to Cologne. At the close of the third day of her journey she entered that beautiful city through 'an avenue, said to be seven miles in length, of lime trees'.[2] She was struck by the magnitude of the city, the number of steeples, and the kindness of a police-officer who, being French, carried her passport himself to a magistrate and had it renewed for the next stage of the journey through Bonn to Coblentz. So that she might spend an evening *en famille* rather than at an inn, he introduced her to a most respectable lady and gentleman (of the old provincial *noblesse*), both French, but 'under the Prussian hard grip'.

[1] Diary MSS. (Berg), pp. 6422–600. Also A.L. (Berg) from FBA to Charlotte Barrett, 27 Sept.–3 Oct. 1815.   [2] See p. 375, n. 1.

Death, misfortune, and oppression had all laid on them their iron hands; they had lost their sons while forcibly fighting for a usurpation which they abhorred; they had lost their property by emigration; and they had been treated with equal harshness by the Revolutionists because they were suspected of loyalty, and by the Royalists because their children had served in the armies of the Revolutionists.[1]

Such were the unhappy vicissitudes of revolution and occupation, which in her very old age Madame d'Arblay incorporated in the curious old rambling stories that her nieces liked to hear. She went to rest in a high, narrow bed, but did not venture to undress or sleep for fear of missing the diligence, which set out at four in the morning. Now she was entering the Germanic lands; nearly all the passengers were Germans, and for the most part she heard only German spoken.

At Bonn she lost her way in a long exploratory ramble, only finding it again by means of a 'hideous little statue' that served her as a landmark—

a deformed little shapeless wooden pigmy, a blue wig painted upon its head, a gilt carved waistcoat, patched with red spots reaching its knees, & large silver Buckles projecting from bright blue shoes—for top & bottom were in exact harmony of colouring. . . . It was designed for the holy Infant![2]

At the posting-inn 'the coach was just departing! The Horses harnessed, every passenger entered, & the Drivers with their whips in hand extended! Oh my God! what an escape!'[2]

The road now led not by zigzag or circuitous ways but directly to Trèves, and Fanny's spirits rose. Looking out over the Rhine she found herself in 'regions of enchantment'. She saw 'Mountains, Towers, Castles, Fortifications, half-demolished; & interspersed with Trees, Hills, valleys, plains, elevations covered with vineyards, thick woods of Lime Trees, country seats, new plantations, & picturesque villages . . . hanging woods of exquisite beauty . . . prospects eternally diversifying'.[2]

The diligence reached Coblentz at ten o'clock at night, and the Prussian official, whose office it was to give out passports, had retired for the night. The conveyance for Trèves was to set out at the usual hour of four in the morning, and as usual it did not set out again for a week. The rain descended heavily,

[1] See p. 375, n. 1. [2] See p. 376, n. 1.

the night was dark, but Madame d'Arblay was scarcely to be stopped now. The passport, if she could obtain it, would take her to Trèves, her journey's end, and all her heart's desire. Enlisting the help of a boy of thirteen or fourteen, she made her way to the police-office. After repeated knockings, the door opened, and 'an ill-favoured man, more asleep than awake, appeared'.

But no sooner had I put forth my paper, & named my passport, than he rudely shut the door in my face, drawing back without uttering a word.

Horror struck—the waning night darkling before me—& the fatal delay menacing a weeks durance in the distant, unknown, unfriendly city. I scarcely kept my feet. I tottered, & held by something, I know not what, that I caught at the Portico.

So much for what such an occasion required. Then she knocked again, and when the porter again appeared, she gave him two francs 'to shut up his beginning voice of brutality' and told him she needed only a signature. The tip was effective. 'He shut us out, in the street, & in the Rain' but soon returned with word that the paper must be signed first by the Prussian Commandant. Fanny and the youth had now to find the Prussian guard-house. It was also closed up without a sentinel in sight. Again Fanny battered at the door, but luckily this time M. le Commandant was a young and impressionable officer who, moved by her story, signed her paper and offered to escort her back to the first officer. In spite of the servant's demur that his master was sound asleep and unwell, the young officer went upstairs, and Fanny followed. The housekeeper, 'a quaint muffled-up old German', trotted in amazement by her side, but did not dare to rouse the personage within the bedroom. The officer, however, rapped at the door, and Fanny rapped also, calling out at the same time that she had come from 'an intimate friend of General Kleist'. The name again wrought wonders; the young officer was permitted to enter with pen and ink, and the paper was signed. Back at the booking-office Fanny put down her last half-napoleon and her gold repeater. When the clerk heard her explanations, he said that her fare could be collected at Trèves. 'Excellent, feeling, benignant German!'

At four in the morning she climbed into 'a queer German carriage' resembling a cart and travelled for two days still up the Moselle valley. 'We stopt for the Night to my great misery in the middle of the *afternoon* in a small village, comfortless, dirty, & save of women & children, uninhabited.' The Prussians treated all the dwellers of the land as a conquered people, 'swearing, storming, throwing away with wanton violence every thing they did not want, & seizing without mercy every thing that was to their taste'.[1]

At length, on Monday evening, July 24, she arrived at Trèves. She had been six days on the road, including one whole night of travel, one day beginning at three o'clock in the morning, and four beginning at four. It was six days since she had heard from M. d'Arblay. The letters he wrote to her had arrived at Brussels after her departure, but they may still be read: '*au nom du Ciel, ma chère Fanny, arrive, arrive! — rejoindre et consoler ton malheureux ami.*'[2]

As her conveyance drove in, M. d'Arblay's valet, a staid old German, usually very soberly composed, broke into a run. 'How I shook at his sight!' But the good creature reassured her instantly. The surgeons had said that the danger was over. In triumphant relief over tragedy averted and evils conquered she was now 'in gaiety of spirits, unbounded!' Her husband's *calèche* was waiting to take her to his door. She knew that she was expected. 'I therefore permitted myself to enter his apartment at once.' 'What a meeting of exquisite felicity! to Both!'[1]

There was no room for Madame d'Arblay in the house where her husband was quartered, but the next day an arrangement was made with Madame la Grange, an impoverished lady of condition, for board and lodging 'upon the pic-nic plan'. Now Fanny went to live in a straggling Gothic fabric at the end of a dark and dingy street, an old habitation, spacious, 'curious & dismal'.[1] There was an immense open chimney in her bedroom, and she could see broken panes, loose boards, and crevices everywhere. As she composed herself to rest, she might have recalled a paragraph written a few weeks previously in one of her letters to Mrs. Waddington:

I am tranquil in nothing during this wandering, houseless, emigrant life. This is no siècle for those who love their home, or who have a home to love. 'Tis a siècle for the adventurous, to whom Ambition always opens resources . . .[3]

[1] See p. 376, n. 1.   [2] See p. 372, n. 2.   [3] See p. 375, n. 1.

There was an interlude when she could enjoy drives in her husband's *calèche* over the Roman roads to every historical and 'beautiful & curious spot in the vicinity of the ancient city on the Moselle'. The antique Roman baths reminded her, probably, of Bath and took her wishes homeward, but she could also enjoy the moment—visits to a humpbacked little mantua-maker, excursions in a small boat up the Moselle, the wild scenery of the Saar valley, and the pure, clear, balsamic air.[1]

Meanwhile M. d'Arblay and his staff employed themselves in attempts to obtain their letters of recall. This proved difficult. Though the mission on the frontier was now quite null and M. d'Arblay incapable of duty even if it were not, yet

the mighty change of affairs so completely occupied men's minds, as well as their hands, that they could work only for themselves and the present: the absent were utterly forgotten.[2]

At length, however, the Duc de Luxembourg, formerly captain of the company of Guards to which M. d'Arblay had belonged, secured all the 'ceremonies of recall', papers authorizing his retirement, the brevet of his promotion to the rank of Lieutenant-General, as conferred by the King at Ghent, and, finally, passports that would allow him to travel through France.

About the middle of September the d'Arblays left Trèves in their own *calèche*. In a formal journal, written up some eight or ten years later, Madame d'Arblay described the return journey through occupied France. The General was depressed by his own helplessness, the wounds that refused to heal, and presently at having to present a passport of 'All the Allies' in order to enter his own country or pass through it.

Though he was glad to see the Monarchy restored, he had hoped that it would have come about by 'the work of the French themselves'. The travellers passed first through a Prussian encampment, then on to Châlons where the Russians kept posts like sentinels along the high road. Presently Fanny saw the Emperor of all the Russians emerge from an old house, and she thought he looked more like 'a jocund young Lubin, or country esquire, than an emperor, a warrior, or a statesman'. They stopped three or four days in Metz, then again at Meaux, where the camps became English.

[1] See p. 376, n. 1.   [2] See p. 375, n. 1.

All converse between us now stopped involuntarily, and as if by tacit agreement. M. d'Arblay was too sincere a loyalist to be sorry, yet too high-spirited a freeman to be satisfied. I could devise nothing to say that might not cause some painful discussion or afflicting retrospection, and we travelled many miles in pensive silence—each nevertheless intensely observant of the astonishing new scene presented to our view, on re-entering the capital of France, to see the vision of Henry V revived, and Paris in the hands of the English.[1]

In Paris the d'Arblays met old friends—Madame de Maisonneuve and her brother General Victor de Latour-Maubourg, M. de Lally-Tollendal, la Princesse d'Hénin, la Princesse de Poix, Baron de Larrey, M. de Lafayette, Madame de Latour du Pin, and many others. These friends had 'wrought themselves, by innumerable kindnesses', Fanny said, into her affections, and she did not tell them just then that she and her General were debating a future residence in England. Fanny thought she had given France a fair trial.

I can never tranquillize my mind with ideas of perfect and permanent safety—as yet in that Volcanic Country; though he assures me all *he sees* is sound and healthy. But he sees with his wishes—and I think with my terrors.[2]

She was determined to take her 'poor Boiteux' to Bath where he might convalesce in quiet and in peace.

On the eve of setting out for England Fanny went round to all she could reach of her intimate acquaintances, to make, as it proved, a last farewell. M. de Talleyrand, who came into Madame de Laval's drawing-room during her visit of leave-taking, reminded Fanny of Juniper Hall, Mickleham, and Norbury Park, and it all seemed much more than twenty-two years ago.

Oh what days were those of conversational perfection! of wit, ingenuity, gaiety, repartee, information, badinage, & eloquence![2]

Finally the General's *calèche* was in the courtyard, and Fanny in a flood of tears left her 'dear, dear, invaluable Madame de Maisonneuve, . . . musing, melancholy, & afflicted' in the empty yard.[2] The leave-taking was sad, and the passage home was 'in full & terrible union' with their '*jarred* & unstrung feelings; there was a continued storm of the loudest winds &

¹ See p. 375, n. 1.   ² See p. 376, n. 1.

roughest waves'.[1] In spite of 'the fury of the elements', Fanny always preferred the deck, but this time her chevalier could not help her. Again she was nearly senseless with seasickness, and when a boat was sent out from Dover for passengers both she and the General had to be carried from boat to boat and thus ashore. It was less than a year since they had crossed tempestuous waters to France, but the year, being that of Napoleon's return, the Hundred Days, and Waterloo, had been scarcely less tempestuous on land. M. d'Arblay was never to recover from its strenuous exertions and 'grievous accidents'. This, however, was still for the future. On October 18 Fanny wrote to Mrs. Locke from Dover:

Last night, my ever dear friends, we arrived once more in Old England. . . . I cannot boast of our health, our looks, our strength; but I hope we may recover a part of all when our direful fatigues, mental and corporeal, cease to utterly weigh upon and wear us.[2]

Because of the wounded leg they were still travelling in their own *calèche*, and on the way to London stopped at Deptford 'to see my dear Brother Charles, whom—alas, alas! I never saw more! for our next—& Last! three years were spent at Bath, whither he never came'. As ten years later Fanny sat writing up the events of 1815 and the journey home, the pain that smote at her heart with recollections of this visit can almost be felt again in the old papers: 'O my dear Charles! how little, I thank Heaven did I then conceive I saw your affectionate Face for the last Time on Earth!'[1]

At Sablonière's Hotel in Leicester Square they met Alexander, who had been staying with James, then James himself. In the two weeks they remained there Fanny was granted two royal audiences, and she managed visits to both Esther and Charlotte, at that time in worse health than the survivors of Waterloo. The strenuous journey had opened the General's wounds again, and Fanny wished only for a quiet inexpensive place where he could 'recruit'. 'Terribly mangled by events of all sorts, public & private',[3] they set off on November 2 for Bath, there to fix their 'winter's Tent'.[4]

---

[1] See p. 376, n. 1.   [2] See p. 375, n. 1.
[3] A.L. (Berg) from FBA to CBFB, 20 Oct. 1815.
[4] A.L.S. (Osborn) from FBA to CB, Jr., 22 Nov. 1815; A.L. (Berg) from FBA to Mary Port Waddington, 19 Dec. 1815.

XV

REQUIEM

(1815–1818)

I had always believed such a sentence would at once
have killed me.
MADAME D'ARBLAY, 1818[1]

BATH was not new to Madame d'Arblay, but she had never
thought it so beautiful—'Hills rising above Hills, here
smiling with verdure, there shadowed by woods' and
terminating almost every street.[1] Besides its 'luxurious beauty'
and the benefit of the hot springs, Bath had 'a thousand coaxing
recommendations to folks of small pecuniary means'.

No carriage is requisite; the market is good & reasonable. . . . Town
& Country are united; Health, or pleasure bring hither sooner or
later almost everybody; it is a good resort of Foreigners; all the
eminent artists visit it occasionally: To walk in the streets is as safe,
easy, & clean as to walk in a courtyard. The people are so honest,
so innocent that Bars & Bolts, even at night, seem superfluous.[1]

Fanny hoped that the General would make Bath his ultimate
residence.

There is no place I have yet seen where the inconveniences of a
limited fortune are so lightly felt, nor where the people at large are
so civilized. . . . Equippage, servants, Table, Jewels, though *here* as
everywhere, very desirable, are not *here* requisite. *Respect* does not
hang either upon the lackey or the attire; and admission is as easy
without the one, as reception is good or bad without the other.
There is something nearer to independence from the shackles of
fortuitous circumstances in the society of *Bath* than I have ever
witnessed elsewhere.[1]

She found also that she still had acquaintances in the city—
people she had known 'an hundred years ago' when she had
'spent 3 months at Bath with the *ci-devant* Mrs. Thrale & the

---

[1] Diary MSS. (Berg), 1818; letters (Barrett) from FBA to Princess Elizabeth,
Mrs. Locke, Lady Keith, members of the Burney family, and others, occasionally
with the replies, copied in General d'Arblay's hand into a Letter Book, 1815–16.
Also 2 A.L.S. (PML) to JB, 22 Nov. 1816, 19 Jan. 1817; A.L.S. (Osborn) to CB,
Jr., 22 Nov. 1815.

present Lady Keith'.[1] She wrote sportively to Princess Elizabeth about

4 gentle Females, who, even in those ancient days were already yclept votaries of Diana, yet who, in this City of Elysia are kept in perfect preservation: & Mrs. Holroyd, Mrs. Francis, Mrs. Harriet Bowdler, & Mrs. Benson, all 4 renowned not alone for *Bluism* and Dianism, but with equal truth, & greater merit, for high principles & active charity. The good & learned Dr. Harrington, too, a friend, contemporary, & correspondent of my late honoured Father, still mixes, I am told with the World to hear Musick & meet familiar connections, and therefore, as your R.H. will perceive, *mes liaisons,* when I *come out* will not begin, at least, precisely among Hebes & Ganymedes! & such examples will save me, it is to be hoped, from any dangerous errors through giddiness![1]

In Bath also in the autumn of 1815 was Mrs. Thrale-Piozzi herself, and, though Fanny had not seen her for nearly thirty years, on her first round of visits she ventured to call. Mrs. Piozzi received her in a small back room.

She was in mourning, & stood up, stiff, silent, & with an air of petrifying coldness—I was moved, I own, strongly moved at her sight, by the remembrance of all her former fondness . . . but though my first impulse was ready to throw me into her arms, her frigid mien & manner soon chilled every feeling, & restored me to a composure on a par with her own. A few stammering words & embarrassed attempts at discourse, soon therefore were superseded by conversation on general subjects, tame, common, & uninteresting. None of her native spirits broke forth, nothing that bordered upon gaiety, much less upon satyre, not a sally, not a repartee escaped her. . . . I stayed a full hour; but there was no brightening up on her side, though I tried that there should be on mine.

I have never seen her since! though she resides not above 20 houses in a straight line from my dwelling. She has called, however, & I have returned her call, but we were both absent from our homes.[1]

Though Fanny made, as she said, 'every possible overture', two years passed before another meeting took place, and then on November 17, 1817, Fanny wrote excitedly to Lady Keith, 'I have something to communicate, curious, interesting, & wonderful'. This was a second call on Mrs. Piozzi.

At the sound of my name, she came hastily from her Boudoir to receive me in the *grand sallon*, I was, as I always am, from a con-

[1] See p. 383, n. 1.

trariety of conflicting recollections, much removed from being natural, or at my ease—but she was so embarrassed so agitated, she could not utter a word, but through the difficulty of respiration that belongs to an asthma.[1]

After the difficult beginning each seemed to recover.

She took me to her Boudoir, seated me on the sofa, fetched me a hand screen, & entered into a most spirited conversation, with all her old facility, & pleasantry, & singularity. I exerted myself in my turn, to the utmost, to let her see '*I feared no colours*', & you would have been much amused . . . for we talked, both of us, in Dr. Johnson's phrase '*our best*' but entirely as two strangers, who had no sort of knowledge or care for each other, but were willing each to fling & to accept the gauntlet, *pour faire la belle conversation*. She interrogated me concerning France under B—, I made several enquiries of the state of Italy previous to the Revolution. My anecdotes, which could not help being new to her, as they were chiefly personal, seemed to excite all her curiosity; hers, which were recounted in her characteristic & most peculiarly entertaining manner, were to me highly interesting: yet was all far more like a dialogue, in some old Grammar between una Italiana & une Française, than like the talk of two old friends. . . . Nevertheless, I was so pleased to find again her old gaiety & fertility & originality that I forgot both her dinner & my own, till it grew suddenly darkish, & I hastily rose to be gone, involuntarily exclaiming:

'Heavens how late it must be! they'll think me lost at home— but how could I help it!'

I was flying off; but in a tone changed from all its light merriment, with a sound of affection, she cried:

'Thank you—and God bless you!'

Much surprised, & instantly touched, I turned back, & held out my hand. She gave me hers, & each hand again pressed the other.

'God bless you! she again & still more impressively cried, 'and I thank you!'

Can you wonder—I immediately embraced her; and then hurried away, while she uttered 'I shall wait upon you, & hope soon to see you again!'[1]

A model conversation between 'una Italiana & une Française' as it might be set in an 'old Grammar' was a far cry from the satiric wit and sentiment of the earlier years, but Madame

---

[1] See p. 383, n. 1.

d'Arblay interpreted the last scene as a reconciliation and thought that it stood to the end.[1]

Friends and relatives of the d'Arblays had expected that M. d'Arblay, who had been faithful to the monarchy through its long adversities, would now be rewarded by appropriate promotions and emoluments. At Ghent Louis XVIII had conferred on him the title of *comte*[2] and, in a *brevet de retraite*, raised his military rank to that of Lieutenant-General with a *traitement* of 4,000 francs.[3] The recognition was 'truly cheering to his loyal heart', but so depleted was the French treasury that the payment of even this modest pension was very uncertain. The d'Arblays had not even the security of the scant half-pay.

The expensive apartments that Fanny's niece Maria Bourdois had engaged in Rivers Street had, therefore, to be relinquished. There was the usual difficulty of finding suitable lodgings at a reasonable price, but the d'Arblays finally settled at 23 Great Stanhope Street. This was a location 'free from the bleak of the Hills, the currents of sharp air in the avenues, & the oppressive damps of the Baths'.[3] It was near the Norfolk Crescent and from the back windows of the house there were beautiful views of the hills. Here the d'Arblays remained for almost three years, and these years saw the close of their life together.

Fanny now had some leisure for letter-writing, and the General copied much of the correspondence on critical family affairs or that with eminent personages into a Letter Book.[3] In addition Fanny hoped for an opportunity to resume work begun in Lower Sloane Street after Dr. Burney's death—an edition of his correspondence, that is, of the letters that he had received, for she did not at that time have many of his own and she did not learn until many years later that she could not publish the letters sent to him without the permission of their writers. Before the close of 1815 the 'immense hoard of papers: 3 trunks full, chiefly MSS. & Letters of my dearest Father', had followed from Calais, where they had been left with other baggage until the d'Arblays should have settled for the winter.[2]

---

[1] But see Mrs. Piozzi's comment on this meeting, Clifford, p. 447. Also Lady Keith's comment, Letter Book, above. Also 2 A.L.S. (JRL) from MF to HLTP, 11 Nov. 1815, Aug. 1816.

[2] 2 A.L. (Berg) from FBA to EBB, 1 July 1815, 1 Feb. 1819.

[3] See p. 383, n. 1.

The General was still suffering from his wounds. In the spring Fanny described him as 'always lame, & . . . terribly susceptible of pain & uneasiness at every false or hasty step, & at any uneven ground'.[1] He had not yet agreed to live permanently in England, but on March 30 Fanny wrote hopefully to Alex that Bath promised to agree with his father. 'When he hears *tout va bien* from you, I see his *mind* settle, as well as his consent, to sojourn ultimately in the country in which you will best succeed.'[2] On April 5 her voice took on a note of warning: 'but should you not take such a degree as to enable you to procure Honour & Independence in this country, however tardily, your Father will not relinquish *his own*. Who would ask him? Work, then, my Alex, work—it would break my heart to be separated from *either* of you!'[2]

In the spring the d'Arblays had had joint plans for a summer and autumn in Paris and Joigny, but in the end Fanny thought it necessary to remain with Alex. On August 7, when M. d'Arblay had recovered health and strength for travelling, he set out alone for France.

Alex was now twenty-one years old and in the summer of 1816 his parents, in their different ways, devoted more thought than usual to his future. His mother, with her uncompromising candour, honesty, and realism, her knowledge of youth and of the world, was a relentless judge. Her anxiety for his welfare made her argus-eyed. What worried her was his feverish tendency to work night and day over whatever mental pursuit had caught his fancy and then to lapse into apathy before the assigned tasks were begun. He was without vices, she thought, nor did he run into extravagance or dissipation, being on the contrary a 'most contented creature' with whatever came his way. An incident related by Charlotte Barrett reveals his extraordinary memory, his literary or poetical bent, and his characteristic occupation and manner. 'How do you think I have spent this morning?' he had asked his cousin.

'Not in mathematics, as you ought, I dare say,' answered I; 'No,' said he, 'I have been translating into french verse Pope's lines on the death of an Unfortunate Lady.'—I told him I did not quite

---

[1] 2 A.L.S. (Berg) from FBA to CBFB, 15–24 May 1816, 17 May 1817; Diary MSS. (Berg), p. 6710.

[2] Four letters (Berg) from FBA to AA, 30 Mar., 5 Apr. 1816, 2, 23 May 1817.

remember the English—'Well then' said Alec, in his simple way, 'I had better tell you the English first' so he began, repeated the whole of that long poem most beautifully, & then, *repeated* it again in french, with every line so exactly similar in expression, & thought, & elegance, that I was lost in astonishment & real admiration though I was too cunning to tell him so, because I knew that he ought to have been poking at his mathematics.[1]

In the summer Madame d'Arblay made an effort to introduce her son into society, delighted at last to see him in dancing-pumps, 'his hair fresh cropt & curled' by the perruquier, and, in general, 'more dress & tidying (greatly wanted) and . . . less neglect of *the graces*'.

Malgré ses distractions, et ses gaucheries, il plaît dans ce monde de Bath d'une manière inconcevable. Son *air* de modestie, ou l'idée étudié répandue de ses talens, lui vaut des succès que l'usage du monde même, à son age, et en Angleterre ne lui vaudra . . .[2]

All this was the entrance of the young man into the world, but above all this she was determined that for that summer at least he should not waste his strength and faculties on mathematics, poetry, and chess. On August 8, at her insistence, he was working at Newton and 'sighing & moaning as if digging his own Grave!' By September 18 he had conquered some of the difficulties: '*C'est bien vrai que c'était un grand Homme, ce Newton!*' 'He gives me a new sense.'[2] Later Fanny learned it was only what Alex had accomplished at Bath in the summer of 1816, when, under her watchful eye, he had gone through Newton 'alone & unaided', that later made it possible for him to become a wrangler.[2] By September 30 she had got him on the right road. If only 'with his really mathematical head' he had condescended to do some of this work before, he might have become a senior wrangler. 'At present', she told James, 'he is of opinion, he shall only be in the Gulph!!' Then she drew a weary analogy from James's own work, *The History of the Buccaneers*: 'O la! it takes as long a time now a days to make a Boy a man as to bake porcelain in one of your Philippine Islands—less than 50 years won't do for either!'[3] To be a *high*

---

[1] A.L. (Barrett) from Charlotte Barrett to FBA, Nov. 1815.
[2] 7 A.L.S. (Berg) from FBA to M. d'A, 6–13 Aug., 18, 22 Sept. 1816, 10–16, 18 July, 1 Aug., 2–6 Aug. 1817.
[3] A.L. (PML) from FBA to JB, 30 Sept. 1816.

wrangler was then thought out of the question; yet 'to be *any* Wrangler, was an Honour all over the Kingdom, & an Honour for life; as well as a road to a *fellowship*, which, also, has *no other*'.[1]

Meanwhile in France General d'Arblay also attempted to work out his son's destiny but by a means less arduous, more pleasant, and more remunerative than the courses Fanny had set through honours at the university. His solution was an *arranged marriage*, but this, fortunately or unfortunately, Fanny could not approve. M. d'Arblay had seen in the daughter of one of his old friends an exquisitely beautiful and accomplished young lady of splendid fortune who would be the ideal wife for Alex and a *belle fille* who, he was precipitately certain, must please even the designer of Evelina and Cecilia.[2] So enraptured was he with his plan that he divulged it to the parents concerned before Fanny had had time to express her opinion. The parents had happily concurred and the nuptial negotiations were proceeding apace.

Madame d'Arblay's approval was not, however, so easily obtained. There was first of all her amazement that M. d'Arblay should have returned to *l'ancien régime* in a matter upon which she had so often heard him condemn it. She agreed to guard the secret from Alex; but she knew that he would be quite indignant at any interference with his '*seeing, selecting, chusing, wholly* for himself'. 'No *Englishman*, he always says, would bear to be treated so like a baby!' There was secondly her scepticism about the naturalness or unaffectedness of the young lady. Beauty, accomplishments, resplendent attractions, and even solid principles 'from the high hereditary virtue which ought to run in her veins', Fanny could grant, but if she were *natural and simple*, where was that nature, that simplicity concealed when they saw her in 1802? Did M. d'Arblay not remember her pirouetting before a full-length mirror in a room full of company '*comme une liliputienne aux airs de princesse*'? 'Simple and natural characters [could become] coquettes & *des petites maîtresses*', but of the reverse Fanny had never heard. And Dr. Marchmont proposed no harder tests for Camilla than Madame d'Arblay for '*la petite Augustine*'.

Let us see this young lady in *public* as well as in *private*, ere we risk

[1] See p. 388, n. 2.
[2] 3 A.L.S. (Berg) from M. d'A to FBA, 20 Sept., 12 Oct. 1816, 16 June 1817.

fixing unalterably the fate of our Alexander: let us see her in mixt society, with *young men*, as well as with her Father's *old Friends*, & with *young women*, at the same time; for to judge whether there is any lurking coquetry there must be *competition*.[1]

Further objections were educed from Alex's youth and in-experience, for though, like M. d'Arblay, she

would gladly save a man, as well as a woman, that *savoir vivre* that leads to vice, fraud, or licentiousness, I yet think no man fit to become a Husband, & a Father, in a world so full of vicissitudes, who has himself no more experience or wisdom than the wife & children of whom he should be the Guide & Guardian.[1]

She could not believe further that Alex was adapted to a military life or that he could live happily as a civilian with the girl's parents. Fanny had no doubt that a beauty such as her husband described would have its influence, as beauty everywhere had. 'But could any permanent amendment ensue, from working upon his errors only through his passions? Is it not to be feared that as *they*, the passions, subside, the errors would all peep up again?' In short, Fanny would not 'excite in him any passion whatever, not even of virtuous love', until he had taken his degree, seen something of the world, and reached maturity.

The General wrote dolorously that she had failed to meet his plan with any *concours* or *rapprochement*, but though Fanny could not yield she was stricken with compunction.

With a trembling heart I write, for fearful is the ground upon which I move while I am still ignorant in what I so displeased & afflicted you. Ah, mon ami, how am I grieved to have done either![1]

On November 20 M. d'Arblay had written from Dover that he was at last in England. Fanny had been expecting him ever since his letter of October 31. 'Judge, therefore, what those winds & storms have made me endure! I have almost lost my Eye sight from a nervous seizure, I believe, across the forehead.' She is still 'trembling all over with the long *attente* & affright'. Even Alex had noticed all this and had just then called out: '*Plus de séparations, maman! cela vous tua!*'[1]

In September, 1816, Esther and Fanny had begun a corre-spondence on a 'sacred business', a memorial or monument to

---

[1] Five letters (Berg) from FBA to M. d'A, 28 Sept., 4, 20, 27–29 Oct., 21 Nov. 1816. Also *Diary*, vi. 300–4.

their father.[1] The matter had originated, quite appropriately, with the residuary legatees, but Fanny thought general propriety would direct them to apply to James for counsel. His angry withdrawal from the executorship, however, threw all the action on Charles, to whom with Esther's permission Fanny undertook to write. 'And I promise that, on my part, I shall make no scruple against any offer that may ensue. *My* scruples will all flow in another channel!' To her great joy Charles soon discovered that there was some possibility of placing the memorial in Westminster Abbey and that, in spite of 'the sadness of his poverty', he would pay one-third of the 'abbey exaction'.[1] There were then the usual family discussions, and so many papers that Fanny had to sit down 'like a clerk in office' before she could calculate the expenses (about £20 each), which Charles carried to that '*Cormorant*', the Abbey.[2] Fanny hoped that the design would include a harp, in itself an epitaph—and that the inscription would be in Latin and written, of course, by Charles.[1] Charles, however, said that, according to epigraphic etiquette, Latin would be inappropriate for his father, who had not attended either of the universities, who had written in the vernacular, and who was eminent not as a scholar (that is, a classicist) but as an historian. Charles thought that the epitaph should be in English, and that Fanny should write it. 'I must do the best I can; which, also, shall be the simplest.'[1]

When, however, the epitaph was circulated, few were pleased with the effort. Marianne Francis, who from association with Arthur Young and the Wilberforces was growing more deeply religious every day, thought the lines about dear Grandpapa too worldly, and most of the family shared her opinion.[3] They thought, for instance, that some prayerful sentiment about the future life would be more fitting than praise of Dr. Burney's conversational powers. Marianne worried over the rationalistic souls in her family: 'In what state of mind Dr. Burney died, I know not. I wish it may be like his grandson [Norbury

---

[1] Seven letters (Berg) from FBA to EBB, 9 Sept., 8, 12, 25 Oct. 1816, 22 Feb., 28 Apr., 14 July 1817; 2 A.L.S. (Berg) from CB, Jr., to FBA, 11 Oct. 1816, 12 June 1817; A.L.S. (in the possession of Dr. Percy A. Scholes) to FBA, 19 Feb. 1817.

[2] A.L. (Berg) from FBA to CB, Jr., 24 Feb. 1817. Also Scholes, ii. 274–5.

[3] 2 A.L.S. (Barrett) from Charlotte Barrett to Arthur Young, 27 Dec. 1816, 9 Apr. 1817.

Phillips], who is now, I doubt not, among the angelic Hosts, singing praises to God.'[1] Madame d'Arblay, who had as firm a belief as Marianne in the life everlasting, would have been quite sure that her father had joined the great choirs and concerts above, and she could have argued the case of rational piety and the efficacy of charity and good works against 'enthusiasm' and the personal or 'inspired' intimations of immortality. All this, however, should not enter into the controversy over the inscription, which, as Fanny pointed out, was not for a tombstone to be placed over the Doctor's mortal remains in the Chelsea Churchyard, where the lines would properly have a religious tendency, but for a memorial tablet to be erected in the Abbey, where they were expected to explain his claims to fame in this world rather than his hopes for heaven.[2] Both Charlotte and James had written 'honest expostulation', and Charles also must have made some demur, for a part of Fanny's defence is extant in letters to him.[2] 'The *Tablet for Fame,* & the *Prayer for Salvation,* are certainly two things. One is for celebrity, in Westminster Abbey: the other is for Devotion, in the church yard Tomb stone.' They had set her 'to deliberate so narrowly & minutely' by their 'fears & representations' that she now felt very clear in that matter. With a little reflection she had been able to bring to her support no less an authority than Dr. Johnson, who had not cavilled with 'the omission of the sacred termination' in Pope's memorial in the Abbey. 'Nor has he given it himself to Dr. Goldsmith, who was *buried* at the Temple!!'[2] The barrage of family expostulation probably effected some revisions. The phrase about the Doctor's conversational powers, for instance, seems to have disappeared, and Fanny's lines on her father were at length put in enduring stone in the Abbey.[3]

Late in the year 1816, the authorities at Cambridge found it necessary to inform the d'Arblays that unless Alex intended to proceed to a medical degree he ought not to hold the Tancred Studentship at Caius for the ensuing term.[4] Fanny wrote frantic letters, as usual, to the resourceful Charles, but Charles also, as she said later, had comprehended the exact terms of the

---

[1] A.L.S. (JRL) from MF to HLTP, 13 Apr. 1814.
[2] Seven letters (Berg) from FBA to CB, Jr., 7 Nov. 1816, 12, 16, 23 Mar., 12 Apr., 3–6 May, 3 June 1817; A.L. (Barrett) to the Duchesse d'Hurst, n.d.
[3] See p. 391, n. 2.   [4] See p. 383, n. 1.

studentship no more clearly than she had. In a letter dated November 30, 1816, Fanny explained to the Master of Caius that such was Alex's turn for mathematics that his parents could not 'make him *le médicin malgré lui*' and that he must, therefore, resign the Tancred.[1] The loss, £120, was no little matter to the d'Arblays, though, as Fanny wrote to one of the Princesses, she was not now 'in the same helpless & even affrighted state as when I escaped with him from the Russian conscription', and never, of course, would she forget the Queen's kindness in that emergency.[2]

In all these deliberations with Charles and the college dons, Alex's omissions and irregularities were again fully reviewed. He was transferred, none the less with great kindness, to Christ's, and left Bath with 'a solemn determination to conquer his antipathy to the John Trot plodding path'.[1] This time, apparently, he was able to keep some of his resolves and on March 7 defended his act with great brilliancy. He described the vicissitudes of the debate in an account which the General copied into the Letter Book with meticulous care. Only Alex's welfare had made the father consent to live in England and endure the loss of friends and country, and well it was that some such results should occasionally have repaid that sacrifice.

In the summer the General had been able to collect some arrears in pay, and but for this, Fanny said, the '*great pull*' of Alex's expenses at the University, his father's Paris excursion, and the monument would have 'utterly *lamed* us'.[1] In the winter the General was seriously ill with jaundice, and Fanny remained for the most part at home—a contented and devoted nurse. Mrs. Locke's visit of that year to Bath and her daily visits to the d'Arblays brought back old times and renewed a friendship for life.[3]

In the spring, when the General again went to France, Fanny once more emerged for a round of calls and visits. A view of the d'Arblays as others saw them in the year 1817 is provided in a letter from Mrs. Whalley of Bath to her husband:

Since I wrote last, I have had the pleasure of a visit from Madame

---

[1] Barrett. Also A.L.S. (Berg) from FBA to EBB, 22 Feb. 1817; A.L. (Berg) to CB, Jr., 24 Feb. 1817; a letter (Letter Book, Barrett) to George Cambridge, 10 Mar. 1817; A.L.S. (JRL) from MF to HLTP, 1 May 1817.
[2] See p. 383, n. 1.　　　　　　　　　　　　　　　　[3] See p. 391, n. 1.

d'Arblay. Indisposition in her family, and on my part, had prevented our meeting before. At last she came alone, and a hard rain kept her for an hour and a half. She was extremely entertaining, and, I think, very amiable in her manners. She talked a great deal of Madame de Staël, and on many other amusing subjects. I understand she has given up writing romances, but is now engaged in arranging a variety of papers which old Dr. Burney left, chiefly consisting of his correspondence with literary characters of his time. But it will be two years at least before this mass can be assorted and prepared for the press. General D'Arblay I have never seen. Mrs. Holroyd tells me, that he has been very handsome, and is very clever. The poor man is now a miserable object with the jaundice; and I fear they are far from comfortable in their circumstances, and are living with the greatest economy, to enable them to support their son genteelly at the University.[1]

The correspondence of 1817 between members of Charlotte's family, especially the letters of Charlotte Barrett and Marianne Francis to Arthur Young, was filled with references to their half-brother Ralph (Dolph) Broome, who in spite of medical help, frequent changes of air, and Charlotte's devoted and self-sacrificial care, was almost certainly dying of consumption.[2] His doctor at Richmond had prescribed another change of air—this time that of Devonshire or Cornwall—and in the journey westward with the invalid, the family stopped at Bath.

The two Charlottes had taken rooms at 17 Great Stanhope Street to be near Aunt d'Arblay. Fanny welcomed them with her usual 'active kindness', and what happened there can best be told in her own words as they stand in letters to Esther, Charles, and James—letters (written, as she said, with lightning speed) that will afford the characteristic tenor, manner, and tone of the later family correspondence. What she had to do was to acquaint them with the departure of 'poor dear Ralph'.[3]

What an abrupt end to cares—attentions—tenderness—privations—exertions impossible to be exceeded! . . .

They arrived at Bath on Wednesday Evening. They took 5 Days to come hither from Richmond, Making only one stage a Day. His

[1] Printed, *Diary*, vi. 304.   [2] See p. 393, n. 1.
[3] See letters (Berg) from FBA to EBB, AA, CB, Jr., CBFB, 28 Apr., 2, 3 May and 2 June 1817, respectively. Also A.L.S. (PML) to JB, 28 Apr. 1817; 6 A.L.S. (Barrett) from Charlotte Barrett to Arthur Young, 10 Feb.–26 May 1817; 7 A.L.S. (Barrett) from MF to the same, 6 Jan.–16 Apr. 1817. Robert Southey's epitaph for the youth is on a tablet in Wolcot Church, Bath.

reduced state & inexpressible weakness leaving no other way of
travelling possible. I saw him on Thursday, in his Bed, & in a state
of suffering the most affecting. He told me he was so used to illness
that he did not mind it, except for his *breath*; but that that was so
bad, he could not bear it.—poor dear fellow! his groans & moanings
are still in my Ears! yet on Friday he was better—& suddenly rose
& began to dress himself!—which he had not done for a long time.
I was never so surprised as to find him in the Drawing room, seated
on the sofa! . . . Saturday, however, he kept his Bed all day—& was
very ill indeed. . . .

[Saturday night] he rambled a good deal—& has done for this
great while—but in no manner more alarming than usual. In the
morning, however, the Nurse thought him so wonderfully quiet,
that she leant over to examine him—& saw he was no more! How
easy such an End! not a sigh marked it! . . .

Our excellent sister supports it beyond all my hopes or even ideas.
She thinks him spared a life of continual illness & pain, & is persuaded Heaven has taken him in pity—but though such is her
resignation she has at times great difficulty to struggle on with her
composure. . . .

The poor Mourner sends you her kindest Love, certain of your
sympathy—adieu, my dearest Esther. I write like lightning, I have
so many Letters to add & wished to let you as much as possible into
the state of the case, knowing well your tender feeling for distress such
as this.[1]

Fanny spent every other hour of the day with her sister.

She accepts all we can do with gentleness & a sort of pleasure. . . .
Indeed, I believe that if she had been spared this blow, & kept her
dear Boy, *we* should have lost *her*! for she is almost worn out with
nursing & solicitude.[1]

As Charlotte herself later said, her controlled resignation was
a severe tax on her nerves and health. It was a sin, her religious
daughters told her, to weep or repine, for Dolph, 'the odd
original boy', the joy of her heart, was in Heaven. Fanny could
only marvel at her patient fortitude.[1]

With the candour and confidence characteristic of her correspondence with her sisters Fanny described her dilemmas
and difficulties, and how again, in the summer of 1817, she
had to choose between France and England, husband and son.

[1] See p. 394, n. 3.

M. d'Arblay would be paid only part of his 'pitiful pension' (specifically, one-third of his half-pay) unless he went to receive it on the spot, and his full pay, General as he was, was less than that of an English captain. Fanny longed to accompany him, but on the other hand there was Alexander, who in the next term was to come up for his final examination at Cambridge. Finally the d'Arblays disconsolately agreed that any sacrifice was preferable to leaving Alex to his own devices at such a critical time, and the General, 'whose affairs absolutely force him to France, will go thither, once more, alone'.[1] The plan was that Alex should go with a tutor, Mr. Jacob, and eight or ten Cantabs to Lyme, though by a later decision to Ilfracombe, and Fanny was to go along also to look after his health, prevent games of chess, insist on proper relaxation, exercise, and food, and above all to rouse him early in the morning to read the prescribed texts and authors.

On June 12 the General left Bath intending to spend a day or two with his son, and Fanny warned Alex: 'Let not your excellent Padre arrive at *Cambridge*, to give you his benediction before his excursion, & *there* find you relaxing from all that can pay his various sacrifices!'[2] The General was 'all disposed to hope, affection, & fair rosy thoughts' where Alex was concerned, resting on the opinion that in the end his son would work out a solution in his own way. The gentleness of the General's disposition emerged in almost every line he wrote, though his life and letters were now increasingly tinged with melancholy, the fault he had confessed to Fanny before his wedding-day. From Dover he wrote dolorously about a hard journey and his last wretched evening in England when Alex, whom he expected, did not appear. I have spoken to Alex, Fanny replied,

in the bitterness of my grief that he had caused you such a night, & been able to stay away from you at such a period. He looked dismayed, but *stunned*, rather than culpable.[3]

He confessed that chess had kept him, but since the General

---

[1] A.L.S. (Berg) from FBA to CBFB, 17 May 1817; A.L. (Berg) to AA, 30 May 1817; draft of A.L. (Barrett) to Princess Elizabeth, n.d., and A.L.S. (Barrett) from Charlotte Barrett to Arthur Young, 3 July 1817.

[2] See p. 387, n. 2.

[3] Letters (Berg) from FBA to M. d'A, 12, 14–18 June, 10–16, 18–27 July 1817; A.L.S. (Berg) from AA to M. d'A, 20 June 1817.

had given him his hand in parting he had thought the visit over. Though Fanny had always consoled herself that Alex had not a vice in the world, chess was a vice, she maintained, if it led him to neglect his duties. Confounded, Alex offered 'the only peace offering & reparation in his power', that of 'positively renouncing chess either as a play or a study, till after he has taken his Degree'. 'For the world', added Fanny craftily, 'do not offer him any composition! he would catch at it instantly.'[1] She knew that it was not the time lost in play that did the mischief, but replaying the game by night and considering how he might have moved more scientifically. Mathematical combinations haunted his sleep, robbed him of rest, and made it impossible for him to rise for the day's assignments. And then there was no tearing him from the pursuit he had in hand, whether it be '*La Place*, or *Kean, La Grange*, or *Lord Byron*', or, as at that very moment, a work in algebra, though he owned it 'utterly useless to his Examination!'[1]

On July 1 young d'Arblay and his mother arrived at Ilfracombe. At first they had rooms near the quay, where she could observe ships with their crews at the dock and the activity of the waterside.[2] Soon, however, odours 'not the most salubrious' forced them to seek a new lodging. This also had a view of the sea, which Fanny wished to keep 'in presence, both for its grand style of prospect, & its bracing air'.[3] She thought constantly of a letter that the General had sent to her from Calais: '*La mer, ma chère Fanny, est entre nous, mais bientôt je l'espère nous serons réunis, et d'ailleurs rien ne sera jamais entre nos cœurs —j'en jure par le mien.*'[4] The new quarters were rented from a shoemaker, Mr. Ramsay, a gentle-mannered man, 'but a martyr to frequent acute rheumatic pains, from working—ah, mon ami! late & in bad weather in his Garden!'[3] Fanny listened to his story and thought of its analogue. 'His garden would delight you', she wrote; 'Peas & Beans are intermingled with Roses & Lillies . . . French Beans with Jessamine.'[3] The eldest daughter, Elizabeth, was very handsome with 'the air, manner, voice & speech of one in much higher life'. The second daughter, Mary, was 'gay,

---

[1] See p. 396, n. 3.   [2] *Diary*, vi. 312–70.

[3] Seven letters (Berg) from FBA to M. d'A, 10–16, 18–27 July, 2–7, 8–15, 16–23, 25–31 Aug., 22 Sept. 1817; A.L. (Berg) to EBB, 14 July 1817.

[4] A.L.S. (Berg) from M. d'A to FBA, 16 June 1817. Quoted back in the reply (Berg), 18–27 July 1817.

wild, prating, frolicsome, good-humoured, officious, service-able, & light-hearted', and Madame d'Arblay sometimes took the trouble to transcribe her awkward, unlearned, but good-natured colloquies.[1] Mary was completely captivated by the Burneyan charm, and at a later time Elizabeth Ramsay followed Madame d'Arblay to London, remained with her in the early years of her widowhood, and was willing to remain her companion for life.

Fanny also made fast friends with Alex's tutor Mr. Jacob, 'a handsome, elegant, and highly-cultivated young man',[2] a senior wrangler, whose industry and self-denial she wished Alex would emulate. Alex, however, found him inimitable, but thought how much his father would dote on the tutor 'and how Jacob would like *him*!' 'How the contrast might strike you,' Fanny wrote to her husband, 'he never considers, for he is more truly free from any sensation of Envy than I ever saw yet any human Being.'[2]

Fanny wished to know above all things whether Alex had irretrievably trifled away all possibility of high honours, and Jacob reluctantly confessed that he had. Alex, who might have been *anything*, 'was not *now* in a condition to become a *senior optimist*', and the young tutor, touched perhaps by her anxiety and kindness or won by a manner that had always inspired confidence and confidences, gradually divulged the Cambridge history in full. Alex's neglect of his work exceeded all description! He had worked once for a mathematical prize; a second time for his *act*, 'on which occasion *no one could have done better*'; and a third time at Bath with his mother, when he had studied Newton. After these exertions he stopped short and did 'literally Nothing, though every prospect was fair before him!' While he had good and useful friends among a group of wranglers, he also consorted with an idle set, who

play upon his credulous & inconceivable inexperience, & entice him to *chess* for whole days, & to walks that never end, & to loitering, & poetry, & declamation, & sitting up at night though only to *recite*, never for any other dissipation.[2]

Alex often declaimed for his mother's benefit, for among his gifts was a beautiful and sonorous voice. She knew, however,

that poetry and declamation were as useless as French mathematics or chess for his degree and she had herself observed his
irregular and feverish habits, how he

would never leave off reciting till he had finished a whole poem, or
whole play—never partake of any meal; but go on with whatever
he is about till he feel gnawn with hunger . . . never go to Bed, till
his burnt out candles leave him suddenly in the dark! & then, his
clothes hardly taken off, & no night cap on his head, he rolls himself between the Bedcloaths, falls into a quick sleep of fatigue; but
quickly awakens from it, cold, shivering, or feverish, & recovers it no
more till, next morning when restored & gentle perspiration quiets
his nerves, & attracts back repose—but so late, that to awaken him
disorders him both in frame & in mind![1]

Fanny set herself to correct all this. She called her son at six in
the morning, remained at his elbow in the pleasant drawing-
room at Ilfracombe with the sea in view, saw to it that he ate
when meals were served, that he got exercise in long rambles
over the bleak hills or the precipitous shoreline, and that he
relaxed over light reading rather than over his favourite studies,
which proved more engrossing, absorbing, and exhausting than
those prescribed. She spent restless nights with worried thoughts
of Paris, of Alex, and of the effort to rise promptly at six o'clock.
The work yet to be done was 'inconceivable', and Alex's groans
at the drudgery were proportionate to it.

The son was, in short, as oblivious of worldly success (or the
means to it) as his father, as absent-minded and individualistic
as his mother, with something of the same absorbed mental
preoccupation that had produced *Evelina*. He was, in a way,
as Fanny observed, a caricature of both parents.[2]

Yet Alex himself could hardly have been more heedless than
his mother when, gathering curious pebbles for the General's
geological collection, her mind on Paris and his return, she
allowed herself to be imprisoned by the incoming evening tide
in the furthermost recess or cavern of the Wildersmouth, the
precipitous sides and end of which allowed neither ascent nor
egress except at low tide by the sands at the mouth. The printed
diaries include a graphic account of her discovery of her predicament (how the dog Diane discovered it first and tried to coax,

---

[1] See p. 397, n. 3.
[2] A.L.S. (Barrett) from FBA to Charlotte Barrett, 16 May 1816.

then to pull her mistress along the sands), their frantic search for an exit, Fanny's attempt to scale the precipices, and finally her discovery of a slaty island with a tuft of green grass on top indicating a place of safety above tide-water. Meanwhile a rising storm 'brought forward the billows with augmented noise and violence'. The asylum lessened, and, urged on by the waves behind, she began to climb to the grass.

My hands were wounded, my knees were bruised, and my feet were cut; for I could only scramble up by clinging to the rock on *all fours.*[1]

Having reached about two-thirds of the height of her rock, she could climb no farther.

All above was so sharp and perpendicular that neither hand nor foot could touch it without being wounded. My head, however, was nearly on a level with the tuft of grass, and my elevation from the sands was very considerable.[1]

She must remain standing, for the slabs were too slanting to sit upon, and from her precarious foothold on the slaty slope she tried with her near-sighted glass to see if the waters were abating. To her horror she saw two rocks protruding from the sea disappear. The tide was then rising, and she watched now for a vessel or fishing-boat, intending to signal with her parasol.

All was vacant and vast! I was wholly alone—wholly isolated. I feared to turn my head lest I should become giddy, and lose my balance.[1]

The dog, shivering with fright, tried to reach the sloping slab but slipped backwards instead of forwards. Fanny, watching for a propitious time, holding on with one hand and balancing with one foot above the watery depths, hooked the handle of her parasol in the dog's collar, hauled her forcibly across the slippery slab, and deposited her at her feet (or rather foot, for she had found a place for only one). The effort to stroke and comfort the dog took her attention momentarily from the sea. Soon, however, the waves began to break on the rock, foaming on to meet on the farther side, and she prayed to Heaven to save her from being washed off the pinnacle and drowned in the sea.

[1] See p. 397, n. 2.

The next waves reached to the uppermost end of my chamber, which was now all sea, save the small rock upon which I was mounted! . . . The wind roared around me, pushing on the waves with a frothy velocity that, to a bystander, not to an inmate amidst them, would have been beautiful. . . . A wave, at length, more stupendous than any which had preceded it, dashed against my rock as if enraged at an interception of its progress, and rushed on to the extremity of this savage chamber, with foaming impetuosity. This moment I believed to be my last of mortality! but a moment only it was; for scarcely had I time, with all the rapidity of concentrated thought, to recommend myself, my husband, and my poor Alexander, humbly but fervently to the mercy of the Almighty, when the celestial joy broke in upon me of perceiving that this wave, which had bounded forward with such fury, was the last of the rising tide![1]

She had now only to wait a few hours till the waters receded, baring the sands at the mouth of the cavern. The sunset was resplendent. Then came darkness and a drizzle, but by a pale light reflected from the waters she at length discerned human figures on the promontories enclosing the cove. Lanterns appeared on the ridges and the wild cliff became peopled with figures. When the tide had fallen sufficiently an old seaman made his way down some precipitous path with a lantern in his hand and Alexander close at his heels. Fanny was glad of the lantern and the escorts, for she did not know how she could have groped her way in the dark 'out of this terrible Wildersmouth'.

A few days later an equinoctial gale washed over the grassy tufts and levelled her stony pyramid. Most of it then lay a mere drift of rocks on the floor of the roofless cavern. The place looked so different that she asked a seaman to identify it for her positively. This he did, adding calmly 'that two days later I could not have been saved from the waves'.[1]

On October 5 Madame d'Arblay and her son returned to Bath, and on the 8th the General wrote from Dover: 'All safe, from dear England once more; stay where you are and where, thank God, I shall soon be near you.'[2] Throughout the summer Fanny had found his letters increasingly tinged with '*la sombre mélancolie*'. The golden days of the vintage at Joigny had not after

---

[1] See p. 397, n. 2.
[2] A.L.S. (Berg) from M. d'A to FBA, 8 Oct. 1817.

all cured his ills. At Ilfracombe Fanny had read every reference
to his health or to medical consultations with wild alarm.
But for the folly of abandoning 'everything that has yet been
done, or sacrificed' for Alex's degree,[1] she would have ventured
another annihilating sea-voyage and joined her husband in
Paris. She had had uneasy apprehensions, but she was hardly
prepared for the change. 'He came in a state to occupy every
faculty of my mind and thoughts—altered—thin—weak—
depressed—full of pain—and disappointed in every expectation
of every sort that had urged his excursion!'[2] He was no longer
able to work in his garden in the Crescent Fields or to accompany Fanny on the long walks they had formerly taken in the
hills. The cruel truth was that the gentle chevalier was to die
a tortured death, but to suffer first increasing, prolonged, and
excruciating pain from an obstruction in the bowels.[3] He knew
that his case was hopeless and he prepared for death with the
nobility and heroism that had marked his life. There is a record
of the day that he tried to tell Fanny what the future must be.
She could only hear him with convulsive grief, but he walked
silently away so that she might learn that henceforth she must
bear grief alone. All this, however, is to anticipate; there was
some respite, at least, and first of all an event that galvanized
all Bath into action—a royal visit.

In a letter from Princess Elizabeth Fanny had had personal
notice of the Queen's plans. She rejoiced in the public welcome
and in the splendour of the old Queen and of the Princess. She
described the 'transport' of the public officials (including the
little mayor, not quite four feet tall), the great dinner, and then
the arrival of the express with the fatal tidings of the tragic
deaths of the Princess Charlotte in childbirth and of her child,
the direct heir to the throne.

[The Duke of Clarence] rose from table, and struck his forehead as
he read them, and then hurried out of the assembly with inexpressible trepidation and dismay. The Queen . . . the Princess . . . all
were dispersed in a moment. . . . The transition from gaiety and
exultation was really awful. What an extinction of youth and
happiness![4]

[1] See p. 397, n. 3.   [2] See p. 397, n. 2.
[3] A.L. (Berg) from AA to Charlotte Barrett, 3–4 May 1818; 3 A.L.S. (Barrett)
from Charlotte Barrett to Arthur Young, 6 Mar., 9, 18 May 1818.
[4] See p. 399, n. 2.

On November 24, however, the old Queen returned to see what the Bath waters could do for her health, and she was accompanied, as before, by the Duke of Clarence and Princess Elizabeth. 'I saw them continually', Fanny said, 'and never passed a day without calling at the Royal abode by the Queen's express permission.' With a somewhat different attitude towards royal attendance her niece confirmed her words: 'I hear that the Queen's visit to Bath put all the inhabitants in a fever of curiosity, expence, or attendance. She kept my aunt d'Arblay standing for three hours every morning during her stay & never gave her a pinch of snuff.'[1] According to Fanny's unpublished letters to Lady Keith, she had seen much more of the Princess than she or her niece (as the editor of her diary) ever publicized. Fanny had lived five years at court when the Princesses were young. The Burneyan sportiveness and gaiety attracted these qualities in others, and the Princess Elizabeth, Fanny said, had 'not only a gaiety of humour the most animating & entertaining, but a sweetness of disposition really unalterable'. She had also a 'talent for drawing, for invention, for embellishment' and 'in her fits of gayety, there bursts forth a vein of sportive ideas that would charm you, I am sure, into laughter by the hour'.[2] When later Fanny heard of the plans for her marriage, she lamented the loss to the Queen, to the royal family and, ingenuously, the loss to herself, for

she has honoured me with a confidential attachment, that has long made our conferences when tête à tête, delightful to me. I might say _sotto voce_, the same of her letters.[2]

In a more formal diary she described General d'Arblay's presentation to the Queen at one of the morning levees in the pump-room.

Ill he was! suffering, emaciated, enfeebled! But he had always spirit awake to every call; and just before Christmas, 1817, we went together, between seven and eight o'clock in the morning, in chairs, to the pump-room.

I thought I had never seen him look to such advantage. His fine brow so open, his noble countenance so expressive, his features so formed for a painter's pencil! This, too, was the last time he ever wore his military honours—his three orders of 'St. Louis,' 'the Legion

[1] A.L.S. (Barrett) from Charlotte Barrett to Arthur Young, 12 Jan. 1818.
[2] Copy of A.L. (Letter Book, Barrett) from FBA to Lady Keith, 9 Mar. 1818.

of Honour,' and 'Du Lys,' or 'De la Fidélité'; decorations which singularly became him, from his strikingly martial port and character.

The Queen . . . rose to make her round with a grace indescribable, and, to those who never witnessed it, inconceivable; for it was such as to carry off age, infirmity, sickness, diminutive stature—and to give her, in defiance of such disadvantages, a power of charming that rarely has been equalled. Her face had a variety of expression that made her features soon seem agreeable; the intonations of her voice so accorded with her words; her language was so impressive, and her manner so engaging and encouraging, that it was not possible to be the object of her attention without being both struck with her uncommon abilities and fascinated by their exertion. Such was the effect which she produced upon General d'Arblay, to whom she soon turned. Highly sensible to the honour of her distinction, he forgot his pains in his desire to manifest his gratitude;—and his own smiles—how winning they became! Her Majesty spoke of Bath, of Windsor, of the Continent; and while addressing him, her eyes turned to meet mine with a look that said, 'Now I know I am making you happy!' She asked me, archly, whether I was not fatigued by coming to the pump-room so early? and said 'Madame d'Arblay thinks I have never seen you before! but she is mistaken, for I peeped at you through the window as you passed to the terrace at Windsor.' Alas! the Queen no sooner ceased to address him than the pains he had suppressed became intolerable, and he re-treated from the circle and sunk upon a bench near the wall; he could stand no longer, and we returned home to spend the rest of the day in bodily misery! . . .

Her Majesty and the Princess soon after left Bath; just before Christmas they were gone—that Queen, that gracious Royal Mistress, from me, as it proved, gone for ever![1]

The royal visit of 1817 concluded with royal gifts—books in which the Queen had written Fanny's name with words of peculiar kindness, and a pair of silver camp candlesticks to light evening researches among her father's papers. The General 'looked over every title-page with delight, feeling as I did my-self that the gift was still more meant for him than for me—or rather, doubly, trebly for me in being calculated to be pleasing to him!'[1]

For some time Fanny had been anxious also about her

[1] Manuscript of *Narrative of the Illness & Death of General d'Arblay* (one version in the Barrett, another in the Berg Collection), partially printed, *Diary*, vi. 355-70; A.L. (Berg) from FBA to EBB, 25 Apr. 1818.

brother Charles, for his letters referred to what Fanny took as
menaces—'strange, partial, quick pains in the back of his head,
very alarming. Yet he writes in spirits, & had, thank Heaven,
the best medical help. I will hope, therefore, for the best.'[1] He
wrote joking letters to Fanny about Noddle (his head): 'yet
Noddle has been queer; not better this Noddle of Nolle'.[1] He
felt that he had diagnosed his danger more accurately than the
doctors, and unhappily he was right. On Christmas morning,
1817, he was struck down with apoplexy and lay for half an
hour on the floor of his dressing-room before he was found.
'He recovered in some measure; but the next day a 2d stroke
followed, & he continued insensible' until, on December 28,
he died. Charles's nieces had long worried over his worldliness
and the state of his soul. Now they could only trust that he had

found mercy with his Maker, through the Savior whom I believe he
served with sincerity, though not always with a 'zeal according to
knowledge'.[2]

Fanny was plagued with no such uncomfortable thoughts of his
future. The God that she and Charles served was a very rational
Being. She thought rather of his brave and arduous career, his
gay and buoyant spirit, his fame, and her own great loss.
'Every newspaper & every tongue will peal the knell.' 'Oh, my
dear Alex, I have lost a Friend the most attached, a Brother
the most partial.' 'Ties such as bound us together are not leaseholds, & cannot be renewed.' 'The loss is bitter—bitter sorrow
to me, & will remain so through my life.'[3] In a letter to George
Cambridge she told of the 'laborious work' that her brother
had recently undertaken

at the request, or rather solicitation of the Archbishop of Canterbury, with a view, as I have every reason to believe, on the part of

[1] 2 A.L.S. (in the possession of Dr. Percy A. Scholes) from CB, Jr., to FBA, 19
Feb., 20 Aug. 1817; A.L. (Berg) to FBA, 18 Sept. 1817; letters (Berg) from FBA
to CB, Jr., to EBB, and to CBFB, 21 Aug. 1813, 22 Feb. 1817, 21 Aug. 1818,
respectively; A.L.S. (Osborn) from CB, Jr., to FBA, 6 May 1816.
[2] 2 A.L.S. (Barrett) from Charlotte Barrett to Arthur Young, 12, 24 Jan. [1818];
A.L.S. (Barrett) from MF to the same, 1 Jan. 1818. Also A.L.S. (JRL) from MF
to HLTP, 23 Feb. 1818.
[3] A.L. (Berg) from FBA to CBFB, 28 Mar. 1818; A.L. (Berg) to AA, 30 Dec.
1817; a copy of A.L. (Letter Book, Barrett) to George Cambridge, 12 Feb. 1818.
The letter to Mary Port Waddington is printed in George Paston, 'A Burney
Friendship', the *Monthly Review*, viii (Sept. 1902), 148–62; ix (Oct. 1902), 136–54.

his Grace, to authorize & accelerate higher promotion in the Church; for the Arch. B^p had a partial regard for my poor Brother, of the warmest sort. This work was an examination of the *Fac Simile* of the Alexandrine MSS of the Greek scriptures which the Trustees of the British Museum have been lately engaged in Printing.[1]

'Extreme accuracy, even to the minutest particle', was necessary, the Archbishop had said, and Charles had shrunk from 'so arduous an undertaking from fears of his health'. To Mrs. Waddington Fanny spoke of the confidence that she believed Charles had had in her and of their mutual respect and affection.

His letters, full of trust, love, or pleasantry, were arriving continually. Heavily I mourn him, and shall mourn him through life.[1]

In the winter Charles Parr Burney learned about the youthful crime (the theft of books) for which his father had been expelled in his student days from Cambridge and he wrote to his Aunt d'Arblay as the person among all his relatives who knew most about that 'melancholy transaction'.[2] He had planned to write a Memoir of his father but was now uncertain whether to write it at all or, if so, how to treat the unhappy episode. Madame d'Arblay's reply will probably stand as the definitive statement on the subject. 'True, my dear Charles, There is,—There was a Fault—that sometimes must cast down our Eyes, & which should always instil modesty into our exultation.' Yet the fault was 'JUVENILE as SINGLE', was acknowledged, heavily punished, repented, corrected, expiated, and pardoned. Fanny thought that the incident, once of 'even agonizing interest', would one day be read as 'an obscure old tale' and forgotten.[2] If in this she was mistaken, and the story must cling to Charles in death as in life, it can be told, one may hope, not as an isolated fact, but as part of the pattern of error or sin, repentance and forgiveness, the work of retrieving and overcoming, which gives to the Burney saga its intensely human and humane proportions.

At Cambridge Alex was at last beginning to prepare for the final examinations, sending home tense and vibrant letters best

---

[1] See p. 405, n. 3.
[2] A.L.S. (Berg) from CPB to FBA, 7 Feb. 1818; 2 copies (Letter Book, Barrett) from FBA to CPB, 28 Feb., 14 Mar. 1818.

described as time-tables for studies not yet begun or completed.[1] He was working hard, but at this date no one except
perhaps the General believed that he could emerge with
Honours. On January 27 the results were in the newspapers and
the d'Arblays found his name with eighteen Wranglers beneath
and only nine above him 'after a waste of ill-directed application and an irregularity of study that had made us fear he would
not even be a Senior Optimus!'[2] His mother's memorandum for
the next day read: '*Jany 28th*. This Evening arrived our dear
Wrangler, blyth as a Lark, all juvenile glee, with the rapture of
scarcely hoped for success in the triumph of attaining it, at last,
his own way: Had his judgment, not his propensity, directed his
ardour, he had perhaps been senior Wrangler.'[2] In a day or
two he was to write an examination for a scholarship, and a few
mournful reflections in the General's Diary marked his departure: '*A six heures Alex est reparti pour Cambridge! — le reverrai-je?
Il y doit rester un mois — me retrouvera-t-il?*'[2]

In February Alex was made a scholar of Christ's College; in
March, a Fellow of Christ's. Sometimes he was jubilant: 'An't
I a lucky dog? Hey?'; at other times, much depressed: 'I am
apparently at the summit of all success, and yet I am miserable.'[1]
He was 'a youth of very uncommon ability, & a wonderful
memory';[3] he was an English schoolboy; but, though he was
to reject the title, he was the son of Comte d'Arblay. He was
the son of Madame d'Arblay, but also a son of 'The Two
Nations', and the problems he was to face were by no means
solved, as his mother had hoped, by the high degree that he
had now condescended to attain.

At the close of February Fanny described the General's
sufferings as cruel and unremitting. 'I will enter into no details
of particulars that could only grieve & shock you, unavailingly',
she wrote Charlotte in the same month; 'I well know that could
you serve us, you would not thank me to spare you!'[4] All who
knew Fanny's exceptionally strong feelings and the love-story
of her marriage trembled for the event. Esther, who was now
living at Lark Hall Place near Bath, tried to warn her, and

---

[1] Letters (Berg) from AA to FBA and M. d'A, 21, 26, 28, 31 Dec. 1817, 10
Feb., 5, 10 Mar. 1818. [2] See p. 404, n. 1.
[3] A.L.S. (JRL) from MF to HLTP, 27 Oct. 1819.
[4] 2 A.L. (Berg) from FBA to CBFB, 19 Jan.–24 Feb., 14 Mar. 1818; A.L. (Berg)
to AA, 17 Oct. 1818.

Fanny, understanding that very well, assumed an airiness of
spirit, pretending not to understand. She could not bear the
confirmation of her own fears and tried to bury them deep in
her consciousness. Documents partially printed, *Narrative of the
Illness and Death of General d'Arblay*,[1] describe the preparations
for death at 23 Great Stanhope Street: the relentless progress
of the disease; the grave and forbidding looks of the consulting
surgeon; the General's attempts to speak naturally, calmly,
and helpfully to Fanny about the long separation so painfully
and rapidly approaching. Here also are the last entries in his
diary: '*Et jamais, jamais la vie ne m'a été plus chère! . . . J'attends
pour ce soir ou demain le résultat d'une consultation! . . . La volonté de
Dieu soit faite!*' Or again: '*Et avec quel courage elle supporte ce
qu'elle a à souffrir!*' And finally: '*20th Février — Je sens que je
m'affoiblis horriblement — je ne crois pas que ceci puisse être encore bien
long — Chère* Fanny—*Cher* Alex—God bless you! and unite us
forever! Amen.*' There were then the arrival of the priest and
the administration of the last rites of the Roman Catholic
Church, and finally the dying injunctions to Fanny. She must
join Charlotte.

'She is a genuine character,' he said, & 'Elle m'aime bien.'—I must
approach, also Mrs. Locke & her Amelia: he wished me their
consoling society—I must approach likewise the Queen & the
Princesses:—I must renew my old connexions & friends, & influence,
for the sake of our Alexander. I must also form new ones for his
sake.—

I now dared no longer oppose to him my hopes of his recovery;
the season was too awful. I heard him only with deluges of long
restrained tears, and his generous spirit seemed better satisfied in
thinking me now awakened to a sense of his danger, as preparatory
for supporting its consequence.[1]

She must look after her health and live for Alex. She must go
into the world with Alex, note his inaccuracies, and comment
on them when alone with him. 'He will not want me', Fanny
protested, in deluges of tears. 'He is liked—& can do by himself.' She would much have preferred to go where the General
was going.

On his visit to Paris in the summer (1817) the General had

[1] See p. 404, n. 1.

had the Vernets, father and son, paint his portrait,[1] and Fanny never forgot the comment he made as he stood below it in their drawing-room at Bath: '*Tout le monde dira à Alex qui est sa mère; mais — qu'il n'oublie pas qui a été son Père! C'est pour cela que je lui ai consacré et fait faire ce Portrait.*'[2] With some such thought still in mind as well as concern for Fanny he phrased another request:

'*Parle de moi!*' He said afterwards, 'Parle — et souvent. Surtout à Alexandre; qu'il ne m'oublie pas!'[3]

She perceived his fear that she would be silent about him as she had been about Susan after that tragic death and that the constraint would injure her health and spirits:

'Je ne parlerai pas d'autre chose! *Nous* ne parlerons pas d'autre chose! Mon Ami — mon Ami — je ne survivrai que pour cela!'

On April 22, after witnessing four or five days of agonized suffering, she could deceive herself no longer and wrote in great distress to her son:

Oh my Alex—
my poor Alex—I fear you will arrive too late—but he yet lives—set off therefore immediately—no one has prepared me for what I now prepare you—though I have seen hopelessness of recovery sometimes—but now! Heaven must prepare us both—I see my approaching misery—[4]

Alex was in time. '*O mon Alexandre, je n'espérais pas te revoir — je vous rends grâces, ô mon Dieu! tous mes tourmens sont compensés.*' Alexander was to look after his mother. '*Je ne la laisserai pas seul!*' '*Prends soin de ta mère, Alexandre, mon ami! . . . jusqu'au grand jour qui nous réunira tous trois! Amen! Amen!*'[5]
The narrative resumes with the day and night of concentrated meditation when the warrior shut himself up within himself; then his farewell to Alex; and his farewell to earth (specifically the part of it visible through the large windows—

---

[1] In the possession of Miss Ann Julia Wauchope, Bushey Heath, Herts.
[2] See p. 407, n. 4.   [3] See p. 404, n. 1.
[4] 2 A.L. (Berg) from FBA to AA, 23 Apr., 17 Oct. 1818.
[5] A.L. (Berg) from AA to Charlotte Barrett, 3 May 1818. Also A.L.S. (Barrett) to Mrs. Locke and Mrs. Angerstein, 20 May 1818.

a prospect 'picturesque, lively, lovely').[1] Fanny knew he was
rejoicing to hail 'one more return of Day and Light and Life
with those he loved'. And then the last day, May 3:

About noon, gently awaking from a slumber, he called to me
for some beverage, but was weaker than usual, and could not hold
the cup. I moistened his lips with a spoon several times. He looked
at me with sweetness inexpressible, and pathetically said '*Qui . . .?*'
He stopped, but I saw he meant '*Who shall return this for you?*' I
instantly answered to his obvious and most touching meaning, by
a cheerful exclamation of '*You!* my dearest Ami! *You* yourself! You
shall recover, and take your revenge.' He softly smiled, but shut his
eyes in silence.

Thus ever awake was his tender solicitude for me!—and in the
midst of all his sufferings, his intellects had a clearness, nay, a brightness, that seemed as if already they were refined from the dross of
worldly imperfection.

After this, he bent forward, as he was supported nearly upright
by pillows in his bed—and taking my hand, and holding it between
both his own, he impressively said: 'Je ne sais si ce sera le dernier
mot — mais ce sera la dernière pensée — *Notre réunion!*'—Oh,
words the most precious . . . I fastened my lips on his loved hands,
but spoke not. It was not then that those words were my blessing!
They awed—they thrilled—more than they solaced me. How little
knew I then that he should speak to me no more!

Towards evening I sat watching in my armchair, and Alex remained constantly with me. His sleep was so calm, that an hour
passed in which I indulged the hope that a favourable crisis was
arriving; that a turn would take place by which his vital powers
would be restored, so as to enable him to endure some operation by
which his dreadful malady might be overcome—but—when the
hour was succeeded by another hour, when I saw a universal stillness in the whole frame, such as seemed to stagnate—if I so can be
understood—all around!—I began to be strangely moved. 'Alex!'
I whispered, 'this sleep is critical!—a crisis arrives!—Pray God—
Almighty God! that it be fav—' I could not proceed. Alex looked
aghast, but firm. I sent him to call Payne. I intimated to her my
opinion that this sleep was important, but kept a composure
astonishing, for when no one would give me encouragement, I compelled myself to appear not to want it, to deter them from giving
me despair.

Another hour passed of concentrated feelings, of breathless dread.
His Face had still its unruffled serenity, but methought the hands

[1] See p. 404, n. 1.

were turning cold; I covered them with new Flannel; I watched over the head of my Beloved; I took new flannel to roll over his feet; the stillness grew more awful; the skin became colder.

Alex, my dear Alex, proposed calling in Mr. Tudor, and ran off for him.

I leant over him now with sal volatile to his temple, his forehead, the palms of his hands, but I had no courage to feel his pulse, to touch his lips.

Mr. Tudor came; he put his hand upon the heart, the noblest of hearts, and pronounced that all was over!

How I bore this is still marvellous to me! I had always believed such a sentence would at once have killed me. But his sight!—the sight of his stillness, kept me from distraction! Sacred he appeared, and his stillness I thought should be mine, and be inviolable.[1]

Late in the evening Alexander wrote to his cousin Charlotte Barrett:

All—all is over—my dearest Charlotte!—Tell my dear aunt that it will be better for her not to come directly—my poor mother will be more relieved by her presence after a little interval has elapsed— she can now see no one but me—but she is serene and resigned—tho' utterly wretched.

He is gone to a happier place where wretchedness intrudes not— if ever a soul was prepared for heaven, his was—his agonies were intolerable—incessant—unrelenting—but from the time of my arrival not a murmur, not a complaint escaped him—'twas all heavenly resignation.[2]

'He expired without a struggle in his sleep' so gently

that for a long while my mother could not believe it,—and even now it seems to us a dream that he is gone—but he *is* gone, and we can only pray to rejoin him.[2]

As soon as news of the General's death reached Richmond, Marianne Francis wrote with all haste to Arthur Young:

My poor aunt, who was most tenderly & devotedly attached to him, is no doubt in a state of the bitterest suffering which it is possible to conceive. Perhaps if you were to write her a kind, & *very* gentle & sympathetic letter, (not forbidding her to grieve) she might take it kindly, & it might do her good. . . . I know not what is the state of her mind; but we should all pray that this sharp affliction may be

[1] See p. 404, n. 1.   [2] See p. 409, n. 5.

sanctified to my poor dear Aunt, to whom he that is gone, was so unspeakably dear.[1]

Esther came often to Great Stanhope Street, as Alex said, 'most soothingly & affectionately'. 'Mourn, & Grieve you *must* in a degree as long as life lasts', she later wrote to Fanny. '*All* who *knew* the distinguished & Exalted Character, and truly amiable Qualities of your lamented partner, *do* & *will* sympathize with you—and long deplore his loss.' Yet for Fanny she recommended a 'little *forced* exertion' lest seclusion and tender sorrow should overwhelm her broken heart and ruin her health. 'Take Care my Dear love!'[2]

Tributes to the General's nobility, gentleness and *gentilesse*, his distinguished appearance and merit, and his amiable qualities, abundant in the condoling letters of Fanny's sisters, nieces, and friends like the Lockes, are repeated in the testimony of the attending physician. Mr. Hay had not wished to present a bill, hoping, rather, that his services might have been accepted 'on the score of friendship' for the General. 'For indeed, My dear Sir, I never met with any one I more sincerely loved, esteemed, and respected, nor whose loss I more deeply regretted!'[3]

General d'Arblay lies in his alien grave on the slope of the old Wolcot Churchyard. Across the river valley there is still a view of 'luxurious beauty' much as he had seen it, 'Hills rising above Hills, here smiling with verdure, there shadowed by woods, here undulating to catch the Eye to distant prospects'. Inside the church is a tablet bearing a full account of his honours—as the sole reward of his heroic services and virtues.

> Sacred to the revered Memory
> of Comte Alexandre Jean Baptiste
> Piochard d'Arblay;
> Chevalier de St. Louis; de la Légion d'Honneur;
> du Lys; et de la Fidélité:
> Lieutenant Général des Armées
> et Officier Supérieur des Gardes du Corps
> de S.M. Louis XVIII, Roi de France.

[1] A.L.S. (Barrett) from MF to Arthur Young, 6 May 1818.
[2] A.L.S. (Barrett) from EBB to FBA, 11 Oct. 1818.
[3] 2 A.L.S. (Barrett) from George E. Hay to AA, 27 Apr. 1818, 1 June 1819. He had written 'Settled' on the account, but when repeatedly pressed, sent in a small bill that the d'Arblays doubled in payment. Cf. A.L. (Berg) from FBA to EBB, 1 Feb. 1819.

These Honours, Sole Rewards of his faithful Services
It is easy to Name, and grateful to Record;
But who shall delineate his noble Character?
The Spirit of his Valour, or the Softness of his Heart:
His feeling of Reluctance to leave his weeping Family;
Yet pious Resignation to relinquish this vain World;
His Kindness on the Bed of Torture;
The PURITY of his Integrity: the TRANSPARENCY of his HONOUR;
or the indescribable charm of his Social Virtues!
His shadowy, faded Form
Is deposited in the adjoining Church Yard.
His devoted Wife, and darling Son
Consecrate this poor Tablet to his loved Remembrance;
with devout Aspiration that his own tender Last Prayer
For their Eternal RE-UNION in the blest abode
of Immortal Spirits
May mercifully be accorded
By the ever-living God.
Through the mediation of our Lord Jesus Christ. Amen.
Died 3ᵈ May, 1818. Aged 65.

XVI

'IN AFFLICTION'S NIGHT'

(1818–1828)

'Yet am I here!'
'I often make chateaus in the air that will re-unite us all.'
MADAME D'ARBLAY, 1816[1]

ON the second Sunday after the General's death, Fanny ventured to church. 'I hoped that it might calm my mind . . . but I suffered inexpressibly; I sunk on my knees, and could scarcely contain my sorrows—scarcely rise any more!' 'Oh, mon ami! mon tendre ami! if you looked down!'[2]

The Burneys, aware of the love-story of Fanny's marriage and the depth of her feelings, scarcely expected her to recover quickly, but in about three years she recovered in some measure, and her widowhood was to run on to a term almost equal to that of her marriage—about twenty-four years.

As the General knew very well, the fulfilling of promises to him (including the promise to write up parts of the family history) and her concern for Alex's future were in time likely to recall her from the depressing waste of reminiscence. For the rest, she turned back to the family and to old friends like Madame de Maisonneuve, soon to visit England, Mrs. Locke, now living at Eliot Vale near Blackheath, and Amelia Angerstein, wife of John Angerstein, with a fine house in Pall Mall and the country places of Weeting in Norfolk and Woodlands near Blackheath. A friend of still earlier times and one to prove constant to the end was George Owen Cambridge, now Archdeacon of Middlesex, who with his beautiful wife Cornelia still lived at Twickenham Meadows. The Archdeacon, childless himself, became a useful counsellor and, so far as his clerical powers extended, a patron to the son of the d'Arblays, taking the place of the father and godfathers that Alex had lost.

[1] From a manuscript poem 'To my Mother' (Berg) by Alexander d'Arblay, dated 13 June 1823; A.L.S. (Berg) from FBA to CBFB, 15 May 1816.
[2] *Diary*, vi. 370.

In 1818 the Burney family, born in the mid-eighteenth century, were passing from middle age to the allotted three score years and ten. Esther, now in her seventieth year, had moved with her family to a house near Bath. She was still, between family catastrophes, 'all spirit and vivacity'. Lark Hall Place, filled with music, musical instruments, books, and drawings, was a typical Burneyan household, and the life there ran on with the characteristic illnesses and troubles to its close. Esther's widowed daughter, Maria Bourdois, now in comfortable circumstances from advantageous marriage settlements, also lived in Bath with her sister Sophia.

These family connexions, together with attractive living conditions, might have kept Madame d'Arblay at Bath had not Alex suddenly and unexpectedly expressed a strong desire to live in London.[1] He was thinking of the libraries, 'celebrated people', and his 'scientific friends', and Madame d'Arblay, remembering her own youth, was scarcely the one to quench such interests and plans. She readily agreed, insisting only on fresh air from flowers and fields, that is, a dwelling-place near parks and gardens 'free from dust or carriages'. Exercise in long walks was essential to her. A second difficulty was by no means new—a diminished and inadequate income.[2] 'Ah me!—were That all!'[1]

On October 2 she arrived in James Street and was received by all there—'James at the head—with the most touching affection & commiseration'. 'I have found in that excellent Brother a feeling for me, a sense of my loss that has softened my grief by its tenderness. It will be a real & true comfort to me to be near him for the rest of my days.'[3] She was invited to stay with James and his family all winter, but on October 8, 1818, she moved to 11 Bolton Street, Piccadilly, and there established a home for Alex.[3]

Bolton Street had been chosen for its proximity to Green Park, Hyde Park, and St. James's, with the advantage also of

[1] A.L. (Berg) from FBA to CBFB, 7 July 1818; A.L. (PML) from FBA to JB, 16 July 1818.
[2] Annual account books (Berg) for the years 1819–27 show expenditures of an annual income of about £450.
[3] 2 A.L. (Berg) from FBA to EBB, 2 Oct. 1818, 1 Feb. 1819; 2 A.L. (Berg) to CBFB, 6 Oct., 16 Nov. 1818; and A.L. (Berg) to AA, 6 Oct. 1818. See also Diary MSS. (Berg), pp. 7104–40.

'the spacious gardens of Devonshire House & Lansdowne with those of the Duke of Portland'.[1] The street was clean, quiet, and close enough to Buckingham Gate for James and his wife to visit her on their morning strolls. Fanny in her turn sometimes took morning walks to James Street. On any quiet morning in November, 1818, she used to set out in her widow's bonnet, black gloves (for she could find no muff sufficiently black), and attire of the deepest black, accompanied by the dog Diane and the faithful and devoted 'Squire of Dames', Elizabeth Ramsay of Ilfracombe. The little group could be seen winding its way along the gravel paths of Green Park or sometimes farther afield into the quiet areas of Hyde Park or sometimes near by in Berkeley Square.

In these years it was principally James to whom Fanny liked to turn for comfort and advice, and no one rejoiced more than she over his late literary achievements. In the previous year he had published the last volume of his onerous work *A Chronological History of the Voyages and Discoveries in the South Sea or Pacific Ocean* (in five volumes). In 1818 he was working on his *Chronological History of North-Eastern Voyages of Discovery*, which appeared in 1819. In Bolton Street Fanny amused the author with a story about Esther in the role of literary reviewer navigating his *North-Eastern Voyages* and collecting her criticisms. Neither Esther nor her husband could claim to be '*extremely conversant* with the subject', but they thought

the style not only manly & perspicuous—but glowing in some places—with the *warm* humanity of his own disposition; I like the independence that reigns thro it,—& the better, because it cannot at present clash with his interest,—when I have navigated the work—and collected my criticisms, I shall write to him.[2]

After many years of domestic discomfort James had settled down with his wife in 'harmony & chearfulness & sociability such as it never was till now', said Fanny, 'from the even dawn of their union'.[2] His house in James Street (Buckingham Gate) was the scene of serious games of whist, and a literary haunt well known to Lamb, Hood, Southey, Crabb Robinson, and at one time to Hazlitt, though the latter's adverse criticism of

[1] See p. 415, n. 3.
[2] A.L.S. (Barrett) from EBB to FBA, 22 May 1819; 2 A.L. (Berg) from FBA to EBB, 21 June 1819, 9 Aug. 1820.

The Wanderer soon lost him his *entrée* there.[1] The young letters of Marianne Francis often supplement the *Essays of Elia* in accounts of Captain Burney, 'a dear hospitable, witty fellow', handing his cup for the ninth time to the tea-maker and inquiring whether this was to be his last or his last but one, then resuming his story about the Giant Golumpus, his son young Clumsy, and Mother Godouble.[1] 'The metre and beauty' of James's verse, moreover, exceeded any the eighteen-year-old Clement Francis had lately seen.

> 'Tis very cold
> I shall be bold
> > to say
> And much I doubt
> I shall go out
> > to day.[1]

James's son Martin, a lawyer, had made some mysterious, unfortunate, and unacknowledged marriage ('I have no inclination, God knows,' said Madame d'Arblay, 'to propagate so fearful a history'). An 'odd joker', as Marianne Francis called him, Martin was still living at home and contributing his share of droll entertainment. The daughter of the house, Sally, was idolized by her father, and not without some reason, judged Madame d'Arblay. 'She is really, in all I see of her, as amiable as she is cultivated & *spirituelle*. A more improved young person I never saw.'[2]

Charlotte, in whose genuine kindness M. d'Arblay had thought Fanny would find some comfort, had not yet recovered from the death of her younger son, Ralph Broome. She usually lived in Richmond to be near her daughter Charlotte Barrett (now the mother of five children), but nothing rejuvenated her strength and spirits so much, she thought, as the sea-breezes drawn in with the incoming tide at Brighton. She spent as much time as possible there, sometimes alone, sometimes with the unwilling Marianne Francis, who disliked her mother's nomadic way of life, and often in the Cambridge vacations with her son

---

[1] Manwaring, p. 250; 2 A.L.S. (Barrett) from MF to Charlotte Barrett, n.d., 10 Jan. 1810; A.L.S. (JRL) from CF to HLTP, 1810.

[2] Ten letters (Berg) from FBA to EBB, 30 Aug., 27 Sept., 4 Oct. 1819, 3 Aug., 24 Oct. 1820, 10 Feb., 12 Dec. 1821, 7 May, 14 Oct. 1822, 29 Oct. 1825; A.L.S. (Berg) to CBFB, 15 Oct. [1819]; A.L.S. (Barrett) from Charlotte Barrett to Arthur Young, 5 Oct. 1819.

Clement Francis, who had ruined his health with hard study. He had taken his degree as eighth wrangler at Caius in 1817, was a Fellow of the College, but was to spend his young manhood, 'all the best days of youth & hope with Physicians & Nurses' or in travels to the Continent for change of air. For many years still Charlotte was to be heavily burdened with illness in her family.

Deaths in the Burney family were irreparable gaps in Fanny's life. In the desolation of her early widowhood she often thought with a quick stabbing pain in her heart of her brother Charles and of his imposing, merry, and affectionate presence, his confidence, and his zealous exertions for her. Yet in the remaining members of the family, in the second generation of Burneys now grown up, and in the third generation soon to begin dutiful visits to their great-uncles and great-aunts, Madame d'Arblay was to find new interests and bright consoling company. Calling on Aunt d'Arblay was a somewhat ceremonious matter, but her nieces and nephews found her invariably kind, and, after she had recovered somewhat from her crushing sorrow, still a gay and entertaining companion.

In November after Alex had returned to Cambridge, Madame d'Arblay sometimes found her 'loneliness very terrible', especially in the long evenings.[1] Early in that month Mrs. Locke and Mrs. Angerstein went through the ordeal of a first visit, staying the whole morning to wear away all terror for the next meeting. As yet Fanny could bear solitude better than the social exertion required in visiting. 'Life seems to linger as if Time travelled with leaden feet.'[2] 'On the bald streets breaks the blank day.'

On November 17 Madame d'Arblay recorded the death of Queen Charlotte—'my dear & venerable Royal Mistress, for so many years the brightest as well as highest example of solid & efficient virtue to all her subjects'.[3] In some quarters, according to letters of the time, the old Queen was so much disliked that scarcely anyone went into mourning; in others she was praised for the example she had set in domestic life by being, as

---

[1] A.L. (Barrett) from Charlotte Barrett to Arthur Young, 10 Nov. 1818, 28 Aug. [1819].

[2] See p. 415, n. 3.

[3] *Diary*, vi. 378–80. Also 2 A.L. (Berg) from FBA to EBB, 30 Nov. 1818, 21 June 1819.

St. Paul commanded, a stayer-at-home for fifty years.[1] To Fanny she had been a steady benefactress and friend for over thirty years. On December 2, the day on which Queen Charlotte was interred, Madame d'Arblay attended a memorial service at St. James's Church. 'I wept the whole time, as much from gratitude and tenderness to hear her thus appreciated as from grief at her loss—to me a most heavy one! for she was faithfully, truly, and solidly attached to me, as I to her.'[2]

The records for 1818 close with Christmas Day. 'Alex left me for Richmond. I favoured his going, yet what am I without him?' At church that morning Dr. Andrewes had administered the sacrament. 'He knew, and highly esteemed, my beloved. I wept at the altar irresistibly.'[2] On the first Yule-tide the mourner was inconsolable, and sorrow with its desolate emotions closed the year in tears.

On September 27, 1818, Alex had been ordained a deacon, but in 1819 he was forced to reconsider his career, when his father's friend the Duc de Luxembourg offered him a commission in the French Guards.[3] By this time, however, he was so much interested in theology that his mother had as much difficulty in getting him 'to his meals from the scriptures' as she had had previously in prying him away from mathematics or poetry.[3] Once again he refused the French honours, and at St. James's Church on Sunday, April 11, 1819, his mother saw him ordained a priest in the Church of England.[4] The problem now was to get him a benefice. Only the unkind could laugh at Sally Burney's wicked story about poor dearest Aunt d'Arblay's distress over having sent Alex fifty miles in fruitless pursuit of one bishop only to lose a golden opportunity to pay court to another by walking merely three miles.[5] Nothing could exceed Alex's apathy on the subject, and his stipulation that his first charge must be in or near London must have put an additional spoke in the wheels of preferment. Though churchmen like the

---

[1] A.L.S. (Barrett) from Charlotte Barrett to Arthur Young, 1 Dec. 1818.

[2] See p. 418, n. 3.

[3] A.L.S. (Barrett) from Charlotte Barrett to Arthur Young, 23 Dec. [1818]; A.L. (Berg) from FBA to AA, 27 Sept. 1818; 2 A.L. (Berg) to EBB, 2 Oct. 1818, 24 Oct. 1820.

[4] 2 A.L.S. (Berg) from FBA to EBB, 21 June 1819, 30 Oct. 1820. Also A.L.S. (Barrett) from Amelia Angerstein to FBA, post-dated, 1819; Diary, vi. 381–2.

[5] A.L.S. (Berg) from Sarah Burney Payne to Charlotte Barrett, 22 Sept. 1828.

Bishop of Salisbury, whom Fanny had met in former days at Windsor, were very kind,[1] and though family friends like the Archdeacon of Middlesex and the Rev. George Locke, rector of Lee, introduced him to their clerical superiors and invited him to read lessons or try out his voice in their pulpits, five years passed before they succeeded in procuring him a living—the new chapel in Camden Town.

In these years Madame d'Arblay decided, partly for her son's future as an English clergyman, to drop the French title bestowed on her husband by the French King at Ghent. She herself used the new honour only in signing French documents, petitions or claims addressed to the bank or the War Office, or occasionally in letters to the royal family. She had noticed that her husband's military rank and her own title *la comtesse* had counted with the Princesses. Their kindness was 'all their own, all instinctive, native', and always the same,[2] but they could invite *la comtesse*, wife of General d'Arblay, quite openly to Buckingham Palace, Kensington Palace, Gloucester House, or Frogmore. When her nieces edited the diaries they thought it modest or expedient to suppress this part of Madame d'Arblay's social life, but about fifty long letters from the Princess Elizabeth (the Landgravine of Hesse-Homburg) and a dozen affectionate missives from Princess Augusta, and over 125 notes of invitation or short letters from the Princesses Sophia and Mary Duchess of Gloucester show in what affection the Princesses held the Keeper of the Robes whom they had known in their young girlhood at Windsor and Kew.[3] As for the French honours, Fanny's policy was deliberate. 'Our limited income, & the decided English destiny of Alex', 'motives of economy and love of simplicity', decided her dropping the title, but in duty to her husband's memory and in justice to the King of France, she spoke unreservedly of the distinction conferred.

---

[1] See p. 419, n. 4.

[2] 2 A.L.S. (Berg) from FBA to EBB, 1 Feb., 10(?) Mar. 1819; 2 A.L. (Berg) to CBFB, 2 May, 17 Sept. 1821; A.L. (Berg) to Mrs. Locke, [1824]: 'My return home was cheerful & interesting with my dear Princess Sophia, in spite of Rain, slush, & mud which we waded through . . . in search . . . of country air.'

[3] 47 A.L.S. (Berg) from Princess Elizabeth to FBA, 1 Nov. 1814–6 Sept. 1833; 37 A.L.S. (Berg) from Mary, Duchess of Gloucester, 7 June 1818–25 June 1832; 12 A.L.S. (Berg) from Princess Augusta, 8 Aug. 1819–21 Oct. 1828; and 79 A.L.S. and 13 A.N.S. (Berg) from Princess Sophia, 9 Oct. 1824–29 Jan. 1827.

This much I think may be as useful & honourable to my Alex as *more* might be hurtful; for it makes known how high his honoured *Father* stood in his own country.[1]

Not Yule-tides, but recurring Mays, the anniversaries of the General's death, were marked in the manuscripts, and especially in letters to Esther, with new attitudes towards grief and new resolves to hail the painful month 'with lessened bitterness, & deepened Gratitude'. Most of the General's friends in whom at this time she would have found great comfort were in France. She was delighted, therefore, in May, 1819, to learn that Madame de Maisonneuve would accompany her brother the Marquis de Latour-Maubourg on a diplomatic mission to England.[2] This was to mean gala evenings for Alex, and for Madame d'Arblay the 'infinite consolation' of a visit almost daily when the magnificent ambassadorial equipage stopped at her door. 'My most sweet & constant Mme de Maisonneuve gives me all the time she can spare, & rather partakes than pardons my deplorable dejection.'[3]

New troubles and losses in the Burney family soon, however, commanded sympathy and active exertions. In the summer of 1819 it became apparent that Esther's husband (Charles Rousseau Burney) was facing a painful death.[4] 'How affecting are all your accounts of dear suffering exemplary Mr. Burney!' 'I read them as lessons,' said Madame d'Arblay,

if not Models, to all our Family that I see, as well as to myself. To amuse himself so ingeniously, so patiently, so *wisely*—while others consume their remnant strength in murmurs & apprehensions. . . . Indeed I honour his courage as much, as I grieve at its cause.[3]

In the summer Esther wrote an uncomplaining but objective review of her husband's and her own career and their life together.[4] Rewards were not always commensurate with merit, and though Charles Rousseau was an accomplished musician, he had known many 'heavy disappointments'. The evil was often balanced by the goodness of her own family and that of

[1] See p. 420, n. 2.
[2] 2 A.L. (Berg) from FBA to AA, 10 Feb., 5 Mar. 1819; 2 A.L. (Berg) to EBB, 10 (?) Mar. 1819.
[3] See p. 418, n. 3.
[4] 2 A.L. (Barrett) from EBB to FBA, 22 May, 19 July 1819.

the Worcester Burneys, who made Charles Rousseau's children their own.

At the end of the summer of 1819 Charlotte had returned from Brighton looking astonishingly better. 'She is recovering her spirits, her active life, & her health, & what is not *ir*recoverable of her happiness.'[1] Madame d'Arblay and Alex, visitors at Richmond at that time, were described in their turn by Marianne Francis. Aunt d'Arblay

is a most gentle & pleasant visitor, is quiet, & kind, & easily pleased—so is her son, who is a person of fine abilities, & very amiable, poor dear fellow. He has an astonishing memory, so has his Mother; but it is impaired by trouble, for she is very low, & has by no means recovered the loss of her husband.[2]

Soon news came from Bath of the death of Mr. Burney. The 'dreadfulness' of the malady, said Fanny, was such as to 'ward off murmuring at the final event'. The sisters knew that at the end Esther had prayed for his release,

but of our truly loved Esther, & her affliction, we sate talking with deepest interest & pity half the night—we knew not how to separate, such tender hold of us had the subject.[1]

'The *End* brings to remembrance the *Beginning*', and Fanny thought of Poland Street when Esther was a girl, of Mr. Seton, and of Mr. Burney as 'a shy, modest, embarrassed, half-formed youth'. So she thought of him still, as a person 'really & truly *without* Guile'. She matched kind thoughts with 'active exertions'—an offer of a small loan, which she could spare for some months, even a year, without the smallest inconvenience, and a 'melancholy Bonnet & Cap', which she had worn only thrice, once to church at Bath and twice to the Duchess of Gloucester's.[1]

All these concerns, together with the reproof implicit in Charlotte's recovery and Esther's resigned composure, served to interrupt the monody of recollection and regret, and by 1821 Madame d'Arblay had begun to recover her sense of humour and her old scribbling habits.

James's hearty laughter at her account of her visit to the Court of Chancery, where she had been summoned to collect

---

a legacy of £10, encouraged her to write a hoaxing letter on
the subject to Esther, the co-sharer of the bequest.[1] Her awed
impressions of Lincoln's Inn, the Lord Chancellor, the Accomptant General, the Advocates, and even of the clerks and
copyists may recall Dickens or Leacock, though the humour
of the piece lies in subtleties peculiar to her own character and
situation: her awe of the proceedings and her fear of the Law
and its chicaneries, in no respect lessened by Charles Parr's
warning that in this case the legal costs were likely to amount
to three times the legacy. Her inward trepidation was concealed, however, by a dauntless resolution to '*behave like a man*'
(this 'being my first appearance in that character'). She described her arrival at the Inns of Court with her *entourage*—the
'rustic Damsel' (Ramsay, her maid), and the dog Diane,
capering about her mistress or barking furiously about the legs
of the solicitor. She told of her staunch efforts to gain attention
so that she might inquire into the costs before matters proceeded to ruinous lengths beyond recall and of how she was
foiled by the laconism of the clerks ('those who think they may
. . . say what they wist, to a money'd Man of Business in a court
of Law, have had less experience than *I* have, Now—OR, a great
deal MORE'). Not till all was done could she find any opportunity to introduce the fearsome question of costs, in this case,
as she finally learned, a mere 4s. 6d. 'That is very generous,—&
I feel much obliged,—& whoever complains of the Law, & of
Lawyers, *I* must stand forth to praise & laud them.' At this the
clerks smiled and even the Accomptant General 'quite unbent
his chancery Brow'.[1] To unbend 'gloomy brows' was the usual
effect of the Burneyan charm, and this was the most engaging
(if not the most *useful*) function of the Comic Spirit.

In the winter of 1820–1 Alex's health failed, and his mother,
agreeing with the doctors that he had been brought to his
present weak and emaciated state by excessive mental application, urged him to take a holiday abroad.[2] Off he went, then,
in the third week of July 'with 2 Cantab Friends of great
celebrity in Science & ingenuity, Herschel and Babbage' for
a summer's mountain-climbing in Switzerland.[3] In April

[1] A.L. (Berg) from FBA to EBB, 3 Sept. 1821.   [2] See p. 417, n. 2.
[3] 2 A.L.S. (Berg) from FBA to CBFB, 7, 24 Apr. 1821; 2 A.L.S. (Berg) to
Charlotte Barrett, 21 Aug., 24 Oct. 1821.

Esther, 'heart-stricken, & deeply, dreadfully afflicted' by the death of her daughter Cecilia, took some comfort from Fanny's sympathy and sympathized with her in turn. 'I am broken hearted my Dearest Fanny!'

You know how beloved she [Cecilia] was,—and *I* know how truly you feel for me. . . . And *shocked I am* to think of poor Dear Alex— having had so alarming a relapse—my poor Fanny—what you have suffered—and have to suffer from the delicacy of that sweet youth's frame & constitution, pains me to the heart—for I find the heart can find room for many pangs at the same time.[1]

Alex's cousins told how on this journey (or a previous one) to Dover he had lost both his trunk and *sac de nuit*, which through the honesty of the innkeepers were returned to his home.[2] 'James is absent beyond most folks', Madame d'Arblay had observed, 'save Alexander! who of absence is King.' 'He is certainly what Merlin called "a singular Particular." '[3] Soon he was writing hilariously from Berne, Lucerne, and Dijon, and though he had intended to return in six weeks, at the end of three months he was still in Switzerland. He spent the winter in Paris and returned to England, very much against his inclination, only in the spring. 'Very magnanimous of my aunt', remarked Charlotte Barrett, 'to let him go.'[4]

In 1820–1, as the printed Diary shows, Mrs. Piozzi and Madame d'Arblay carried on a correspondence that seems to have been resumed after the meeting of 1817 in Bath. These letters, with their allusions to Streatham, its people, the beginning and the hey-day of a strange friendship, marked the end. On May 2 Mrs. Piozzi died, according to contemporary testimony, 'in peace & charity with all'. Her wit remained to the last, raising 'unwilling smiles in the midst of the tears they shed for her'. Fanny paid a last tribute of respect to

her fine faculties, her imagination, her intelligence, her powers of allusion and citation, her extraordinary memory, and her almost

---

[1] 3 A.L.S. (Barrett) from EBB to FBA, 25, 28 Feb., 4 Apr. 1821. Cf. A.L. (Berg) from FBA to CBFB, 7 Apr. 1821.

[2] See p. 418, n. 1.   [3] See p. 417, n. 2.

[4] Charlotte Barrett's Letter Book (Barrett), 9 Sept., 4 Oct. 1821; A.L. (Berg) from FBA to EBB, 22 Aug. 1823. For objections see A.L.S. (Berg) from SHB to Charlotte Barrett, 27 Feb. 1821.

unexampled vivacity, to the last of her existence. . . . She was, in truth, a most wonderful character for talents, and eccentricity, for wit, genius, generosity, spirit, and powers of entertainment.[1]

In 1821 Madame d'Arblay was much occupied with events in her brother's house. In April, 1821, Sally, who her aunts and cousins thought might have made a match to raise herself in the world, married a bookseller. This was her cousin John Payne, whom she ruled with a rod of iron, or rather a feather, since, as Madame d'Arblay observed, a feather sufficed. The wedding at St. Margaret's Church, Westminster, was the famous wedding described by Lamb, who caught the blankness of the house, if not the rueful comment of the clan, after the gay and clever girl had left. Sally was said to resemble her Aunt d'Arblay and to have, like her father, 'wit at will'. She was considered as amiable as she was 'cultivated & Spirituelle', 'a clever & delightful creature'.[2] 'She might have made a better match if she had wish'd.' Yet poor Johnny could not help being a tradesman, and he was so generous, and sent his bride such tender letters filled with money that the family was tempted to capitulate with a pun and put the bookseller in their best books.[3]

In 1818–21 Fanny had rejoiced to see James cross the park 'arm and arm with his wife' and to know that all the old discords and enmities were now confined to whist. 'Their looks have lost all the *wear & tear* that so often & so long disfigured them of discontent, gloom, care & discomfort.' In spite of his service at sea and his scientific and historical works on maritime dis-covery, James was still Captain Burney—'an old half-pay Captain' for over forty years.[3] The family had always suspected that his democratic and Whiggish principles and his outspoken criticism of his superiors had clashed with his interests and made 'South Sea Bubbles of all his hopes'. His father knew how

politics had been his ruin—soured his temper; & instead of being an admiral to wch his standing entitled him, set aside by Ld St Vincent, the very man who abetted him in his disloyalty. . . . He was upbraided for his political principles—& laid on the shelf for

---

[1] *Diary*, vi. 389–400; Charlotte Barrett's Letter Book (Barrett).
[2] Manwaring, pp. 264–76; also Annie Raine Ellis, ED, i. lxxiii.
[3] See p. 424, n. 4.

the rest of his life, by the noble admiral, notwithstanding his de-clared partiality for Jacobins—[1]

Both Fanny and James had come a long way, however, since as Second Keeper of the Robes she had asked the old Queen for a ship of twenty-eight guns. As the Captain's geographical publications demonstrated, he was one of the first navigators of the age, and his works made interest for him with the Duke of Clarence, now an Admiral of the Fleet. When James wrote to the Duke soliciting his interest, it was immediately granted, and to this interest, as Mrs. Burney explained in a letter to Sally, was added that 'obtained by your very kind and affec-tionate Aunt D'Arblay with the Princess Augusta'.[2] Fanny was happy to tell how, one day in May, 1821, when she was walking with the Duchess of Gloucester and the Princess Augusta in the Queen's Gardens in Buckingham Palace, some lucky accident in the conversation gave her an opportunity to make James's case better known to the Duchess.[3]

Whatever the concomitant circumstances, the fair winds that combined to waft the troubled mariner home, on the evening of August 14, 1821, James received notice from the Admiralty that a commission had been signed on July 19 appointing him Rear-Admiral on the retired list. On the same evening Mrs. Burney wrote the glad news to Fanny, then on a fortnight's visit to Twickenham Meadows. 'And now be assured of my happy thanks to you, my dear & very steady friend—for it is all, all owing to _you_.'[4] In a few days James sent a boyish report of his good behaviour.

I was tolerably diligent for me. I received notice of the good in-tended, from the Admiralty on Tuesday evening at or after 8 oclock, and before I went to the Admiralty, at 11 oclock next forenoon, was at the Duke of Clarence's door, but he was gone . . . all I could do was to leave a letter and a card![5]

Fanny and Charlotte embraced for joy 'like the two kings in the Rehearsal, again & again', and Fanny wrote to Alex:

[1] A.L.S. (Osborn) from CB to CB, Jr., 31 May 1808.

[2] See p. 425, n. 2.

[3] A.L. (Berg) from FBA to EBB, 23 Nov. 1821. Also A.L.S. (Barrett) from CBFB to FBA, 27 Nov.–1 Dec. 1821; Manwaring, p. 289.

[4] A.L.S. (Berg) from Mrs. James Burney to FBA, 14 Aug. 1821.

[5] A.L.S. (Berg) from JB to FBA, 17 Aug. 1821.

'Doff your Hat, & wave it in the air, on the mountains, & in the vallies, with a loud Huzza! Huzza! Huzza!' 'Health to Admiral Burney!'[1]

In September Fanny was again writing about her brother (in these years her happiest subject): 'Our Admiral enjoys his Honours with philosophy of manner, but with real & great internal satisfaction. So do I for him, God knows.'[2] Nothing could now give her as much pleasure, except perhaps a good benefice for Alex and 'some fair, prudent, *spirituelle* & amiable Damsel's' accepting his hand.[1] And now, God save the Admiral!

Yet in 1820 Fanny had remarked rather ominously:

Our good James is tolerably well; but alas, my dear Esther, by no means as flourishing as last year: I think him changed, & broken; he is weak, & stoops cruelly; but, at times, he retains all his wonted powers of wit & humour, & his parts & understanding are brighter, I think, than ever. God preserve him![3]

With success and happiness, as Fanny afterwards said, she had hoped for James 'a cheerful & agreeable, long old life'. She had hoped that

he would find it extended beyond our dear Father's, because I thought he would avoid the gloomy retirement & seclusion into which that dear Father fell, & which embittered & harrowed & depressed many *years* of the existence that might else, like that of Mrs. Delany, have been lent him for his comfort, & the delight of all his Friends.[2]

All the Burneys thought that James's promotion would lengthen as well as sweeten his days; they did not know, as they afterwards put it, that the measure of his days was full.

Following Alex's departure for Switzerland late in July Fanny had gone on a series of visits, first for a fortnight to Twickenham Meadows, then to Richmond, and finally to the 'fragrant abode' Eliot Vale, near Blackheath, where Mrs. Locke lived.[4] Mrs. Locke was 'a sight of wonder & admiration', said

---

[1] 2 A.L. (Berg) from FBA to AA, 20 Aug., 25 Nov. 1821; A.L.S. (PML) to JB and Mrs. Burney, 1821.

[2] 2 A.L. (Berg) from FBA to CBFB, 17 Sept., 11 Dec. 1821. Also A.L.S. (Berg) from SHB to Charlotte Barrett, 7 Sept. 1821. Also entry in Charlotte Barrett's Letter Book (Barrett), 31 Dec. 1821.

[3] A.L. (Barrett) from FBA to EBB, Nov. 1820.

[4] See p. 423, n. 3.

Fanny, for retaining *beauty* after the flight of youth. Even in 1825 she was still 'in high beauty as well as health—both of mind & body. Wonderful she is, & enchanting, without and within.'[1] It was here on November 17, 1821, that Fanny heard the news of James's sudden death. Mrs. Locke kept her until after the funeral, for, as the sisters agreed, with the baleful wretch Phillips about (whom none of them except James could bear to look upon since Susan's death), how could she have gone to James Street?

The agitation in James Street—the to and fro—and the gloom of your home, without dear Alex, must have killed you, and that wretch being there, what could you have done![2]

Soon, however, Fanny returned to her empty and cheerless house to write Esther all she could learn or remember about James's last days. Esther had asked for particulars, wishing to learn something more about 'this dear & good brother' than that he was lost to her forever.[3] Fanny's heart was so saddened, her head so confused with spasms of nervous pain, that she feared she could not write clearly; and 'yet to write on this subject where there is such true sympathy is all I am fit for'. 'Whatever he had that was imperfect was nothing NOTHING in the scale of his good & excellent qualities. I hardly know how to begin, or what to write, I feel so completely your want to know *all*.' But her efforts to apprise Esther of all the circumstances made her in these years her brother's best biographer. She copied a letter from Susan's daughter (Fanny Raper) telling about the Admiral's last evening, the last of the hospitable parties in the house in James Street. The Admiral was in 'particular good spirits' and

when the company was gone . . . said he should smoke a little before he went to Bed, & desired to have two pipes left for him. The family [Sally and her husband John Payne, who were spending the evening and night there] then retired to rest; but, at about half past one, Mrs. Burney—who is always anxious about the candles when she leaves

---

[1] 2 A.L. (Berg) from FBA to EBB and to CBFB, 13 Mar. 1822, and 24 June 1825.

[2] A.L.S. (Barrett) from CBFB to FBA, 27 Nov.–1 Dec. 1821; A.L.S. from Mrs. James Burney to FBA, 22 Nov. 1821.

[3] A.L. (Berg) from EBB to FBA, 20 Nov. 1821.

him up—went down, & as she was descending the last stairs—she heard him fall![1]

The doctors who were called said it was not apoplexy.

They say that by the constant & too great working of his Brain he has produced an ossification of part of it, and, in age, this becomes brittle; & similar effects have been known before.[1]

Susan's daughter, who, like Alexander, had so many reasons to love the Admiral, desired to see him, while he still lay on the couch in the little parlour.

My poor dear uncle is very little altered, & has a very sweet, calm, & benignant expression on his countenance, & looks as if he only slept.[1]

Madame d'Arblay, who held so many troubled years in memory, was glad to testify at last to the return of happier feelings and to reconciliations that banished all traces of former resentments. James had hung his father's portrait by the fireside in James Street between those of Mr. Crisp and William Windham, and he not only allowed Fanny 'to name our dear Father without reserve, & with the tenderness I have ever felt for him, but he now, occasionally, mentioned him, & with respect & affection, himself'. She felt that James had died at peace and harmony with himself and all the world.

Certainly, great as were his peculiarities, & ill-judged as were some of his actions, from his excentric idea he might hold himself above the controul of opinion, or custom, he yet had a Heart of the noblest nature, formed for even tender kindness, & earnest zeal for those he loved. . . .

I do not believe a heart could be more filled with unmixt good will towards all mankind than that which beat in his heart till one o'clock last Saturday morning.[1]

Of Dr. Burney's family of eight, only four—Esther, Fanny, Charlotte, and Sarah Harriet—now remained to condole with one another. There was great sympathy for Sarah Harriet, whose circumstances were straitened and precarious, whose health was never robust, and whose grief for James must be

[1] A.L.S. (Berg) from Fanny Phillips Raper to FBA, 21 Nov. 1821 (a long letter giving details about the Admiral's death and funeral) partly copied by FBA in A.L. (Berg) to EBB, 23 Nov. 1821. Also A.L.S. (Berg) to EBB, 12–14 Dec. 1821.

'the most heart piercing she has ever endured'.[1] She was still
at Chelsea College in 1820 when she completed her fourth
novel, *Country Neighbours*, but in April, 1821, she had written
to Madame d'Arblay about leaving there and taking a post as
governess.[2] With insufficient health to keep that post she
spent part of the year 1822 in family visits, and then came the
cheering news:

Lord Crewe had been desirous of Miss Burney's taking charge of his
grandchildren, who are wards in Chancery. . . . She is to have a
house in Park Street kept for her; they are placed under her control
quite independently of Lord Crewe. . . . The salary for Aunt Sarah,
Mrs. B. thinks will be £300 a year.[3]

All the family truly 'rejoiced at so comfortable & happy a
prospect for this poor soul'—one 'quite providential in her
present situation'.[3]

Uncertainties about Alex's plans and the fear that he might
return to an 'empty house, even for a night' kept Madame
d'Arblay close at Bolton Street through most of the winter and
up to the end of March, 1821, when that *insouciant* young man
was at length persuaded to return. She knew that since his
arrival in Paris on October 4 he had been cordially entertained
by his father's friends, through whose introductions he was able
to attend the Institutes and meet poets, mathematicians, and
scientists, among them Laplace. With all this Alex turned more
ardently than ever to mathematics and poetry. And he had
confided to Madame de Maisonneuve that he would like two
more years of such intellectual life and liberty '*avant de prendre
un Bénéfice*'.[4]

Fanny's gratification at all this was dimmed in the end with
worries over his future in England. He was in his twenty-eighth
year, and James, the Archdeacon, and even the Paris connexions
felt that he ought not to stay away so long without a '*useful
pursuit* or *ostensible cause*'. 'He should give himself a rank in

[1] A.L. (Berg) from FBA to AA, 23 Nov.–18 Dec. 1821; 2 A.L. (Berg) to EBB,
29 Jan., 13 Mar. 1822.
[2] 2 A.L.S. (Barrett) from SHB to FBA, 7 Dec. 1820, 22 Apr. 1821. Also 2
A.L.S. (Berg) from SHB to Charlotte Barrett, 7 Sept. 1821, 15 Mar. 1822.
[3] Charlotte Barrett's Letter Book (Barrett), letters dated 14, 22 Sept. 1822;
and letters (Berg) from SHB to Charlotte Barrett, 2 Dec. 1823–6 Apr. 1829.
[4] 2 A.L.S. (Berg) from FBA to EBB, 12–14 Dec. 1821, 27 Jan. 1823; letters
(Berg) from Madame de Maisonneuve to FBA, 22 Jan.–28 Mar. 1822.

society, as one of its citizens first—& amuse himself afterwards.'[1]
When Madame d'Arblay discovered at the end of March that
her son was no longer staying with his father's friends but was
'braving the world' by himself at l'Hotel de Tours, she became
alarmed. If you offend society, a time will come, she warned him,

when Resentment will find its vent, in pouncing upon either your
Reputation, your *happiness* or your *Fame*—according to the openings
your progress in life may make for the workings of . . . *scandal,* or
ill will, or *criticism.*[1]

There was a cry against him in Paris, which in England was
kept down by her 'assumed resignation'. And she attempted to
spur him to action. Awake! write! or come![1]

Madame de Maisonneuve and her brother for Fanny's sake
speeded the traveller home.[2] In May he was invited to preach
at Twickenham, and in December in Mr. George Locke's
pulpit in Lee Church. He was amazingly improved and could
not fail, it was thought, of being a distinguished preacher.[3]
Mrs. Locke wrote with characteristic insight and kindness
about his performance,

so highly gratifying to those feelings of pride & vanity by which we
make up for the total lack of all such feelings in the dear highly
gifted & *so dearly* simple preacher.[3]

Not since 1818 had Fanny been so happy.[3]

In 1823 he was asked to preach at one of the early canonical
services at St. Paul's Cathedral and again in June, in the same
pulpit, 'by order of the Bishop of London'. Fanny worried lest
he should put off the preparation till the last night and 'so
mount the rostrum half dead!' Everything depended on that
rostrum, and she was ready to smile at her own ludicrous
behaviour in having gone three times beforehand to view the
'scene of Diction'.[4] When Parliament broke up the Bishops
dispersed, and all hope of a benefice had to subside until they

---

[1] A.L. (Barrett) from George Cambridge to FBA, n.d.; 2 A.L. (Berg) from
FBA to AA, 4 Feb., 25 Mar. 1822.

[2] See p. 430, n. 4.

[3] A.L. (Berg) from Amelia Angerstein to FBA, 26 Dec. 1822; A.L. (Berg) from
Mrs. Locke to FBA, [Jan.] 1823; A.L.S. (Berg) from FBA to Charlotte Barrett,
30 Dec. 1822.

[4] Diary MSS. (Berg), Feb. 1823. Also 3 A.L. (Berg) from FBA to EBB, 6 May,
21 June, 16 Oct. 1823.

were called together again. Though the sermons were highly
praised, the design succeeded only partially, because through
one misadventure or another Alex was kept from thanking the
right people or presenting himself presentably at the right time
to the relevant Bishop. Evidently the shining hour passed. No
one, according to the family comment, could have been more
indifferent or apathetic than the young man himself. On Goose
Day in September he went on a delightful jaunt to Dover,
Ramsgate, Margate, Sandgate, and Folkestone. In November
he joined his mother at Brighton, where she had taken rooms
for a month's happy visit to Charlotte Broome.[1]

It was almost two years since Fanny had seen so much of this
'sister—Friend—crony & Favourite'.[2] There were stories still
about the sensation she caused among the gentlemen, who made
it a practice to drink her health in three times three, and a
report, which Esther heard three years later, about the effect
of her charms on a particular gentleman.[3] Charlotte was much
concerned about her son, now a nervous tubercular patient
requiring exacting care. With all this, said Fanny, she never
spared trouble or cost to serve a 'Friend, Acquaintance, or even
stranger'. 'A kinder heart never beat in a human bosom, nor
one of higher probity or sounder principle.'[2]

One month of Charlotte's company and the change of air
had quite set Fanny up again and she began to feel that she
might live for a long time. 'I now think there is an organic con-
formation for Longevity, that demands the continuation of
exertions for which our Earthly career seems designed.'[2] She
was now able to keep the promises she had made the General
to write up such events as her presentation in 1814 to Louis
XVIII,[4] her travels from Brussels to Trèves (a journey then
nine years in the past), and her adventure of 1817 on the cliffs
of Ilfracombe. These formal journals, along with two or three
drafts of 'The Illness and Death of General d'Arblay', composed
from memoranda and memory, comprise nearly 300 pages or
over three-fourths of the sixth volume of Austin Dobson's

<hr />

[1] See p. 431, n. 4.

[2] 2 A.L.S. (Berg) from FBA to CBFB, 2 July, Oct. 1823; A.L. (Berg) to EBB,
23 Dec. 1823; A.L. (Berg) to Charlotte Barrett, 9 Dec. 1823.

[3] A.L.S. (Barrett) from EBB to FBA and CBFB, 17 Oct. 1828.

[4] See introduction to Diary MSS. (Berg), pp. 6422–600: 'Trèves—written
present Sept. 12, 1824.'

PLATE IV

Journal-letter written by Fanny Burney and edited by her some thirty years later

edition of the *Diary and Letters*. These formal diaries, her current
correspondence, onerous editorial work on the vast collection
of Burney papers, including Dr. Burney's correspondence and
her own and that of Susan, and finally a three-volume work,
Memoirs of Doctor Burney, occupied the lonely evenings in Bolton
and Half Moon Streets from 1822 till 1832, when she reached
her eightieth year.

In December young d'Arblay was invited (probably through
the influence of Archdeacon Cambridge, who was a prebendary
at Ely) to preach in Ely Cathedral; and Charlotte Barrett, then
living at Ely, wrote a long letter to Aunt d'Arblay about dear
Alex's performance there. The congregations of three churches
had assembled in the Cathedral. Presently the Bishop, preceded
by his sword-bearer, ascended the Throne, and from the
Cathedral pulpit the slim, dark-eyed son of Madame d'Arblay
preached such a beautiful sermon that the ladies were 'in
raptures' and similar admiration was reported on the part
of the gentlemen. At tea, by special request, he regaled
the company with one poetical sermon after another, for in
these years, by writing poetry and sermons alternately, Alex
was becoming something of a poet-preacher.[1] Fanny longed to
see him in a benefice and she longed to see him chained, *well*
chained, of course; but the bride

must be eminently pleasing to win his heart; she must be eminently
literary to keep his society; she must be eminently œconomical to
sustain his Fortune, & she must be eminently sweet tempered to
bear with his eccentricities.[2]

Unfortunately Alex fell in love without reference to the
specifications. The girl of his dreams was Caroline Angerstein,
granddaughter of Mrs. Locke, daughter of the elegant Amelia
and her husband the wealthy John Angerstein, at whose London
house and country homes Alex was often a guest. A glimpse of
the young people is given in Amelia Angerstein's charming
apology to Madame d'Arblay for keeping Alex over his birthday
while his 'precious mother' sat alone in her lonely house in
Bolton Row. The day was very much like former days at
Norbury Park, where conversation and a walk through the

[1] A.L.S. (Barrett) from Charlotte Barrett to FBA, 15 Dec. 1823.
[2] 2 A.L.S. (Berg) from FBA to CBFB, 2 July 1823, 25 Oct. 1828; A.L. (Berg)
to EBB, 16 Oct. 1823.

wood and meadows seemed to make all guests—from the most
serious artists to a gay laughing girl like Lucy Fitzgerald—
superlatively happy. The evening had begun with 'an exquisite
treat of *poetry*' and then Alex had continued with one of
Molière's plays. Mrs. Angerstein had not seen him look so
bright and strong and robust since his '*Westhumble childhood*';
Mr. Angerstein, who took great pleasure in his society, thought
the same, and to compensate somewhat for the delay, he would
order his carriage to take Alex half-way home.[1]

Tensions developed in January, 1824, when Caroline Angerstein fell dangerously ill with some excruciatingly painful
infection and with groans and screams called for death, while
the frightened young people, her brother and his friends,
waited distractedly on the staircases or wandered in the empty
drawing-rooms below. For a fortnight Alex remained with the
others, to Fanny's horror, an uninvited guest at Brandon Hall.
He must leave at once, she told him. 'Indeed, my Alex, you
must make an effort to quit a spot where you are a real *intruder*,
since unasked, however leniently treated, or indulgently *liked*—
if not *pitied*.' And he must not come by *post* like one distracted,
for he is neither a declared nor an accepted lover, 'whose
despair, like that of a Husband or a Father, or a Brother, is but
legitimate'. And not for the world is he to come away without
seeing his host and hostess to beg for commands or commissions
that he might execute in London. But how could the feckless
Alex 'watch & cherish & foster another'? Difference in fortune
will now make more difference than ever before because of
necessaries for 'so delicate a frame'. Alex may be certain that
there can be

no happiness with deprivations of habituated comforts where there
is not Health. . . . The one who misses may *bear*,—but that is not
Happiness!—& the one for whom the change was made may adore
& be grateful, but must lament & be frightened, & that is not
Happiness neither![2]

With arduous family nursing Caroline recovered, and in the
spring Alex, still true to his heart's desire, wrote to his mother
asking her to speak to Mrs. Angerstein about his wishes. This

---

[1] A.L.S. (Berg) from Amelia Angerstein to FBA, 18 Dec., n.y.
[2] Four letters (Berg) from FBA to AA, 6, 9, 14 Jan., 12 Apr. 1824; A.L. (Berg)
to EBB, 27–29 Jan. 1824.

was the most important moment of his life, but his letter was
already tinged with despair.

My dear mother,

I solemnly request you to be so kind as to make known to Mrs.
A—n the state of my feelings with respect to Miss A—n, together
with my present hopes and chances of rising in my profession,—as
I do not think I can ever have so favourable an opportunity as the
present, being precluded from speaking myself to Miss A—n by
the state of her health; and because any further delay wd. be ascribed
to want of *empressement*, whereas hitherto it has only been a principle.

Under these circumstances, I pledge myself to bear as manfully
as I can any disappointment, and at all events not to make you
chargeable with that which, in all human possibility, is already
decided, and only awaits its completion or negation in the event
being made known to us.

At the same time, my feelings at this moment are in a state of
ungovernable anxiety, which may make me talk a great deal of
nonsense backwards and forwards; but of this I beg you *to take no
account*, only bearing in mind that the whole is *at my peril*, as you will
only be acting by my *express desire* and earnest request.

And whether I am to succeed or fail in this most important
moment that in my life yet occurred, you alone, my dear Mother,
can enable me to bear success without madness, or disappointment
without despair.

Ever your affectionate son
Alex^r d'Arblay

11 Bolton Street
Piccadilly
Monday morning, May 24, 1824.[1]

How Madame d'Arblay coped with this mission does not
appear. Speculations about human action are hazardous, but
if the Angersteins were unwilling to trust their daughter to
Alex's fortune and prospects, Madame d'Arblay, in the pride
that made her stiffly independent rather than abject, would be
quick to anticipate and accept such objections. Alas for the
young Comte d'Arblay (and, perhaps, the youthful Caroline)!
Report had it that at Ely she had seemed susceptible enough
to the preacher-poet and very willing to listen to a declaration.[2]
Alex gained his first experience as a parish priest in March,

---

[1] A typed copy (Barrett).
[2] A.L. (Barrett) from Charlotte Barrett to FBA, n.d.

1824, when Jacobs, his former tutor, asked him to relieve Mr. Lockhart in the two parishes of Stone and Hartwell in Buckinghamshire for three weeks. Fortunately for the record, Fanny went along also. Visual pictures are infrequent in Fanny's writing, but here she supplied one of Alex waiting in his surplice at the antique door of the church of Stone to officiate at an infant's funeral. The church stood 'on an eminence, with the town at its foot, & high hills, rather bleak, in every other part of the view'. The infant's coffin was carried by 'four young maidens in long red cloaks' from the top of a distant hill into the valley, and then up again to the reach of the church-yard, and at the end of the procession came 'the poor Father, in tattered garments', holding another child by the hand. The young clergyman went out with measured pace to the gate of the churchyard,

then led the way back, reading occasionally some sentences of scripture; & his bare head & meditative turn of features gave him a very poetical appearance, though by no means a dramatic or irreligious one—*au contraire*, he was deeply impressed by the cere-mony, which he performed for the first time.[1]

The only clerical disaster worth recording was Alex's forgetting on one Sunday to give out the banns, but this was speedily remedied on the following Sunday when the impatient bride-elect took care to seat herself where she could jog the clerk 'to jog the Parson'. When Alex apologized a little later, the clerk grinned: 'I don't think the Man cared much, sir—but, Mister Lockhart would be main angry, for he's very pertickler.'[1]

In Alex's thirtieth year (1824), he was at length brought into notice and favour. On March 28 the Bishop of London heard him preach and recommended him to Dr. Moore, the vicar of St. Pancras, who, after listening to a trial sermon, offered him the new chapel at Camden Town. As curate, Alex was to be responsible for parish duties over a wide district (according to Fanny, for a population of 80,000) with an emolument of £200 per year with £50 deducted for living quarters.[2] Madame

---

[1] 2 A.L. (Berg) from FBA to AA, 2, 12 Feb. 1824; 2 A.L. (Berg) to Charlotte Barrett, 1824; A.L.S. (Berg) from AA to CPB, 27 Mar. 1824.
[2] 2 A.L. (Berg) from FBA to Charlotte Barrett, 2 Sept., 14 Oct. 1824; 2 A.L.S. (Berg) to EBB, 10 June, 1 Sept. 1824; 3 A.L. (Berg) to CBFB, 5 July, 4 Oct. 1824, 13 Mar. 1828; A.L. (Berg) to Mrs. Locke, 18 [July 1824]. See also Charles E. Lee, *St. Pancras Church and Parish* (1955), ch. viii.

d'Arblay was only mildly elated. She hoped that Alex could live for part of each week, at least, in Bolton Street, for 'he will not, (under a *very good living*, & a wife, to boot) give up London, its Literature, Science, improvements, society, Libraries, & public places, to live completely in a Fauxbourg, that is neither Town nor Country'.[1] She always thought of Camden Town as a Fauxbourg between St. Pancras and Hampstead, though she could not but admire the lovely prospects extending to Regent's Park, Hampstead, Highgate, Primrose Hill, and Kentish Town.[1] In a candid letter of June 19 to Esther she revealed deep misgivings about her son's career. 'It is not his capability that I can doubt—*that* would be affectation, but it is his *absence* and his *carelessness*.'

He is so unused to controll, so little in habits of punctuality, so in-different to the customs of the World, & so careless of inferences, opinions, & consequences, that I cannot but tremble to see him advanced at once, to the whole duty of a New Church in a new Parish, with the complete charge of the District—without some previous practice as an attendant Curate.[1]

No such observations, however, were allowed to appear in her letter of June 17 to Alex, then in Paris. The offer was very flattering, since unsolicited, and, as their clerical friends thought, 'a first step to high & solid Church preferment'—to heights other than Hampstead Hill.[2]

The next notable event was the consecration of the new chapel. On that day (July 15) Madame d'Arblay was a guest in the vicar's pew, and steadfast beside her, Archdeacon Cambridge. As the 'mitred carriage' approached, the folding doors were flung open, and presently the Bishop emerged from the vestry, then 'a body of the Clergy', the twelve parliamentary trustees, the Chancellor, the churchwardens, clerks, beadles, and vergers, and with the procession a tall, slight, dark young man drooping along the way—Alexander d'Arblay, son of Lieutenant-General Comte Jean Baptiste Piochard d'Arblay and Frances Burney, his wife. Fanny was considerably pained to see her son's dejection, then grew quite frantic with anxiety when, after the morning service was read and the third verse of the hymn preceding the sermon was sung, no preacher

---

[1] See p. 436, n. 2.
[2] A.L. (Berg) from FBA to AA, 17 June 1824.

appeared in the pulpit. 'Mr. Wesley ran & re-ran over the keys with *fugish* perseverance', Mrs. Moore looked about expressively, and the Archdeacon 'quite shook' with the fear that Alex had either lost his sermon, or had thought of a new conclusion. The Bishop's glance fell on the vicar's pew and on the little lady with the anxious frightened eyes (this must be the famous Madame d'Arblay, Fanny Burney, who had written *Evelina* and *Cecilia* nearly half a century ago). The delay was the verger's fault after all, but when the 'new camdenite' appeared to give the preliminary prayer his voice was scarcely audible. Then 'feeling his voice, or recovering from some tremor', his mother thought, he gave out the text 'with a fullness of tone' she supposed must have carried it to Hampstead.

The instant all was over, the kind Archd^n gave me his hand, with a cordial shake, saying 'I give you Joy!'

The committee of trustees spoke with Mrs. Moore, who later turned to Fanny. 'I hope you have been gratified, Mme d'Arblay, for every body else has.' In the vestry also everyone was gratified:

Dr. Moore . . . said dauntlessly, without waiting to be informed first of the Bishop's opinion, 'My lord, I hope you have been gratified?' 'I have been highly gratified,' he answered; & it is the second time Mr. d'Arblay has given me gratification.[1]

No sooner had the long quest ended than the Archdeacon began to devise means of saving the new shepherd and his charge from 'those occasional aberrations of mind which belong to men of ardent imaginations, & cause them to forget the immediate object on which their attention should be fixed'. The Archdeacon advocated

a steady middle aged man servant of rather methodical habits not a fine gentleman or a *genius* but with a head like a wooden Dutch clock that can strike the hours and quarters, and who must be allowed to sound them (respectfully) in his master's ears.[2]

Fanny too thought that Alex's adjutant should be *middle-aged*, not a raw boy, who will be always playing at marbles in your absence; nor a young second hand fop, who will wear your shirts &

---

[1] See p. 436, n. 2.
[2] A.L.S. (Barrett) from George Cambridge to FBA, 12 June 1824; also A.L.S. (Berg) from FBA to AA, 17 June 1824.

cravats for you, & then wonder they are always in want of renewal; nor a gawky country lad, who will always be running to the ale house,[1]

but a reliable handy man who would be willing to work and lay a little money by for his old age. In mid-August Fanny took lodgings near Alex's apartments at 49 Park Street or Park *Row* (as she thought it ought to be called, since it was open in front to Regent's Park). In November she left him in charge of a very kind couple to whom she was forever grateful for shaking him out of deep slumber when the chapel bell began to ring, or for waiting with a greatcoat at the door to tell him when it was raining.[2]

What Alex needed was a wife. Esther had suggested a Miss Margland—the disagreeable governess in *Camilla*—as a suitable helpmeet. Fanny quite approved. 'Your recommendation of a good steady woman about 40, with strong nerves, a large stock of Patience, is a portrait the most judicious possible for my belle fille.' Alex, who had always appreciated his Aunt Burney's fund of wit, had shouted with laughter. 'I wish you could as easily reform as you can entertain him!'[3]

The Burney correspondence of the ensuing years provides various glimpses of young d'Arblay and the vicissitudes of his career. The French affairs were not yet settled, and from 1824 to 1829 he was often in Paris with difficulties about an indemnity. 'Now it is the Religion; now, the country; now the Birth, and now the Benefice.' And now he has secured the indemnity *in full*, and his mother fears that he will spend it, as he did Dr. Burney's legacy, on books.[4] Now Aunt Broome is as angry as possible with him for coming home with an Elzevir edition rather than the new coat she thought he needed; and now he has been seen in a drawing-room somewhere in something beyond the peak of fashion—in a *gold* coat. The reigning complaint, however, was about a negligence in dress that, in Charlotte Barrett's opinion, kept 'poor Alex a curate and a bachelor to this moment'. And then Madame d'Arblay could never be easy about his health. He was 'thinner than the

---

[1] See p. 437, n. 2.   [2] See p. 436, n. 2.
[3] Diary MSS. (Berg), scraps, box vii.
[4] Seven letters (Berg) from FBA to EBB, 10 June 1824, 7 June, 29 Oct., 10 Dec. 1825, 28 June 1826, 16 Feb., 12 June 1828. Also 4 letters (Berg) to CBFB, 2–4 Oct. 1824, 13 Mar., 25 Oct. 1828, 14 Dec. 1829.

thinnest', still subject to burning fevers and lethargies. Often
he sat up all night, versifying the Psalms or writing society
verses, or on Saturday night, till dawn, composing his sermon
for the morning. 'I can never quit him', Madame d'Arblay
wrote to Esther, who in the summer of 1825 had wished for
company by the seaside. 'I can never quit him with ease of
mind, for more than a few days while I still witness his un-
conquerable incurability in the care of his Health, his affairs,
his arrangements, his Engagements, even his *attire*!' Again he is
'in excellent looks', as Sarah Harriet thought in 1828. She has
heard 'by a side wind, & from a quarter not to be distrusted'
that he 'dresses like a gentleman and goes into good society,
and is remarked for his clever countenance; and in favour with
all those he gets into conversation with'. In the same year Sally
Payne was wishing with all her heart that the Bishops would do
something for him. 'I believe he really at present performs his
clerical duties very completely and without any *forgets*. He
certainly is not only a charming companion, but grows more &
more so every time we see him.' She wished also that he could
be 'made aware how much his dear mother's health depends
now on her mind being kept perfectly easy, and he would be
better pleased to be told so by my aunt Broome, and more
convinced, than by anything a cousin could say'. In 1829 Esther
had caught a glimpse of him before he set out for Dover, 'and
to you [Charlotte], I must say—how sorry I was to see how *old*
he looked, his poor mother in a most anxious state about him &
his affairs'. Fanny was often in a 'most anxious state' or 'sadly
annoyed' about his careless ways; and his gay letters, at least
those extant, seem little calculated to allay solicitude—a letter
of 1834, for instance, telling about his travels to Buxton, when
he stood at the back of a stage-coach and, 'pelted by the pitiless
storm' all the way, arrived thoroughly soaked.

Being quite knocked up by my journey, I resolved to cut it & go
quickly to bed. What was my vexation to find the next day that this
was *the* great ball of the season—& that the Spencer party were all
there, along with Miss *Byron* (the daughter of the great lord) a
charming & most interesting girl—whom I had felt most curious to
see & who took her leave the next day. So as usual . . . I arrived
'just in time to be too late'.[1]

[1] See Note M, p. 494.

Sally Payne added cheerful postscripts to Alex's letters from Buxton telling her about gay jaunts and parties in which Alex is 'the delight of us all, the life of the house'. Unfortunately a Miss Sheridan was leaving, but 'Alex is easily consolable in such cases'.[1]

These accounts are impressionistic merely, describing passing or drifting events; like the flotsam marking a wreck, they are insignificant, meaningless in themselves, but meaningful perhaps as symptoms of something amiss—something that in the end served to nullify high potentialities, purpose, and endeavour. The crisis in Alex's affairs, however, was deferred until 1835, when he had reached his forty-first year.

Meanwhile a succession of Burneys passed and repassed in dutiful visits to Aunt d'Arblay in Mayfair: Susan's daughter, Fanny Raper, 'still a Hebe of freshness & beauty'; Sally Payne, 'all spirit & pleasantry & agreeability'; Dick Barrett, an Eton schoolboy, bearing messages from his mother and grandmother; Charles Parr Burney, now the third Dr. Burney; Maria Bourdois, from whom Fanny had been alienated for six years over the decision to leave Bath, all of which, however, 'passed from my mind & memory, at sight of her changed & really touching expression of distress'. Among the Worcester Burneys 'known & loved in happy days' was Rebecca Sandford, another nonpareil: 'round & around we may all look ere we see so sweet a character'.[2] Faithful also to former times was Edward Francesco, who year after year came on Sunday for tea, usually accompanied by his niece Fanny Burney. So gentlemanly was his appearance that Madame d'Arblay did not guess, until Esther told her, how very economical he had need to be. Fanny was scandalized. 'Can it be possible such should be the result of a Life, of Talents, & of virtues like his!' 'How shamefully ill must he have been paid for his innumerable as well as beautiful Works!' The subject spurred her to a long reflective letter on her gifted cousin, his talents and modesty, or rather 'invincible diffidence' that amounted to *obduracy* in his resistance to all suggestions that sought to push his works into notice or 'bring his merit forward'.[3]

[1] See Note M, p. 494.
[2] 2 A.L. (Berg) from FBA to CBFB, 30 July 1821, 13 Mar. 1828; 2 A.L. (Berg) to Charlotte Barrett, 9 Dec. 1823, 2 May 1825; three letters (Berg) to EBB, 8 July 1824, Feb. 1825, 8 Dec. 1826.
[3] 2 A.L. (Berg) from FBA to EBB, 8 July 1824, Dec. 1826.

The letters of the twenties, at least those free of crushing bereavements and troubles, were still occasionally shot through with flashes of the comic spirit, and among them were the letters dealing with the vexed problem of domestic help.

The Demoiselle Holmes did not hit my fancy at all. I thought she had a species of bold countenance, which was not rendered more timid by an almost immediate enquiry whether I did not keep a Footman, & the plump remark, in answer to my negative—'Why that's but awkward.' 'And *dull*, too?' quoth I—which surprised from her a good hearty & honest laugh. Whereupon I recommended to her to apply for a place of more convivial agreeability; & she smiled more sedately, & curtsied respectfully, & we parted, very good friends.[1]

Visitors to Bolton Street included friends faithful to other days: Madame d'Arblay's 'old Intimate Blue crony, Sir W. W. Pepys'; Mrs. Hoare (Sophy Thrale); and Lady Templetown, who often called on her way to visit Mrs. Locke at Eliot Vale, sometimes taking Fanny along with her. In the year 1826 Sir Walter Scott came to see the 'celebrated authoress of *Evelina* and *Cecilia*' and found 'an elderly lady, with no remains of personal beauty, but with a simple and gentle manner, a pleasing expression of countenance, and apparently quick feelings'.[2]

There was laughter in Bolton Street when in October, 1826, Charlotte returned from a year's sojourn in Italy and France, where she had accompanied her invalid son Clement for change of air.[1] All the family were amazed that Sister Broome, the most English of the Burneys in habits and prejudices, should have liked France so well. Fanny had been especially uneasy, but now she

embraced her with a thankfulness & pleasure unspeakable—Her terrible illness & danger, so far from Home—from us All . . . had impressed me with so much apprehension & concern . . . that I had never yet received her sight with such full Joy.[3]

She noted that Charlotte had adopted some Paris fashions and looked delightful—'quite *pretty*, were it not for those faithless

[1] 3 A.L. (Berg) from FBA to Charlotte Barrett, 7 Apr., 2, 11 May 1825; 2 A.L. (Berg) to EBB, 29 Oct., 30 Dec. 1825.

[2] J. G. Lockhart, *Memoirs of Sir Walter Scott* (5 vols., 1900), v. 72–73. Also A.L.S. (Berg) from EBB to CBFB, 25 Oct. 1829.

[3] A.L.S. (Berg) from FBA to EBB, 25 Oct. 1826.

first runners away of the graceful effect, to common beholders, of sportive gaiety'. Fanny intended to suggest that Charlotte should have these 'drawbacks to the pleasures of risibility' mended, but in spite of them, according to Charlotte's grand-daughter, Julia Barrett, then about seventeen years old, there was much risibility in Bolton Street. All the family remarked on Julia's beauty. Madame d'Arblay thought her a 'most lovely companion, without & within', and 'simple, unaffected, affectionate, useful, & pleasing'.[1] Julia, in her turn, indus-triously commented on evenings in Bolton Street.

'We go to Aunt d'Arblay every night & have the pleasantest possible evenings with her. She tells such amusing stories as you well know—sometimes repeats poetry—takes off all the curious people she used to know, &c. that you can easily imagine how pleasant it is!' 'Alex makes Grandmama as angry as possible with him every night, by bringing home some new book he has bought in the day, while none of her persuasions can induce him to buy a new coat.' Sometimes Mrs. Angerstein called, and Julia had never seen anyone 'so elegant as she is!' Sometimes Cousin Edward came to tea. Once he had allowed Julia to look at his drawings. 'The Girls' School' was 'most beautiful and full of fun'. 'Drawing taught in all its Branches' included capital sketches of 'drawing a long Bow' and drawing straws and teeth. He had also written and illustrated a new set of adventures for John Gilpin. 'Notwithstanding the fun & absurdity of the ideas, [they] are so extremely beautiful, that one is never tired of looking at them.' They were 'equal to Hogarth, in Humour, & to Cipriani in taste', and Julia could not understand Edward's excessive modesty. One could never be tired of looking at such drawings, and yet nothing, no one, could be as entertaining as Aunt d'Arblay. 'All her merry stories set her, & us laughing for the hour together, but some-times in the midst of her _grave_ ones, Grandmama falls asleep, & when she wakes again, Aunt d'Arblay insists upon my telling all the story over again, up to the point where Grandmama fell asleep—Only fancy how appalling! to have to tell Aunt d'Arblay's stories before her face!'[2]

[1] See p. 442, n. 3.
[2] A.L.S. (Barrett) from Julia Barrett to Charlotte Barrett, 31 Oct. 1826. Also A.L. (Barrett) from CBFB and Julia Barrett to Henrietta Barrett, n.d.

In 1828 Alex, dissatisfied with his accommodation in 11 Bolton Street, persuaded his mother to move to 1 Half Moon Street, where he could have a large and well-lighted study. This dwelling was opposite the Green Park and still near the squares that Fanny liked for their walks and fresh air. She was still within half an hour's summons of the 'gracious & beloved Princesses' and easily accessible to members of the family who happened to come on brief visits to London.

The years 1828 and 1829 marked two family casualties in the deaths of Esther's daughter Fanny Burney, authoress of *Tragic Dramas* (1818), and of Charlotte's son, Clement Francis, Fellow of Christ's College, Cambridge. 'He has lived, & looked like one dying, except for partial intervals', said Fanny, 'for many years.' 'But those who remain to mourn such premature bereavements must surely—surely be pitied—felt for to the Heart's Core.'[1]

In 1828, the year of the death of the Queen of Würtemberg (the Princess Royal of Great Britain), Madame d'Arblay, having scarcely herself recovered from some illness, went 'Mobbled, & Muffled, & Hooded' to pay a consolatory visit to Princess Sophia at Kensington Palace. She could sometimes see herself as well as others as 'a Figure of Fun' and still in a sad world enjoy laughter, even at her own expense. And so she arrived, at the age of seventy-six, at Kensington Palace—

to the no small wonder, no doubt,—& probably Horror, of the Heralds preceding my ushering into Presence,—who, having received orders to take care I caught no cold, came forward as the royal vehicle drove up to the Gates, Two pages with a large umbrella in front, & two footmen to each touch an Elbow in the rear,—& two underlings spreading a long carpet from the coach steps onward to the Hall, . . . & all, no doubt, inwardly sniggering when they saw it was for such a Figure of Fun! However, I am always so well pleased when I can be beguiled into a little simper myself, that I am ever ready to rejoice when I can produce a sly smile, or an honest Grin, or an unguarded Horse laugh in any of my neighbours.[2]

In the autumn of 1829 Esther spent a month with Fanny,

[1] A.L. (Barrett) from EBB to FBA and CBFB, 17 Oct. 1828; A.L. (Barrett) from FBA to CBFB, 31 Mar.–1 Apr. 1828; A.L.S. (Berg) from Charlotte Barrett to FBA, 9 May 1828; A.L.S. (Berg) from FBA to CBFB, 19 Feb. 1829. Also letters (Barrett) for the years 1825–30.

[2] A.L.S. (Berg) from FBA to CBFB, 25 Oct. 1828.

well pleased at finding her so well ('& grown quite plump').[1] This was a joyous interlude; yet apart from such visits, Madame d'Arblay often found the evenings very lonely, for 'evening society in London is very difficult to be obtained'.

It requires an expence quite ruinous with regard to vehicles—even where the visits are to Friends whose cars are at one's command: for though the Horses may prance to and fro with disinterested obedience, their drivers & Back attendants would wear aspects terribly grim if made to partake of the same exalted self-privation.[2]

Bath was the place where indigent 'Female *Elegant* society' could live with 'dignity and independence'. In Bath one might still call for a chair, but in London chairs were 'nearly exploded' and so rarely demanded as to be enormous in price.[2] In the evenings then, at least when her eyes would permit, Madame d'Arblay pored over 'pale & melancholy' manuscripts and, writing on, augmented them by the ream.

[1] See p. 442, n. 2.
[2] A.L.S. (Berg) from FBA to EBB, 7 June 1825.

XVII

MEMOIRS

(1828–1832)

I have very long known that my Father *designed* & *wished* &
bespoke me for his Editor.
MADAME D'ARBLAY, 1820[1]

THE editing of Dr. Burney's papers was begun in 1797, when
after the death of Mrs. Burney the Doctor himself undertook to re-read and destroy sections of his correspondence.
Madame d'Arblay was then living at West Humble, but on
visits to Chelsea she was invited to help her father with the task.

From the time of the death of my mother-in-Law, he put the key
of his Bureau of private Letters & papers into my hand, & began
employing me to examine, read, preserve, or destroy his long
accumulation. This was our constant occupation, *I* reading, & he
listening, during the fortnight or 3 weeks I spent with Him at that
time: & when I left him for dear, dear Westhumble, he told me I should
renew it every visit I made;—& so I did, in the few intervals in
which we were tête à tête from that period before my departure for
France. But they were rare, & our joint rummage did not extend,
I think, beyond his early Letters.[1]

In 1802 Fanny joined her husband in Paris, and when with
the course of the Napoleonic wars the Doctor began to despair
of her return, he chose Charles as his editor, 'conceiving him,
next to myself, most acquainted with his literary habits, intentions, & wishes'.[1] On her reappearance in 1812, however,
Charles relinquished the work with very good grace 'considering
the very erroneous ideas he had formed & nourished' of its
pecuniary value.[1] She discovered that during her ten years'
absence, the Doctor had not gone further

than with his correspondence with my Mother in Law, & all her
Letters & papers, & those of Bengal Richard; of all of which I never

---

[1] A.L.S. (Barrett) from FBA to EBB, 20 Nov. 1820. Also A.L.S. (Osborn) from
CB to Christian Latrobe, [1796]; 2 A.L.S. (Berg) from CB to CB, Jr., [1796]; to
FBA, 2 Dec. 1796: 'I have burned near 500 long letters to my *late* dear partner,
wch she c^d not find in her heart, poor soul, to destroy.'

found a single vestige. All else, he amused himself in sorting & arranging, but destroyed not a line; not even an invitation to dinner.[1]

But when she was again at Chelsea, the Doctor

again put his key into my hands, & pointed to the Pigeon holes in which were the packets he bid me read to him. We went through the Letters of Mr. Greville, from the commencement of that early intercourse,—all of which were clever, but many disputative, quarrelsome, & highly disagreeable. He did not preserve above 3 or 4.[1]

Most of the review of 1812 was given to the Doctor's verses

& to bits & scraps of his memoirs, pointed out by himself—& which, taken separately, & selected, & apropos to some current subject, or person, read agreeably,—when read by Himself, & consequently intermixt with anecdotes & recollections that rendered them interesting—as was every thing he ever related.[1]

In 1814 Fanny had taken rooms in Lower Sloane Street in order to be near her Father, but through various unpropitious circumstances the editorial work was neglected.

He meant I should go through his whole stores, *to* him & *with* him; I meant & wished it also, most sincerely; but he had no sleeping room for me at the College; our Evenings, therefore, were necessarily very short,—& I lived more at Charles's & with Charlotte than at the College; & my own work, promised to the publick, by Longman, at a stated period, without my consent,—through some mistake—entangled my time so dreadfully that the progress of our manuscript researches was slow & scarcely perceptible.[1]

Fanny's family concerns, the slowness of her recovery from her operation, the writing of *The Wanderer*, and finally the Doctor's failing strength prevented prolonged or serious work on the manuscripts. In April of 1814 Doctor Burney died. In his will no provision was made for the deposition or editing of his memoirs and correspondence—an omission that Fanny said had astonished her, 'considering the unexamined state of his private memorandums, & the various papers that could not have been spread, even in a general Family review, without causing pain, or confusion, or mischief'.[1] By general consent of the family the trust devolved upon her, and any proceeds

[1] See p. 446, n. 1.

realized from the publication of the papers were to be shared with Esther as a residuary legatee.

When the d'Arblays set out for Paris in 1814, they took the Doctor's papers with trunks of family letters and journals; and at their precipitate flight on the return of Napoleon from Elba, prominent among Fanny's worries were the hoards of manuscripts left to the vicissitudes of war.[1] Everything was safe, however, as the d'Arblays found on their return from Trèves late in 1815, and the trunks of papers were again packed up to follow them to England and to Bath.[2] There the d'Arblays again set up a troubled household, but it was not until the summer of 1817 at Ilfracombe that Fanny found leisure for a serious examination of her father's Memoirs.[3] In 1814 she had expected that she would need only to make an abridgement,

which I thought would contain 3 Volumes in octavo; & to select his correspondence to the amount of 3 more, which would rapidly sell the whole, in chusing them from the names of Garrick, Diderot, Rousseau, Dr. Warton, Dr. Johnson, Mr. Mason, Horace Walpole, Lord Mornington, Mr. Crisp, Mr. Greville, Mrs. Greville, Lady Crewe, Mr. Bewley, Mr. Griffiths, Mr. Cutler, M[rs] Le Noir, Lord Macartney, Lord Lonsdale, Duke of Portland, Mr. Canning, Mr. Windham, Mr. Wesley, Mr. La Trobe, Mr. Walker, Mr. Burke, Mr. Malone, S[r] J. Reynolds, Mr. Seward, Kit Smart, Mrs. Piozzi.[4]

Could anyone read such names, she thought, '& not conclude that the Press would cover them with Gold'?[4] At Ilfracombe she found that she had been deceived.

Doubts, & strong ones, had, indeed, occurred, from my occasional view of the state of the Repository, in hunting for some secret Letters & papers of Mr. Broome, which Charlotte most earnestly claimed from me, & helped me to seek: but it was at Ilfracombe, in 1817, that my definitive disappointment took place. In reading the Memoirs *de suite*, with a red pencil in my hand, for little erasures & curtailings, I soon unhappily, discovered that they really were so unlike all that their honoured writer had ever produced to the

---

[1] 2 A.L.S. (Berg) from FBA to EBB, 8 Apr., 1 July 1815.

[2] A.L. (Berg) from FBA to Mary Port Waddington, 19 Dec. 1815.

[3] See drafts of letters (Berg) from FBA to Princess Elizabeth, June 1817, in which she says she is engaged in 'rummaging, sorting, selecting, preserving or destroying the innumerable mass of MSS. of every description left by my dear Father. He seems to have burnt nothing.'   [4] See p. 446, n. 1.

Publick, that not only they would not have kept up his credit & fair
Name in the literary World, if brought to light, but would certainly
have left a cloud upon its parting ray—attended by a storm of disapprobation, if not invective, upon the Editor who,—for a fortnight's
quick profit from his earlier established celebrity, had exhibited her
faded Father's faded talents.—A fortnight, I say; because, the first
curiosity satisfied, the Memoirs would have sunk to waste, & have
been heard of no more.[1]

Fanny little knew how much 'curiosity *un*satisfied' was to lament
this work, but it was the content, not the loss, that she thought
lamentable.

All the juvenile voluminous MSS. are filled with *literal* nurses' tales,
—such as, narrated by himself, were truly amusing, as his vivacity
& quickness & ready Wit rendered every thing that passed his lips:
but on paper, & *read*, not *recited*, they were trivial to poverty, & dull
to sleepiness. What respected his family, mean while, was utterly
unpleasant—& quite useless to be kept alive. The dissipated facility
& negligence of his Witty & accomplished, but careless Father; the
niggardly unfeelingness of his nearly unnatural Mother; . . . all these
furnish matter of detail, long, tedious, unnecessary,—and opening
to the publick view a species of Family degradation to which the
name of Burney now gives no similitude.

In coming to the epoch of Manhood, I had hoped to find some
interesting details, & descriptions, relative to our dear & lovely own
mother: but from whatsoever cause, he is here laconic almost to
silence. 3 or 4 lines include all the history of his admiration & its
effects. Whether these were recollections too melancholy for his
nerves, or whether the intensity with which he had once felt on this
subject had blunted his remnant sensibility, I cannot determine—
but he gives his whole paper at this time to enormous long paragraphs & endless folio pages, upon the City electioneering for
organs & concerts, & Stanley's rivalry, & Fraser's, & local interests
of the day, now sunk for every memory, & containing nothing that
could either benefit or amuse a single Reader by remaining on
record.

Then follow various cahiers on Norfolk & Lynn, with some more
agreeable style of writing,—but still upon people not generally
known, nor ever described with circumstances that may create a
running interest for them. All is detached, vague, & unknit into
any consistence.

At last comes London; & Then all the great names I have

[1] See p. 446, n. 1.

mentioned to you begin to occur: & here I had the full expectation
of detail, anecdote, description, & conversation, such as to manifest
these characters in the brilliant light of their own Fame, & to shew
our dear Father the carressed, sought, honoured & admired Friend
of such a constellation: for such he was & as much loved & esteemed
as if he had been universal Patron of them all.—

But alas, what a falling off ensues!—He contents himself with
naming all these people, saying where they met, mentioning the first
day he made acquaintance with them; where they dined together—
the Day, the Week—the month, the year—& then stops short, to
go to some other date for some other such encounter. There is little
more than copying the minutes of engagements from his Pocket
Books, made at the time his memory was full & gay, & when he
purposed dilating upon every name & circumstance in his Memoirs, as he did, on the moment, in his discourse to his family or
friends.[1]

This was Madame d'Arblay's summary of the twelve closely
written *cahiers* of the Doctor's Memoirs. Her editorial work was,
by her own standards, conscientiously thorough. Since 'the dear
indefatigable author' revised and rewrote some of the *cahiers*
three times over, so she read and re-read the variant versions
'to ascertain whether there were any difference in the narra-
tions & any choice to be taken', holding 'it right not to destroy
a line unexamined'.[1]

By November, 1820, she had perused the Memoirs throughout with 'the most sedulous attention' and had gone over them
a second time,

in marking & separating every leaf, or passage, that may be usefully,
or ornamentally, Biographical. While all that I thought utterly
irrelevant, or any way mischievous, I have committed to the Flames.
Whatever admits of any doubt, or demands any Enquiry, I have
set apart.[1]

She considered it 'not nothing' in the present state of her health
and spirits

to have dissected this multifarious work, & to have removed all that
appeared . . . peccant parts, that might have bred fevers, caused
infectious ill-will, or have excited morbid criticism or ridicule.[1]

She had seen 'how much evil might have accrued from its

[1] See p. 446, n. 1.

falling into other hands, less aware of various allusions' than she was, and her mind was 'considerably easier'.

By this time she had also read other parts of the voluminous archive.

The enormous load of Letters, Memoirs, documents, mss: collections, copies of his own Letters, scraps of authorship, old pocket Books filled with personal & business memorandums, & fragments relative to the History of Musick, are countless, fathomless![1]

Among 'common & useless' material there was much that was 'edifying, secret, or interesting'. 'The inspection, were it made by a person out of the family', she rightly judged, 'would be curious & entertaining', but to her, 'from concomitant recollections, losses, & regrets', it was often very painful.[2] By 1828 Esther also had read packets of the papers in question. When she agreed with her sister on their nature and worth, Fanny 'felt lightened of one of the heaviest burthens' on her mind,

& from that time, thought no more of the matter, but continued burning the collection as fast as I had leisure to re-read, & consider over what bits & scraps ought to be rescued from the flames, for some *ultimate* short record, preceding such few Letters as could be selected that were promising of any general interest.[3]

Of the 'bits & scraps' of Dr. Burney's Memoirs that escaped the flames there are at least 135 fragments extant.[4] Though the skeleton of one *cahier* still survives, the remains include for the most part leaves or parts of leaves cut from the original *cahiers*, pieces written and often rewritten from margin to margin in the fine vertical handwriting of the Doctor's old age. These bits were in Madame d'Arblay's opinion the purple patches, and as such were allowed to survive, but 'curious & entertaining' they most certainly are, especially the anecdotes drawn from the life of Bath and London in the forties. These are at once vignettes of Burney's laughing gifted young manhood and little set-pieces or distillations of eighteenth-century life as vividly clear as Dutch paintings imagined in miniature. A few of the anecdotes referring to Fanny herself are printed in the three-volume work on her father that she ultimately produced. Another category of material partially utilized in the

[1] See p. 446, n. 1.   [2] See p. 448, n. 3.
[3] 2 A.L. (Berg) from FBA to EBB, 16 Feb. 1828 and n.d.
[4] See Ch. I, p. 1, n. 3.

work and still surviving in manuscript is the series entitled 'Characters Extracted from various writings of my dearest father'.[1]

What seems to be lost besides curious vignettes of eighteenth-century life is detailed information about the musical and theatrical worlds, musicians and actors, together with amusing anecdotes, facts, and scenes relating to the Doctor's youth, which, as is frequently the case, remained more clearly etched in his aged memory than later events. Still extant, for instance, is his account of a luxurious journey with his daughter Esther in 'an admirable Diligence' from Paris to Lyons in 1766. He named and described the other passengers—a lady of the *noblesse*, a *visconte*, a brigadier, a major of the Guards, a literary gentleman, and a rich merchant from Lyons. He recounted parts of their conversation, and he could easily have filled a volume, he said, 'in describing the persons & things which occurred in this agreeable voyage, they are still so fresh in my memory, though more than 40 years have elapsed since it took place'.[1] This journey was taken not in 1764, as has been supposed, but during a subsequent and very lively visit to Paris in 1766. Even those leaves that remain will serve to set parts of the record straight.

However the loss may be deplored, Madame d'Arblay's motives are clear. She would not exhibit her 'faded Father's faded talents' for a fortnight's profit. She would not publish the material or risk its being used by others in a manner 'disagreeable to all his Race'. After Charles's death she thought of giving the papers to Charles Parr, but, though she could trust his 'honour' and 'delicacy', she knew

he *could* not have found time, & *would* not have found patience, for such a revisal as would have kept to his own breast the innumerable memorandums, &c. that might most grotesquely, from one secretary or amanuensis to another have got dancing about in the World.[2]

Both Charles and Fanny had expected the Memoirs to be in the style of the Italian and German Tours, but she thought that after investigations like hers he would have agreed that the material could 'reflect no additional lustre' on their father's

[1] A scrap among Dr. Burney's Memoirs (Berg) annotated by FBA.
[2] See p. 446, n. 1.

'bright literary character, but might diminish its radiance, as has been the case with various posthumous publications'.[1] She was persuaded, besides, that the Doctor himself

> would have made all these omissions . . . had he written these memoirs while still living in the World.—And Then—he would have given to what remained the Zest of observation, Conversation, & anecdote.[2]

Four years later, therefore, in her researches of October 10, 1824, she was delighted to come across a comment on the Memoirs, written by her father himself, that seemed to support the opinions she had formed.[3] The Doctor had feared that the records he had kept of his 'numerous invitations' as entered at the time in his Pocket Books and lately transferred to the Memoirs might prove 'very dry & uninteresting' without some account of

> the conversations, bon mots, or characteristic stories told by individuals, who struck fire out of each other, producing mirth & good humour—when these short entries were made I had not leisure for details, & now memory will not supply them!

He could only hope that the Memoirs would be taken, at the worst, as

> *vain boasts* of notices & favours, rec^d from eminent & worthy persons; not of transactions too corrupt & depraved to be termed *human frailties*, or amiable *weaknesses*.

Madame d'Arblay seized on the 'truly sagacious' paragraph as a vindication of the policy she had already chosen out of 'conscientious tenderness to the true Fame' of her gifted father,

> who had he a little earlier commenced his memoirs would have made them one of the best & most edifying works of the present age.[3]

Difficulties also arose over the publication of the second part of the archive—Doctor Burney's correspondence. In 1814 Madame d'Arblay thought that she had only to select letters sufficient to fill three volumes in octavo and that the mere names of such correspondents as Rousseau, Garrick, and

---

[1] See p. 451, n. 3.   [2] See p. 446. n. 1.
[3] In two drafts (Berg).

Dr. Johnson, would ensure a sale. The papers, however, were disappointing and her researches

fatiguing, in general, past all description, for my dear Father has kept, unaccountably, All his Letters, however uninteresting, ceremonious, momentary, or unmeaning. The Few I find that are not fit to light candles, even from the greatest names, is really incredible. They are chiefly invitations, or arrangements of *rendez-vous*. I speak of the Letters of the Great in Rank; those of *Friends* I have not yet begun. Those of great Authors are concise, & upon some accidental occasion.[1]

Few could judge of the toil of reading 'through Bag after Bag' of such letters wholesale. She estimated that it would take about three years to read through the collection.[2]

However, Speed the Plough! my Eyes are better, though still cruelly weakened—Who can wonder?—but I go on as industriously as they will permit me; &, I conclude by surmizing that about 3 years hard reading, for myself, will finally produce about 3 quarters of an hour's reading to my Lecturers. Such, however, as the poor little Book may one Day be, should I live, at last, to edit it, its net profit shall most scrupulously be shared between the Residuary Legatees.[1]

The responsibility was one 'of great plague & perplexity & privacy' but a sense of duty drove her on.

If it were not, as it is, a business of Conscience, there is no advantage I would not gladly relinquish to get rid of so toilsome, perplexing, unwieldly & harassing an occupation.[1]

She would do all she could to prevent the less creditable leaves of the family history or family tree from 'dancing about in the World'.

Such were the editorial policies that she pursued for nearly ten years as she read and selected letters from her father's accumulated stores. By the opening of 1828 she had chosen and edited enough letters for two or three volumes, and was about to send them to a copyist, when she was informed of statutes, passed while she was in France, that classed letters as literary works and protected their authors as owners of copyright.[3] 'To

---

[1] See p. 446, n. 1.

[2] For the present distribution of Dr. Burney's correspondence see Bibliography of MSS. (Appendix B).

[3] Madame d'Arblay's informants were Harriet Bowdler and Mrs. Maltby of Bath. See A.L. (Berg) from FBA to EBB, 16 Feb. 1828. Cf. G. S. Robertson, *The Law of Copyright* (Oxford, 1912), p. 134, for a court ruling of 1813.

collect & select & arrange the *correspondence*' had always been her intention, but, strangely enough, that turned out 'the thing least easy to accomplish'.[1] Since the assortment comprised, for the most part, letters written to rather than by Doctor Burney, it could not be printed (at least not without permissions difficult or impossible to obtain), and all her plans were again thrown into confusion. She thought the rulings just, but deplored the bad luck that had kept her in ignorance of them so long, for all the years, indeed, that she had been 'chronologizing, erazing, & preparing a volume, or two, or three for the press'. She was at liberty, of course, to publish her father's letters, but of these she had only a few. His letters to herself or to other members of the family on family troubles or concerns she would not have dreamed of printing, and except for first drafts of letters of high ceremony or of letters of his very old age, later transcribed by an amanuensis, the Doctor had left few copies of his lively and entertaining epistles.

This was a set-back. It is not nothing, as she might have put it, to have prepared two or three volumes for the press and to discover at the age of seventy-six that one must close the book and begin all over again.

In 1828 she was faced with an ultimatum that if she did not intend to publish a life of her father, the authors of the 'Literary Biographical works' would have to attempt it.[1] She consulted friends who gave an opinion coinciding with her own—that it was her 'bounden Duty' to prepare her father's annals, which otherwise might 'be mangled in a manner disagreeable to all his Race'.[1] True, many of the *cahiers* were now in ashes, but she could resurrect or restore their contents from her 'own full sources & retentive memory, & most confidential repositories'. The biography required only her 'own exertions of mingled intellect & memory—& enough too, God knows!', she added, '& perhaps beyond Both'.[1] Remembering how in the completion of *Cecilia*, *Camilla*, and *The Wanderer* she had been hurried on by both press and public, she decided now to work secretly. In 1828, to the surprise of all beholders, she had been granted a new lease of health, and in February of that year she confessed to Esther that she had begun to write. She was informed that all other hands were discouraged 'from the certainty that, *should*

[1] See p. 451, n. 3.

such be the case, no one living had such materials,—not from
his own mss—which might be transferable, but from personal
memory', and the booksellers 'generously & respectfully' agreed
to wait.[1]

By 1831 she had completed the work, and though she wished
to have it published posthumously, Charles Parr Burney
thought it ought to appear at once so that his aunt could reply
to criticisms or questions that neither he nor any of the Doctor's
grandsons could answer.[2]

In 1832, Madame d'Arblay's eightieth year, *Memoirs of
Doctor Burney* appeared in three volumes, but no memory of her
earlier work or consideration for weight of years or sorrow was
allowed to temper the virulence of the adverse criticisms it
excited, both public and private. The cruellest of these was an
article of some eighteen pages in the *Quarterly Review*, wherein
Croker developed his thesis that the octogenarian effort, partly
destroyed by Madame d'Arblay, could hardly have been 'more
feeble, anile, incoherent, or "*sentant plus l'apoplexie*," than that
which she has substituted for it'.[3] According to Croker, the parts
in the Doctor's own words

though occasionally somewhat inflated, appear simple and natural
in the midst of the strange *galimatias* of pompous verbosity in which
his daughter has enshrined them.[3]

He culled risible examples of 'pompous verbosity', among
them one described as 'a curiosity in its kind', since it contained
what he thought must be the longest adjective in the language.

And not here ended the sharp reverse of this altered year; scarcely
had this *harrowing* filial separation taken place, ere an assault was
made upon his conjugal feelings, by the *sudden-at-the-moment-though-
from-lingering-illnesses-often-previously-expected* death of Mrs. Burney,
his second wife. [The hyphens and italics are Croker's.][3]

If Madame d'Arblay had not been so well meaning and so
aged, even her friends might have thought that she deserved
such strictures not for her style but for her *choice* of styles, that is,
for abandoning the lively and competent prose that, as some of
her letters of the time and later show, she still had at her com-

[1] See p. 451, n. 3.
[2] Draft of A.L. (Berg) from FBA to Rebecca Burney Sandford, Oct. 1832.
[3] xlix (Apr. 1833), 97–125.

mand, for the curious language of the *Memoirs*. She had always been at her best in familiar letters or in fictitious familiar letters (like those in *Evelina*), where she could give free play to her observation, to playfulness, tenderness, or satire, and, in the epistolary novel, to a fifth ingredient, invention. A formal biography, however, was neither a letter nor a novel nor a journal, and it required, as she undoubtedly assumed, something quite different in manner. The curious prose of the *Memoirs of Doctor Burney* was probably developed in an effort to aggrandize the subject, and in an allied effort to *depersonalize* the vast mass of highly personal, private, informal or colloquial, particularized, and often embarrassing material of the familiar writings of the Burneys. Circumlocution and euphemisms were less likely to give offence in biography than was detail, and according to the eighteenth-century critical tenets on which Fanny was brought up, generalizations, even if more remote from the subject, could be more valid than any of the particulars from which they are derived. The biography of her father was a high theme and she undoubtedly hoped to treat it as such, little suspecting that the circumlocutions with which she bridged and abridged embarrassing material, her abstracts, and large generalizations could one day be read as ludicrous pomposities. In 1814 Hazlitt had said that he saw in *The Wanderer* 'no decay of talent, but a perversion of it',[1] and though his critical acumen cost him James's friendship and many a game of whist in James Street, his criticism was neither unjust nor unkind. With regard to style, at least, it is as applicable to the *Memoirs* as to *The Wanderer*.

Not content, however, with denouncing the literary style of the *Memoirs* Croker proceeded to attack Madame d'Arblay's character or motives for writing, accusing her of deceit, falsehood, and inordinate vanity. Under a pretence of writing the Doctor's *Memoirs* she had written her own. 'We have a strong suspicion', said Croker, 'that it was *because* her father's autobiography did not fulfil *this* object, that *it* has been suppressed.'[2] He complained that the story of the publication and success of her own *Evelina* was given a disproportionate space in the work, and alleged that vanity and egotism had dictated her choice of

[1] The *Edinburgh Review*, xxiv (Feb. 1815), 320–33.
[2] See p. 456, n. 3.

material and that vanity had driven her to pretend that she was only seventeen when *Evelina* was published. Croker had taken a journey to King's Lynn and triumphantly ascertained Madame d'Arblay's age from the parish registers (one would have supposed we were 'rival Beauties', she commented) though he could have learned from the Preface (or apologia) to the first edition of *Evelina* that it was Evelina and not Fanny who was supposed to be seventeen when that novel appeared.

Space allotments in the *Memoirs* were not, indeed, measured with mechanical impartiality, but the disproportionate space given to the production and success of *Evelina* may be blamed partly, at least, on Sir Walter Scott, for it was at his request that she wrote down the wonderful story in detail.[1] From the far-away days when Susan and Mr. Crisp greedily importuned her for journal-letters, a request was the spur that most readily set her to writing. Even when she knew that her journals were likely to be circulated widely, she wrote more easily and with greater sureness, charm, and humour when she had one interested reader in mind. What Croker said about vanity may, according to Fanny herself, be allowed; 'All is vanity!' But all attacks on her veracity she strongly resisted.

Contemporary accounts of the Burneys often included much erroneous matter. In 1817 M. d'Arblay, transcribing some account of the Doctor and his family from a Parisian publication, *Biographie des Hommes vivants*, complained of being '*fatigué en diable avoir copié tant d'erreurs*'.[2] In biographical sketches like the preface to the 1814 edition of *Evelina* or in critical reviews like that of Croker himself on *The Wanderer*,[3] the ages of Evelina and Fanny Burney were often confused, but there is no evidence that the mistake originated with the Burneys or that, with all their pride and delight in the wonderful story of *Evelina*, they attempted to perpetuate the erroneous detail. If it be asked why Fanny did not then correct such errors, the answer is that it was her consistent policy to avoid literary quarrels. She had not grown up in her father's house and lived for months at a time at Streatham (to say nothing of visits to Strawberry Hill, Bolt Court, Hampton House, Twickenham Meadows, and Chessington,

<hr>

[1] *Diary*, vi. 410–11; *Memoirs*, ii. 122–3.
[2] A.L. (Berg) from M. d'A to FBA, 25 June 1817.
[3] The *Quarterly Review*, xi (Apr. 1814), 123–30.

or of mornings in the bookstalls or assembly rooms at Bath or Brighton) without hearing, at one time or another, all there was to hear about the literary squabbles of her age and the half-century before and without deciding, for her part, to avoid public disputes and rude warfare with reviewers or critics, 'let them say what they will'. She was pleased with a 'Retort Sarcastic' that her nieces Charlotte Barrett and Fanny Raper had drawn up, but, though she was later to regret it, her first reaction to Croker's attack was typical of the policy she had pursued all her life ('I Shrink from a war of that—or any other kind—in periodicals').[1]

Young d'Arblay had also begun a defence of his mother. Drafts of a composite defence still exist,[2] but plans for publishing it came to nothing—perhaps because of Alex's procrastination, new objections on Fanny's part, or the fears that inexperienced writers like her nieces may well have had in coming to grips with Croker. They knew that truth alone would not suffice for such a combat. For some years Madame d'Arblay thought very little about the malicious aspersions, but in the last months of her life they rose again to plague her, and on July 30, 1839 (about five months before her death), she again referred to Croker's 'Defamation'.

I can use no softer term than Defamation for the least attack upon my veracity and now, once more awakened to my original feeling, I poignantly regret that I did not at once answer it or let my dearest Alex, who could not even name my wanton calumniator but with trembling emotion.

Honesty she always believed 'the first attribute of the noblest work of God'.[3]

It was probably in a dutiful sense of what was owing to her aunt's character, or of what she remembered of Alex's intentions, that Charlotte Barrett, as one may gather, found courage to write to Thomas Babington Macaulay asking him to undertake the vindication. Copies of his reply were sent to various members of the Burney family and still survive:

Nov. 21, 1839
Though I had not the honour of knowing Mr. Alexander d'Arblay

---

[1] A.L. (Berg) from FBA to CBFB, 26 July–1 Aug. 1833.
[2] In both the Berg and the Barrett Collections.
[3] A.L.S. (Berg) from FBA to Charlotte Barrett, 30 July 1839.

I know the works of Madame d'Arblay well, and have read them over & over with constant delight. I should be glad to have an opportunity of shewing my gratitude to a writer from whom I have derived so much innocent pleasure. But I really do not think that I should serve her by noticing the article in the Quarterly Review. Her place in public estimation will be fixed, not by what other people may write about her but by what she has written herself. What would her old friend Dr. Johnson have gained by answering Kenrick? What did Pope gain by engaging in a conflict with Cibber? And what has Madame d'Arblay to gain by a controversy with Croker? In truth the article in the Quarterly Review has long been utterly forgotten while Evelina and Camilla are just as much read as ever.

I earnestly hope that your excellent relation will feel that the only wise course is to meet attacks such as that to which you refer with silent contempt.

I have the honour to be Madam
Your obedient humble servant
T. B. Macaulay.[1]

Holograph scraps of paper show that in the last months (perhaps weeks) of Madame d'Arblay's life, as she wrote down final messages for those she loved and final directions about her will, papers, letters, and keys, her wavering thoughts turned once more to Croker's malicious aspersions: 'Tell Macaulay I honour him for his manly & upright way of speaking of Dr. J . . . I wd have gladly accepted my vindication from his hand. . . . My father was much struck . . . that falsehood & calumny . . . without being stopped & taken up w^d surely increase like a snowball.'[2] She could not know that this calumny on her veracity would resemble a snowball chiefly in having melted away, as Macaulay had said, many years before.

And yet not entirely. Madame d'Arblay had not worried quite in vain. Long after her death Croker's article was quoted at length in a fresh attack of 1862 by Mrs. Waddington's daughter, Lady Llanover. This appeared in the editorial comment on Madame d'Arblay in the sixth volume of *The Autobiography and Correspondence of Mary Granville, Mrs. Delany; with*

---

[1] Copies in both the Berg and the Barrett Collections. Macaulay's letter is referred to in A.L.S. (Berg) from SHB to Anna Wilbraham Grosvenor, 9 Mar. 1843: 'Charlotte Barrett sent it to me, & I think it was written either to her or Fanny Raper'.

[2] Holograph scrap, Diary MSS. (Berg), box viii.

interesting reminiscences of King George III and Queen Charlotte, published in 1861–2.[1] When Mrs. Waddington learned in 1817 that Madame d'Arblay was reading through parts of the Burney correspondence with a view to publication, she anxiously requested that her part of it, the packets of confidential missives that she had written to Fanny since 1789, be returned to her.[2] Fanny complied, if rather dryly; but whether Mrs. Waddington was thinking of her tearful lamentations about Philip Goldsworthy or about something else, she was very uneasy about the Burney publications, and before the *Diary and Letters of Madame d'Arblay* (1842–6) appeared she had formally requested that her name should not appear in it. Charlotte Barrett also complied, and the long biographical letters that Madame d'Arblay wrote to Mrs. Waddington appear under the caption 'Madame d'Arblay to a Friend'.

All this was to come later, but even in 1832 Mrs. Waddington and her daughters found cause for displeasure in the paragraphs (*Memoirs*, iii. 45–55) that seemed to suggest that their aunt Mrs. Delany was a pensioner or something of a pensioner of the Duchess of Portland, and they sought to deny any such dependence. Madame d'Arblay, soon apprised of their displeasure through members of the Burney family then in Italy,[3] turned in great consternation to her masses of papers in a search for old letters to support what had seemed to her a fact known to many. She appealed also to Mrs. Ann Agnew, Mrs. Delany's confidential servant, housekeeper, and amanuensis, whose garrulous and circumstantial replies, docketed in Madame d'Arblay's aged handwriting 'Letters from Ann Agnew, amanuensis & lady's Maid to Mrs. Delany. To be kept for authenticating Dr. Burney's Memoirs', still survive to serve precisely that purpose.[4] They remain to corroborate facts, very

---

[1] vi. 125–8, 263–4, 271–3, 278–9, 316–20.

[2] See A.L. (Barrett) from FBA to Mary Port Waddington, 22 Aug. 1817; and A.L.S. (Berg) to the same, 12 July 1821.

[3] A.L. (Berg) from Charlotte Barrett to FBA, 21 Apr. 1833; also joint A.L. (Barrett) from CBFB and Charlotte Barrett to FBA, 26 Sept. 1834: 'Dr. Jenks who knew Mrs. Waddington at Rome, thought her extremely flighty in the head— half deranged . . . and this excited state of mind may perhaps account for her being querulous on the subject of that work which in reality so much exalts Mrs. Delany's name & character'.

[4] 3 A.L.S. (Barrett) from Ann Agnew to FBA, 18 Mar., 21 Nov. 1834, 13 Jan. 1835. For a contemporary letter giving the same information see Diary MSS. (Berg), 1785–6; also A.L.S. (Berg) from FBA to SBP, 6 July 1798.

well known in court circles at the time of the death of the Duchess of Portland, that had moved King George and Queen Charlotte to grant Mrs. Delany a pension of £300 with an invitation to live at Windsor.[1] If it were not for the invidious attack on Madame d'Arblay's veracity, and if veracity were not one of the indispensable requirements in a journalist or diarist whose writings are to be taken seriously as social or biographical records, then this unworthy controversy revolving about the contents of the hampers that the Duchess of Portland sent or brought to St. James's Place could be forgotten. But if truth be challenged and the challenge still remembered, then it must be shown and conceded that, as the burden of proof has it, the hampers were not empty. Madame d'Arblay spoke truly even if, with all her good intentions (and her intentions were never more respectful than here), somewhat unguardedly and inadvisedly.

A comparison of the mass of Burney manuscripts with the letters, journals, and memoirs that Madame d'Arblay prepared for the press will show that she often suppressed painful episodes of the family history. While such omissions necessarily result in distortion, the evidence is that she did not fabricate or invent. While she did not always tell the full truth about some of the family difficulties, sins, and errors, she did not tell untruths. As a biography, therefore, the *Memoirs* is limited by the point of view and the selection of material, but within its limits it is authoritative, and more authoritative than anything else written on Dr. Burney, or likely to be written. It is based on knowledge that no other biographer can hope to have. Unlike later biographers, she had no need to argue from analogy as to what must have happened, or to make deductions and inferences that may follow the laws of reason but frequently diverge from the historical facts.[2] Man is a creature richly compounded of elements, deeps, and motives other than reason, as it takes no heap of manuscripts to show.

There were cavillers also within the Burney family or among its near connexions. There was first the Reverend Richard Allen Burney (son of Esther and Charles Rousseau), Rector of Rimpton, in Somerset, who in 1807 had made a successful

---

[1] See Note N, p. 494.

[2] See Note O, p. 495.

application to the College of Arms for Armorial Bearings and who seemed more sensitive than other Burneys about his descent from the humble Sleepes. In 1830 he begged his cousin Alex d'Arblay to stop the publication of the *Memoirs* or to persuade Madame d'Arblay to burn them 'for reason of their avowing the undignified Birth' of her mother, his grandmother Esther Sleepe. 'The tendency of this age is to respect individuals . . . without reference to their ancestry', courteously replied the son of Comte d'Arblay. Even if his mother could 'be persuaded to throw into the fire the fruit of her so great labour, which has solaced many a weary & many a solitary hour, are you sure that the subj^t w^d drop, & that no one in this scribbl^g age w^d take it up?' He recalled the lady in Lafontaine 'who broke her mirror for being too faithful, & then found a mirror in each fragment'.[1] Richard had appealed also to Charles Parr Burney to stop the publication of the work, but Charles Parr thought that the honour of the family could safely be trusted to his famous aunt, *la comtesse* d'Arblay, who in some respects had most to lose from its dishonour. Richard explained that, though he had been married some twenty years, he had neglected up to this time to explain the humble strains in his lineage to his wife. He may also have felt embarrassed about the statement he had submitted to the College of Arms regarding 'James Sleepe, Gentleman'. Madame d'Arblay probably knew nothing of this last, but with her wide experience in 'worldly difficulties' and her tolerance for most human failings, she sympathized with Richard in his marital quandary. In October, 1832, just before the advertisement of the *Memoirs* was released, she wrote to Mrs. Sandford asking her to mediate between Richard and his wife or Richard and the author of the forthcoming *Memoirs*.[2] She would have herself obliged him with any kindness in her power, and she had endeavoured, she said, 'to find means for sinking the name that causes him so much uneasiness', but she had endeavoured in vain. 'None occur that are not big with mischievous incitement to libellous malice.' 'Mystery provokes inquiry.'

[1] A draft of a letter (Berg) from AA to Richard Allen Burney, 8 Sept. 1830, edited and annotated by FBA, 3 May 1838. Also A.L.S. (Berg) from FBA to Mrs. Sandford, as on p. 456. n. 2.

[2] See p. 456, n. 2.

My *Mother*, my thrice honoured Mother was, I believe, of angelic mould, without & within: & I have painted her as such, neither from fancy, nor remembrance, but from M:S:S: both in prose & verse of my dear Father, & Richard, like myself, may be proud, not ashamed,—when once his passing difficulties are over,—in hoping that such blood may be circulating in *his* veins, & in those of his fine children.[1]

There was also the Reverend Stephen Allen (son of Dr. Burney's second wife) who thought the Doctor's financial indebtedness to this wife insufficiently stressed, if not misrepresented, and that Madame d'Arblay had not paid sufficient honour to her stepmother. Madame d'Arblay took great care in her replies to Stephen's charges of 'erroneous statements', substantiating the facts that he had questioned by pertinent excerpts from her father's papers. Her letters on the subject, kind, polite, and conciliatory in tone, and firm, well ordered, and well reasoned in exposition, would serve, if printed, not only to document the *Memoirs*, but to counterbalance or offset them as samples of her octogenarian style. She was now over eighty years old, but her grasp of idiom and idea was as strong as her grasp of the pen, which swept in straight lines as clearly, firmly, and legibly as ever from margin to margin, from top to bottom of the usual four pages.

Were we to meet, half an hour, as your son well observed, might bring us to the same way of thinking; for the documents I could produce, & the circumstances I could unfold, would lead you to comprehend the motives of my *Belief*, & either settle *you* to allow its justice, or call forth reasons against it to which *I* ought to yield.[2]

Though she had not painted her father's second marriage in colours to recall the widow, or widower, of Ephesus, she had hoped that her respectful account of her stepmother would have given Stephen 'Gratification, not chagrin'. 'If our dear Mrs. Rishton had been alive, how different would have been her view of my recital! of its constant respect, & occasional kindness!' Stephen had missed the stormy days in St. Martin's Street, and he could not, in any case, be expected to judge impartially. Neither, perhaps, could Fanny, but looking backward at old unhappy far-off things, she had tried, she said, to do justice to

[1] See p. 456, n. 2.
[2] Two drafts of letters signed (Berg) from FBA to the Rev. Stephen Allen, [1833].

her stepmother's beauty, intelligence, and literary acquirements. She had 'always admired & esteemed her good qualities,
which were manifold & charming'.[1]

The original Memoirs, as far as one can make out, included
chronological accounts of the interesting, the great, and the
odd, whimsical, and lovable people that the Doctor knew. His
daughter followed his plan. The *Memoirs of Doctor Burney* is
largely a chronological series of character-sketches drawn partly
from the Doctor's Memoirs and correspondence and partly
from her own recollections of personages that they both knew
well and had perhaps discussed. As she had once pointed out,
whereas Esther and even Susan had married and left home
before their father was 'dubbed a Public man', her own

incipient career of Notage took place just as *his* was at its meridian:
for the second volume of his History of Music, & my own second
work, Cecilia, came out in the same year. We basked, therefore,
in public sunshine at the same time, & were tied together in innumerable little incidents.[2]

These were the years when he liked to take Fan in his hand and
call on Dr. Johnson, Sir Joshua, and many others, and when his
heart leapt up in pride and gratification to see her lionized at
the blue parties by men even then famous. These halcyon days
together with the long years preceding them, when she had
worked as his amanuensis in the study at St. Martin's Street,
were the periods of her father's life that she knew best and that
with all their associations occurred most vividly to her when she
wrote about him. It was natural that she should describe these
years at great length rather than such periods of his life as she
knew only at second hand. It was natural also that the vignettes
of Garrick, Dr. Johnson, Mr. Crisp, Mr. Twining, and those
friends that the Doctor and his daughter had in common
should have been more fully detailed than those she did not
know, and that much space should have been given to one or
two like Mrs. Delany who played a much larger part in her own
life than in her father's. It might be pointed out also that her
brothers and sisters (except perhaps Susan) had little mention;
that family catastrophes, the sorrows caused at different times
and in different ways by the Doctor's sons, James, Charles, and
Richard, are *sunk*, as she would say; that the point of view is

[1] See p. 464, n. 2.   [2] See p. 451, n. 3.

hers, not his (though perhaps never opposed to his); that the *Memoirs* is not by modern standards an adequate biography, and that it might more properly be entitled 'Memoirs of the Doctor and his Daughter'. All this, together with adverse criticism of the execrable style, may be allowed. Yet the work included incidents and vignettes that no longer exist elsewhere in the records, and, as has been pointed out, it is authoritative in a way none other can ever be.

Madame d'Arblay would not, perhaps, have grieved very much over modern criticism of her own work, as long as it could grant, as it can, that the *Memoirs* is what she meant it to be—a loving and faithful record of

the progress of a nearly abandoned Child, from a small village of Shropshire, to a Man allowed throughout Europe to have risen to the head of his profession; and thence, setting his profession aside, to have been elevated to an intellectual rank in society, as a Man of Letters—

'Though not First, in the very first line'
with most of the eminent men of his day.[1]

[1] *Memoirs*, i. ix.

XVIII

THE WORLD OF LIGHT

(1832–1840)

. . . and I alone sit lingring here.

THE years 1832–3 were to take high toll of the surviving members of the Burney family and their connexions, and in view of the losses soon to occur it was fortunate for Madame d'Arblay and for Charlotte Broome that for most of the year 1832 they were within comfortable visiting distance of each other, the one at 1 Half Moon Street, the other at Number 36. Two years previously Charlotte Barrett had taken her younger daughter, Henrietta, to Italy for her health, and at the close of 1831 the elder Charlotte settled down at Half Moon Street in order to be near her sister. Her 'chief object & comfort', said Marianne Francis, was to be close to Aunt d'Arblay. 'She seems not to covet any other company.'[1]

The sisters could support each other, therefore, when on February 17, 1832, they received the sad but inevitable news of Esther's death at Bath. Sarah Harriet, who was also in Italy, wrote with great concern for Fanny:

How little dare I think of my own sorrow, when I reflect upon that which you must feel! The habits of confidence and attachment of so many years—the recollections of past times, when in your girlhood you were companions, and when life, tricked out in its gayest colours was opening before you—the subsequent unfeigned admiration with which each looked up to the talents of the other—the similarity of affection that united you both so strongly to the other dear Sister you so much earlier lost—All, all these are links which when thus torn asunder, must make you feel to the very quick the keenness of the wound you now suffer.[2]

Esther's 'rarely mixt qualities of Heart & Talents', her 'gay exertions', and the wit and buoyant spirits that had lightened

---

[1] A.L.S. (Berg) from MF and A.L.S. (Berg) from MF and CBFB to Charlotte Barrett, 15 Aug., 4 Nov. 1831; and 7 letters (Berg) from MF to CBFB 6 May 1829, 1, 25, 26 Aug., 1, 3, 14 Sept. 1831.
[2] A.L.S. (Berg) from SHB to FBA, 30 Mar. 1832.

her own difficult way and that of others had long been com-
memorated in Fanny's writings. There were no elaborate
tributes at this time, perhaps because Charlotte, to whom Fanny
would naturally have written, was near enough for consolatory
visits and reflections.

Scarcely had Charlotte Broome had time to reconcile herself
to the first loss of the year when she was told of the death of her
daughter Marianne Francis.

In 1827 Marianne had secured a house of her own at Kingston-upon-Thames. Often she was called on to aid her mother's
migrations from lodging to lodging in Richmond, London, and
Brighton, but whenever she could be spared she retired to the
'settled abode', where she had assembled her possessions—
books in many languages, music, her own musical compositions,
and her musical instruments including an organ—'a very complete & beautiful instrument' on which on one occasion she
played from ten in the evening until, without her noticing it,
the candles had burned low in their sockets and daylight had
come in at the windows. She established 'infant schools' and,
when she could obtain permission, read and prayed in work-
houses and prisons. She tried also to show her cousins and
friends the way of salvation; not content any more than was
Rowland Hill, her mother said, to go to Heaven herself, she
wished them to go too. In the thirties she had come to consider
Armstrong and Irving as the two 'wonderful lights & Luthers
of the day', giving full credence to the gibberish heard in
Irving's congregation as inspired voices or warnings of the
coming judgements or the Second Coming.[1] She had tried in
vain to persuade Alex d'Arblay to hear the voices, and his
orthodox comment on the phenomena may still be read in his
published sermon *The Apostolic Gift of Tongues, contrasted with
some modern claims to inspiration* (1832). Marianne's evangelical
zeal had sometimes tended to estrange her from her family, but
Charlotte Barrett, writing in great grief from Rome, wished to
honour her sister's memory, her kindness, and her faithfulness
to God.

[1] Letters (Berg) from MF to Charlotte Barrett, 1826–32; 2 A.L.S. (Barrett)
from CBFB to Charlotte Barrett, 11–13 May, 26–29 June 1832; A.L.S. (Barrett)
from Charlotte Barrett to Henry Barrett, 6 Apr. 1832; A.L. (Barrett) from Julia
Barrett to Charlotte Barrett, 12 Aug. 1833; A.L.S. (Osborn) from Edward F.
Burney to CPB, 7 Apr. 1832.

My dearest Marianne was a redeemed child & servant of God. . . .
She lived to her Savior on earth & devoted her time and her excellent
powers & talents to promoting his service.

Charlotte wished to distinguish between the part of Marianne's
faith that was 'firm & sincere and scriptural' and the credence
her sister had lately given to the inspired voices in Mr. Irving's
congregation.

Whether *she* was right or mistaken in believing this to be a super-
natural work she knows now—and whether *we* are right in thinking
it, as I do, a delusion, we shall know hereafter.[1]

On April 5, 1832, the remains were interred in the main aisle
of All Saints at Kingston-upon-Thames. Edward Francesco
Burney, who with Martin Burney, Henry Barrett, and John
Payne had represented the family, afterwards reported to
Charles Parr that the service was 'conducted in a handsome
and respectful manner' and had 'seemed to cause a great
sensation at Kingston'.[1] And now Charlotte Broome had lost
three of her four children—Ralph, Clement Francis, and
Marianne. 'I find such poignant regrets in looking *back*, that
I now endeavour not to look back at all.'[1]

Later in the spring one of the Worcester cousins, Elizabeth
Warren Burney, died at Rimpton,[2] and in the summer of 1832
the death of Mrs. James Burney added to the year's sum of
sorrow and regret. The Admiral's biographers remember her
not as Mrs. Battle, but rather as a small exquisite figure in black
velvet and gold lace, with a pale face, and tiny feet in French
slippers. She had always the respect and sympathy of her
Burney in-laws, and in turn she had found Fanny an 'ever loved
& esteemed sister & friend' from the time when, a good fifty
years before, she had first beheld her 'in the little back parlour
in St. Martin's Street'.[3] Said to have been rather cold in manner,
Mrs. Burney must have had a warm heart and very generous
and spacious powers of forgiving. Her funeral was in some
respects a curtain call, for among the mourners, like a ponderous
and sinister villain appearing for a last bow at the end of a

---

[1] See p. 468, n. 1.　　　　　[2] See the Worcester Journal.
[3] A.L.S. (Berg) from Mrs. James Burney to FBA, 22 Nov. 1821; Manwaring,
p. 286.

tragedy long since played out, came Molesworth Phillips. He was now seventy-six years old, the last survivor of Cook's expeditions, and, faithful still to old memories, he had come to pay his last respects to Admiral Burney's widow, requesting at the last to be buried in the Admiral's grave. To Fanny, bending over her most 'secret repositories', re-reading with dim, aged, tearful eyes the closely written records of Susan's broken life, he was still her sister's murderer.

Had her life been less grievously affected by secret afflictions, I think she might still be where I *am*![1]

Fanny Raper, who was much moved by the memories that her aunt's funeral excited and by the unexpected meeting with her father there, met him again accidentally in Hyde Park. She could only wish that he might be touched by 'redeeming grace', the wonderful effects of which, like Marianne, she had so often witnessed in the dissenting chapels, but she was happy to think that he was more amenable than formerly to such thoughts. He had read the sermon she had sent him and had, indeed, written one of his own. On September 11, 1832, the year the black cholera spread throughout England, Lieutenant-Colonel Phillips, having suffered 'all the agonies of that direful disease', passed on to his reward.[2]

At the close of this year or the beginning of the next, Fanny Raper had also to mourn for her brother William Phillips, who died in some ship somewhere at a foreign wharf or on the wide sea. All the family had made plans and conjectures about dear William, 'but the possibility of losing him never occurred'.[3]

In Half Moon Street Fanny and Charlotte, afflicted in varying degrees by the family losses of the year, comforted each other till the autumn of 1832, when Fanny was again thrown into the 'profoundest grief' at the last illness of Mrs. Locke of Eliot Vale, whom she had long considered, next to Mr. Crisp, her greatest friend outside the Burney families. The 'threatened separation' could not be for long 'in *Time*, but in Feeling there

---

[1] A.L. (Berg) from FBA to EBB and A.L. (Berg) to CBFB, 6 May 1823, 12 June 1834.

[2] See A.L. (Berg) from Fanny Phillips Raper to her daughter Minette (Mrs. Nugent) Kingston, 12 Sept. 1832. For biographical details see scrap-book (Berg), *Fanny Burney and Family, 1653-1890.*

[3] A.L. (Berg) from Charlotte Barrett to Henry Barrett, 18 May 1833.

is no calculation for the seeming duration of even a minute that is spent in affliction'. 'What a year this has been!'[1]

In February, 1833, the heartbroken report reached Half Moon Street and Brighton that the three years' trial of the air at Pisa, Lucca, and Rome had failed. Henrietta Barrett had died on January 31, 1833.[2] Her grandmother Broome, who had borne the cost of the long experiment, could only conclude that, with the other 'poor darlings' lost to her, Henrietta was safe in Heaven. Though neither Charlotte nor Fanny in their expressions of sympathy breathed a word about their own aged needs and longings, it must have been a relief and joy to both when in June, 1833, Charlotte Barrett and Julia returned to England. Mr. Barrett was living at Brighton (4 Burlington Street), and when the Charlottes joined him there Madame d'Arblay was again left alone.

In June, 1833, Madame d'Arblay was eighty-one years old, and Charlotte seventy-one, but the sojourn of the latter in London and the cessation of work on the manuscripts and *Memoirs* had done Fanny a world of good. Marianne Francis used to tell of typical evenings in Half Moon Street with Madame d'Arblay talking 'in her animated, hand clasping, energetic French way',

telling her long curious stories till she is quite hoarse, and dr Mama fast asleep but jumpˢ up every now & then in her sweet way, to fall in with the current of the remarks, answerˢ in her sleep.[3]

The confidence of the sisters in each other and their unison of heart and sympathy were complete. In 1833–4 Madame d'Arblay was 'remarkably well—wonderfully!'[4] In the summer of 1833 she was again taking long walks and she had paid two visits to the Princess Sophia at Kensington Palace. The nieces

---

[1] Sermoneta, pp. 351–4; A.L. (Berg) from FBA and CBFB to Charlotte Barrett, 19–27 Feb. 1833; A.L.S. (Osborn) from FBA to CPB, 12 Apr. 1832.

[2] See series of letters (Berg and Barrett) from Charlotte Barrett to CBFB, to Henry Barrett, and others, dated Hastings, Boulogne, Pisa, Lucca, and Rome, Apr. 1829–Mar. 1833; also A.L.S. (Berg) from CBFB to Charlotte Barrett, 19 Feb. 1833.

[3] A.L.S. (Berg) from MF to Charlotte Barrett, 22 May [1832].

[4] Seven letters (Berg) from MF to CBFB, 29 Mar., 30 July, 16, 23 Nov. 1833, 1 Jan., 3 Feb., 31 May 1834. Also A.L. (Berg) from FBA to Charlotte Barrett, 3 Nov. 1833; A.L.S. (Berg) and A.L.S. (Barrett) from Julia to Charlotte Barrett, 6 Aug. 1833 and 28 July 1834.

and nephews calling in those years did not know when they
had found her 'so brisk in every way'. In 1833 Charlotte
Broome, in London again on business, spent the month of September in Bolton Street. In November Sarah Harriet returned
from Italy 'looking younger & brighter & better, in all ways,
than when she went abroad'.[1] And Fanny was always glad to
welcome another caller of these years, her godson Dick Barrett,
now a student at King's College, Cambridge. Frequently sent
on errands to Half Moon Street by his mother or grandmother,
he soon earned his great-aunt's approval by his manly appearance and principles and, presently, her sympathy for the
trouble he had with his eyes. In the end she was to make him
her residuary legatee.

All this was very pleasant. With the production of the *Memoirs*
and family journals, old trusts had been fulfilled. With bright
hopes of the hereafter, the loss of friends and relatives could be
borne, and the last decade of Madame d'Arblay's life might
have run on peacefully to a close had it not been for Alex and
her continued fears about his health and his career. Years ago
when General d'Arblay had wished his son to accept a commission in the French Guards and to make a French marriage,
he had not failed to point out to Fanny that the alternative
would probably be an obscure curacy in England, a position
that Alex with his disposition and temperament would be forever incapable of improving—and the General's words had
already proved prophetic.

In spite of efforts to obtain a better living or a lectureship in
London, Alex was still at Camden Town. In 1831–2 he was
absorbed in scholarly interpretations and then in the versifica-
tion of the Psalms—a work still extant in manuscript.[2] In 1830
he published a funeral sermon on the death of His Majesty
King George IV, which he had preached in Camden Chapel, St.
Pancras, on Sunday, July 18, 1830. The work, called *The Vanity
of all Earthly Greatness*, was gratefully dedicated to the Venerable
Archdeacon of Middlesex, in whose pulpit the author had first
attempted 'to defend the cause of eternal truth'. Thereafter he
published *A Discourse on the New Year* (preached in Camden

---

[1] See p. 471, n. 4.
[2] Berg and Barrett Collections. For d'Arblay's theories on poetry see A.L.S.
(Barrett) from AA to MF, 18 Jan. 1831.

Chapel, St. Pancras, January 1, 1832); *The Apostolic Gift of Tongues, contrasted with some modern claims to inspiration* (1832); *The Path of the Just . . . two discourses occasioned by the death of W. Wilberforce* (August, 1833); *Apostolical Preaching considered in a Farewell Discourse* (preached on Sunday, March 20, 1836, in Camden Chapel); and *The Preaching of St. Paul* (a discourse delivered on November 27, 1836, in Ely Chapel, Holborn). These sermons, with a poem *Urania* (1833) and a treatise on whist, seem to complete the corpus of his printed work. Of all these perhaps the theme suggested by the death of King George IV, 'the vanity of all earthly greatness', seemed to touch the most responsive chords in the preacher and call forth his best powers of rhetoric.

Those sable garments which I behold—these trappings of woe which I touch—the muffled peal of bells, and the solemn minute-guns we have heard during the week—the momentary suspension of trade in the most bustling metropolis of Europe—the fallen countenances of those flatterers whose destiny hung on departed greatness—the eager joy of those sycophants, who crowd to worship the rising sun—all tell us that DEATH hath been busy here,—that the *dust* which was once a *king*, hath joined the royal tenants of the tomb, ashes to ashes, earth to earth—that God is great, that man is nothing, that *all is vanity*!

Like Solomon, George IV had found by its bitter fruits that pleasure is vanity. The poet-preacher would not, however, 'rake up every error which Charity would cover with a veil—that veil we shall *all* wish drawn over our sins, in the dark hour that levels the subject and the Prince!' Rather, the congregation were to heed the warning attending a monarch's fall to the grave.

He . . . is levelled with the meanest of the mean,—when the worm fattens upon the lord of the earth and the viceregent of the Deity—

Survey, in your mind's eye, the map of this mighty empire . . . see the ocean groaning under the burden of those vessels that bear the commerce of the world, braving polar snows and equatorial fires—see the tributary homage . . . behold the two Indies dropping into England's lap their illimitable and exhaustless treasures. . . . Survey all this, and ask—where is the brow to which all this bowed? . . . Go, ask the grave—it is his sister! Ask the worm—it is his brother!

In 1833 because of Alex's long absences in Paris 'a party was forming for a complaint' to the Bishop of London.[1] In 1834 there was a minor flurry in Half Moon Street when the curate, having had to cut short a vacation at Bath and Rimpton, arrived at the last moment to fill in a *questionnaire* sent by the Bishop of London concerning the ministry at Camden Town and its duties and emoluments. 'He had not much to relate', his mother dryly observed,

that would excite Parliamentary Enquiry or Reprimand,—or Dissenting envy or ill will. But he did not get his document filled up till the *last* minute—the *very* last that the Bᴾ named—& that has kept me in water not quite cold till only yesterday![2]

Charlotte could be depended on for sympathy and humorous advice on such vexations. Though Alex was a man of letters the Bishop was a 'man of Fetters', and since the 'tiresome Queries' were likely to be put every year,

it might save Alex a labyrinth of bothers & puzzles and worries if he were to keep a copy of the answer he has now sent, to poke into this time twelvemonth, as a refreshment to the pangs of memory— for, as to the 'pleasures of Memory' I'll be bound for it Mr. Rogers never introduced these torments from the Bishop to the curate.[2]

Much depended on the impression the curate made on the new Bishop, and Aunt Broome's warnings and 'hints' relayed through Fanny about a dinner to which Alex was invited at Lambeth Palace betray her misgivings as to the characteristic and costly failings of that young man. He ought to wear his clerical costume—'Black, & all Black—except the neck cloth'—

& not to exceed 3 Glasses of wine—& no Beer—only water, instead —He used to say that wine made him rampant. . . . & if the Bᴾ has a wife, I wᵈ charge him to pay her all the attention opportunity permits in this visit—& to *converse* with her—but not talk of *plays* & *operas* or Balls—this Bᴾ taking to him might make his fortune—[2]

Two weeks later Charlotte wrote to inquire whether or not Alex had called and left a card, a *Camden* card

—or I think he will never have another invitation from Him— . . . only he shd. go in clerical costume, in case he shd. meet the Bᴾ just coming out—[2]

---

[1] A.L. (Berg) from FBA to AA, 9 Feb. 1833.

[2] Three letters (Berg) from FBA to CBFB, 29 Mar. 1833, 12 Jan.–3 Feb., 31 May 1834; 4 A.L. (Barrett) from CBFB to FBA, 11–13, 27 Feb., 10 Mar., 26 Apr. 1834.

Apparently Alex seldom in his life lacked or heeded such advice. Whether or not he made a late or feckless appearance with his card and unluckily met the Bishop coming out, we do not know; but no rich living fell to his lot. As Esther had said, he was 'an unlucky wight'. Though in March Fanny could report that he was doing exactly what all the family would have directed— reading the long service every morning during the last week of Lent and composing and delivering a series of lectures to end on Easter eve—yet from this time, whether through weariness or boredom or lack of strength or because of some special discouragement, his efforts seemed to cease. This was the tenth year of his curacy at Camden Town with a salary of £200 (less £50 for living quarters) and the fortieth year of his life.

He is well, however, thank God! though thin! thin! thin! & he is furnishing his new Lodging of 3 closets with all the elegance in his power—&—alas all the Expense not in his *present* power![1]

In January he had visited his cousin at Rimpton. In July he had gone to some fête of Miss Thrale's at Sevenoaks, which was to include a great charity ball.[2] In September he joined the Paynes at Buxton and was the life of gay parties there with the Spencers. In October he was at the White Horse Hotel at Brighton, where he received a warning letter from his mother about the mischief 'excited by so quick a disappearance after an understood *stationary* arrangement'. In reply he had to ask her for seven pounds so that this time he could pay his bill before leaving.

I will repay you faithfully as soon as they give me my last quarter's salary due the first of this month. This is much better than borrowing from Mr. Barrett, as it wd. be a bore to get a name for a knack at borrowing wherever I go.[2]

Meanwhile his mother was shocked to learn from Arthur Barrett that the Barretts had not seen him.[2] What then was he doing by himself at the White Horse Hotel? Long ago Fanny had feared that her son might 'dwindle into incurable Langour from supine self-indulgence & inertia'. And now, ill herself, she

---

[1] See p. 474, n. 2.
[2] 2 A.L.S. (Barrett) from Julia to Charlotte Barrett, 1, 28 July 1834; three letters (Berg) from AA to FBA, 14, 19 Sept., 23 Oct. 1834; A.L. (Berg) from FBA to AA, 20 Oct. 1834.

felt neglected; and she wrote a series of notes to 'young Heed-less' calculated to shock him into an awareness of his duties and responsibilities.[1]

The *locus* of his social interests for 1835 was Dover. Sarah Harriet had heard of a Mrs. Bolton there, 'wife of a Dr. of that ilk', who, because of some disability, was 'carried on an inclined plane to people's houses of an evening', but who was reported to be 'very handsome, immoderately clever, an Astrologer, even, that draws out, or draws up (which should I say?) Nativities; and is, besides, poetry-mad, & has conceived a mad fancy for Alex d'Arblay'.[2] On January 23 Sarah Harriet said that Alex had gone to Dover to pay this Sybil a visit. A letter of his mother's, dated February 5, duly reported his return 'in high health & spirits, but thinner than ever', and his sitting up 'till 3 or 4 in the morning, making society verses'.[3] All this was gossip; but then an unsigned copy of part of a letter written by some friend from Dover on April 4, 1835, seems to have instituted a more significant turn of events—Alex's introduction to Mary Ann Smith.

My friend M.A.S. is very good & we often talk of you—I am con-vinced if you liked her & popped, you would be accepted—but I am no matchmaker—I never disguise the truth from either party, more especially when both are my friends—if I held out to you she was a genius, I should lie—nor is she enthusiastic—her nature is formed in a different mould—but no one that I ever saw in the shape of her structure & character, possesses a rarer combination of amiabilities, & plenty of talent if called forth—her judgment is good & sound, and all she does is well principled & steady—there now—do you not intend giving us a look ere we leave—we may never meet again under such happy circumstances—The steamboat runs regularly to Dover & comes in one hour less than the coach—so come next week if possible—contrive to give the booby's the slip—[4]

Alex was soon at Dover again, and before the end of April wrote enthusiastically to his mother: 'I would give Worlds you could see her! I think her the person above all others I yet have met

[1] A series of short notes (Berg) from FBA to AA, 1834–6. For the earlier warning, A.L. (Berg) from FBA to AA, 25 Nov.–18 Dec. 1821.

[2] A.L.S. (Berg) from SHB to Anna Wilbraham Grosvenor, 23 Jan. 1835.

[3] A.L. (Berg) from FBA to CBFB, 5 Feb. 1835.

[4] A copy of a letter (Barrett) annotated: 'Extract of a letter of Mr. B., rec'd April 4, 1835.'

with that you, my madre, would prefer for me.' Madame
d'Arblay was somewhat startled at the precipitancy with
which 'so solemn an engagement' had been entered into
'without the smallest knowledge, on either side, of each other's
principles, Temper, or mode of life'. She would have objected
had the girl been a Dissenter or a Republican. There difference of opinion is mortal, but as it was, she sent her felicitations,
her 'delighted & tenderest Benediction, my dearest dearest
Alex'.[1]

Mary Ann Smith must have run something of a gauntlet in
Half Moon Street, when she first met the aged Madame
d'Arblay, who even in her mid-eighties impressed new acquaintances as a very 'clever woman', whose 'chief cleverness consists
in great discernment of character'.[2] All, however, went well—
more than well. 'I have seen the young lady', Fanny reported to
Charlotte, '& she has put me in Heaven! so much I like her!—
so much that love is the only proper word!' As Charlotte said,
it was 'indeed balmy & softening in the midst of difficulties' that
Mary Ann Smith had won Madame d'Arblay's heart, as she
had Alex's, in the first interview.[2] 'She, indeed, appears to me
a real treasure of sound sense, good principles, & governed
though strong sensibility.'[3] Mary Ann, praised as a model of
patience and goodness, had need of all such qualities, for Alex,
now forty-one, seemed ready to quit the struggle. New difficulties, specified and unspecified—impediments that Charlotte
had heartily prayed might be removed—proved insurmountable.

To begin with, Camden Chapel (with its £200 less £50 for
living quarters) was 'quite insufficient for his hoped for establishment'. Before July, 1835, he had made up his mind to resign
and was seeking, as his mother wrote Charles Forster, 'some
church, chapel or Lectureship in London for alas! his terrible
malady of absence becomes so serious, as to unfit him for most

---

[1] 2 A.L. (Berg) from FBA to AA, n.d., 1 May 1835.

[2] 2 A.L. (Berg) from FBA to CBFB, 10, 18 July 1835; A.L.S. (Barrett) from
CBFB to FBA, n.d. [1835]; A.L.S. (Barrett) from Julia to Charlotte Barrett, 12
May 1836.

[3] 2 A.L. (Berg) from FBA to CBFB, 8 July 1835, 17 Feb. 1837; A.L.S. (Barrett),
12 Oct. 1835. For Miss Smith's connexions and the approval of Brooke Greville,
who thought that she would become 'a very general favourite' in the Burney
family, see A.L.S. (Berg) from SHB to FBA, 31 Aug. 1835. Also A.L.S. (Barrett)
from Charlotte to Henry Barrett, 10 Sept. 1835.

of the duties that belong to the Parish Priest!'[1] Worse still—
whether from mental or physical fatigue, world weariness, or
some new discouragement, some chronic weakness or secret
debilitating indulgence—all his purposes, resolves, and motives
for action sank into an incurable lethargy or apathy, from which
he could not be roused. When he stayed away from Half Moon
Street, his mother thought him alienated even from her, and
through the winter of 1835–6 she continued her series of reproachful notes. 'Turn—turn—yet turn—if not irreclaimable,
if not, for no cause under Heaven, secretly alienated!' 'Mes
yeux! My prescription!' 'Mes pauvres yeux!' 'Your unheard of
neglect!'[2]

She tried to reach him with words, summons, reproaches,
and the call of duty that might jostle him into action, but he
could no longer try to do what she thought he ought to do. He
retreated farther into some world of thought within himself,
leaving the women to comfort each other. 'Were I constantly
with him', wrote Mary Ann Smith to Fanny, 'to rouse him
into action'—for

few such lights are sent into the world & much will be required of
them—however pleasant it may be to live in an ideal world of our
own, Heav'n is not won by speculation—*daily* & *deeply* do I deplore
an influence that has sunk into apathy so fine, so noble a mind—but
he will recover dearest Mad^me D'Arblay & be again the comfort to
you he has been & to me he will ever be *all* & *every* thing—I am glad
he has called on Dr. Moore.[3]

And she asked permission to lock away a sympathetic letter
from Madame d'Arblay that had in its turn cheered and comforted her. On March 20, 1836, Alex preached his last sermon
at Camden Chapel. He was still a Fellow of Christ's College
and seems to have spent part of the summer at Cambridge;
yet the letters that his mother sent there were often returned by
his friends, for no one seemed to know where he was. Charlotte
hoped that he would 'turn over a new leaf', but Fanny's extant
letters of April and June, addressed to him at Christ's College
or the British and Continental Coffee House, Cornhill, reflect

<hr>

[1] A.L.S. (Berg) from FBA to the Rev. Charles Forster, 1836; A.L. (Osborn) to
CPB, 12 May 1836; A.L. (Berg) from CPB to FBA, 13 July 1835.
[2] See p. 476, n. 1.
[3] A.L.S. (Berg) from Mary Ann Smith to FBA, 30 Jan. 1836.

her growing consternation at his apathy and neglect or his real
or fancied alienation. 'Is it from *worn out affection* or from indifference?' 'If all I write to *Jostle* only *hardens* your remnant
feelings, I had best stop & *literally* leave you to your fate.'[1] Aunt
Broome could hardly bring herself to believe that Alex could
fail to return to

his tender mother's kind roof, or, in being more with her in the day
time—independently of his love for you, it seems as if he must do so,
for his *own peace of mind*.[2]

On June 2 Charlotte Barrett expressed her relief that Alex had
at last written to his mother, along with conjectures (perhaps
no more valid than those that could be hazarded today) on the
source of the trouble.

It was shameful for him to keep his poor dear mother so long in
misery—he knows very well how anxious she is—and *anybody* would
have been miserable at not hearing from him for so long a time.
But I think he has been some where else besides Cambridge
otherwise how should his Cambridge Friends have sent letters to
him in London? I am sadly afraid he has some *chère amie*—many
people suspect as much from his conduct. It would be far best to
marry Miss Smith directly. The Arch[dn] says Dr. Moore was very
glad to get him out of his Chapel & the arch[dn] heard, probably from
Dr Moore, that it was the *general wish* of his Parishioners that he
should leave it. although this friendly minority of 90, induce poor
Alex to fancy he was duped. He has been his own dupe, as we all
are, in most cases.[2]

The pitiable claims of a ragged verger and other representations
from the Parish with which occasionally Madame d'Arblay had
to deal were recurring signs of Alex's fitful stewardship.

All his life his mother, unconforming herself, had tried to
make him conform and shoulder responsibility by appeals to
his conscience and his feelings. A despairing letter of this time,
written with the candour and simplicity that his cousins had
so often attributed to him, betrayed unhappy guilt-complexes
about responsibilities that he could no longer meet but that
still had the power to torment him. Already he was more than

[1] See p. 476, n. 1.
[2] Joint A.L.S. (Berg) from CBFB and Charlotte Barrett to FBA, 30 June 1836;
also A.L.S. (Barrett) from Charlotte Barrett to CBFB, 2 June 1836.

'half in love with easeful death', ready to quit upon the mid-night.

> O I am very unhappy
> I know not what to say
> I will dress & come—

le deep deep gloom has laid hold of me & God knows if I shall ever shake it off——The more I pine in solitude the worse it grows Poor generous May! Her fresh heart her happiness ought not to be put at stake upon me whose spirit is broken whose soul is fled.

How I admire her & the more I admire—how I feel wretched at the impossibility of *now* doing her justice as she deserves And yet ought I not to try? Ought I to give myself up for lost without at least an effort? NO! . . . O that I had gone to Brighton directly—Perhaps the change of air & of scene could have made me another man. . . . I have taken to my bed frightfully of late—I find it more & more irksome to leave it—

Everybody remarks how thin & haggard I grow—& at times I have heard this with a reckless indifference & almost a wish for a release—

O that I could put my mind in a firmer attitude O my dear dear mammy how beautiful your patience your forbear-ance has been—How unworthy I feel of it—how it cuts me to the soul. Why have I fled from you—who alone can even attempt to cure me?—O it is a madness—a delusion without a name.[1]

Meanwhile George Cambridge, doggedly faithful to the last, asked Alex to undertake the ministry of Ely Chapel, and on October 21, 1836, Fanny was writing in jubilation and thank-fulness to Charlotte. 'The Arch[d] has been exquisite in judgment, delicacy, wisdom as well as in true kindness.'

The chapel is *decidedly* given to Alex, in a manner the most affec-tionate & cordial, by the Archdeacon, who, it seems, has it in his Gift! 'Tis Ely Chapel in Ely Place, Holborn—*Not* just what one might wish, for position!—but what ever is?[2]

Alex also was grateful. This was the second appointment that he owed primarily to his mother's old friend, and he dedicated to him, as he had his first published work, the sermon preached on Advent Sunday, November 27, 1836, on the re-opening of Ely Chapel, Ely Place.

[1] A.L. (Berg) from AA to FBA, n.d.
[2] A.L. (Berg) from FBA to CBFB, 21 Oct. 1836.

As I dedicated to you the first-fruits of my pen, it was natural that I should inscribe to you also this beginning of the after-harvest, since, after a short retirement, I am now resuming my sacred duties at the call of the same partial friend under whose auspices I first began them.

In spite of fatalistic misgivings about the outcome, he could not, with any sense of his calling, refuse the post.

When you proposed to me to take charge of Ely Chapel, I was well aware of the arduousness of the undertaking. I knew that, lost in a recess, it attracted no notice from passers by, and was unknown to many in its immediate neighbourhood. I knew that, since it had been closed, other places of worship had sprung up, and had drawn off those who formerly attended there. But I knew also that, while large subscriptions were collecting for building new temples to the Lord, this ancient house of prayer could not long remain neglected, without furnishing a handle to the enemies of the church. I did not think myself at liberty to shrink from a possible chance of being useful. The bark is now launched, I fear, against wind and tide; but the issue is not in the hands of him who plies the oar, but of that viewless Spirit, whose breath alone can swell the sail.[1]

The ancient house of prayer, the beautifully proportioned Ely Chapel, was reopened late in the autumn of 1836. It was still damp and cold in the drear December of that year, and people said, probably erroneously, that a 'malarious fever' lurked about it. After the Christmas services Alex came down with influenza and a high fever, and Madame d'Arblay, who had nursed him through a thousand fevers, somehow knew that this time he would not recover. By 'his express wish she did not go to his Bedside', and his cousin Charles Parr sent messages to relatives and friends that Alexander wished to be left to himself.[2] On January 19, 1837, he died. The son of Madame d'Arblay was buried near his father the Comte Alexandre d'Arblay in Wolcot Churchyard in Bath, and the eulogies and tributes extant in

[1] See the dedicatory letter (19 Dec. 1836) published with the sermon *The Preaching of St. Paul* (a discourse delivered on 27 Nov. 1836 at Ely Chapel).

[2] See A.L.S. (Barrett) from Cornelia (Mrs. George) Cambridge to Charlotte Barrett, 20 Jan. 1837; a reference in A.L.S. (Barrett) from Julia Barrett Thomas to Charlotte Barrett (5 June 1837) to a letter (now lost) from Alex's favourite cousin Minette Raper (Mrs. Nugent Kingston) to Julia as above; A.L.S. and draft of A.L. (Berg) from Charlotte Barrett to FBA, 1837; and A.L.S. (Barrett), 21 Jan. 1837. Also A.L.S. (Berg) from SHB to Anna Wilbraham Grosvenor, 23 Feb. 1837.

family letters of the time all praise his 'pure & unoffending
spirit', 'his sweet and guileless temper, "in wit a Man—simplicity a child"—his brilliant talents—high powers of mind—
noble intellect—his bright & varied & original conversation'—
'& his many agreeable & engaging qualities, so clever & en-
livening! & so artless & candid!'[1] His devout cousins thought
that the 'change must be unspeakably blessed', since it came

when he seemed to be peculiarly prepared—perhaps he had never
been more conscientiously endeavouring to serve God—more nobly
& piously willing to put forth his best exertions for that high purpose,
and to employ his fine powers of mind in a way that might do good
to others, though the field was narrow and unpromising for his own
worldly advancement.[2]

Among the reflections on Alex's character and career were the
apt thoughts that occurred to his Aunt Broome. Though she
pitied her 'poor, dear, excruciated, hard hard tried sister', she
thought the early end a blessing. 'Oh, my dearest—as this poor
darling was no match for the World, it seems a mercy for him to
be taken to Heaven.'[3] When Fanny, struck by a ring of truth in
the sentence, asked for an explanation, Charlotte tried to elaborate her meaning. She had meant that Alex, 'so pure in his own
intentions', was 'no match for the World, and must have been
liable to perpetual troubles and impositions that none but his
exemplary, foreseeing tenderest of Mothers could foresee in time
to *prevent*'.[3]

Tho' we are in deep sorrow for our *own* loss—as we loved him dearly
—as to this dear lamented, noble minded as he was in *reality*, he was
so artless, so unsuspicious—so unable to cope with the World & its
ways—that—for a moment at a time—when only meditating on that
poor darling *exclusively*—I regard it, as a Mercy in the Almighty to
have taken him to Heaven, while watch'd & cherished as he continued to be by his precious mother, who understood him better
than all the world besides. In Heaven we hope & pray to meet him—
& time is getting on—[3]

With the candour, confidence, and openness characteristic of

[1] See p. 481, n. 2.
[2] A.L.S. (Berg) from Charlotte Barrett to FBA, 1837.
[3] 2 A.L.S. and A.L. (Barrett) with copies Diary MSS. (Berg), box viii, from
CBFB to FBA, 18 Jan., 12 Feb. 1837, and n.d.; 2 A.L. (Berg) from FBA to CBFB,
31 Mar., 11 Apr. 1837.

Fanny's long correspondence with her sisters, she penned a pained reply.

You thought it a *mercy* he was taken while yet watched & cherished in this world of which he so little knew how to combat the ways and arts—

I could read no more! I had often, transiently admitted that idea —but recoiled from it with shuddering . . . anguish—but its force & truth now seized me resistlessly—yet affected me so poignantly— that I could not dwell on it nor know what to do with myself for agony at the thought, That it was best he was withdrawn from me!— so I put the letter down . . . & finally, my own tenderest & often wisest beloved, though always humblest—*hear* & receive my own acknowledgement, that I believe you are right![1]

It was said that 'after the first tremendous burst of grief' Madame d'Arblay had seemed 'almost supernaturally sup- ported', most 'wonderfully sustained under her bitter trial'.[2] Charlotte thought her 'a pattern of Resignation to the Divine Will', but the private diaries and notebooks of the time with their changed handwriting and broken syntax will show, quite apart from the sentiments expressed, the shattering effects of the loss. 'All others, though dear to me before, & dear to me ever, were enjoyed with him, & seemed somehow, intermingling with his existence.'[3]

1837. On the opening of this most mournful—most *earthly* hopeless, of any and of all the years yet commenced of my long career! Yet, humbly I bless my God and Saviour, not hopeless; but full of gently- beaming hopes . . . of the time that may succeed to the dread in- fliction of this last irreparable privation, and bereavement of my darling loved, and most touchingly loving, dear, soul-dear Alex.[4]

In February Fanny was writing to Charlotte about Mary Ann Smith, who had offered to come and live with her. Madame d'Arblay considered it 'almost barbarous to listen to a plan of such a nearly sublunary funeral of so much merit', but when she learned that Alex had planned or agreed to the arrangement and that for this reason, among others, Miss Smith wished to carry it out, she gave a glad consent. 'Her

[1] See p. 482, n. 3.   [2] See p. 481, n. 2.
[3] A.L. (Berg) from FBA to CBFB, 12 July 1837; A.L. (Berg) to Charlotte Barrett, 22 Aug. 1837; A.L.S. (Berg) from SHB to FBA, 13 June 1837.
[4] *Diary*, vi. 415.

sweetness & goodness to *solicit* so heavy a charge and my
Alex's delight she tells me when she proposed it—how soothing!
how healing!' 'It has moved me to the soul!'[1]

New plans required a new place of residence, and in the
spring and summer she was oppressed with the prospect of
moving her effects and the hoard of manuscripts, now greatly
augmented by Alex's large library, manuscript works, and
papers ('I have some little comfort of pride in his Library, &
the credit it did him'). 'How will you, my dear soul, get through
the fatigue of a removal?' wondered Sarah Harriet. 'Such an
enterprise is always harassing: but ten times worse in sickness
& sorrow.'[2] The extraordinary exertions, mental and physical,
that Fanny had been capable of making throughout her long
life were usually followed by feverish illnesses. So again in July
and August she was very ill, but on August 22 well enough to
report that she was better, though 'the last time Dr. Holland
thought all over & my kindest friends thought they took their
last leave. Laborious was my recovery & only obtained by high
living, & strongest wines & even brandy! My pulse was so
sunk as to be hardly felt. Yet am I here!'[2] Her own surprised
commentary on her continued survival recurs like a stanzaic
refrain through the late troubles of her four score years and
eight. By August 27 she had moved to 112 Mount Street.
Through the summer Charlotte Broome had been attempting
to lure her to Brighton.

> Still, my Charlotte & myself keep thinking that—when all is done
> that can be done—& 'nought but dead silence, & a grim repose'
> remains—it may be *possible* for you to come to *me*—where you need
> not see a soul, unless by *choice*—having a comfortable bedroom entirely
> unmolested—the sea air—& air from the Downs, blowing in, when-
> ever the window is open, to brace the constitution—a garret for
> your maid—& your two Charlottes always at hand—I am unable
> to take a journey to town—obliged on keeping my room—so, I try
> to support my spirits with this plan—[3]

Early in November Fanny set off, and since she could not now
be hurried home by an erratic youth who might return to a cold

---

[1] A.L. (Berg) from FBA to CBFB, 17 Feb. 1837. Miss Smith's name was suppressed in the printed diaries at her own request and that of her brother, who
thought it 'an impropriety for a young unmarried woman to be mentioned in print'.
See A.L.S. (Barrett) from Mary Ann Smith to Charlotte Barrett, 2 Dec. 1841.

[2] See p. 483, n. 3.   [3] See p. 482, n. 3.

house in her absence, she remained for a month. 'She passed that month', Charlotte Barrett wrote,

with her sister secluded from all visitors except that sister's family, on whom the wisdom of her observations, counsel, & habits, and the extreme kindness & benevolence of her spirit made an impression that will never be effaced.[1]

Fanny in turn paid her tribute to her sister Charlotte Broome: 'Dear excellent Charlotte! more of worth, goodness, purity of character, & rectitude of conduct, never yet united in any one person.' In seventy-odd years not a doubt had risen between them to demand

even an explanation. For mistakes, for short memories, for errors in passing transactions, we have often *demanded satisfaction*—though not at Chalk Farm! but for tenderness, fond feelings, reciprocations of Love, our account is not yet ended, & has never been broken.[1]

The visit had done her a world of good. Even her eyes were 'really mended & braced by my kind visit to Brighton & Brightoneers'.[1] Her new dwelling in Mount Street was still near the parks, and to her physician's astonishment she was able to resume her walks in Berkeley Square.

As her Memorandum Book of 1838 shows, she still observed January 6, the date of Susan's death, as a day of prayer and remembrance. Mary Ann Smith did not come to live in Mount Street until March,[2] and though the morning calls of her nieces and faithful friends like Mrs. Angerstein brightened the early part of the day, the loneliness of the evenings, Fanny said, broke her down. The mornings were filled, besides, with the closing business of life—new clauses for her will and the disposal of manuscripts. Alex's papers were 'a chaotic heap of *literary litter*', and the task of sorting was often agonizing, awaking regrets and keeping old troubles alive. Every paper and every chattel brought her son to mind with abrupt recollection.

I would fain make him my theme—yet without this agony. Make it with a serenity that should only brighten remnant life by its prospect—not its inflexible regret.[2]

[1] A.L. (Berg) from FBA to EBB, 7 June 1825; to CBFB, 11 Dec. 1837; Diary MSS. (Berg), box viii.
[2] Memorandum Books (Berg); 2 A.L.S. (Berg) from FBA to CBFB, 6 Mar. 1838, 20 Apr. 1838. Also the reply, A.L.S. (Berg) from Charlotte Barrett to FBA, [1838].

Were *they* disposed of—these myriads of hoards of MSS.—I might enjoy a more tranquil resignation. I might think of my Alex without that perturbation that makes the thoughts of Him so tragic![1]

Her notebooks and diaries of the year record the days on which sacks of letters and papers were consigned to the fire. She asked the Charlottes for advice about the residue.

Shall I Burn them? at once—or shall I, & can I so modify a division as to spare for future times various collections that may be amusing & even instructive?—Certainly were I younger & could here wait for the examination—but such is not the case.[1]

A failing in her sight terminated about twenty years' reading in the Burney and d'Arblay papers. 'My eyes will work at them no more!'[1]

Meanwhile, as Sunday came round at Brighton, Charlotte wrote a long letter to Fanny. This was a pleasure, for she had for some time cultivated the illusion that she was in her sister's company when she wrote to her.[2] On minor troubles, including the vexed problem of servants, she could still produce a pun or two: 'I believe Caps & Captains engross the minds of those under 40, & *after* "fat fair & forty," they are subject to being Deaf, Dummy & obstinate.' The letters of the sisters in these years were often solemn pacts to keep to the 'medical nourishment'—the diets and nostrums that they devised and prescribed for each other—wines 'recommended by the Faculty', 'Tops & Bottoms—jellys—Gingerbread nuts—Bisquit & Currant Jelly—Spunge Bisquits dip'd in *light* wine'. Each was to remember the 'tender claims' of the other, eat, and avoid the end of most old ladies, as they diagnosed it—death by starvation. '*Recruit* is so necessary to Nature in its decline.' They knew that the end could not be very far away. As Fanny wrote to Charlotte, 'we must Both . . . be prepared to know that a separation here MUST come however long we may be spared the anguish!' All hope must be in 'a permanent re-union' here-after. And she repeated what she had formerly written to Esther, 'we must hold ourselves prepared to *give* or to *receive* from each

[1] See p. 485, n. 2.
[2] A.L. (Berg) from FBA to Charlotte Barrett, [1835]; four letters (Berg) from FBA to CBFB, 5 Feb., 14 Dec. 1835, Mar. 1837, 22–27 Aug. 1838; letters (Barrett) from CBFB to FBA, 11 May 1834, 3 Apr. 1837(?), 17 Jan., 15 June, July 1838.

other *one* of the bitterest afflictions that remain to our lots' but 'unless we are together at the time, we must bear it in absence!' They were past the time when, with such apprehensions on the mind, they could journey to each other.[1]

Charlotte Broome, however, had set her mind on one more journey. 'Ungenteel' as it was, she preferred London in the summer because the streets were clean then and the days long. As usual she wished to be near her sister. The scarcity of lodgings and the high prices of the coronation year made some difficulty, but finally convenient rooms were found at 22 Mount Street, Grosvenor Square, and in August, 1838, Charlotte made her last journey to London town. 'The sight of her sister to whom she was fondly attached seemed to revive her', Charlotte Barrett later wrote, 'but after a few weeks a sudden and rapid attack came on, and in two days all was over.'[2] Of all the sorrows Charlotte Barrett had known, this was the deepest:

My dear mother's tender and constant affection—her faithful counsel—and her indulgent assistance, had been so long my comforts that it seems like a cutting up of life to lose her. . . . Alas *hers* is a loss that no time will soften, and I feel it every day—nearly every hour.[2]

Charlotte's was 'a simplicity of goodness', Fanny had always said, 'totally unconscious of its own worth',[3] and to Fanny, even more than to her niece, this loss was a cutting away of life. Sarah Harriet, now an invalid herself, also grieved in her invalid chair at Bath: 'The loss of my sister Broome was a heavy blow to me! I loved her warmly & fondly,—perhaps, the best of any of my family.' Like everyone else, she pitied Fanny for the 'heavy addition to her cup of sorrow'. 'Poor thing! she has gone through sorrows that in anticipation she herself and we all should have thought, must have demolished her.'[4]

Bereft not only of her two Alexanders, but also of the last of the 'original progeny' of the Burneys, the last tie, as she said, to native 'original affections', Fanny was now indeed, by all

---

[1] See p. 486, n. 2.

[2] A.L.S. (Barrett) from CBFB to FBA, July 1838; draft of A.L. (Barrett) from Charlotte Barrett to Mrs. Aufrère, 15 Nov. 1838. The death certificate states that Charlotte Ann Broome, gentlewoman, died of sporadic or bilious cholera on 12 Sept. 1838, aged 75 years. See also A.L.S. (Barrett) from SHB to Charlotte Barrett, 17 Apr. 1839, and the reply, 4 May 1839.

[3] See quoted back in A.L. (Berg) from Charlotte Barrett to FBA, 29 Jan. [1835].

[4] A.L.S. (Berg) from SHB to Anna Wilbraham Grosvenor, 22 Mar. 1839.

Burney standards, alone. Old friends like George Cambridge
or Mrs. Angerstein, the faithful Mary Ann Smith playing gently
on the piano, relatives including Edward Francesco, Fanny
Raper, the Barretts, or Colonel Henry Burney, who helped so
much with the practical problems of the last years—all these
could ease but not prevent her essential loneliness. A new diary
for 1839 hailed 'Another baneful January!'

One more melancholy year let me try—since for some hidden mercy
it seems granted me—hidden—for all Life's happiness is flown with
my Alexander—dearly as I yet—as ever—Love many—& some still
with the warmth of a Heart open to the sacred feelings of the tenderest friendship.[1]

In this month, whatever the reason, she moved or was moved
from 112 Mount Street to 29 Lower Grosvenor Street at the
corner of Davies Street ('I am *bodily* better certainly but worn
with removing at this season—in my shattered state & in
this month—this baleful—yet let me hope blessed month!').[2]
Notebooks with written records of her resolves indicate how
much her strength lagged behind her mind and will. Yet on
her eighty-seventh birthday (June 13, 1839) she could report
having made a rough assortment of Alexander's papers and
a rough catalogue of *all* manuscripts,[3] a new will or a codicil to
a will already made, and she had written asking Charlotte
Barrett if she would like to be her executrix. 'I do not ask *will*
you *consent*—but should you *like* it?'[2] She was pleased with
Colonel Burney's wish that she should be godmother to his
infant son, who was to be christened Alexander d'Arblay
Burney so that, in spite of Alex's death, the d'Arblay name
might remain in England.[4]
    The broken sentences of her last writings show the effects, as
her physician put it, of 'a head over-worked, and a heart over-
loaded'.[5] Her wandering thoughts as traced rather blindly over
the old papers formed a kaleidoscope in which Macaulay,
Croker, Dr. Burney, Alex, Amelia Angerstein, Sarah Harriet,
and the Princesses mingled shiftingly, the connexions lost in

[1] A holograph notebook (Berg) for 1839. Also Diary MSS. (Berg), box viii.
[2] A.L. and A.L.S. (Berg) from FBA to Charlotte Barrett, 8 Jan., 30 July 1839.
[3] This useful list fills a *cahier* (Berg).
[4] A.L.S. (Berg) from SHB to Anna Wilbraham Grosvenor, 22 Mar. 1839.
[5] *Diary*, vi. 406.

complicated trains of association. She could no longer accept royal invitations, though events near the throne were still of interest. The young Queen Victoria had been deluded into a wrong opinion and measure and 'though not blameless, is extremely to be pitied'. 'There is some mystery in the terrible calumny, to which the poor young innocent & inexperienced Queen is doubtless a Dupe.'[1]

Later Charlotte Barrett was to ask her cousin Fanny Raper for a character of their famous aunt for a preface to the *Diary and Letters of Madame d'Arblay*. Susan's daughter, who could look back half a century to the days of her childhood at Mickleham, when her aunt had come from court in a beautiful gold cap and Norbury had stood weeping at the gate when she left, tried to make her appraisal true:

a passion for writing . . . innate conscientiousness, strength of mind, self denial, rectitude of principles, precision of judgment, keenness of apprehension, depth of feeling and warmth of heart formed the basis of her character; to which was added generous appreciation of the merit and character of others; discriminate selection, humorous clear-sightedness, every power of heart and intellect.[2]

Charlotte's daughter thought rather of her aunt's adherence to 'the strait path of duty', of her memory and her imagination. 'If any one was entitled to confide in talents or yield to the guidance of imagination, she might have claimed that privilege.'[3] Madame d'Arblay had been brought up in an age that tried to distinguish between reason and passion, but '*the Passions*', she said, ought to be subdued to Patience,

for that, I begin to think, is more properly their Superior than Reason, which, in many cases, finds it hard not to join with them.[4]

Orthodox in most of her thinking, she had yet a realistic knowledge of human nature, and there was probably little in human conduct that could now surprise her. Orthodox or conventional also in her conformity to the proprieties, in the major issues of her marriage and her career there must have been few who,

---

[1] See p. 488, n. 2.   [2] Barrett.
[3] Draft of a letter (Berg) from Charlotte Barrett to Miss Morton, 6 Jan. 1840; 3 letters (Barrett) from Charlotte to Henry Barrett, 20 Nov., 4, 7 Dec. 1839; A.L.S. (Osborn) from Charlotte Barrett to CPB, 4 Jan. 1840; *Diary*, iv. 416–18.
[4] Diary MSS. (Berg), box viii; *Diary*, iv. 164. Also A.L.S. (Berg) from Cornelia (Mrs. George) Cambridge to Charlotte Barrett, 29 Oct. 1838.

while keeping a respectable place in society, conformed less to the patterns of their status.

In November, 1839, Madame d'Arblay became so ill and weak that Charlotte Barrett came from Brighton to be with her and remained six weeks.[1] At one time Dr. Holland, judging that the end must be near, desired Miss Smith 'to write & prepare Mrs. Angerstein for the worst'.[1] The Archdeacon came to read the prayers appointed for the sick, but Madame d'Arblay could not admit him. Her nieces and Charles Parr also tried to read to her, but her mind was straying, wandering far away, perhaps far above, so that it was impossible to enlist her attention. 'We attempted it once or twice, and she said, "My dear, I cannot understand a word—not a syllable—but I thank God, my mind has not waited till *this* time." She often appeared to be praying—her hands clasped and her eyes lifted up.'[1] She appeared to be praying, but sometimes, very probably, in accordance with the long habits of her life in sleeplessness and sickness, she was going over long poems or pieces of music. When the poet Rogers, who was sitting with her a few weeks before her death, asked if she remembered the lines from Mrs. Barbauld's *Life* that he had repeated to her, she replied, 'Remember them! I repeat them to myself every night before I go to sleep.'[2]

> Life! we've been long together,
> Through pleasant and through cloudy weather:
> 'Tis hard to part when friends are dear;
> Perhaps 'twill cost a sigh, a tear;
> Then steal away, give little warning,
> Choose thine own time,
> Say not Good Night, but in some brighter clime
> Bid me Good Morning.[2]

And yet, such was the strength of her constitution, that, as Mr. Barrett predicted, she again recovered. The end was deferred until the beginning of the year 1840, prolonged by some spiritual strength, significantly enough, as the mystical may say, to January 6, the date of Susan's death, the anniversary of which since 1800 she had kept for communion with Susan and others who had gone before her into the world of light. 'In

---

[1] See p. 489, n. 3.   [2] Austin Dobson, *Diary*, vi. 420 n.

humble but cheerful hope I look upwards with aspiration to go where she *is*—& where—my dearest Charlotte, what a Paradise does not mental anticipation form for our Futurity!'[1]

'Her kindness remained as ever,' Susan's daughter said, 'though it became more and more distasteful to her to receive us—she could not endure the exertion of speaking.' After she had slept a little, one of her attendants remarked that she had wanted rest. '*I shall have it soon, my dear*', she replied with confidence, and at half past one o'clock on the morning of January 6, 1840, she departed in peace, perfectly aware of her approaching end. Her nieces reported her last words: 'I know I am dying, but I am willing to die; I commit my soul to God, in reliance on the mercy & merit of my redeemer.'[2] Mingled with these words about her own future were directions to the executors of her estate, instructions to Charlotte Barrett, Colonel Burney, and her lawyer about keys to the boxes where her papers were to be found.

The remains were to be interred in Alexander's grave in Wolcot Churchyard in Bath. By railway now, as well as by coach and 'post chariot', representatives of the different branches of the Burney family made their way to Bath. There in the presence of James's son, Richard's son, Charles's grandson, Susan's daughter, Charlotte's daughter and grandson, the faithful Mary Ann Smith, and other mourners, Madame d'Arblay was interred with her son. The grave of the brave chevalier is near by on the slope over which the fresh winds blow from the hills surrounding the city of hills, where one of the dramas of her life was played to a close and where long and long ago she had come as Fanny Burney.

[1] A.L. (Berg) from FBA to CBFB, June 1834.
[2] A.L. (Berg) from Fanny Phillips Raper to Charlotte Barrett, [6 Jan. 1840]; A.L.S. (Barrett) from Charlotte Barrett to Richard Barrett, 9 Jan. 1840; A.L.S. (Berg) to Henry Barrett, 11 Jan. 1840.

NOTES

Note A, p. 5. According to the registers (Harleian) of St. Vedast, Foster Lane, 'Esther yᵉ Daught' of Mʳ Sleepe by . . . his Wife was Borne May yᵉ 19th & Baptized yᵉ 9th day of June 1723. By Mʳ Wm Bayley.' Since the names *James* and *Foster Lane* (as supplied in n. 2, p. 4) rule out the alternative possibility of the date 1 Aug. 1725, as entered in the registers of St. Michael le Quern for the birth of a Hester, daughter of *Richard* Sleepe, the St. Vedast date may be taken, tentatively at least, for the birthday of Esther Sleepe Burney.

Note B, pp. 65, 66, 88, 89. Ten letters or drafts of letters written by Fanny Burney to the bookseller Thomas Lowndes are preserved in a grangerized edition of *Diary and Letters of Madame d'Arblay* (6 vols.), a work richly illustrated with valuable autographs. I am indebted to their former owner, Mrs. Atherton Cumming, and her daughter Miss Elmer Cumming, direct descendants of the Burneys, for the privilege of a day's reading in this work, and to them and the present owner, John R. G. Comyn, Esquire, for permission to quote the letters here. The ten letters were published by Walter Frith, 'Autour d'Evelina, some unpublished letters of Fanny Burney', the *Cornhill Magazine*, xviii (Apr. 1905), 454–65. Letter No. 1 bears a postmark. The others may be either drafts of letters or letters sent by messenger and retrieved.

Note C, pp. 65, 66, 67, 87, 88. This folder is preserved among the Barrett Papers (BM) and contains 7 A.L.S. (dated) from Thomas Lowndes to Mr. King or Mr. Grafton, to be called for at the Orange Coffee House; and 2 A.L. from FB (in feigned writing) to Mr. Lowndes, Bookseller, Fleet Street. The letters are numbered, edited, and sometimes marked with the signs used in the Diary MSS. No. 7 is printed in ED, ii. 213; Nos. 1–6 are shown in facsimile in Constance Hill, *The House in St. Martin's Street*, pp. 87–109.

Note D, p. 73. In the Osborn Collection. The volume includes occasional poems on events occurring in Cambridge and Shinfield in 1777–8. The dates of the poems indicate that Charles remained in Shinfield throughout December 1777, and for part of the next year, e.g. 'On the death of Peter Floyer, esq., of Shinfield Place, Berkshire' [4 Dec. 1777]; 'On the Bells at Shinfield Church, hung in 1778'; 'A Farewell to Shinfield', 1778.

Note E, p. 73. A poem of 207 verses (Osborn) entitled 'A Letter to F. J. H. W.' (apparently Francis John Hyde Wollaston, who had been at the Charterhouse with Charles). The poem is annotated by Charles: 'Feb. 3, 1778. Not sent—The Reason will never be forgotten, so need not be set down!' What happened is probably indicated by a letter (Osborn) written by Francis Wollaston (the father of the brilliant Wollastons) to Charles, 3 Feb. 1783, firmly discouraging any further friendship between Charles and his sons ('I think it right for your sake as well as my own & my family not to renew our acquaintance').

NOTE F, pp. 73, 74. See the Burney–Twining correspondence (BM), especially letters from Mr. Twining to CB, 17 Dec. 1777, 28 July, 19 Dec. 1778, 28 Dec. 1781, 5 May, 18 Sept., 28 Nov. 1782, 27 Jan., 19 Feb., 5 July 1783, 3 Feb. 1784, all of which touch on Charles's problems. Other letters in this correspondence indicate that Madame d'Arblay was not alone in wishing to suppress painful episodes in Charles's early career. See the correspondence of 1881 between members of the Burney family and Mr. Richard Twining, who was then arranging the Twining correspondence for publication. In this correspondence it is suggested that Mr. Richard Twining may see 'the propriety of omitting' letters written by Charles Burney (Mus. Doc.) on 23 Dec. 1777, 1 Dec. 1778, 22 Oct. 1780, in which 'there are allusions to a very painful matter'.

NOTE G, pp. 182, 184. *Thraliana*, ii. 739, 760. Cf. Clifford, p. 225, n. 2: 'I am convinced from the moment of the nuptials she showed him all my Letters, & probably attributed to me every obstacle that he found in his way.' Also a copy of the same letter, Letter Book (Osborn): 'It is the common mode upon such occasions by which the "fond married loves" repair their cruelties & hesitations; & the counsellors who, however urged to openness, have declared adverse sentiments, are almost uniformly sacrificed at the hymeneal shrine.' Also Dr. Burney's comment (*Memoirs*, iii. 380–1): 'The old rancour, or ill-will, excited by our desire to impede the marriage, is totally worn away. Indeed, it never could have existed, but from *her* imprudence in betraying to him that proof of our friendship for *her*, which ought never to have been regarded as spleen against him, who, certainly, nobody could blame for accepting a gay rich widow. What could a man do better?' This was in 1807, but the rancour, of course, had not worn away. See Clifford, p. 414, n. 1.

NOTE H, p. 205. Much that Fanny wrote about Colonel Digby has been deleted from the printed journals but may be read in the Diary MSS. (Berg). In June 1842 Julia Thomas and Minette Kingston (Charlotte Barrett's daughter and cousin) were reading the proof-sheets of the *Diary and Letters* and busily scratching out sections about 'Digby's jilting'. See A.L.S. (Barrett) from Julia Thomas to Charlotte Barrett, 9 June 1842: 'If you can cut out a volume of Digby, it will be an improvement.'

NOTE I, pp. 214, 215. See fragments of 4 pages cut from Fanny Burney's Court Journal (Barrett), 30 Apr., 7 May [1790]; also A.L.S. (Berg) from FB to CB, Jr., 2 Aug. [1790]; A.L.S. (PML) from FB to JB, 1 Sept. 1790; A.L.S. (Barrett) from Jacob Bryant to FB, 24 June 1790; A.L.S. (Osborn) from CB to CB, Jr., 21 July 1790; A.L.S. (Osborn) from CB, Jr., to FB, [1790]; 6 A.L.S. (Osborn) from FB to CB, Jr., 21 May, 10, 26 June, 9, 17, 26 July 1790; and 5 A.L.S. (Osborn) on the subject of the Memorial from G. I. Huntingford, J. Carliol, Henry Kett, J. Winstanley, and Dr. Hay to CB, Jr., 14, 28 Apr., 16, 25 May, 14 July 1790, respectively. One page of the Memorial showing a long list of signatures still survives (Osborn). See also a copy of a very frank letter about Charles from FB to William Windham, Diary MSS. (Berg), scraps, box iv, together with Windham's reply. For Charles's hopes for the Headmastership of the Charterhouse see Diary

MSS. (Berg), May 1791 (pp. 4281–90). For Susan Burney's comment, Journal-letters (Berg), 1790–1.

NOTE J, p. 279. Two drafts of letters signed (Berg) from FBA to the Rev. Stephen Allen, [1833]. See also Scholes, ii. 149–52. Cf. Maria Rishton's remarks in A.L. (Barrett) to FBA, 24 Dec. 1796: 'And no infirmities of Temper or other frailties of Human nature are remembered on such an Occasion and indeed I believe latterly extreme sufferings added to the quantity of Laudanum that she constantly took at times caused a Temporary derangement from the extreme irritability of her Nerves—God Bless your dear Father for his Goodness to her!'

NOTE K, p. 291. A.L.S. (Berg) from CBFB and MF to Charlotte Barrett, 29 July 1817: 'The James Street arrest was for House rent for his wife. wch he had tried to elude by telling the creditors that she was not his wife, only a sham marriage, & the Landlord was on the point of turning her out of doors, only she brought them certificates of the marriage. . . . There was another writ . . . and it is understood he is now in prison.' Also A.L.S. (Barrett) from Charlotte Barrett to Arthur Young, 7 Dec. 1819; and A.L.S. (Osborn) from CB to Lady Crewe, 26 Sept. 1801. For other biographical details see the scrapbook (Berg) 'Fanny Burney and the Burneys'.

NOTE L, p. 342. Passages about Mrs. Ireton can be matched with suppressed or unpublished passages in the Burney MSS. referring to the second Mrs. Burney. Cf. 'Mrs. Ireton was reclining on an easy chair, still disordered from her voyage, though by no means as much in need of assistance for her shattered frame, as of amusement for her restless mind' (*The Wanderer*, i. 68–69) with comments on Mrs. Burney's restlessness of mind (Diary MSS. [Berg] suppressed fragments, Aug. 1782 and A.L. [Berg] from FBA to SBP, 24 Aug. 1792) including the comment: 'She wants more amusement to keep off the foul fiend than any human being I ever saw.' Also cf. Mrs. Ireton's quarrels with her son, her sarcasms ('splenetic witticisms'), and her contemptuous method of referring to people whose names she pretends to have forgotten, with Charlotte Burney's remarks (ED, ii. 311).

NOTE M, p. 440. A.L.S. (Barrett) from Julia Barrett to Charlotte Barrett, 8 Nov. [1826]; A.L. (Berg) from Charlotte to Henry Barrett, 13 Aug. 1832; A.L.S. (Berg) from SHB to Charlotte Barrett, 25 Apr. 1828; 2 A.L.S. (Berg) from Sarah Burney Payne to Charlotte Barrett, [1828] and 22 Sept. 1828; A.L.S. (Berg) from EBB to CBFB, 25 Oct. 1829; A.L.S. and A.L. (Berg) from AA with postscripts by Sarah Burney Payne to FBA, 14, 19 Sept. 1834; A.L.S. (Berg) from FBA to EBB, 7 June 1825.

NOTE N, p. 462. Mrs. Agnew's assertion (quoted in corroboration by Lady Llanover, *Autobiography*, vi. 316–17) that at the death of the Duchess of Portland three of Mrs. Delany's nephews offered to come to her rescue seems to be an unconscious admission that the death of the Duchess had brought about a crisis in Mrs. Delany's pecuniary affairs. Fanny often referred to Mrs. Delany as 'the *most* exalted of female characters I ever knew' and later cited her 'angelic' attitude towards the Duchess of Portland and those who wished to help her as a model for Susan and others in the

Burney family who displayed stiff-necked pride in seasons of need. For example, see A.L.S. (Berg) from FBA to SBP, 6 July 1798.

NOTE O, p. 462. The evidence of the manuscripts revises the deductions of Dr. Percy A. Scholes, i. 105–6, ii. 226, 232, 355. Parish registers correct dates in Scholes, i. 46, ii. 143, 235, 239. Emily Hahn in *A Degree of Prudery* (1950) errs in the unfortunate assumption (pp. 177–8) that 'Mrs. Thrale leaped to the wrong conclusion' about Fanny Burney and her relations with George Cambridge and that it was 'Mr. Cambridge, elderly father of Mr. George Cambridge' (and not the young man) who absorbed Fanny Burney's thoughts in 1784–6.

APPENDIX

THE BURNEY MANUSCRIPTS:
A TENTATIVE SUMMARY

1. The manuscripts of
    Diary and Letters of Madame d'Arblay (7 vols., 1842–6), *c.* 7500 pp.
    The Early Diary of Frances Burney, 1768–78 (2 vols., 1889), 780 pp.
    Holograph manuscripts originally belonging to the Diary MSS. (above) but for the most part discarded or suppressed by Madame d'Arblay herself or subsequent editors, *c.* 1,000 pp.

    Journals or Journal-letters at some time separated from the Diary MSS.: M. d'Arblay's courtship. Catalogued as Diary, 8 April–9 May, 1793, *c.* 54 pp.
    Accounts of a surgical operation. Catalogued as A.L.S. to Esther Burney, 12 March, 1812, *c.* 15 pp.
    Adventures at Ilfracombe in 1817, 32 pp.
    The illness and Death of General d'Arblay. Catalogued as Diary, 17 Nov., 1819–9 March, 1820, *c.* 128 pp.

2. Manuscripts of Madame d'Arblay's novels:
    A draft of *Evelina* (incomplete), *c.* 104 ff.
    Cecilia (incomplete), *c.* 274 ff.
    Camilla (incomplete), *c.* 47 ff. in Madame d'Arblay's hand; *c.* 685 ff. in General d'Arblay's.

3. Manuscripts of Madame d'Arblay's unpublished plays:
    'The Witlings', *c.* 63 ff.
    'Edwy and Elgiva', *c.* 139 ff. Also 29 ff. of additional MS. material in General d'Arblay's hand and that of Madame d'Arblay.
    'Elberta', 152 ff.
    'Hubert De Vere', 53 ff.; a second draft, 55 ff.
    'The Siege of Pevensey', 120 ff.
    'A Busy Day', 185 ff. in General d'Arblay's hand with corrections by Madame d'Arblay. Also notes for revisions.
    'Love and Fashion', 181 ff. with additional notes (15 ff.).
    'The Woman-Hater', 243 ff.; also a second draft, 100 ff. and additional notes (50 ff.).

4. Manuscripts of *Memoirs of Doctor Burney* (incomplete), 17 ff. Also 'Characters extracted from various writings of my dearest father', 26 ff.

5. Miscellaneous holographs, notes, suggestions for plots, dialogue, character-sketches for novels and plays, 417 pieces.

6. Thirty-five holograph notebooks, *cahiers* (various sizes), including account books, memorandum books, extract books, commonplace-books, and registers of manuscripts (in Madame d'Arblay's hand).

7. Manuscript verse:
   'Content! Thou real, and only bliss', 1 folio.
   'To Doctor Last', 1 folio.
   'Verses from the French of Voltaire', 1 folio.
   'Willy', 29 pp. (a French translation in General d'Arblay's hand).

8. Sixteen themes by Fanny Burney or General d'Arblay (1792–3), 31 ff.

9. Holograph translation of Fontenelle's *Entretiens sur la pluralité des mondes*, 96 ff.

10. Drafts and copies of legal documents, wills, contracts.

11. Four large scrap-books containing genealogical tables, prints, and letters (recatalogued in the correspondence to follow).

12. General d'Arblay and his son Alexander d'Arblay: literary fragments, translations, verses, historical sketches, diaries, notebooks, legal documents.

13. Dr. Charles Burney (1726–1814): mutilated fragments cut from his own Memoirs, *c.* 104 pieces.

14. Journals and Journal-letters by Susan Elizabeth Burney Phillips, 1786–93, 1797; 3 notebooks, *c.* 1,272 pp.

15. Journals and Diaries kept by Marianne Francis, 1803–21, 18 folders, *c.* 690 pp.

16. Odds and ends, keepsakes, and matter characteristic of family archives.

17. FAMILY CORRESPONDENCE (24 letter-boxes):

Letters written by Charles Burney, Mus.Doc. (1726–1814)		*c.* 127
„	Charles Burney, D.D. (1757–1817)	32
„	James Burney, Rear-Admiral	22
„	Frances Burney d'Arblay	929
„	Susan Elizabeth Burney Phillips	244
„	Charlotte Ann Burney Francis Broome	24
„	Sarah Harriet Burney (novelist)	198
„	Esther Burney Burney	10
„	the second generation of Burneys:	
„	Charles Parr Burney (1785–1864)	25
„	Charlotte Francis Barrett	84
„	other Barretts	19
„	Clement Francis	27
„	Alexander d'Arblay	58
„	Sarah Burney Payne	19
„	Marianne Francis	115
	to Marianne Francis (including 79 from Arthur Young)	124

FAMILY CORRESPONDENCE (*cont.*):

Letters written to Frances Burney d'Arblay

	by Hester Lynch Thrale Piozzi	184
	„ Madame de Maisonneuve	121
	„ the Royal Princesses	175
	„ others of the French or English nobility	26
	„ Maria Allen Rishton	52
	„ General d'Arblay	160
	„ others (exclusive of family letters as above)	309
Letters written by or to other Burneys (exclusive of above)		19

THE BRITISH MUSEUM

THE BARRETT COLLECTION OF BURNEY PAPERS (Egerton 3690–708) obtained in 1952 (see the *British Museum Quarterly*, xviii, June 1953).

Frances Burney d'Arblay:
  Fragments from the Court Journals (1786, 1789, 1790), 18 ff.
  Early draft of part of *Camilla*, 49 ff.
  Draft of an introduction to *Cecilia*, 3 ff.
  Verses addressed to members of the family, 9 ff.

Susan Burney Phillips: Journal-letters (1780–9), 350 ff.

Mrs. William Locke: A Journal often referring to the Burneys, 76 ff.

Burney Correspondence:

Letters written	by Charles Burney, Mus.Doc. (1726–1814)		*c.* 28
	to Charles Burney (as above) chiefly from		
	the Rev. Thomas Twining		*c.* 100
	by Charles Burney, D.D. (1757–1817)		*c.* 20
	„ James Burney		*c.* 3
	„ Frances Burney d'Arblay		*c.* 223
	„ Susan Elizabeth Burney Phillips		*c.* 30
	„ Charlotte Ann Burney Francis Broome		*c.* 100
	„ Sarah Harriet Burney		*c.* 30
	„ Esther Burney Burney		*c.* 15
2nd and 3rd	„ Charlotte Francis Barrett		*c.* 215
generation of	„ Marianne Francis		*c.* 190
Burneys	„ Julia Barrett Thomas Maitland		*c.* 80
	„ miscellaneous Barretts		*c.* 30
	„ Alexander d'Arblay		*c.* 5
	„ Richard Barrett (uncatalogued)		
Letters written to	Frances Burney d'Arblay (exclusive of		
	family letters as listed above):		
	by Mr. Samuel Crisp		*c.* 30
	„ Hester Lynch Thrale Piozzi		*c.* 25
	„ Maria Allen Rishton		*c.* 30
	„ miscellaneous		*c.* 250

A trunkful of uncatalogued Barrett Correspondence (letters, &c., 1860–90); legal documents, certificates, copies of wills, &c.

THE BURNEY PAPERS (Add. MSS. 936–9, 39303), and others.
Fragments of Dr. Burney's Memoirs (Add. MSS. 48345).

THE OSBORN COLLECTION

(The private collection of Mr. James M. Osborn of Yale University)

Letters written by Charles Burney, Mus.Doc. (1726–1814)	*c.* 440
to Charles Burney (as above)	*c.* 334
by Charles Burney, D.D. (1757–1817)	*c.* 205
to Charles Burney (as above)	*c.* 491
by Charles Parr Burney (1785–1864)	*c.* 62
to Charles Parr Burney (as above)	*c.* 469
by Frances Burney d'Arblay (including 13 copies in General d'Arblay's hand)	*c.* 118
to Frances Burney d'Arblay (excluding some 90 letters by Charles Burney, Mus.Doc. and D.D. as above)	*c.* 23
by and to other Burneys	*c.* 56

Susan Burney Phillips: Journal-letters (1787–8), *c.* 500 pp.

Charles Burney, Mus. Doc. (1726–1814):
'Astronomy, An Historical and Didactic Poem', bk. 1, 9 ff.
'The Trial of Midas, the second, a tale', 50 ff.
A notebook of verse, 42 ff.

Memoirs, 6 scraps and the mutilated remains of a notebook, *c.* 23 pp.
Musical notebooks, 6 in number, containing musical memoranda.
Holograph manuscripts of verses, occasional poems, elegies, and anniversary poems addressed to members of the family.

Charles Burney D.D. (1757–1817):
Three notebooks of verse, autobiographical and occasional.
Numerous documents belonging to members of the Burney family.

THE JOHN RYLANDS LIBRARY, MANCHESTER

Letters written by Charles Burney, Mus.Doc. (1726–1814)	15
„ Frances Burney d'Arblay	10
„ Marianne Francis	163
„ Clement Francis	22
„ Charles Burney, D.D. (1757–1817)	3

For the correspondence of Hester Lynch Thrale Piozzi, of which most of the Burney letters above form a part, see Dr. M. Tyson, *Hand-List of Additions to our English Manuscripts* (1935); Dr. F. Taylor, *Supplementary Hand-List of Western Manuscripts* (1937) and *Hand-List of Additions* (1937). See also James L. Clifford, *Hester Lynch Piozzi (Mrs. Thrale)* (1941), appendixes D, E.

THE BODLEIAN LIBRARY, OXFORD

Letters written by Charles Burney, Mus.Doc. (1726–1814) 24
    ,,   Charles Parr Burney (1785–1864) 125
    ,,   other Burneys 12

THE PUBLIC LIBRARY, ARMAGH

1. Copies of 27 Journal-letters written by Susan Elizabeth Burney Phillips to her sister Frances Burney, 1787–8. Copies by Henry Augustus Johnston from letters lent to him in 1881 by Susan's granddaughter Mrs. Nugent Kingston.

2. Transcripts of 52 Journal-letters, as above, 1795–9. Copied by the Rev. David Wauchope.

Some of these were sketchily printed by R. Brimley Johnson in *Fanny Burney, and the Burneys* (1926). The originals are for the most part in the Barrett Osborn, and Berg Collections, but there are copies of letters here, the originals of which are not at the moment to be found.

THE PIERPONT MORGAN LIBRARY, NEW YORK

1. A Letter Book containing 45 letters from Frances Burney d'Arblay to her brother, James Burney, and 11 letters to other members of her family.

2. Letters, documents, memorials, by and to James Burney, Rear-Admiral.

THE LIBRARY OF THE NATIONAL PORTRAIT GALLERY

A grangerized edition of *The Early Diary of Frances Burney, 1768–78* (in 7 vols.) and of the *Diary and Letters of Madame d'Arblay* (in 16 vols.), illustrated by prints of contemporary scenes, reproductions of oils and miniatures, and transcripts of letters written by or to or about members of the Burney family. By Leverton Harris.

THE LIBRARY, WINCHESTER COLLEGE

In the Huntingford Correspondence (the Wiccamica Collection), at least ten letters from Charles Burney, D.D., to Bishop Huntingford.

THE HENRY E. HUNTINGTON LIBRARY AND ART GALLERY, SAN MARINO, CALIFORNIA

'Consolatory Extracts Daily Collected or Read' in the year 1800 by Madame d'Arblay; and six Burney letters.

THE YALE UNIVERSITY LIBRARY, NEW HAVEN

Eight Burney letters; a commonplace-book, 1793–7, in General d'Arblay's hand including his translation of Madame d'Arblay's verse-narrative 'Willy'; and 'An Anecdote for the Life of Dr. Johnson', 2 ff., by Charles Burney, Mus. Doc.

THE BOSTON PUBLIC LIBRARY

Four Burney letters.

PRINCETON UNIVERSITY LIBRARY
Five Burney letters.

THE KING'S LYNN BOROUGH MUSEUM
Three Burney letters.

THE PUBLIC RECORD OFFICE
One Burney letter.

NORTHWESTERN UNIVERSITY LIBRARY
Two Burney letters.

OTHER PRIVATE COLLECTIONS

A FAMILY COLLECTION: the possession of Miss Ann Julia Wauchope, at Howton, Bushey Heath, Herts., the great-great-granddaughter of Charlotte Ann Burney Francis Broome (and the great-great-grandniece of Madame d'Arblay), who, along with her brother, the late David Wauchope, Esquire, inherited most of the Burney manuscripts now in the Berg Collection, the NYPL, as well as the Barrett Collection of Burney papers recently placed in the British Museum. See the *British Museum Quarterly*, xviii (June 1953), 41–43. Miss Wauchope still possesses interesting letters, portraits, miniatures, first editions of Burney publications, and mementoes (including a watch that Queen Charlotte gave to Fanny Burney and a sampler worked by Esther Sleepe). This is the residue of the vast archive that Madame d'Arblay willed to her niece Charlotte Francis Barrett and that, much augmented, came down more or less intact in the Barrett family until the year 1924, when the first division was made in the papers.

A FAMILY COLLECTION: formerly in the possession of Mrs. Atherton Cumming, the daughter of Charles Burney, Esquire, and now the property of her grandson, John R. G. Comyn, Esquire, consisting of a grangerized edition of the *Diary and Letters of Madame d'Arblay*. Among the illustrations in this grangerized edition are:

Letters written by Charles Burney, Mus.Doc. (1726–1814)	4
to Charles Burney (as above)	19
by Frances Burney d'Arblay	22
to Frances Burney d'Arblay	22
by other Burneys	30

In this collection there is also, Charles Parr Burney, a commonplacebook.

Dr. Percy A. Scholes, Oxford: documents incorporated in his *The Great Doctor Burney* (2 vols., 1948). This material includes transcripts of letters, about 70 originals, and a typescript of 'A Journal of the Worcester Burneys', *c.* 190 ff.

Mr. John Sparrow, Warden of All Souls College, Oxford:

Letters to Charles Burney, D.D. (1757–1817)
from Samuel Parr   *c.* 110
other Burney items   *c.* 60

Mr. and Mrs. Donald F. Hyde of Somerville, New Jersey:

Letters or drafts of letters by Charles Burney, Mus.Doc.(1726–
1814)   *c.* 19
by Charles Burney, D.D. (1757–1817)   *c.* 5
by Frances Burney d'Arblay   *c.* 3

Mr. Richard Border, Pulborough, Sussex:
Letters by Charles Burney, Mus.Doc. (1726–1814)   *c.* 3
to Frances Burney d'Arblay from Pacchierotti   *c.* 12

Professor F. W. Hilles, Yale University:
A part of Fanny Burney's Court Journal (*c.* 53 pp.).
Burney letters.   *c.* 15

Mr. Brooks Shepard, Librarian of the School of Music, Yale University:
Letters by Charles Burney, Mus.Doc. (1726–1814)   *c.* 6

The Carl H. Pforzheimer Library (Hidden Brook Farm, Purchase, N.Y.):
Letters to Charles Burney, D.D. (1757–1817).   *c.* 4

Miss Stella M. Alleyne, Cuckfield, Sussex: a small collection of Burney letters (lately dispersed at auction).

INDEX

For Libraries and Collections of Burney manuscripts see Appendix, pp. 496–502. For details about letters sent to or received by members of the Burney and d'Arblay families see the footnotes. (Senders and recipients of such manuscript letters are not in general indexed.) For abbreviations, see p. xvi.

PRINTED IN GREAT BRITAIN
AT THE UNIVERSITY PRESS, OXFORD
BY CHARLES BATEY, PRINTER TO THE UNIVERSITY